Macmillan
Encyclopedia of
Computers

Editorial Board

Editor in Chief

Gary G. Bitter
Arizona State University

Editors

Gordon B. Davis
University of Minnesota

Diana J. Gabaldon
Arizona State University

William I. Grosky
Wayne State University

Cathleen A. Norris
University of North Texas

M. D. Roblyer
Florida A. & M. University

Macmillan

Volume 1

Encyclopedia of Computers

Gary G. Bitter
Editor in Chief

Macmillan Publishing Company
New York
Maxwell Macmillan Canada
Toronto
Maxwell Macmillan International
New York · Oxford · Singapore · Sydney

UNIVERSITY OF FLORIDA LIBRARIES

Copyright © 1992 by Macmillan Publishing Company
A Division of Macmillan, Inc.

All rights reserved. No part of this book may be reproduced or
transmitted in any form or by any means, electronic or mechanical,
including photocopying, recording, or by any information storage and
retrieval system, without permission in writing from the Publisher.

Macmillan Publishing Company
A Division of Macmillan, Inc.
866 Third Avenue, New York, NY 10022

Maxwell Macmillan Canada, Inc.
1200 Eglinton Avenue East, Suite 200, Don Mills, Ontario M3C 3N1

Macmillan, Inc., is part of the Maxwell Communication Group of
Companies.

Library of Congress Catalog Card Number: 91-45339

Printed in the United States of America

Printing number
    3 4 5 6 7 8 9 10

Library of Congress Cataloging-in-Publication Data

Macmillan encyclopedia of computers / Gary G. Bitter, editor in chief.
        p.   cm.
      ISBN 0-02-897045-4 (set). — ISBN 0-02-897046-2 (vol. 1). — ISBN
  0-02-897047-0 (vol. 2)
        1. Computers—Encyclopedias.   I. Bitter, Gary G.
  QA76.15.M33   1992
  004′.03—dc20   91-45339
                                                      CIP

The paper used in this publication meets the minimum requirements of
American National Standard for Information Sciences—Permanence of
Paper for Printed Library Materials. ANSI Z39.48–1984.

Editorial and Production Staff

Philip Friedman
Publisher

Elly Dickason
Editor in Chief, Macmillan Reference

David Eckroth
Executive Editor

Jonathan Wiener
Project Editor

Karin K. Vanderveer
Assistant Editor

Josephine Della Peruta   William Drennan
Copy-editors

Steven van Leeuwen
Proofreader

Cynthia Crippen
Indexer

Lynn Constantinou
Production Manager

Contents

PREFACE

The *Macmillan Encyclopedia of Computers* is an up-to-date two-volume work on computers. Although invaluable to any reader, the *Encyclopedia* is targeted to students and other nonspecialists. The purpose of the *Macmillan Encyclopedia of Computers* is to provide an authoritative comprehensive work on all aspects of computers. The *Encyclopedia* was written by leaders in computer science, information systems, and computer education.

The *Macmillan Encyclopedia of Computers* contains more than 200 articles explaining the role of computers in our world and giving a comprehensive account of computers with a factual overview. The topics covered include the broad spectrum of computers in government, education, industry, and business. Hardware and software topics include history, design, and the role each has played in our lives. Careers, computer systems, programming languages, applications, and the future are explored from various aspects. Each article has been carefully researched and includes references as well as a reading list. Figures and illustrations are included as appropriate.

The *Encyclopedia*'s articles are arranged in alphabetical order and vary in length. The lives of important figures in the history of computers are presented in 500-word capsule biographies, whereas overarching topics such as ethics and computers or use of computers in education receive 5,000 words or more. An entry on a key subject such as scientific applications of computers is typically 3,000 words long; in addition, 2,000-word articles are devoted to each of several facets of the topic (astronomical use, biological use, chemical use, mathematical use, meteorologic use).

The List of Articles in this volume may be consulted to ascertain whether a particular subject is the topic of an article. Furthermore, small capitals are used within each article to identify words and phrases that form the titles of other articles. Thus, a reader interested in computer "understanding" of human language could start with the broader notion of NATURAL-LANGUAGE PROCESSING or with an entry on a more specific concept such as SPEECH TO PRINT or SPEECH SYNTHESIS AND RECOGNITION. Another approach would be to begin with an article on a historical individual such as Alan TURING, or on a particular application such as KNOWLEDGE BASES AND EXPERT SYSTEMS. All these articles are linked to one another by cross-references. Finally, the Index provides page-number citations for the key words of every topic covered in the *Encyclopedia*.

A two-volume reference work clearly has no hope of saying the last word on a subject as vast as computers. Nor should an encyclopedia article seek to expand the boundaries of its discipline in the same way as a journal article or symposium presentation. Encyclopedias exist to make the present fund of information accessible to readers in many categories, including students, teachers, writers, and those who are simply curious. Most articles in this *Encyclopedia* include a list of references as a starting point for further investigation.

A project such as the *Macmillan Encyclopedia of Computers* is a major undertaking requiring the cooperation of many people. I was fortunate to have Gordon Davis, Diana Gabaldon, Cathie Norris, Bill Grosky, and M. D. Roblyer as editors. Their unfailing dedication and energy provided the best written articles available. They worked with authors to ensure carefully written articles. This difficult task of providing clear, relevant information was done on a strenuous timeline. The reviewers of the articles provided needed input and validity checks. Finally, David Eckroth, Jonathan Wiener, and Elly Dickason of Macmillan Publishing Company made the entire project possible. Of course, the support of my wife and sons will never be forgotten.

GARY G. BITTER

LIST OF ARTICLES

LIST OF ARTICLES

LIST OF CONTRIBUTORS

Abbey, Beverly
University of North Texas
Mainframe Computer Manufacturers
(Appendix)

Agrawal, Dharma
North Carolina State University
Hardware: Computer Architecture

Akritas, Alkiviadis G.
University of Kansas
Symbolic Computation

Allais, David C.
Applied Tactical Systems of Washington
Bar Code Systems

Amer, Tarek
University of Florida
Auditing in Computer Environments

Analyti, Anastasia
Michigan State University
Query Processing in Databases

Anneberg, Lisa
Lawrence Institute of Technology
Parallel Computing

Applegate, Lynda M.
Harvard University
Executive Information Systems

Asbrand, Deborah
Writer
Games, Computer; Microcomputers (Personal
Computers)

Bailey, Andrew D., Jr.
University of Arizona
Auditing in Computer Environments

Baumbach, Donna
University of Central Florida
Hypermedia; Hypertext

Becker, Gary H.
Consultant
Copyright Laws

Bozeman, William C.
University of Central Florida
Microcomputers (Personal Computers);
Spreadsheets

Brazel, Anthony J.
Arizona State University
Meteorological Use of Computers

Brengle, Marte
Writer
Forth; Information Services

Brittain, David L.
Florida Department of Education
Windows

Brumbaugh, Ken
University of North Texas
Icons

Burns, Roy B.
Ernst & Young
Retailing, Computer Use in

Campbell, Margaret J.
Writer
Literary Analysis, Computers in

Canaday, Kathlyn
University of North Texas
Microcomputer and Minicomputer
Manufacturers (Appendix)

xvii

Cawley, Jeffery L.
Northwest Analytical
Workstations

Chakravarthy, C. V.
Stevens Institute of Technology
Data Compression and Fractals

Cherrington, J. Owen
Brigham Young University
Accounting Use of Computers

Cho, Namjae
Boston University
Processing Methods

Clark, Larry
Monell Chemical Senses Center
Biological Use

Clinton, Janeen
FDLRS–Alpha Center
Disabled, Technology for the

Concepcion, Arturo I.
California State University, San Bernardino
Operating Systems

Conrad, Michael
Wayne State University
Cybernetics and Natural Computing

Conrady, Denis
University of North Texas
Modula-2

Cooper, Robert B.
Florida Atlantic University
Queueing Theory

Coorpender, Ray
University of North Texas
Aerospace, Computer Applications in

Coyer, Shahnaz Y.
University of Minnesota
Voice Mail

Dalal, Rajiv
Citicorp Technology Office
Banking, Computer Use in

Davidson, Gayle V.
University of Texas at Austin
Interactive Computer Systems

Davis, Gordon B.
University of Minnesota
Information Requirements Determination;
  Management Information Systems

Deavours, Cipher A.
Writer
Cryptography

Dede, Christopher J.
University of Houston
Home, Computers in the

Deppe, Paul R.
Arvin Cal-Span
Hardware: Hardware Interfaces

Dewdney, A. K.
University of Western Ontario
Chaos Theory

Dewhirst, Donald L.
Writer
Solid Modeling and Finite Element Analysis

DeWitt, John K.
Arizona State University
Biomechanics and Computers

Dewitz, Sandra
University of Texas at Austin
Systems Development Life Cycle

D'Onofrio, Marianne J.
Central Connecticut State University
Academic Degree Programs

Early, Grady
Southwest Texas State University
Airline Reservation Systems

Elieson, S. Willard
University of North Texas
Telecommunications Companies (Appendix)

LIST OF CONTRIBUTORS

Engler, Pamela
Florida Department of Education

Equity Issues and Computers

Everest, Gordon C.
University of Minnesota

Computer-Aided Software Engineering

Ferratt, Thomas W.
University of Dayton

Careers in Information Systems

Fifhause, Al
The United Methodist Church

Religion, Computer Uses in

Fotouhi, Farshad
Wayne State University

Database Management

Gabaldon, Diana J.
Arizona State University

Scientific Applications, Computer Technology
in

Galletta, Dennis F.
University of Pittsburgh

Office Automation

Garson, G. David
North Carolina State University

Social Science Applications of Computers

Ginzberg, Michael J.
Case Western Reserve University

Decision Support Systems

Goldstein, David K.
Boston University

Processing Methods

Golshani, Forouzan
Arizona State University

Nonstandard Database Systems; LISP and
PROLOG

Good, Phillip I.
Claremont College

Mathematical Use of Computers; Statistical
Applications of Computers

Hall, Sheldon T.
Writer

Database Programming; Languages,
Very-High-Level; Report Generators

Hamilton, Scott
The Manufacturing Guild Ltd.

Manufacturing Resource Planning

Hansen, Barbara
Digital Dispatch Inc.

Viruses

Hawkins, Donald
AT&T

Videotex

Hawn, Walter
Writer

Databases, On-line; Typesetting; Word
Processing

Hill, Arthur V.
University of Minnesota

Operations Management

Hillman, Donald
Lehigh University

Information Storage and Retrieval

Hirst, Graeme
University of Toronto

Natural-Language Processing

Hoff, Gary L.
Writer

Medical Imaging, Computer-Assisted;
Medical Informatics

Hofstetter, Fred
University of Delaware

Arts, Computers in the

Holcomb, Terry L.
University of North Texas

Multimedia

LIST OF CONTRIBUTORS

Hoot, James
State University of New York at Buffalo
BASIC

Huntsberger, Terry
University of South Carolina
Visualization Techniques

Ives, Blake
Southern Methodist University
Strategic Applications of Information
Technology

Jackson, Allen
University of North Texas
Health and Fitness, Computer Applications in

Jacob, Tom
University of North Texas
Data Structures

Jacobstein, Neil
Cimflex Teknowledge
Artificial Intelligence in the Automotive
Industry

Jajodia, Sushil
George Mason University
Distributed and Heterogeneous Database
Management Systems

Jalics, Paul J.
Cleveland State University
Performance Evaluation

Jansma, Andrew
Dakota State College
Electronic Document Image Processing and
Management

Jarvenpaa, Sirkka
University of Texas at Austin
Presentation Graphics

Jazayeri, Mehdi
Hewlett-Packard Laboratories
Compilers; Programming Language Design

Johnson, William R.
Writer
Religion, Computer Uses in

Jordan, Eleanor
University of Texas at Austin
Systems Development Life Cycle

Kandel, Abraham
University of South Florida
Knowledge Bases and Expert Systems

Kauffman, Robert J.
New York University
Financial Services, Computer Use in

Kaur, Devinder
University of Toledo
Parallel Computing

Kearsley, Greg
George Washington University
Authoring Languages, Systems, and
Environments

Kelton, W. David
University of Minnesota
Simulation

Keuffel, Warren
Writer
Languages, Computer

Khailany, Asad
Eastern Michigan University
Database Design, Automated

King, John Leslie
University of California, Irvine
Organization of the Information Systems
Function

King, William R.
University of Pittsburgh
Planning of Information Systems

Knezek, Gerald
University of North Texas
Direct Screen Manipulation

Koltes, Scott J.
Digital Dispatch Inc.
Viruses

Korel, Bogdan
Wayne State University
Software Engineering

Kraemer, Kenneth L.
University of California, Irvine
Government, Computers in

Lambert, Joanne
University of North Texas
Interactive Video Manufacturers

Lambert, Robert
Walt Disney Pictures and Television
Animation, Computer

Lee, J. A. N.
Virginia Polytechnic Institute and State University
Hacking

Lehman, John
University of Alaska
Documentation

Lehman, Lisa M.
Writer
User Documentation

Lidtke, Doris K.
Towson State University
History of Computing; Computing Associations (Appendix)

Lieberman, Henry
Massachusetts Institute of Technology
Object-Oriented Programming

Locatis, Craig
National Library of Medicine
Authoring Languages, Systems, and Environments

Lockwood, Diane
Seattle University
Cost/Benefit Analysis of Computer Use

Lomerson, W. L.
University of North Texas
Computer Peripheral Manufacturers

Lorents, Alden C.
Northern Arizona University
Business Use of Computers

Luger, George F.
University of New Mexico
Artificial Intelligence

March, Salvatore T.
University of Minnesota
Data Modeling, Logical

Mark, Robert M.
Manufacturers Hanover
Trading, Computer Use in

Marlowe, Howard
Marlowe & Company
Political Uses of Computers

Marsh, Tony P.
Arizona State University
Biomechanics and Computers

Martin, Worthy
University of Virginia
Image Processing

McBane, Donald A.
Clemson University
Marketing and Marketing Research, Computer Use in

McConnaughey, Janet
Writer
Journalism, Computers in

McCubbrey, Donald J.
University of Denver
Electronic Data Interchange

McDougle, Kenny O.
Pittsburg State University
Sports, Computer Applications in

McGregor, John D.
Clemson University
Data Entry

LIST OF CONTRIBUTORS

McKibben, Loretta
University of Oklahoma

APL; Astronomy, Computers in; Aviation, Computers in; FORTRAN; Geology, Computers in

McLean, Scott P.
Arizona State University

Biomechanics and Computers

McNamara, Joel·
Writer

Pascal

Meadows, Catherine
U.S. Naval Research Laboratory

Military Use of Computers

Mehrotra, Rajiv
University of Kentucky

Robotics

Mejabi, Olugbenga O.
Wayne State University

Manufacturing Engineering, Computers in

Miller, Tomas A.
Arizona State University

Meteorological Use of Computers

Mitchell, William J.
Harvard University

Architecture, Computer Uses in

Moseley, Warren
Writer

Ada

Muncy, James A.
Clemson University

Marketing and Marketing Research, Computer Use in

Murthy, S. N. J.
Central Michigan University

Hardware: Computer Systems

Myers, John L.
National Trust for Historic Preservation

Lists; Printing Technologies

Nadel, Bernard A.
Wayne State University

Algorithms

Navin chandra, D.
Carnegie-Mellon University

Artificial Intelligence in Engineering Design

Neill, James R.
Florida Department of Education

Electronic Mail

Nordeen, Jon K.
Dayton Hudson Corporation

Credit Systems

Norris, Cathleen A.
University of North Texas

Ergonomics

Norvelle, Ronald L.
Florida A. & M. University

Desktop Publishing

O'Shaughnessy, Douglas
Université du Québec

Speech Synthesis and Recognition

Ouchi, Glenn I.
Laboratory PC Users Group

Chemical Industry, Use of Computers in the; Laboratory Information Management Systems

Pangaro, Paul
Pangaro Incorporated

Cybernetics and Artificial Intelligence

Panko, Raymond R.
University of Hawaii

End User Computing

Pennington, J. B.
Tennessee State University

Real Estate Industry, Use of Computers in the

LIST OF CONTRIBUTORS

Perrolle, Judith A.
Northeastern University
Social Impacts of Computing

Pijawka, David
Writer
Hazardous Waste Management, Computers in

Pitterle, Michael E.
University of Wisconsin, Madison
Pharmacy Practice, Use of Computers in

Poirot, James L.
University of North Texas
PL/I; Supercomputer Manufacturers
(Appendix)

Pramanik, Sakti
Michigan State University
Query Processing in Databases

Putnam, Frederick A.
Laboratory Technologies Corporation
Data Acquisition Boards

Quinn, Clark N.
University of Pittsburgh
Hardware: Screen Design

Rahimi, Morteza A.
Wayne State University
Organizing Institutional Information Systems
Infrastructure

Rajlich, Vaclav
Wayne State University
Ethics and Computers

Rana, S. P.
Wayne State University
Local Area Networks; Networks, Computer;
Wide Area Networks

Riccardi, Gregory A.
Florida State University
Supercomputers

Rifkin, Glenn
Writer
Speech to Print

Roblyer, M. D.
Florida State University
Education, Computers in

Rossow, Conrad
Minnesota Mutual Insurance Company
Insurance, Computer Use in

Russell, Jack
Writer
ALGOL 60 and 68

Savenye, Wilhelmina C.
Arizona State University
Joysticks

Schaffer, J. David
Philips Laboratories
Machine Learning

Schlereth, Hewitt
Writer
Navigational Use of Computers

Schlieve, Paul L.
University of North Texas
Computer-Aided Design and Manufacturing

Schrum, Lynne
Writer
Computer Component Manufacturers

Sengupta, A.
University of South Carolina
System Reliability

Sethi, Ishwar K.
Wayne State University
Pattern Recognition

Shin, Kang G.
University of Michigan
Real-Time Systems

Singh, Harpreet
Wayne State University
Parallel Computing

Singhal, Mukesh
Ohio State University

Distributed Computing

Smith, Gerald
University of Minnesota

Decision Making

Snyder, James R.
University of Minnesota

COBOL

Soesilo, J. Andy
Writer

Hazardous Waste Management, Computers
in

Sood, Arun K.
George Mason University

Hardware: Computer Design; Hardware:
Memory Design

Spencer, Donald D.
Writer

Babbage, Charles; Boole, George; Bricklin,
Daniel; Byron, Augusta Ada; Cards,
Jacquard and Hollerith; Careers in
Computing; Cray, Seymour; Dijkstra,
Edsger W.; Eckert, J. Presper; Gates,
William H. (Bill); Hollerith, Herman;
Hopper, Grace Brewster Murray; Jacquard,
Joseph-Marie; Jobs, Steven Paul; Kemeny,
John G.; Kurtz, Thomas E.; Leibniz,
Gottfried Wilhelm von; Mauchly, John
William; Norris, William C.; Pascal, Blaise;
Turing, Alan Mathison; von Neumann,
John; Wirth, Niklaus; Wozniak, Stephen G.

Spoor, James E.
Spectrum Human Resource Systems

Human Resources, Use of Information
Technology in

Sprowl, James A.
Fitch, Even, Tabin, & Flannery

Legal Applications of Computers

Straub, Detmar W.
University of Minnesota

Security, Information Systems

Stubblefield, William A.
University of New Mexico

Artificial Intelligence

Taylor, Harriet G.
Louisiana State University

Keyboards

Ting, T. C.
University of Connecticut

Access Control

Varshney, Pramod K.
Syracuse University

Coding Theory; Information Theory and
Coding

Vogel, Douglas R.
University of Arizona

Cooperative Work Systems

Waldon, Jefferson L.
Writer

Geographic Information Systems

Walker, Roy O.
University of Illinois

Law Enforcement, Computers in

Wallace, F. Layne
University of North Florida

Sound, Computers and

Wallace, Susan R.
University of North Florida

Menus

Wand, Yair
University of British Columbia

Data

Ward, Allen C.
University of Michigan

Constraint Reasoning in Mechanical
Engineering Design

Watne, Donald A.
Portland State University

Information Systems Quality and Control

LIST OF CONTRIBUTORS

Watt, Daniel Lynn
Educational Alternatives
Logo

White, James
University of South Florida
Binary Numbering System

Winsor, Phil
National Chiao Tung University, Taiwan
Music, Computer Applications in

Wojtkowski, W. Gregory
Boise State University
Prototyping

Wojtkowski, Wita
Boise State University
Prototyping

Woolverton, Michael
Thunderbird College
Farming, Computer Use in

Wybo, Michael D.
University of Minnesota
Security, Information Systems

Yakal, Kathy
Writer
Fax; RPG

Yap, Chee Sing
National University of Singapore
Remote Work

Yaprak, Ece
Western Michigan University
Parallel Computing

Young, Jon
University of North Texas
Videodiscs

Zeigler, Bernard P.
University of Arizona
Simulation Languages

A

ACADEMIC DEGREE PROGRAMS

Some segment of the work force must be educated as information systems (IS) specialists, prepared to use information technology to achieve the goals of organizations. Another segment must be educated as computer science specialists to develop and maintain computer and information technologies. A third segment must be educated as software engineering specialists to build software programs and tools to program use of computer and information technologies. Academic degree programs that provide the education necessary to prepare specialists in information systems, computer science, and software engineering are discussed in this article.

INFORMATION SYSTEMS

Some of the first academic degree programs for information systems were developed in the late 1960s. In 1990 more than 450 programs in North America provided preparation in information systems, with degree programs usually found in business schools. Many of these schools focus on both undergraduate and graduate education; some, on one level only. The programs are in a variety of departments. A sampling of some of the names given to departments preparing people in this area includes Management Information Systems, Information Systems, Information and Decision Sciences, Computer Information Systems, Decision Sciences, Management Science and Information Systems, and Accounting and Information Systems. The International Conference on Information Systems (ICIS), established in 1980, provides a yearly forum for academicians and others interested in information systems

to discuss research and curriculum issues related to their discipline.

Curriculum guidelines and recommendations for information systems began to be published in the early 1970s. The first were published by two major professional organizations, the Association for Computing Machinery (ACM) and the Data Processing Management Association (DPMA). Some institutions have adopted either the ACM or DPMA guidelines in developing their academic degree programs; other institutions have used both sets. Both professional organizations were developing new sets of curriculum guidelines and recommendations in the early 1990s. The DPMA was developing the DPMA Model Curriculum for a Four-Year Undergraduate Degree in information systems (DPMA 1991), based on the philosophy that such programs should be easy to develop, maintain, and update. It was developed using a methodology that can be replicated as the knowledge base evolves. The model provides a framework for implementing a variety of academic degree programs in information systems, depending upon the institution's resources and philosophy. This curriculum is designed to develop the learner's ability to conceptualize, design, and implement high-quality information systems. It emphasizes systems theory, problem solving, and software engineering.

The DPMA curriculum is designed around seven knowledge clusters (see Figure 1) considered necessary to cover the knowledge needed by all IS graduates. The IS body of knowledge is comprised of computer concepts, organizational concepts, information technology, and systems theory and development (see Table 1). These areas are subdivided into approximately 250 items or knowledge units, which are mapped to the

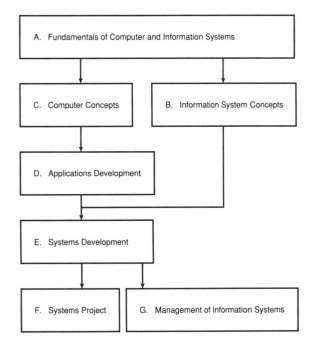

FIGURE 1. Knowledge clusters in the DPMA curriculum model. From "Information systems: The DPMA model curriculum for a four-year undergraduate degree," p. 14. Copyright 1991 by the Data Processing Management Association. Reprinted by permission.

seven knowledge clusters within each of the knowledge areas. The knowledge units are mapped to the knowledge clusters by determining the level of depth of competency required in each cluster. A knowledge unit may appear in more than one cluster at different levels of competency. Courses are then derived from the knowledge clusters. Descriptions for the nine courses suggested for IS graduates are shown in Table 2. Suggested elective courses in the DPMA curriculum include IS Professionalism and Ethics, Information Center Concepts and Management, Audit and Security Management, Telecommunications and Distributed Processing, Implementation of PC Network Systems, Office Automation Systems, GDSS/EMS/ ESS (Group Decision Support Systems/Electronic Mail Systems/Executive Support Systems), Decision Support Systems/Expert Systems, Software Engineering, Alternative Analysis and Design Methodologies, Computer Graphics, System Simulation, Software and Hardware Architecture, Advanced Database Concepts, and Human–Computer Interaction.

TABLE 1. The DPMA Model Curriculum

1.0 Computer Concepts
    1.1 Computer Architectures and Hardware
    1.2 Algorithms and Data Structures
    1.3 Programming Languages and Applications Development Facilities
    1.4 Operating Systems
    1.5 Data and Computer Communications

2.0 Organizational Concepts
    2.1 Organization Theory
    2.2 Information Systems Management
    2.3 Decision Theory
    2.4 Organizational Behavior
    2.5 Project Management
    2.6 Change Management
    2.7 Legal
    2.8 Professionalism

3.0 Information Technology
    3.1 Database
    3.2 Information Retrieval
    3.3 Artificial Intelligence (AI)
    3.4 Computer Assisted Systems Engineering (CASE)

4.0 Systems Theory and Development
    4.1 Systems Theory
    4.2 Systems Development
    4.3 Development Techniques
    4.4 Information Systems Planning
    4.5 Information and Function Analysis
    4.6 Information Systems Design
    4.7 Systems Implementation and Testing Strategies
    4.8 Types of Information Systems

Source: DPMA 1990.

The body of knowledge and methodology proposed by DPMA are adaptable to the development of both associate and advanced degree programs. The programs can range from those emphasizing computer technology to those concentrating on managerial approaches to information systems. The methodology provides a global approach to information systems curricula development.

The importance of supporting curricula comprised of general education, professionalism, and ethics, as well as communications course work, is emphasized in the DPMA curriculum model.

The ACM curriculum recommendations for information systems provide another example of academic preparation for those

TABLE 2. Course Descriptions from the DPMA Curriculum

IS-1 Fundamental Concepts of Information and Computer Technology

Use a desktop computer with current important end-user software to solve problems within an organizational environment. Includes coverage of software and hardware components, operating system concepts, information structures, and formal problem-solving techniques. Includes supervised laboratory exercises.

IS-2 IS Concepts

Identify managerial/organizational information needs. Describe the role of IS in management, including current professional practices and methodologies. Includes presentation of systems theory, decision theory, organizational models, types of IS, IS planning, and IS development.

IS-3 Computer Concepts

Describe the function and architecture of computer hardware and software technologies. Includes data and instruction representation, networks, operating system functions, and programming languages. Includes supervised structured laboratory exercises.

IS-4 Application Design and Implementation

Use information systems techniques to solve managerial and organizational problems of limited complexity. Includes solving formal analytic problems and implementing solutions using IS development techniques with a procedural language. Includes supervised structured laboratory exercises.

IS-5 Application Development

Use information systems techniques to solve managerial and organizational problems of limited complexity. Emphasizes CASE tools, quality assurance and testing, and interactive systems. Includes supervised structured laboratory exercises.

IS-6 Systems Development 1

Use information systems methodologies to solve enterprisewide managerial and organi-

(continued)

TABLE 2 (cont.)

zational problems. Students will use systems design methodologies to develop single-user system, including using database. Includes supervised structured laboratory exercises.

IS-7 Systems Development 2

Use information systems methodologies to solve enterprisewide managerial and organizational problems. Students will use systems design methodologies to develop multiuser system, including using database. Includes project management techniques, security techniques, and system testing and implementation. Includes supervised structured laboratory exercises.

IS-8 Systems Project

Solve an information system problem using project management and IS methodologies. Apply project management techniques in a group project environment. Develop systems documentation, implement system, and present completed project report.

IS-9 Management of IS

Demonstrate a comprehension of the principles and concepts involved in the management of organizational information systems resources. Includes CIO functions, information systems planning, legal and professional issues, and strategic impact of information systems.

Source: DPMA 1990.

wishing to specialize in computerized organizational information systems. The program is based on the premise that graduates will be employed in positions involving organizational information systems. Graduates will be able to

1. assist in defining and planning information systems;

2. elicit information requirements for applications and assist in designing the systems;

3. implement information systems applications;

4. manage information systems development and operation.

Graduates will also be able to work in functional area positions and general management positions. Because of the organizational context in which IS graduates will work, the curriculum structure assumes an understanding of organizations and their processes and functions. Information systems personnel often assume the role of change agents, for whom communication and human relations skills are vital. Graduates must be prepared to assist in using information systems to achieve organizational goals and in being competitive in a global business environment.

Information systems graduates must have knowledge in three important areas: (1) organizational knowledge and interpersonal skills, (2) information systems concepts and processes, and (3) information systems technology (computer hardware, systems software, and application software).

The ACM information systems program prescribes a set of courses that address each of these areas. The program addresses both undergraduate and graduate education in information systems. Its recommendations for undergraduate education evolved from those for the post–bachelor's degree program. The general structure of information systems curricula is given in Figure 2.

The graduate-level program provides two options: (1) the MBA or MIS major, preparing a student to become an information systems designer (see Figure 3), and (2) an MIS minor, preparing a student to become an information systems analyst (see Figure 4). The information systems designer is responsible for specifying hardware and software requirements in designing information systems. The suggested program for learners preparing for careers as information systems designers is a ten-course sequence (five courses in information systems technology and five in information systems concepts

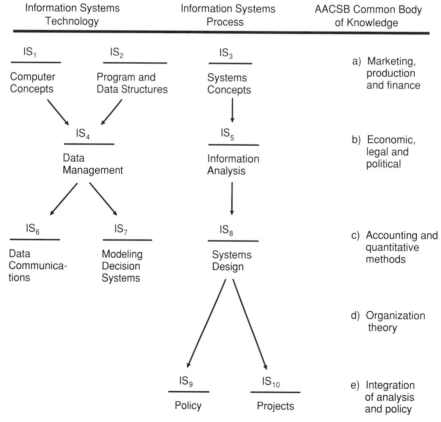

FIGURE 2. General structure of information systems curriculum (undergraduate and graduate levels). From Nunamaker et al. 1983, p. 83. Copyright 1983 by the Association for Computing Machinery, Inc. Reprinted by permission.

Semester

	IS$_1$	IS$_2$	IS$_3$	
1st	Computer Systems Concepts	Program, Data and File Structures	Systems and Information Concepts in Organizations	
2nd	IS$_4$ Data Management	IS$_5$ Information Analysis		
3rd	IS$_6$ Data Communications, Networks and Distributed Processing	IS$_7$ Modeling and Decision Systems	IS$_8$ Systems Design	
4th	IS$_9$ MIS Policy	IS$_{10}$ System Development Projects		

FIGURE 3. Master's-level program for systems designers. From Nunamaker et al. 1983, p. 85. Copyright 1983 by the Association for Computing Machinery, Inc. Reprinted by permission.

and processes). The information systems analyst is the liaison between users and information systems specialists and helps the user to define the information system's requirements. For those preparing as information systems analysts, the suggested program is a four-course sequence.

Whether a program of studies in information systems emphasizes the DPMA or the ACM curriculum model or a combination, the context in which information systems graduates will work requires that programs of study emphasize an understanding of organizations and their management or

require this as a prerequisite. Such prerequisite knowledge may be defined in a variety of ways. One is to follow the American Assembly of Collegiate Schools of Business (AACSB) accreditation standards.

An ACM curriculum revision was expected in 1992. As it took shape, its structure followed the 1980s curriculum but reflected developments in data communications, support systems, and expert systems, dividing information system development processes into one course for simple, standalone applications and a second for large integrated applications.

IS$_3$	IS$_2$	IS$_5$	IS$_8$
Systems and Information Concepts in Organizations	Program, Data and File Structures	Information Analysis	Systems Design

FIGURE 4. MBA/IS area of emphasis. From Nunamaker et al. 1983, p. 85. Copyright 1983 by the Association for Computing Machinery, Inc. Reprinted by permission.

COMPUTER SCIENCE

Nearly 1,000 college and universities in the United States offer degrees in computer science. Recommendations for computer science program curricula first began to appear in 1965. A recent report, *Computing Curricula 1991* (Association for Computing Machinery and IEEE Computer Society 1990), contains recommendations for a variety of programs, such as those in computer science, computer engineering, computer science and engineering, and informatics. This report represents a joint effort of two major professional societies—the ACM and the Computer Society of the Institute for the Education of Electrical Engineers (CS-IEEE). The task force responsible for this report was charged with pre-

senting recommendations for the design and implementation of undergraduate curricula in computing.

An overview of the proposed undergraduate program in computing is summarized in Figure 5. Nine major subject areas are identified as being important for programs with computing as their focus (see Figure 6), including subject matter considered essential for all undergraduate curricula in computing. This subject matter is presented as a set of common requirements that ensure that all students understand computing. They are organized as knowledge units, which are organized by subject area (see Table 3) and consist of items that can be combined to form courses to meet an institution's priorities. The same knowledge units

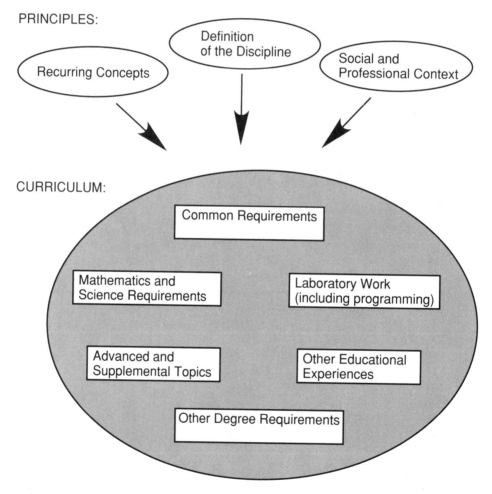

FIGURE 5. A complete curriculum and its underlying principles. From *Computing curricula 1991—A report of the ACM/IEEE-CS joint curriculum task force*, p. 17. Copyright 1991 by the Association for Computing Machinery, Inc. Reprinted by permission.

Subject Area
Algorithms and Data Structures
Architecture
Artificial Intelligence and Robotics
Database and Information Retrieval
Human-Computer Communication
Numerical and Symbolic Computation
Operating Systems
Programming Languages
Introduction to a Programming Language (optional)
Software Methodology and Engineering
Social, Ethical, and Professional Issues

FIGURE 6. The subject areas. From *Computing curricula 1991—A report of the ACM/IEEE-CS joint curriculum task force,* p. 22. Copyright 1991 by the Association for Computing Machinery, Inc. Reprinted by permission.

TABLE 3. Knowledge Units Identified as Essential by the ACM/IEEE Task Force

AL: Algorithms and Data Structures
  AL1: Basic Data Structures
  AL2: Abstract Data Types
  AL3: Recursive Algorithms
  AL4: Complexity Analysis
  AL6: Sorting and Searching
  AL7: Computability and Undecidability
  AL8: Problem-Solving Strategies
  AL9: Parallel and Distributed Algorithms

AR: Architecture
  AR1: Digital Logic
  AR2: Digital Systems
  AR3: Machine-Level Representation of Data
  AR4: Assembly-Level Machine Organization
  AR5: Memory System Organization and Architecture
  AR6: Interfacing and Communication
  AR7: Alternative Architectures

AI: Artificial Intelligence and Robotics
  AI1: History and Applications of Artificial Intelligence
  AI2: Problems, State Spaces, and Search Strategies

DB: Database and Information Retrieval
  DB1: Overview, Models, and Applications of Database Systems
  DB2: The Relational Data Model

HU: Human-Computer Communication
  HU1: User Interfaces
  HU2: Computer Graphics

(continued)

TABLE 3 (cont.)

NU: Numerical and Symbolic Computation
  NU1: Number Representation, Errors, and Portability
  NU2: Iterative Approximation Methods

OS: Operating Systems
  OS1: History, Evolution, and Philosophy
  OS2: Tasking and Processes
  OS3: Process Coordination and Synchronization
  OS4: Scheduling and Dispatch
  OS5: Physical and Virtual Memory Organization
  OS6: Device Management
  OS7: File Systems and Naming
  OS8: Security and Protection
  OS9: Communications and Networking
  OS10: Distributed and Real-Time Systems

PL: Programming Languages
  PL1: History and Overview of Programming Languages
  PL2: Virtual Machines
  PL3: Representation of Data Types
  PL4: Sequence Control
  PL5: Data Control, Sharing, and Type Checking
  PL6: Run-time Storage Management
  PL7: Finite State Automata and Regular Expressions
  PL8: Context-Free Grammars and Pushdown Automata
  PL9: Language Translation Systems
  PL10: Programming Language Semantics
  PL11: Programming Paradigms
  PL12: Distributed and Parallel Programming Constructs

SE: Software Methodology and Engineering
  SE1: Fundamental Problem-Solving Concepts
  SE2: The Software Development Process
  SE3: Software Requirements and Specifications
  SE4: Software Design and Implementation
  SE5: Verification and Validation

SP: Social, Ethical, and Professional Issues
  SP1: Historical and Social Context of Computing
  SP2: Responsibilities of the Computing Professional
  SP3: Risks and Liabilities
  SP4: Intellectual Property

Source: ACM/IEEE 1990.

may be included in more than one course. Thus the common requirements are not presented in a set of discrete courses.

Depth of study is ensured by advanced/supplemental topics within the nine subject areas. The curriculum should provide depth of study in several of these areas. This study is achieved through completion of several additional courses determined by the institution. Topics considered very significant include those listed in Table 4.

Mastery of computing requires not only an understanding of the major subject areas but also an understanding of the processes that professionals in computing use: theory, abstraction, and design. These processes are included throughout the common requirements. Laboratory work is also incorporated and is used to reinforce the integration of the processes of theory, abstraction, and design with subject matter. Theory is used in devel-

TABLE 4. Supplemental Topics Identified as Significant by ACM/IEEE

Advanced Operating Systems
Advanced Software Engineering
Analysis of Algorithms
Artificial Intelligence
Combinatorial and Graph Algorithms
Computational Complexity
Computer Communication Networks
Computer Graphics
Computer-Human Interface
Computer Security
Database and Information Retrieval
Digital Design Automation
Fault-Tolerant Computing
Information Theory
Modeling and Simulation
Numerical Computation
Parallel and Distributed Computing
Performance Prediction and Analysis
Principles of Computer Architecture
Principles of Programming Languages
Programming Language Translation
Real-Time Systems
Robotics and Machine Intelligence
Semantics and Verification
Societal Impact of Computing
Symbolic Computation
Theory of Computation
VLSI System Design

Source: ACM/IEEE 1990.

oping and understanding the underlying mathematical principles that apply to computing. Undergraduates are often introduced to theory within an introductory mathematics course, followed by course work designed to provide a study of algorithms (complexity theory), architecture (logic), and programming languages (formal grammars and automata). Abstraction, rooted in the experimental sciences, is used in developing models for potential algorithms, data structures, architectures, and the like. Experiments are designed to test hypotheses about these models, about alternative design decisions, or about the underlying theory itself. Undergraduates are introduced to abstraction through class and laboratory work. Models are presented that require analysis and inquiry into the limits of computation, the properties of new computational models, and the validity of unproven theoretical conjectures. Design, rooted in engineering, is used in developing a system or device to solve a problem. Undergraduates are introduced to design by studying existing designs and by designing systems or devices. Through laboratory projects, students learn to evaluate alternatives, costs, and performance of the designs they and others create, considering real-world constraints.

The computing curriculum also exposes students to associated cultural, ethical, legal, and societal issues. In addition, twelve important, recurring concepts are incorporated into the curriculum.

Computing Curricula 1991 provides sample curricula for computing professionals as well as for well-rounded professionals who may not necessarily be pursuing a career in computing but who have a strong interest in it and who wish to combine computing with another discipline.

The rapid growth of computing and in high technology prompted the National Science Foundation (1988) to sponsor a study for development of an expanded taxonomy of computer specialist occupations. It includes computer scientist, computer hardware engineer, computer software engineer, telecommunications specialist, systems programmer, systems analyst, programmer, computer operations specialist, technical support specialist, and computer trainer.

SOFTWARE ENGINEERING

Software engineering is the process whereby engineering, scientific, and mathematical principles, methods, and tools are applied in a disciplined fashion to produce quality software systems economically. Software engineers are specialists with skills in engineering, design, management, science, and mathematics. They can build software systems to meet users' needs and to maintain these systems. Their task spans the software system life cycle. More specifically, software engineers are architects of complex systems, eliciting systems requirements, setting specifications, and designing, verifying, implementing, testing, documenting, and maintaining complex and large-scale software systems.

The first three academic degree programs in software engineering were developed at the graduate level in the late 1970s. In 1985 three additional graduate-level programs were established. Since 1985, approximately twelve programs have been initiated or are under development.

The Software Engineering Institute (SEI), established at the Carnegie Mellon Institute in December 1984 under a contract from the Department of Defense, has as its primary mission the advancement of software engineering. One of the strategies being implemented to fulfill its mission is the promotion of software engineering education. Recent efforts of the SEI resulted in recommendations for the core content of a master of software engineering program. Twenty-one content units (see Table 5) have been identified as important for incorporation into a graduate degree software engineering program. Design of these units into courses was a task undertaken by participants at the 1988 SEI Curriculum Design Workshop (Ardis and Ford 1989). Six semester-length courses were designed; these included (1) Software Engineering, (2) Specification of Software Systems, (3) Principles and Applications of Software Design, (4) Software Generation and Maintenance, (5) Software Verification and Validation, and (6) Software Project Management.

The proposed curriculum also includes a project experience component, such as a

TABLE 5. Content Units Recommended by SEI

The Software Engineering Process
Software Evolution
Software Generation
Software Maintenance
Technical Communication
Software Configuration Management
Software Quality Issues
Software Quality Assurance
Software Project Organizational and Management Issues
Software Project Economics
Software Operational Issues
Requirements Analysis
Specification
System Design
Software Design
Software Implementation
Software Testing
System Integration
Embedded Real-Time Systems
Human Interfaces
Professional Issues

Source: Ford 1990.

cooperative program with industry, representing at least 30 percent of the students' work. Suggested electives can be categorized into five areas: software engineering subjects, such as software development environments; computer science; systems engineering; application domain; and engineering management. Figure 7 shows the structure of the proposed graduate program based on the six core courses. This structure depicts the spiral or recurring approach to the learning process. Material is presented several times. Each presentation builds on the previous one and thus increases the depth of knowledge in a given area. The undergraduate curriculum provides students with the basics of computer science and programming. The six recommended core courses build on the basics by adding depth, formal methods, and programming concepts associated with systems engineering and control and management activities. Further depth and an opportunity for specialization are provided through electives and project experience.

Since a limited number of students pursue a master's degree, providing software engineering education only at the graduate level does not address the need for software

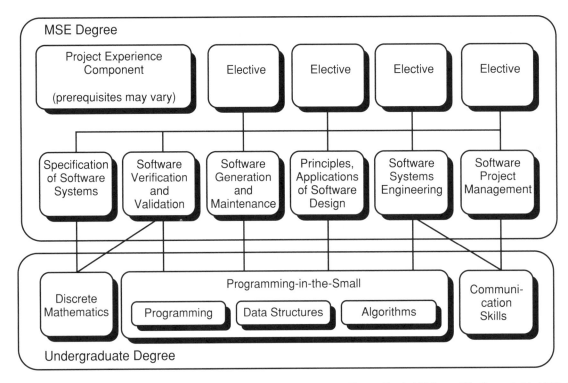

FIGURE 7. Master of software engineering curriculum structure. From Ford 1991, p. 27. Copyright 1991 by Carnegie Mellon University. Reprinted by permission.

engineering professionals. The 1990 *SEI Report on Undergraduate Software Engineering Education* (Ford 1990) presents a justification for software engineering as a legitimate engineering discipline at the undergraduate level. The report describes a strawman curriculum and assumes it should have the same basic structure as for other branches of engineering. Other curriculum design considerations are as follows:

1. The curriculum should be reasonably close to the accreditation guidelines of both the Accreditation Board for Engineering and Technology (ABET) and the Computing Sciences Accreditation Board (CSAB), as compatible. (ABET is the accrediting agency for engineering programs; CSAB, for undergraduate curricula in computing. Therefore these organizations may accredit software engineering programs in the future.)

2. The curriculum should incorporate the most up-to-date software engineering knowledge appropriate at the undergraduate level.

3. The curriculum should incorporate the material defined by the ACM/IEEE-CS joint curriculum task force to be common to all undergraduate computing curricula.

4. The curriculum should reflect appropriate pedagogical considerations, such as those in an engineering curriculum.

The ABET guidelines (see Figure 8) and the CSAB guidelines (see Figure 9) were

Requirement	ABET Content Category
25%	Mathematics and Basic Sciences
25%	Engineering Sciences
12.5%	Engineering Design
12.5%	Humanities, Social Sciences
25%	Electives

FIGURE 8. ABET accreditation guidelines for engineering programs. From Ford 1990, p. 55. Copyright 1990 by Carnegie Mellon University. Reprinted by permission.

Requirement	CSAB Content Category
22.5%	Mathematics and Sciences
33.3%	Core and Advanced Computer Science
27.5%	Humanities, Social Sciences, Arts, Other
16.7%	Electives

FIGURE 9. CSAB accreditation guidelines for computer science programs. From Ford 1990, p. 56. Copyright 1990 by Carnegie Mellon University. Reprinted by permission.

carefully considered in arriving at the proposed software engineering undergraduate curriculum structure. The proposed curriculum structure for software engineering (see Figure 10) organizes required content into four major categories: (1) mathematics and basic sciences, (2) software engineering sciences and software engineering design, (3) humanities and social studies, and (4) electives.

The software engineering curriculum structure deviates from the ABET requirements by shifting one course from the mathematics and science category to the electives area. It differs from the CSAB requirements in that it includes somewhat more technical material in the major field. Another difference is that the arts are not explicitly included with the humanities.

The SEI report examines the validity of the software engineering curricula structure by examining the potential curriculum content in each category.

The mathematics and science content should prepare students to be competent in a technological society and with the appropriate foundation for subsequent software engineering courses. Recommended mathematics and science requirements are shown in Figure 11.

The software engineering sciences should provide a bridge between mathematics or basic science and software engineering practice. Knowledge of these sciences should permit a software engineer to reason about the artifacts he or she intends to build before they are built. It should allow the engineer to design a software system that does not crash the first time it is implemented. Software engineers need a type of science that permits confidence and predictability in software systems; this kind of science should provide analytical tools or capabilities for the software engineer. The curriculum need not have engineering science and engineering design segregated in different courses. The content of the curriculum could be grouped into four categories: (1) software analysis, (2) software architectures, (3) computer systems, and (4) software process. Fourteen courses are suggested to provide the content in the four areas listed above. Rough sketches of these fourteen courses are given in the 1990 SEI report along with a proposed course sequence. In addition, within the 1990 SEI report appendix the SEI strawman courses are mapped to the ACM/IEEE-CS curriculum knowledge units, indicating in which SEI courses the ACM/IEEE-CS curriculum knowledge units are covered in most detail. The SEI report also suggests some goals for the liberal education component of a software engineering curriculum.

Requirement	Semester Hours	Content Category
22.5%	27	Mathematics and Basic Sciences
37.5%	45	Software Engineering Sciences and Software Engineering Design
25%	30	Humanities, Social Sciences
15%	18	Electives

FIGURE 10. Curriculum structure for software engineering. From Ford 1990, p. 56. Copyright 1990 by Carnegie Mellon University. Reprinted by permission.

Subject	Courses
Discrete mathematics	2
Probability and statistics	1
Calculus	2
Numerical methods	1
Physics	1
Chemistry	1
Biology	1

FIGURE 11. Mathematics and science requirements. From Ford 1990, p. 59. Copyright 1990 by Carnegie Mellon University. Reprinted by permission.

References

Ardis, M., and G. Ford. 1989. *1989 SEI report on graduate software engineering education* (CMU/SEI-89-TR-21). Pittsburgh: Software Engineering Institute, Carnegie Mellon University; Alexandria, Va.: Defense Technical Information Center.

Association for Computing Machinery and IEEE Computer Society. 1990. *Computing curricula 1991—A report of the ACM/IEEE-CS joint curriculum task force.* New York: IEEE Computer Society Press.

Data Processing Management Association (DPMA). 1991. Information systems: The DPMA model curriculum for a four-year undergraduate degree (draft). Park Ridge, Ill.: DPMA.

Ford, G. 1990. *1990 SEI report on undergraduate software engineering education* (CMU/SEI-90-TR-3, ESD-TR-90-204). Pittsburgh: Software Engineering Institute, Carnegie Mellon University; Alexandria, Va.: Defense Technical Information Center.

————. 1991. *1991 SEI report on graduate software engineering education* (CMU/SEI-91-TR-2, ESD-TR-91-2). Pittsburgh: Software Engineering Institute, Carnegie Mellon University; Alexandria, Va.: Defense Technical Information Center.

National Science Foundation. 1988. *Profiles —Computer Sciences: Human Resources and Funding* (NSF No. 88-324). Washington, D.C.: NSF.

Nunamaker, J. F. Jr., J. D. Couger, and G. B. Davis, eds. 1983. Information systems curriculum recommendations for the 80s: Undergraduate and graduate programs—A report of the ACM curriculum committee on information systems. In *ACM curricula recommendations for information systems, vol. II,* pp. 77–101. New York: ACM.

For Further Reading

American Assembly of Collegiate Schools of Business. 1991. *The American Assembly of Collegiate Schools of Business standards for business and accounting accreditation approved by the membership of the American Assembly of Collegiate Schools of Business.* St. Louis: AACSB.

————. *1990–92 AACSB Accreditation Council Policies, Procedures, and Standards.* St. Louis: AACSB.

Association for Computing Machinery. 1983. *ACM curricula recommendations for computer science, vol. I* (ACM no. 201831). New York: ACM.

————. 1983. *ACM curricula recommendations for information systems, vol. II* (ACM no. 201832). New York: ACM.

Barnes, B. H., and J. B. Rogers. 1991. Computing curricula 1991: Its implications for software engineering education. Unpublished manuscript. Washington, D.C.: Computer and Computation Research.

Carlyle, R. E. 1989. Salary survey: What are you worth? *Datamation* 35(19):22–30.

Davis, G. B., and M. H. Olson. 1985. *Management information systems: Conceptual foundations, structure, and development,* 2nd ed. New York: McGraw-Hill.

DeGross, J. I., G. B. Davis, and M. Alanis. 1989. *1989 directory of management information systems faculty in the United States and Canada.* New York: McGraw-Hill.

Frand, J. L. 1990. *Preparing business schools to meet the MoIS challenges of the 1990s: A syllabus book of the IBM Management of Information Systems 1985–1990 grant program.* Los Angeles: University of California Information Systems Research Program, The John E. Anderson Graduate School of Management.

Frand, J. L., L. Bouchard, L. N. Ray, M.L.H. Roldan, and N. G. Sutcliffe. 1990. *Preparing business schools to meet the MoIS challenges of the 1990s: A summary report of the IBM Management of Information Systems 1985–1990 grant program.* Los Angeles: University of California Information Systems Research Program, The John E. Anderson Graduate School of Management.

Parnas, D. L. 1990. Education for computing professionals. *Computer* 23(1):17–22.

Source EDP. 1991. *1991 computer salary survey and career planning guide.* Irving, Tex.: Source EDP.

Marianne J. D'Onofrio

ACCESS CONTROL

Access control protects data and programs in computer, database, and communication systems by ensuring that all access to stored objects is authorized. The effectiveness of access control depends on two premises: proper identification and authentication of the user, and correct specification and control of the access rights of the user. The first premise guarantees that no person is able to acquire the access rights of another. The second premise regulates reading, writing, and deleting of data to protect against unauthorized disclosure and modification.

Concern with regard to protecting valuable and sensitive information has increased as the use of computers becomes widespread. The study of access control has evolved rapidly since the 1970s, but the field is still unsettled. Data security issues have social, political, and economical as well as technical ramifications. The inevitable conflict between the individual's right to privacy and society's need to know and process information has been recognized. (See also ETHICS AND COMPUTERS.)

Technical studies of access control include access control policy formulation, user identification and authentication, access control to stored objects, control of information flow from one stored object to another, inference control of confidential data in statistical databases, and encryption of data stored in files or transmitted on communications channels. Recently, research on computer VIRUSES that distort data and disturb systems has been urged.

ACCESS CONTROL POLICY

An access control policy specifies desired protections against accidental and malicious threats to data secrecy, authenticity, and system availability. An access control mechanism is a particular implementation or design capable of enforcing the policy. The distinction between policy and mechanism permits independent discussions of the access requirements of a system and the way in which these requirements may be fulfilled. To protect sensitive information, the government assigns information to restricted classes and grants security clearances to individuals. A user is permitted to read only the information classified at a level equal to or lower than the individual's clearance level. Such classified information is protected by law; therefore, control of access to the information is often referred to as the *mandatory* access control policy. Independent of this requirement is the *discretionary* access control policy that specifies the rights of each user to have access to certain categories of information based on the user's need to know as defined by the application organization. A user is allowed access only to information that satisfies both access control policies.

USER IDENTIFICATION AND AUTHENTICATION

The fundamental principle of access control is that no person should be able to acquire illegitimately the access rights of another. The system must first know who is requesting access and must authenticate the individual's claimed identity. This is accomplished by identification and authentication procedures at the log-in time that require identification and password before permitting the user to proceed. User passwords can be changed and are controlled by the user. Some systems require users to change the password after a designated number of entries, and store user passwords as ciphertext that cannot be deciphered even by the systems staff. Advanced systems may use other personal characteristics such as fingerprints for authentication.

ACCESS CONTROL TO STORED OBJECTS

One of the common methods to control access to stored data is the use of an access matrix. All legitimate users and stored data objects are the active and protected entities of the matrix; rows correspond to users and columns correspond to data objects. An entry for a particular user and data object lists the access rights or privileges of the user for the data object. A control monitor prevents the user's programs from accessing a data object when the entry does not include the right. The data objects typically include files, databases, segments of memory, and programs. The rights typically include "read," "write," "add," "delete," and "execute." Most existing systems have some form of privileged mode that allows certain users full access to the whole system.

An authorization list is often used with a single object to list its legitimate users and their associated rights. It is typically used to protect owned objects. For example, the owner of a file has the sole authority to grant and revoke the access rights of other users. Locks and keys may be implemented within the list structure to provide additional flexibility and control. On the other hand, a capability list may be used to grant a user access rights to objects. A capability in the list specifies an object and a set of rights for the holder of the list. Once the capability list is granted to a user, the user's access to an object need no longer be validated by searching an authorization list.

An abstract data type encapsulates data objects and operations that manipulate the objects in a small protected domain. These objects can be accessed only through predefined operations. Use of the encapsulation concept, object-oriented languages, and database systems can implement access control constraints on data objects. A capability list provides an attractive tool for implementing abstract data types because the objects required by a program can be linked to the program by capabilities.

Multilevel data security systems have been developed for protecting sensitive government information. Within such systems, each stored object is associated with a classification label and each user is assigned a clearance label. Access is permitted only when the classification of the object and the clearance of the user are appropriately matched. Audit trails are available to record user data access activities in order to detect potential abnormalities and to hold the user accountable, since no access controls can be absolute.

Application-dependent data security is based on the user's responsibility and role in the organization. Access controls are usually implemented in query processing systems. In such systems, each user is provided with a set of restrictions that define the user's rights to certain categories of information. A user's query is modified on the basis of these restrictions before access to the database is permitted. User role–based data security is designed to handle complex and diversified access constraints often required by commercial organizations.

FLOW CONTROL OF INFORMATION BETWEEN STORED OBJECTS

Confidential data can be leaked indirectly in a multiuser system. The need to share data and programs in a database or network system creates a considerably more complex data security requirement. A user may obtain access rights from the owner and then pass them to other persons without the consent of the original owner. A legitimate user program may access a data object and later pass its contents to other programs. A "Trojan horse" (program that damages the systems on which it runs) or a computer virus lurking inside a program can perform harmful functions to copy or destroy data, and viruses may also copy themselves to contaminate or infect other data files or programs.

Flow controls deal with the rights of dissemination of access privileges and data contents. A program can be confined or made memoryless so that it cannot retain or leak its parameters. Processing of classified information may be restricted to one security level at a time, and information flow between levels is rigorously controlled. Data content is permitted to flow only within a class or upward. Flow of information can be either direct or implicit through a third party. For example, the content of A may be revealed by the condition of an if-statement when the passing of information from A to B is regulated by the if-statement. A *covert channel* is one that is not intended for information transfer but is necessary in order for the system to process the data. Covert channels must be identified and controlled, and information flow should be permitted only through legitimate channels.

INFERENCE CONTROL OF CONFIDENTIAL VALUES IN STATISTICAL DATABASES

Statistical databases such as census data are designed to prevent access to sensitive individual data while permitting users to obtain statistics about the population. A clever user can deduce confidential individual information by correlating different but overlapping statistics. Inference controls make such deduction difficult.

The ways in which statistics are released are means for controlling inferences. Macrostatistics provide only a limited subset or a normalized sample of all statistics. Microstatistics consist of individual data records, but they can be processed only by programs that have predefined query sets. Therefore, no assumptions can be made about the programs that process the data. Protection mechanisms may be applied to microstatistics by removing identification information, adding random noise to the data, suppressing highly sensitive data, deleting records with extreme values, or placing restrictions on the size of the query. The resulting statistics may be slightly distorted for higher levels of data security. Controls that provide a high level of security are not always practical for general-purpose database systems. Conflicts between the need for flexibility in statistical studies and the need for protecting individual data have been recognized.

ENCRYPTION TECHNIQUES

Encryption of confidential data stored in databases or transmitted on data communications channels is often used to protect sensitive information. Two basic types of ciphers—transpositions and substitutions—are often used in combination. (See also CRYPTOGRAPHY.)

In a simple cryptographic system, the owner of the file selects a cipher and gives the key either directly or through a secure channel to legitimate users. When the enciphering and deciphering keys are different, the system is called an *asymmetric* cryptographic system. Using this asymmetric concept, public-key systems have been developed in which each user has a public key in an open directory and a private key known only to that user. The sender obtains the receiver's public key from the directory to encrypt the plaintext and the receiver uses the private key to decrypt the ciphertext. The digital signature that authenticates the sender's message works in reverse. The sender encrypts a signature using the private key, and the receiver uses the sender's public key to decrypt and confirm the ciphered signature of the sender. In a cryptographic system, keys may be leaked through a number of possible means. Advanced systems can change keys after each message is transmitted, and automated key management systems may be implemented centrally or distributively in a computer network system.

References

Bell, D. E., and L. J. LaPadula. 1973. *Secure computer systems: Mathematical foundations and model,* ESD-TR-73-278. Bedford, Mass.: The MITRE Corporation. A formal description of the U.S. Government's mandatory access control policy.

Denning, D. E., and P. J. Denning. 1979. Data security. *Computing Surveys* 11(3): 227–49. A comprehensive discussion with an exhaustive bibliography.

Denning, D. E. 1982. *Cryptography and data security.* Reading, Mass.: Addison-Wesley. A good reference source on data security.

Department of Defense. 1985. *Department of Defense trusted computer system evaluation criteria,* 5200.28-STD. Washington, D.C.: Department of Defense. An official reference for secure computer systems evaluation.

Dobkin, D., A. K. Jones, and R. J. Lipton. 1979. Secure database: Protection against user inference. *ACM Transactions on Data-*

base Systems 4(1):97–106. A general description of protection methods for statistical databases.

Linden, T. A. 1976. Operating system structures to support security and reliable software. Computing Surveys 8(4):409–45. A comprehensive description of several common operating systems' control structures.

Merkle, R. C. 1980. Protocols for public key cryptosystems. In Proceedings of 1980 Symposium on Security and Privacy, pp. 122–33. Oakland, Calif.: IEEE Computer Society. A detailed illustration of public-key systems.

Simmons, G. J. 1979. Symmetric and asymmetric encryption. Computing Surveys 11(4):305–30. A comprehensive coverage of encryption methods.

Stonebraker, M., and E. Wong. 1974. Access control in a relational data base management system by query modification. In Proceedings of 1974 ACM Annual Conference, pp. 180–86. San Diego, Calif.: Association for Computing Machinery. A description of query modification techniques.

Ting, T. C. 1988. A user-role based data security approach. In C. E. Landwehr, ed. Database security: Status and prospects. Amsterdam: Elsevier Science Publishers. An introduction to user-role-based access controls.

T. C. Ting

ACCOUNTING USE OF COMPUTERS

Accounting consists of the record-keeping functions within an organization. Any time the organization buys or sells a product, pays its employees, or incurs an obligation, a business transaction has occurred. Accountants record, classify, and summarize these transactions. Eventually, the results are reported to a variety of people including investors, creditors, governmental agencies, and management. These people use the information contained in the reports to make important decisions such as whether to invest or loan money to the company, how much tax to assess, and changes that need to be made within the organization to operate more profitably. Therefore, accounting is a service function that provides relevant information about the activities and profitability of the company to a variety of users.

The techniques accountants have used to record, classify, summarize, and report business transactions have varied over time with advances in technology. The earliest accounting records identified were recorded on stone tablets or stone walls. Later, Egyptians recorded their business transactions on papyrus scrolls. Journals and ledgers with handwritten entries were the standard for many years. Significant changes began to occur when Herman Hollerith introduced the punched card in 1890 (see CARDS, JACQUARD AND HOLLERITH). The card was initially used by the U.S. Census Bureau. It worked so well that Hollerith left the Census Bureau and organized his own company. Eventually, his company was merged into what is known today as International Business Machines.

The computer is the most recent advance in technology that accountants have adopted to record, process, and report business transactions more efficiently. Computers are far more efficient and more accurate than human processors, punched cards, or any other technology previously used. This greater efficiency has enabled accountants to keep pace with the changing business environment.

Several changes have demanded the speed and efficiency of computer processing. First, business enterprises and institutions have become larger and more diverse. Divisionalized enterprises, huge conglomerates, multinational organizations, and giant government agencies are the rule rather than the exception. The size and complexity of organizations demand more formal methods of internal and external communication. Managers can no longer keep up-to-date on operating conditions of the enterprise on an informal basis.

Second, the pace of business activity has accelerated so that time to respond to opportunities and react to difficulties has been shortened. The need for timely information alerting management to developments inside and outside the organization has become more pressing.

Finally, the social environment in which businesses and institutions operate has shifted toward increasing government regulation and increasing demand for disclosure of financial and operating data. Without computer processing, accountants would not be able to handle the vast amount of data processing required by most medium- to large-sized organizations.

HOW ACCOUNTANTS USE COMPUTERS

The computer is central to almost every activity performed in accounting. These activities can be broadly classified into (1) financial reporting, (2) specialized reporting for management decision making, and (3) income tax reporting. Each of these areas is explored in more detail.

Financial Reporting

Business operations can be subdivided into cycles. Owners invest money in the company. Part of the money is used to acquire operating assets such as land, buildings, and equipment and part is used to acquire merchandise or provide services that are sold to customers. Merchandise or services are eventually sold, cash is collected, more merchandise is purchased, and the cycle continues. These transaction cycles have traditionally been identified with individual components of the accounting system. Typical cycles include the following:

1. Purchasing and payment cycle: Merchandise is purchased, goods are received, and an account payable to the supplier is created. Eventually, the supplier is paid for the merchandise.
2. Inventory and warehouse cycle: A record must be kept of the inventory on hand. If the inventory is used as an input to a manufacturing process, production control, calculation of unit production cost, and finished goods inventory control are relevant issues.
3. Sales and collections cycle: When merchandise is sold to a customer, an account receivable is created. Processing sales orders, maintaining a record of accounts receivable, shipping, cash collections, and sales analysis are included in this cycle.
4. Payroll and personnel cycle: Relevant information must be maintained on employees. Employees must also be paid for their services. Payroll processing, payroll taxes, personnel management, and pension plans are integral parts of this process.
5. Capital acquisition and management cycle: This cycle includes capital stock management, working capital management, management of long-term investments, fixed-asset management, and cash management.

These cycles are combined through the general ledger. Once the general ledger has been updated for the transactions recorded in each of the cycles, general-purpose financial statements are prepared. These statements, including income statement, balance sheet, and statement of cash flows, are distributed to investors, creditors, and other individuals outside the organization. They are also used as a basis to prepare income tax returns to state and federal governments.

Traditionally, computer systems have reflected this cycle approach. Individual computer files and programs were written for each cycle or for individual components within a cycle. Early computer programs were written specifically for one company. This was costly and inefficient. General-purpose software is currently available from numerous software companies for most financial reporting functions. Some of the more common applications include general ledger, accounts receivable, accounts payable, payroll, inventory, fixed assets, and cost accounting. Accountants have played and continue to play a significant role in selecting, installing, and operating these applications.

The current trend in financial accounting and reporting is to develop integrated systems with common databases. With this approach, business transactions are entered into the common database once and shared with relevant users throughout the organization. Accountants assist in building and using these large-scale databases. This role includes building controls into the system to maintain database accuracy and integrity.

Specialized Reporting for Management Decision Making

Management can obtain from the general-purpose financial statements some of the information they need to operate the business and make good management decisions. Frequently, however, there is a need for specialized management information. This may be for normal recurring-type decisions or for one-time decisions. Normal recurring decisions include budgeting, variance analysis, and operations control. One-time decisions include dropping a product line, capital investment analysis, and determining the appropriate product mix. Management looks to accountants to provide the needed information.

Some of the data that accountants need to provide useful information to management are contained in the company's computer files. There are a variety of database query languages that accountants can use to retrieve relevant data. If the data are located in a database at a distant location, communication hardware, software, and lines may be used to transmit data to the local site. If the data are located in a large computer database, they may be downloaded for processing and analysis on a mini- or microcomputer. Additional data may need to be collected and entered into the computer to assist with the analysis. Once the data are collected and in a form that the computer can process the accountant has a variety of software choices for the analysis. Some of the options most commonly used are summarized below:

Generalized packages. Generalized software packages include spreadsheets, database management systems, and statistical packages. Electronic spreadsheets are one of the most popular software packages for accountants because they simulate a columnar worksheet typically used by accountants. Numerous packages have emerged over the years, all of which have the same processing capabilities: inputting data into rows and columns, performing arithmetic calculations with the data, and defining relationships

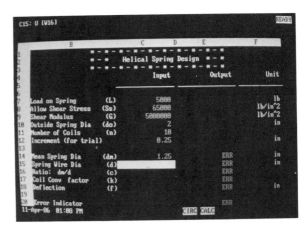

FIGURE 1. Lotus: spreadsheet screen with rows, columns, and data. *Courtesy Lotus Development Corporation.*

between the data. Figures 1, 2, and 3 illustrate data analysis using a Lotus spreadsheet. Figure 1 shows how data are entered into the spreadsheet in rows and columns. The data can be manipulated and summarized into graphs and reports as illustrated in Figures 2 and 3.

Database management systems (DBMS) software provides the user with an easy means of defining the structure of a collection of data, designing video screen formats for inputting data, maintaining the data, and producing reports. The DBMS software may suffice for the total application development effort in some cases; however, more complex situations may require interfacing DBMS files with other packages or programs custom

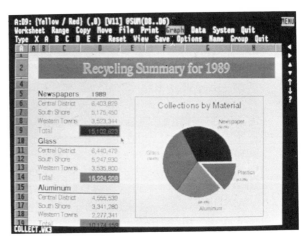

FIGURE 2. Lotus: graph screen. *Courtesy Lotus Development Corporation.*

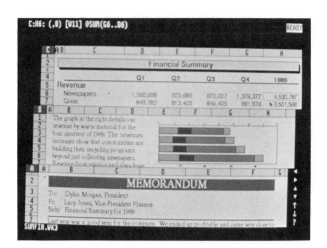

FIGURE 3. Lotus: screen with financial summary, graph, and memorandum. *Courtesy Lotus Development Corporation.*

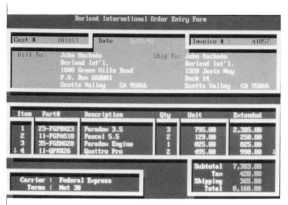

FIGURE 5. PARADOX: order entry form and part of database table. *Courtesy Borland.*

written by the user. Figures 4, 5, and 6 illustrate some of the typical screens encountered when using PARADOX, a popular database software package. Figure 4 shows the relational database in the background with a query in the center of the screen. Figure 5 contains a typical input screen for entering data into the database. Data from the database can be extracted using a query, manipulated, and summarized into a report or a graph as illustrated in Figure 6.

Statistical packages are available for all computer sizes from micro to mainframe. They perform most statistical analyses including regression analysis, correlation analysis, and analysis of variance.

Special accounting applications. There are a variety of software products for specific accounting applications. Budgeting, for example, is a process that accountants and management perform on a regular basis. Programs to assist with the budgeting process have been developed and are marketed by a variety of software companies. Consolidation of financial statements is another specialized accounting application.

Custom programs. If a generalized software package or a special accounting application can be used, it is generally less costly and more efficient. Sometimes, however, the problem is so unique that a custom program is required. The accountant may write the program or be assisted by a computer programmer. Third-generation languages such as COBOL, FORTRAN, C, BASIC, APL, or PL/I are frequently used.

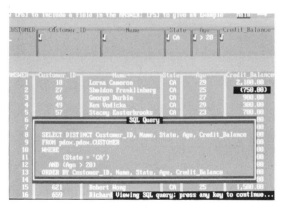

FIGURE 4. PARADOX: relational database with SQL query. *Courtesy Borland.*

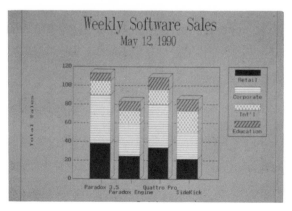

FIGURE 6. PARADOX: graph screen. *Courtesy Borland.*

Income Tax Planning and Preparation

Most individuals and almost all business organizations are required to file an income tax return annually. Approximately 35 to 40 percent of most certified public accountant firms' revenue comes from assisting individuals and organizations with tax planning and with preparing tax returns. Tax accountants use the computer in three main ways: tax return preparation, tax research, and tax planning.

Tax return preparation. Software packages are available for use on microcomputers or on computer networks that can be accessed with a terminal, modem, and communication lines. These software packages accept from the accountant important information about the organization or individual filing taxes. W-2 wages, interest income, dividend income, itemized deductions, and exemptions are the types of data that the accountant enters into the program. The program calculates the tax liability and prepares the tax return that is submitted to the federal or state government.

Tax research. The tax code becomes more complex with each new revenue act passed by Congress. An accountant must not only know the tax code, but also must be able to identify Internal Revenue Service (IRS) rulings and court cases that are relevant to a particular tax problem. Tax libraries that contain these items have been computerized and offered through a variety of services. Most of them contain a full text of the IRS code, treasury regulations, judicial cases, and revenue rulings. The accountant forms a search request that consists of a code section or key words that relate to the tax problem under consideration. The computer searches through the computerized tax library and identifies all the code sections, regulations, cases, and rulings that fit the search request. The accountant is on-line with the computer so that the request can be modified to expand or reduce the breadth of the search. Once the desired information has been located the accountant can print it for documentation and future reference.

Tax planning and analysis. Accountants use the computer for a variety of tax planning and analyses. Estate planning, gift planning, retirement planning, and differences between accounting methods selected for financial reporting and tax reporting are examples of the computer analyses performed in this area. For example, an accountant may be asked by a client to determine how much retirement income will be received each month if $2,250 is invested in an Individual Retirement Account (IRA) each year for the next 20 years at an 8 percent interest rate. Some specialized packages can be purchased for these analyses, but generalized accounting packages or customized programs are frequently used.

IMPACT OF COMPUTERS ON ACCOUNTING CONTROLS

One of the responsibilities of accountants is to verify the accuracy and integrity of the data, data processing, and reported information. Prior to computer processing, accountants relied on a trail of paper documents to support the development of financial reports. Responsibilities were separated among individuals so that the work of one person verified the accuracy of the work of another person. By computerizing the accounting process the computer has removed much of the trail of paper documents by storing all of the data in computer files and has replaced most of the people. Controls are still important, but the computer does much of the controlling.

Verifying the accuracy of the data as they are entered into the computer is an important control point. If bad data are entered into the computer, the files will be incorrect and financial reports will be misleading. The accountant and the computer work together to perform edit checks and control totals on the input data to verify their accuracy.

Many controls are built into the computer programs to verify the accuracy of the processing. Accountants work with computer programmers and systems analysts to identify the controls that are required and to test for their accuracy prior to installing the programs for accounting use.

THE LINK BETWEEN ACCOUNTING AND COMPUTER SCIENCE

Accountants rely on engineers for the development and maintenance of computer hardware. Accountants rely on computer scientists and information systems personnel for the development of much of the computer software. This includes computer operating systems, utility routines, assemblers, compilers, and communication software. Accountants use the hardware and software developed by engineers and computer scientists to develop and operate business and accounting applications.

For Further Reading

American Institute of Certified Public Accountants (AICPA), Computer Applications Subcommittee. 1984. *Introduction to microcomputer processing capabilities: A management advisory services special report.* New York: AICPA.

Clark, F. J. 1986. *The accountant and the personal computer.* Englewood Cliffs, N.J.: Prentice-Hall.

Computers in Accounting. New York: Warren, Gorham & Lamont. This journal has ten issues per year. Each issue has several good articles on computer applications for accounting data processing.

Cushing, B. E., and M. B. Romney. 1990. *Accounting information systems.* 5th ed. Reading, Mass.: Addison-Wesley.

Jensen, D. L., ed. 1985. *Information systems in accounting education.* Columbus: Ohio State University.

Perry, W. E. 1982. *The accountant's guide to computer systems.* New York: Wiley.

Sommerfield, R. M., G. F. Streuling, R. L. Gardner, and D. N. Stewart. 1989. *Tax research techniques.* 3rd ed. New York: AICPA.

Tutton, J. 1987. Computer accounting—The way forward. *Accountancy,* Mar., pp. 149–50.

Wilkinson, J. W. 1985. *Accounting and information systems.* 2nd ed. New York: Wiley.

Wilson, A. 1987. Accounting with expert systems. *The Accountant's Magazine,* July, pp. 18–19.

J. Owen Cherrington

ACOUSTICS

See Sound, Computers and

ADA

The Ada programming language began development in the 1970s at the initiative of the Department of Defense (DoD), to aid with the software crisis in complex military systems. Software for complex military systems is usually late, costs more than originally estimated, does not work to original specifications, is unreliable, and is difficult and costly to maintain. Furthermore, several other problems were associated with the general software crisis:

- Software costs increased while hardware costs decreased.
- Software maintenance nearly tripled original development costs.
- Error corrections were extremely costly.
- Software tasks were becoming more complex, but no adequate tools existed to deal with the problems.
- Support tools for each machine were different.
- Software was not reusable on different systems.
- There existed a lack of adequate management and software development tools.

The DoD therefore decided that a language was needed to reduce software development and maintenance costs, to provide portability of software and programmers, and to encourage sound software engineering practices for applications such as multi-level security and embedded computer processing. For these reasons, the DoD sponsored the development of the Ada programming language. Through a combination of modern software engineering methods (structured design and programming, top-down development, strong data typing, object-oriented techniques, and modularity) and common support tools, the DoD sought to develop software that was reliable, maintainable, less costly over the life cycle, and portable.

1. *Reliable.* The software can detect and possibly recover from an error or failure conditions in operation, and special measures have been taken to prevent errors in analysis, design, and code implementation.
2. *Maintainable.* The software product has been constructed such that the structure and organization of the system are clear. Modification of the system can be done with relative ease.
3. *Less costly over the life cycle.* Cost reduction occurs only over the life of the product. Ada is concerned primarily with projects of long duration that will be modified and enhanced continually. Cost savings during development, if any, are "icing on the cake." Ada provides a set of automated tools to aid software developers at various phases during the life cycle. Examples include compilers, linkers, loaders, code auditors, and programming support libraries.
4. *Portable.* The use of Ada will promote the movement of software from one type of computer to another (provided that each computer has an Ada compiler) because the language has been standardized, and because implementation dependencies can be localized or isolated.

PRIMARY APPLICATIONS

Ada is a general-purpose, high-order programming language with considerable expressive power. The Ada programming language was designed to support a wide variety of applications hosted on a wide variety of computing systems. Some examples of these applications include systems programming, real-time programming, data processing, and software being developed by project teams. Ada was initially designed to support software development for embedded computer systems. Embedded computer systems form a part of larger, primarily computational systems, such as weapons systems. The applications that Ada was designed for require real-time control of many concurrent processes, automatic error recovery and fail-safe execution, and interfaces to many complex nonstandard input/output devices.

The Ada language contains features that are specifically intended for functional decomposition and data abstraction. These techniques are used during the development of large software systems to reduce the amount of detail needed to understand them. Ada also concentrates the programmers' attention on the design and planning of software interfaces. As a result, programmers should be able to spend more time on the early phase of software design, and less time on the software integration and testing phases.

With Ada, program modules are organized into various types of entities referred to as packages, tasks, and subprograms. This form of organization improves clarity and allows tight control over the visibility of names.

The Ada language is modular in both a logical and a physical sense. Ada's logical modularity associates specific operations with each data type and tightly controls the visibility of variables. It also ensures that changes to the implementation part of a module do not affect other routines that use a module, as long as the module interface specification remains constant. From the management point of view, the modern software engineering principles embodied in Ada provide increased control over the design process.

Software written in Ada should be simpler to maintain than that written in FORTRAN because of its readability and understandability. Ada lessens the problems of finding software errors and correcting them (because of its readability). Ada is also expected to improve software reliability because of the extensive checking that occurs at both compile time and run time. Ada is especially important because it supports object-oriented development. An object is a container that holds data (e.g., constants and variables). In addition to a value, every object has a property called type, which defines the kind of data that the object may hold. An object can accept only values that fit the definition for its type.

ADA FEATURES

Ada has several features to encourage the expression of reusable software components. The features include combinations of packages, subprograms (procedures and functions), and tasks called program units. All program units have a similar form, consisting of the specification and the body.

1. *Specification.* The specification describes what the program unit does. This information is "visible" to (can be referenced by) this and other program units.
2. *Body.* The body details how a program implements an algorithm or structure. This information is "hidden" from (cannot be directly referenced by) other program units.

Reliability is increased because interface (specification) errors can be easily detected. Maintainability is increased because changes to the implementation (body) can be done without affecting user program units. During the development of Ada, emphasis was placed on program readability over ease of writing. For example, the rules of the language require that program variables be explicitly declared and their types be specified. The syntax of the language avoids the use of encoded forms in favor of more English-like constructs.

THE PACKAGE

The Ada package is a basic structuring unit that groups functionally related data and program units (encapsulation). The package provides for reusable software components, and increases maintainability because the

effect of changes made to the code can be localized. Packages provide the ability to do the following:

- Write huge programs (such as embedded systems) that can be understood piece by piece.
- Divide a programming project among teams independently. This is important because embedded systems are typically developed by large teams of tens or even a few hundred people. If each had to be aware of the others' work, total chaos would result.
- Write general software components that can be incorporated into many programs. As algorithms and data structures are used in many different embedded systems, software costs can be reduced by plugging these general software components into new systems instead of building the components from scratch each time. A package is a collection of related entities including variables, type declarations, procedures, and functions. Packages are the basic building blocks of large programs. Unlike a subprogram, a package does not exist to be executed.

A package provides a collection of computational resources that may be used by one or more other program components. These resources (the variables, type declarations, procedures, and functions) should be placed in the same package if they are closely related and are meant to be used in conjunction with each other.

A package has two features: the interface and the implementation. In Ada, a sharp distinction is drawn between the interface of a package and its implementation. The interface explains how the entities provided by the package to the outside world are to be used. The implementation explains how these entities work externally. Only the interface of a package is relevant to the user of the package. The package interface includes (among other things) the following:

- Declarations of variables available to all users of the package. A package may provide variables that can be set or examined by all users of the package.

- Types defined in the package for use outside the package. A package may define new types or subtypes. Program units using the package may refer to these types or subtypes in variable and subprogram declarations, for example.
- Procedure names, parameter names, and parameter types for procedures defined in the package for use outside the package.
- Function names, parameter names, parameter types, and result types for functions defined in the package for use outside the package.

The package implementation includes (among other things) the following:

- The algorithms for all procedures and functions described in the interface.
- Subprograms used internally by those procedures and functions, but not called directly from outside the package.
- Types and variables used internally to implement the procedures and functions described in the interface.

A package has two parts: (1) The package specification is essentially a list of declarations of entities to be used outside the package, and (2) the package body describes the implementation.

THE TASK

Tasks are entities whose executions proceed in parallel. Each task can be considered to be executed by a logical processor of its own. Different tasks (different logical processors) proceed independently, except at points where they synchronize. Some tasks have entries. An entry of a task can be called by other tasks. A task accepts a call of one of its entries by executing an accept statement for the entry. Synchronization is achieved by rendezvous between a task issuing an entry call and a task accepting the call. Some entries have parameters. Entry calls and accept statements for such entries are the principal means of communicating values between tasks.

Tasks allow multiple threads of control. A task operates in parallel with other parts of the program. It is written as a task specification, which specifies the name of the task and the names of formal parameters of its entries, and a task body, which defines its execution. A task unit is one of the kinds of program unit. A task type is a type that permits the subsequent declaration of any number of similar tasks of the type. A value of a task is said to designate a task.

RENDEZVOUS

When either a called task or its caller arrives at a rendezvous point, the one that arrives first waits for the other one. During the rendezvous (the execution of the statements in the accept) the caller is suspended. The caller resumes execution after the rendezvous is completed.

EXCEPTIONS

This section defines the facilities for dealing with errors or other exceptional situations that arise during program execution. Such a situation is called an exception. To raise an exception is to abandon normal program execution so as to draw attention to the fact that the corresponding situation has arisen. Executing some actions, in response to the arising of an exception, is called handling the exception. An exception declaration declares a name for an exception. An exception can be raised by a raised statement, or it can be raised by another statement or operation that propagates the exception. When an exception arises, control can be transferred to a user-provided exception handler at the end of a block statement or at the end of the body of a subprogram, package, or task unit.

CONTROL FLOW

When an exception is raised, normal program execution is suspended. If there is a handler for the exception in the innermost frame, control is transferred to it. If there is no handler, the exception is propagated up to the frame that caused the frame incurring the exception to be invoked—the caller in the case of a subprogram, or the surrounding frame in the case of a block. If a handler is found there, it is executed. If not, the exception is propagated up one more level. If no handler is found in the program, the underlying operating system terminates the program (and can take other actions such as issuing error messages). When a handler is found, the execution of the handler replaces execution of the frame containing the handler (and any lower-level frames).

SUBPROGRAMS

There are two kinds of subprograms: procedures and functions.

- Subprograms enable programmers to modularize programs.
- Subprograms enhance software readability.
- Subprograms enhance software maintainability.
- Subprograms are analogous to FORTRAN subroutines and functions, but are more rigorous.
- Subprograms provide an abstract name for some algorithm or computation.
- Subprograms separate the implementation of the algorithm from the specification of its interface.
- Subprograms avoid duplication of code executed in more than one place.

PROCEDURES

Procedures define a sequence of actions, and are invoked with a procedure call.

FUNCTIONS

Functions define a computation that returns a value. The value may be of any type. Functions terminate on execution of a return statement.

GENERICS

A generic is a program unit that is either a generic subprogram or a generic package. Generic units permit programmers to parameterize subprograms and packages to form templates of units. Nongeneric subprograms or packages can be obtained from these templates. These resulting units are said to be instances of the original generic unit. A generic unit is declared by a generic declaration. This form of declaration has a generic formal part declaring any generic parameters. An instance of a generic subprogram is a subprogram, and an instance of a generic package is a package. As generic units are templates, they do not have the properties that are specific to their nongeneric counterparts. For example, a generic subprogram can be instantiated but it cannot be called.

The first form of generic parameter declaration declares generic formal objects. The type of a generic formal object is the base type of the type denoted by the type mark given in the generic declaration. A generic parameter with several identifiers is equivalent to a sequence of single generic parameter declarations. A generic formal object has a mode that is either in or out. In the case of the absence of a mode, the mode "in" is assumed. A generic parameter declaration that includes a generic type definition or a private type declaration declares a generic formal type. A generic formal type is considered to be distinct from all other (formal or nonformal) types.

EXAMPLES OF ADA CODE: IMPLEMENTATION OF THE STACK DATA TYPE

For the implementation of the stack data type, several functions and procedures must be defined:

Procedure Push	Push an item onto the stack.
Procedure Pop	Pop the top item off the stack.
Function Is_Equal	Return true if two stacks are the same.
Function Depth_Of	Return the current number of items on the stack.
Function Is_Empty	Return true if there are no items on the stack.

Function Top_Of	Return the item on the top of the stack.
Procedure Clear	Remove all the items (if any) from the top of the stack and make the stack empty.
Procedure Copy	Copy the items from one stack to another stack.

In this example, a stack object is represented as a linked list, in which each node contains a single item as well as a pointer to the next node. In Ada, this type can be written as

```
type Node is
  record
    The_Item  :  Item;
    Next      :  Stack;
  end record;
```

Here is an implementation of each operation in Ada. For procedure Clear, we need to set the stack object to point to null:

```
procedure Clear  (The_Stack  :  in out
    Stack) is

begin
    The_Stack := null;
end Clear;
```

To push an item on the stack, we first create an object of type Node using an allocator. The node record is then given the value of the item, and the Next component is set to point to the beginning of the list. We then point the stack object to this new node:

```
procedure Push (The_Item : in Item;
    On_The_Stack  :  in out Stack ) is

begin
    On_The_Stack := new Node' (The_Item →
    The_Item,
    Next → On_The_Stack);

exception
    when Storage_Error →
      raise Overflow;

end Push;
```

For the Pop operation, we just throw away the first node:

```
procedure Pop (The_Stack : in out Stack) is

begin
    The_Stack := The_Stack.Next;

exception
    when Constraint_error →
      raise Underflow;

end Pop;
```

For the Copy procedure, we first check for the case in which the source stack is empty. If the stack is empty, we set the destination stack to null also. Otherwise, we create new nodes in the target stack corresponding to nodes in the source stack. We also declare two local variables as indices into the source and destination stacks to make sure that the items are copied in the correct order.

```
procedure Copy (From_The_Stack : in
    Stack;
    To_The_Stack : in out Stack) is

    From_Index : Stack := From_The_Stack;
    To_Index    : Stack;
begin
  if From_The_Stack = null then
    To_The_Stack := null;
  else
    To_The_Stack := new Node' (The_Item
      →
      From_Index.The_Item,
      Next      → null);
    To_Index := To_The_Stack;
    From_Index := From_Index.Next;

    while From_Index /= null loop
      To_Index := new Node' (The_Item →
        From_Index.The_Item,
        Next      → null);

      To_Index := To_Index.Next;
      From_Index := From_Index.Next;
    end loop;
  end if;
exception
    when Storage_Error →
      raise Overflow;

end Copy;
```

In the function Is_Equal, we again must declare two local variables to use as indices into the left and right stacks. Next, we go through the items in both stacks. If at any point a match does not exist, we return false. We repeat this loop until the Left_Index is null. If the Right_Index is also null, then both stacks had the same depth, and the function terminates normally.

```
function Is_Equal (Left : in Stack;
    Right : in Stack) return Boolean is

  Left_Index    : Stack := Left;
  Right_Index   : Stack := Right;

begin

  while Left_Index /= null loop
    if Left_Index.The_Item /=
    Right_Index.The_Item then
      return False;
    end if;

      Left_Index := Left_Index.Next;
      Right_Index := Right_Index.Next;
  end loop;

    return (Right_Index = null);

exception
  when Constraint_Error →
    return False;

end Is_Equal;
```

The function Depth_Of visits every item of the stack just like the function Is_Equal; however, instead of testing for similarities, we just increment a counter, so that we will know how many items are on the stack.

```
function Depth_Of (The_Stack :   in Stack)
    return Natural is

  Count  : Natural   := 0;
  Index  : Stack := The_Stack;

begin

  while Index /= null loop
    Count := Count + 1;
    Index := Index.Next;
  end loop;

  return Count;

end Depth_Of;
```

The function Is_Empty will return true if The_Stack is not pointing to any node:

```
function Is_Empty (The_Stack   : in Stack)
    return Boolean is

begin

  return (The_Stack = null);

end Is_Empty;
```

The function Top_Of simply returns the value of the item in the top node of the stack:

```
function Top_Of (The_Stack   : in Stack)
    return Item is

begin

  return The_Stack.The_Item;

exception
  when Constraint_Error →
    raise Underflow;

end Top_Of;
```

This package body of the implementation of a basic stack can now be compiled into a library of reusable software components, which is one of the most powerful features of the Ada language.

SUMMARY

Ada is a general-purpose, high-order programming language with considerable expressive power. The Ada programming language was designed to support a wide variety of applications as well as a wide variety of computing systems. It combines the best of practical language constructs with a combination of sound software engineering fundamentals. It is the combination of these features that makes Ada such a powerful computer language.

For Further Reading

Ada Information Clearinghouse Newsletter. This quarterly publication is a powerful resource on the Ada language. It is free and can be obtained from Ada Information Clearinghouse, c/o IIT Research Institute, 4600 Forbes Blvd., Lanham, MD 20706-4320.

Booch, G. 1987. *Software components with Ada: Structures, tools, and subsystems.* Menlo Park, Calif.: Benjamin/Cummings.

———. 1987. *Software engineering with Ada.* Menlo Park, Calif.: Benjamin/Cummings.

———. 1991. *Object oriented design with applications.* Redwood City, Calif.: Benjamin/Cummings.

Foreman, J., and J. Goodenough. 1987. *ADA adoption handbook: A program manager's guide.* Pittsburgh, Pa.: Carnegie Mellon University, Software Engineering Institute, technical report, CMU/SEI-87-TR-9, Version 1.0. Excellent resource on all phases of adopting and using Ada.

Lee, K. J., and M. S. Rissman. 1989. *An object-oriented solution example: A flight simulator electrical system.* Pittsburgh, Pa.: Carnegie Mellon University, Software Engineering Institute, technical report, CMU/SEI-89-TR-5.

Warren Moseley

ADAPTIVE DEVICES

See Disabled, Technology for the

ADVERTISING

See Marketing and Marketing Research, Computer Use in

AEROSPACE, COMPUTER APPLICATIONS IN

Aerospace is defined as the Earth's atmosphere and the space beyond considered as a whole. The exploration of space began in the late 1950s, with computers involved as essential tools in every stage of the process. Today, computers used in support of aerospace operations range from small microcomputers used for word processing, planning, and data management to large mainframe computers for sophisticated in-formation and control systems. This article examines the use of computers at the U.S. National Aeronautics and Space Administration (NASA) as a representative sample of computer applications in aerospace organizations worldwide.

Computer applications at NASA can be summarized as follows:

Microcomputers:
- Electronic mail.
- Word processing.
- Spreadsheets.
- Database management.

Minicomputers:
- Computer-aided drafting.
- Computer-aided design and engineering.
- Computer graphics and word processing.

Mainframes:
- Payroll.
- Budgets.
- Shuttle operations (configuration management).
- Launch control.
- Software development.

Special applications:
- Electronic printing.
- Electronic publishing.
- Photographic process monitoring.
- Modeling/design.
- Simulation.
- Instrumentation/data logging.
- Telemetry.

COMPUTER-AIDED DESIGN AND ENGINEERING

NASA uses two computer-aided engineering graphics software packages, PLAID and TEMPUS, which model objects like Space Station modules and the astronauts who will work in the Space Station environment. By studying the graphic models, specialists can find ways to ensure that the people in space interact efficiently and safely with machines. Unusable designs can be modified quickly and easily before scale models are ever built. PLAID is also useful for Space Shuttle mission planning and spacewalk simulation. The supporting hardware for these programs is a VAX 11/785 computer with a micro-VAX workstation networked to the main VAX.

Future planning is only part of the role of the computer in space travel. The astronauts, engineers, and technicians who operate the Space Shuttle rely on the launch processing system, onboard systems, and the Shuttle Data Processing Complex, all highly automated systems with programs using billions of calculations. These computerized systems are unique to space flight.

COMPUTERS RELATED TO THE SPACE SHUTTLE

Launch Processing System

At Kennedy Space Center in Florida, the launch processing system (LPS) is the computer-controlled overseer for prelaunch checkout and sequencing of the launch countdown of the Space Shuttle. The Space Shuttle, which carries people, equipment, laboratories, and satellites to and from Earth orbit, consists of an orbiter about the length and weight of a DC-9 jetliner, a huge external tank carrying propellants for the orbiter's main engines, and two solid rocket boosters. The external tank is the only component that is newly fabricated for each mission.

During assembly and checkout the LPS monitors the solid rocket boosters, external tank, Space Shuttle main engines, and the complex systems of the orbiter through extensions called hardware interface modules (HIMs). More than 20,000 test parameters exist for just the ground-support equipment of the Space Shuttle.

The LPS consists of three major subsystems: checkout, control, and monitor; central data; and record and playback. The large-scale host computers are Honeywell 66/80s. The checkout, control, and monitor subsystem hardware is produced by Martin Marietta. The distributed minicomputers are Model 245 machines produced by Modular Computer System, Inc.

Checkout, Control, and Monitor Subsystem

The checkout, control, and monitor subsystem consists of operator-manned consoles in the firing rooms, minicomputers, a data transmission system, a data recording area, HIMs, a common data buffer, and front end processors.

Each subsystem operator position in a firing room has its own keyboard and visual display system. The information the human operator needs to make her or his decisions is displayed on screens resembling home color TV sets. Charts and diagrams are shown, pointing out where the unexpected condition exists, and using different colors to indicate the degree of urgency. A "red" signal means that immediate human attention is needed to prevent possibly serious consequences.

All consoles are orchestrated to work together on major tasks through an integration console at the front of the firing room. The small computer with each console has an on-line disk storage capacity of 5 million words to hold all the test procedures to be conducted by that operator and his or her assistants.

A master console in the firing room provides the controlling link for transfer of the real-time software from the central data subsystem, where it is compiled, to the network of up to 100 parallel minicomputers and microprocessors throughout the LPS. Approximately 430 minicomputers are used during a regular launch.

Central Data Subsystem

The central data subsystem consists of four large-scale computers that store test procedures, vehicle processing data, a master program library, historical data, pretest and posttest data analyses, and other data. These computers make an immense amount of data immediately available to the smaller computers of the checkout, control, and monitor subsystem, which have much less storage capacity.

The central data subsystem has two major interfaces. The real-time interface receives the vehicle and ground support control and monitor subsystem. The video simulation interface provides simulated programs in the firing rooms without actually having a Space Shuttle to test against.

Record and Playback Subsystem

The primary function of the record and playback subsystem is to record unprocessed Space Shuttle instrumentation data during tests and launch countdowns. These recordings can then be played back for posttest analysis when firing room personnel wish to troubleshoot Space Shuttle or LPS problems.

COMPUTERS USED ON BOARD THE SPACE SHUTTLE

The Space Shuttle contains five identical general-purpose computers (GPCs). The hardware and software are redundant so that the avionics system, which controls most of the Space Shuttle systems, can withstand multiple failures. Four of the computers are designated to run the primary avionics system software (PASS) and one computer is known as the backup flight system (BFS). The PASS and BFS are coded with different software although they perform the same guidance navigation and control (GNC) functions. This is to protect against a generic PASS software failure (undetected software errors). The PASS computers can run a variety of software programs such as GNC, systems management (SM), or payloads operation. During the noncritical phases of the mission, the PASS computers can be loaded or reconfigured to contain these programs as desired. During ascent and entry PASS has no system management capabilities. The BFS general-purpose computer runs GNC and SM software concurrently. Backup flight system management is a subset of the capabilities of PASS management required for dynamic flight. The fifth computer acts as a backup flight control system during ascent and entry. The backup flight system is powered off on orbit. It can be quickly activated and assume orbiter control if the PASS GNC software should fail or cannot maintain control of the orbiter.

The five computers are interconnected through digital data buses. During critical flight phases, such as ascent and entry, the PASS computers operate as a cooperative, redundant set to perform GNC tasks. Critical GNC sensor data, available to all redundant set GPCs, are independently verified by each GPC.

Each of the computers operating in a redundant set operates in synchronized steps and cross-checks results of processing about 440 times per second. If a computer operating in a redundant set fails to meet the synchronization requirements for redundant set operations, it is removed from the set.

The Space Shuttle computer is a modified model of an IBM AP-101, an extension of the System/4 PI line that IBM developed for aerospace application. Each computer has 106,496 words (36 bits per word) of memory and is composed of two parts: a central processing unit (CPU) and an input/output processor (IOP). The CPU performs all the arithmetic and logic operations for both parts; it controls the flow of data into and out of the main memory and controls the activity of the IOP. The CPU is capable of performing fixed-point binary and fractional operations and floating-point hexadecimal fraction calculations. The CPU uses a microprogrammed instruction set of 154 instructions. For typical Space Shuttle programs, the CPU can perform approximately 400,000 operations per second. Both the CPUs and IOPs are in enclosures measuring 7½ inches high by 10⅛ inches wide by 19½ inches long; each weighs 57 pounds.

The five CPUs and IOPs are located in the crew compartment middeck avionics bay and are cooled by fans. By today's standards, the computers are not very fast, but their advantages rest in their size (that of a bread box) and their ability to withstand the rigors of space flight.

COMPUTERS USED FOR LANDING THE SPACE SHUTTLE

The microwave scan beam landing system (MSBLS) provides highly accurate three-dimensional position information to the orbiter to compute steering commands to maintain the spacecraft on the nominal flight trajectory during the landing phase, beginning approximately 15 kilometers (8 nautical miles) from the runway at Edwards Air Force Base in California or the Kennedy Space Center in Florida.

The orbiter landing system is composed of three independent MSBLS sets. Each set consists of a Ku-band antenna, a radio frequency assembly, and a decoder assembly. Each Ku-band transmitter–receiver, with its decoder and data computation capabilities, determines the elevation angle, the azimuth angle, and the range of the orbiter with respect to the MSBLS ground station.

The orbiter MSBLS initially acquires the ground station while the orbiter is on the heading alignment circle at an altitude of approximately 4,300 meters (14,000 feet). Final tracking occurs at the terminal area energy management automatic landing interface at approximately 3,000 meters (10,000 feet) and 15 kilometers (8 nautical miles) from the MSBLS ground station. Angle and range data from the MSBLS are used by the guidance, navigation, and control system from acquisition until the orbiter is over the runway approach threshold at an altitude of approximately 30 meters (100 feet). From this point to touchdown, radar altitude provides elevation (pitch) guidance.

Although the computerized landing system is available to astronauts returning from space missions, Space Shuttle commanders have the option of bringing in the spacecraft in manual mode. In 1983, a head-up display (HUD), similar to the displays used on military aircraft, was installed in the Space Shuttle *Challenger* and later incorporated into the Shuttle fleet. The HUD helps the crew fly to exactly the right spot for landing, which is particularly important when heavy payloads are aboard and braking and rollout are important considerations.

The HUD is a set of two small glass screens, an optical combiner, positioned such that when the crew looks out the window they see through the glass all essential instrument data and landing information without ever taking their eyes off the real world as they swoop down and glide in for their landing. This system eliminates the moment of *transition,* as pilots call it, when they shift their attention from the instruments that have guided them through poor visibility to that point in the approach where they can see the runway and use visual, out-the-window references for control to landing. Images are generated by a small cathode ray tube and passed through a series of lenses before being displayed to the crew on the combiner glasses as lighted symbology. The HUD computer will also generate a simulated runway until the spacecraft breaks through any cloud layers obscuring the real runway.

MISSION CONTROL CENTER COMPUTERS

Space Shuttle flights are monitored and controlled from NASA's Mission Control Center at the Johnson Space Center in Texas. The Shuttle Data Processing Complex provides the processing of command, trajectory, and telemetry functions. The complex includes five IBM 308X-class machines, one dedicated to classified data processing, one dedicated to nonclassified data processing, and three capable of supporting classified or nonclassified data processing and associated support equipment. The two dedicated machines are designated as flight support hosts (FSHs) and the other three are designated as real-time hosts (RTHs). The three RTHs provide support for the Space Shuttle real-time command and control functions for secure and nonsecure missions. The remaining host functions are supported by the two FSH computers, one designated as the Space Transportation System (STS) FSH and the other designated as the Department of Defense (DOD) FSH. A control monitor isolation system prevents configuration of equipment processing classified data to equipment processing nonclassified data.

Host 1 is the STS FSH, and it is an IBM 3081-K with 32 megabytes of storage. Attached to it are two communications controllers allowing it to communicate with on-site and off-site facilities. Also attached are thirteen magnetic tape drives and ten disk drives with a capability of storing 25,200 million bytes of data. Hosts 2, 3, and 4 serve as the RTHs and are IBM 3083-JXs with 32 megabytes of storage each. Attached to each are two disk drives capable of storing 5,040 million bytes of data.

During flight operations, one RTH supports the mission operations computer functions; during mission-critical periods a second RTH supports the dynamic standby computer function. The capability exists to switch computer functions in 400 milliseconds should the mission operation computer fail.

The host computers perform the following functions in support of the Shuttle data processing:

- *Network communications.* This subsystem sets up the interface controller to receive data from the worldwide tracking network and to separate and route telemetry and tracking data to the proper destination.
- *Trajectory.* During launch and landing procedures, radar tracking data samples are received and processed from remote tracking sites. The radar data are converted to vehicle position and velocity. Flight controllers can view the trajectory computed from radar data and that calculated by the onboard computers and telemetered down. Both are compared with nominal trajectory. If the predefined maneuver is inadequate, a new one is computed for uplink to the onboard computers.
- *Telemetry.* These programs can receive measurements from onboard sensors or onboard computers of orbiter telemetry data and from tracking site recorders. The subsystem converts these raw data to engineering data for viewing by the flight controllers. Each parameter can be checked against predefined limits and an out-of-limit condition is clearly shown on the displays. An audible alarm is triggered for critical conditions. Flight controllers can request several historical parameters at a time or a plot to represent trends.
- *Telemetry data retrieval and reduction.* Processed telemetry data are continuously stored on both magnetic tape and disk. Every 4 hours, a standard set of historical reports are generated and placed on microfiche.
- *Command and control system.* This subsystem formats and uplinks data to the onboard computer systems. Flight controllers use this subsystem to send real-time commands to onboard systems such as the ones

configuring the communication system. In this way, flight controllers can back up the crew functions or relieve the crew of tasks more of concern to ground controllers.

Other support programs include the software checkout system and the hardware checkout system. Other functions within the RTH and FSH computers support reconfiguration of the Mission Control Center, maintenance of program libraries, collection of statistics, configuration management of workstations, and validation and tracking of message traffic to and from the host workstations across a local area network.

COMPUTERS FOR SIMULATIONS

Every manned space flight requires intensive preparation. Astronauts and flight controllers take part in "dress rehearsals" for each mission. A high-fidelity simulated mission environment provides training in the interaction between the crew and mission control personnel, responses to stressful situations, flight replanning, validation of flight procedures and plans, ground uplink, and evaluation of system performance. This concept of integrating crew and flight control team simulations was first established during Project Mercury and has evolved through all manned-flight programs since then.

In the Shuttle Mission Simulator (SMS) computer facility there are thirty-two computers that serve the fixed base simulator and the motion base simulator. The host computers are two large-scale UNIVAC 1100/44 computers that contain the majority of the simulation math models. Each computer is in a 4 × 2 configuration, with four computational arithmetic units and two input/output units. The UNIVAC 1100/44 is capable of executing an average simulation mix of approximately 2 million operations per second. One computer is assigned to each station—the fixed base simulator and the motion base simulator.

The support computer consists of 20 Perkin-Elmer 8/32 minicomputers, which gather and transfer data as well as house the math models for tracking, telemetry, and communication simulations. The execution capability of the Perkin-Elmer 8/32 is approximately 350,000 operations per second; however, the input/output and computational capabilities of these units are not identical and vary according to the task performed.

The simulation interface device houses the flight general-purpose computers (GPCs) for the two crew stations and data-handling equipment that interfaces with the simulation interface device intelligent controller. Real GPCs must be physically present because they are too fast to be simulated by the UNIVAC. The GPCs are IBM AP 101 computers, just as they are on board the Space Shuttle. The difference between the Space Shuttle GPCs and the SMS GPCs is that the Shuttle GPCs have a nonvolatile memory and an iron ferrite core, whereas the SMS GPCs have a volatile memory and a monolithic core.

AMES CENTER SUPERCOMPUTER

The world's most powerful supercomputer, capable of crunching out a quarter of a billion calculations a second, operates at the NASA Ames Research Center in Mountain View, California. Project officials for the Numerical Aerodynamic Simulation (NAS) system emphasize that NAS is not a set of computer hardware, but an evolving capability comprising people, skills, powerful central processors, a nationwide communications network, and a range of computation, scheduling, and output devices.

The NAS program is being used primarily for aeronautical research and development of new generations of ultrahigh-speed aircraft. The Cray 2 supercomputer with a 256-million-word memory can tackle the most demanding aerodynamics computations ever attempted. The NAS features high-speed processing networks with workstations, graphics capabilities, and long-haul satellite and land-line communication links between research centers.

A national network allows off-site scientists, at 27 locations, access to the system via satellite or high-speed terrestrial lines. More than 250 scientists and engineers use the system.

The NAS building is equipped with an array of systems for the optimal functioning of the computers. The 90,000-square-foot structure has a 14,000-square-foot central computer room, bronzed windows that dim entering sunlight, and a climate-cooling system twenty-eight times more powerful than that in a normal office building of the same size.

The major research projects selected for the NAS focus on aerodynamics and hypersonic flight research. The high-speed supercomputers are used to solve complex aerodynamical equations so that aircraft configurations can be tested by "flying the aircraft in the computer." The NAS reduces both the time and the costs of developing new aircraft. Other NAS projects include astrophysics, weather modeling, computational chemistry, and other large-scale computational problems.

Ray Coorpender

AGRICULTURAL USE OF COMPUTERS

See Farming, Computer Use in

AIRLINE RESERVATION SYSTEMS

In the United States alone, in 1989, there were approximately 450 million airline passengers, almost one and one-quarter million passengers per day. On the average, it is as if each of the approximately 250 million residents of the United States takes almost two airplane trips per year. By the year 2000, the International Air Transport Association (IATA) estimates that there will be some 800 million airline passengers per year in the United States and some 2.2 billion airline passengers per year globally. Passenger demand is so great that almost all airlines have turned to computerized reservation systems (CRSs) to keep track of their passengers.

Several hundred commercial airlines operate worldwide, but there are fewer than a dozen major CRSs that are used in travel agencies. All systems handle all large airlines and dozens of smaller ones. The major systems are listed here:

- SABRE (Semi-Automatic Business Research Environment), installed in 1961 and located in Dallas, was developed by IBM for American Airlines (AA). SABRE is the grandfather, both temporally and conceptually, of modern systems. It was first marketed to agencies in 1976.
- PARS (Passenger Airline Reservation System), founded by Trans World Airlines (TWA) with later participation by Northwest Airlines, and DATAS II, developed by Delta Airlines, have been merged into Worldspan.
- System One (Houston), developed by Eastern Airlines, was historically the fourth system to be developed (after SABRE, Apollo, and PARS) and serves Texas Air (Continental Airlines and Eastern), which owns 50 percent of the system. General Motors, via Electronic Data Systems (EDS), owns the other half.
- Apollo (Rosemont, Ill.) is owned by Covia, which is controlled by United Air Lines (UAL). Other partners are Alitalia, British Airways, KLM, Swissair, USAir, and Air Canada.
- Gemini (Toronto), the principal system serving Canada, is being rewritten using Apollo technology. Covia owns one third of Gemini.
- GETS is owned by several smaller airlines with little money. It is based on Gabriel, a system created by the Société Internationale de Télécommunications et Aéronautique, a company that provides communications services for international airlines.
- Amadeus (Madrid) is owned primarily by Air France, Iberia Airlines, Lufthansa German Airlines, Scandinavian Airlines System (SAS), and some minor partners elsewhere in Europe and in Africa and Asia. Amadeus derives from System One technology.
- Galileo (Swindon, England) is owned primarily by Alitalia, British Airways, KLM Royal Dutch Airlines, Swissair, Covia, and,

again, minor partners elsewhere in Europe. United Air Lines has an interest in, and access to, Galileo, which derives from Apollo technology. (Most other national carriers in Western Europe use Amadeus or Galileo, thus pushing out such older systems as Travicom [England].)
- Abacus, based in Singapore, derives from PARS, and serves Cathay Pacific and Singapore Airlines.
- Infini, a joint effort of Abacus and All Nippon Airways (ANA) for use only in Japan, was in the planning stages in the early 1990s.
- Fantasia, based in Sydney, Australia, serves Qantas Airlines.
- Axess and Able serve, respectively, Japan Air Lines (JAL) and ANA.

Customer demand and operational efficiency explain the links in ownership of existing systems. For example, Abacus and Worldspan own 5 percent of each other so that Abacus' link to Infini will provide access to Japan for Worldspan. Increased linkage is expected. Amadeus is actively seeking CRS partners for clients who want links in the United States and Canada. And System One has been asked by SERTEL, the transportation ministry of Mexico, to automate the Mexican airlines' reservations systems.

Each linkage development in the CRS industry points to increased globalization of service. Although it is anticipated that more rather than fewer systems will exist by the end of the century, it is expected that all systems will be increasingly interconnected as airline traffic grows. These interconnections should increase the ease with which our ever more mobile population can make travel arrangements through local travel agents or directly through airlines.

BACKGROUND

But what is a CRS? The short answer is that it is simply a very large database (see DATA) accessed by a very large telecommunications network. But it wasn't always that way. In the 1920s, a prospective airline passenger reserved a seat by calling, or visiting, the appropriate airline at the airport, where the passenger's name was entered on a paper list or, possibly, even a seating chart. In the 1930s, airlines often had offices downtown. The seating chart went from the office to the airport when the office closed for the day. The airlines thrived as the telephone industry thrived.

OVERBOOKING

When nonmilitary traffic boomed in 1945 immediately after World War II, overbooking became a problem because, although it was as easy to telephone to cancel a reservation as to make that reservation, almost no one did so. The no-show problem became so acute that, in 1946, a penalty system was implemented. This system failed primarily because of noncompliance by several airlines. Another penalty system, implemented in 1954 on coach travel, also failed for the same reason. A $3 charge on passengers who failed to cancel reservations was instituted in September 1957. Although this plan did serve to reduce the number of no-shows, it came under severe attack by mid-1958 by several airlines who claimed that the no-show penalty system was too costly to administer and that it had already served its purpose as a psychological club to deter no-shows.

By the late 1950s, however, the problem of overbooking was so critical, because of the lost revenue associated with empty seats, that IATA stepped in. Effective April 1, 1958, it announced, outgoing international passengers on airlines serving the United States, Canada, Mexico, and Cuba would be required to pay for their tickets at least 72 hours in advance of their flight, or within 48 hours after the airline had confirmed their reservation. In addition, passengers out of the United States or Canada were required to confirm continuing or return reservations within certain periods. Clearly it had become imperative that there be a seat for every passenger who wanted one and a passenger in every seat; however, as pressure mounted for the airlines to ensure some absolute minimum number of empty seats, the prob-

lem of overbooking, particularly on some vacation routes, increased. But compensation to bumped passengers was rarely adequate. In the early and mid-1960s, this compensation was limited to a range of $5 to $40 based on 50 percent of the price of the affected ticket.

Overbooking remained a live issue through the 1960s, 1970s, and 1980s, however, particularly during holidays. As passengers learned that airlines overbooked, they began making multiple reservations to increase their chances of actually getting a flight. Various rules were proposed, adopted, modified, or abandoned over the years. At present, an oversold flight's passengers are bumped in a particular order that is headed by volunteers. Voluntarily and involuntarily bumped passengers are compensated, based on the price of their ticket, and given free tickets on an alternate flight to their destination. (A flight is overbooked if reservations exceed seat capacity. A flight is oversold if more customers actually show up at departure time than can be accommodated by the aircraft; that is, a flight can be overbooked but, if there are enough no-shows, not oversold.)

THE BEGINNING

During the 1950s, the time required to reserve a seat increased. Seat reservations were still made by telephone, but the paper seating chart gave way to an electronic signaling system, connected to a central reservation office, which ticket agents used to clear available space with other cities served by the same flight.

One such system, installed in July 1952, reduced the time required to reserve a seat and more closely controlled the airline's inventory of seats. In this system, ticket agents determined seat availability by inserting a destination plate into a handset and pressing buttons to specify the date of the flight and the number of seats desired. If the requested seats were available, a small light bulb on the handset turned on. In effect, this system merely used electronic signals to replace oral messages, and electronic rather than manual methods in filing and searching for information.

Another system, Transactor, developed by Trans Canada Airlines (TCA) and Ferranti Electric, Ltd., in 1957, simplified the reservation process through use of an IBM-size mark sense card. Such moves into unit-record equipment became more critical as, for example, Trans Canada Airlines' reservation system grew to 3.5 million separate transactions required to process 250,000 Trans Canada Airlines passengers each month.

During the late 1950s and the 1960s, reservation systems became more automated. Early in 1958, United Air Lines installed an electronic system built around two IBM RAMACs (Random Access Methods of Accounting and Control). The system could handle 60 million reservations per year by keeping a running inventory of seat reservations on approximately 1,000 flights per day. Connected to eighty U.S. cities via private telephone lines or leased teletype lines, each RAMAC had a random-access memory unit consisting of a stack of fifty 2-foot-diameter, double-sided disks revolving at 1,200 rpm. Resembling a high-speed jukebox, each of the unit's disks could hold 100,000 characters, so each RAMAC could hold 5 million characters. Although the changeover to RAMAC cost them some $150,000 plus $19,000 per month IBM rental fees, United Air Lines operated the system for only about 2 years before installing a completely new system.

Also, early in 1958, Braniff Airlines connected its teletype network directly to a reservation system built by Teleregister Corporation. The first of its kind in the industry, the system consisted of magnetic drum storage capable of holding data on up to 60,000 flights up to 6 months in advance, although Braniff required data on only 250 flights per day for 31 days in advance. Teleregister's system, RESETRON (REServations by ElecTRONics), was powered by two processors that ran simultaneously and in parallel to provide cross-checking capability. Teleregister operated this system for other airlines such as Trans World Airlines, which retained domestic flight data for 31 days in advance and overseas data for up to 6 months.

THE BIRTH OF MODERN COMPUTERIZED RESERVATIONS SYSTEMS

In late 1961, American Airlines installed SABRE running on dual IBM 9090s (highly modified 7090s). The largest electronic data processing system ever devised for business use, SABRE linked 1,100 reservation sites in sixty-one cities over 10,400 miles of leased telephone lines and could handle 7,500 seat reservations per hour. Conceptually, the system was quite simple. If a customer requested a ticket from New York to Chicago, the ticket agent selected from a file an information card that showed all New York–Chicago flights and inserted it into the agent's console. When the agent pushed buttons for the date requested and the number of seats, the console displayed lights next to all flights that had that number of seats left. The agent then pushed the "sell" button and used the console typewriter to enter the passenger's name, home and business phones, and time limit for ticket pickup. All information was displayed on the console printer. During the entire interchange, the 9090 monitored the actions of the ticket agent to ensure against error. The immediate advantage to American Airlines of SABRE was to make canceled space available for resale within 3 seconds. This enhanced ability to manage its seat inventory helped American Airlines increase ticket sales to cover much of SABRE's $5 million per year rental/maintenance cost.

SABRE reduced the work load required to handle ticket sales, seat inventory, and passenger records. It was the first CRS that captured, electronically, the two most important reservation records: the passenger name record and the seat inventory. Previously, such information was maintained manually on cards. With each American Airlines city maintaining seat inventories for its originating flights, a reservation might require twelve people, twelve or more procedural steps, and two or three hours of work.

Also in 1961 Air France installed AIRS (Automatic Integrated Reservation System). Designed to record information on all seats (empty, reserved, or waiting list) on some 9,000 Air France flights scheduled up to 6 months in advance, AIRS depended for its memory on six 300-track drums and sixty magnetic tapes. Developed by two International Telephone and Telegraph (ITT) affiliates in Europe, AIRS allowed Air France's 500 ticket agents to process seat assignments almost simultaneously. AIRS had a 5-second response time for inquiries about any of several hundred thousand passengers recorded at any given time. British Overseas Airways Corporation (BOAC) used a similar system that was also developed by a European subsidiary of ITT.

Another 1961 installation was Instamatic, which was developed by Teleregister for United Air Lines. Instamatic, claimed at the time to be the largest integrated electronic data processing system in the business world, was installed on June 2, 1961. It allowed 3,000 United Air Lines ticket agents in 100 locations to confirm reservations in less than 1 minute, a considerable reduction from the 45 minutes required earlier. Located in Denver, the system was linked to the ticket agents with some 12,000 miles of communications circuits.

Some airlines tried to limit the need for complex reservation systems, however. TWA and Allegheny offered a no-reservation service on some northeastern flights. In this scheme, passengers simply showed up at the airport to buy a ticket for the next available flight in much the same way that passengers board other public transportation vehicles such as municipal buses.

In late 1964, after almost 10 years of planning, Pan American Airways (Pan Am) installed PANAMAC 1, which, running on dual, specially adapted IBM 7080s, linked 114 Pan Am cities on six continents. The system handled 75,000 requests per day for reservations and information as well as various in-house bookkeeping chores. In late 1974, Pan American upgraded to PANAMAC 2 running on dual IBM 370/158s under IBM's specially designed operating system Airline Control Program (ACP).

In early 1965, Scandinavian Airlines System installed the first Europe-wide reservations system and the world's first remote-load control system. SASCO, running on two IBM 1410s with 1301 disk storage, served twenty cities in twelve countries. Additional,

though slower, access to the system was provided by some 4,000 teletype machines around the world.

In late 1965, British European Airways began installation of Beacon (BEA COmputer Network) using dual Univac 494s with a 4.8-microsecond cycle time and 32K 30-bit words of primary memory. In 1968, British Overseas Airways Corporation installed IPARS (International PARS) running on IBM 360/65s. In 1974, British European Airways and British Overseas Airways Corporation merged to form British Airways, whose reservations system, Travicom, and its business subsystem, BABS (British Airways Business System), ran on dual IBM 370/168s and, by the late 1980s, accounted for about 90 percent of ticket sales in England.

One of the most ambitious computerized systems of the 1960s was Trans World Airlines' PARS, installed in mid-1968. Designed to handle both fully automated, centralized reservations and a total management information system (MIS) (see MANAGEMENT INFORMATION SYSTEMS), PARS ran on a dual-processor Burroughs D830 computer system using JOVIAL for the reservation system and COBOL for the MIS function. PARS was linked to more than 2,000 computer terminals via a nationwide telecommunications network. Because of the D830's processing speed of 4 million operations per second, each agent terminal had essentially instantaneous access to 650 million characters of flight and passenger information stored on forty disk file systems. One of the most important characteristics of PARS was the elimination of almost all written records. The MIS function provided management reports that contained summaries of flight information, but written records concerning specific passengers or flights were no longer required. Passenger and flight data were stored on disk for several months in advance. Within days of the landing of a particular flight, that set of data was deleted to make room for passenger information for future flights. Passenger information grew more complex as well. PARS eventually allowed Trans World Airlines to record seat assignments, automobile rentals, hotel/motel reservations, and even special meal instructions. Trans World Airlines also used PARS to plan flights, make flight movement reports, and schedule crews and meals.

A similarly ambitious system was PNR (Passenger Name Record) developed by Eastern Airlines. Installed in July 1968, PNR ran on three IBM 360/65s, a changeover from a Univac 494 system. Billed as the "world's largest and newest" reservation system, PNR had storage for over one million passenger records by using each system's 524K primary storage, three large core storage units (over 6 million characters each), twenty 2314 disk systems (over 200 million characters each), 676 movable disk packs (over 25 million characters each), and twenty-four nine-track tape drives. Eastern had obtained PARS from IBM in 1966. After extensive modification, which included the addition of PNR capability to PARS, Eastern renamed its system Programmed Airlines Reservation System One, later shortened to System One. By 1971, Eastern was already planning a changeover to dual IBM 360/195s, the largest IBM computers at the time; however, Continental Airlines also claimed that its SONIC (Systemwide On-line Network for Information Control) was the first CRS to use third-generation computers (dual IBM 360/65s) and was also the first to use cathode-ray tubes (CRTs) rather than hard-copy printers for its ticket agents.

EQUIPMENT UPGRADES

The late 1960s saw several switchovers to third-generation machines. American Airlines phased in dual IBM 360/65s for SABRE. Alitalia opened ARCO (Automatic Reservations and COmmunications) also using the IBM systems. Later, in 1972, Alitalia added an IBM 370/155 to its triple 360/65s and added freight control to ARCO. Delta Airlines phased in Deltamatic 2. Western Air Lines initiated Acu-Res on dual IBM 360/65s. Trans World Airlines had planned to switch PARS to triple Burroughs D830s; however, software development problems resulted in TWA ultimately moving to IBM 360/65s. United Air Lines switched to triple Univac 1108s to handle messages, material

control, and flight information and planning, but moved their airline reservations to PARS on IBM 360/65s. Pacific Southwest Airways switched to dual NCR Century 200s. Even Aeroflot, in 1968, installed a Minsk-23 computer in Moscow, a move that reduced from 5 to 6 hours to only a few minutes the time required to respond to telegraphed reservation requests from other Russian cities. In the early 1970s, a Siren-1 system capable of handling all departures from Moscow (up to 1,100 flights over a 30-day period) replaced the Minsk-23 (up to 500 flights over a 20-day period). In 1975, Aeroflot added a Univac 1106-2, running Air France software, for international flights. In the late 1980s, however, Aeroflot contracted with SABRE to market Aeroflot's international flights.

During the 1970s, a number of new systems were installed, and most existing systems were substantially upgraded. In 1970, Japan Air Lines (JAL) installed JAL-COM 2, which allowed ticket agents to sell space on any Japan Air Lines international flight. JALCOM 2 ran IPARS (International PARS) on dual IBM 360/65s. JALCOM 2 was preceded by JALCOM 1, which still handled domestic Japan Air Lines flights.

Cathay Pacific Airways entered the CRS market in 1971 with CPARS (Compact PARS), a less complex (and less expensive) alternative to IPARS. Designed to serve small or regional airlines, CPARS was, by 1975, being used by Braathens-SAFE (Norway), VASP (Brazil), Gulf Air (Bahrain, Qatar, Oman, and the United Arab Emirates), and Avianca (Colombia). The original dual IBM 360/30s were replaced in 1973 with a single IBM 370/135.

In North America, several smaller airlines used Continental Airlines' SHARES (SHared Airline REservations System). Based on PARS technology and running on dual IBM 360/65s, SHARES served Air California, Aeromexico, Alaska Airlines, Aloha, British Caledonian, Frontier, Hughes Airwest, Mexicana, Ozark, Piedmont, and Wien Air Alaska as well as Continental.

In 1976, United Air Lines introduced Apollo, its travel agency CRS. By the end of the 1970s, United Air Lines had upgraded to an IBM 3033, American Airlines to an Am-dahl V/7 and later to a V/8, Trans World Airlines to an IBM 3033, and Eastern to dual IBM 3033s. Eastern's 3033s carried System One; its old 360/195s were used to run reservations systems for Southern, Air West, Ozark, and Piedmont. By the late 1980s, System One had twenty IBM mainframes, mostly 3090s, in four data centers to handle System One traffic.

EUROPE

In mid-1987, a group of 21 airlines in Europe realized the difficulty of achieving the agreements necessary to institute a single European CRS. One reason given was equipment incompatibility, although there were political considerations as well. Most European airlines used either IBM or Unisys (Burroughs/Univac merger) mainframes; a common system would, presumably, have to use a single supplier. Accordingly, the airlines split into two groups to develop two separate systems, Amadeus and Galileo, a solution more satisfactory, perhaps, than a single system (because of increased competition), but certainly preferable to six or ten or even twenty-one CRSs.

TRAVEL AGENTS

Historically, CRSs had been reserved for use by each airline's own ticket agents or, in the case of interline passengers, by connecting airlines' ticket agents. From the late 1960s through the mid-1970s, there was industry-wide interest in a single CRS to handle reservations for all airlines; however, it finally became clear that agreements between industry members (because of competitiveness fears) and the federal government (because of antitrust fears) could not be forged. In 1967, the airlines decided to increase productivity by allowing access to their own individual systems by travel agents. Leading the pack as usual, American Airlines tied eighty-seven travel agents and businesses to SABRE in late 1967, thus perhaps precipitating the interest of other airlines in the travel agent and business market. By the mid-1970s, both United Air Lines and American

Airlines had established a significant presence in the burgeoning travel agent market.

Initial acceptance of automation by travel agents was relatively slow. In February 1979, only 2,000 of some 14,000 registered travel agents were automated. By June 1980, about 4,000 agents had joined one of the CRSs. By late 1983, about 80 percent of 22,000 agents had joined a CRS, with about 14,000 of these joining Apollo or SABRE and accounting for up to 60 percent of airline bookings and ticketings. By the late 1980s, about 95 percent of all travel agents had signed on to one of the five major CRSs. Of these 35,000 agents, about 36 percent had joined SABRE, 25 percent Apollo, 18 percent System One, 12 percent PARS, and 9 percent DATAS II. Each of these agents had an average of nearly four terminals.

For Further Reading

AA computer to handle 7,500 bookings an hour. *Airlift,* Dec. 1959, 23:23.

Airlines plan common reservation system for travel agents. *Management Services,* Sept. 1967, 4:11.

Davies, R. E. G. 1972. *Airlines of the United States since 1914.* Washington, D.C.: Smithsonian Institution Press.

Donoghue, J. A. 1983. Reservations systems likely to be disciplined. *Air Transport World,* Sept. 1983, 20:24–25, 29–30.

Edwards, M. 1978. British Airways provides supersonic response with global data system. *Communications News,* Aug., 15:38–41.

Emme, E. M., ed. 1977. *Two hundred years of flight in America.* San Diego, Calif.: American Astronautical Society.

Feldman, J. M. 1984. Airlines pondering future dealings with travel agents. *Air Transport World,* July, 21:19–20, 23, 26–27.

———. 1989. Global CRS: Choosing up sides. *Air Transport World,* Aug., 26(8):32–38.

Gifford, D., and A. Spector. 1984. The TWA reservation system. *Communications of the ACM* 27(7):650–65.

Jakubauskas, E. B. 1958. Adjustment to an automatic airline reservation system. *Monthly Labor Review,* Sept., 81:1014–16.

Jenkins, W. E. 1969. Airline reservation systems. *Datamation*, March, 15:29–32.

Maulsby, G. F. 1971. Planning and implementing a major systems conversion. *Data Processing Magazine* 13:26–29.

McLellan, V. 1979. Airlines cope with a crisis. *Datamation* 25:78, 80–81.

McWilliams, G. 1988. Data are passengers at System One. *Datamation* 34:90.

———. 1987. PS/2 flying high in reservations systems. *Datamation* 33:24–26.

Minini, D. J. 1969. Implementing the very large applications-software package. *Datamation* 15:141–42, 144.

New airline data processing system to handle 180,000 reservations per day. *Computers and Automation*, July 1961, 10:3B–4B.

Pan Am to open worldwide reservations system. *Computers and Automation*, Dec. 1964, 13(12):54.

Rek, B. 1987. Computer reservations controversy spreads. *Interavia*, Aug. 1987, 42:819–20.

SABRE—Electronic airlines reservation system. *Systems*, June 1967, 8(6):23–25.

SABRE—Realtime benchmark has the winning ticket. *Data Management*, Sept. 1981, 19:26–28.

SAS reservations system links 12 European countries. *American Aviation*, March 1965, 28:59–60.

Snow, A., and B. A. Weisbrod. 1982. Consumer interest legislation: A case study of Nader v. Allegheny Airlines. *Journal of Consumer Affairs* 16:1–22.

Solberg, C. 1979. *Conquest of the skies.* Boston: Little, Brown.

Strong speaker line-up for Geneva CRS symposium. *Interavia*, April 1988, 43:292.

Tipton, S. G. 1947. *The air transportation industry.* Boston: Bellman.

TWA takes giant step toward automation. *American Aviation*, Feb. 1966, 29:67–68, 70.

Grady Early

AIRPLANES

See Aviation, Computer Use in

ALGOL 60 AND ALGOL 68

Algol stands for algorithmic language, and, as the name implies, it is used for expressing algorithms (or problem solutions) to a computer. The basic purpose for developing Algol was to have a language tool that would lend itself to the solution of complex, computational processes with a high degree of structure. Such a language tool would make the program development and program correction (debug) process easier than it had been with less structured languages such as FORTRAN. Algol was developed by an international group of computer people between 1957 and 1960. Several improvements and modifications have been made in Algol since 1960, but what became known as Algol 60 was basically formed as it was published in the May 1960 issue of the *Communications of the Association for Computing Machinery (ACM)* in the article entitled "Report on the Algorithmic Language Algol 60," edited by Peter Naur. Algol 60 is a precursor to the more recent Algol 68, which was published in 1969. There were seven representatives including Peter Naur who held a final preparatory meeting at Mainz, Germany, in December 1959 to prepare a final report on Algol. At the same time, in the United States, anyone who wished to was requested to send changes or corrections to the *Communications of the ACM*, where the changes would be incorporated and published. These comments and the report previously mentioned became the basis for Algol 60.

The committee responsible for Algol 60 continued deliberations through the 1960s, and it soon became apparent that Algol 60 contained several features that could be improved. Some of the suggested improvements included better handling of input and output (transput) especially with regard to alphabetic character strings, additional syntax options for loop structures, the inclusion of the CASE command, and others. As a result of the various deliberations, Algol 68 was developed to include the aforementioned improvements, and was defined in "Report on Algorithmic Language Algol 68," by A. van Wijngaarden, B. J. Mailloux, J. E. L. Peck, and C. H. A. Koster, and subsequent to their efforts, several other groups worked on various compilers for the Algol 68 language. The most successful of these projects is the Algol 68R compiler developed by a team at the Royal Radar Establishment, Malvern, England. The Algol 68 language grew somewhat in popularity, especially in the academic community, because of its ability to state lengthy and involved problems in a structured way. Although the concepts of structured programming and modular program design were still in their infancy at the time the Algol 68 language was developed, the language syntax made use of these methods better than any other language during the 1960s. The structured programming concept means that a program should be designed using a prescribed set of programming structures (sequence, selection, and repetition) and should avoid where possible the use of the GOTO command. Modular design means that a program should be broken down into functional units to simplify the programming process.

PRIMARY APPLICATION

The primary application of the Algol language is in the solution of complex, computational processes that often involve iterative processes, that is, many problems in science and engineering. For example, the process of determining the factorial of a number requires successive determinations of products until the multiplier is reduced to one (i.e., the factorial of 5 is $5 \times 4 \times 3 \times 2 \times 1$). As mentioned, Algol is a precursor to the more popular and modern Pascal and C languages; therefore, the basic syntax of many of the Algol commands is quite similar to those of Pascal and C. The Algol language compiler works well with computers that have a limited memory size because of its "dynamic memory allocation" feature. With this feature command blocks (or segments of commands) can be set up so that certain variable areas can be shared by other command blocks, thus saving memory space. This feature was especially attractive during the 1960s and early 1970s when memory was extremely expensive. Also, applications re-

quiring mathematical functions and very complex problems requiring many levels of program detail and conditions were easily solved using this structured language.

EXEMPLARY SYNTAX

The syntax of Algol is discussed on the basis of the basic symbols of the language, arithmetic expressions, program construction, loops, conditions, and transput.

Basic Symbols of the Language

The basic symbols of Algol include the letters of the alphabet in both upper- and lowercase. The digits consist of the values 0 through 9. Other symbols include $+ - \times / ^\wedge . , : := ; ( ) [ ] = < >$.

Numbers

A number is represented in its general format with a sign and a scale factor to the base 10. The value $+5.456712_{10}-4$ illustrates an Algol number in scientific notation. A number can also be stated as integer or real. Examples of integer values are 45, 567, -555, and $+344$. Examples of real numbers are 0.6644, 3.14, $+0.710$, and -3.00002.

Identifiers

An identifier is a name given to represent a memory area; they are usually called variables. An identifier may contain any sequence of letters or numbers, but must contain at least one letter. There is no limit to the size of an identifier, and the name can be chosen freely; however, the following sequences of letters may not be used as identifiers as they are reserved for special purposes. This is only a partial list of Algol-reserved words:

abs	exp	sqrt	arctan
ln	sin	sign	entier

Arithmetic Expressions

The arithmetic expression (or assignment statement) is constructed from numerical constants and identifiers (or variables). The assignment of numerical values is handled by the use of the assignment symbol ":=". The variable identifier is to the left and the expression is to the right of the assignment symbol. The statement would appear in the form V := E, where V represents the assignment variable and E represents the expression. A few examples of the arithmetic expression or assignment statement follow.

```
VOLUME := 3.14 × RADIUS ^ 2 × HEIGHT;
CIRCUM := PI × DIA;
COMMISSION := SALES × .03;
```

Construction of a Program

A program consists of declarations and statements. A declaration is the part of the program that further defines a variable and is nonexecutable. A statement is an executable command given to the computer. The statements of the computer are divided up into simple statements and compound statements. A simple statement has the form V := E, and a compound statement has the form

begin S;···S; S **end**

Note that the compound statement starts out with the word *begin* and ends with the word *end.* The statements within this block are delimited by a semicolon except for the last one before the "end" statement. As a program will have both declarations and statements the program has the form

begin D; D;···D; S;···S; S **end**

where D stands for any declaration and S represents any statement. The program is divided into two parts: (1) the declaration part followed by (2) the statement part. Figure 1 presents as an example a complete program that reads a computer record that contains a radius of a circle and then computes the circumference and area using the appropriate formula. Subsequently, the radius, circumference, and area are printed.

Loops

Practically any program will need to repeat the execution of a set of commands. It is rare

```
begin  real r, circum, area;
    read (radius) ;
    circum  := 2 X pi X radius;
    area := pi X radius X radius;
    print (radius, circum, area)
end
```

FIGURE 1. A program that computes the circumference and area of a circle.

that a program will perform a single calculation and then stop as shown in Figure 1. The typical problem application involves the execution of the same set of commands a number of times. This looping process is necessary in many different situations. For instance, a number of records in a payroll file must be processed one after the other to produce paychecks, or an iterative process is necessary on a *single variable* supplied to the computer. For example, determining the factorial of the number 7 will require six iterations to complete the computation ($7! = 7 \times 6 \times 5 \times 4 \times 3 \times 2 \times 1$). The first iteration multiplies 7×6. The second iteration multiplies this first product 42 (7×6) by 5. This continues until the multiplier is reduced to one. The repetition or loop process is represented in Algol using a controlled loop structure. A variable is introduced as the controlled or loop variable, and the contents of the loop variable will control the number of iterations. The general form of the statement is

for V := E **step** E1 **until** E2 **do** S

where V is the loop variable, E is an expression representing the initial value of V, E1 is an expression representing the increment value of V, and E2 is an expression representing the maximum value of V. An expression can be a single constant value, the name of a variable itself, or a more complex arithmetic expression. The statement after the "do" command, represented by S, is to be executed until the maximum condition (E2) occurs. The identifier S could represent a single statement or a compound statement. An example of the general form previously discussed is

for ctr := **1 step 1 until max do S**

where *ctr* is the variable to increase, varying it from one, increasing it by one (step value) until the variable called *ctr* is greater than the content of the variable called *max*. Figure 2 illustrates a simple looping procedure where the program reads in a value and determines its factorial. This idea has been previously discussed as an application that requires an iterative process. The identifiers called VAL, MAX, and ANS are declared integers. The value is read to an identifier called VAL. The original value VAL is stored at an identifier ANS, which becomes the accumulator that will hold the sum of the products. This assignment places the first value into the accumulator. The value called VAL is saved away at another variable called SAVEVAL in order to print the original value later (as VAL is altered inside the loop, it loses its original value and it is not available for printing). The identifier called MAX is set equal to one less than VAL (i.e., if the value is 7 then it will require six iterations to determine the factorial). MAX contains the maximum number of iterations. The statements within the loop cause the current value to be multiplied by one less than the current value, and their product is accumulated into the ANS identifier. Then the content of VAL is decreased by one so that the appropriate value will be available in VAL for the next time through the loop when VAL is again multiplied by one less than itself.

```
begin
  integer val, max;
  read (val) ;
  max  := val − 1;
  ans  := val ;
  valsave := val ;
  For ctr  := 1 step 1 until max do
    begin
      ans := ans X (val − 1) ;
      val := val  − 1
    end;
  print (valsave, ans)
end
```

FIGURE 2. An Algol program that determines the factorial of a number.

Conditional Statements

The comparison of two values is often an integral part of a computer program. Certain processing activities are carried out only under certain conditions. For example, a value may be tested to be sure it is a number before using it in a subsequent calculation, or an identification code (e.g., a student classification code that contains 1, 2, 3, or 4) must be a specific value before a calculation is carried out. The various forms of the conditional expression follow.

format 1   **if** condition **then** statement;
format 2   **if** condition **then** statmt1 **else** statmt2;

In a computer application involving shipment of goods, the shipping charge may be based on the distance it is shipped. An example describing this calculation follows:

Example in   if distance < 500
Algol 60   then chg := .08
                      else chg := .12;

Example in   if distance < 500
Algol 68   then chg := .08
                      else chg := .12
                  fi

The example in Algol 68 shows the use of the "fi" statement (endif).

Transput

The process of reading data and printing data is first discussed as it applies to Algol 60, and then this discussion is followed by alternative print formatting using Algol 68. The simplest form of the read statement has already been used in Figure 1. From Figure 1, the command

read (r);

causes a value to be read from an input record into a memory area identified by the identifier called *r*. The command

read (NUM, TYPE, A, B);

reads four values from an input record into four memory areas specified by the identifiers NUM, TYPE, A, and B. The record must contain four separate values, and they must be delimited by either a space or a comma. A sample record to be read by the read statement above might look like the one that follows:

0030, 1, 50.0, 10.0

The 0030 is read into the identifier called NUM, the value 1 is read into the identifier TYPE, the value 50.0 is read into the identifier A, and the 10.0 is read into the identifier B.

The print command is shown in its simplest form as follows:

print (NUM, TYPE, A, B, AREA)

This command causes the contents of the identifiers NUM, TYPE, A, and B to be printed on a single line. A typical line of printed output as a result of the execution of the statement above might appear as

0030 1 50.0 10.0 500.0

The data from the identifiers are printed in the same order as shown in the print command. A drawback of the Algol 60 print command is that alphanumeric string data must be printed with the use of an accompanying format statement. This is a very cumbersome limitation of Algol 60. Algol 68 does allow the printing of string data within the print command itself. For example, the following print command of

print (NUM, "RECTANGLE", A, B, AREA);

would print essentially the same as shown before except that it prints the string constant "RECTANGLE" after the NUM identifier. Also, both input and output can be handled through formatted transput. For an excellent reference on the subject of formatted printing, as well as other advanced features of the language, see Brailsford and Walker (1979).

An Example Using Algol 60

Figure 3 is a simple Algol 60 program that reads *n* records that contain a geometric figure number, type, and two values that

```
begin
  integer n ;
  read (n) ;
  for i := 1 step 1 until n do
    begin  real a, b;
          integer num, type;
          read (num, type, a, b);
          if type = 1 then
            begin
              area := (a x b);
              print (num, a, b, area)
            end;
          else
          if type = 2 then
            begin
              area := pi x ((a / 2) ^2;
              print (num, type, a, area)
            end;
          else
          if type = 3 then
            begin
              area := a x b / 2;
              print (num, type, a, b, area)
            end;
    end;
end
```

FIGURE 3. An Algol program that calculates and prints the areas of geometric figures.

represent two sides of a figure. In the case of a circle, it reads the diameter only into the identifier called A and identifier B is unused. Once the values are read, it determines the kind of geometric figure by examining the TYPE identifier (1=rectangle, 2=circle, and 3=triangle), and then performs the appropriate calculation to determine the area of the figure. The figure number, the type, the sides (or diameter in the case of a circle), and the area are printed on separate lines for each record.

ALGOL 68 ENHANCEMENTS AND DIFFERENCES FROM ALGOL 60

Algol 68 contains several features not found in Algol 60. Algol 68 contains more elaborate handling of transput (input and output). Algol 68 also allows the use of formatted transput, which means that the format of the line can be described within the print statement itself. Moreover, Algol 68 handles the reading and printing of character data much more easily than its Algol 60 precursor through the use of the **readf** and **printf** commands. The Algol 68 compiler is much more efficient and more transportable to other machines (especially the Algol 68C compiler), and the language contains a CASE statement that is not available on the older compiler.

An Example Modified for Algol 68

Figure 4 illustrates the same program shown in Figure 3 using Algol 60 except that it uses the WHILE command, prints character data without the use of a format statement, uses the fi (endif) and od (enddo), and employs a more popular structured programming method that involves the preread/postread technique. The program illustrated in Figure 4 allows processing of an undetermined number of records through the use of a "program switch." The program switch is an identifier ENDFLAG and looping is controlled by the contents of this variable. As long as the content of ENDFLAG is equal to 0 (WHILE ENDFLAG = 0 DO) the looping process continues and additional records are processed. The last record in the file is a delimiter or sentinel record that contains −9999 in the identifier NUM. When this record is sensed, the ENDFLAG identifier is set equal to one. Once the content of END-FLAG is changed to something other than zero the processing loop is terminated and the program ends. Note that there is a matching "fi" command for every "if" in the program.

```
begin
  real a, b;
  integer n, num, type;
  endflag := 0;
  read (num, type, a, b) ;
  while endflag = 0
  do
   if type = 1 then
     area := (a x b) ;
     print (num, " rectangle ", a, b, area) ;
   else
     if type = 2 then
      area  := (pi x ((a / 2) 2) ;
      print  (num, " circle", a, area);
     else
      if type = 3 then
        area := a x b / 2;
        print (num, "triangle", a, b, area)
      fi
     fi
   fi
   read (num, type, a, b) ;
   if num = −9999 then endflag := 1
   fi
  od
end
```

FIGURE 4. An Algol 68 program that determines the area of geometric figures, prints character string data, uses the fi (endif), and uses a structured programming approach using a preread and postread.

ADVANTAGES AND DISADVANTAGES

Although Algol never gained universal acceptance in industry, the language paved the way for more powerful and structured languages such as Pascal and C. A major *advantage* to Algol is that it lends itself to structured programming and modular design. No other language at the time had as elaborate a WHILE command, block structure, or CASE command. The CASE command is a special case of the if...then...else command, which provides a mechanism for multiple conditional testing on a single variable. This command is especially useful when an identification code is tested for several possible values, and based on the value, a separate action is taken. At a time when memory was very expensive, the major advantage to Algol was its dynamic storage allocation feature previously discussed. The Algol 68R compiler version has a very fast compilation time with an extensive set of mathematical functions.

A major *disadvantage* of the Algol language that kept it from being accepted universally is its lack of transportability among computer types and computer brands. Although the language contained features that allowed easy use of structured programming techniques, it remained rather complex and required much time to learn as compared with other languages such as FORTRAN (formula translator) and COBOL (common business oriented language). One distinct disadvantage of Algol is its primitive input and output handling capability, especially with character data; and although the language has been enhanced in this area, file handling is more difficult than with languages such as COBOL and PLI.

Reference

Brailsford, D., and A. N. Walker. 1979. *Introductory Algol 68 programming.* New York: Wiley.

For Further Reading

Baumann, R., M. Feliciano, F. L. Bauer, and K. Samulson. 1964. *Introduction to Algol.* Englewood Cliffs, N.J.: Prentice-Hall.

Lindsey, C. H., and S. G. van der Meulen. 1981. *Informal introduction to Algol 68.* Amsterdam: North-Holland.

McCracken, D. D. 1962. *A guide to ALGOL programming.* New York: Wiley.

McGettrick, A. D. 1978. *Algol 68: A first and second course.* London: Cambridge University Press.

Jack Russell

ALGORITHMS

Around 350 BC the Greek mathematician Euclid invented a procedure for finding the greatest common divisor of two positive integers. This is considered to be the first nontrivial algorithm ever devised. The term *algorithm* comes from the name of the ninth-century Persian mathematician Mohammed al-Khowârizmî, which in Latin became Algorismus. He is credited with providing the step-by-step rules for adding, subtracting, multiplying, and dividing decimal numbers.

In designing an algorithm we must make some assumption about the allowed set of basic actions from which the algorithm may be built, as well as about the entities that may be manipulated by these actions. For example, an algorithm for robot control might involve entities such as wheels, arms, and cameras and actions such as moving forward, reversing, and turning. An algorithm for drawing pictures may involve entities such as lines, circles, and rectangles and use actions such as shrinking, expanding, and rotating.

PROGRAMMING LANGUAGES

The language used for expressing the relevant algorithmic actions and entities may be simply some natural language such as English, or it may be formalized for use on a computer, in which case we have a *programming language.* (See Pratt, 1984, for a good survey.) In the latter case, the actions and entities correspond respectively to the "instruction set" and the "data types" of the programming language. An algorithm becomes a *program* or a *coded algorithm* when it is written in a specific programming language. Coded algorithms have the advantage of being precise and unambiguous, but at the cost of details that sometimes obscure the forest for the trees. With algorithms expressed in natural language, the converse tends to be true: their structure is transparent but details are ambiguous. As a compromise it is often convenient to write algorithms in a *pseudolanguage* or in *pseudocode,* a semiformal notation, often intermediate between an existing programming language and some natural language. Below we use a pseudolanguage based largely on Pascal, and most of the language constructs described below are for this Pascal-like language.

Pascal is one of the many different programming languages that have been designed to handle the wide variety of instruction sets and data types needed for different applications and different styles of programming. It is a rather general-purpose, yet quite compact and elegant, language. These features have made it currently one of the favorite languages in which to teach introductory computer science courses. Other programming languages are FORTRAN, designed largely for doing scientific numerical calculations, and COBOL, intended for business programming. LISP was designed for "symbolic" computation based on list processing. APL was designed for matrix computation. The relatively recent and revolutionary language PROLOG was designed for computing deductively with logical facts and rules. LISP and PROLOG are popular for artificial intelligence applications. SmallTalk is intended for "object-oriented" programming where problem solving is modeled as a process of interaction between various "objects." This language is also popular for artificial intelligence as well as for general programming of simulations.

DATA TYPES

Most programming languages provide as basic data types *integers* (such as 1, 2, -1, 0), *real numbers* (such as 1.23, -3.5) to some fixed degree of precision, and *characters* (such as "A," "B," "$") . Many programming languages also allow for structuring these basic data types into *data structures* such as *multidimensional arrays*. For example, a sequence of ten related integers could be stored in a one-dimensional array $A[i]$ of integer components, with index i ranging from 1 to 10. The sixth integer for example could then be referenced as $A[6]$. (Such a one-dimensional array is used below.) A table of 100 characters could be stored in a two-dimensional array $B[i, j]$ of character components, with indices i and j each ranging from 1 to 10. The character in the third row and fifth column of the table would be $B[3, 5]$. Examples of other useful data types and data structures provided by various programming languages are *Booleans, complex numbers, sets, character strings, records, linked lists,* and *files.*

COMMANDS

To manipulate such basic data types and data structures a programming language must provide a repertoire of actions or a command set. At the most basic level are the operators for the built-in data types, such as addition, subtraction, multiplication, and division for integer and real numbers, and concatenation for character strings to make longer strings. There are also usually "Boolean" operators for checking if certain relations hold between values. For example, the expression $x < y$ has value true if the value of x is less than the value of y; otherwise it has value false. At a higher level are the programming statements

from which programming modules such as *procedures* and *functions* are built. And at a still higher level is the mechanism for combining such modules, through invocations of each other, into an overall program. Particularly important for elegant program design is the ability of a module to call itself recursively. Not all programming languages provide this capability.

Perhaps the simplest programming statement is the assignment statement, such as $x := 3$. The latter statement assigns the value of the expression on its right, in this case just 3, to the variable on its left, in this case x. A variable such as x corresponds to a location in memory with the corresponding name. Such simple statements may be executed in sequence by formatting them sequentially (left to right, top to bottom) on the page. For example the sequence temp := x; x := y; y := temp swaps the values of variables x and y by first placing the value of x in variable temp, then placing y in x, and then temp in y. Note the use of semicolons to make clear the separation between statements. The semicolon may be thought of as an implicit "and then do" statement.

Control structures are programming language constructs that allow the programmer to specify the "flow of control," or the order of execution of statements, in a program. The above *linear sequencing* of statements in their order of appearance in the program is the simplest kind of control structure, and is provided in some form by all languages. Another common control structure is *conditional sequencing* or *branching*, where the next statement to execute can be made dependent on the value of some intermediate result in the computation. CASE, IF-THEN, and IF-THEN-ELSE statements are three common types of statement for achieving branching. For example, IF $x < y$ THEN return(x) ELSE return(y) returns the minimum value of x and y.

Programs containing only sequential and conditional sequencing control structures can prescribe processes of at most some fixed length, as no part of such an algorithm is executed more than once. *Iteration* or *looping* statements provide control structures for prescribing processes of arbitrary length. Three such statements in Pascal are the FOR,

WHILE, and REPEAT statements. For example, FOR $j := 1$ TO n DO sum := sum + $A[j]$ adds all the numbers from $A[1]$ to $A[n]$ for arbitrary n, putting the value in variable sum, which supposedly has been set initially to have value zero.

PROCEDURES AND FUNCTIONS

In designing any but the simplest algorithms it is important to be able to *abstract* groups of statements into modules, whether named or unnamed. Such abstraction facilitates the designing, writing, understanding, debugging, and updating of a program. Unnamed modules are achieved by the BEGIN-END statement, which allows a sequence of statements placed between BEGIN and END keywords to appear in place of a single statement. Named modules are of two types, functions and procedures, depending on how their results are returned. Unlike with unnamed modules, the statements constituting a procedure or function module do not actually appear where they are to be used. Rather they are written somewhere (only once) and are invoked elsewhere (possibly many times) by a simple call to the corresponding module's name with appropriate parameters. We will see examples below.

Procedure modules are grouped between the keywords PROCEDURE and END, and allow the statements so grouped to appear effectively in place of a single statement. Function modules are grouped between the keywords FUNCTION and END. Syntactically, calls to procedures are statements, whereas calls to functions are used as parts of expressions (in a statement), essentially like functions in mathematics. For example, a function MaxMin1 for finding the maximum and minimum numbers in an array $A[i]$ of length n may be written as in Figure 1 in terms of two subfunctions Max and Min.

MaxMin1 works by iterating through the components of array A and, for each new component, updating the record of the largest (Most) and smallest (Least) components so far. Comments, an important but oft-neglected part of program writing, appear at the right starting with %. Note the use in MaxMin1 of a compound BEGIN-END statement. Note also that we assume that MaxMin1 (as well as MaxMin2 below) can return a pair of values (Most,Least). A given problem may often be solved by many different algorithms. For example, the above MaxMin1 algorithm achieves its goal via iteration or looping, using a FOR statement. A *recursive* algorithm, with no iteration, is also possible, as in Figure 2.

MaxMin2 works by breaking array A into a first half and a second half, applying itself recursively to get the maximum and minimum of each of these halves, and returning as the maximum and minimum for its input array, respectively, the maximum of the two halves' maxima and the minimum of

```
FUNCTION MaxMin1 (A, n);
Most := A[1];                          % Initializing Most to equal A[1].
Least := A[1];                         % Initializing Least to equal A[1].
FOR j := 2 TO n DO                     % Looping through the other array elements. . . .
  BEGIN
    Most := Max(Most,A[j]);            % updating Most by a call to function Max.
    Least := Min(Least,A[j]);          % updating Least by a call to function Min.
  END;
return(Most,Least);                    % Returning the overall maximum and minimum in A.
END.
FUNCTION Max(x,y);
IF x > y THEN return(x) ELSE return(y);
END;
FUNCTION Min(x, y);
IF x < y THEN return(x) ELSE return(y);
END;
```

FIGURE 1. MaxMin1, an iterative algorithm to find the greatest and least numbers in an array.

```
FUNCTION MaxMin2(A, start,end,L);
IF L = 2                                          % Nonrecursive part.
   THEN IF A[start] > A[end]
      THEN return (A[start],A[end])
      ELSE return (A[end],A[start])
   ELSE BEGIN                                      % Recursive part. Find max and min . . .
      (max1,min1) := MaxMin2(A,start,start+L/2-1,L/2);   % of 1st half of A[start] to A[end], and
      (max2,min2) := MaxMin2(A,start+L/2,end,L/2);       % of 2nd half of A[start] to A[end].
      return(Max(max1,max2), Min(min1,min2));            % Return max of 2 max's and min of 2 min's.
         END
END.
```

FIGURE 2. MaxMin2, a recursive algorithm to find the greatest and least numbers in an array.

the two halves' minima. The recursion terminates when the subarray being scanned is only of length $L = 2$, in which case the maximum and minimum can be found directly. To simplify the splitting process, MaxMin2 assumes that the length of the initial array is a power of 2, so that all recursively produced sublists are of even length and can thus be split into two equal-length halves as above. The initial call is MinMax2(A,1,n,n) for a list of length n stored in $A[1]$ to $A[n]$.

As here, a recursive algorithm is one that solves a problem by applying *itself* to solve subproblems of the original problem (and similarly for the subproblems) and appropriately combining the results. It corresponds to an important general strategy for problem solving called "divide and conquer," which often provides a natural and elegant solution method, even though it may not necessarily be the most efficient method. In any case, a recursive algorithm is often a good place to start. From this a more efficient nonrecursive version may often be developed by stages if desired. Recent research has attempted to automate this transformation process. See, for example, Paull (1988).

COMPLEXITY ANALYSIS

It is important to be able to estimate the cost of using an algorithm to solve problems. This is especially so when there are two or more algorithms applicable to a given class of problems, because one would like to choose the most efficient algorithm (which may very well vary with the particular problem in-

stance being solved). Below we use Π to denote a problem class, π for an individual problem instance, and Π_n for the nth subclass of instances.

The main measures of algorithmic cost, also called algorithmic complexity, are the amount of time the algorithm takes to run, called time (or runtime) complexity, and the amount of computer memory it requires, called space complexity. Other measures may also be relevant, such as length and clarity of the code, but usually these are of secondary importance and cannot be analyzed as rigorously as space and time complexity. We concentrate on algorithmic time complexity analysis below.

A full time complexity analysis of an algorithm *Alg* would give the actual run time $T(\pi)$ of the algorithm as a function of the problem instance π being solved. This can be expressed as the sum of the time $T_s(\pi)$ that it takes for each statement s of the algorithm to be executed in solving that instance. And $T_s(\pi)$ can be expressed as the product of t_s, the time it takes statement s to execute once, by $N_s(\pi)$, the number of times it is executed in solving instance π. Thus, $T(\pi) = \Sigma_{s \in \text{Alg}} T_s(\pi) = \Sigma_{s \in \text{Alg}} t_s N_s(\pi)$.

In practice it is usually sufficient to obtain an expression for $N_s(\pi)$ for only the statement s that is executed most in the algorithm. Accordingly, we henceforth drop the statement subscript s in our notation. Also, it is not usually necessary (or even possible) to obtain $N(\pi)$ as a function of each instance π, but rather only as a function of some feature(s), say n, of problem instances. For example, for algorithms that sort lists we may not need the complexity as a function of the actual list π sorted but only as a function of the list's length $n = length(\pi)$. A problem parameter such as n partitions a problem class Π into subclasses; all instances π with the same value of the parameter n would be considered as being in the same subclass Π_n.

Within such a subclass, instances, although having the same value for n, will nevertheless usually have different complexities. Thus, an analysis in terms of n means that we no longer have a unique complexity $N(n)$, as we did for the "exact-case" complexity $N(\pi)$ for a given instance; rather, we have a range of such exact-case complexities N for a given n. The highest such value is called the worst-case complexity $N^w(n)$ for subclass Π_n; the lowest is the best-case complexity $N^b(n)$; and the average is the expected complexity $\overline{N}(n)$. Figure 3 shows these relationships graphically; $p_n(\pi)$ and $q_n(\pi)$ there denote two possible probability distributions for the instances in each subclass Π_n. As seen in the figure, the expected complexity usually varies with the assumed probability distribution of the instances in a subclass.

Let us see how the above ideas apply for the two MaxMin algorithms above. The most executed operations in MaxMin1 are the comparisons $x > y$ and $x < y$ of subroutines Max

and Min respectively, and both these are executed equally often for a given instance. So we use as our measure of complexity for MaxMin1 the sum of the number of $x > y$ and $x < y$ comparisons, which we denote by $N^{(1)}$. Because in MaxMin1 there is a total of two comparisons at each loop cycle (that is, for each value of the loop index $2 \le j \le n$), we have that

$$N^{(1)}(n) = \sum_{j=2}^{n} 2 = 2n - 2$$

For MaxMin2 the sum of the number of comparisons can be expressed by the following recurrence equation or difference equation:

$$\begin{aligned} N^{(2)}(n) &= 1 \text{ for } n = 2 \\ &= 2N^{(2)}(n/2) + 2 \text{ for } n > 2 \end{aligned}$$

This is because MaxMin2 does a single comparison when $n = 2$. For larger n it breaks a list of length n into two sublists each of length $n/2$, each thus requiring $N^{(2)}(n/2)$ comparisons in the corresponding recursive subcalls, and in addition two more comparisons are done in processing the answers to these recursive subcalls. The above recurrence equation has solution $N^{(2)}(n) = 3n/2 - 2$, as can be verified by substituting back into the recurrence. Note that, as here, it is often

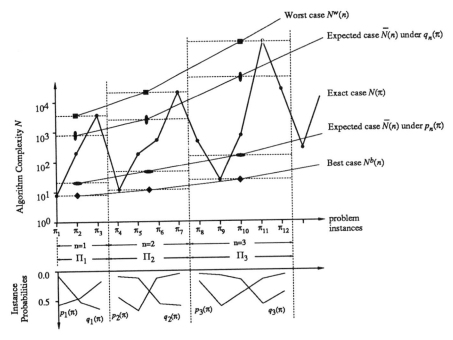

FIGURE 3. Exact-case, best-case, worst-case, and expected-case complexities of an algorithm.

most natural (though not essential) to use a recursive expression in deriving the complexity of a recursive algorithm, whereas a summation expression is most natural for deriving the complexity of an iterative algorithm.

As $3n/2 - 2$ is always less than $2n - 2$, we see that MaxMin2 is always better than MaxMin1 (at least in terms of the number of comparisons performed), and in fact its advantage, $n/2$, increases with list length n. Usually, an algorithm complexity comparison is not as cut and dry as the one presented here. There is usually a range in which one algorithm is best, then a crossover point at which the other algorithm becomes best. Note also that for either MaxMin1 or MaxMin2, the count N is clearly the same for all problem instances (all lists) of the same size n. For either algorithm, the best-case, worst-case, and expected-case values of $N(n)$ are thus the same for a given n, and equal the exact-case value of all instances in the corresponding subclass Π_n. In the general case, depicted in Figure 1, this is not so, and one must decide whether to compare algorithms in terms of their best-case (optimistic), worst-case (pessimistic), or expected-case ("realistic") complexities, and in the last case one must also decide on which probability distribution to assume for problem instances.

We have covered some of the basic ideas in the design and analysis of algorithms. Many more fascinating issues, which space precludes here, remain to be discussed. Harel (1987) extends the above ideas and provides an excellent introduction to the field of "algorithmics" in general.

References

Harel, D. 1987. *Algorithmics—the spirit of computing*. Reading, Mass.: Addison-Wesley. A comprehensive and deep, yet highly readable, account of the field of algorithmics. Perhaps the best introduction to computer science for the intelligent beginner.

Paull, C. M. 1988. *Algorithm design: A recursion transformation framework*. New York: Wiley-Interscience. Hard reading, but provides some wonderful unity to the field of algorithm design.

Pratt, T. W. 1984. *Programming languages, design and implementation*, 2nd ed. Englewood Cliffs, N.J.: Prentice-Hall. A comprehensive discussion of the principles of programming languages. Includes good high-level discussions of the languages FORTRAN, COBOL, PL/I, Pascal, Ada, LISP, SNOBOL, and APL.

Maurer, S. B., and A. Ralston. 1990. *Discrete algorithmic mathematics*. Reading, Mass.: Addison-Wesley. An excellent introduction to the mathematics necessary for the design and analysis of algorithms.

For Further Reading

Sedgewick, R. 1988. *Algorithms*, 2nd ed. Reading, Mass.: Addison-Wesley. An excellent survey of contemporary algorithms, including searching, sorting, geometric, graph, and mathematical algorithms.

Bernard A. Nadel

ANIMATION, COMPUTER

Computer animation is the art of producing and presenting a sequence of electronic images in rapid succession to give the illusion of movement.

Animated sequences or pictures seen in commercials, Saturday morning cartoons, and motion-picture films typically involve tens of thousands of hand-drawn pictures. For every minute of animation on television, over 1,500 individual drawings must be produced to create a smooth, animated sequence. Artists can speed up this process greatly with the assistance of computers. The computer also allows the artist to create certain types of special effects and complex artwork that would be difficult or tedious to produce by hand.

Computer animation can involve flat moving images (two-dimensional or 2-D animation) or complex objects with shape, depth, and texture (three-dimensional or 3-D animation).

Computer animation requires more

FIGURE 1. Example of an animated ball bounce. Computers can assist in calculating and plotting this motion. *Courtesy Pixar; reproduced by permission.*

powerful hardware and software than computer graphics. In addition to re-creating the color and detail of an electronic graphic image, computer animation systems must play back a quantity of frames quickly and smoothly enough—typically at thirty frames per second—to create the illusion of motion. Artists and programmers usually produce computer animation on high-end personal computers, on workstations, or on graphics terminals attached to mainframe computers.

To create a simple 2-D animation on a computer, the animator draws an outline of the object or character on the screen, usually using a *graphics tablet* and a *stylus* or a mouse. Once the drawing has been entered into the computer, it can be stretched, erased, enlarged, reduced, or repeated at will.

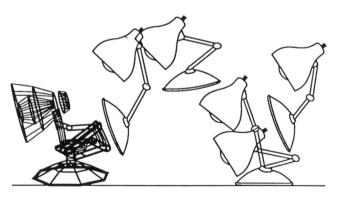

FIGURE 2. Motion of more complex objects, such as this lamp figure, involves a combination of machine calculation and artist intuition. The leftmost image is a wireframe model. *Courtesy Pixar; reproduced by permission.*

The animator first draws the basic steps of motion of the object, called *keyframes.* These are the places in the sequence where movement begins or ends, and enough intermediate poses to indicate the path or pattern of motion. For instance, for a ball bouncing off the floor, keyframes may indicate the starting point of the fall, the point at which the ball hits the floor, and the maximum height of the rebound. If the motion is simple enough, the computer can calculate the intermediate steps of motion in a process called *inbetweening.* Inbetweening complex motion can require very powerful computer software and hardware because of the number of variables involved in calculating the changes from one frame to the next. Often, animators opt to combine hand-drawn work with computer graphics in a process called *computer-assisted animation.* This takes advantage of both the human intuitiveness of describing moving images on paper, and the speed and flexibility of computer-defined motion.

The computer can assist in the coloring of animated sequences as well. Through the use of *painting* and *rendering* software, flat line drawings and dimensional computer models (i.e., three-dimensional objects) can be colored and shaded to give shape and form to the electronic images.

A two-dimensional animation is commonly seen in television cartoons, where characters appear as flat figures against flat background pictures. By painting and shading characters to give them the appearance of depth, and by using multiple overlapping background elements, some illusion of depth and dimensionality is achieved. Though much of this work is still drawn and painted by hand today, computers are sometimes used for special effects or to add color to black-and-white animated images.

A 3-D or *dimensional* animated sequence begins with the artist designing a static framework of the object to be moved, a technique called *modeling.* Computer models, like most computer graphics, can be created within the computer using a variety of methods. The most common is *geometric construction,* wherein the artist or programmer uses a tablet or keyboard to instruct the computer to create simple geometric forms—spheres and cubes, for instance. These shapes can be modified and combined to create complex objects. A car model might be constructed by combining and modifying several rectangular solids to form the "body" and cylindrical solids to form the "wheels."

Shapes of real-world objects can be transferred into the computer by *digitizing* pictures or drawings. In this process, the computer animator uses a *digitizing stylus* to locate points on paper drawings or blueprints. The stylus transmits relative locations of points on the drawing into the computer, forming a flat computer image. The computer can combine front, top, and side views of an object into a dimensional computer model. Special styluses designed for work with miniature plastic or clay models are sometimes used to translate the dimensions of physical objects into computer coordinates.

Pictures and drawings can also be digitized and brought into the computer using optical scanners, videocameras, and lasers.

Once a model is constructed in the computer, the animator must define its motion. The model's motion is partly defined by the animator and can be partly based on calculations produced by the machine. For instance, a bouncing ball falls and rebounds from the ground based on the laws of gravity. A computer animator can set the path of the ball on the screen using keyframes, then allow the computer to employ known laws of physics to calculate the way gravity causes the ball to accelerate and bounce back. This is called *constraint-based motion.*

Complex objects and movements can require very detailed instructions from the animator. Computer animation of a horse running would involve construction of a computer model of a horse, with joints and moving parts of the horse designed into the model to allow realistic movement. The computer animator repositions the computer model of the horse step by step, setting the direction of movement for each part—head, neck, legs—then stores each new position in the computer. When the computer is directed to play back the images in sequence, the dimensional model of the horse animates.

Animators occasionally use *live-action reference* footage to study the motion of real objects as an aid to designing computer-animated sequences. Through a technique called *motion capture,* some systems transfer motion information of an object directly from a videotape to the computer model.

An important part of making computer animated models look real is *rendering.* Rendering adds color, shading, and texture to each frame of the animated sequence. Once a model is constructed, the animator can select appropriate colors from a computer color palette. Even simple personal computers offer choices of millions of colors; more powerful workstations can span billions of colors. *Texture mapping* allows the colors added to an object to mimic textures of the real world. Instead of uniformly brown wood, for instance, the animator may design or photograph a sample surface of woodgrain and instruct the computer to apply this "color" over the computer model.

Computer animation allows artists to control other attributes of the appearance of moving objects as well. The animator can define the position of an imaginary light source falling on a computer-modeled object. This technique, called *shading,* can vary as the object moves to add to the illusion of depth and dimension. *Transparency* and *reflectivity* also can be used to make animated objects appear as clear as glass or as shiny as a metal ball.

Once an animator has created a moving sequence on the computer, the sequence can be saved on computer disk or tape for future playback, or it can be recorded on videotape or videodisc. *Digital film recorders* also allow the sequence of electronic images to be transferred one frame at a time to motion-picture film.

Computer animation is useful in *design,* where simulations of moving parts—the whirling blades of a jet engine, for instance —can help detect problems before manufacturing begins. *Motion analysis* is also useful in sports and in medicine. Athletes can compare videotapes of their own hurdle jumps with computer-animated sequences to help improve technique. Physicians can use simulations of blood flow through the heart to understand the causes of heart valve failure and blood clots better.

Scientific visualization is another important application of computer animation. The flow of fluid through a turbine or the way air passes over the wing of a supersonic aircraft are complex concepts to study on paper. Computer animation allows engineers and scientists to experiment with various designs and allows the computer to display the result as dynamic models. (See also VISUALIZATION TECHNIQUES.)

Motion-picture and television productions commonly use computer animation to create special effects. The computer can quickly calculate changing perspectives of objects and backgrounds, allowing illusions of motion not easily achieved by conventional cameras or hand-drawn art. Computer animation can also be *combined* with live-action film or video to achieve a unique visual effect, mixing the real world with imaginary elements. This technique is commonly used in television commercials and in some feature films.

Computer animation hardware and software continue to improve. As these systems become more powerful and the images more realistic, they are evolving as commonplace visualization tools for artists and engineers to add to the traditional methods of drawing and painting animated images.

For Further Reading

Armstrong, W., M. Green, and R. Lake. 1987. Near-real-time control of human figure models. *IEEE Computer Graphics and Applications* 7(6):52–61.

Badler, N. I. 1982. Human body models and animation. *IEEE Computer Graphics and Applications* 2(9):6–7.

———. 1987. Articulated figure animation. *IEEE Computer Graphics and Applications* 7(6):10–11.

Computer images. 1989. *The National Geographic.* October.

DeFanti, T., and C. A. Csuri. 1985. Art and animation. *IEEE Computer Graphics and Applications* 5(7):31.

Girard, M. 1987. Interactive design of 3D computer-animated legged animal motion. *IEEE Computer Graphics and Applications* 7(6):39–51.

Lasseter, J. 1987. Principles of traditional animation applied to 3D computer animation. *Computer Graphics* 21(4).

Magnenat-Thalmann, N., and D. Thalmann. 1985. *Computer animation: Theory and practice.* New York: Springer-Verlag.

———. 1985. An indexed bibliography on computer animation. *IEEE Computer Graphics and Applications* 5(7):76–86.

———. 1985. More an evolution than a motion problem. *IEEE Computer Graphics and Applications* 5(10):47–57.

Reynolds, W. C. 1983. Computer animation with scripts and actors. *Computer Graphics* 16(3):289–96.

Smith, T. G. 1986. *Industrial Light and Magic: The art of special effects.* New York: Ballantine Books.

Thomas, F., and O. Johnson. 1984. *Disney animation: The illusion of life.* New York: Abbeville Press.

Robert Lambert

APL

APL (A Programming Language) is an interactive, mathematically structured programming language used primarily for problem solving. Used in its most elementary mode, APL functions as a sophisticated calculator; used to its fullest extent, APL is a powerful mathematical problem-oriented programming tool. An interpreted language, APL allows the use of subprograms, but does not support the concept of the "main body" of a program.

Mathematics is the queen of the sciences, and a language unto itself; all other sciences, including physics, astronomy, and chemistry, use mathematical concepts and methods to study natural phenomena. As an example, physicists typically use *matrices,* or special arrays of numbers, to solve complex equations of motion. A mathematical solution exists for various manipulations of a matrix and, depending on the size of the matrix, involves a series of calculations. As the dimensional size of an array increases, so does the complexity of the manipulation and calculations. A typical solution of a matrix, such as calculating an inverse, is sometimes given as a programming project for students of computer science, and involves creation of a computer program just for that often formidable task. In APL, the inverse of a matrix may be found interactively by the user in a direct way with the use of only one operator. In languages such as FORTRAN, the user would typically rely on a library of subroutines that may need to be modified to obtain the same result.

This use of special operators to perform such vector and matrix operations on arrays of values or variables is what sets APL apart from most of the other programming languages. APL's similarity to algebraic notation allows operations that ordinarily are not expressed in a concise manner with conventional symbols; algorithms are thus described in a very efficient manner. For users of mathematics, APL offers a comfortable command syntax that is similar to the notation with which they are familiar. Thus, APL offers the mathematician, statistician, and engineer a "language" that bridges mathematical abstractions and computer syntax.

As in mathematics, the philosophy of APL is to use simple, nonverbal symbols to denote operations (rather than key words, which do not exist in APL). For example, the addition of two matrices, which would require two or more loops and a program consisting of a dozen or more statements in other programming languages, is simply "A + B" in APL. More than eighty symbols are available. APL also allows the creation of compound signs, in which new symbols may be created by combining others and given a unique meaning by the user. The ability to create new compound symbols renders APL programs much smaller than equivalents in other, more verbose programming languages.

In APL the algorithm for solution of a mathematical matrix operation is contained in a single operator rather than in a subroutine. Mathematicians and scientists find this useful in solving complex problems without having to do an excessive amount of programming. APL offers a wide range of operators, and also allows the user to define operators as needed. These operators are represented by a single character, mostly from a special character set. Because of this special character set, the use of APL requires specific graphics hardware and software.

APL is a very concise and powerful programming language that can be simple to learn. The simplification of data structures offered by APL's adept handling of arrays is its greatest strength. Data declarations, the bane of many a new programmer, are rarely required because so many computer operations are describable by single operators.

The APL user may learn operators as they are needed, without getting acquainted with the entire language. This is an advantage for the new user, who can quickly learn simple operations in a few minutes. For instructors who wish to teach mathematics rather than programming, APL is an ideal choice for interactive learning, as students learn mathematical concepts through the operators rather than by traditional programming techniques.

Developed in the late 1950s and early 1960s by Kenneth Iverson, APL originally began as mathematical notation rather than a programming language. *A Programming Language*, which Iverson published in 1962, is the founding work on which APL is based. At APL80, the International Conference on APL held June 24–26, 1980, Iverson summed up his philosophy:

> Notation, and mathematical notation in particular, is an important tool of thought. [The] advantages possessed by programming languages (executability and universality) can be combined, in a single coherent language, with the advantages of mathematical notation.

Further, in *A Programming Language*, Iverson discusses his ideas for a new language for the expression of algorithms in a concise and precise manner:

> Most of the concepts and operations needed in a programming language have already been defined and developed in one or another branch of mathematics. Therefore, much use can and will be made of existing notations. However, since most notations are specialized to a narrow field of discourse, a consistent unification must be provided. For example, separate and conflicting notations have been developed for the treatment of sets, logical variables, vectors, matrices, and trees, all of which

may, in the broad universe of discourse of data processing, occur in a single algorithm. (Iverson 1962, pp. 1–2)

Iverson designed APL for human understanding and information, rather than to instruct a computer and conform to its limited character set.

An experimental time-sharing system for the IBM System/360 was used for APL initially, hence the APL/360 version of the language, and APL was implemented as an interactive language in 1967. Efforts to standardize the language have been made since the early 1970s, and in the past few years new versions of APL have been developed, such as APL2, APL Plus, and Sharp APL2. Improvements include the ability to access other software, particularly relational databases, such as SQL and DB2, and programs written in other programming languages, such as FORTRAN. This is especially important because of the large number of scientific and mathematical libraries of existing programs in FORTRAN. Personal computer versions are available, and software interfaces allow APL to work with software such as STATGRAPHICS, to allow for statistical analyses and graphic presentation of data.

For Further Reading

Anscombe, F. 1981. *Computing in statistical science through APL.* New York: Springer-Verlag. Technical uses in statistics.

Curth, M. A., with H. Edelmann. 1989. *APL: A problem-oriented introduction.* West Sussex: Ellis Horwood Limited.

Iverson, K. E. 1962. *A Programming Language.* New York: Wiley. The original book in which specifications for the language were first outlined.

Loretta McKibben

ARCHITECTURE, COMPUTER USES IN

Historically, architects have used handmade drawings and three-dimensional scale models to record design ideas, to communicate proposals to clients, and to specify construction work to be executed. The basic idea of computer-aided architectural design is to substitute a digital representation stored in computer memory for traditional drawings and models. This digital representation describes (at some appropriate level of abstraction) a proposed building's geometry and materials. Usually it is constructed incrementally, as design decisions are made and modified, through use of specialized editing tools provided within a highly interactive graphic environment. It can be used throughout the design process to generate displays, reports, and analyses as required for particular purposes, and it can eventually be archived to form a permanent, definitive record of the completed design. Exploitation of the capabilities of digital representations can yield efficiencies through elimination of time-consuming and error-prone manual processes, expand the domains that architects explore in search of solutions, and generate higher levels of confidence in proposals through performance of more extensive and sophisticated analyses.

GEOMETRIC DESCRIPTION OF BUILDINGS

The most fundamental issue in implementation of a computer-aided architectural design system is choice of a method of geometric description. This choice determines the domain of designs the system will be able to handle, the types of displays it will be able to produce, the repertoire of editing operators it may provide, the variety of analysis and reporting operations it will be capable of supporting, and the computational resources that will be required for acceptably responsive performance. Different architects operating in different contexts have different requirements, preferences, and resource constraints—suggesting that different ways of making the trade-offs are implicit in choosing among available approaches to geometric description of buildings.

Methods of geometric description may be based on two-dimensional or three-dimensional Cartesian coordinate systems and may take points, lines, surfaces, or solids as their primitives. This yields seven basic possibilities, as follows:

	Two-Space	Three-Space
Points	pixel images	voxel models
Lines	line drawings	wire frames
Surfaces	polygon plans	surface models
Solids		solid assemblies

The idea of a pixel image representation follows directly from that of a two-dimensional, finite, integer Cartesian coordinate system. A value specifying some spatial quality is simply associated with each addressable point in the plane. For display, these values are interpreted as pixel intensities or colors. Thus, for example, a floor plan may be represented by serial-numbering the constituent rooms, associating a serial number with each point to specify the room within which that point is located, and employing a color-coding scheme for display of the plan as a mosaic of colored room shapes. Similarly, the site for a building may be represented by describing numerically elevation, soil conditions, hydrological conditions, vegetation, and so on at each point. The generalization to voxel models of three-dimensional spatial configurations (similar to the voxel models used in medical imaging) is straightforward: A value is associated with each addressable point in a three-dimensional, integer, Cartesian coordinate system. Quadtree and octree techniques may be employed to reduce the very large storage demands that these types of representations tend to make.

LINES

Outside of some specialized applications in site analysis and interior space planning, however, such exhaustive, point-by-point descriptions of spatial configurations are rarely necessary or appropriate in practice. Since buildings normally consist of areas and volumes that are (for practical purposes) homogeneous between well-defined boundaries, it is usually far more effective to de-

scribe them in terms of the properties and relationships of spatial boundaries. These boundaries form a hierarchy: Zero-dimensional points bound one-dimensional lines, these lines bound two-dimensional surfaces, and these surfaces bound three-dimensional volumes.

The simplest type of representation based on this abstraction strategy is a two-dimensional plan, section, or elevation consisting of straight lines, arcs, and other curves arranged on a planar surface. Each straight line is represented by its end-point coordinates, and instances of other types of curves are specified by means of additional parameters that describe shape between the end points. The associated repertoire of editing operators provides (at least) for inserting, deleting, extending, and trimming lines of various types; forming line relationships such as parallels, perpendiculars, and tangents; grouping lines into selectable subshapes; and copying and transforming these subshapes. Systems based on this type of data structure, and oriented toward input, editing, storage, and hard-copy production of precisely constructed line drawings are conceptually and functionally related to traditional manual drafting practice, are usually classified as computer-aided design/drafting (CADD) systems, and are in widespread practical use in architectural offices.

A wire-frame model consists of lines in three-dimensional space. The data structure and editing operators of a wire-frame modeling system are closely analogous to those of a two-dimensional drafting system, but the viewing system must additionally provide for projection of lines onto a two-dimensional display surface (see Figure 1), and the interface must incorporate some technique for specifying locations in the three-dimensional coordinate system. Procedures for producing the parallel and perspective projections normally used by architects simply apply appropriate rules for converting three-dimensional end-point coordinates of lines in the model into two-dimensional end-point coordinates of lines in the projected drawing. Specification of points in space is accomplished through use of standard drafting operators in specified construction planes, or

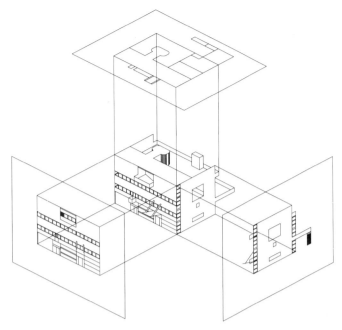

FIGURE 1. Projection onto picture planes to produce various architectural drawings from a single three-dimensional model.

through use of special hardware for three-dimensional coordinate input.

SURFACES

Wire-frame models can represent the essentials of a building's geometry in elegantly sparse and economical fashion, but they are too radically abstracted to serve as the bases for generation of sophisticated displays and analyses. In particular, they contain insufficient geometric information to allow automatic removal of hidden lines in projected views, or the production of shaded renderings. This can be remedied by extending the data structure to record not only associations of points to specify lines, but also associations of lines in circuits that bound closed surfaces. Thus a building is represented as a collection of surfaces (rather than as a collection of lines)—much as in a cardboard or chipboard physical model. In the simplest case the surfaces are all planar, and any curved surfaces are approximated by small planar facets. More sophisticated systems also provide parametrically described cylindrical surfaces, spherical surfaces, spline sur-

faces, and so on. The two-dimensional equivalent of a surface model is a map or plan represented as a mosaic of polygons.

Three-dimensional surface models provide the bases for realistic simulation and detailed exploration of a proposed building's visual qualities. Through use of appropriate surface-sorting techniques they can be used to produce perspective views in which hidden surfaces are removed. If a direction of incident light is specified, then it is straightforward to produce simple shaded views by calculating surface normals and shading surfaces in accordance with Lambert's cosine law. Photorealistic renderings of both exteriors and interiors can be produced by introducing additional surface and lighting parameters and calculating surface intensities by means of ray-tracing or radiosity procedures that take account not only of light directly incident on surfaces but also of light interreflection between surfaces in a scene—so reproducing extremely subtle effects (see Figure 2). These renderings can be matted into scanned or video-captured images of sites, so that the building is convincingly shown in context. Animated sequences can be produced by rendering successive frames corresponding to the positions of a camera moving through the building.

FIGURE 2. A ray-traced rendering of an architectural interior.

SOLIDS

The idea of boundary representation can be carried one step farther by recording the associations of surface facets that enclose solids. Thus a building is represented as a collection of solid "building blocks"—much as in a wooden or polystyrene physical model. Typically, a solid modeling system provides a vocabulary of parametric solid primitives (box,· cylinder, prism, solid of revolution, etc.), operators for inserting and deleting solids, geometric transformation operators for assembling them in space, and spatial set operators (union, intersection, subtraction) for building complex solid shapes from simple ones. The spatial set operators suggest an alternative way of organizing the data structure—as a constructive solid geometry (CSG) tree in which shapes are described as Boolean combinations of simpler shapes (see Figure 3). In architectural applications of solid modeling techniques, solids may be used to represent both physical elements such as columns and slabs and enclosed voids such as rooms. An architect can employ the available operators to shape and assemble construction elements and spaces in a very direct, sculptural way.

Since an assembly of solids is a geometrically complete description (in the sense that it is always possible to determine whether an arbitrarily specified point is within an arbitrarily selected solid), volumes, centroids, and surface areas can be calculated, arbitrary sections can be cut, and inadvertent spatial clashes between elements can be detected. Furthermore, material properties can be associated with solids so that their structural and thermal properties can be analyzed— typically by means of finite-element methods. Finally, the properties of joints and connections between solids can be described so that structural, kinematic, and other analyses of assemblies of solids can be performed. Thus the advantage of the solid-assembly approach to building description is that it supports integration of a wide range of useful applications. The disadvantage is that implementation of general, robust, responsive systems of adequate capacity raises challenging software engineering problems and

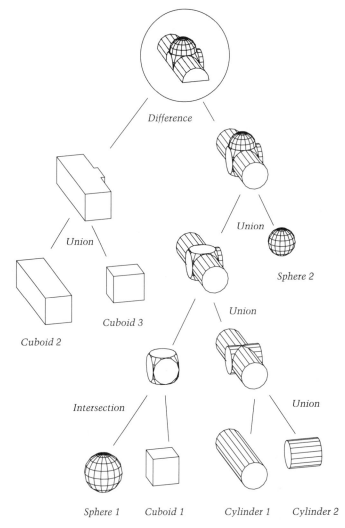

FIGURE 3. A CSG tree for a simple architectural composition.

makes high demands on computational resources.

ARCHITECTURAL VOCABULARIES

Whatever geometric description method is used, computer-aided architectural design systems can often take advantage of the fact that buildings are usually composed of multiple instances of standard elements drawn from a fairly restricted vocabulary. The database can thus be divided into two parts: a catalog file that contains detailed descriptions of vocabulary elements, and a project file that contains parameter values specifying instances of these elements located in a particular design. (So, for example, a CADD system might maintain a catalog of standard drafting symbols, and a solid-assembly system might maintain a catalog of standard three-dimensional construction elements.) Factoring the data in this way allows nonredundant, extremely compressed description of projects. Maintenance of pointers from instances to corresponding detailed descriptions provides for efficient expansion of the project file into a fully detailed building description; conversely, maintenance of pointers from catalog description to instances allows efficient compilation of bills-of-materials and cost estimates.

DESIGN TASK AUTOMATION

Architectural design is, in general, a trial-and-error process of developing alternative proposals for consideration, subjecting these proposals to analysis and criticism, modifying proposals in response to analysis results and critical feedback, and so on until a satisfactory proposal emerges. The final proposal is developed and documented in detail, and the usual end product is a set of working drawings and specifications that serves as the basis for a construction contract, construction planning and management, and the actual construction work. After a building has been constructed, as-built drawings are frequently produced for use in facility management and to provide the starting point for planning any future modifications. The subtasks that must be performed during the course of this process may be grouped into three broad classes: documentation tasks, analysis and evaluation tasks, and synthesis tasks.

DRAWING AND IMAGE PRODUCTION

The simplest CADD systems focus narrowly on documentation tasks—input, editing, and maintenance of project databases, and production of drawings from these databases. (They are closely analogous in function to basic word processing systems, with the difference that the former deal with

geometric rather than text data.) They usually emphasize efficiency in performance of two-dimensional graphic editing operations and versatility in document production capabilities. Since databases for major architectural projects are large and complex, these systems are increasingly seen as specialized database management systems with graphic interfaces and graphic reporting capabilities. Mostly they are used to replace manual drafting at the design development and documentation stage of a project, with the objective of shortening the time spent at this stage and reducing costs. (Production of working drawings has traditionally been the most time-consuming and expensive part of an architectural design process, so there is considerable incentive to seek efficiencies through use of computer methods.)

Systems with three-dimensional surface modeling and rendering capabilities are mostly used to produce renderings and animations that help designers and their clients to visualize proposals. Thus they automate the documentation work traditionally performed by perspective delineators and architectural model-makers. They may be used to generate quick, simple perspectives and isometrics that designers need in order to study the visual and spatial properties of alternatives, or to produce more detailed and realistic renderings of more developed proposals for presentation to clients.

DESIGN ANALYSIS

Many different types of analyses of a proposed building's cost and performance must be performed during the course of a design project, and most of these can be automated. Structural consultants analyze loads and stresses and compute member sizes, mechanical consultants perform energy analyses and size heating and cooling plants and ducts, acoustic consultants compute reverberation times and other properties of auditoriums, lighting consultants analyze distributions of light energy and artificial illumination requirements, cost consultants take off quantities and produce cost estimates, and so on. These analyses range from quick, rough calculations based on approximate or highly aggregated data performed at an early stage to give an indication of a proposal's feasibility, to detailed and accurate simulations performed to provide rigorous validation of a fully developed proposal. Simple spreadsheet models are often used to produce preliminary feasibility analyses, but highly specialized, frequently very sophisticated programs are employed to generate detailed simulations, analyses, and estimates. Analysis programs can be standalone applications, but their use becomes much more efficient, and sources of potential error are eliminated, when input data can be extracted automatically from the database of a computer-aided architectural design system.

AUTOMATED DESIGN SYNTHESIS

The most ambitious approach to computer-aided architectural design is to attempt implementation of systems that automatically synthesize proposals that satisfy specified requirements. This is difficult, since problems of selecting and arranging spaces and construction elements to satisfy functional and aesthetic requirements tend to be ill-defined and combinatorially explosive. There has been a great deal of research on automated architectural design synthesis, but only limited practical success in some specialized domains—layout of floor plans for circulation efficiency, layout of high-rise office building cores, or layout of parking bays to fit the maximum number of cars into a given space, for example. Automated design synthesis software typically depends on some combination of efficient generation of relevant alternatives for consideration, effective use of known constraints to limit trial-and-error searching, and exploitation of specialized knowledge about particular design problem domains to direct the search for a solution in promising directions.

INTEGRATED COMPUTER-AIDED ARCHITECTURAL DESIGN SYSTEMS

A particularly important advantage of the digital building descriptions maintained by computer-aided architectural design systems is that they can support both vertical and horizontal integration of design processes. Vertical integration is achieved by providing various design professionals involved in a project (architects, structural engineers, mechanical engineers, landscape architects, interior space planners, etc.) with immediate access to current, definitive project data. Horizontal integration is achieved by maintaining a project database through time, and using it to support successive design and construction activities—for example preliminary design, design development and documentation, construction management, and in-use facility management. Integration may be achieved either by providing data transfer links between different systems used by different design team members at different stages, or by integrating applications around a single, central, definitive database. Either way, integrated computer-aided architectural design systems have much greater potential advantages than those oriented to automation of just one task (such as drafting of working drawings, rendering of perspective views, or cost analysis), since they allow the cost of input and maintenance of a digital building description to be offset by the benefits of many applications, and since they greatly reduce the communications overhead of the design process.

IMPACTS ON ARCHITECTURAL PRACTICE

Prototype computer-aided architectural design systems were first implemented in the early 1960s, and mainframe-based systems with refreshed-vector graphic displays found some limited practical application in the late 1960s and early 1970s. When relatively inexpensive 16-bit minicomputers (such as the DEC PDP-11) and storage-tube displays became available, these provided platforms for implementation of documentation-oriented systems that were successfully employed in many large architectural and architecture/ engineering organizations. (Costs were high, so these systems made economic sense only where there was a large volume of documentation work to be handled.) Minicomputer-based systems were supplanted at the end of the 1970s by systems that took advantage of the capabilities of 32-bit superminicomputers and raster graphic displays to provide more fluid and responsive interfaces, greater capacity, faster performance, and integration of wider ranges of functions. The emergence of inexpensive personal computers running the DOS operating system provided the opportunity to mass-market simplified systems to thousands of small architectural and engineering consulting firms. By 1990, use of computer systems to perform documentation and many analysis functions had become commonplace in both large and small architectural offices, the computer-aided architectural design software market had become highly competitive, and graduates from professional degree programs in leading schools of architecture were expected to possess substantial expertise in applying computer technology in design.

Traditionally, architecture has been a highly labor-intensive profession, heavily dependent on accumulated personal experience and on the crafts of drawing and modeling by hand. Many people were attracted to it because they enjoyed these crafts. Architectural fees were usually based (either directly or indirectly) on the number of hours spent on a project. The growing use of computer-aided architectural design technology is producing a fundamental structural change: Architectural firms are becoming more capital-intensive, more reliant on knowledge recorded in the form of programs and databases, and more dependent for their competitiveness on strategic investment in computer technology. The first effect to be felt was reduction of the handicraft component of design through replacement of manual drafting by computer drafting, but the introduction of new tools to support the complex and intellectually demanding tasks of design proposal synthesis and evaluation is a development of far greater long-term importance.

For Further Reading

Crosley, M. L. 1988. *The architect's guide to computer-aided design.* New York: Wiley.

Greenberg, D. P. 1989. Light reflection models for computer graphics. *Science* 244: 166–73.

Kalay, Y. E. 1989. *Modeling objects and environments.* New York: Wiley.

Mitchell, W. J. 1977. *Computer-aided architectural design.* New York: Van Nostrand Reinhold.

———. 1989. Architecture and the second industrial revolution. *Harvard Architecture Review 7.*

———. 1990. *The logic of architecture.* Cambridge, Mass.: The MIT Press.

Mitchell, W. J., and M. McCullough. 1991. *Digital design media.* New York: Van Nostrand Reinhold.

Mitchell, W. J., M. McCullough, and P. Purcell, eds. 1990. *The electronic design studio.* Cambridge, Mass.: The MIT Press.

Radford, A., and G. Stevens. 1987. *CADD made easy: A comprehensive guide for architects and designers.* New York: McGraw-Hill.

William J. Mitchell

ARTIFICIAL INTELLIGENCE

[Artificial intelligence is the one field of computer science that can be said to have had the most impact on the outside world. Many fields not now considered to be part of artificial intelligence, such as PATTERN RECOGNITION *and* ROBOTICS, *originally were so considered. As they matured and became more precise and algorithmic in nature, they gradually left the fold. The general article that follows gives an introduction to the field and provides insights into why this occurred. Knowledge Bases and Expert Systems introduces what some consider the most profitable practical application of the field and presents one author's view of where this field is heading. Application of expert systems to medicine is one of the topics addressed in Medical Informatics. One of the most intriguing areas of artificial intelligence is that of devising artificial learning systems. The article Machine Learning discusses the current state of the art in this area. Mechanical language translation has been a dream of scientists for many years. Natural Language Processing introduces us to this field. Finally, the articles Artificial Intelligence in Engineering Design and Artificial Intelli-*

gence in the Automotive Industry *present applications of artificial intelligence to very practical fields of engineering endeavor.*]

Artificial intelligence (AI) is that branch of computer science concerned with the study of knowledge representation and search. Its goals are the creation of computer programs that behave in an intelligent fashion, and the use of computational models to understand intelligent behavior in humans, machines, and societies.

In expanding this definition, we examine AI from three different perspectives:

1. Historical. AI is considered a subdiscipline of computer science. Although the roots of AI include an older tradition of philosophical and psychological efforts to understand the nature of intelligence, AI as a discipline began with the creation of the computer, as seen in the following section.

2. Methodological. Traditionally, artificial intelligence has emphasized the use of symbolic data structures to represent knowledge of a domain, formal rules of inference to manipulate these structures, and search algorithms to apply this knowledge to problem solving. This methodology is examined in the second group of the following sections.

3. Application. Progress in AI is driven by a number of difficult and important application areas, including natural-language understanding, expert systems, intelligent problem solving, planning, and learning. This article concludes with an outline of these applications.

COMPUTERS, THE TURING TEST, AND THE ORIGINS OF ARTIFICIAL INTELLIGENCE

Although the eighteenth, nineteenth, and early twentieth centuries saw the formalization of science and mathematics, it wasn't until the creation of the digital computer that AI became a viable scientific discipline. By the end of the 1940s, electronic digital computers had demonstrated their potential to provide the memory and processing power required by intelligent programs. It was then first possible to implement formal reasoning systems on a computer and to test empirically their sufficiency for exhibiting intelligence.

One of the first papers to address the question of machine intelligence was written in 1950 by the British mathematician Alan TURING. "Computing Machinery and Intelligence" (Turing 1950) is important both for Turing's conjecture that intelligence is open to a formal characterization, independent of a biological brain, and for his response to arguments against the possibility of automating intelligence.

While Turing had already given computing machines a precise characterization through his definition of the *Turing machine,* he recognized that intelligence itself was not amenable to such mathematical axiomatization. To circumvent the difficulties of defining intelligence, Turing proposed a behavioral evaluation of intelligent programs, called the *imitation game* and now referred to as the *Turing test.* This test measures the performance of an allegedly intelligent machine against that of a human being. The test places a human and the computer in rooms apart from a second human, the *interrogator.* The interrogator communicates with them by means of a textual device such as a computer terminal and attempts to distinguish the computer from the human on the basis of answers to questions asked over this device. If the interrogator is unable to distinguish the machine from the human reliably, then, Turing argues, the machine must be regarded as intelligent.

Important features of the Turing test are the following:

1. It gives us an objective notion of intelligence—that is, the behavior of a known intelligent being (the human) in response to a set of questions. This standard allows us to determine whether the machine is intelligent, while avoiding questions about the "true" nature of intelligence.

2. It prevents us from being sidetracked by confusing currently unanswerable questions relating to whether the machine uses the "appropriate internal processes" or whether the computer is actually "conscious."

3. As a blind test, it eliminates any bias in favor of the human over the machine by forcing the interrogator to focus entirely on the content of the answers.

The Turing test has played an important role in the development of AI. Besides giving theoreticians a criterion for recognizing an intelligent program, it also gives applications designers a basis for evaluating software performance. Expert systems, for example, are usually validated by comparing the performance of the program to that of a human expert on a common set of problem instances. The MYCIN program, for instance, was evaluated by letting a group of practitioners blindly evaluate the diagnoses provided by MYCIN and a group of human practitioners on ten actual meningitis cases (Buchanan and Shortliffe 1984).

Artificial intelligence is unique among the sciences in tracing its beginnings as a formal discipline to a specific place and time. The Dartmouth Summer Research Project on Artificial Intelligence was held in 1956 and was the first gathering of researchers who had written computer programs exhibiting some form of intelligent behavior. A brief description of several of the invited presentations at this workshop and other early research will provide a perspective on the state of the art in AI in the late 1950s and early 1960s. This work is also important in that it established many of the core concerns of contemporary AI.

Arthur Samuel's checkers player (Samuel 1959) used a number of techniques first developed in the field of operations research. These include *hill climbing, mini–max search,* and the use of an evaluation polynomial to rate board states. This program was remarkable in a number of ways: It was the first example of a machine learning program, improving its performance by changing its evaluation function and by storing board states and their evaluations for future use. Through these techniques, the program learned to play an excellent game of checkers; more importantly, the techniques Samuel developed remain a vital part of MACHINE LEARNING methodology. In addition, the program was impressive for its use of sophisticated representational and memory management techniques to overcome the limitations of 1950s hardware.

Herbert Gelernter (1963) developed a geometry theorem–proving program that successfully proved many theorems from high-school geometry texts.

Newell, Shaw, and Simon, then researchers at the Carnegie Institute of Technology, presented their Logic Theorist (Newell and Simon 1963a). They also presented some interesting research comparing a run of their computer program proving mathematical theorems with traces of human subjects solving the same theorems. This comparative research is arguably the beginning of work in cognitive science, the use of computer programs as a tool for modeling human cognition. EPAM (Feigenbaum 1963) was another early cognitive program that attempted to model the way in which humans memorize and index sets of nonsense syllables. EPAM was developed by Edward Feigenbaum, one of Herbert Simon's students; Feigenbaum was later to play an important role in the development of the first expert systems and of the Stanford AI research laboratory.

Newell and Simon's General Problem Solver (GPS) (Newell and Simon 1963b) was the first effort to provide a unified theory of human cognition in the form of a computer program. The GPS assumed that any problem could be solved by a general method of heuristic state space search.

It was also at the Dartmouth conference that John McCarthy selected the name *artificial intelligence* for the new field of research. The word *artificial* was selected for its literal meaning: to make (the Latin verb *facere*) by skilled effort (*ars, artis,* the root for the English *artist* and *artisan*). McCarthy's early contribution to AI was the design of the LISP (LISt Processing) language. Over the years, LISP has been the single most important tool for AI research and development.

These early results were collected in the book *Computers and Thought* (Feigenbaum and Feldman 1963). The continuing royalties from this collection still fund the Computers and Thought Award, presented biannually at the International Joint Conference on Artificial Intelligence (IJCAI). Technical conferences such as IJCAI and the yearly American Association for Artificial Intelligence (AAAI) conference continue to serve as the primary forums for research in AI. In addition, communication among AI researchers has been promoted by numerous books and by technical journals, including *Artificial Intelligence, The AI Magazine, Computational Intelligence,* and *Cognitive Science.*

THE METHODOLOGY OF MODERN ARTIFICIAL INTELLIGENCE

If there is any unifying principle to current work in AI, it is the *physical symbol system hypothesis* (Newell and Simon 1976, p. 116):

> A physical symbol system consists of a set of entities, called symbols, which are physical patterns that can occur as components of another type of entity called an expression (or symbol structure). Thus a symbol structure is composed of a number of instances (or tokens) of symbols related in some physical way (such as one token being next to another). At any instant of time, the system will contain a collection of these symbol structures. Besides these structures, the system also contains a collection of processes that operate on expressions to produce other expressions: processes of creation, modification, reproduction and destruction. A physical symbol system is a machine that produces through time an evolving collection of symbol structures. Such a system exists in a world of objects wider than just those symbol expressions themselves.

Newell and Simon then state the physical symbol system hypothesis:

> A physical symbol system has the necessary and sufficient means for general intelligent action.

This hypothesis states the underlying assumptions of AI in a succinct form and, in addition, outlines the methodology of "mainstream" work in AI:

1. Represent the important objects and relationships in the problem domain as sentences in an appropriate formal language.

2. Define operations that transform these sentences in ways that reflect the semantics of the problem domain. For example, these operations may be atomic actions that a robot may take in the world, or rules in an expert system or logical reasoning system.

3. Problem instances consist of a description (in the language of step 1) of the given data or starting conditions of the instance (the start state) and a description of the desired solution (the goal state).

4. Search the space of sentences produced by applying these operations to legal expressions to find a series of operations that lead from the starting state to the goal state.

The next section will examine the implementation of this methodology in more detail.

PROBLEM SOLVING AND STATE SPACE SEARCH

State space search is based on the assumption that any problem can be solved by searching through a space of appropriately defined operations on formal sentences. These operations define a space of partial solutions called the *state space.* The technique of solving problems by searching this space is called state space search: the search for a series of operations that transform the starting state into the required goal state.

Much early work (1960 through the mid-1970s) in AI was devoted to developing state space search as a general problem-solving method. This methodology was successfully applied to a variety of fields, including mathematical theorem proving, planning, and problem solving. This work focused on finding languages that could adequately describe classes of problems and strategies for efficiently searching the resulting space. Many of these strategies, such as means–ends analysis, were *heuristic* in nature—that is, they provided intelligent guidance through the space while not guaranteeing that such guidance would always produce an optimal problem solution. Heuristics are further examined in the following section.

In developing the methodology of state space search, the first-order predicate calculus was often chosen as a general language for describing problem states. First-order predicate calculus, because of its roots in mathematics and formal logic, provides well-understood, logically sound, and complete

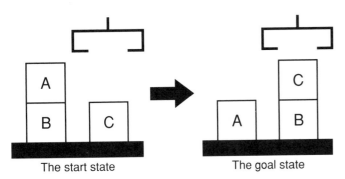

FIGURE 1. Two states of the blocks world.

inference rules. It can also be shown that predicate-calculus-based theorem provers are *Turing complete*—that is, any process that could in principle be formalized can be formalized using predicate calculus. This further strengthened its appeal as a general language for intelligent systems.

For example, suppose we would like to apply the methodology of state space search to find a series of actions to transform a starting state into a desired goal (see Figure 1).

The start state of the world is described using predicates:

block(a).	block(b).	block(c).
clear(a).	clear(c).	ontable(b).
ontable(c).	on(a,b).	inhand(nil).

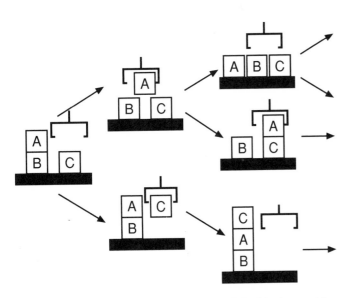

FIGURE 2. The search space of the blocks world.

Similarly, we describe the goal state:

block(a).	block(b).	block(c).
clear(a).	clear(c).	ontable(b).
ontable(a).	on(c,b).	inhand(nil).

The operations that the robot can perform are also described using predicate calculus. These operations consist of *preconditions*, which define circumstances under which the operation may be performed; an *add list* of sentences that are true when the operation completes; and a *delete list* of things that are no longer true when the operation completes. Some of the operations given our block-stacking robot include:

    pickup(X):
        Preconditions: clear(X) ∧ inhand(nil)
        Delete list: clear(X) ∧ on(X, Y)
        Add list: inhand(X)

    stack(X,Y)
        Preconditions: clear(Y) ∧ inhand(X)
        Delete list: clear(Y) ∧ inhand(X)
        Add list: inhand(nil) ∧ on(X,Y)

In addition, the planner has rules for inferring additional properties of the blocks world descriptions. Such a rule might allow the program to infer when a block is clear:

$$\forall \; X \; block(X) \land (\neg \exists \; Y \; block(Y) \land on(Y,X)) \rightarrow$$
$$clear \; (X)$$

This rule states that for all X, if X is a block and there does not exist a block Y, such that Y is on X, then X is clear. Note that much of the power of predicate calculus comes from the use of variables (X,Y) to define general rules and operations such as those given above.

Given this description of the blocks world domain, we may solve problems by searching the state space to find a series of moves that transforms the beginning state into the goal state, as in Figure 2.

As this example shows, search-based problem solving may be adapted to a variety of problem domains. By establishing the methodology of knowledge representation and state space search, this early work provided a framework for AI. This research explored a number of search strategies that continue to be used today, including *forward search*, in which problem solving begins with data and searches forward to find a solution, and *backward search*, in which the search process begins with the desired goal and works back to the given data. Other strategies explored at this time include *depth first search, breadth first search,* and *best first search.* These strategies are described in more detail in Luger and Stubblefield (1989).

PRODUCTION SYSTEMS

Another important AI technique to emerge from this early research was the *production system architecture* (see Figure 3). The production system is a control method that has proven particularly important for implementing search algorithms, designing expert-system-building tools, and modeling human performance. The production system provides pattern-directed control for an inferencing system; a rule is used when and if it matches a state of the problem-solving process. A production system consists of three components: a set of *production rules,* a *working memory,* and a *recognize–act control cycle.*

1. Production rules. A production rule is a condition-action pair that describes a single chunk of problem-solving knowledge. The condition part of the rule defines when the rule matches a state of a problem-solving process. When the condition matches a problem state, the rule may be *fired,* performing the associated action. Production rules are often represented in an "if . . . then . . ." syntax.

2. Working memory. This contains a description of the current state of the problem-solving process. The contents of working memory are matched against the conditions of the production rules, producing a set of *enabled* productions.

3. The recognize–act control cycle. This is straightforward: The current state of problem solving is maintained as a set of patterns in working memory. These patterns are matched against the rules to produce a

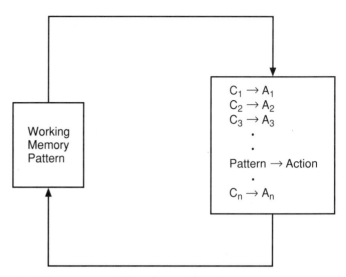

FIGURE 3. A production system. Control loops until working memory pattern no longer matches the conditions of any productions.

set of enabled rules, called the *conflict set. Conflict resolution* is the process by which the production system selects a rule from this set. This rule is then *fired.* Its action modifies the contents of working memory, and the cycle repeats. This continues until recognition produces an empty conflict set. At this point the system stops and the problem solution is in working memory.

Newell and Simon used production systems to model human problem solving in pioneering research done at Carnegie Mellon University in the 1960s and 1970s. In their approach, production rules represented the knowledge and skills a human being might possess. These might be rules for playing chess, solving physics problems, or diagnosing diseases. Working memory represents the human's short-term memory or attention at a given time in the problem-solving process. Thus the production system may be interpreted as modeling the activation of skills or chunks of knowledge by the human's current focus of attention, and the application of those skills to problem solving.

The production system has proven an effective architecture for the implementation of AI programs for a number of reasons, including the following:

1. Ease of implementing state space search. The successive configurations of working memory correspond to neighboring states in a space. The firing of rules implements a transition between states.

2. Pattern-driven reasoning. This simplifies the implementation of opportunistic problem-solving strategies, as required by AI. It allows a highly flexible control structure in which the needs of a problem situation determine what is done next, rather than a previously specified procedural ordering.

3. Representational flexibility. We may use any language to represent production rules as long as it supports pattern matching; for example, a production system could be used to implement the planner of the previous section.

4. Flexibility of control. The production system supports a variety of search strategies. By placing the given data of a problem in working memory and matching conditions against these data, the production system reasons in a forward fashion. By placing a goal in working memory and matching against rule conclusions, the production system implements backward reasoning. In addition, by modifying the conflict resolution strategy, the system can implement a variety of heuristically based strategies.

For more information on production systems see Luger and Stubblefield (1989) and Waterman and Hayes-Roth (1978).

STRONG METHODS AND THE RISE OF KNOWLEDGE-BASED SYSTEMS

The major focus of this middle period (1960 through the early 1970s) of AI research was on the development of general architectures for intelligent problem solving. The production system is an example of this orientation. Another focus of this work was on the use of *heuristics* to control search. Search-based problem solving is plagued by the large number of states in interesting problem spaces. As a search algorithm moves into a space, the number of states tends to increase exponentially. Consequently, intelligent problem

solvers must have some way of effectively guiding the search process.

A heuristic is any problem-solving method that improves the efficiency of a problem solver (Pearl 1984); in a production system, for example, a heuristic may be used to select a rule in conflict resolution. However, this increase in efficiency has a price: Heuristic search may sacrifice the quality of solutions or even the ability of the problem solver to find a solution in every instance. Means–ends analysis, as discussed above, is an example of a heuristic. While it is effective in choosing an operation that reduces the syntactic difference between the current state and the goal, it may break down in certain situations. Consider a situation in which the current problem state is such that any solution must temporarily *increase* the difference between this state and the goal. Means–ends analysis cannot select an operator in these situations.

During this middle period, the emphasis was on finding general principles of intelligent behavior. Consequently there was much work on finding heuristics, such as means–ends analysis, that might prove effective across a variety of domains. These heuristics do not use knowledge of a specific domain to guide search; instead, they examine syntactic properties of the representations. Means–ends analysis does this by reducing the syntactic differences between states. Another general heuristic might favor production rules that reduce the number of patterns in working memory.

However, research showed that general, syntactic methods, called *weak methods,* were limited in their ability to solve problems. In trying to extend search-based problem-solving methods to domains of human expertise, such as organic chemistry or medical diagnosis, researchers realized that humans relied on knowledge that was specific to those domains. These heuristics are called *strong methods* and underlie the development of *knowledge-based systems,* also known as *expert systems.*

MYCIN (Buchanan and Shortliffe 1984), a knowledge-based system for diagnosing bacteremia and spinal meningitis, is an early example of a knowledge-based system. Rather than relying on weak methods, the designers of MYCIN emphasized the construction of a large base of specific diagnostic knowledge. This knowledge base was represented as "if . . . then . . ." rules. A typical MYCIN rule is the following:

if (a) the infection is primary-bacteremia, and

(b) the site of the culture is one of the sterile sites, and

(c) the suspected portal of entry is the gastro-intestinal tract

then there is suggestive evidence (0.7) that infection is bacteroid

Note that this rule, unlike weak heuristics, is useful *only* for diagnosis of bacteremia. These rules are applied to problem instances by an *inference engine*, essentially a production system that matches rules with the facts of a specific case.

Knowledge-based systems have proven effective in practical domains for a number of reasons. By using AI techniques such as pattern-directed search, they were able to solve problems that were too complex or irregular to lend themselves to traditional programming techniques. Knowledge-based systems are able to explain their reasoning by listing the sequence of rules used in solving a problem; this increases their usefulness and understandability. By applying large amounts of knowledge to problems, they achieved high levels of expertise in a variety of problems that were long considered proprietary to human experts.

Knowledge-based systems, based on such general problem-solving techniques as state space search, production systems, and logical representation, represented an important shift of emphasis for AI. Instead of looking for general principles of intelligent behavior, researchers began to focus on methods of acquiring and representing the knowledge used by humans in problem solving. This shift of emphasis has raised a variety of issues that continue to be the focus of ongoing research. How may we determine the specific knowledge used by a human in solving a problem? Humans are notoriously inarticulate about their actual thought processes; consequently, knowledge acquisition remains a difficult problem. Knowledge-based systems explain their reasoning; how

may these explanations be best organized and presented? Expert systems, in spite of many current claims, are not human experts; what are the limits of the formalization of knowledge?

Finally, because knowledge-based systems require extremely large amounts of knowledge for most domains, researchers have focused a great deal of energy on the development of languages that simplify the acquisition, organization, and application of this knowledge. The study of *knowledge representation* has emerged as a central concern of modern AI.

Research in knowledge representation is driven by the needs of knowledge-intensive problem solvers such as expert systems. Natural-language understanding, or the problem of getting machines to understand human languages, has also placed demands on knowledge representation. Representation languages including logic, rules, frames, and objects provide AI programmers with a powerful set of tools for building knowledge bases. These techniques are also formalized in a number of commercial software packages that simplify program development. A particularly powerful class of these programs are *hybrid tools*, which provide the programmer with multiple representation languages, typically rules and frame/objects; different inferencing techniques such as inheritance or rule-based reasoning; multiple search strategies such as forward and backward search; and a rich set of tools for constructing user interfaces and debugging programs. *Readings in Knowledge Representation* (Brachman and Levesque 1985) provides a valuable introduction.

ALTERNATIVE ARCHITECTURES FOR INTELLIGENT PROGRAMS

While the main thrust of AI research has been toward developing more expressive representations and inference strategies, another school of research has focused on alternatives to the explicit representation of problem-solving knowledge. *Parallel distributed processing*, or *PDP*, refers to models of computation that use large numbers of relatively simple computational units, working in combination, to produce powerful results (Rumelhart and McClelland 1986).

Neural networks are typical of this approach. Patterned after the low-level architecture of biological brains, neural networks consist of large networks of artificial neurons. Like biological neurons, these elements are extremely simple: They accept signals from other neurons; these inputs are augmented by weights on the input lines. Each element computes a function of these weighted inputs and, depending on the result of this calculation, either sends a signal to other neurons or remains quiet. Through the patterns of connections in the network and the ability of neurons to stimulate or

inhibit each other, these systems demonstrate powerful collective behaviors.

Figure 4 illustrates a simple type of neural network called a *perceptron* (Rosenblatt 1962), as it might be used in a computer vision system. The inputs to the network are sets of pixels from the image. The outputs are classifications of the image. Through the system of weights and the pattern of connections, the network is able to compute a mapping from the features of the image onto an appropriate classification.

These systems show promise for complementing representation-based AI. For example, since the computation is spread out over many elements, parallel distributed ap-

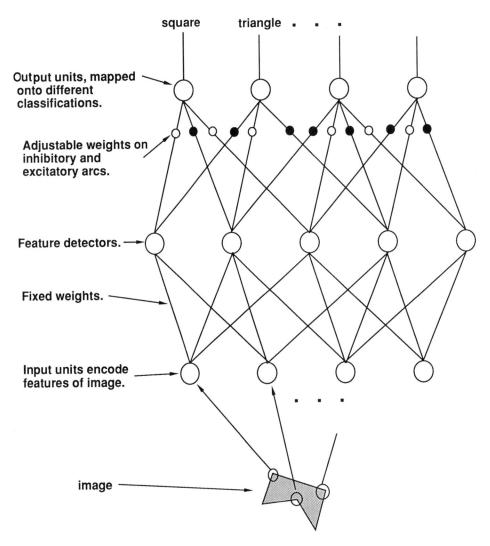

FIGURE 4. A simple three-layer perceptron with one hidden layer.

proaches can draw conclusions in spite of the presence of significant amounts of noise in the data. Also, progress has been made in developing algorithms that allow PDP systems to learn from experience by, for example, adjusting the weights on the connections in a neural net.

SURVEY OF APPLICATION AREAS

Artificial intelligence is driven by a number of important and demanding application areas. While it is impossible to be exhaustive in the scope of a single encyclopedia entry, a brief survey of these applications is essential to any discussion of AI.

Automatic theorem-proving (Wos et al. 1984) is one of the oldest areas of AI, tracing its origins past Newell and Simon's Logic Theorist to the philosophical work of Russell and Whitehead. Work in theorem proving continues, focusing on the development of more sophisticated models of mathematical reasoning and on extending techniques to a wider range of application areas. In particular, theorem proving has found success in the design and validation of logic circuits and the verification of computer programs.

Knowledge-based systems (Luger and Stubblefield 1989, Waterman 1986) include some of the most successful applications of AI techniques. Knowledge-based systems have been written in fields as diverse as medical diagnosis, industrial process control, geology, and engineering design. Current issues in knowledge-based systems include knowledge representation, knowledge acquisition, and the design of intelligent user interfaces.

Planning (Fikes et al. 1972) addresses the problem of finding a series of actions that will reach some goal. While robotics is the most obvious application of planning technology, these techniques have also found application in such areas as the design of manufacturing processes and the planning of scientific experiments. Planning is complicated by the necessity of representing changes in a world over time. Also, since such applications as robotics require interaction with the real world, planners must deal with noise and error, allowing for detection and correction of plan failures. Another important issue for planners is the *frame problem*: How can a planner anticipate the side effects of a given action?

Natural-language understanding (Allen 1987, Winograd 1983) is one of the most challenging areas of AI research. The goal of creating computer programs that can effectively communicate in human language is an old one. While there have been impressive successes in highly constrained areas of discourse, general language understanding remains elusive. The problem is with the large amounts of knowledge required to understand even simple sentences. Consequently, natural-language understanding has driven, and continues to motivate, research in knowledge representation and the semantics of human language.

Machine learning (Kodratoff and Michalski 1990, Michalski et al. 1983, Michalski et al. 1986) addresses the problem of creating computer programs that can learn from their own experience, by observation, or by interpreting high-level advice. In addition to work in parallel distributed processing, considerable work has been done in symbol-based learning, focusing on the use of prior knowledge to guide learning in new domains.

Knowledge representation and reasoning (Brachman and Levesque 1985) continues to be a vital area of research, focusing on the development of representation languages that capture the full range of knowledge, and the development of sophisticated models of representational semantics.

Cognitive science (Collins and Smith 1988, Newell and Simon 1972) continues with the goal of using computer programs as a tool and a metaphor for understanding human cognition. This field blends AI with psychology, philosophy, linguistics, neuroscience, anthropology, and other disciplines in an effort to understand the functioning of the human mind at neural, cognitive, and social levels.

Other important application areas include common-sense reasoning and naive physics, game playing, computer vision, intelligent tutoring systems, the design of intelligent user interfaces, automatic programming, the design of symbolic programming languages, and the simulation of complex systems. All of these areas are the focus of active, ongoing research and promise to enrich the field of AI for years to come.

THE FUTURE OF ARTIFICIAL INTELLIGENCE: KNOWLEDGE MEDIA AND AUTONOMOUS AGENTS

The effort to produce intelligent problem solvers has led to the development of knowledge-based systems—programs that use explicitly represented knowledge to solve problems and explain the reasoning that led to those solutions. This approach has proven its viability through several successful programs; however, a number of limitations and unfulfilled promises remain. The difficulties in acquiring and organizing sufficient knowledge, along with the likely impossibility of ever proving that such a knowledge base is actually correct, suggest that we should emphasize the creation of intelligent apprentices and assistants, rather than autonomous intelligent agents. Some researchers, such as Weizenbaum, have questioned the morality of letting machines make decisions in such intimately human domains as law, politics, and business (Weizenbaum 1976).

Thus the current generation of intelligent machines may be seen as extending rather than replacing our own intellects. However, work will continue on designing machines that are capable of functioning as independent autonomous agents. A range of applications, such as space exploration or the use of robots to perform tasks (such as nuclear reactor maintenance) that are too dangerous for humans, could benefit greatly from the development of such machines.

Another path of development accepts the possibility that computers may be inherently limited in their ability to achieve humanlike intelligence and focuses on the development of intelligent assistants. One of the exciting and revolutionary potential outcomes of this research is the development and growth of electronic knowledge media.

While most contemporary electronic media are highly efficient at storing large amounts of factual information—for example, in databases—they are limited in capturing knowledge. Knowledge requires complex organization; representations such as frames, objects, and rules can capture the complex structure of human knowledge. Knowledge is dynamic; an expert, either a human or a machine, can apply the appropriate expertise to specific problem instances. Knowledge is flexible; it can be applied freely to a class of problems. Knowledge changes; knowledge-based systems allow frequent updates through the addition of new rules to the knowledge base.

Knowledge-base technologies promise the development of media for storing, transmitting, searching, and applying dynamic knowledge, just as books allow us to transmit more static information. As knowledge representation techniques progress and standards evolve, we will see formal knowledge become a marketable commodity. It is possible to envision the development of *knowledge utilities*, supplying knowledge bases to subscribers, much as contemporary utilities supply water and power. These changes in the transmission and use of knowledge will provide science, business, and government with powerful tools for progress as well as dangerous opportunities for their abuse.

Artificial intelligence reflects some of the oldest concerns of Western civilization in the light of modern computational technology. The notions of rationality, representation, and reason are now under scrutiny as perhaps never before, since computer scientists demand to understand them operationally, even algorithmically. At the same time, the political, economic, and ethical situation of our species forces us to confront our responsibility for the effects of our artifices. The interplay between applications and the more humanistic inspirations for much of AI continues to inspire hosts of rich, challenging questions.

General references for AI include *The Encyclopedia of Artificial Intelligence* (Shapiro 1987) and *The Handbook of Artificial Intelligence* (Barr et al. 1989). Our discussion of the historical foundation of AI is taken from *Artificial Intelligence and the Design of Expert Systems* (Luger and Stubblefield 1989), where a more detailed discussion of the algorithms and representations of AI is available.

References

Allen, J. 1987. *Natural language understanding.* Menlo Park, Calif.: Benjamin Cummings.

Barr, A., P. Cohen, and E. A. Feigenbaum. 1989. *The handbook of artificial intelligence,* vols. I–IV. Menlo Park, Calif.: Addison-Wesley.

Brachman, R. J., and H. J. Levesque, eds. 1985. *Readings in knowledge representation.* Los Altos, Calif.: Morgan Kaufmann.

Buchanan, B. G., and E. H. Shortliffe, eds. 1984. *Rule-based expert systems: The MYCIN experiments of the Stanford Heuristic Programming Project.* Reading, Mass.: Addison-Wesley.

Collins, A., and E. E. Smith, eds. 1988. *Readings in cognitive science.* Los Altos, Calif.: Morgan Kaufmann.

Feigenbaum, E. A. 1963. The simulation of verbal learning behavior. In E. A. Feigenbaum and J. Feldman, eds. *Computers and thought.* New York: McGraw-Hill.

Fikes, R., P. Hart, and N. Nilsson. 1972. Learning and executing generalized robot plans. *Artificial Intelligence* 3(4):251–88.

Gelernter, H. 1963. Realization of a geometry theorem proving machine. In E. A. Feigenbaum and J. Feldman, eds. *Computers and thought.* New York: McGraw-Hill.

Kodratoff, Y., and R. S. Michalski, eds. 1990. *Machine learning: An artificial intelligence approach,* vol. III. Los Altos, Calif.: Morgan Kaufmann.

Luger, G. F., and W. A. Stubblefield. 1989. *Artificial intelligence and the design of expert systems.* Redwood City, Calif.: Benjamin Cummings.

Michalski, R. S., J. G. Carbonell, and T. M. Mitchell, eds. 1983. *Machine learning: An artificial intelligence approach.* Palo Alto, Calif.: Tioga.

———. 1986. *Machine learning: An artificial intelligence approach,* vol. II. Los Altos, Calif.: Morgan Kaufmann.

Newell, A., and H. Simon. 1963a. Empirical explorations with the Logic Theory Machine: A case study in heuristics. In E. A. Feigenbaum and J. Feldman, eds. *Computers and thought.* New York: McGraw-Hill.

———. 1963b. GPS: A program that simulates human thought. In E. A. Feigenbaum and J. Feldman, eds. *Computers and thought.* New York: McGraw-Hill.

———. 1972. *Human problem solving.* Englewood Cliffs, N.J.: Prentice-Hall.

———. 1976. Computer science as empirical inquiry: Symbols and search. *Communications of the ACM* 19(3):113–26.

Pearl, J. 1984. *Heuristics: Intelligent search strategies for computer problem solving.* Reading, Mass.: Addison-Wesley.

Rosenblatt, F. 1962. *Principles of neurodynamics.* New York: Spartan.

Rumelhart, D. E., and J. L. McClelland. 1986. *Parallel distributed processing.* Cambridge, Mass.: The MIT Press.

Samuel, A. L. 1959. Some studies in machine learning using the game of checkers. *IBM Journal of Research and Development* 11: 601–17.

Shapiro, S. C., ed. 1987. *The encyclopedia of artificial intelligence.* New York: Wiley.

Turing, A. A. 1950. Computing machinery and intelligence. *Mind* 59:433–60.

Waterman, D. A. 1986. *A guide to expert systems.* Reading, Mass.: Addison-Wesley.

———, and F. Hayes-Roth, eds. 1978. *Pattern directed inference systems.* New York: Academic Press.

Weizenbaum, J. 1976. *Computer power and human reason.* San Francisco: W. H. Freeman.

Winograd, T. 1983. *Language as a cognitive process: Syntax.* Reading, Mass: Addison-Wesley.

Wos, L., R. Overbeek, E. Lusk, and R. Boyle. 1984. *Automated reasoning: Introduction and applications.* Englewood Cliffs, N.J.: Prentice-Hall.

George F. Luger
William A. Stubblefield

ARTIFICIAL INTELLIGENCE IN THE AUTOMOTIVE INDUSTRY

The automotive industry in the United States, Europe, and Japan demonstrated a strong and early interest in applying ARTIFICIAL INTELLIGENCE (AI) techniques to its operations. This article focuses on applications of KNOWLEDGE BASES AND EXPERT SYSTEMS, but the industry has also utilized other subfields of AI such as machine vision, NATURAL-LANGUAGE PROCESSING, MACHINE LEARNING, and neural networks. Evidence of interest in AI was apparent by the early 1980s, when several of the largest U.S. automotive companies, such as General Motors and Ford, made direct multimillion-dollar investments in new AI startup companies such as Teknowledge, Inc., The Carnegie Group, and Inference Corporation.

The rationale for automotive industry investments was that AI was a critical new technology that promised to revolutionize every aspect of the manufacturing process. Given the strategic importance of technical knowledge in competitive advantage, none of the automotive companies wanted to be left behind. This basic idea proved correct; AI is strategic and knowledge-based technology works. Productivity improvements, measured in speedup of work tasks, in the order-of-magnitude (10×) range and occasionally in the two-orders-of-magnitude (100×) range are commonly reported in the literature (Feigenbaum et al. 1988). Knowledge-based systems have been successfully applied to automotive design, manufacturing, service, planning, scheduling, diagnosis, quality control, configuration, process control, risk analysis, and distribution problems.

In spite of the diversity of automotive AI applications, many of the projects undertaken were essentially proof-of-concept demonstrations. Most of these demonstrations were technical successes, but fewer than half of them made it into day-to-day automotive operations. Equally important, the real economic leverage in applying knowledge-based systems is in doing things smarter, not just automating current practice (Ernst 1990). A recent 5-year study of the world automotive industry by MIT underscored the importance of process improvements by comparing the historical U.S. focus on machine automation with the Japanese focus on lean production (Womack et al. 1990). For AI applications to provide sustained competitive advantage in the automotive industry, project selection must be driven by the need for fundamental business process improvements with knowledge systems technology used as an enabling factor.

EXAMPLE APPLICATIONS

Diagnosis of machines on the automotive production line was one of the earliest and most successful applications of knowledge-based systems. General Motors (GM) sponsored the development of the Charley system, named after a retiring vibration expert named Charley Amble (Bajpai and Marczewski 1989). The Charley system reads the vibration signature of rotating equipment on the plant floor and recommends action on periodic maintenance of the equipment. The system has been fielded for several years and has been successfully installed in over 40 GM plant sites.

Ford sponsored an application called the Fuel Injector Diagnostic System (FIDS) that assists grinding machine operators in the diagnosis of fuel injector needle grinding problems. The FIDS, like most diagnostic expert systems, provides clarification, standardization, encoding, and retention of the diagnostic expertise of line personnel. It reduces downtime by reducing the time required to diagnose problems. It captures daily maintenance information and distributes the collected diagnostic expertise equally to all shifts throughout the organization.

Navistar (Feigenbaum et al. 1988) built a truck configuration system to capture a customer's unique requirements for custom trucks, taking into consideration materials, assembly lines, and compatible options. The system contains over 6,000 rules on truck configurations and constraints. It is in operational use and has increased product quality and decreased both delivery time and cost of production.

Toyota (Feigenbaum et al. 1988) built a diagnostic expert system called Atrex that supports central service center technicians in assisting field service technicians in diagnosing and repairing cars. Toyota's strategy centralizes confidential corporate knowledge. Toyota decided to place most of its emphasis on making more reliable automobiles, rather than ever more sophisticated methods of repairing them.

Chrysler developed an expert system to aid in the debugging of an engine dynamometer test facility. The system incorporates the diagnostic knowledge of instrument development and test engineers in several modules. The modules include engine exhaust emissions, temperature, strain gauge pressure and torque, and spark advance measurements. Chrysler claims that the system helps end users to quickly investigate and repair instrument failures.

CONCLUSION

A critical observation regarding the operational automotive AI applications delivered to date is that the AI-specific component of the application typically represents 15–25 percent of an overall systems solution. For AI to be effective in complex automotive applications it must be integrated with standard systems and software engineering techniques, communications networks, corporate database technologies, and standard application platforms.

It is now clear that while AI technology is powerful and even revolutionary, its incorporation into standard automotive operations will be a function of (1) end user education about the benefits of the technology and (2) the ability to integrate and deliver the technology effectively into industrial application environments. Effective delivery will require greater ease of use and lower costs to build, modify, and maintain knowledge bases over the application life cycle.

Overall, the largest barriers to effective application of knowledge system technology in the automotive industry are educational and organizational, not technological. Several factors are operating together to overcome this problem. The number of visible, successful applications grows each year. The number of people in the automotive industry with direct experience with the technology is increasing rapidly. Finally, technology innovations such as embedded systems and task-specific tools make knowledge systems progressively easier to apply effectively. The best is yet to come: intelligent manufacturing of smart cars that sense their passengers and their environment, and aid in driver navigation and decision making.

References

Bajpai, A., and R. Marczewski. 1989. Charley: An expert system for diagnosis of manufacturing equipment. In H. Schorr and A. Rappaport, eds. *Innovative applications of artificial intelligence*, pp. 148–58. Menlo Park, Calif.: AAAI Press.

Ernst, R. G. 1990. Why automating is not enough. In J. Stark, ed. *Handbook of manufacturing automation and integration*, pp. 17–23. Boston: Auerbach.

Feigenbaum, E., P. McCorduck, and H. P. Nii. 1988. *The rise of the expert systems company.* New York: Times Books.

Womack, J. P., D. T. Jones, and D. Roos. 1990. *The machine that changed the world.* New York: Rawson Associates.

Neil Jacobstein

ARTIFICIAL INTELLIGENCE IN ENGINEERING DESIGN

Designing is the act of devising an artifact that satisfies some useful need—in other words, performs some function. Designing is pervasive in many human activities; for example, an engineer conceiving of a new type of toaster, a financial manager configuring a profitable portfolio, or a chef concocting a new dish. Underlying these design tasks is a core set of principles, rules, laws, and techniques that the designer uses for problem solving.

Designers are constantly producing newer and better artifacts. In the modern competitive world, they are under constant pressure to turn out new and innovative products quickly. To improve the productivity of designers, computer-aided design tools have been developed. In the short term, these efforts have focused primarily on automating the more routine and tedious tasks involved in design. Of the two major phases of a design process, *conceptual design* and *detailed design,* tool-building efforts have concentrated mainly on the latter phase. Applications have been limited to tasks such as computer-aided drafting, solid modeling, numerical optimization, simulation, and analysis. These systems are popularly called *computer-aided design* systems.

Conceptual design is much harder to automate. Conceptual design is the process in which (1) needs are identified, (2) a problem is formulated, (3) specifications are laid out, (4) appropriate solutions are generated through the combination of some basic building blocks, and finally (5) an evaluation is carried out (see Figure 1). Conceptual design, unlike analysis, has no fixed procedure and involves a mix of numeric and symbolic reasoning. Design automation (DA) systems, in general, use some form of search to find an artifact that satisfies a given set of design specifications. For all practical purposes, the solution space is too large to enumerate fully. For this reason, special techniques are used to control and direct the search for solutions.

This article presents a review of some of the newer DA systems. For a complete review of the DA literature, see Tong (1987) and Navin chandra (1990). Following is a selection of approaches to design automation with a description of actual systems that use these approaches to solve real design problems.

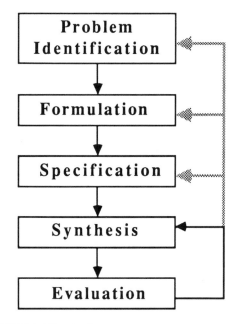

FIGURE 1. The design process.

PRODUCTION RULES

Rule-based approaches can be applied to those design domains where all the procedures are well understood and all the decision points are known beforehand. In this approach, IF-THEN rules are used to partition, refine, and specify the design. A good example of rule-based design is the R1/XCON (McDermott and Steele 1981) system in use at Digital Equipment Corporation. R1 configures computers based on customer requirements. It determines components to be placed in the central processing unit (CPU), the panels to be put in the cabinet, and the floor layout.

SEARCH TECHNIQUES

Search techniques have been successfully applied to a variety of design problems. Though very general in its applicability, search is a slow and inefficient method of finding solutions. Much of the research in this field is directed toward finding clever methods of reducing the size of the search space. Two popular search techniques are generate and test, and constraint-directed search.

Generate and Test

At the simplest level, designs can be generated by the *generate and test* paradigm (Lindsay et al. 1980). The idea is to generate design alternatives and to test them against the given specifications. When the first consistent solution is found, the process stops. No DA system uses this paradigm. This is because it is often possible to evaluate an artifact even when it is only partially designed, allowing for early detection and elimination of design problems.

Generate and test procedures may also be set up to work in stages. If a design problem is expressed as a collection of variables, then assigning a value to a variable corresponds to a stage in the process of synthesizing complete solutions. In this process of synthesis, as shown in Figure 2, partial designs are fed into a synthesis mod-

FIGURE 2. The staged generate-and-test process.

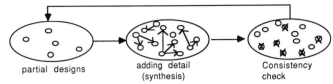

FIGURE 3. Constraint checking in a staged search process.

ule, where details are added. Incomplete detailed designs reenter the loop and go through the process until completion.

Constraint-Directed Search

One can search for design solutions in a treelike fashion, checking for consistency during the synthesis process rather than at the end. Examples of techniques that use this approach are depth-first search (Golomb and Baumert 1965), breadth-first search, and constraint-directed search (Fox 1983). This basic idea is used extensively in design automation systems. Figure 3 shows how a consistency check is introduced in the basic synthesis process.

For example, consider the task of laying out furniture in an apartment. We are given the shape and size of the apartment and the shapes and sizes of the various pieces of furniture (see Figure 4). Next, we set up requirements (constraints): The desk should be next to the window, the cabinet should be about 3 feet from the desk, etc. Search can start by selecting one item (e.g., the desk) and finding all suitable placements for it; this step is called *expansion*. Next, the constraints are used to reject alternatives that don't satisfy the requirements; this step is called *pruning*. The search continues by selecting another piece of furniture and finding placements for it. The process of expansion and pruning is continued until one finds a solution in which all the pieces of furniture have been placed and all the constraints are satisfied.

REFINEMENT TECHNIQUES

A special class of design techniques relies on refinement operators to convert a given de-

sign specification into a design description. Refinement can be carried out incrementally or hierarchically.

Incremental Refinement

Incremental refinement is the process of converting an artifact specification into an artifact description by applying a series of correctness-preserving operators. Every time an operator is applied to a specification, detail is added uniformly over the entire specification.

This paradigm has been used for program design (e.g., PECOS project [Barstow 1979]). For example, a program specification in LISP-like pseudocode could be transformed into actual LISP code through the application of refinement operators. The real advantage of using incremental refinement lies in domains where the final artifact is semantically equivalent to the representation language used. In program design the speci-

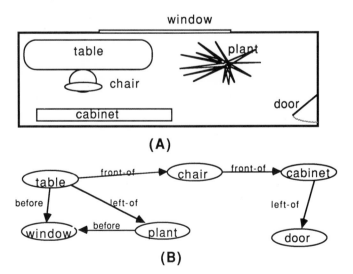

FIGURE 4. The room layout problem.

fication and the final artifact are both in LISP and are semantically equivalent. Semantic equivalence, on the other hand, is low in physical artifact design. This makes it harder for one to develop refinement operators that conserve the semantic correctness of the representation.

Hierarchical Refinement

Hierarchical refinement is the process of decomposing a given artifact specification into subparts. The process continues by decomposing the different subcomponents independent of each other. The process continues until the subcomponent specifications at the leaves of the search tree correspond directly to primitive components (e.g., gates). The search process can be viewed as an AND-OR tree, where each refinement step produces an AND node, which means that a component is composed of some subcomponents taken together. The OR nodes represent choices between or among different refinement operators applicable to a component. After each branching, a test for correctness and completeness is made. Examples of this approach are two DA systems, DESTINY (Sriram 1987) and VEXED (Steinberg 1987).

One of the major assumptions of the hierarchical refinement method is that of subcomponent independence, or at most, loose coupling among the subcomponents. The problem with the independence assumption is that design decisions made in different subcomponents can interact unfavorably, thus leading to wasted effort. Many different techniques for reasoning about control and the intelligent use of constraints have been developed to solve the problem.

THE USE OF AGENTS AND SPECIALISTS

Design problems often involve distributed expertise. Two exemplary DA systems—AIR-CYL (Brown and Chandrasekaran 1986) and PRIDE (Mittal et al. 1985)—are built using this paradigm. The basic idea is to factor the design knowledge into agents (usually in a hierarchy), which are used to solve the problem in a collective, cooperative fashion, where each agent is responsible for some aspect of the design.

In AIR-CYL the basic agent is called a specialist. Each specialist contains alternative plans. Plans, in turn, contain sequences of steps. A step contains information about how to calculate and check some design parameter and also contains knowledge about what could be done in case of constraint failure. During the design process, specialists receive requirements from parent specialists. Based on the requirements, the specialist chooses a particular precoded plan and follows the steps in the plan. If a step fails, a failure suggestion is passed up to the specialist that called it. For example, a step that calculates piston-seal width might fail because none of the available seals is as thin as the one needed. The corresponding suggestion is "Increase piston thickness."

The other system, PRIDE, designs paper paths for photocopiers. It decides on the paper trajectory, number of rolling stations, and other paper-handling equipment that make up the paper path. Like AIR-CYL, PRIDE also uses constraints, steps, plans, and advisory mechanisms. PRIDE, however, does not use advice blindly. The program takes the stored advice and does a problem analysis in the light of the advice context. In this way, PRIDE is able to generate modification suggestions over and beyond the actual static knowledge it possesses.

CASE-BASED REASONING

Case-based reasoning (CBR) is one of the newer and more promising design techniques. It is the problem-solving paradigm wherein previous experiences are used to guide problem solving (Kolodner et al. 1985). Cases similar to the current problem are retrieved from memory, and the best case is selected from those retrieved and compared with the current case. The precedent case is adapted to fit the current situation, based on the identified differences between the precedent and the current case. Successful cases are stored so they can be retrieved and reused in the future. Failed cases are also stored so they will warn the problem solver of potential difficulties and help recover from failures.

Case-based problem solving is founded on the premise that a machine problem solver uses its experiences (cases) in solving new problems instead of solving each new problem from scratch. CBR can also help the problem solver by providing memories of past failures and solutions, which can be used to detect impending problems and identify possible repair strategies without working from scratch (Navin chandra 1991, Sycara and Navin chandra 1991).

CONCLUSIONS

Artificial intelligence (AI) techniques have been applied to a wide variety of design problems. As design is a very rich domain, it has provided a forum for the integration of several AI techniques such as machine learning, search, analogy, qualitative reasoning, case-based reasoning, and expert systems. Hence the design domain has served not only as an application area for AI but also as a means of developing new ideas in AI.

References

Barstow, D. 1979. An experiment in knowledge-based automatic programming. *Artificial Intelligence,* August, pp. 73–119.

Brown, D. C., and B. Chandrasekaran. 1986. Expert systems for a class of mechanical design activity. In D. Sriram and B. Adey, eds. *Proceedings of the First International Conference on AI Applications in Engineering.* Southampton: Computational Mechanics.

Fox, M. S. 1983. Constraint-directed search: A case of job shop scheduling. Ph.D. thesis, Carnegie-Mellon University.

Golomb, S. W., and L. D. Baumert. 1965. Backtrack programming. *Journal of the ACM,* pp. 516–24.

Kolodner, J. L., R. L. Simpson, and K. Sycara. 1985. A process model of case-based reasoning in problem solving. In *Proceedings of IJCAI-85,* pp. 284–90.

Lindsay, R., B. Buchanan, E. Feigenbaum, and J. Lederberg. 1980. *Applications of artificial intelligence for chemical inference: The Dendral project.* New York: McGraw-Hill.

McDermott, J., and B. Steele. 1981. Extending a knowledge-based system to deal with ad hoc constraints. In *Proceedings of the Seventh International Joint Conference on Artificial Intelligence.* Los Altos, Calif.: William Kaufmann.

Mittal, S., C. Dym, and M. Morjaria. 1985. PRIDE: An expert system for the design of paper handling systems. In C. Dym, ed. *Applications of knowledge-based systems to engineering analysis and design,* pp. 99–116. New York: American Society of Mechanical Engineers.

Navin chandra, D. 1990. *Innovative design systems: Where are we and where do we go from here?* Technical Report CMU-RI-TR-90-01. Pittsburgh: Robotics Institute, Carnegie Mellon University.

———. 1991. *Exploration and innovation in design: Towards a computational model.* Berlin: Springer-Verlag.

Sriram, D. 1987. *Knowledge-based approaches to structural design.* Southampton: Computational Mechanics.

Steinberg, L. I. 1987. Design as refinement plus constraint propagation: The VEXED experience. In *Proceedings of the Sixth National Conference on Artificial Intelligence,* pp. 830–35.

Sycara, K., and D. Navin chandra. 1991. Index transformation techniques for facilitating creative use of multiple cases. In *Proceedings of the Twelfth International Joint Conference on Artificial Intelligence.*

Tong, C. 1987. Toward an engineering science of knowledge-based design. *Artificial Intelligence in Engineering* 2(3):133–66.

D. Navin chandra

ARTS, COMPUTERS IN THE

Computers have so altered the discipline of music that they are required for accreditation by the National Association of Schools of Music. Art students who cannot use illustration software are unemployable as graphic artists, who commonly spend 80 percent of their time editing artwork on computer screens. Choreography, lighting, set design, and animation software has permeated theater and dance. Enabling this rapid change in the way musicians and artists work is a powerful combination of desktop hardware and software that allows computers to create any sequence of sounds and any juxtaposition of colors, and synchronize the two.

Computer music has come a long way since Max Mathews made the first digital sound on an IBM 704 mainframe in 1957. Just as word processing revolutionized writing by making it easy to edit text, so also has the computer helped composers and arrangers replace static sheets of staff paper with musically active computer screens.

There are music printing programs that let you play a song into a personal computer and print the notes on music paper; editors that let you modify the performance before you print it; computer-based instruction programs that teach how to read notes and play a music keyboard; and ear-training lessons that sharpen your ear so you can improve your music playing and arranging skills. Instead of rewinding and splicing tape, studio

musicians are using personal computers to record and edit instantly any note and to mix sound tracks with split-second precision.

The computer music field was held back during the 1960s and 1970s by a lack of standardization. Music software programs worked well with the sound generator for which they were designed, but programs often required different synthesizers. There was no guarantee that computer music keyboards would be compatible with later models in the same product line, much less with brands made by other vendors.

To solve this problem, synthesizer manufacturers began to formulate a standard to make music keyboards interchangeable. After much discussion, the Musical Instrument Digital Interface (MIDI) standard was adopted in 1983. The MIDI standard lets music keyboards exchange performance information and send messages describing what is being played to and from personal computers.

The MIDI standard inspired such confidence among manufacturers and consumers that, in only a few years, millions of MIDI keyboards and synthesizers were sold to homes, schools, and musicians. The standard allows these devices to be connected to per-

FIGURE 1. Music notation software transcribes music played on the keyboard in real time. *Courtesy Coda Music Software.*

sonal computers. To quote the famous film soundtrack composer Frank Serafine (Mace 1985):

> In the past, musicians went into recording studios with a drummer, a bass player, a guitar player, and then you would lay down tracks on a multitrack recorder. MIDI is allowing me to go in and compose with drums, bass, guitar, and piano, as if I had a multitrack recorder. But the advantages of it are that I can go in and I can edit. I can step through all my sequences and go in and maybe take out a couple of bars here and there. Before, it would be ridiculous to chop tape.

Just as MIDI lets music be transported across a wide variety of hardware and software programs, so also are there graphics standards that permit artwork to be imported and exported. The most commonly used graphics standards are Tagged Image File Format (TIFF), Computer Graphics Metafile (CGM), and Encapsulated PostScript (EPS). The successful graphics artist knows how to use these standards to move graphics from platform to platform and enhance artwork with the tools available in specific graphics programs.

Until recently, the Macintosh had the undisputed lead as a platform for desktop graphics. Windows PostScript has enabled graphics programs just as powerful to be created for IBM personal computers and compatibles.

Desktop graphics programs let artists display objects as wire-frame outlines for quick editing, use Bezier curve tools to re-shape the objects, blend colors to create

FIGURE 2. Artwork generated with the graphics program CorelDraw. *Courtesy Corel Systems Corp.*

custom palettes, use graduated fills to create special effects and gradient backgrounds, embellish drawings with calligraphic pens, layer objects and move them from foreground to background, blend one object into another by automatically drawing the intermediate shapes between the two, wrap text around the objects, kern the text, and fit the text to a curved path.

Some graphics programs come with clip art libraries including more than a thousand images. Another way of getting existing artwork onto a computer screen is through color scanning; 24-bit color scanners now provide more than 16 million true colors on the computer screen. Raster-to-vector conversion software translates scanned images into wire frames for object-oriented editing.

No single program supports all of these features; large graphics production houses employ staff members adept at specific programs, and the artwork is passed from artist to artist for adding special effects. For example, one artist can add color three-dimensional shading to a monochrome drawing made by a designer with a computer-assisted design (CAD) program.

The results can be output to film recorders for producing 35-millimeter slides, divided into color separations for offset printing, or used on screen with computer projectors for lecture presentations. Some graphics programs include slide-show sequencing software that can display one picture after another automatically during a presentation.

For artistic purposes, it is generally acknowledged that computer art still is in its infancy. To quote Robert Riley, curator of media arts at the San Francisco Museum of Modern Art (Andres 1990): "Somebody made a paintbrush once by pulling hair out of a horse and tying it to the end of a stick. The software programs are at that stage. The horse is a very valuable assistant to the artist."

Andy Warhol and David Hockney have both used microcomputers to create artistic works. Computer art by Barbara Nessim, Sheriann K-Sun Burnham, and Barbara Joffe is beginning to attract attention from serious art dealers and collectors. As Riley appropriately quipped, computer art is not an oxymoron. Indeed, the computer-generated movie *Tin Toy* by Pixar won an Oscar in 1989. Pixar's animation production group was able to create a three-dimensional model of a baby's body by merging clay figures with a skeleton description. Special Pixar software called Renderman fit the body model to an animation of the skeleton to allow the baby to move and flex. Animating the baby's face required the definition and functional grouping of more than forty facial muscles.

In 1990, sixty years after its opening, the Museum of Modern Art (MOMA) in New York City mounted an exhibit of computer-generated imagery by Matt Mullican, a California artist best known for banners and posters displaying symbols of God, heaven, and fate. Using a massively parallel computer called the Optomystic Connection Machine 2, he generated views of an allegorical city that MOMA displayed on a dozen 3 × 4-foot transparencies mounted in light boxes; a nearby TV monitor took viewers on a tour of the city. Another permanent exhibit of computer art has been installed at the Fine Arts Museum of Long Island, which teaches seminars on computer imaging and provides hands-on experience with graphics software.

Desktop art programs are highly effective when their output is used in hypermedia programs that combine graphics images and musical sequences into artistically powerful multimedia presentations. Any part of any image can be defined as a hot spot that, when selected, can trigger any other graphic or audio excerpt. The essence of hypermedia is the linking of objects, which can consist of text, image, full-motion video, videodisc slides, audio compact discs, or MIDI sequences. When a word in a document is linked to an object, the document is called a hypertext; when part of a picture is linked, it is called a hyperpicture; when a bullet on a text slide is linked to a multimedia object, it is called a hyperbullet.

For example, the University of Delaware's PODIUM software provides the user with instant access to thousands of digital images, videodisc slides, motion sequences, and digital audio clips. The presenter uses any word processor to type an outline of the presentation, and the PODIUM program creates a hypermedia web with navigation tools. By selecting an item on the presentation overlay, the user can show instantly any slide or motion sequence in any order. The word processor interface lets the PODIUM user easily synchronize digital audio and video events; all music on audio compact discs can be accessed down to a seventy-fifth of a second.

Hypermedia programs are enabling presenters to take advantage of the powerful music and graphics editors discussed in this article and to combine them into powerful multimedia presentations. Multimedia will be as important to computing in the 1990s as the personalization of computers was in the 1980s, and both art and music are playing key roles in its evolution.

Art and music combine in videodiscs. Each side of a 12-inch videodisc holds 54,000 broadcast-quality images that can be viewed as still slides or in full-motion video with digital audio. All of the operas produced by the Metropolitan Opera in New York and Covent Garden in London are being pressed onto videodisc. Symphonies, concertos, piano music, a large collection of jazz, and dozens of musicals are available. Performers, conductors, and ordering information are listed by Schwartz (1989).

Videodiscs also contain the works of Pablo Picasso, Andrew Wyeth, Bill Viola, Ansel Adams, and Phillip Pearlstein. The National Gallery of Art is available on videodisc; 1,600 still images span eight centuries and include masterpieces by da Vinci, Monet, Renoir, and Matisse. The *Vincent van Gogh* videodisc puts at the user's fingertips hundreds of paintings by van Gogh. The van Gogh videodisc comes with an index that lists the paintings according to period; by creating a hypermedia outline based on this index, the user can access any painting within a second. Narration by Leonard Nimoy can also be accessed on audio track A; excerpts from van Gogh's letters are on audio track B. Ordering information for art videodiscs can be found in *The Videodisc Compendium* (Emerging Technology Consultants, Inc., P.O. Box 1244, St. Paul, Minnesota 55112).

Although growth has been slow, the fields of theater and dance are also being affected by computers. Computer-assisted design software is used to design theatrical sets. Dance notation programs are being used to choreograph footwork in Labanotation and Benesh Movement Notation, and three-dimensional animation software plays the choreography on computer screens. Choreographers can view the dance from different audience perspectives and make changes prior to enactment by a human player. The complexity of modeling human movement and the artistic nature of dance present significant challenges to theatrical software developers.

It should also be pointed out that computers are aiding appreciably in the management of arts programs. For example, box office software such as BOCS, Ticketmaster, and RITA facilitates ticketing and marketing in the performing arts. Museums are using hypermedia systems for database applications, cataloging, and public access information systems. Marching band software lets band directors design shows and print charts for each member of the band, compressing what was once weeks of manual labor into a few hours of computer use. Score editors let conductors extract parts, transpose them into the proper keys, and print sheet music with ease. Inventory programs keep track of uniforms and instruments.

The computer has altered substantially and irreversibly the professions of musician and artist. To prepare future musicians and artists for work in the information age, it is critically important to include computer use in their education at all levels. Notable is the magnet school program in the DuPont Manual High School in Lexington, Kentucky, where computers are used to teach students fine art techniques as well as commercial art forms. The San Jose Unified School District has developed an extensive MIDI program in education to encourage the use of computers and peripherals in classroom music instruction; the teachers are trained at San Jose State University's Department of Music, which has developed a complete K–12 curriculum.

Computer artists and musicians are challenging the limits of what can be done with computers in the realms of sight and sound, and the result will be more interesting applications, better-looking screens, powerful multimedia applications, and new art forms. The decade ahead can anticipate the emergence of camps and styles of computer art, analogous to the movements that formed in painting and music through the ages.

For further information, see the scholarly journals *Computers and the Humanities*, *Dance Notation Journal*, *Computer Graphics*, and *Computer Music Journal*, and the trade monthlies *Keyboard Magazine* and *Electronic Musician*.

References

Andres, C. 1990. Computer painting: Is it art yet? *MacWeek* 4(18):29.

Mace, S. 1985. Electronic orchestras in your living room. *InfoWorld* 7(12):31.

Schwartz, E. 1989. *The educators' handbook to interactive videodisc.* Washington, D.C.: Association for Educational Communications & Technology.

For Further Reading

Heck, M., D. Green, and D. Green. 1990. King of the draw: Windows PostScript illustration programs raise the stakes against Macintosh standards. *InfoWorld*, 20 Aug., pp. 51–73.

Hofstetter, F. T. 1988. *Computer literacy for musicians.* Englewood Cliffs, N.J.: Prentice-Hall. Includes a bibliography.

Madison, C. 1990. Technology changes how top design firms work. *MacWeek* 4(18):34.

Politis, G. 1990. Computers and dance: A bibliography. *Leonardo* 23(1):87–90.

Fred Hofstetter

ASCII

See Binary Numbering System

ASTRONOMY, COMPUTERS IN

Astronomy, the oldest of the observational sciences, dates back to the ancient Egyptians and Mayas and chronicles the attempts of humans to understand and make sense of the heavens. In recent decades, computer technology, coupled with telescopes and other modern observing instrumentation, has served to revolutionize astronomy, the science of observing the stars, galaxies, and planets, as well as the newer, related field of astrophysics, which applies theoretical physics to astronomical objects.

HAND CALCULATIONS AND THE BIRTH OF MODERN ASTRONOMY

In the late sixteenth century, the brilliant observational astronomer Tycho Brahe built a sophisticated observatory at Uraniborg, Denmark, and recorded over 20 years of precise data concerning the positions of the planets. All measurements were taken with hand instruments and painstaking care, and were the most accurate to that date. Johannes Kepler, who worked for Brahe and took over his results after Brahe's death in 1601, used this set of data to formulate his Laws of Planetary Motion, arrived at through hand calculating the orbit of the planet Mars. The first two laws were published in 1609, and the third, 9 years later. Kepler discovered, among other things, the elliptical shape of planetary orbits. Kepler's untiring devotion to his work fostered the birth of modern observational astronomy.

The same calculations that Kepler made to plot accurately the orbit of Mars from its observed position, or any other planet in our solar system, now would take a matter of hours, rather than Kepler's years, with the use of computers to reduce and plot planetary data.

VISIBLE LIGHT AND THE ELECTROMAGNETIC SPECTRUM

Detailed visual exploration of the universe began in the early 1600s when Galileo observed the heavens with his small telescope, capable of resolving the crescent phase of Venus and the satellites of Jupiter and Saturn. In this century, photographic plates used with telescopes have allowed astronomers to keep pictorial records of planets, stars, and other astronomical phenomena. Photographic plates allowed for long-exposure photos, which reveal details in the range of visible light that the human eye could never discern alone with even the largest telescopes.

Today, charge-coupled devices (CCDs), the semiconductor analog of photographic plates, allow astronomers and astrophysicists to put pictorial information into a digital format. A CCD is usually composed of about a quarter million microscopic, light-sensitive diodes in a rectangular array from 1 to 10 millimeters on a side. With the CCD, as well as conversion of photographic plates to digital format, astronomy has entered the realm of image processing, in which an image of an astronomical object is composed of pixels, or tiny dots, each assigned a numerical shade of gray. Highly efficient, CCDs provide an accuracy in telescopic observations unimagined in the 1950s and 1960s. Their sensitivity can improve an older telescope's ability to detect faint objects by up to eight times. Digital images may be enhanced by computer processing to bring out detail, a capability unheard of in the days of photographic plates.

The image of the dedicated astronomer, peering intently into the telescope and pointing the instrument by hand, is no longer relevant to the larger telescopes or even to those belonging to some amateurs. Computers typically control the guidance of telescopes; they automatically point the instruments in the proper direction under the guidance of digitized star maps of an accuracy heretofore unattainable. Modern astronomers are more likely to be seated at a computer console, typing in commands and sharing what the telescope "sees" via a high-resolution graphics monitor!

After the 1930s the science of astronomy was revolutionized by the addition of information previously invisible and unknown. Energy is radiated by celestial objects in electromagnetic radiation of different wavelengths, of which visible light is only a small part. The human eye senses only a limited range of the electromagnetic spectrum. Other information about celestial objects in the universe remained unstudied until the invention of techniques and detectors sensitive to the different wavelengths of light.

In 1930, Karl Jansky discovered that radio noise was emanating from the center of our galaxy, the Milky Way, in the direction of the constellation Sagittarius. But it was not until after World War II that the science of radio astronomy was finally born. Radio telescopes can detect cold clouds of gas in space that do not emit visible light, where stars are typically born, as well as extremely hot gas associated with exploding stars and the centers of galaxies.

Unfortunately, radio telescopes have low resolving power, and radio astronomers use a technique called *interferometry* to make many radio telescopes resolve as one. Computers play a vital role in coordinating these telescopes, and radio interferometry would not be possible without them. The Very Large Array, located near Socorro, New Mexico, consists of seventeen radio telescopes on a Y-shaped track that may be moved as needed for resolution of different objects. Radio astronomers have even gone so far as to use the Earth itself in very-long-baseline interferometry (VLBI), coordinating radio telescopes on different parts of the globe to function together to obtain higher-resolution images. Results from these types of observations are not immediately usable, but must be processed first by computer image processing techniques.

The Earth's atmosphere absorbs other segments of the electromagnetic spectrum; particularly ultraviolet light, X rays, some parts of the infrared, and short-wavelength radio waves. Also, the atmosphere sometimes interferes with astronomy in the visible wavelengths because of weather, water vapor in the atmosphere, and other types of distortion. Space-based astronomy, the sending of astronomical instruments into space, above the atmosphere, via rockets or the Space Shuttle, overcame atmospheric interference. The most significant astronomical instruments sent into space thus far include the International Ultraviolet Explorer (IUE), launched in 1978; the Einstein Observatory or HEAO 2, launched in 1978 and used until 1981 to observe X-ray emissions; and the Hubble Space Telescope (HST), launched in

1991 by the Space Shuttle to observe in the infrared and visible regions of the spectrum.

The Hubble Space Telescope, proposed in 1972 by NASA, is the ultimate orbital telescope with its 96-inch mirror; it is unfettered by Earth's unpredictable atmosphere. Computer controlled, the HST was designed to ''see'' with up to ten times the resolution of the largest ground-based telescopes, and to glimpse the edge of the knowable universe.

The first images from the HST were disappointing, at best. Unfortunately, design errors in the primary or secondary mirrors had compromised, at least temporarily, the telescope's potential, and NASA engineers and scientists worked to correct the problem with the telescope's mirrors. A shuttle mission was scheduled for 1993 to replace the HST's Wide Field and Planetary Camera with one that fully corrects the defect. Other instruments were to be installed to correct the optics of other detectors, and restore the HST to performance levels near those of the original design. At that time, we hope, the Hubble Space Telescope will peer to the edge of the universe, as well as enable astronomers to get a closer look at astronomical phenomena nearer to Earth.

NASA's Gamma Ray Observatory (GRO) was launched in April 1991 by the Space Shuttle *Atlantis,* and carries four massive detector instruments. Gamma rays are high-energy emissions from cataclysmic cosmic events that occurred near the dawn of time. Gamma rays tell us much about black holes, quasars, pulsars, and nucleosynthesis, and cannot be detected on Earth.

IMAGE PROCESSING AND ASTRONOMICAL DATABASES

The digital data taken from astronomical detectors and telescopes are stored in computer databases for retrieval and manipulation. Each data file represents the equivalent of one old-fashioned photographic plate, with data stored according to the $x-y$ coordinates on the detector and computer screen. Ground-based telescopes are linked directly to a computer to record the information.

Space-based telescopes and detectors must have onboard computer systems that store the data, then use radio waves to transmit the databases, one at a time, to ground-based computers. "Raw" images of celestial objects are processed on mainframe computers to remove signal noise and other defects.

Color images are not detected directly; a color image is a combination of several images, each composed of shades of gray, and filtered into red, blue, or green. The filters reveal the variances in color, which are reconstructed digitally on the computer.

Digital astronomical data are stored on magnetic tape, or may be transferred to compact-disk read-only memories (CD-ROMs). As an example, during the visit of Halley's Comet in 1986, data were archived in various International Halley Watch centers throughout the world, such as the Center for Spectroscopy and Spectrophotometry at Arizona State University. Spectral data obtained from ground-based and space-based telescopes and detectors were transmitted from scientists all over the world, converted to standard format, and archived onto CD-ROMs. These sets of disks containing all of the spectrographic data on Halley's encounter are available to scientists for study in a compact, easy-to-use format.

DATA REDUCTION AND ANALYSIS

Besides using computers to obtain images of celestial objects, astronomers and astrophysicists use computers in a variety of other ways, including graphical display of data, data reduction, solution of equations that attempt to explain physical phenomena, and mathematical data analysis. Data from stars emitting radiation in specific patterns, such as pulsars and binary stars, are more easily studied when graphically displayed and analyzed. The way an astronomer uses a computer may be as individual as the astronomer, customized to specific projects and needs. Gone are the days when scientists laboriously hand-calculated variables in hundreds of equations to obtain meaningful

results. Johannes Kepler would certainly appreciate the computer.

Some data, such as the spectral signature of stars, are best expressed in graphical form. Different types of stars, from hot, young, blue ones to older cool, red stars, emit various types of radiation at different wavelengths and possess different, predictable spectral types and signatures, which are evident when the light from an individual star is split by a spectrometer or spectrograph. (The colors you see when sunlight is split by a prism are a result of the Sun's spectrum of visible light.) Annie Jump Cannon and her colleagues at Harvard Observatory proposed the classification scheme for stellar spectra that was adopted internationally in 1910. Thousands of stellar spectra were classified by "eye" by Cannon and other young women. Today, a star's spectrum is quantified by wavelength emission, which enables more precise classification and study than could be imagined by Cannon and her colleagues.

COMPUTER MODELING

Although astronomers are mostly observational scientists, obtaining and studying data from astronomical objects, theoretical astrophysicists strive to unlock the underlying physical processes by using the laws of physics to create "working" models of astronomical phenomena. Because of the enormous amounts of computation involved in their work, computers are an essential tool to astrophysicists.

Computer models of, for example, a star's interior and the processes occurring there can be created from known physical parameters and then studied for results. The results obtained from such a model can then be compared with those for an actual star. This comparison yields information about both the star and the accuracy of the equations and assumptions used to create the model.

The advent of new graphics and display technology, coupled with the capabilities of superconducting computers, has enabled astrophysicists to make three-dimensional models of the known universe, as well as regions near our own galaxy. By plotting the distribution of galaxies throughout the universe, scientists have discovered much about galactic clusters and the large-scale structure of the universe. Most interesting is the finding that the universe is not uniform; rather, it has a "soap bubble" appearance, with vast regions containing little matter interspersed with huge clusters of galaxies.

THE FUTURE

The impact of computers and semiconducting detector components on the sciences of astronomy and astrophysics has been revolutionary. Amateur astronomers, who have long contributed to important astronomical observations and discoveries, are also beginning to benefit from the use of computers and CCD technology on a smaller scale. One thing is certain: advances in computer technology, coupled with newer and more sophisticated telescopes on the ground and in orbit, will certainly continue the evolution of humanity's understanding of the cosmos.

For Further Reading

Periodicals

Both *Astronomy* and *Sky and Telescope* occasionally have articles on charge-coupled devices and the use of computers for amateur astronomers. Both are highly recommended.

Aviation Week and Space Technology, the "watchdog" of the aviation and space industries, publishes up-to-the-week information about astronomical spacecraft, launches, and other topics.

Books

Burgess, E. 1982. *Celestial Basic: Astronomy on your computer.* Berkeley, Calif.: Sybex. A book of BASIC programs for the amateur astronomer.

Seeds, A. 1990. *Foundations of astronomy.* Belmont, Calif.: Wadsworth. An introductory, college-level astronomy textbook.

Loretta McKibben

AUDITING IN COMPUTER ENVIRONMENTS

"Auditing is the systematic process of objectively obtaining and evaluating evidence regarding assertions about economic actions and events to ascertain the degree of correspondence between those assertions and established criteria and communicating the results to interested users" (American Accounting Association 1973). Generally, an independent person (i.e., the auditor) carries out the task of objectively obtaining and evaluating evidence. The auditor can be internal or external to the organization, depending on the intended audience and purpose of the audit.

There are three types of audits. An operational audit is concerned with reviewing any part of the organization's operating procedures to evaluate the efficiency and effectiveness of those procedures. A compliance audit seeks to determine whether the auditee is following prescribed policies and procedures. A financial statement audit is concerned with establishing that management's assertions concerning the economic activities of the firm, as represented in the financial statements of the firm, conform to accepted practices.

To accomplish the intended purpose of each type of audit, assertions must be specified, criteria must be established, and objective evidence must be available on which to base a comparison of the assertions with the established criteria. Internal auditors are most often associated with the first two types of audit, although external auditors can participate in audits of this nature as well. The interested reader should consider the wealth of published literature available from the American Institute of Certified Public Accountants (AICPA 1990) and the Institute of Internal Auditors (IIA 1989) in pursuing these issues. Given the space available and the specific focus on auditing in computer environments, this article concentrates on the most prominent audit activity: financial statement audits by external auditors for use by third parties outside the firm under audit.

FINANCIAL STATEMENT AUDITS

Two general observations are necessary to focus this discussion. First, every audit is, by economic necessity, a sampling of the underlying events and supporting evidence. The audit will have been designed to reduce the risk of a material error being present in the reported financial statements, but not to ensure absolute accuracy. Thus, the statements may have minor (i.e., not material) inaccuracies, and there will still be some risk that a material error could be present even after a competently planned and executed audit. Second, the auditor must choose from many possible evidential sources and evidence-gathering techniques in planning an efficient and effective audit. For example, the auditor may expend substantial time and effort in testing a firm's system of internal control for effectiveness. If it is found to be effective, the auditor will consider reducing direct substantive tests of the balances reported in the financial statements. For example, where control over sales, receivables, and cash collections is particularly effective, the auditor may reduce the number of confirmation requests sent to customers asking them to confirm the balance shown as due and included in the financial statements. Although many choices have to be made, the degree to which the auditor decides to rely on the internal control systems of the firm is fundamental.

COMPUTERIZED ENVIRONMENTS

In a computerized environment, the auditors' responsibility is to evaluate the auditee's internal controls and the results of processing accounting data. These responsibilities are as follows (Cash et al. 1977):

1. Understanding the system
2. Verifying phases of processing
   A. General controls
   B. Application controls
3. Verifying results of processing

When significant accounting functions are handled by computing systems, the auditor must first gain an understanding of the system. The extent of subsequent testing related to verifying the phases of processing and the results of processing depends on the auditor's judgment based on an understanding of the system. In a well-designed system the auditor may expend substantial resources in verifying the phases of processing and reduce the extent of testing related to verifying the results of processing. If the system is not well designed or does not function effectively, the auditor may expend few or no resources in testing the phases of processing and concentrate resources directly on verifying the results of processing. The choice of audit plans is a matter of audit judgment; however, auditing standards do require that the auditor gain an understanding of the system and do not allow complete reliance on tests of systems controls (i.e., all audit plans include some level of substantive testing).

INTERNAL CONTROL AND THE PHASES OF PROCESSING

An internal control system is the set of procedures and policies established to provide reasonable assurance that organizational objectives will be achieved, in compliance with laws, regulations, and ethical guidelines relevant to the organization (AICPA 1989a, 1989b; American Accounting Association 1973; IIA 1989). Effective internal controls provide protection of organization resources (including information) from hazards and abuse, as well as promote operational efficiency. With respect to the information under audit consideration, the general objectives of an internal control system are to ensure reasonably that recorded information is valid and complete, properly authorized, and properly classified and summarized. If a system of internal control is in place and operating effectively in meeting these objectives, then the organizational information under audit can be considered reliable. As noted above, the auditor may be justified in spending considerable time in evaluating an organization's system of internal controls where they are expected to be effective.

THE COMPUTER AND INTERNAL CONTROL

There are two broad classifications of internal control procedures and policies that cover the phases of processing. General controls cover the computer and data processing activities within an organization as a whole, including the operations of the computerized data processing activities, computer programming procedures, hardware controls, and access to the computing facilities. Application controls relate to the input, processing, and output of a given computer application (e.g., the processing of billing or payroll).

General Controls

General controls are pervasive in that they impact on the auditor's ability to rely on application controls. Weaknesses in general controls can affect application controls in all application areas. The first set of general controls is organizational in nature and outlines the organizational structure and responsibilities of computing personnel. A key general control of this nature is separating personnel responsible for important computing activities. Proper separation of responsibilities requires that two or more individuals collude in order to perpetrate a fraud or hide an error, thus making it more difficult for any single individual to commit an act of fraud. Separating personnel involved in application systems analysis and programming from personnel responsible for computer operations is generally considered a critical separation of duties. An analyst or programmer who can gain access to computer operations during applications processing could make unauthorized changes in applications programs. Likewise, a computer operator who has unrestricted access to program copies and related documentation could also implement unauthorized changes. Authority and responsibility should also be clearly separated among the functions of transactions authorization, file library maintenance, and data control. In addition to separating duties, all computing personnel should be carefully supervised and regularly evaluated. These general controls not only help protect valuable information resources, but also promote organizational efficiency.

Another aspect of general control involves data security. These controls are designed to avoid theft, physical destruction, and unauthorized access to organizational data. Elementary controls such as secured facilities, labeling of tape and disk storage media, and maintenance of backup copies help avoid the misplacement, loss, or destruction of data. A data recovery plan and procedures should also be coupled with backup facilities to ensure recovery can be efficiently and effectively accomplished. Applications of cryptology may also be appropriate for particularly sensitive data.

General controls can also be implemented in the computer hardware circuitry. For example, a parity bit is often added to the set of bits used to represent data. Parity bits are used by various hardware devices such as tape storage units to detect errors in the circuitry when a bit is lost or added because of equipment malfunction. Likewise, data transmission can be verified by an "echo check" verifying that the signal received by a component matches the source data.

Application Controls

The general controls discussed above focus on the computing system environment as a whole. Application controls are specifically targeted on the input, processing, and output of a given computerized application such as customer billing. Input controls are intended to ensure that all input is fully accounted for and that input is complete and accurate. They form the first level of control defense against data input errors. Input controls include control and hash totals, field checks, limit checks, check digits, and document counts. In addition, input controls include the effective design of hard copy forms and/or computer screens for data entry, with the objective of verifying the validity and completeness of data at entry.

Processing controls are focused on ensuring that all authorized input is processed as intended and that no unauthorized input is processed. Processing controls include batch and hash control totals, limits checks, and suspense files designed into the transaction processing programs.

Output controls are put into place to ensure the accuracy, completeness, timeliness, and proper distribution of processed output, whether the output is on screen, in printed form, or on magnetic secondary storage. Output should be initially screened for obvious errors in format and content. A standard format can be used as a reference in completing this format check. All output should be immediately routed to a controlled area for distribution to authorized persons. Output control totals (e.g., a batch record count) should be compared and verified with input control totals. Finally, formal procedures should be in place to systematically record, report, and correct errors discovered in output.

As may be evident from the inclusion of the same controls under input, processing, and output, it can be difficult to categorize a particular control mechanism as an input, processing, or output control. Similar control mechanisms may be used for each activity. It is sometimes useful to classify controls as preventive, detective, or corrective. Preventive controls are designed to prevent an error or problem from occurring, detective controls are intended to discover control problems soon after they occur, and corrective controls are established to remedy problems that are discovered through detective controls. General controls in the computer environment are mainly designed to be preventive and apply to all application areas. Application controls generally used to prevent errors include passwords; turnaround documents; and input validation checks such as validity tests, logic tests, and control totals. Detective controls include similar data transmission controls, control registers, and control totals. Corrective controls include the specific processes for correcting detected errors and providing adequate audit trails for error correction.

TECHNIQUES FOR VERIFYING THE PHASES OF PROCESSING

The auditor has essentially two choices in auditing the phases of processing in a com-

puter environment. The auditor can ignore the computer by auditing around the computer, or the auditor can audit through the computer in an attempt to understand the processing activities directly. In auditing through the computer, the auditor will invariably audit with computer assistance (i.e., the auditor will use computing to audit the computer processes). In auditing around the computer, the auditor may choose to use computing technology to aid in this effort or resort to traditional manual methods. The use of computing technology to aid in the audit is often referred to as auditing with the computer. These distinctions become evident as each option is discussed.

Auditing Around the Computer

Auditing around the computer is the traditional approach to auditing a computerized information system. Under this approach the processing components of the system are in effect treated as a "black box." That is, the auditor does not examine the actual processing that takes place, but rather examines only the input and output of the system. The idea is to calculate manually the expected results of computer processing for some set of test data (artificial or actual input), then compare those results with the actual results of computer processing (i.e., output). The key assumption is that if the actual output matches that which was manually calculated as expected output, then processing itself is correct and all output is reliable.

Auditing around the computer is inexpensive and easy, and requires minimal knowledge of the computing technology or methods. This approach does, however, have a significant limitation in that it does not allow any inference about how and whether the processing system handles a specific transaction or error that was not included in the example input/output. For example, in a classic case, a bank's accounting programs properly handled all overdrawn bank accounts except the system programmer's account. Unless the test data included the system programmer's account, no test data technique would likely discover this error.

Auditing Through the Computer

Auditing through the computer is an approach intended to "open" the black box and examine the processing operations of the system. Table 1 lists several techniques generally considered appropriate for auditing through the computer and summarizes the advantages and disadvantages of each. The details of the most common techniques are discussed below. Each technique should contribute to an understanding of the processing activities if it is to be considered a through-the-computer audit technique. The key assumption is that if the processing system is found to be well designed, including adequate controls, and operating effectively, then output can be accepted as reliable. The advantage of auditing through the computer is that it allows the auditor to examine directly how the processing system handles different classes of transactions, including transactions with specific types of errors. This approach is, however, relatively expensive to implement and generally requires a significantly more complete understanding of the computer processes to be examined.

The first listed and most common technique is the "test deck" or test data technique. Under this technique a set of audit test transactions are prepared by the auditor. These transactions will be designed to contain both valid transactions and transactions with predetermined errors and irregularities. The test transactions are processed through the auditee's system, generally during a dedicated audit test run. The output from this test run is then compared with predetermined results for the test transactions. If the application program under examination processes every transaction correctly, including the predetermined errors and irregularities, the auditor infers the existence of the appropriate functioning controls. This technique is probably best restricted to batch processing systems.

Two other common techniques used to audit through the computer are the integrated test facility (ITF) technique and the embedded audit module technique. These two techniques are better suited for on-line processing systems, because testing of the system can take place concurrently with actual processing. The integrated test facility technique is an extension of the test data technique except that the test transactions created by the auditor are processed concurrently with actual (live) transactions of the organization. The test transactions are specially coded so the system can identify them and print the results of their processing separate from the actual transaction output. The coding also facilitates the removal of the effects of these test transactions from actual reports. This technique allows the auditor to examine and test the same processing steps as those applied to live transactions. Therefore, the auditor has no doubt that the computer operations being tested are those used in daily processing.

Embedded audit modules are special portions of a given application program that monitor and collect data for the auditor. As live transactions enter the system they are processed by the application program and the audit module contained in that application program. If a transaction meets some predetermined condition, it is copied onto an audit log for auditor review. For example, transactions with dollar amounts in excess of prescribed limits (these should have been identified by a preventive input control) will be detected and copied to the audit log. Therefore, the audit module actively monitors all transaction or transactions over selected times and reports those having special audit significance. The embedded audit module technique can also allow the monitoring of processing not related to individual transactions, such as unauthorized attempts to access the system. It is, however, a costly and complex technique to implement.

Space does not permit discussion of the other less common techniques noted in Table 1; however, careful consideration of a number of them will show that they still require a "black box" inference by the auditor. Even the ITF technique discussed above does not enable the auditor to observe the actual operation of the control mechanism. Some techniques generally classified as through-the-computer techniques might better be classified as auditing with the computer. Both the test deck (data) and ITF techniques may best be classified in this manner. Parallel simulation is also such a technique. In a

TABLE 1. Summary of Techniques and Tools Used to Audit Through the Computer[a]

Technique	Description	Synonyms	Advantages	Disadvantages
Test data	Test transactions prepared by auditor and processed during a dedicated audit run	"Test deck"; a related term is "test data generator"	Little technical expertise; increased process logic examination by data designer; effective if the variety of conditions is limited	Only preconceived conditions are tested; almost impossible to design comprehensive test data for complex systems; time consuming; lacks objectivity
Integrated test facility (ITF)	Test transactions processed along with live processing	"Minicompany," "dummy company," "auditor's central office," "extended test data method"	Tests system in a regular processing mode; only moderate degree of technical expertise required; other advantages parallel those of test data	Removing test data from system may cause destruction of client files; use of different or special process logic; other disadvantages parallel those of test data
Embedded audit module	Special portions of application program collect audit data for later review		Most complete monitor of transactions; ongoing monitor of transactions; ability to monitor nontransaction processing	High level of computer knowledge required; costly and complex to implement
Parallel simulation	Auditor-created programs to simulate processing functions in parallel with client's program		Allows independence of auditor from client personnel; facilitates examination of a larger number of transactions; only moderate level of technical expertise required	This technique is an automated version of the "around-the-computer" technique and has the same disadvantages as that technique, except that it handles substantially larger samples (for a given time or process it may handle the population of transactions).
Flowchart verification	Examination of logic schematics (flowcharts) of program code	Related term is "automatic flowcharting routine"	Improved readability over code checking; logic interpretability is improved	State-of-art of automatic flowcharters not sufficiently developed; cumbersome and time consuming if manual; another language

(continued)

TABLE 1. Summary of Techniques and Tools Used to Audit Through the Computer[a] (cont.)

Technique	Description	Synonyms	Advantages	Disadvantages
Tagging and tracing (TT)	Tags input data and displays relevant info at key points during processing	"Tagging and picture taking," "tracing marked data"; "audit indicator" and "snapshot" are specific implementations of this technique	Use of actual data; can be more effective when used in combination with ITF	May also require special process logic not normally used; no guarantee that all logic paths are traversed; risk of code violation when entry points are known
Mapping	Logically traces paths of processing to determine if all critical paths are traversed	"Missed branch indicator," "control monitors," "logic supervisors"	Refers auditor to undesirable code; examines process logic; once developed, easy to implement; can be used in conjunction with other techniques	Interpretability of output; high process overhead; preprocessing may camouflage malicious code
Concurrent processing	Detects exceptional or unusual conditions during audit run	"Continuous processing," "concurrent auditing," "continuous auditing by exception"	Designed to detect "exception" conditions when they occur; can be used in conjunction with "threat monitoring" routines of a security system	Does not examine process code; most systems detect only anticipated "exceptions"
Controlled processing or reprocessing	Auditor independently tests and verifies auditor copy of software, then processes client data		Allows auditor to check for consistency of processes used during and at end of audit; technical expertise required	Does not verify process code directly; it is assumed another technique is used
Program code checking	Detailed analysis (line-by-line) of software program code	"Program listing verification," "desk checking," "code checking"	Process logic examined in detail; auditor is intimately aware of process code content	Very high level of expertise required; very time consuming; practical only in relatively simple systems

Adapted from Cash et al. 1977.

[a]The value, advantages, and disadvantages of any verification technique ultimately must be examined in the context of specific audit circumstances including noncomputerized controls. Thus, the existence of disadvantages relative to a technique does not preclude it from being the "best" alternative in the circumstances at hand. Relevant issues include auditor expertise, timing, cost, and available alternatives yielding acceptable results.

parallel simulation, the auditor writes a program intended to emulate critical aspects of the client's program, for example, payroll processing. The auditor then processes actual client transactions through the auditor's emulator. If the results agree with the client's processing and all error conditions are properly handled, the auditor infers proper computer control. This really amounts to using the computer (i.e., auditing with the computer) to audit around the computer.

VERIFYING THE RESULTS OF PROCESSING: AUDIT SOFTWARE

Auditors use computers to support a variety of audit activities, including risk assessment, program planning, workpaper preparation, statistical sampling, use of expert systems, and a rapidly expanding group of decision support systems intended to create more efficient and effective audits. The most common method of utilizing the computer to aid the auditor in verifying the results of processing is through the application of generalized audit software packages (GASPs).

Generalized audit software packages are computer programs used by the auditor to review, retrieve, and operate on information stored in the client's computer files. Generalized audit software packages perform many of the mechanistic audit functions that have traditionally been carried out by junior auditors or clerical personnel. These tasks include extracting or retrieving data from the auditee's electronic files, performing calculations with data (e.g., calculating price and quantity extensions for customer invoices), summarizing data to provide a basis of comparison (e.g., summarizing salaries for comparison with total payroll), selecting statistical samples, and performing necessary mathematical calculations. These program packages are usually developed by software development firms or large auditing firms and are designed to be easy to use. It should be noted that GASPs do not examine the application programs of the organization. Therefore, GASPs are not a substitute for the techniques used to audit around or through the computer. In addition, GASPs still have limited

capacities in complex data structures typical of on-line databases.

INCREASING USE OF COMPUTERS

The increased role of the computer in accounting and management information processing dramatically affects the task of the auditor. Although the basic objectives of the audit are the same whether a manual or computerized system is in place, the introduction of the computer requires the auditor to adapt to the changed form of the audit trail and resulting output formats. This has generally required that the auditor adopt computer technologies to support the auditor in performing the audit and in evaluating accounting information systems.

There has been rapid expansion in the use of the computer to support audit activities and auditors (Bailey et al. 1988). The introduction of decision support systems to support risk analysis, audit program planning, and general and specific financial and business data relevant to the audit and workpaper control has been impressive. The unanswered questions are perhaps even more impressive. The interested reader is referred to Bailey et al. (1988).

References

American Accounting Association. 1973. *Studies in accounting research 6: A statement of basic auditing concepts.* Sarasota, Fla.: American Accounting Association.

American Institute of Certified Public Accountants (AICPA). 1989a. *Statements of auditing standards no. 48: The effects of computer processing on the examination of financial statements.* New York: AICPA.

———. 1989b. *Statements of auditing standards no. 55: Consideration of the internal control structure in financial statement audits.* New York: AICPA.

———. 1990. *Statements of auditing standards.* New York: AICPA.

Bailey, A. D., Jr., L. E. Graham, and J. V. Hansen. 1988. Technological development and EDP. In A. Rashad Abdel-Khalik and I. Solomon, eds. *Research opportunities in* accounting: The second decade, chap. 3, pp. 57–94. Sarasota, Fla.: American Accounting Association.

Cash, J. I., A. D. Bailey, Jr., and A. B. Whinston. 1977. A survey of techniques for auditing EDP-based accounting information systems. *The Accounting Review* 52(4).

Institute of Internal Auditors. 1989. *Standards for the professional practice of internal auditing.* Altamonte Springs, Fla.: Institute of Internal Auditors.

For Further Reading

Arens, A. A., and J. K. Loebbecke. 1988. *Auditing: An integrated approach.* Englewood Cliffs, N.J.: Prentice-Hall.

Cashin, J. A., P. D. Neuwirth, and J. F. Levy. 1986. *Cashin's handbook for auditors.* 2nd ed. New York: McGraw-Hill.

Murphy, M. A., and X. L. Parker. 1989. *Handbook of EDP auditing.* 2nd ed. New York: McGraw-Hill.

Sawyer, L. B., and G. E. Sumners. 1988. *Sawyer's internal auditing: The practice of modern internal auditing.* Rev. ed. Altamonte Springs, Fla.: Institute of Internal Auditors.

Wilkinson, J. W. 1986. *Accounting and information systems.* 2nd ed. New York: Wiley.

Tarek S. Amer
Andrew D. Bailey, Jr.

AUTHORING LANGUAGES, SYSTEMS, AND ENVIRONMENTS

Authoring systems and languages are programming tools used to develop interactive software. As interactive software has been used mainly in education, authoring systems and languages are most closely associated with the development of computer-based instruction; however, because interactive software is now common in many other areas such as entertainment, point-of-sale, and decision support systems, authoring systems and languages are no longer used exclusively for education.

The major characteristic of an interactive program is that it can process user input and provide a contingent response. In the early days of computing (circa 1950–1970) most programs ran in batch mode and no information was output until after a program finished running. This was unsatisfactory for educational programs, and work began in the 1960s to develop computer languages that allowed user input while the program was running.

Special-purpose programming languages called authoring languages were designed specifically to make it easier to create interactive programs. Supporting graphics and color as well as *multimedia* presentations (e.g., audio and video) are considered essential capabilities of authoring languages. Recording user responses so that the student's progress can be analyzed is another important feature.

By the end of the 1970s, dozens of authoring languages were available (cf. Barker 1987, Kearsley 1982). Some were designed for large mainframe systems; others were specific to micro- or minicomputers. Most authoring languages ran only on a particular computer system (e.g., COURSEWRITER, TUTOR), although a few were implemented on a range of different machines (e.g., PLANIT, PILOT).

In the late 1970s, the first authoring systems began to appear (cf. Crowell 1988, Fairweather and O'Neal 1984, Pogue 1982). Authoring systems are program generators. By filling in predefined fields and selecting options from menus, it is possible to create a program without any formal programming. Authoring systems provide three major benefits. First, they allow individuals (instructional designers, teachers) without any programming background to create instructional software. Second, they significantly reduce the amount of debugging required because the program generated by the authoring system is free of programming errors. Third, by virtue of not requiring programming skill and debugging, authoring systems allow programs to be created in much less time.

During the 1980s, both authoring languages and systems continued to evolve and become more powerful, matching the additional capabilities of the personal computer systems becoming available at that time. Even though more and more developers used authoring systems, there was still heavy use of authoring languages and programming languages to create *instructional software*. Although authoring systems provided many benefits, they did not offer the full flexibility and fast execution possible with authoring or programming languages. Most commercial vendors offered authoring tools having both an authoring system and an underlying authoring language. This made it possible to create programs using either the system or the language depending on the instructional need and the author's programming skills.

In the mid-1980s, the first authoring environments began to emerge. Authoring languages and systems are tools for the development of a program; authoring environments are automated tools that cover a much wider range of the instructional development process, including the analysis of what to teach, the design of lessons, and evaluation. Authoring environments provide software tools for all the activities involved in creating interactive instruction, not only the creation of programs (cf. Kearsley 1986, Merrill and Li 1989, Russell et al. 1987). Figure 1 summarizes the history of authoring software just outlined.

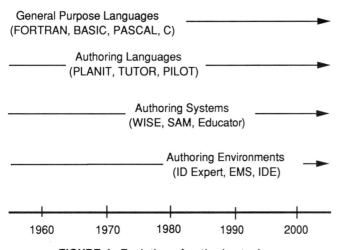

FIGURE 1. Evolution of authoring tools.

The history of authoring tools mirrors the general trends in the software world. The progression from specialized programming languages to systems to environments can be seen in many other application areas (e.g., engineering, simulation, business). Authoring systems are similar in a number of ways to other kinds of software such as prototyping tools, screen builders, and desktop presentation (slide show) programs. As most programs today are interactive and involve graphics and color, authoring tools have become a major component of software development in areas besides instruction.

MAJOR FEATURES

Authoring languages and systems are probably best understood by examining their features. In the case of authoring languages, these features are parameters that could be specified in a line of program code; in the case of authoring systems and environments, they are usually options or parameters selected from menus.

Text Editor

At a minimum, an authoring tool allows the entry and modification of text strings, including insert, delete, move, and copy. Most programs also allow the positioning of text at any desired location on the screen. Selection of font size and style is common, as is choice of text color and highlighting. Some authoring tools also provide a character editor that allows the creation or modification of new text characters or "sprites" to be used in the program.

Graphics Editor

Most current authoring tools include some type of graphics editor that allows the drawing of basic forms such as lines, circles, boxes, arcs, and freehand shapes. Other typical options are fill (with color or patterns), rotate, copy, move, resize, erase, and change line thickness or color. Most graphics editors also allow images to be imported from another program.

Animation

Many authoring tools include an animation option that allows text or graphics objects to display in a timed sequence. The option lets the author specify the path and timing of the movement.

Sound Editor

A sound editor allows sound effects or musical sequences to be created and modified. In some cases, the sound editor allows for synthesized speech or digital sound sampling.

Device Driver

Many authoring tools allow computer control of a videodisc or compact disk read-only memory (CD-ROM) player. Drivers are programs that give authors the ability to locate a specific frame and/or play a prescribed number of frames. Speed of play (slow, fast, single frame) and direction (forward, backward) can also be specified.

Answer Processing

All authoring programs provide some kind of answer-matching capability including exact match, numerical answers only, ignorable characters, upshift/downshift, *and/or* combinations, and spelling tolerance. Most authoring programs also allow for touch or mouse input. Some provide built-in formats for different types of questions such as true/false, multiple choice, and fill in the blank.

Branching

A variety of branching options are provided by authoring programs, usually tied to the results of the answer match. This can include various types of conditional branches (e.g., if answer correct, if third try, if *n* seconds elapsed) as well as loop structures or subroutine calls. Branching options allow for feedback messages and different lesson sequences to be displayed.

Variable Handling

Most authoring systems allow use of variables to store input text strings (e.g., the student's name) or values to be used in calculations (e.g., scores). Authoring programs also typically include system variables such as date, time, and input buffer that can be used by the author.

Student Recordkeeping

At a minimum, most authoring systems provide for the automatic collection of student responses in a data file. Many have report generation capability, displaying student responses or scores by individual or group (class). More sophisticated systems provide test item analysis and detailed student progress reports.

File Management

All authoring programs allow some level of file management options in terms of saving, loading, copying, renaming, erasing, and printing programs (lessons) created as well as access to the various editors mentioned earlier. Many recent authoring systems allow lesson files to be manipulated by moving icons around the screen. File management options may also include the ability to switch back and forth between authoring and run-time mode and the ability to create a student run-time version of a program that can be delivered on computers not having the authoring software.

Course Management

Some authoring systems provide higher-level organization capabilities that allow the author to select or specify certain instructional strategies to be used in a program or to define the configuration of the system for which the program is being developed. There may also be routines that allow course components to be integrated with other application programs.

EXAMPLES

Some examples of the major types of authoring tools currently available are discussed in this section. The programs mentioned are considered representative of a particular kind of authoring tool and are not being endorsed or recommended.

Mainframe Tools

Most companies use a large mainframe and terminals for their computer-based education activities and require an authoring tool that can be used in this kind of computing environment. Phoenix (Goal Systems International, Columbus, Ohio) is an authoring language that is widely used in this setting. Phoenix supports primarily the kinds of page-oriented displays possible on mainframe terminals, although there is a "micro" version of the language that allows uploading/downloading with the host mainframe. There are also a number of authoring tools that run on UNIX-based mainframes. CAST (Global Technology Inc., Chicago, Illinois) and Authology (CEIT Systems, San Jose, California) are examples.

Personal Computers

The largest category of authoring tools comprises those developed for personal computers, especially MS-DOS machines. The most commonly used and oldest authoring languages available for personal computers (PCs) are PILOT (PC Pilot, Washington Computer Services, Bellingham, Washington) and TENCORE (Computer Teaching Corp., Champaign, Illinois). A version of PILOT has been available for every major PC beginning with the Apple II (cf. Starkweather 1985). Many of the more recent authoring systems for PCs tend to be visually oriented and use icons and graphic controls. Examples are Icon Author (AIMtech, Nashua, New Hampshire) for MS-DOS machines and Course of Action (Authorware Inc., Bloomington, Minnesota) on the Macintosh. Probably the most successful authoring tool to date (on any computer) has been HyperCard from Apple. As this program is given away with every Macintosh purchased, it is widely available. HyperCard combines both an authoring system and an authoring language (called AppleTalk) and is therefore both easy to use and powerful.

Multimedia Workstations

There are many authoring systems available that have been specially developed for multimedia workstations (usually a PC linked to a videodisc or CD-ROM player). Popular examples include OASYS (Online Computer Systems, Germantown, Maryland) and QUEST (Allen Communication, Salt Lake City, Utah). Although most PC-based authoring tools support some level of multimedia capability, authoring tools specifically designed for this purpose support a wider range of editing features and hardware configurations.

Proprietary Systems

All of the authoring tools mentioned so far run on major brands of computers; however, there also exist authoring tools that run only on a proprietary computer system and are designed to take advantage of the special capabilities of that system. The best-known examples are the TUTOR author language designed for the PLATO system (including touch panels and high-resolution graphics) and the authoring language and system used with the TICCIT system (featuring color, video, and learner-controlled lessons). The WISE authoring system for the WICAT computer system is another recent example.

ISSUES

A number of theoretical and practical issues associated with authoring tools are discussed in this section. They include selection, usage, portability, licensing, and instructional flexibility.

Selection

Given the large number of authoring tools commercially available and the variety of possible features, selecting the best or most appropriate tool for a given instructional application is difficult. A number of different selection strategies have been proposed. The simplest method is to rate authoring programs according to the presence or absence of various features, ranking those features more important for a desired application (Locatis and Carr 1985). Another possibility is to compare different authoring systems in terms of efficiency when used to create the same lesson (Hillelsohn 1984) or based on cognitive processing demands for authors (Locatis and Carr 1988). A more comprehensive approach applies these efficiency measures to standard authoring tasks to estimate the authoring tool's flexibility and power (MacKnight and Balagopalan 1989).

Usage

Another aspect related to the design and selection of authoring tools is the intended or actual user. Even though authoring languages are specially designed for interactive applications, they still involve programming. Authoring systems, on the other hand, are intended to be used by individuals without programming background. They can still, however, be complicated to use. Rode and Poirot (1989) report that relatively few teachers use authoring systems and those who do generally have more experience designing interactive software. Authoring systems tend to be used by instructional developers who are well trained in the instructional design and development. Regardless of how effective the authoring tool is, development of interactive software requires a significant understanding of instructional design (Kearsley 1984). This can be a limiting factor in the value of an authoring tool.

Portability

One practical factor limiting the selection of authoring tools is that most developed originally on one computer will not run on another type of machine. This is a function of different operating systems and machine capabilities such as graphics, input devices, and storage media. Lack of portability across different computers reduces the cost-effectiveness of courseware development and is one of the factors that contribute to the high cost of many programs. To develop programs that can run on a variety of different computers, a general-purpose programming language is often used, as this is least likely to be machine specific. Authoring systems and environments tend to be unique to a specific computer system, although there are a few that run on multiple types of computers.

Licensing

Most authoring languages, like general-purpose programming languages, have a one-time purchase price and license. Authors are free to develop and distribute as many programs as they wish with no additional cost involved. Many authoring systems, however, require a royalty fee for every run-time copy of a program that is created or require authors to purchase extra run-time software for each lesson to be distributed. As few authors or companies want to pay a royalty for a program they create or be perpetually dependent on vendors for run-time software, this licensing consideration has discouraged many would-be users. Futhermore, authoring systems are often priced much higher than authoring languages of comparable power.

Instructional Flexibility

One of the major theoretical issues in the use of an authoring tool is the extent to which it facilitates or constrains the development of good computer-based learning materials. Most authoring languages are neutral in this respect as they do not contain any built-in instructional theory; however, authoring systems and environments do tend to embody certain instructional models or logics. For example, a test template may allow only multiple-choice format, making the use of open-answer or fill-in-the-blank questions difficult. On the other hand, some authoring systems provide instructional templates that encourage the author to use a broader selection of learning strategies. Authoring tools should make it easier for developers to be creative rather than limit their options.

FUTURE DEVELOPMENTS

At least five factors are likely to shape the future development and use of authoring tools. Two factors, mentioned earlier, are the wider use of interactive programs beyond the realm of education and the emergence of authoring environments that cover the entire scope of instructional development, not only the program generation step. The impact of both of these trends is to make authoring software of interest to many more people than has been the case historically.

A third major trend that has already been alluded to is the increasing emphasis on multimedia authoring tools. With the increased use of videodisc and CD-ROM systems (including DVI and CD/I technologies), there is a greater need for sophisticated authoring tools that can work with these systems. Because of the complexity of creating interactive multimedia presentations, tools that can simplify the development process are likely to be in demand.

A fourth trend is smarter software. Artificial intelligence (AI) continues to be applied to a wide variety of computing applications including education (e.g., McFarland and Parker 1990, Poulson and Richardson 1988). One of the limiting factors in developing intelligent tutoring systems has been the lack of suitable authoring tools (Kearsley 1988). Currently, AI languages such as LISP and PROLOG must be used, restricting development to authoring teams that have such expertise. On the other hand, expert system shells (i.e., authoring programs for creating expert systems), such as VP Expert, Insight, and First Class, are widely available and have resulted in the widespread exploration of that form of AI in education (e.g., Lippert 1989). As more authoring tools are developed for other aspects of AI, it is likely that their features will be integrated into tools for developing instructional software.

Finally, as more instructional designers and teachers have formal training and experience in creating interactive software and exposure to authoring programs during their course work, the use of authoring tools is likely to increase.

In summary, it seems likely that future authoring software will become much broader in scope and more powerful in capabilities. Authoring tools are likely to emerge as a major software category, considerably outgrowing their humble beginnings as relatively obscure programs for creating simple instruction.

References

Barker, P. G. 1987. *Author languages for CAL.* Basingstoke: Macmillan.

Crowell, P. 1988. *Authoring systems.* Westport, Conn.: Meckler Publishing.

Fairweather, P., and F. O'Neal. 1984. The impact of advanced authoring systems on CAI productivity. *Journal of Computer Based Instruction* 11(3):90–94.

Hillelsohn, M. 1984. Benchmarking authoring systems. *Journal of Computer Based Instruction* 11(3):95–97.

Kearsley, G. 1982. Authoring systems in computer-based education. *Communications of the ACM* 25(7):429–37.

———. 1984. Instructional design and authoring software. *Journal of Instructional Development* 7(3):11–16.

———. 1986. Automated instructional development using personal computers. *Journal of Instructional Development* 9(1):9–15.

———. 1988. Authoring systems for ICAI. In D. H. Jonassen, ed. *Instructional designs for microcomputer courseware.* Hillsdale, N.J.: Erlbaum Associates.

Lippert, R. C. 1989. Expert systems: Tutors, tools, and tutees. *Journal of Computer Based Instruction* 16(1):11–19.

Locatis, C. N., and V. H. Carr. 1985. Selecting authoring systems. *Journal of Computer Based Instruction* 12(2):28–33.

Locatis, C. N., and V. H. Carr. 1988. Using a lesson-element keystroke-oriented approach for estimating authoring tool efficiency. *Journal of Computer Based Instruction* 15(1):23–28.

MacKnight, C. B., and S. Balagopalan. 1989. An evaluation tool for measuring authoring system performance. *Communications of the ACM* 32(10):1231–36.

McFarland, D., and O. R. Parker. 1990. *Expert systems in education and training.* Englewood Cliffs, N.J.: Educational Technology Publications.

Merrill, M. D., and Z. Li. 1989. An instructional design expert system. *Journal of Computer Based Instruction* 16(1):90–94.

Pogue, R. E. 1982. The authoring system:

Interface between author and computer. *Journal of Research & Development in Education* 14(1):57–67.

Poulson, M. C., and J. J. Richardson. 1988. *Foundations of intelligent tutoring systems.* Hillsdale, N.J.: Erlbaum Associates.

Rode, M., and J. Poirot. 1989. Authoring systems—are they used? *Journal of Research in Computing in Education* 22(2):191–98.

Russell, D. M., T. P. Moran, and D. S. Jordan. 1987. The instructional design environment. In J. Psotka, L. D. Massey, and S. A. Mutter, eds. *Intelligent tutoring systems: Lessons learned.* Hillsdale, N.J.: Erlbaum Associates.

Starkweather, J. A. 1984. *A user's guide to PILOT.* Englewood Cliffs, N.J.: Prentice-Hall.

For Further Reading

Merrill, M. D., Z. Li, and M. K. Jones. 1990. Second generation instructional design. *Educational Technology* 30:34–39.

Olson, M. J. 1989. The expert media system. *Journal of Interactive Instruction Development* 3:3–10.

Greg Kearsley
Craig Locatis

AUTOMATIC TELLER MACHINES

See Financial Services, Computer Use in

AVIATION, COMPUTERS IN

In the early days of flying, there was only the pilot and the plane. Planes were small, sometimes equipped with metered gauges providing the pilot with information about the craft: amount of fuel remaining, altitude, attitude. Flights across country or oceans were risky business; it was easy to get lost or caught in a down draft or wind shear. The weather could change from sunny skies to clouds to a raging thunderstorm or snow storm. A pilot could easily get lost, having only visual landmarks such as towns, highways, rivers, and mountain ranges to find the way. Early pilots were true pioneers; bravery was a strict requirement for successful flying.

Today, anyone can board a commercial jetliner and fly just about anywhere in the world, in comfort. Today's pilots have sophisticated weather forecasts to guide them, navigational aids beyond the wildest dreams of early flyers, and persons on the ground tracking their progress. Military pilots push the limits of human endurance in high-performance aircraft, even eluding the enemy's radar. Astronauts ride the most sophisticated flying machine ever, the Space Shuttle; they are propelled into low Earth orbit by the shuttle's powerful rocket boosters and then land the spacecraft like any other glider plane at the end of the mission. None of these modern aviation miracles would have been possible without computers.

Historically, designing an airplane has involved thousands of calculations. And the more complex the airplane, the more calculations needed during the design phases. One reason for these calculations is the ever-present problem of aircraft "flutter," which results from the destructive disturbance of the atmosphere as a wing moves through it. Too much flutter and too little structural strength are a sure recipe for disaster. After the 1930s, as aircraft speed increased, this problem became more acute. As in many areas of engineering, a theory existed that could help scientists to calculate the effects of flutter and to make the changes needed to avoid it; however, the calculations might require the time of dozens of workers, or human calculators, for days, or even months.

Northrop Aircraft was an early pioneer in the use of computers in the aerospace industry. In the first years of the Cold War between the United States and the Soviet Union, Northrop was involved in the *Snark* guided missile project and the *Flying Wing* manned bomber, both of which included many major design innovations. The computational aspects of these projects spurred Northrop into early use of computers, even though neither project was successful for the company.

In the 1940s, IBM developed a series of calculators for business applications that operated on punch cards and vacuum tubes. Though much larger than a standard mechanical calculator, these calculators were much faster. Engineers at Northrop Aircraft used one of these calculating machines to solve their flutter problems, and prompted IBM to introduce the card programmed calculator, which was welcomed by aerospace companies. This calculator could perform simple arithmetic quickly, but could not store programs internally.

Since that time, the computer and its applications in the aviation industry have evolved. Most dramatic for early aerospace travel was the use of the first electronic "chips" in the Apollo missions to the Moon, in which integrated circuits were integral to guidance and navigational systems. The need for computing speed, capability, and accuracy combined with space and weight savings was first solved definitively by Jack Kilby of Texas Instruments and Robert Noyce of Fairchild Semiconductor, who invented the integrated circuit within 6 months of each other in late 1958 and early 1959. An integrated circuit combines many transistor and resistor components on a single semiconducting chip of silicon.

From the Apollo era to the mid-1970s, computers became smaller, more powerful, and easier to use, and their applications in the aerospace industry increased. One of the most important ways in which computers have contributed to the aerospace industry since that time is in the area of computer-aided design/computer-assisted manufacturing (CAD/CAM).

In the initial phase of aircraft design, many drawings are made of prototypes; these are examined by engineers and changed as they see fit. A small prototype of an aircraft design is built from design specifications, then tested extensively in wind tunnels for flightworthiness. Before computers were used to make these drawings, changes to design "specs" meant starting over with hand-drawn blueprints. Computer-aided design allows the designer to store drawings of an aircraft, retrieve them, and make changes without completely redrafting them. Wind tunnels are still used, both actual and computer-simulated, but hand-drawn specifications are on their way out. Computer-drawn specifications of the aircraft are used through to the production phase; every nut and bolt on the aircraft are indicated in the CAD drawing. As more manufacturers acquire CAD/CAM technology, computers will continue to play an increasing role in this area.

The Stealth series of aircraft, which includes the B-117 bomber used extensively in the Persian Gulf War against Iraq, are the first aircraft for which design and manufacture were accomplished mostly by the aid of computers. The B-117 was designed on a computerized drawing board using CAD, and specifications for its components were drawn using CAM tools, in which direct fabrication was specified by computers. Doubtless the strange shape of the B-117 is due to computer analysis of the behavior of radar waves as they strike a plane's fuselage, though this information is still classified by the U.S. Air Force.

ONBOARD SYSTEMS

In the past two decades, computers have played an increasing role in the cockpit. Avionics, which relay information about the aircraft and flying conditions to the pilot, have become more complex and accurate as a result of microcircuitry and complex programming. Navigational aids allow larger aircraft to almost fly themselves with great accuracy, independent of the weather and visual flight references such as landmarks. Onboard systems instantly relay to the pilot information concerning the craft, including status of engines, fuel lines, and environmental systems for passengers.

Sophisticated computer programs can even check a pilot's progress and issue warnings in dangerous situations, for example to "pull up" when too close to the ground or to "dive" to avoid a collision with other aircraft.

A good general rule applies to onboard systems: the more high-performance the aircraft, the more computerized equipment there is on board. High-performance fighter aircraft are capable of high-speed dives and maneuvers that would kill a human, so pilots must stay on guard to keep within human endurance limits. Computers cannot, however, replace the fighter pilot's skill and expertise in battle situations. Some human guidance is still called for.

Onboard telemetry units on the Space Shuttle constantly relay information to its computers, indicating exact altitude and course. These systems have to be complex, as the Space Shuttle becomes a glider after reentering the Earth's atmosphere, and has only one chance to land on the runway. The shuttle's successors, the so-called intercontinental transports or "space planes," will be as far advanced beyond the shuttle as the shuttle was beyond many earlier planes. Capable of taking off like any other plane yet achieving Earth orbit, these spacecraft of the future will fully use computer technology in design, manufacture, and execution.

PILOT TRAINING

Pilots of Amelia Earhart's day received a few lessons from another pilot and then flew solo to prove their "stuff." Today's pilots of commercial and high-performance jet aircraft receive training in normal flying, as well as in procedures for emergencies, without ever leaving the ground!

Thanks to computers and advanced video graphics, a pilot can spend hours in a flight simulator, gaining many years of valuable flight experience. In fact, most commercial pilots are required to spend a certain number of hours in a simulator per year. Simulators can be programmed to mimic the flight characteristics of almost any plane, replete with every conceivable disaster from engine failure to landing gear that do not retract. Today's pilots are much more prepared and better trained thanks to computer technology.

AIR TRAFFIC CONTROL

As commercial air traffic grew in the 1950s and 1960s, so did the need to monitor that traffic in the air. Computers conveniently evolved during this period, and became able to handle the complex job of keeping track of who is flying where in the skies. The Federal Aviation Administration (FAA) holds the responsibility of overseeing and directing our nation's air traffic safety.

Two types of air traffic control centers monitor civilian and military aircraft: the air traffic control center (ATCC), and the tower control stations at all large airports. Tower air traffic controllers monitor the aircraft during take off and landing. Computers aid these controllers in keeping track of incoming flights and directing them into orderly traffic patterns. Outgoing flights are similarly monitored.

Air traffic controllers stationed at ATCCs around the country do not monitor takeoffs and landings. Their duty is to monitor in-flight traffic between airports, and they are aided by large computerized radar screens that indicate the altitude, speed, and bearing of all aircraft within a specified zone, which would be impossible to calculate manually.

Like pilots, computer simulators are used to help air traffic controllers learn their profession. In January 1991, the FAA unveiled a new $10 million control tower simulator at the Mike Monroney Aeronautical Center in Oklahoma City, where all new air traffic controller candidates are trained. Three computers generate images of aircraft landing, taxiing, and taking off; the trainee observes the images and manipulates from a realistic tower control booth. The computer-generated planes have imaginary pilots that respond to the air traffic controller's spoken commands rather than to keyboard input. Mock crashes train controllers to handle the real-life disasters they may encounter. Of course, errors made by controller trainees in this simulator do not endanger real aircraft, crew, or passengers.

THE FUTURE

As the aerospace industry has evolved and become more complex, so has its dependence on computers. Though many tasks in design and manufacture that require human judgment and expertise may never be completely accomplished on the computer, computers will probably continue to have an expanded role in all aspects of aviation and aerospace pursuits.

For Further Reading

Aviation Week and Space Technology, a weekly magazine that provides up-to-the-minute insights into aviation and aerospace concerns.

Ceruzzi, P. E. 1989. *Beyond the limits: Flight enters the computer age.* Cambridge, Mass.: MIT Press.

Loretta McKibben

B

BABBAGE, CHARLES

Charles Babbage was born on December 26, 1791, in Teignmouth, Devonshire, England. From the very beginning, he showed a great desire to inquire into the causes of things that astonish children's minds. On receiving a new toy, Charles would ask, "Mamma, what is inside of it?" Then he would carefully proceed to dissect it and figure out how it was constructed and what made it work. All throughout his career, he continued to have a curious and questioning mind. This curiosity played a significant part in the development of many of his famous ideas.

He was one of the two surviving children of Benjamin Babbage, a wealthy banker, and Betty Plumleigh Teape, both descended from well-known Devonshire families. Babbage's parents were affluent and he had the opportunity to attend private schools.

After a succession of private tutors he entered Trinity College, Cambridge, in 1810. At Trinity College, Babbage's studies led him to a critical examination of the logarithmic tables used to make accurate calculations. He was well aware of the difficulty and tediousness of compiling the astronomical and nautical tables and dreamed of a machine that would one day calculate such tables. At Trinity College, he proved to be an undisciplined student, constantly puzzling his tutors. He was often annoyed to find that he knew more than his teachers. But in spite of his outward displays of rebellion, he was already on his way to absorbing the advanced theories of mathematics.

In 1815, Babbage, John Herschel, and other contemporaries founded the Analytic Society. Its purposes were to emphasize the abstract nature of algebra, to bring continental developments in mathematics to England, and to end the state of suspended animation in which British mathematics had remained since the death of Sir Isaac Newton.

After receiving his master of arts degree from Trinity College in 1817, Babbage plunged into a variety of activities and wrote notable papers on the theory of functions and on various topics in applied mathematics.

In 1822, Babbage designed his difference engine, considered to be the first automatic calculating machine. Based on the recommendation of the Royal Society, he was able to obtain a grant from the British government that permitted him to work on this machine. The difference engine was to be a special-purpose device, constructed for the task of preparing mathematical tables. After 8 years of work, Babbage lost interest and abandoned this machine and turned to the design of the analytical engine.

In 1833, Babbage conceived his analytical engine, the first design for a universal automatic calculator. He worked on it with his own money until his death. Babbage's design had all the elements of a modern general-purpose digital computer, namely, memory, control, arithmetic unit, input, and output. The memory was to hold 1,000 words of fifty digits each, all in counting wheels. Control was to be by means of sequences of Jacquard punched cards. The very important ability to modify the course of a calculation according to the intermediate results obtained, now called conditional branching, was to be incorporated in the form of a procedure for skipping forward or backward a specified number of cards. The arithmetic unit, Babbage supposed, would perform addition or subtraction in 1 second while a 50×50 multiplication would take about 1 minute. Babbage spent many years developing a mechanical method of achieving simultaneous propagation of carries during addition to eliminate the need for fifty successive carry cycles. Input to the machine was to be by individual punched cards and manual setting of the memory counters. Output was to be punched cards or printed copy. Although Babbage prepared thousands of detailed drawings for his machine, only a few parts were ever completed.

The description of Babbage's ideas would not be adequate without mention of Augusta Ada BYRON, Countess of Lovelace, who was acquainted with Babbage and his work. Her writings have helped us understand this work and contain the first descriptions of programming techniques.

An oversensitive and tactless person, Babbage was unpopular with many of his contemporaries. By the end of his life, he was disappointed by his failure to bring his principles within sight of completion; however, Babbage was actually attempting the impossible with the means at his disposal. He was a man born a hundred years ahead of his time. He died in London on October 18, 1871, surrounded by the drawings, cogwheels, and fragments of his hopeless, halffinished dream.

Babbage is thus the grandfather of the modern computer, and although this was not understood by his contemporaries, Babbage himself was probably aware of it.

For Further Reading

Bernstein, J. 1981. *The analytical engine.* New York: William Morrow.

Halacy, D. 1970. *Charles Babbage.* New York: Macmillan.

Hyman, A. 1982. *Charles Babbage: Pioneer of the computer.* Princeton, N.J.: Princeton University Press.

Donald D. Spencer

BANKING, COMPUTER USE IN

The use of computers by banks has significantly changed the way banks operate. Only three decades ago, banks used to hire hundreds of clerical staff whose only job was to calculate manually the end-of-day balances for all customer bank accounts. This process not only was tedious and required concentration, but also was very prone to errors. The introduction of computers to perform this task efficiently eliminated these clerical positions. Computers were able to do the same job more quickly and very accurately. The infusion of computer technology into the banking industry has not yet reached some of the less developed countries, where the manual process still exists.

Banks depend heavily on computer systems not only for their day-to-day operations but also as a means to make them more competitive with respect to other banks and financial institutions. Computers are used to deliver financial products to customers more efficiently, more quickly, and more cheaply than before.

CONSUMER BANKING

When most people think of a bank, they mean consumer banking or branch banking (also called retail banking). The consumer banking business provides customers with a wide variety of financial products ranging from checking and savings accounts (demand deposits) to credit cards and traveler's checks. Most of these services are provided through tellers within a branch. Recently, however, banks have started to deliver these products through their automated teller machines (ATMs). Automated teller machines are computers that provide account balance information, dispense cash and traveler's checks, allow cash and checks to be credited to accounts, transfer money between various accounts, and allow certain bills to be paid. All these functions can be activated on proper and valid identification of a customer. Access to these services is usually provided 24 hours a day to customers by ATMs located outside of branch premises.

The impersonal nature of using an ATM has some advantages. For instance, when applying for a loan, most people prefer not to describe their financial circumstances to a stranger (banks' customer service representatives) and would rather deal with a machine. So some banks are allowing customers to make small loan applications at ATMs, with immediate responses (approval or rejection).

The increasing popularity of ATMs is evidence of the decreasing level of fear of using computers. Banks are now poised to introduce the next wave of electronic banking—home banking. The idea is to provide customers with access to their bank from their homes. This is being achieved by integrating computers into ordinary home appliances, such as television sets, and allowing customers to access their accounts using this enhanced "terminal." Citibank recently introduced its own version of the home banking terminal, the enhanced telephone (ET). This device looks very much like an ordinary telephone except that it has a small built-in screen and keyboard. It ordinarily functions as a telephone, but when a special key is pressed, it automatically dials the bank's computers and allows the customer to query his or her account. The enhanced telephone provides the same functions as an ATM, except for dispensing cash and traveler's checks and making cash and check deposits.

Computers are also helping to streamline operations within banks. With the introduction of magnetic ink character recognition (MICR) technology, banks have been able to process the huge amounts of checks and other financial paper much more rapidly and accurately. Magnetic ink character recognition technology uses special ink to print account numbers and other information on checks so that computers with appropriate scanning devices can read and recognize the characters. Combining this technology with handwriting recognition technology will eliminate the need for a human operator to input manually a check's account number and dollar amount.

CORPORATE BANKING

The corporate banking function within a bank serves corporate clients with their short- and long-term finance needs, including cash management (also known as treasury management), securities trading, foreign exchange transactions, and loans. Banks use computers to reduce the cost of providing these services to their clients. Some of the major banks handle from $100 to $300 billion a day for their corporate clients. Keeping track of such amounts of money requires very fast and accurate processing of transactions, and this is one area where computers excel.

Corporate clients, like individual customers, also may want to know the state of their accounts at any given moment. To facilitate quick and accurate access to this information, banks allow their major corporate customers' computers to access the banks' computers directly through communications networks with full provision for security.

Future trends in the corporate banking industry include providing global corporate clients with a financial view of their company at any time, in any currency. This requires banks to keep track of all financial transactions that may be taking place worldwide and to present the state of these transactions to their clients, 24 hours a day.

SOCIETAL IMPACTS

The use of computers in the banking industry has allowed banks to provide financial services rapidly and inexpensively to a large number of geographically dispersed people. Customers are no longer limited to accessing their money at times determined by banks; they are now able to access their accounts 24 hours a day, 7 days a week.

The widespread use of computers in the banking industry has led to the phenomenon of credit systems. As computers are able to keep accurate records on customers' financial profiles, banks frequently pass such information about customer accounts to credit bureaus, which, in turn, provide credit reports on customers to the banks. Credit reports provided by these systems, however, are not the only criteria used by banks to determine "good" versus "bad" customers.

Exploiting economies of scale for technology enables large banks to provide their services more cost-effectively than small banks. This appears to be a factor in the trend toward large banks.

[*See also:* Financial Services, Computer Use in.]

For Further Reading

Ritter, L., and W. Silber. 1986. *Principles of money, banking and financial markets.* 5th ed. New York: Basic Books. Highly recommended as an introduction to the world of banking.

                                    Rajiv Dalal

FIGURE 1. Example bar code.

BAR CODE

Over the past 20 years, the bar code has become widely used in commerce, industry, and government. Those little black and white parallel lines link computer databases with many types of business transactions. This article explains how information can be represented in a bar code and why bar code scanning is increasingly favored over other techniques for capturing transaction data. It continues with a discussion of some important uses of bar code in stores and factories.

AN IDEA WHOSE TIME HAS COME

Although bar codes were patented as early as 1949, they did not come into practical use until about 1970. Prior to that time, the special-purpose electronic devices required for scanning and decoding printed bar patterns had been prohibitively expensive. Today, bar code scanners are greatly improved and considerably cheaper than they were in the early 1970s.

A bar code symbol consists of alternating dark and light parallel lines that are logically arranged to encode information. An example of how this may be accomplished is presented in Figure 1. Here we see the characters "123" represented in two-of-five bar code. Note that the bars are either narrow or wide. We associate the binary value zero with the narrow bars and the value one with the wide bars. Each character is encoded in five bars, of which exactly two bars are

wide. This two-of-five rule allows us to encode the ten digits as follows:

Character	Code
1	10001
2	01001
3	11000
4	00101
5	10100
6	01100
7	00011
8	10010
9	01010
0	00110

Any single defect in the printing or scanning process could make one of the wide bars appear to be narrow, or vice versa; however, such a defect would not result in incorrect data, because the affected code group of five bars would no longer contain two wide bars. A data error can occur only if there are two complementary defects within a code group.

We note that the data characters (123) in Figure 1 are bounded on either end by "start" and "stop" patterns. If the bar code symbol is scanned from left to right, the bar sequence is 110 . . . 101; scanned from right to left the sequence is 101 . . . 011. Depending on which start/stop sequence is encountered, the scanner interprets the five-bar groupings in a forward or backward fashion. This allows the bar code symbol to be correctly scanned in either direction.

The two-of-five bar code discussed here was one of the earlier arrangements and has been largely superseded by more modern symbologies. (A bar code symbology, or language, is simply a set of rules for encoding information.) Contemporary symbologies are more space efficient than the old two-of-five, while providing equal or better data security. These advantages are accomplished by using more complicated encoding rules. Some symbologies can represent letters of the alphabet and special characters as well as numbers. The more widely used symbologies and their primary areas of application are listed here:

UPC	Retail—North America
EAN	Retail—international
Codabar	Libraries
Interleaved two-of-five	Warehousing
Code 39	Industry and government
Code 128	Industry and commerce

Most printing processes for ordinary text and graphics can easily be adapted to print bar code also. Thus, any item that is labeled with human-readable information can be bar-coded with minimal expense. When the bar code is scanned, a focused beam of light is moved across the symbol. The reflected light is converted to an electrical signal that alternates between a lower and a higher voltage as the beam moves across the bars and spaces. A small, special-purpose computer built into the scanner analyzes the scan signal according to rules for decoding the particular symbology. This decoded information is then typically arranged in some standard digital format, such as ASCII (American Standard Code for Information Interchange), and transmitted to a general-purpose computer.

Bar code scanners may be hand-held by a human operator, or they may be permanently mounted above or beside a conveyor belt. The hand-held types include wands, touch scanners, and laser scanners. Because of the data security built into the standard bar codes, scanning is quite accurate. Data error rates on the order of one error per 3 million characters scanned are typical. This contrasts with keyboard data entry, which commonly involves one error for every 300 characters keyed. Compared with the traditional technique of capturing data using handwritten forms and keyboard entry, bar coding is far more economical, faster, and more accurate.

BAR CODE IN THE SUPERMARKET

Careful planning and broad voluntary agreements between food manufacturers and retailers underlie the success of retail systems with bar code scanning. The familiar UPC bar code symbol on peanut butter jars and soft drinks does not contain the price. The symbol simply represents a unique product whose price and description can be retrieved from a database stored in an on-site computer.

Here is how the system works. In 1971, food retail associations in the United States, along with manufacturers of packaged goods, agreed on a numerical code for identifying products. Each manufacturer was assigned a unique five-digit (later amended to six-digit) number by a central numbering authority (currently the Uniform Code Council in Dayton, Ohio). Each unique product intended for sale in the supermarket was then given its own five-digit number by the manufacturer. For example, the Seven-Up Company's number is 078000, and they have assigned number 00079 to the 12-ounce can of Diet 7-Up. This product is uniquely identified by the eleven-digit number 07800000079.

A new bar code symbology called the UPC symbol was developed in 1973 for use on retail products. Compared with the two-of-five bar code in Figure 1, UPC is much more complicated. Each digit is represented by only two bars and two spaces, but the bars and spaces have four possible widths. The standard UPC symbol contains twelve digits, including the six-digit manufacturer's number, the five-digit product number, and a check digit that ensures accurate scanning. A special provision of UPC applies to numbers that contain long strings of zeros. For these numbers, a smaller bar code called a zero suppression symbol can be substituted.

The UPC symbol for Diet 7-Up is shown in Figure 2. From left to right, the first two bars are called the left guard pattern. Each successive code pattern (space, bar, space, bar) represents the digit printed under it. The last three bars are the right guard pattern. The small 5 at the right is the check digit value.

At the checkout counter, a laser scanner

FIGURE 2. UPC symbol.

built into the counter "looks" up at packages as they are dragged above it. When a six-pack of Diet 7-Up is scanned, the scanner logic obtains the message 780790 and expands it into the equivalent eleven digits. This eleven-digit message is immediately transmitted to the in-store computer containing the product database. The eleven-digit product numbers form a key field that is rapidly searched for a match. When the data are retrieved, they show that 7-Up is normally sold in units of six, unless the clerk keys some lesser quantity to indicate a broken six-pack. The price and description are displayed to the consumer and printed on his or her receipt, all in less than 1 second.

The UPC system provides for faster checkout, ensures pricing accuracy, and reduces store operating costs. Scanning of data facilitates accurate stock control and reordering and helps store management evaluate their merchandising programs.

BAR CODE IN INDUSTRY

Managers of manufacturing processes depend on detailed information gathered and entered into computerized databases. Traditional clipboard-to-keyboard techniques are being supplanted by bar code in leading edge industries such as aerospace, automotive, electronics, and pharmaceutical manufacturing.

Automobile manufacturers require that their suppliers label containers of parts and raw materials with bar code labels that meet exacting standards of form, content, and quality. Prior to shipping material, the parts supplier notifies the car factory of the exact contents of each container using a direct computer-to-computer transfer of data. When the material is received, two bar code symbols on the carton are scanned. One symbol identifies the supplier; the other identifies the specific container. All other aspects of the receiving transaction can now be handled by computer without human intervention.

Inside the automobile plant, major components such as engines and transmissions are bar-coded to identify their unique serial numbers, as well as their part number identity. When these major parts are installed, their bar codes are scanned and matched with the unique vehicle identification number. This confirms to the computer controlling the assembly operation that the right engine was put in the right car. Furthermore, it constructs an accurate configuration record of each vehicle, which can be used to manage any special maintenance or recall activities.

CONCLUSION

There is a vast and growing body of knowledge on the technology of bar code and the many ways it is used to speed the flow of accurate information into computer systems. An excellent source of information is AIM, a trade association that specializes in bar code and related techniques: AIM USA, 634 Alpha Drive, Pittsburgh, PA 15238; telephone: (412) 963-8588. Information concerning any aspect of bar code in retail and retail distribution can be obtained from the administrator of the UPC code and symbol: Uniform Code Council, 8163 Old Yankee Road, Dayton, OH 45458; telephone: (513) 435-3870.

For Further Reading

Collins, D. J. 1990. *Using bar code.* Duxbury, Mass.: Data Capture Institute. Covers a broad range of bar-code–related topics.

Palmer, R. C. 1989. *The bar code book.* Peterborough, N.H.: Helmers Publishing. An excellent textbook on the technical aspects of bar code.

David C. Allais

BASIC

Of all high-level computer programming languages used in the elementary and secondary schools today, BASIC (Beginners All-purpose Symbolic Instruction Code) is the most popular. BASIC was developed in the early 1960s by Dr. John KEMENY and Dr. Thomas KURTZ of Dartmouth College. Unlike other programming languages of the time, BASIC was developed primarily for interactive use with on-line devices such as the cathode ray tube (CRT) and teletype terminals. Since its inception, BASIC has made a major impact on computer programming in the United States and abroad.

BASIC offers a number of advantages over other programming languages. First, as the name itself implies, BASIC was developed specifically for simplicity. With very little direction, a beginner can create reasonably powerful programs in a very short time using only a few of BASIC's program language statements and system/editing commands. Because of its relative ease of use for the inexperienced, BASIC has achieved a well-deserved reputation as a programming language for the non–computer professional.

"BASIC" BASIC

With the use of only a few statements/ statement pairs such as PRINT, INPUT, GOTO, IF . . . THEN, LET, and END, working versions of most typical programs can be created. These simple, commonly understood words are used in BASIC programming as follows:

PRINT   As the command implies, "PRINT" instructs the computer to "print" something. Printing is commonly accomplished by either a CRT or a printer.

INPUT   INPUT statements tell the user that a requested response must be made on the keyboard before continuing. Consider this program sequence:

```
10    PRINT "WHAT IS YOUR NAME";
20    INPUT $
```

When the preceding program is run, the screen will indicate

WHAT IS YOUR NAME?

Before continuing, the program user must "type in" (input) a response from the keyboard.

GOTO   BASIC programs include a listing of commands that are to be carried out in ascending order. Thus, the command on line 10 is executed before that on line 20. The GOTO command, however, instructs the program to proceed to any specified location. As is demonstrated in the following program sequence, the GOTO command is an especially powerful programming tool.

```
10    PRINT "THE LUNCH ESSENTIALS: PIZZA
      AND POP."
20    GOTO 10
30    END
```

When the preceding program is run, the computer will print

THE LUNCH ESSENTIALS: PIZZA AND POP.

After printing the line 10 command, the program proceeds to line 20, which directs the program back to line 10. Such programs will keep printing until the computer either is shut off or malfunctions. When a program requires a computer to print a line in this manner, it is referred to as an "infinite loop."

IF . . . THEN   This command allows the program to "branch" to a specified location depending on a response. Think about this program sequence:

```
10    PRINT "HOW OLD ARE YOU";
20    INPUT A
30    IF A > 18 THEN 60
40    PRINT "SORRY CHARLIE, NO CAR FOR
      YOU!"
50    GO TO 70
60    PRINT "CONGRATULATIONS! YOU
      HAVE JUST WON THE NEW CAR OF
      YOUR CHOICE!"
70    END
```

When the preceding program is run, the screen would read:

HOW OLD ARE YOU?

If the user typed in "16," because 16 is not greater than (>) 18, the screen would respond:

SORRY CHARLIE, NO CAR FOR YOU!

If, on the other hand, the user typed in "19," which is greater than 18, the computer would respond:

CONGRATULATIONS! YOU HAVE JUST WON THE NEW CAR OF YOUR CHOICE!

Although determining where to pick up your new car might be a problem, using the "IF . . . THEN" statement to make other programs similar to this is not.

LET   LET allows the programmer to assign given values to variables. This feature is especially helpful with programs requiring mathematical formulas, or in solving equations.

PUTTING IT ALL TOGETHER

The following example shows how a simple program can be developed using just a few of the basic vocabulary, syntax, and numeric capabilities of BASIC.

```
COMPUTER ADDING MACHINE
10    PRINT "TYPE IN TWO NUMBERS AND I
      WILL ADD THEM FOR YOU."
20    PRINT "TYPE YOUR FIRST NUMBER"
30    INPUT FIRST
40    PRINT "NOW TYPE IN THE NUMBER
      YOU WANT ME TO ADD TO THE
      FIRST NUMBER"
50    INPUT SECOND
60    PRINT FIRST + SECOND: "IS THE SUM"
70    PRINT "DO YOU WANT TO ADD TWO
      MORE NUMBERS?"
80    PRINT "TYPE 1 for YES OR 2 for NO"
90    INPUT X
100   IF X = 1 THEN 10
110   PRINT "LET ME KNOW WHEN I CAN
      ADD AGAIN FOR YOU."
120   END
```

When the above program is run, the first two lines in the program (10 and 20) result in the words:

TYPE IN TWO NUMBERS AND I WILL ADD THEM FOR YOU.
TYPE YOUR FIRST NUMBER.

The INPUT statement (line 30) tells the computer to wait until a number is typed. Line 40 prompts the user to type a second number. Line 60 instructs the computer to perform the arithmetic operation requested and report the sum. If the user types "1" in response to the question printed by the computer in accordance with lines 70 and 80, line 100 directs the program back to line 10 to begin again. If "2" is selected, the program concludes with the message:

LET ME KNOW WHEN I CAN ADD AGAIN FOR YOU.

PROS AND CONS

Much of BASIC's simplicity for programmers is attributed to the convenience of typing a command line directly into the computer and having on-line program edit capabilities. This *interactive* feature is a major contrast to the laborious processes (typing data cards, inputting cards, and waiting for output error message sequences) bemoaned by pre-1970s computer programmers. Because of the ease of direct communication between the computer and the user, BASIC is universally perceived as being among the more "friendly" (i.e., easier to use) of today's programming languages.

In addition to its classic simplicity and user friendliness, more recent versions of BASIC include capabilities for relatively sophisticated graphics, music, color, and sound programming. BASIC also allows for arithmetic and Boolean operations on numeric as well as character strings.

BASIC has also achieved a great deal of its popularity because it is "free"; that is, it comes with IBM and IBM-compatible personal computers when they are purchased. This "built-in" feature is sometimes perceived as a cost savings as other language software can be a considerable expense.

In spite of its basic simplicity and overall popularity among beginning programmers, BASIC is not without real or perceived problems. Perhaps one of the most criticized aspects of this language is its "unstructured" nature. This nature may be perhaps better understood by imagining if this volume were written in a language without traditional punctuation marks. Furthermore, imagine a new mark being developed that would require the reader to move ahead or behind several pages to locate the next sentence to be read. Such a task would make even a paragraph difficult to understand, let alone a volume of this magnitude. Thus, BASIC programs are generally perceived as a numbered list of instructions rather than as a list of specific procedures. This potential, critics argue, discourages beginning students from approaching programming in a more structured "top-down" (general-to-specific) planning style, which most programming experts favor. Such "bad habits" emerging from its *unstructured* programming potential encourage a preference for teaching programming with the use of more structured computer languages (e.g., Pascal).

Another problem that has affected the use of BASIC somewhat is that although there is a universally accepted set of standard rules for the language, individual manufacturers have slightly differing modifications, which causes confusion from company to company (e.g., IBM BASIC differs, although only slightly, from the Apple version of BASIC). As relatively minor as these modifications may be, they can present annoyances to beginners.

Despite the aforementioned criticisms, BASIC remains a high-level programming language that continues to offer interactive and relatively simple programming access to both beginning and intermediate users. In spite of its drawbacks, at least in the near future, BASIC appears destined to continue as a leading introductory computer language.

For Further Reading

Baron, N. S. 1986. *Computer languages—A guide for the perplexed.* Garden City, N.Y.: Anchor Press/Doubleday.

Bateson, R. M., and R. D. Raygor. 1985. *BASIC programming for the Apple computer* (G. Bitz, illus.) St. Paul, Minn.: West.

Boillot, M. and W. Horn. 1983. *BASIC.* 3rd ed. St. Paul, Minn.: West.

Brodzinski, I. F., and R. D. Greenwood. 1984. *Enjoying BASIC—A comprehensive guide to programming.* New York: Harper & Row.

Conley, W. E. 1982. *BASIC for beginners.* Princeton, N.J.: Petrocelli Books.

Cook, S., M. McNiff, and R. Thomson. 1980. In L. Poole, ed. *Practical BASIC programs.* Berkeley, Calif.: Osborne/McGraw-Hill.

Cox, M. J., and K. B. Sullivan. 1986. *Structuring programs in Microsoft BASIC.* Boston: Boyd & Fraser.

Emmerichs, J. 1984. *The programmer's toolbox.* Beaverton, Oreg.: Dilithium Press.

Grillo, J. P., and J. D. Robertson. 1981. *Techniques of BASIC.* Dubuque, Iowa: W. C. Brown.

Haigh, R. W., and L. E. Radford. 1983. *BASIC for microcomputers: Apple, TRS-80, PET.* New York: Van Nostrand Reinhold.

Hennefeld, J. 1981. *Using BASIC—An introduction to computer programming.* Boston: Prindle, Weber & Schmidt.

Kemeny, J., and T. E. Kurtz. 1980. *BASIC programming.* 3rd ed. New York: Wiley.

Mandell, S. K. 1983. *Computers and data processing today with BASIC.* St. Paul, Minn.: West.

Pardee, M., and M. Waite. 1982. *BASIC programming primer.* 2nd ed. Indianapolis, Ind.: H. W. Sams.

Poirot, J. 1983. *Apple BASIC.* Austin, Tex.: Sterling Swift.

Silver, G. A., and M. Silver. 1984. *Simplified BASIC programming for microcomputers.* New York: Harper & Row.

Siragusa, C. R. 1983. *Introduction to programming BASIC—A structured approach.* 2nd ed. Boston: PWS.

Steiner, J. P. 1984. *The standard BASIC dictionary for programming.* Englewood Cliffs, N.J.: Prentice-Hall.

Thompson, R. G. 1981. *BASIC, a first course.* Columbus, Ohio: C. E. Merrill.

Worland, P. 1989. *Introduction to BASIC programming: A structured approach.* 2nd ed. Boston: Houghton Mifflin.

James L. Hoot

BINARY NUMBERING SYSTEM

Any number system based on two digits is called a *binary* numbering system. Knowledge of the binary numbering system used in computers is fundamental to an understanding of how computers work. Binary numbers, also called *base two* (or *radix two*) numbers, are used in computers both to represent *data* (quantities and characters) and to signify *instructions* to the central processing unit (CPU). Binary numbers, together with Boolean logic, also provide the means with which computers are able to make decisions.

DENARY NUMBERING

In everyday life in Western society, the *denary* numbering system, also called *base ten* or the *decimal system*, is used to count and to perform computations. Quantities less than ten are represented in the denary system using one of the ten digits, 0 through 9. Quantities larger than ten are represented by aggregating the ten digits using a convention called *place value*. Even grade-school children recognize that to represent the next quantity after 9, a "1" digit is placed to the left representing "one group of ten," and then counting resumes in the place on the right, beginning with the digit "0" (see Table 1). When 99 is reached, a third place is required representing "groups of one hundred." The

TABLE 1. Place Value in Denary and Binary

Denary				Binary							
1000	100	10	1	128	64	32	16	8	4	2	1
			0								0
			1								1
			2							1	0
			3							1	1
			4						1	0	0
			5						1	0	1
			6						1	1	0
			7						1	1	1
			8					1	0	0	0
			9					1	0	0	1
		1	0					1	0	1	0
		1	1					1	0	1	1
		1	2					1	1	0	0
		.	.					.	.	.	.
		.	.					.	.	.	.
		.	.					.	.	.	.
		9	9		1	1	0	0	0	1	1
	1	0	0		1	1	0	0	1	0	0

values of the places are called *powers* of ten. One thousand ($10 \times 10 \times 10$) is ten to the third power (10^3), one hundred (10×10) is ten to the second power (10^2), ten is ten to the first power (10^1), and one is ten to the zero power (10^0).

In everyday life it is easy to forget that the use of ten digits is almost an entirely arbitrary choice. There is nothing special about base ten except that human beings have ten fingers, which may account for its common use. Useful systems of numeration can be built using two, ten, sixteen, or any number of digits. Among the numbering systems used by various human societies throughout history are base five, base twelve, base twenty, and even base sixty.

BINARY NUMBERING

Electronic computers have only two "fingers," so they use a base two system instead of a denary system. Computers have only two digits to work with because the physical devices used to represent those digits have only two states. In the typical modern electronic computer, transistors are used to represent these digits, also called *bits*. The transistor's low-voltage state is called *zero*, and its high-voltage state is called *one*, thus establishing the core of a base two system.

The digits are exhausted in binary counting much sooner than they are in base ten. Only after counting nine objects is one forced to invoke place value in base ten. In binary, place value must be used after counting only one object. A "1" digit is then placed to the left, representing "one group of *two*," and counting resumes in the place on the right, beginning with the digit 0.

Because the digits are exhausted so frequently, binary numbers are longer than their base ten equivalents. This fact makes binary a poor choice for human beings to use. Most human beings have difficulty remembering numbers larger than five to nine characters. Fortunately, computers are very fast and have very accurate memories, so the problems that humans encounter working in binary are trivial for computers. Apart from this major difference, working with binary numbers is remarkably similar to working in base ten. With practice, even relatively slow and fallible human beings can learn to compute binary numbers with remarkable ease.

OPERATING WITH BINARY NUMBERS

The value of a denary number can be shown by expanding it as illustrated in this example:

$$5,907 = 5 \times 1,000 + 9 \times 100 + 0 \times 10 + 7 \times 1$$

A binary number can be similarly expanded to reveal its denary value. Note that powers of two must be used in the expansion instead of powers of ten (see Table 2). To find the denary equivalent of 101101, for example, the number may be expanded as illustrated here:

$$101101 = 1 \times 32 + 0 \times 16 + 1 \times 8 + 1 \times 4 + 0 \times 2 + 1 \times 1$$
$$= 32 + 8 + 4 + 1$$
$$= 45 \text{ (denary)}$$

A denary number can be converted to binary by dividing or subtracting with powers of two. The binary equivalent of denary 53 is computed below as an example, using the subtractive method. The process starts by identifying the largest power of two that can be subtracted from 53, and then subtracting each successive smaller power of two from the remainder.

$$53 - 32 = 21$$
$$21 - 16 = 5$$
$$5 - 8 = \textit{won't subtract}$$
$$5 - 4 = 1$$
$$1 - 2 = \textit{won't subtract}$$
$$1 - 1 = 0$$

TABLE 2. Powers of 2

2^0	=	1
2^1	=	2
2^2	=	4
2^3	=	8
2^4	=	16
2^5	=	32
2^6	=	64
2^7	=	128

Therefore,

$$53 = 1 \times 32 + 1 \times 16 + 0 \times 8 + 1 \times 4$$
$$+ 0 \times 2 + 1 \times 1$$
$$= 110101 \text{ (binary)}$$

Binary addition is very similar to denary addition except that the place value convention of "carrying" must be done more frequently. Examine this addition example (recall that in binary $1 + 1 = 10$):

```
        (111)← (carries)
        110101
      + 101110
      ─────────
       1100011
```

Procedures also exist for performing binary subtraction, multiplication, division, and other operations.

REPRESENTING CHARACTERS

To store characters in a computer's memory, codes are used that assign each character a specific reference number. For microcomputers, the most commonly used character code is the American Standard Code for Information Interchange (ASCII). In ASCII, the letter "A" is referred to with the binary number 01000001, which equals denary 65. Table 3 provides some additional examples. Note that lowercase letters such as "a" have unique codes and that numerals (the characters for the digits) such as "1" also have codes. In mainframe and minicomputers, another code called the Extended Binary-Coded-Decimal Interchange Code (EBCDIC) is often used. In EBCDIC, "A" is 11000001 (denary 193). Additional examples of EBCDIC are also given in Table 3. Whatever the system used, the assignment of code numbers to characters is mostly arbitrary, with the exception of order. The fact that the code for "A" is one less than the code for "B" means that code numbers can be used to

TABLE 3. Partial Character Code Table

ASCII	EBCDIC	Character
01000010	11000010	"B"
01100001	10000001	"a"
00110001	11110001	"1"
00111111	01101111	"?"

alphabetize and perform other actions on characters. Coding of characters is one reason that computers' memories are addressed in *bytes* (groups of 8 bits). The eight digits in a byte allow the storage of numbers up to denary 255, consequently allowing the coding of up to 256 (0–255) characters, a number sufficient to include all upper- and lowercase characters of the English alphabet, all English punctuation symbols, all the basic numerals, and other characters as well.

SIGNIFYING INSTRUCTIONS

The CPU of any computer has a finite repertoire of primitive instructions that it is able to perform. Binary numbers are used to tell the CPU which instruction to perform. Machine/assembly code programs do this directly by sending binary numbers to the CPU. English-like high-level programs written in languages such as BASIC or Pascal must first be translated to binary numbers by an interpreter or a compiler. As is the case with character codes, there is no single universal standard for instruction codes. The specific number used to refer to a given instruction varies with the design of the CPU. On the IBM System/370 mainframe computer, for example, the binary number 00011010 (denary 26) signifies to the CPU to add two numbers stored in memory locations called *registers*. The Intel 8086/8 family of microprocessors (commonly used as microcomputer CPUs) perform a comparable operation when instructed with the binary number 00000001 (denary 1).

USING BINARY NUMBERS TO MAKE DECISIONS

Computers make decisions with *Boolean logic*. The basic operators of Boolean logic (AND, OR, NOT) use binary input to produce decisions in binary form. For example, in the decision *if a person is female AND the person is grown, then the person is a woman*, the result (person is a woman) is true (1) only when both conditions are true: female = true (1) AND grown = true (1). If either condition is false (0), then the result is false. Computers

TABLE 4. AND Gate Logic

Condition 1 (Input 1)	Condition 2 (Input 2)	Result (Output)
False (0)	False (0)	False (0)
False (0)	True (1)	False (0)
True (1)	False (0)	False (0)
True (1)	True (1)	True (1)

use circuits called *logic gates* to evaluate such Boolean expressions. In the case of an AND gate, there are two inputs and one output, all of which are expressed in binary form. Table 4 shows the logic pattern of an AND gate. When such a gate is used to evaluate the truth of the Boolean expression *If binary numbers had NOT been devised AND Boolean logic had NOT been developed, then computers would NOT exist as we know them today,* the result is *TRUE.*

For Further Reading

Augarten, S. 1984. *Bit by bit: An illustrated history of computers.* New York: Ticknor & Fields.

Gillie, A. C. 1965. *Binary arithmetic and Boolean algebra.* New York: McGraw-Hill.

Hellwig, J. 1969. *Introduction to computers and programming.* New York: Columbia University Press.

Millington, T. A., and W. Millington. 1971. *Dictionary of mathematics.* New York: Barnes & Noble Books.

System/370 reference summary. 1984. 6th ed. Poughkeepsie, N.Y.: IBM Corp.

Troutman, A. P., J. A. White, and F. Breit. 1988. *The micro goes to school: Instructional applications of microcomputer technology.* Pacific Grove, Calif.: Brooks/Cole.

James White

BIOLOGICAL USE OF COMPUTERS

Accessibility of computers to biologists via powerful personal computing systems, along with recent developments in microcircuit technology, has been a critical factor important for advances in biological research; however, this accessibility is only a recent occurrence. In the early 1970s, technically adventurous biologists at research institutions were entering data into mainframe computers by keypunch cards. Analyses of all but the most rudimentary types required extensive programming. Such skills were beyond the fundamental training of the majority of biologists, and for the most part, data were directly read from chart recorders and analyzed with pencil and paper, slide rule, or, for the more technically oriented, a calculator. Automated data acquisition was not the normal situation for most independent laboratories.

The late 1970s saw personal computers creep into laboratories, but they were few in number because of the expense, and considerable programming skills were still necessary for even the most routine tasks. As the price of personal computers continued to decline and performance and software capabilities increased, more personal computers found their way into the laboratories to the point where, now, multiple machines per investigator are not uncommon. With the development of menu-driven software, increasingly miniaturized fast processors, and a variety of commercially available analog-to-digital interface boards, it became easier to integrate sensors into the computer system, making data acquisition a simpler task.

Although the tasks for which biologists use computers are myriad, a few examples will best illustrate how tabletop processors can facilitate research. In the laboratory, a biologist may examine prepared specimens under a light or electron microscope. Historically, images from light microscopes were traced to paper via projection tubes and the morphometric data were either mechanically measured or placed into computer memory via digitizing pads. This labor-intensive task is prone to error. Recent advances in mathematical models and computational power of computer workstations have allowed biologists to use computers for data acquisition and image analysis. High-resolution video images are acquired directly from prepared specimens from light microscopy or images from electron micrographs and read into the computer's memory. The digital image can then be analyzed for predefined patterns, or edited to enhance resolution. In this way, features of the cell or tissue, that is, size, shape, and number of objects of interest, can be quantified. The human eye and brain can do this task quite easily, but only through large numbers of computations via a variety of algorithms can this be done by machine. The advantage of automating something so easily done by our own neural circuitry is a matter of convenience and improved efficiency. The computer will automatically screen for those objects specified by the biologist and provide any number of vital statistics on the composition of the specimen. A microdriver on the stage of the microscope, under computer control, can move the slide so that the specimen is automatically and systematically examined. The advantage of such systems is their ability to objectively find defined objects repetitively and without fatigue. Thus, numerous histological or clinical specimens can be processed without error in an efficient manner.

As we have seen, prepared tissue can be analyzed in any number of ways; however, one difficulty in traditional techniques employed to investigate living tissue is that the electrodes used, no matter how small, always are large relative to the scale of the cell, and the act of measurement itself often disrupts the integrity of the cell. Image analysis can be used to circumvent this constraint. Live images can be scanned in real time, and individual cells can be viewed while physiological processes are quantified. Such analysis is not normally possible with conventional memory available to computers, but with optical write-once, read-many (WORM) disk drives, gigabytes of memory are available to an individual investigator during the course of an experiment.

One area of considerable interest to neurobiologists is how stimuli begin the chain of events that result in an electrochemical signal being sent to the brain. The permeability of the cell membrane to calcium is an important feature of this process. Using phosphorescent dyes injected into cells that have an affinity for calcium, the biologist can trace the influx of calcium across the cell membrane. The amount of calcium traversing the membrane can be quantified by the brightness of the image. The amount of phospho-

rescence on a millisecond time scale and the pattern of illumination within the cell can tell investigators much about ion channels within the cell membrane. Photoaffinity labels can be attached to any number of chemicals involved in cell processes. Thus, where and when certain parts of the cell are activated and under what physiological conditions certain processes occur can be investigated without disrupting the integrity of the cell.

In fact, any image can be quantified. The applications can be varied. Some investigators have used marked points on individuals' faces to quantify facial expressions in response to social cues or odor stimuli. Other investigators use densitometry to quantify electrophoretic gels or 2-deoxyglucose images of neurobiological tissue. Electrophoresis is often used to make inferences about the composition of proteins and the underlying genetic processes responsible for the manufacture of proteins. Cells stained for 2-deoxyglucose activity are useful as an index of cell metabolism.

Computers are also useful for biological research areas other than image analysis. The ability to acquire data has often limited biologists in their ability to investigate phenomena. For the physiologist this meant physically reading instruments and counting grids on chart recordings; however, recent advances in insertable computer cards and software have made the task of communicating between measurement instruments and the computer easier. This ability to acquire data on-line has made possible our ability to monitor numerous physiological processes in real time. Combined with the appropriate multitasking software, the visual image of the experiment in graphic form can be displayed on screen as the experiment progresses, while the computer samples data from the various measurement instruments in the background. This on-line monitoring of the experiment and preliminary ability to interpret trends graphically allow the investigator to keep better track of an experiment. In this way the number of individual preparations may be kept to a minimum.

The increased computational power of personal computers also has allowed the development of increasingly sophisticated graphics programs. The ability to visualize the processed data is the first important step in data analysis. Plotting data by hand is time consuming, and plotting the data in different formats without the aid of computers is sometimes impractical. With computers, once entered, the data can be visualized in a variety of ways almost instantaneously with little effort.

Gaining access to the data also is difficult without computers. Large amounts of data are virtually intractable without the aid of the computational power of a microprocessor. By hand, even a simple t statistic can consume considerable time for large datasets. Although biologists managed to survive prior to hand calculators and computers, great productivity and access to sophisticated statistical analysis were beyond the reach of the average investigator. Menu-driven software for complex analyses has allowed biologists to analyze data for complex and subtle patterns in more than three dimensions within seconds, rather than weeks.

The computational power of modern desktop computers allows investigators to carry out simulations without actually having to physically perform experiments. Once the mathematical algorithm is known, the different variables of the model can be changed to determine how the system responds as a whole. Biochemists involved in the pharmaceutical industry have used this technique to model the performance of drugs on biological systems and generate hypotheses about what a receptor may look like. This chemical structure–behavioral activity approach also has been used by physiological ecologists to discover nonlethal chemical repellents for birds and mammals. Repellents are useful management techniques where wildlife and human interests conflict. For example, vertebrate repellents can be incorporated into granular pesticides to reduce the risk of accidental ingestion by birds and mammals. Granular pesticides are important because they represent the only way to adequately protect crops in a no-till agriculture system. Limiting tillage is important for the minimization of erosion of fertile soil and general soil conservation. Similarly, computational power is needed to track wildlife populations using demographic data. Such

models set harvests so that yields can be sustained.

Other areas of field biology where computers can be used are a bit more arcane. Biophysical ecology is the study of how micrometeorological conditions may affect an animal's behavior or physiology. Such information is of interest in developing an understanding of the evolutionary selective forces shaping the limits to geographic distributions of plants and animals. To a small lizard the sun-baked expanse of a few meters might as well be the Sahara Desert because of the hostile thermal environment. Thus, the few hundred square meters of the lizard's territory consists of a mosaic of habitats that may restrict activities such as foraging and limit access to potential hiding places or sites where eggs may be laid. The only way of knowing what the thermal landscape looks like is to measure it. The more measurements spatially and temporally placed, the better the picture will be. Biophysical ecologists typically use data-logging instruments to record such data automatically from thousands of sampling points. These data are stored in small portable modules, which are subsequently picked up from the field and linked to personal computers where the information can be processed.

Radiotelemetry is the remote recording of data from a transmitter. Telemeters can convey positional information or data on the activity or physiological status of an animal. In some cases it is important to know where an animal goes and how much time it spends at a given location. For migrating species, this information is important because it can tell us what habitats are vital to the species and it can be useful for setting policy on habitat preservation. In the most dramatic cases the animal may travel thousands of miles, crossing international boundaries. Here signals from the transmitter can be picked up via satellite and the information transferred to the end user. Many such animals can be simultaneously monitored if each animal is broadcasting its signal on a different frequency. Knowing the position of the animal is only the first step in the process. If conservation is an end goal, then the habitat of centralized locations must be quantified. The simplest way of doing this is to have biologists physically go to these locations and survey the areas. But resources may be finite and manpower limited. An alternative is to characterize the habitats of interest via satellite imagery. A surprising amount of detail about the vegetative habitat structure can be gained in this way.

The slow incorporation of computers into biological science may itself reflect demographic processes. New investigators entering the field tend to be more computer literate than their established counterparts. As these investigators gain stature, the integration of biology and technology will become more complete.

For Further Reading

Anker, L. S., P. Jurs, and P. A. Edwards. 1990. Quantitative structure retention relationship studies of odor-active aliphatic compounds with oxygen-containing functional groups. *Analytical Chemistry* 62: 2676–84.

Cooper-Smith, R., and M. Leon. 1989. Glucose-6-phosphate dehydrogenase activity in the olfactory system of the young rat— An enzyme histochemical study using computerized image analysis. *Journal of Comparative Neurology* 289:348–59.

Derenzo, S. E. 1990. *Interfacing: A laboratory approach using the microcomputer for instrumentation, data analysis, and control.* Englewood Cliffs, N.J.: Prentice-Hall.

Freeman, W. J., and B. Baird. 1987. Relation of olfactory EEG to behavior: Spatial analysis. *Behavioral Neuroscience* 1d:393–408.

Ransom, R., and R. J. Matela. 1986. *Advances in plant science,* vol. 1: *Computer graphics in biology.* Portland, Ore.: Dioscorides Press.

Royet, J. P., G. Sicard, C. Souchier, and F. Jordan. 1987. Specificity of spatial patterns of glomerular activation in the mouse olfactory bulb: Computer-assisted image analysis of 2-deoxyglucose autoradiograms. *Brain Research* 417:1–11.

Shaw, D. M., and S. F. Atkinson. 1990. An introduction to the use of geographic information systems for ornithological research. *Condor* 92:564–70.

Larry Clark

BIOMECHANICS AND COMPUTERS

Biomechanics is the study of the structure and function of biological systems through application of mechanical principles. The most commonly studied system is the human body. This area of research includes exercise and sport, ergonomics, engineering, and medicine. Qualitative measures are frequently applied to "solve" human movement problems. Coaches constantly strive to improve the technique of their athletes. A secretary might try different keyboards for a computer to find the one that "feels" the best. Although descriptive techniques are invaluable, quantification of movement is essential to gain a better understanding of why humans move the way they do.

Four major areas where the computer has made a significant impact in the field of biomechanics are field research, laboratory research, administration, and instruction (Miller 1989). The portability and self-contained nature of the microcomputer have permitted better field analysis. Researchers are now able to collect data in an environment familiar to the subject rather than in a laboratory. Larger and faster computers (mainframes and workstations) have increased the ability to perform complex mathematical analyses, and researchers can now collect, process, and analyze more substantial quantities of numerical data.

TYPES OF ANALYSIS

In biomechanics two primary types of analysis occur: kinetic and kinematic. Kinetic analyses involve direct measurement of the forces responsible for motion. Kinematic analyses focus on describing motion in terms of position, velocity, and acceleration. Kinetic variables may then be derived through a process known as inverse dynamics.

Most recording devices used in biomechanical research produce a continuous electronic (analog) signal (Miller 1989). The computer cannot store this signal in its raw form; rather, it must be converted into a numeric or digital form. By use of an analog-to-digital (A/D) converter, the analog signals can be "sampled" and converted to a series of numbers (Miller 1989, Winter 1990). This has increased the speed and accuracy of data collection and analysis dramatically. Each sample can be thought of as a "picture" of the original signal. Because the signal changes with time, taking more "pictures" (or increasing the sampling frequency) will produce a better representation. This process is known as "analog-to-digital" conversion.

Kinetic Analysis

Force platforms are elaborate scales using strain gauges or piezoelectric elements to measure forces (Gowitzke and Milner 1988, Grieve et al. 1975, Winter 1990). For example, as weight is placed on a force platform, the electrical signal flowing through the sensing elements is changed in proportion to the amount of force the elements experience. The resistance change affects the amplitude of an alternating current. This analog signal is amplified and stored on the computer via the A/D converter for future analysis. The force platform is used to measure the ground reaction forces during walking, running, or any portion of a movement that can be confined to a small area on the ground.

Research in muscle and joint function, including strength, fatigue, and range of motion, has been assisted by a device known as a dynamometer. Software controls the dynamometer, which manipulates the velocity and range of motion of a limb for a variety of different movements. The machine functions in three modes: isokinetic (constant velocity), isotonic (constant force), and isometric (no motion). It is commonly used in the areas of rehabilitation, conditioning, and sports medicine. For example, torque curves during a leg extension–flexion exercise can aid the biomechanist in diagnosing strength deficiencies or rates of muscle fatigue.

The study of the electrical signals produced by muscles, electromyography, is an-

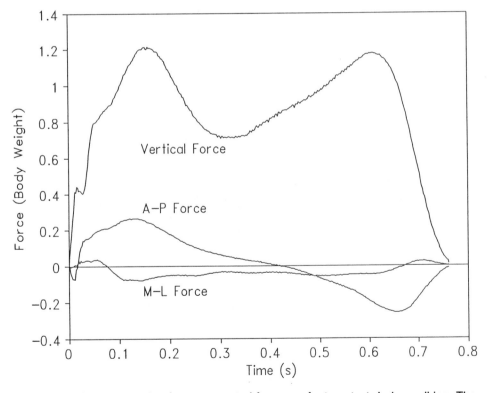

FIGURE 1. Ground reaction force generated from one foot contact during walking. The anterior–posterior (A-P) force acts along the length of the foot while the mediolateral force acts across the foot. Note that the vertical force is the largest one acting on the foot and can reach values of two times body weight.

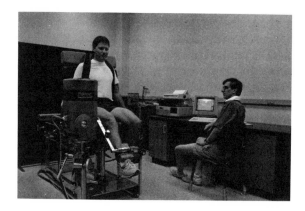

FIGURE 2. A dynamometer setup to test quadriceps and hamstring muscle strength during knee extension and flexion.

other area of research in biomechanics (Gowitzke and Milner 1988, Grieve et al. 1975, Winter 1990). Electromyograms (EMGs) are useful in the attempt to understand the control of posture or movements such as walking or cycling. The EMG electrode also outputs an analog signal, thus

requiring the use of the computer and A/D converter for collection of the data.

Kinematic Analysis

Imaging techniques are the conventional way of studying the kinematics of human movement (Gowitzke and Milner 1988, Grieve et al. 1975, Miller 1989, Winter 1990). Modern tools for data collection include video, 16-millimeter film, and optoelectronic devices. Early imaging systems were based on cinematography. Analyzing 16-millimeter film of a task involved a time-consuming process called manual digitizing. By projecting the image onto graph paper, one could determine the x and y coordinates of points on the image (usually marking the endpoints of body segments) by hand. Tracking these points through subsequent frames allowed researchers to calculate the positions of individual segments through time. From these points, a stick figure diagram could be created to display the movement. Velocities and

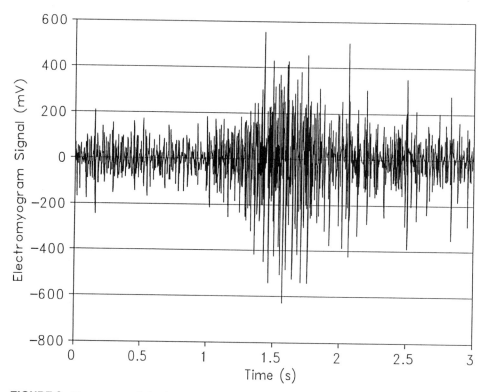

FIGURE 3. Unprocessed electromyogram signal from the vastus medialis muscle during a resisted knee extension.

accelerations of body segments could be calculated and used to identify characteristics of the movement pattern.

Advances in imaging and recording technology led to the development of motion analysis systems (Gowitzke and Milner 1988, Grieve et al. 1975, Winter 1990). These projected the filmed images onto calibrated "digitizing tablets." A hand-held device then precisely located the coordinates of a point and used a computer to store the data on disk, saving a great deal of time in the analysis process.

More recently, advances in video technology have led to the development of video systems (Peak Performance Technologies, Ariel Performance Analysis Systems, and Expert Vision) where computers are the integral link between data collection and analysis (Gowitzke and Milner 1988, Miller 1989). Instead of 16-millimeter film, a video tape provides a record of the task to be digitized. This is a more cost- and time-effective medium for collecting data.

The video cassette recorder (VCR) is linked to the computer through a video "frame grabber" board and specialized software that allows the computer to control the operations of the VCR. The frame grabber board reads the information for one frame of the video tape and displays it on a video monitor. The video monitor has a resolution of 1,024 columns and 1,024 rows, providing more than 1,000,000 points on the screen. Each point in the image can be defined by a pair of x, y coordinates marking the specific location on the video monitor. To digitize a point manually, a mouse is used to move a cursor to the point on the image and then mark it. The computer then stores these coordinates.

Automated systems are a recent development in video analysis, significantly decreasing processing time (Gowitzke and Milner 1988). Points of interest on the subject are marked by reflective tape. Preliminary information is input, allowing the computer to look in a specific portion of the screen for individual points that are distinguished from the background by the intensity of light reflected from them. This eliminates the need for the user to move the cursor to each point of interest. The computer then automatically tracks these contrasting bright spots from frame to frame.

Several types of automated systems (Watsmart, Selspot) rely on optoelectronic devices using infrared emitters and charge-coupled devices in special cameras to record points of interest in digital form (Gowitzke and Milner 1988, Winter 1990). These systems are comparable to the automated video system except that the visual record of the task is eliminated. The cameras transmit the digitized coordinates directly to the computer, with software controlling the entire process.

DATA PROCESSING

On completion of data collection, it is usually necessary to reduce and process the data further to a more interpretable form. In a university research setting many of these processes are performed by software written by the researchers. Often, research groups strive to create a library of general programs that can be used directly or modified for a specific project.

Elimination of "noise" from numerical data, known as smoothing, is a universal problem that has been significantly reduced by applying complex algorithms that "smooth" the raw data (Gowitzke and Milner 1988, Miller 1989, Winter 1990). Noise can be defined as extraneous signals that

FIGURE 4. Stick figure diagram from digitized coordinates during walking on a treadmill.

tend to clutter and hide the true signal. Smoothing is achieved through various mathematical schemes ranging from filtering routines that eliminate specific frequencies from a dataset to sophisticated interpolation (splines). The smoothing routines can be relatively simple, yet still involve an enormous amount of calculation.

With image analysis numerous errors (digitizing errors, camera distortions) can be introduced into the data during the collection procedure. Therefore smoothing routines, similar to those used to "clean up" electrical signals, are used to average out these random errors. By use of the processed data, kinematic information such as velocity and acceleration can be generated with more precision.

MODELING

An alternative direction of research in the study of human movement is mathematical modeling. Computer simulations of models of the human body provide quantitative data similar to those from kinetic and kinematic analyses (Grieve et al. 1975, Winter 1990). Sophisticated simulations require the use of computers to perform the necessary mathematical analyses. Much of the progress in this area is due to the advances in computer technology from engineering, automobile, aerospace, and medical research.

Biomechanists model the human body by approximating it as a series of rigid segments connected by joints able to move in a constrained way (Winter 1990). Complex mathematical equations that describe the operation of muscle and tendon can be added to the model to control the movement of the segments. As the intricacy of the model increases, the mathematical equations that govern the dynamics of the movement increase rapidly. The usefulness of a small microcomputer is quickly outgrown; however, mainframes and supercomputers are suited to the task of processing large datasets.

The new supercomputers, performing up to 100 million instructions per second (mips), use vector processing to accelerate the output of the numerical data. Some personal workstations are capable of 33 mips. By comparison a 386 computer with a math coprocessor can do approximately 7 to 8 mips. This speed equates to significant time savings, even when a personal computer (PC) is used. For example, deriving, coding, and error checking the dynamic equations of motion for a three-segment planar model of the lower limb can take 2 months using hand calculations. With a PC and software such as Autolev, it is possible to perform the same tasks in less than 1 hour. More complex models that may require 8 months of work can be completed in 3 to 4 hours. The PC software derives the equations and writes the code in FORTRAN, a language suited to scientific calculations using large arrays. The software for the workstations is typically written in C, as UNIX, the operating system used by many workstations, is also written in C.

One of the main advantages of the fast workstation is the ability to animate the numerical results in real time. A substantial volume of data can be compressed into an easily understood format whereby the researcher can view the results and make changes accordingly. For example, a model of the arm may be built to study motion of the elbow joint using the biceps brachii and triceps muscles. For more detailed analyses more muscles can be added. The workstation and the supercomputer can be linked through a network so that they work together, one to do the number crunching and the other to display the results.

Although there will never be an alternative to analysis of actual motion, some desirable benefits are associated with the use of computer simulations of movement. Perhaps the most important of these is the "what if" paradigm. For example, the biomechanist may ask "what if" an amputee was to use a heavier or lighter artificial limb. The weight and other physical characteristics of the limb segment in the model can be altered and the effects of these changes on the walking pattern examined. In this way many different limbs may be quickly evaluated without the chance of injury to a human subject. Using more complex models that include muscles, the sports biomechanist can ask "what if" a high jumper were able to increase the strength of the lower limb muscles and therefore produce more force during the takeoff. Would a greater height be possible?

STATISTICS

Although typical experiments provide numerous datasets, it is difficult to assign a useful meaning to these data without some form of statistical analysis. For this purpose comprehensive statistical routines have been developed (SPSS, SAS, STATPRO). Thus the PC and mainframe assist the researcher in the final analysis and interpretation of data, arguably the most challenging facet of the entire research process.

ADMINISTRATION AND INSTRUCTION

As biomechanics is a research-oriented field, written records are of major importance for its advancement as a science (Miller 1989). Use of the computer as a word processor has led to faster preparation of manuscripts and reports for scientific literature. Communication between professionals in the field through electronic mail networks is another distinctive application of the computer. Educational instruction in biomechanics has been aided by such programs as PLATO, and microcomputers have allowed students to experience the research process in more detail.

References
Gowitzke, B. A., and M. Milner. 1988. *Scientific bases of human movement.* 3rd ed. Baltimore, Md.: Williams & Wilkins.
Grieve, D. W., D. Miller, D. Mitchelson, J. P. Smith, and A. J. Smith. 1975. *Techniques for the analysis of human movement.* London: Lepus.
Miller, D. 1989. Microcomputers in biomechanics research and applied settings. In J. S. Skinner, C. B. Corbin, D. M. Landers, P. E. Martin, and C. L. Wells, eds. *Future directions in exercise and sport science research.* Champaign, Ill.: Human Kinetics.
Winter, D. A. 1990. *Biomechanics and motor control of human movement.* 2nd ed. New York: Wiley-Interscience. Comprehensive overview of area.

Scott P. McLean
Tony P. Marsh
John K. DeWitt

BOOLE, GEORGE

George Boole was born on November 2, 1815, in Lincoln, England, the son of a poor shoemaker. Boole attended only elementary school and a small commercial school before going out to work as an assistant teacher at the age of 15. He spent 4 years teaching at two different elementary schools. Coming from a stratum of society in which people were not expected to attend a university and, in fact, were discouraged from it, Boole had to educate himself entirely on his own. He was self-taught in mathematics and opened his own school in Lincoln when he was 20. During scant leisure time, Boole read mathematics journals in the Mechanics Institute, founded about that time for science education. There he wrestled with material written by mathematicians Isaac Newton, Pierre-Simon Laplace, and Joseph-Louis Lagrange, and began to solve advanced problems in algebra. His first paper, "The Theory of Analytical Transformation," was published in 1840 in the *Cambridge Mathematical Journal.* This paper and one published the following year, on the theory of linear transformations, were the precursors of the theory of invariance, without which there would have been no relativity theory. The papers impressed other mathematicians so much that they urged him to go to Cambridge. But Boole, now responsible for his aging parents, turned the idea down.

In 1844, he discussed how methods of algebra and calculus may be combined in an important paper in the *Philosophical Transactions of the Royal Society.* The same year he was awarded a medal by the Royal Society for his contributions to analyses. Boole soon saw that his algebra could also be applied in logic.

In 1847, he published a pamphlet, *Mathematical Analysis of Logic, Being an Essay Towards a Calculus of Deductive Reasoning*, in which he argued persuasively that logic should be allied with mathematics, not philosophy. On the basis of his publications, Boole in 1849 was appointed professor of mathematics at Queen's College in Cork, Ireland (despite his lack of degrees), and for the first time experienced relative security. He remained at the college for the rest of his life.

In 1854 Boole published *An Investigation of the Laws of Thought, on Which Are Founded the Mathematical Theories of Logic and Probabilities*. This book, along with his 1847 publication, described his ideas and made him the father of modern symbolic logic. His logic, called Boolean algebra, was not realized until the latter part of the nineteenth century.

Boolean algebra is really an explanation of binary, zero–one logic. In the formula $x \cdot x = x$, the only numeric solutions in Boolean algebra are 0 and 1. If you represent a condition of no current flow in a circuit by 0 and a condition of current flow in the circuit by 1, then other Boolean formulas are possible:

$$1 + 1 = 1$$
$$0 + 1 = 1$$
$$0 + 0 = 0$$
$$1 \cdot 1 = 1$$
$$0 \cdot 1 = 0$$

Boolean algebra led to the design of electronic computers through the interpretation of Boolean combinations of sets as switching circuits (see also BINARY NUMBERING SYSTEMS).

Because Boole demonstrated that logic can be reduced to very simple algebraic systems, it was possible for Charles Babbage and his successors to design mechanical devices that could perform the necessary logical tasks.

The year after he wrote his *Laws of Thought*, he married Mary Everest, niece of Sir George Everest, for whom Mount Everest

is named. The Booles had five daughters. The children were a testimonial to his ideas. His third daughter, Alice, made extraordinary mathematical discoveries without any formal mathematical training. The fourth, Lucy, also without any college education, became a lecturer in chemistry and head of the chemical laboratories at the London School of Medicine for Women. The youngest daughters published several novels and some music.

Boole died on December 8, 1864, after he persisted in lecturing after being caught in a bone-chilling rain, and so contracted a cold that turned into pneumonia.

Boole's name is a household word among computer scientists and mathematicians. His influence on the development of computers and their rules of operation was unique, and yet he is virtually unknown outside these fields.

For Further Reading

Harmon, M. 1975. *Stretching man's mind: A history of data processing*. New York: Mason/Charter.

Donald D. Spencer

BRICKLIN, DANIEL

Daniel Bricklin was born in Philadelphia, Pennsylvania, on July 16, 1951. He grew up there, attending Solomon Schechter Day School. In 1969, he enrolled at the Massachusetts Institute of Technology (MIT) and began studying mathematics, switching in the middle of his junior year to computer science. Bricklin graduated from MIT in 1973 with a bachelor of science degree in electrical engineering and computer science. While at MIT, he worked a great deal with a graduate student named Bob Frankston. The two agreed they would go into business together one day.

Bricklin wanted to stay close to computers, so in the fall of 1973, he started working for Digital Equipment Corporation (DEC) near Boston. His first task there was to program a wire-service interface to a newspaper typesetting system. He also worked on computerized typesetting and obtained much experience with visual display screens and editing. His most important job at DEC was as project leader of the company's first word processing system, WPS-8, one of the earliest word processing programs. Bricklin wrote a large part of the program's code, as well as the functional specifications.

In 1976, he became a senior systems programmer for Fas Fax Corporation, manufacturers of electronic cash registers. While here, he worked closely with the firm's hardware designers and learned something about running a small business. He left there in 1977 and that fall entered graduate school in business at Harvard University.

Bricklin wanted to start a small business and, while at Harvard, he hoped to learn the "secrets" of doing this. There was a great deal of time to daydream in his classes. One day in the spring of 1978, he came up with the idea of the electronic spreadsheet. He imagined the electronic calculator, the word processor that would work with numbers. Could not a small computer speed up the calculations required in solving business problems? Bricklin was a programmer who wanted to apply his programming skills to creating a kind of electronic blackboard that would perform calculations automatically.

Bricklin and Frankston got together and decided they would work on an electronic spreadsheet in Frankston's attic in Arlington, Massachusetts. One of the most difficult and important ideas was how to label where something was. Bricklin decided that the simplest way was to use a grid coordinate system. As people usually think in letters and numbers, he labeled the top with letters and put numbers down the side. Bricklin used his experience working with interpreters to view VisiCalc as a programming language.

In the fall of 1978, Bricklin and Frankston made a deal with Dan Fylstra that they would produce this electronic spreadsheet and he would publish it through his small home computer publishing company, called Personal Software (Personal Software even-

tually became VisiCorp). Bricklin and Frankston named their company Software Arts.

In January 1979, working versions of VisiCalc were shown to Apple Computer, Inc., Atari Corporation, and other personal computer companies. A. C. Markkula, a third owner of Apple Computer, Inc., said "Hmm, interesting checkbook program—you market it yourself, we're not interested." The first VisiCalc ad appeared in the May 1979 issue of *BYTE Magazine.*

The news of VisiCalc spread rapidly. By May 1981, VisiCalc sales had exceeded 100,000 units. In 1983, cumulative sales topped half a million units. The success of Software Arts continued until 1984 when it entered into an extended legal battle with VisiCorp over the rights to VisiCalc. In the spring of 1985, Bricklin left Software Arts to be a consultant at Lotus Corporation for a short time. In November 1985, Bricklin formed a new company, Software Garden.

[*See also:* Spreadsheets.]

For Further Reading
Lammers, S. 1986. *Programmers at work,* pp. 131–51. Redmond, Wash.: Microsoft Press.

Donald D. Spencer

BROKERAGE USE OF COMPUTERS

See Financial Services, Computer Use in

BUSINESS USE OF COMPUTERS

Computers were first used commercially in organizations starting with the UNIVAC I in 1951. The UNIVAC I was used by the Census Bureau in tabulating census results in 1951 and by companies such as General Electric and General Mills for accounting and payroll applications in the mid-1950s. Computers were used primarily for transaction processing systems in the late 1950s and early 1960s.

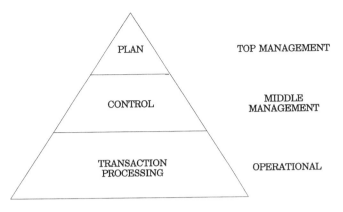

FIGURE 1. Information systems pyramid.

A transaction is the recording of an event or the recording of information on some entity. Maintenance of these recordings or records was the prime application for the computer for the following reasons: (1) They were rule-based systems that could easily be defined by a computer program. (2) The same tasks would be repeated for each record. (3) Once the rules were defined and tested, the

computer could repeat the tasks with high speed and accuracy.

Examples of some of the first transaction systems using computers are payroll (time cards), banking (checks), inventory (issues and receipts), and billing (invoices and payments). These systems were referred to as data processing (DP) systems or electronic data processing (EDP) systems.

The use of computers expanded in the later 1960s and early 1970s to include more reporting for management control and planning. An example of a control report is a listing of customers who are behind in paying their bills or of customers who have accumulated balances that are beyond their credit limit.

Implementation of systems to support higher levels of management became more complex. The rules for these systems are not as well defined. The rules can be different from manager to manager, from month to month, or depending on a number of other variables. These systems depend more on external data, which come from outside the organization, than on data from within the organization. Examples of external data would be economic data, census data, and market share data.

Systems that support management use for decision making and planning are called information systems, MANAGEMENT INFORMATION SYSTEMS, and DECISION SUPPORT SYSTEMS. The pyramid in Figure 1 shows the various levels of systems, their target levels of management, and the different labels used for these systems.

Computers are used in most organizations to support the primary functions of the organization. These functions include (1) financial planning and control, (2) marketing and distribution, (3) production, (4) human resource management, and (5) communication. The systems are either developed by programmers and analysts within the organization or purchased from software vendors. Most of the information systems are designed around databases that can support the transaction processing requirements and the management reporting for decision-making needs. Figure 2 shows the interrelationships of these major subsystems.

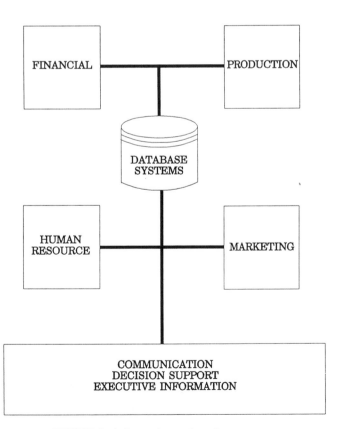

FIGURE 2. Information subsystems.

FINANCIAL PLANNING AND CONTROL

Most Organizations

The financial transaction processing systems in most organizations include the following subsystems.

General ledger. The general ledger is the overall set of revenue, expense, asset, liability, and equity accounts for an organization. All financial activity (payments, deposits, purchases, sales) is recorded in some way using forms, documents, and journals. These transactions are summarized on a periodic basis and posted to the general ledger. The general ledger maintains the current balances for all accounts, and it is used to produce the financial statements (balance sheet and income statement) at the end of each reporting period. A number of general ledger software systems are available that are applicable to businesses of any size and hardware platforms of any size (microcomputer-based systems, minicomputers, mainframes).

Purchasing/accounts payable. All organizations need to purchase material, supplies, and products. Service organizations (doctors, lawyers, barbers, hospitals, universities) purchase supplies and equipment that they use in their daily activities. Production organizations (contractors, factories) purchase supplies and equipment and, in addition, purchase products that go into the production of new products to be sold. The transaction systems (purchase orders, invoices, payments, receiving documents) record each event in appropriate journals and ledgers. The cash disbursements journal maintains detail information on each payment, and the payables subsidiary ledger maintains balances on how much the organization owes to each vendor. The computer information system supporting this function is referred to as the procurement subsystem. It is closely interconnected with the materials requirements subsystem.

Sales and receivables. Most organizations are in the business of selling some product or service. Each sale generates data such as the amount, date, name of purchaser, item purchased, and mode of payment. These transactions are recorded on documents and forms such as sales orders, invoices, and payment records. Each sales transaction is posted to the sales journal, cash receipts journal, or accounts receivable subsidiary ledger, depending on the type of sale. The subsidiary ledger maintains the current balances for each customer who buys products on account and pays on a periodic basis. Computer software to support these functions is used by most organizations. The sales subsystem has a close interrelationship with the marketing subsystem.

Payroll. Payroll in many organizations is the largest financial system in terms of money spent. It requires the maintenance of much information, and it is tied to many other information subsystems. Larger organizations have set up a separate department, referred to as human resource management. The payroll system is a responsibility of this department and is described under the human resource management heading.

Asset management. Computer information systems are used to maintain the equipment and property records of an organization. Records are maintained on the cost, location, accumulated depreciation, and life of assets such as buildings and equipment.

Treasury systems. Organizations that borrow money or get their funding through stock have systems to maintain records on who owns the stock, the number of shares, and the amount of dividends and interest paid. These systems are used to communicate with the stockholders on a periodic basis regarding financial status, annual meetings, and voting for items at the annual meeting.

The transaction processing systems described above generate and maintain data in databases used for planning and control. Most of these subsystems include management reports and query systems that assist managers at all levels. Larger organizations have financial subsystems that produce information for upper-level management decision support, planning, and control. These are described below.

Large Organizations

Budgeting and cost control. Budgeting is the process of setting up a plan for how much money will be spent by area and category. Once budgets are set up, there is a need to report on a periodic basis how much has been spent and to flag areas that appear to be out of control. Management can use these reports to take action to cut costs or modify the plan.

Financial planning. Most organizations need to maintain a cash flow plan (money coming in and going out). Timing is very important. Financial obligations (bills) need to be met on a timely basis; otherwise the organization can jeopardize its credit rating. Excess cash should be either invested in the organization through expansion and/or improvements or invested in instruments (certificates of deposit, notes) that earn interest. Information systems are used to estimate cash needs, forecast cash surplus, and maintain the current status of all cash deposits.

MARKETING AND DISTRIBUTION

Computer-Based Transaction Processing Systems Maintained for Marketing

Sales order processing. This system records the sale of each item, including the item number, description, quantity, price, date, taxes, and, in some cases, name of purchaser. In some organizations this may be done by a computer-controlled cash register. In other organizations it may be done by filling out a form on the screen of a personal computer or terminal.

Invoicing is billing the customer for the sale. In some cases the sales order and invoice may be the same. In other cases the only record of the sale is in the form of a cash register and/or credit card receipt. Sales on account normally are recorded through invoices that provide information to the accounts receivable system.

Shipping. Organizations that provide products through phone and mail orders have a shipping system that coordinates the packaging and delivery of the product to the customer. Information is maintained on orders filled, orders to be filled, mode of shipment, date shipped, shipping costs, and carrier.

Computer-Based Systems Used to Support Marketing Management Information Systems and Decision Support Systems

Marketing research. Systems gather data on customers, customer needs, customer satisfaction, potential new products, and potential new markets. These data are used to develop marketing plans. Data are collected and maintained on the industry to analyze market potential, market share, and competitive advantage.

Performance systems. Organizations maintain information systems on customer and product profitability, response time in meeting customer needs, inability to meet customer needs, and customer satisfaction. These systems are used to respond to problems that may lead to losing customers or losing sales.

Sales forecasting and trends. Information systems are developed to maintain data on industry, economic, population, and other trends that may have an effect on sales. These systems help predict estimated demand for products, reporting on sales in units and dollars for each product by month. This information is used to plan the production, inventory, and financial requirements for future months.

Advertising. Information systems are used to analyze advertising strategy and performance. Analysis is done on different types of media (radio, TV, magazines, newspapers, billboards) as to cost, numbers and types of people reached, and effect on sales.

PRODUCTION

All organizations are involved with the production of some good or service. Larger organizations require a number of subsystems to maintain information on the production process. Some of the computer-based transaction processing subsystems are as follows.

Product specifications. Organizations that produce complex products use engineers to draw up product specifications. These specifications are maintained by an information system that keeps track of how the product is built and what parts are used to build it. This is called a bill of materials. The information in this subsystem is used to support production, scheduling, inventory, and cost. Engineers use a variety of software packages to support this function. They are referred to as computer-aided design (CAD) and computer-aided engineering (CAE). (See also COMPUTER-AIDED DESIGN AND MANUFACTURING.)

Production scheduling. Computer systems are used to analyze total demand for a product (orders from customers and forecasted demand) and to provide a production plan for each component that goes into the product. The system uses information from the product specifications subsystem to determine the various components, the person(s) responsible for each component, the quantity, and the production sequence. The objective is to fill all the orders and not end up with surplus products.

Materials requirements planning. The heart of the production system is maintaining data on what is currently in inventory, what needs to be ordered, when it needs to be ordered, and how much needs to be ordered. This subsystem gets information from production scheduling, production specifications, and suppliers. Information is maintained on vendors, products, costs, and shipping data. Purchase orders are produced by the system to obtain components in synchronization with the production schedule. In some cases the purchase order goes directly through communication lines from the organization's computer to the vendor's computer (see ELECTRONIC DATA INTERCHANGE).

Quality control and inspection. Information systems are used to track the products from production into inspection and to maintain data on reject rates, reject reasons, and status of previous rejected products. This information is used to correct problems in production, to control costs, and to increase customer satisfaction.

Cost control and reporting. In most organizations the primary costs are associated with producing the product or service. Information systems are used to track the cost of labor and material going into producing the product or service for every step or task. This information is used to determine product profitability, to design more efficient approaches to the production process, and to monitor cost trends.

HUMAN RESOURCE MANAGEMENT

(See also HUMAN RESOURCES, COMPUTER USE IN).

Payroll. Payroll systems are very adaptable to computer systems because of the volume of data, the many rules, and the repetitive work that is done week after week. Hundreds of software packages are available to support payroll for small and large computers and for small and large organizations. Some of the software is specifically designed for industries with special rules. Most organizations have employees who are paid on a periodic basis. Much information is recorded each pay period in connection with paying an employee. Hourly employees record their hours on time cards. Data are maintained on state, federal, and social security taxes. Most organizations offer benefits (health insurance, dental insurance, retirement plans) for which a part of the cost is deducted from each check and forwarded to the companies supplying the benefits. Quarterly and annual reports are made to state and federal agencies. Payroll can be complex in some organizations because of the rules regarding shift time, overtime, holiday time, and high-risk tasks.

Benefits. Systems are required to maintain information on the various benefits that are a part of each employee's fringe package. These include health insurance, dental insurance, retirement plans, vacation time, sick time, personal-leave days, credit unions, stock incentives, education and training, and profit incentive plans. The information and rules maintained by these systems can vary significantly, depending on the type of employee, length of service, and the plan selected by the employee.

Career path management. Many organizations have information systems to help them maintain data on each individual's objectives, skills, training, and performance measures. These systems can be used to support the task of managing the work force in a number of its aspects, such as (1) assisting management in looking at the strengths and weaknesses in the work force, (2) looking at skills existing and needed for a new project, (3) planning future training needs, (4) budgeting for education, (5) planning for promotion and pay increases, and (6) planning recruiting needs.

Minority management. Information systems are used to maintain data on hiring minorities, analyzing current minority status, and analyzing minority percentages in the labor market.

COMMUNICATION

The primary use of computing in organizations today is in communicating information from one function to another, from one employee to another, and from one organization to another. All of the information subsystems are integrated. Information created in one subsystem is used by another subsystem. All of the subsystems are in some way connected to the financial subsystems.

Computer systems support this integration in a number of ways. Common databases are used to share data between subsystems. Networks are used to connect everyone by means of terminals, microcomputer-based systems, network servers, and communication links. Software is available to assist users in connectivity, communication, and workstation environments. Some examples of the software in the communication subsystem follow.

Electronic mail. ELECTRONIC MAIL (e-mail) is used in organizations to send messages to individuals or groups. The messages are composed on terminals or personal computer-based terminals and sent to others with terminals. Receiving terminals normally notify the user that a message has arrived. Most systems allow the users to view the messages in any order; file them by subject, date, or sender; respond by typing a note on the same message; print the message; and purge files of past messages. Electronic mail makes it easy and fast to communicate with groups of people, because any message and response can be available to anyone in the group.

Calendar management. Calendars for each individual can be maintained at their terminals and be accessible from other terminals. This facilitates the scheduling of meetings by anyone on the system, using software that can scan the calendars to find common open times for the attendees.

Document management. Central filing systems can be maintained electronically, so that everyone on the network can have access, when necessary, to documents produced by others. This allows one filing system for many workers and makes it easier for groups to work on common documents, such as a training manual or procedures manual. All members of the group are able to view the latest version of the manual at any time. When the manual is complete, it can be referenced electronically or printed on high-speed laser printers.

Electronic reference. Large volumes of data such as catalogs, encyclopedias, dictionaries, phone books, and plane schedules can be accessed using optical disk technology (compact-disk read-only memory [CD-ROM]).

Executive information systems. Top management in organizations use terminals and executive information system (EIS) software to report on key summary data about the organization. The reporting is often done with color graphics that display the data in the form of charts and graphs. The executive can interact with the system, selecting the data, time periods, and type of chart. The executive can also give the system "what if"–type questions, for example: "What effect will a higher interest rate have on the organization?" (See also EXECUTIVE INFORMATION SYSTEMS.)

For Further Reading

Eliason, A. L. 1983. *Online business computer applications.* Chicago: SRA.

Hirschheim, R. A. 1985. *Office automation—A social and organizational perspective.* New York: Wiley.

Holsapple, C. W., and A. B. Whinston. 1987. *Business expert systems.* Homewood, Ill.: Irwin.

McConn, C. E. 1989. *Business computer systems—Design, programming, and maintenance with case studies.* Englewood Cliffs, N.J.: Prentice-Hall.

McLeod, R., Jr. 1990. *Management information systems—A study of computer-based information systems.* New York: Macmillan.

Nash, J. F. 1989. *Accounting information systems.* Boston: PWS-Kent.

O'Brien, J. A. 1990. *Management information systems—A managerial end user perspective.* Homewood, Ill.: Irwin.

Parker, C. S. 1989. *Management information systems—Strategy and action.* New York: McGraw-Hill.

Perry, W. E. 1987. *The information center.* Englewood Cliffs, N.J.: Prentice-Hall.

Summers, E. L. 1989. *Accounting information systems.* Boston: Houghton Mifflin.

Wilkinson, J. W. 1989. *Accounting information systems—Essential concepts and applications.* New York: Wiley.

Alden C. Lorents

BYRON, AUGUSTA ADA

Augusta Ada Byron was born in London on December 10, 1815, to George Gordon Byron, better known as Lord Byron, and Anne Isabella Milbanke Byron. Anne and Lord Byron separated a little over a month after the birth of their daughter; Lord Byron then left England, never to return. Ada, as she was known in the family circle, married William, eighth Lord King, in 1835, and 3 years later became known as the Countess of Lovelace.

"I hope that the gods have made her anything save *poetical*—it is enough to have one such fool in a family." The comment came from the pen of Lord Byron. The great English poet and ladies' man was referring to his only legitimate daughter, 7-year-old Ada, and the time was 1823, the year before his death, at 36.

Ada was well tutored by those around her (British logician Augustus De Morgan was a close family friend), but she hungered for more knowledge than they could provide. She was actively seeking a mentor when Charles BABBAGE, the noted English mathematician and inventor, came to the house to demonstrate his difference engine for her mother's friends. Then and there, Ada resolved to help him realize his grandest dream: the long-planned but never constructed analytical engine. Present on that historic evening was Mrs. De Morgan, who wrote in her memoirs: "While the rest of the party gazed at this beautiful instrument with the same sort of expression and feeling that some savages are said to have shown on first seeing a looking glass or hearing a gun, Miss Byron, young as she was, understood its workings and saw the great beauty of the invention."

Ada and Babbage became close friends, writing to each other regularly on topics that ranged from the design of machine tools to the latest society gossip. There is little doubt from these letters that Babbage was rather in love with the beautiful young countess whose mind so closely matched his own. Ada, however, was only in love with Babbage's analytical engine.

The analytical engine was what we would now call a programmable computer, with an almost infinite capacity for changes in its program. The machine, which depended on the interaction of hundreds of accurately machined gear wheels, was never actually built; however, this did not prevent Ada and Babbage from establishing the procedures for how the machine would work when it was finally completed.

General Luigi Menabrea, a celebrated

Italian engineer and general, was shown the prototype of the analytical engine. On returning to Italy, he wrote a technical account of the machine in French. Ada, while preparing an English translation of this publication, added many footnotes and appendices. This translated paper, the only one of Ada's that was saved, was the best description of the computer that was to be written for almost a hundred years. It was through Ada's writings that the understanding of the analytical engine was preserved into the twentieth century.

She also had the idea that she and Babbage, surely the most distinguished mathematicians of their generation, could create a scheme to calculate the odds on horse races, the profits to go to the development of Babbage's analytical engine. In her effort to develop a mathematically infallible system for betting on the ponies, she had to pawn her husband's family jewels twice to pay off blackmailing bookies.

By preparing the instructions needed to carry out computations on Babbage's calculator, Ada became the world's first computer programmer. The U.S. Pentagon has honored Ada Byron by naming a computer language after her—ADA. This language, which is similar to the language Pascal, is designed to be used on Department of Defense systems. Ada is now a registered trademark of the U.S. Department of Defense.

On November 27, 1852, at the age of 36, the exact age at which her father, Lord Byron, had died, Ada died of cancer. She was buried in the Byron vault at Hucknall Torkard church in Nottinghamshire. At her own wish, she lies at the side of her father.

For Further Reading

Evans, C. 1984. *The making of the micro.* London: Harrow House.

Donald D. Spencer

CAD/CAM

See Computer-Aided Design and Manufacturing; Solid Modeling and Finite Element Analysis

CADD (COMPUTER-AIDED DESIGN/DRAFTING)

See Architecture, Computer Uses in

CARDS, JACQUARD AND HOLLERITH

[*This article discusses the development of the punched card as a medium for data storage and input. It begins with the invention of a punched card system in the nineteenth century to automate the process of weaving, and continues with the adaptation of the punched card to the tabulating machine and the computer.*]

JACQUARD CARDS

Intricate patterns and figures are woven in cloth with a *drawloom,* a device invented in the Far East and brought to Europe during the Middle Ages. In this drawloom, or loom, a cord was tied to each warp thread; these cords were knotted into groups so that the right ones could be raised together. The weaver had an assistant called a *drawboy,* who sat on top of the loom and pulled the cords, following a sequence given by a paper diagram of the pattern. The regularity of the

pattern depended entirely on the reliability of the drawboy, who was only an apprentice and tended to tire of the hard, monotonous work. Attempts were eventually made to eliminate the need for a drawboy on top of the loom. The first stage, introduced in the seventeenth century, was to control the cords with levers worked by an assistant who stood beside the loom where the weaver could see him.

France was an early leader in elegant weaving, and a number of inventors had sought ways to automate the process and so lower the cost.

In 1725, the inventor Basile Bouchon devised a method of selecting the cords automatically. Each cord was threaded through a needle. Every time the shuttle was about to be passed through, a cylinder punched with rows of holes, one for each needle, was slid along to touch the row of needles. A roll of paper was wound around this cylinder; the sequence of the pattern was recorded on this in the form of holes fitting over those on the cylinder. If a needle met a hole, it passed into the cylinder, through it, and was not moved.

If it met an unpunched space, it was forced outward by the movement of the cylinder. The assistant now pressed a pedal, operating a device that caught the needles that had been moved and pulled the cords attached to them. The shuttle was then passed through, the roll of paper was wound forward one space, and the cycle began again. This device eliminated mistakes, but still required the services of an assistant. Furthermore, the paper kept tearing. Three years later, in 1728, the French inventor Falcon improved the loom, replacing the paper roll with an endless chain of stiff punched cards strung together, and making the various pattern-weaving operations automatic. This technique was later adopted for use in the first successful machine to operate from punched cards.

The next step was taken in 1745 by a watchmaker, Jacques de Vaucanson. He built an experimental loom in which the movement of the cylinder pulled the cords directly, without the need for an assistant. But the machinery that worked this arrangement was so complicated and unreliable that the idea never caught on.

Not long after this, Joseph-Marie Jacquard was born. During a checkered career in which he fought for both sides in the French Revolution, he invented an automatic net-making machine. This gave him a reputation that caused him to be summoned to Paris to overhaul Vaucanson's original loom. He immediately set out to produce a workable version.

Jacquard designed a loom controlled by punched cards (Figure 1). A separate card was used for each passage of the shuttle. A hole punched at a particular position on the card indicated that a certain warp thread was to be lifted. A position where a hole could have been punched, but was not, indicated that the corresponding thread was not to be lifted. The pattern to be woven was "programmed" by punching the cards appropriately.

Jacquard did not invent the punch card-controlled loom, but he improved on previous versions so much that his was the first automated loom to achieve widespread commercial success. By 1812, there were 11,000 Jacquard looms in France alone (Figure 2).

A particularly famous tapestry of Jacquard himself hung in drawing rooms all over Europe and England. Approximately 24,000 punched cards had been used to drive the loom to weave it. One of these tapestries found its way into the possession of Charles BABBAGE, who saw in Jacquard's punched card device a means of controlling and storing numbers for his analytical engine.

HOLLERITH CARDS

Herman Hollerith is widely known as the person who originated the punched card. Although he adopted the original idea from Jacquard, the modern punched card closely resembles Hollerith's invention.

In 1879, Hollerith was employed by the U.S. Census Bureau. He started work on a machine for mechanically tabulating population statistics. Later he developed a tabulating system that used electrical contacts for the sensing of holes and provided a method for sorting punched cards. His first card measured 6⅝ × 3¼ inches (16.8 × 8.25 cm) and contained twenty-four columns, each with twelve punching positions. Hollerith's punched cards and tabulating equipment were first used for the tabulation of the 1890 census.

Data cards were punched with holes on spots indicating particular information, such as employment. To obtain the total number of men working in factories, for example, the data cards were placed one by one over mercury-filled cups. The machine dropped rows of telescoping pins onto the surface of the card. Wherever there was a hole, a pin dropped through the hole into the mercury, thus completing an electrical circuit and activating a switch. The closing switch caused a

FIGURE 1. A punched card used in Jacquard's automatic loom. An endless chain of these cards rotated past the needles of the loom. As the cards moved by, only the needles that matched holes were able to penetrate, and their threads determined the pattern.

FIGURE 2. A silk weaving factory around 1830, where an early version of the Jacquard loom is being used. Jacquard used punched cards to determine the pattern to be woven. *Courtesy Camelot Publishing Company.*

needle on a dial to jump one or more spaces, depending on the information on the card. When all of the cards were passed through the machine, the desired answer showed directly on the dial.

Hollerith formed the Tabulating Machine Company to build and sell his tabulating machine. In 1911, Hollerith's company merged with other companies to form the Computing-Tabulating-Recording Company (C-T-R), which later became the IBM Corporation. From the early twenty-four-column card, the IBM card developed into forty-five columns. The forty-five-column card was used by the Census Bureau until 1940. By 1924 the first eighty-column equipment was

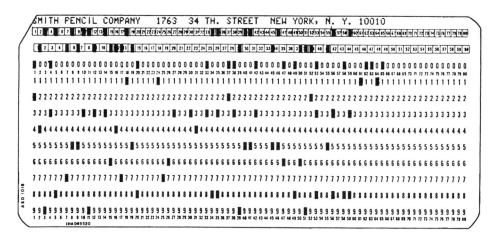

FIGURE 3. IBM eighty-column card format. *Courtesy Camelot Publishing Company.*

developed, almost doubling the card capacity.

Today, the most popular size of card measures 7⅜ × 3¼ inches (19.6 × 8.25 cm) with eighty columns of twelve punch positions (Figure 3). Each column represents one letter, number, or other symbol, depending on the pattern of holes in that column. The computer reads the cards when they are passed through a card reader, which can flip through cards at a rate of up to 2,000 cards per minute. Each card passes between a light source and a row of solar cells, which detect the location of the holes in the card. The pattern of holes is thus transformed into a pattern of electrical signals. The card reader sends these signals to the computer, where they are translated into machine instructions. If many data will be generated by a program, and these data will subsequently be read by another machine, it is possible to have the output of the computer punched directly on cards by a machine called a card punch.

Many designs are used for the mechanics of card reading and punching equipment. Attention is focused intently on handling the cards in a gentle manner. If the edge of a card becomes slightly damaged, it can cause a severe jam in the reading mechanism, which in turn can interrupt the processing of a very powerful piece of computing equipment.

Because the presence of a punch or a pencil mark can be sensed in a similar manner, optical readers can read cards that have intermixed punches and marks. This is a useful attribute in that prepunched cards can be used in many applications, such as job ticket accounting and inventories by department, where the common information is prepunched and the specific information is added by hand.

In 1969, IBM announced a ninety-six-column card for use with some of their computer systems (Figure 4). The card measures 3¼ × 2⅝ inches (8.25 × 6.67 cm) and stores ninety-six characters of information. The card uses small round holes, rather than the rectangular holes of the eighty-column

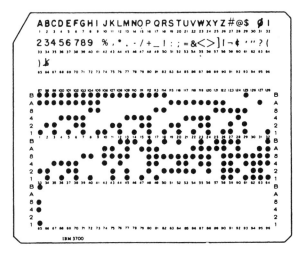

FIGURE 4. IBM ninety-six-column card format.

card. Space is available in three rows at the top of the card to allow for a printout of the data stored on the card. The data are stored, as punched holes, in three rows of thirty-two columns each. Only six rows are used to represent a character or a number. Multiple punches are used to add up to a numeric value; that is, the 1, 2, and 4 rows will be punched to indicate a value of 7. This saves space compared with the format used in the eighty-column card, which uses a decimal format for numeric data.

The two main advantages of punched cards are permanency of records and easy grouping of records. As the environmental conditions for cards are found in all computer installations, cards may be retained for long periods, thereby eliminating the necessity to keypunch the same data every time they are needed. As every card is a record in itself, all the necessary information required for one transaction can be contained in the fields of one card, permitting all similar transactions to be readily grouped.

The late 1960s and early 1970s also saw the introduction of devices designed to replace the card as a storage medium for input of transactions into a computer. These devices and advanced techniques have become increasingly dominant, with the use of cards being sharply reduced but not yet eliminated.

For Further Reading

Augarten, S. 1984. *Bit by bit*, p. 64. New York: Ticknor & Fields.

Becker, J. 1973. *The first book of information science*. Oak Ridge, Tenn.: United States Atomic Energy Commission.

Fang, I. E. 1988. *The computer story*, pp. 19–21. St. Paul, Minn.: Rada Press.

Fernbach, S., and A. Taub. 1970. *Computers and their role in the physical sciences*, pp. 33–36. New York: Gordon & Breach.

Giarratano, J. 1982. *Foundations of computer technology*. Indianapolis, Ind.: Howard W. Sams & Co., Inc.

Moreau, R. 1984. *The computer comes of age*, pp. 12–14. Cambridge, Mass.: MIT Press.

Donald D. Spencer

CAREERS IN COMPUTING

Computer and information technology is a field that is leading the way toward a society that will rely more and more on information. As this field goes through what seems to be an almost continual period of change, employment opportunities also change.

As a career, the computer field offers the excitement of exploring new frontiers and the challenge of participating in the building of a new information society. When most people think of jobs in the computer field, they usually think of systems analysts, programmers, computer operators, and data entry operators. These positions are well known. The computer field, however, courts a host of people with various talents, from managers and design engineers to teachers and writers; from sales representatives, scientists, and computer service technicians to librarians and word processing operators. If you are a doctor, a lawyer, an engineer, a mathematician, an architect, a police officer, a teacher, an accountant, a stockbroker, an artist, or a businessperson, the industry beckons you also to combine your knowledge with computer skills. Furthermore, you can choose the business or industry in which you want to work. If you are interested in teaching, there is plenty of opportunity for you to teach in colleges, secondary schools, and elementary schools.

If you are interested in research and developing new techniques or products, there is plenty of opportunity for you. If you are interested in business, you can choose almost anything from banking to department store management. Businesses of all kinds and sizes, whether international corporations or small businesses, engineering or farming, offer opportunities for people interested in the computer field. If you like to create fine art, you can use sophisticated computer drawing systems to aid you in your work. In fact, there are four major groups of employers that hire computer-trained personnel:

- Organizations that use computers as part of their business operations

- Companies that manufacture computer equipment or develop software packages
- Service organizations that sell time on their computers and offer a variety of computer services
- Businesses that market a variety of such services as training, personnel recruitment, equipment leasing, and equipment sales (computer stores)

Some computer professionals specialize in a segment of the job market. Computer-related jobs are particularly plentiful in technical industries, such as manufacturing plants, the aircraft industry, and toy manufacturing, and in information industries, such as insurance and banking. It is common for an individual to move, for example, from one engineering firm to another; this person would be specializing, in effect, in the engineering or scientific aspects of the computer industry. There are many areas of specialization: computer graphics, accounting, information communications, publishing, education, banking, research, software development, medicine, transportation, artificial intelligence, process control, police work, science, sales, music, fine art, writing, and aerospace are but a few examples.

Women, take notice. The computer field is a good place for women. More women earn higher salaries in computer-related jobs than in any other technical or business occupation. Many women occupy positions as managers, systems analysts, programmers, data entry operators, sales representatives, college instructors, writers, secondary and elementary school teachers, computer operators, computer graphics artists, word processing operators, and software developers. Today many women find that the computer industry is an excellent career area, and in the future it should be even better.

Many disabled workers find positions in the computer field as programmers, word processing operators, computer graphics artists, and software developers. Modifications to the equipment have helped make this possible. The physically disabled direct computers by using special keyboards or pointing devices; the blind use Braille terminals. Both computer manufacturers and user companies sponsor training programs for the disabled. According to many case studies, the efforts have paid off with productive, loyal employees.

Some computer professionals prefer working for computer manufacturers. They are developing software, helping to design and produce new hardware products, training customers, writing technical manuals, selling machines and services, and maintaining the equipment. Other people like free-lance work. There are, for instance, a large number of free-lance programmers, systems analysts, computer graphics specialists, consultants, computer instructors, and software developers who enjoy the freedom of working where they wish and controlling their own work hours. Many free-lance people work at home or for small computer-related consulting or software development firms.

In recent years the microcomputer industry has introduced many new job opportunities into the marketplace. Rather than pursuing a traditional computer job in an industry or business, an individual can now join a firm that uses microcomputer systems for a variety of applications. Microcomputer systems have also introduced a variety of home-based jobs: moonlight programming, software product development, part-time computer store sales representative, microcomputer system repair, part-time teaching, and so on. Whether you are a high school graduate or a mathematician, an artist or a salesperson, an engineer or a teacher, there is a job in the computer field to suit your unique skills and abilities. In a time when people throughout the world feel unsure about employment, the computer industry is experiencing phenomenal growth, with a consequent booming demand for people with computer-related training.

In addition to jobs for computer professionals, there will also be millions of new jobs in occupations that have felt the impact of computers. For example, people who operate word processing machines or who operate a police information database have computer-related jobs. Thousands of businesses, hospitals, police departments, government agencies, schools, libraries, banks, advertising agencies, and other organizations are computer users. These organizations need qualified people to operate their computers and related equipment.

Advancements in artificial intelligence will continue to cause many job descriptions to change. For example, secretaries will have to adapt to the "talking typewriter." Meteorologists will have to use expert systems for weather forecasting. Teachers will be expected to use intelligent computers for teaching. Librarians will have to use databases that consist of expert systems.

IS A COMPUTER CAREER RIGHT FOR YOU?

One exciting feature of the computer field is the remarkable variety of choices in careers. There are many different ways for you to be involved. You may (1) design, build, or maintain computer equipment; (2) design programs that instruct computers how to solve problems; (3) apply computer technology to problems in business, education, or government; (4) work independently or as part of a team; (5) find interesting jobs almost anywhere in the world; and (6) undertake research and development.

Educational requirements may range from a high school diploma to a doctorate, depending on the specialty. Most computer people find that a college diploma offers better training and greater career opportunities.

What personal characteristics and skills do you need? A keen interest and curiosity about computers and their applications are sure indications that you should pursue the field. As in many vocations, you will need good oral and written communications skills, a sense of responsibility, and an ability to reason logically. Many professional positions require specialized knowledge of mathematics, engineering, or business as well as a knowledge of computer equipment and applications programs.

EDUCATION AND TRAINING

Career opportunities depend strongly on your education and training. Having careful-ly evaluated your talents and interests, you can choose your educational goal and decide whether you are interested in vocational training, community college, college or university, or graduate school.

Vocational programs are available in many high schools. Vocational school graduates are trained for such jobs as data entry operators, word processing operators, or computer operators. Community colleges and junior colleges usually offer a variety of computer-related courses. Some offer a 2-year associate degree in computer science or information systems. Some colleges also offer 1-year certificate programs to train word processing operators, computer graphics specialists, and computer operators. Credits earned at a 2-year college can often be transferred to a bachelor's program at a 4-year college or university. A community college education may enable you to obtain a beginning job, and an employer may be willing to pay for additional education.

Universities and colleges offer bachelor programs that can qualify you for many computer-related positions, including computer graphics specialist, systems analyst, computer programmer, customer engineer, design engineer, sales representative, college instructor, and secondary school teacher. They provide curricula that can qualify you for graduate school. They also provide interdisciplinary curricula that let you combine your computing interests with studies in other fields. You could major in robotics engineering with a supplementary specialty in computer science or obtain a fine arts degree with a supplementary specialty in computer graphics.

Most graduate programs at universities require a bachelor's degree in a computer-related discipline. Many graduate students obtain a master's degree while working part time. A master's degree will qualify you for a highly skilled job with an entry salary about 30 percent higher than that obtainable with a bachelor's degree. It also may qualify you to teach in a college program. A doctoral degree will qualify you for university faculty positions and for senior research positions in research laboratories, with another 30 percent increment in starting salary.

YOUR JOB POTENTIAL

You can enter the computer field directly from high school as a data entry clerk or computer operator and receive on-the-job training while attending college. You can be a programmer, then a systems analyst, and work up to manager. You can even open your own computer store or start a software development company. You can be trained in computer maintenance and repair in the military service, or you can study electronics at a community college or technical school and then get on-the-job training from a computer manufacturer or open your own computer repair business. You can earn a bachelor's degree in electrical engineering, help design computer equipment, then become a chief designer or project manager. You may become a computer science instructor and teach in college, secondary school, or elementary school, or for computer manufacturers and other business organizations.

Although there are many paths in computing, many computer people obtain a bachelor's degree in a technical field such as computer science, information science, or engineering before entering the job market. Some continue on into graduate school, working toward a master's or doctoral degree; a few work toward these graduate degrees while also working as a computer professional. Many employers encourage additional education by paying for all or part of it.

CAREER OPPORTUNITIES

For persons who use computers as part of their job responsibilities, career paths can be almost infinite. That is, the careers of users will follow the needs and opportunities of the mainline industries or professions they follow. For instance, suppose a teacher masters the use of computers for student record keeping or computer-assisted instruction. This person still will be guided in career choices by developments in education. The same will apply to architects, health professionals, robotic engineers, accountants, or others who work in computer-dependent fields.

By contrast, those who choose to become computer professionals can look for a series of challenging opportunities that center around the development and operation of computer systems.

Some of these opportunities are listed here. A detailed description of these jobs are discussed in the section CAREERS IN INFORMATION SYSTEMS.

- Data entry operator
- Data control clerk
- Program/file librarian
- Computer operator
- Systems programmer
- Database administrator
- Telecommunications specialist
- Security officer
- Electronic data processing auditor
- Applications programmer
- Systems analyst
- Manager

Although the jobs listed are those most quickly identified with computer technology, they are not the only ones in the field. Nor are they necessarily the most important. If there are analysts, programmers, and operators, then there must also be teachers to instruct people to use computer equipment, sales representatives to sell the equipment, design engineers to develop new hardware products, and so on. The following descriptions are of other key computer-related positions.

- Computer graphics artist
- Computer-aided design technician
- Design engineer
- Computer service technician
- Sales representative
- Word processing operator
- Instructor/teacher
- Technical writer
- Computer consultant
- Project Leader
- Contract programmer
- Robotic engineer
- Robot technologist/technician
- Mathematician
- Statistician

- Chemist and physicist
- Computer service bureau operator
- Manufacturing factory worker

Computer Graphics Artist

If you have an interest and talent for both art and computer science, you might consider a position as a computer graphics artist. Computer-generated imagery is used in architecture, medicine, government research, training for pilots and other specialists, and simulation and special effects for film and television. Computer graphics programmers combine a knowledge of design and programming to develop graphical databases that create pictures in two, sometimes three, dimensions. Some images cannot be easily distinguished from art forms produced by more traditional means. Computer graphics animators use their skill to generate cartoon animation by computer, thereby eliminating the need for tedious frame-by-frame, hand-drawn pictures. Computer graphics artists also produce graphs and charts for business uses. Computer graphics art is one of the hottest careers of the 1990s, reports a survey conducted by *Money* magazine. The career of computer graphics artist appeared third on a list of the fifteen fastest growing, lucrative, challenging, and prestigious professions for the next decade.

Computer-Aided Design Technician

The computer can do more, better, and faster designing than traditional design methods. Whether in the design of buildings, airplanes, automobiles, toys, bridges, engine parts, complex computer circuitry, or other products, computer-aided design (CAD) will affect education, employment, and ways of work more than any other single technology. The demand for CAD technicians will increase during the 1990s and will require some kind of postsecondary vocational or technical training, which for the most part is not now available. Computer-aided design, coupled with computer-aided manufacturing (CAM), represents one of the largest and most well-established uses of computer graphics. Computer-aided design personnel use computer workstations to design a tremendous range of things. Computer-aided manufacturing personnel use the results of CAD work to manufacture parts.

Design Engineer

Design engineers find practical applications for the ideas and discoveries of chemists, physicists, and mathematicians. When you see a finished computer product, whether it is a microcomputer or a disk drive unit, an engineer was involved somewhere in its creation. The computer industry employs many electrical, mechanical, and industrial engineers. Electrical engineers are engaged in the research and development of new computer products such as disk drives and circuit board designs. They also solve complicated electrical problems associated with new products. Mechanical engineers work on the design of products such as keyboards and microcomputer cases. Industrial engineers are concerned with the way people, machines, and materials are used together to manufacture computer equipment. Engineers are employed in the research development laboratories of major computer manufacturers, research institutions, and government agencies. A bachelor's degree is necessary for all beginning engineering positions; many engineers also have master's and doctoral degrees.

Computer Service Technician

The people who maintain and repair the machines in a computer installation are called computer service technicians (also called customer engineers, field engineers, or maintenance technicians). Every equipment manufacturer needs technicians because it is the manufacturer's responsibility to keep equipment working well. If computers are maintained properly and repaired promptly, they will last many years. When a computer system breaks down, the technician determines the cause as quickly as possible. This often takes many hours or days because large computer installations are very complex. The problem may occur in the central processing unit, or it may be a hardware or software problem. There may be a defect in the disk unit, input terminal, printer, or any of the other devices connected to the central processing unit. Applicants for jobs as computer service technicians should have a high school education and a strong interest in anything electrical, electronic, or mechanical. Two years of technical training or experience after high school or a college education are also required. The ability to read electrical and mechanical blueprints and to handle tools skillfully and the desire to solve problems are also among the major qualifications. Technicians are also expected to present a good appearance and possess a pleasing personality. Once hired by a computer manufacturer, the technician applicant is trained by the manufacturer. This usually consists of classroom instruction and on-the-job training.

Sales Representative

Sales representatives for a computer manufacturer usually work out of a regional office serving a large city and its surrounding areas. They contact potential buyers of computer equipment and visit their offices to make a sales presentation. A sales representative must know his or her equipment well and be able to show prospective customers how this equipment differs from that of other computer equipment manufacturers. Sales representatives spend a considerable amount of time traveling to sales prospects. They prepare sales proposals, handle routine sales paperwork, stay up-to-date with the changes in their company's products, keep abreast of the products produced by competing companies, and prepare financing arrangements for customers. A college education is necessary for obtaining a job as a computer manufacturer sales representative. Systems analysts, programmers, engineers, and computer science teachers make excellent sales representatives because their technical knowledge is useful in talking with potential customers.

Word Processing Operator

A word processing operator specializes in preparation of textual documents. This work may be done by secretarial or administrative personnel. In addition, many word process-

ing specialists work on catalogs, parts lists, sales literature, company newsletters, and other documents needed to run an organization. Word processing techniques are also vital to desktop publishing. This activity involves preparation of publications required to run an organization and to communicate with its marketplace. In the past, publishing activities required specialized, outside services for design, typesetting, and printing. Recently, capabilities needed to prepare graphic materials, set type, and output attractively printed documents have been incorporated into microcomputer hardware and software. Word processing and electronic publishing techniques make organizations more responsive to demands of their own organizations and of the markets they serve.

Instructor/Teacher

Over 1,000 programs in computer education are offered at community colleges and 4-year universities across the country. Computer science programs are also beginning to appear in thousands of elementary and secondary schools. Instructors are needed at all levels to develop a program of study, give lectures, assign readings, supervise laboratories, administer exams, and evaluate students' work. Some systems analysts, programmers, engineers, scientists, and technical writers are also part-time instructors. These people teach many of the evening computer science courses offered by universities, colleges, and technical schools. Beginning college instructors usually have at least a master's degree in computer science or a related field. Assistant, associate, or full professors generally have obtained doctorates or are doctoral candidates. Computer science instruction at the elementary school level is usually presented by elementary school teachers who have had some in-service computer science training. Some large high schools use computer science instructors; smaller schools often assign computer science instruction to math or science teachers.

Technical Writer

Computer manufacturers, software development companies, large businesses, and government departments employ thousands of technical writers. Technical writers produce the necessary reference manuals, training manuals, programming manuals, books, and reports associated with computer equipment and software. They also help prepare technical proposals for new computer installations, applications programs, and research projects. As the demand for technical writers grows, new positions will require increased knowledge of sophisticated documentation techniques. A working knowledge of hardware, applications, and programming languages will also be important. Technical writers with an awareness of various advertising techniques will be an asset to companies marketing data processing services or hardware. To be a successful technical writer of computer publications, you should have some training in computer science, good communications skills, and writing ability. Many systems analysts, programmers, scientists, managers, and teachers are also part-time writers.

Computer Consultant

Many businesses and organizations occasionally require specialized talents and services that are not available from their own personnel. Rather than hire new people to handle these positions, many businesses engage outside consultants on a temporary basis. Consultants may be engaged to (1) conduct feasibility studies; (2) advise company personnel on the design of a specific system; (3) design a system; (4) develop computer programs; and (5) teach a seminar, workshop, or class to company employees. As more and more small businesses acquire computer systems, opportunities for consultants to supply services and expertise will continue to grow. Many consultants have a bachelor's degree; many hold advanced degrees.

Project Leader

A project leader or project manager has the personnel and budgetary responsibility of a specific information processing project. The project leader oversees the work of a team and makes sure everyone is working together toward the proper development of a project. A principal goal is to coordinate all the tasks involved in producing a specific hardware or software product. A project leader is an experienced information processing professional with management ability. Project leaders need not have been programmers themselves, but they must thoroughly understand programming and systems design. In some companies a project leader bounces from one project to another; in others an employee assumes the role of project leader only for the length of a specific project. The minimum education for a project leader is a bachelor's degree in computer science or a related field.

Contract Programmer

From time to time many businesses and organizations need temporary programmers to produce programs. They are called contract programmers, independent programmers, or free-lance programmers. Contract programmers are engaged to develop specific programs and are paid by the hour. They have little job security, as they travel from job to job and company to company. Sometimes, however, job assignments can require the contract programmer to remain at one job location for one or more years. Contract programmers can gross as much as $70,000 a year for their 40-hour weeks and often much more, if they work overtime. Contract programmers are usually well-educated, experienced, and highly motivated professional programmers who have developed good reputations and business contacts within the industry. Businesses use contract programmers because they do not currently have equivalent expertise on the payroll or because they need additional programming personnel for a short period. Contract programmers often have to travel far from home and must be able to adjust to working in new environments and living in a new city, often for weeks, months, or years at a time.

Robotic Engineer

Only recently has any area of engineering been labeled a glamour field. In fact, the engineer is usually a "behind the scenes" member of the team, solving problems and seeking quicker, better, and less expensive ways of operating a plant. A robotics engineer, therefore, seeks ways in which to design, build, and use robots for improved productivity, quality, safety, and cost savings. The engineer will have many interactions with management concerning cost proposals, efficiency studies, and quality control reports. Quite frequently a degree in engineering will lead to a management position, possibly manager of robotics or director of automation, if the particular organization is large enough. Should you choose to pursue an engineering degree, you not only have the option to work with the overall manufacturing process, but also the opportunity to climb the corporate ladder into various management positions. Like most other engineering programs, a degree in robotic engineering takes 4 to 5 years of university or college study. Many institutions now offer graduate study in robotics, too. It is estimated that approximately 70,000 jobs will be created in robotics by the mid-1990s.

Robot Technologist/Technician

Robot technologists and technicians are in great demand in many industries. Truly, a good robot program cannot be instituted unless the ideas, analyses, and plans of the engineer can be carried out. The job of a technologist/technician then is to implement the ideas of the engineer as well as improve them when applicable. The technologist/technician serves as a liaison between the engineer and the robot application. They are "the doers," the "hands on" members of the "robot team." It has been estimated that an additional 25,000 robot technicians will be needed by the mid-1990s.

Mathematician

As a tool, mathematics is essential for understanding and expressing ideas in the natural and social sciences. Mathematicians not only study mathematics; they use it to solve practical business or scientific problems. Theoretical mathematicians advance the field by developing new principles and establishing new relationships among existing principles. Applied mathematicians use mathematics to develop theories, techniques, and approaches to solving practical problems in business, engineering, government, and the natural and social sciences. Mathematicians are involved with working out many of the problems that are created in designing computer circuits and making different computer components compatible. Mathematicians work closely with systems analysts and programmers in developing solutions to complex applications programs.

Statistician

Statistics keep us informed as a society and can even help us understand the characteristics of our world and the people in it. Statisticians are the people who devise ways of obtaining the figures, oversee the research, and interpret the numerical results of surveys and experiments once they are in. Over half of all statisticians can be found in private industry, mainly in manufacturing, business, finance, and insurance companies. About one third work for federal, state, or local governments. Others work in colleges and universities and nonprofit organizations.

Chemist and Physicist

Chemists make up a large group of scientists employed in the manufacturing of computers. Most people know that the job of a chemist is to study and find practical ways of using all kinds of different substances, but few are aware of the important work chemists do in the processing of microminiature circuits inside computers. These circuits, which carry electronic impulses, are formed during a chemically controlled photographic process. Physicists study the fundamental forces and laws of nature to enhance our understanding of how the world works and to increase our ability to use those fundamental forces in productive ways. Solid-state physics, which deals with the behavior of solid matter, led to the development of transistors and microminiature circuits; these, in turn, paved the way for the development of many new computer products.

Computer Service Bureau Owner

Not every company has its own computer, but most companies do need the kind of service—data processing, mass mailing, and so on—that computers offer. Out of this need has grown the computer service bureau. Not only is much capital required to set up a service bureau, but a keen knowledge of the existing market for computer services and a plan for gaining and keeping one's share of it are also essential.

Manufacturing Factory Worker

Designing computers will do little good if they cannot be manufactured and delivered to the customer. Today, robots and automated assembly techniques are used in the manufacturing process. The manufacturing jobs involved include everything from assembling the electronic components and circuit boards to packaging the products in shipping cartons. In some instances, the work is typical factory operations; however, it may be more tedious than usual because it involves working with many very small parts.

Other Occupational Titles

Among the newer computer-related job titles are artificial intelligence technician, computer law specialist, fiber-optics technician, information broker, knowledge engineer, laser technician, and robot trainer.

LICENSING AND CERTIFICATION

Four-year college programs, as well as advanced degree programs, have been established to meet the demand for computer science and information processing professionals. Two-year associate degree courses and 6-month to 1-year courses also offer preparation for differing levels of programming and for data entry positions. Some 4-year institutions offer special programs in computer graphics, artificial intelligence, robotics, and information technology, and some companies offer on-the-job training for selected employees.

In addition to formal or on-the-job training, some people in information processing also have professional certification offered through the Institute for Certification of Computer Professionals. Headquartered in Chicago, the Institute is an independent organization of data processing professionals who are working to improve industry standards by offering tests for certifying data processing managers and programmers. Those who pass the appropriate half-day examinations receive a Certificate in Computer Programming (CCP) or Certificate in Data Processing (CDP).

For Further Reading

Cetron, M. 1984. *Jobs of the future.* New York: McGraw-Hill.
Computer graphics career information handbook. 1989. New York: ACM SIGGRAPH.
Snelling, R. O., and A. M. Snelling. 1989. *Jobs! What they are—Where they are—What they pay.* New York: Simon & Schuster.
Spencer, D. D. 1984. *A guide to computer careers.* New York: Macmillan.
Winkler, C. 1983. *The computer careers handbook.* New York: Arco Publishing.

Donald D. Spencer

CAREERS IN INFORMATION SYSTEMS

This article presents various career opportunities in the information systems field. The first section describes a variety of job possibilities grouped into three areas: those that focus on working with the technology of information systems, those that bridge the gap between this technology and people who use this technology in their work, and those that involve managing. A career is broader than a job; the second section discusses potential careers within the information systems field and offers suggestions on managing one's career.

Why should anyone consider a career in

information systems? Compared with all occupations in the 1990s, the U.S. Bureau of Labor Statistics expects growth in systems analysis and computer programming positions to be much greater than average, and growth in computer operations positions to be greater than average. (See Table 1 for a complete list of jobs.)

Although growth in the number of jobs such as that experienced and expected in the information systems field could make a career in this field attractive, other factors are also important. Such factors include an individual's interests, the expected competition from others entering the field, and salary. The descriptions of various job and career

possibilities provided below should make it easier to assess the fit with one's interests. Recent studies, summarized by Mawhinney et al. (1988), suggest that the number of U.S. college students going into computer-related majors is declining, indicating that demand should exceed supply for a number of jobs in the United States during the next few years. Finally, reported salaries of various information systems jobs have increased over time. For example, the average salaries of systems analysts reported in the *Datamation* salary surveys increased by more than 30 percent between 1984 and 1989, and average salaries for application programmers went up about 40 percent (see Carlyle 1989).

TABLE 1. Information Systems Job Titles

Corporate Staff[1]	Database Administration[3]
Vice President	Manager
Director of DP/MIS	Database Administrator
Technical Services Manager	Datacom/Telecom/Connectivity[3]
Information Center/Data Center Manager	Manager
Director of Security	Analyst
Systems Analysis[2]	Network Engineer
Manager	Network Administrator
Senior Systems Analyst	Computer Operations[3]
Lead Systems Analyst	Manager
Systems Analyst	Shift Supervisor
Junior Systems Analyst	Lead Computer Operator
Applications Programming[2]	Computer Operator
Manager	Microcomputer/Workstation Manager
Lead Application Programmer	Production and Input/Output Control[3]
Senior Application Programmer	Supervisor
Application Programmer	Lead Production Controller
Intermediate Application Programmer	Scheduler
Junior Application Programmer	Control Clerk
Systems Analysis/Programming[2]	Data Entry[3]
Manager	Supervisor
Lead Systems Analyst/Programmer	Operator
Senior Systems Analyst/Programmer	Office Automation[4]
Systems Analyst/Programmer	Word Processing Supervisor
Intermediate Systems Analyst/Programmer	Word Processing Operator
Junior Systems Analyst/Programmer	Microcomputer User Services Specialist
Operating Systems Programming[3]	Other[4]
Manager	Specialists
Senior Systems Programmer	Consultant
Intermediate Systems Programmer	PC Evaluator
Junior Systems Programmer	

[1]Jobs in this area focus on managing.
[2]Jobs in this area focus on managing and bridging the gap between information technology and people who use this technology.

[3]Jobs in this area focus on managing and working with the technology of information systems.
[4]Jobs in this area vary in focus.
Source: Carlyle 1989.

JOB POSSIBILITIES

A variety of jobs exists in information systems. These jobs span the range of occupational levels, from clerical and operations through technical and professional to managerial. The first set of jobs described below has a technology focus, involving work with computer or communications hardware (i.e., equipment), software, or data. Many of these jobs require specialized knowledge or skill. The second set of jobs described below focuses on bridging the gap between information technology and people having specialized knowledge or skill in other areas who seek to apply this technology to their work. These jobs require knowledge or skill not only in information technology but also in applying the technology to help other people do their work. The final set of jobs described below involves managing in the information systems field. Although technical knowledge and skill are important in entry-level management positions, managerial knowledge and skills become increasingly important in higher management positions.

Jobs with a Technology Focus

Information systems in organizations are developed to serve a serious business purpose; nevertheless, they are built with technology that is fascinating in and of itself to some people. Over time, the technology has changed and, likewise, so have the challenges and rewards of learning and mastering the new technology.

Although some people find information systems technology fascinating, others take a more utilitarian view. They want the technology to work when they use it. They want it to compute accurately, to store and retrieve data as needed, to route messages properly, and generally to help them do their work better without their having to worry about how the technology works.

Helping others do their work better without their having to worry about how the technology works is an underlying role of the jobs described here as having a technology focus. Having fun with or mastering the technology is a potential reward.

Some jobs focus on operating computers, including providing and controlling the data used during operation. People in these jobs are responsible for maintaining the equipment, scheduling the work to be completed, entering and verifying data, running computer programs as scheduled, checking that all data have been entered and processed accurately, and cataloging and controlling programs or files of data. Workers in this area include computer operators, data entry operators, data control clerks, and program/file librarians.

Other jobs focus on assuring that computers, individually and in networks, and databases are appropriately available and accessible. People in these jobs typically have higher levels of knowledge, skill, or responsibility than those in operations jobs. Workers in this area include systems programmers, telecommunications specialists, database administrators, security specialists, and electronic data processing (EDP) auditors.

As the technology changes, jobs with a technology focus change. Fifteen years ago, data entry operators were known as keypunch operators because of the equipment used for data entry; database administrators virtually did not exist. The growth of the personal computer since the early 1980s has created new specialties such as telecommunications/data communications in local area networks. New or different jobs are likely to emerge in the future. Some organizations now have technology specialists whose job is to research and evaluate new technologies. More detailed descriptions of a few jobs with a technology focus are presented below.

Data entry operator. This clerical job involves using keyboarding skills to enter symbols (alphabetic, numeric, or special characters) onto a computer-readable medium, such as magnetic tape or disk. An operator may be responsible for converting source data into appropriate codes (e.g., converting U.S. state names into two-letter codes) and comparing keyed data to a source document to detect and correct errors. Keying speed and accuracy are important performance measures.

Data control clerk. A data input clerk reviews the data needed to run a computer program (e.g., to generate grade reports in a school system) to verify that all the appropriate data are available and ready for the job. A data output clerk reviews the data, or messages about the data, generated by a job to verify the data as complete, accurate, and in conformance with normal expectations. Documentation provided by others (e.g., an application programmer or systems analyst) forms the basis for the review. If problems are found, the clerk is responsible for initiating actions to address them.

Program/file librarian. This clerical job involves cataloging and maintaining a library of computer programs, data files, and the media (e.g., tapes and disks) on which they are stored. In larger installations, the volume of programs and associated documentation, files, and storage media can be considerable. The librarian is responsible for controlling access to all of these items through check-in and check-out procedures and for entering new items and removing items no longer needed.

Computer operator. A computer operator is responsible for the operation of one or more computers and associated peripheral devices, such as printers, disk drives, and tape drives. For routine jobs (e.g., payroll processing) the operator will use instructions prepared by others (e.g., the payroll application programmer) to set up the computer and peripheral devices to run the jobs. While the computer is running, the operator is responsible for monitoring messages from the system and taking appropriate action, such as changing disk packs, mounting different tapes, terminating a job, or starting a new job after resetting the system. Computer operators do not usually need a college degree. Experience with a specific OPERATING SYSTEM is an important factor in a larger installation. Obtaining a job without prior experience and learning on the job is more likely in a smaller installation.

Systems programmer. A systems programmer works with the operating system (i.e., the program that manages the uses of the computer) rather than application programs (i.e., the programs that do what users want). Thus, a systems programmer examines the performance of the computer system, given a particular set of hardware components and application programs, and seeks ways to make it work more efficiently rather than working with those desiring to use information technology to support their work. When a new version of the operating system is installed or changes are made to the system configuration (i.e., the specific combination of hardware components at a given installation), the systems programmer is responsible for fine-tuning the operating system to keep all the parts of the system working together well. This technology-focused work requires programming skill and, perhaps, a computer science degree.

Database administrator. As organizations recognize the value of data as a critical resource, the database administration function will become more important. The technology-focused work of database administration requires a background similar to that of a systems programmer. This work revolves around the database management system (DBMS) software and the way data records are stored and accessed in much the same way that systems programming revolves around the operating system and system configuration for a specific installation. This work includes installing new versions of the DBMS, reorganizing the way data records are stored and retrieved to improve system performance, and revising the database structure and how various users view and access the database as the data needs of the organization are redefined.

Telecommunications specialist. As more interconnected systems are implemented and changes in communications technology occur, the need for specialists knowledgeable in the telecommunications arena should continue to grow. Networked computer systems make it possible for people to communicate and compute when and where they need to. Many networks manage voice, data, graphics, and full-motion video communications. A telecommunications specialist helps make networked computer systems perform efficiently and with the proper security and controls. One form of telecommunications specialist, whose role is to work with the networking software and hardware to optimize network performance, is similar to a systems programmer.

Security officer. This high-level officer is responsible for protecting the assets found in computer-based information systems. Normal and unusual risks must be assessed and addressed by this officer. An example of a normal security measure is the implementation of training programs for employees (e.g., data entry operators) to teach them proper procedures (e.g., for entering accurate data). An example of a security measure for an unusual risk is the establishment of a disaster recovery plan (e.g., what is to be done to back up data on a regular basis and how the backup data will be used to return to normal operations in the event of a disaster such as a flood or fire). This officer should have strong knowledge of the technology of information systems as well as processes for risk assessment and avoidance in this arena.

Electronic data processing auditor. An information system should be audited not only after it has been implemented but also while it is being developed. A postaudit is designed to assess how well a system meets its intended purpose and to determine how well the system implements controls that guard against errors and losses. The EDP auditor participates in system development to assure that system developers understand accounting principles and audit requirements and take them into account. A competent EDP auditor must know accounting, auditing, and information systems, particularly business applications.

JOBS THAT BRIDGE THE TECHNOLOGY AND THE USER

As noted above, some people in organizations take a utilitarian view of information systems technology. They want it to help them do their work better without their having to worry about how the technology works. They need information systems specialists to help them specify the requirements for the support that information systems technology will provide for their work; to design and develop (or acquire) the technology to meet those requirements; and to help train them to use the technology and answer questions.

The information systems specialists who help bridge the gap between the information systems technology and the user of the technology occupy a variety of jobs. Systems analysts help elicit the requirements for a new or revised information system. These requirements specify what the system should be capable of doing to support the user's work. Systems analysts also specify the design of the system (i.e., how the system should meet the requirements). Application programmers develop the computer programs (i.e., software) according to the specified design. Trainers explain how to use software developed by application programmers within the organization or purchased from software vendors. Finally, user support specialists answer questions about the hardware, software, and data that arise as the installed information systems technology supports users in performing their work.

The development of information systems often requires a team effort. In some organizations, the division of labor among team members leads to higher degrees of specialization than in others. For example, the systems analysis function may be divided between information analysts, who focus on specifying the system requirements, and system designers, who focus on specifying the design to meet the requirements. In other cases the systems analysis and computer programming functions may be performed by the same person, known as a programmer analyst. In still other cases an organization may hire consultants to perform one or more of these functions required for systems development.

Jobs in information systems may be found in other organizations besides those that develop or acquire information systems to support their own employees' work. Organizations that provide systems development consulting services, such as systems analysis, computer programming, and training, employ people to provide these services to clients. Software vendors and organizations that develop software on contract hire people for the same kinds of purposes. People in these kinds of positions may be known as consultants, software engineers, and instructors.

As technology and organizations change, jobs that bridge the technology and user evolve. The tools and technologies available for systems analysis and design, computer programming, and training have changed considerably in the last fifteen years. Computer-assisted software engineering (CASE) tools are examples of such tools. Organizational desires to integrate data across different work areas (e.g., marketing, engineering, production, and finance) and integrate hardware and software from different vendors have required a different mix of knowledge and skills among team members working on systems development projects. Developments in artificial intelligence and expert systems have led some organizations to hire specialists to bridge the gap between these technologies and users whose work the new technology supports.

More detailed descriptions of the key jobs that bridge the gap between technology and users are presented below.

Applications programmer.   Once the needs of a user have been determined and a system designed to meet those needs, an applications programmer uses the specified system design to write computer programs to satisfy user needs. Programmers must know a computer language (e.g., COBOL or Focus) and how to program (i.e., code statements) in that language. Some programming tasks can now be performed by CASE tools or automated code generators, but these tools do not re-

place programmers; instead, they make it possible for programmers to be more productive as they write, test, and debug programs. Although a college degree is not necessarily required by all employers, an individual with college work in programming and business is likely to be an attractive candidate for a position as a business applications programmer. Individuals with coursework in engineering or science instead of business are more likely to be attractive candidates for more specialized positions as technical applications programmers. Some employers promote computer operators into programming positions if they take programming coursework. Some employers require prospective systems analysts to start as applications programmers.

Systems analyst.   The role of a systems analyst may be divided into two tasks. The first task is to understand the requirements of the user and help articulate them. This task requires an ability to understand the requirements from a business perspective and a knowledge of information technology so that *what* the user wants can be specified within the context of the technology. User requirements include the information needed, the speed with which it should be provided, the volume of processing needed in a given time period, and the kinds of computing and communication capabilities needed. The analyst usually needs to understand and document the user's work, the current information system support for that work, and problems the system has in supporting the user's work, before specifying what the new system should do.

The second task is to design programs, files, input forms, output formats, and hardware requirements. This task requires an ability to specify *how* to meet the user requirements. In some organizations the first task is performed by an information analyst and the second by a system designer. In some organizations systems analysts/programmers perform both tasks, as well as applications programming.

A systems analyst must be able to communicate effectively with people in the information systems area as well as people in the user area. An applications programmer with experience working in a specific user area could become a systems analyst for that area. Employers seek college graduates familiar with programming and having knowledge of computer systems. For example, a degree in management information systems (MIS) is desirable for work in a business environment. For information analysis positions working with managers, employers may seek M.B.A. graduates in MIS.

JOBS THAT INVOLVE MANAGING

The information systems area needs managers for the various types of people, projects, and resources that comprise this important function within organizations. As people gain experience in the jobs described above, they may move through different levels of responsibility. The top-level managers in information systems are vice-presidents and directors of MIS. The term *Chief Information Officer* (CIO) is used to identify the highest executive in the information management function.

Managers need a mix of technical, human relations, and conceptual skills. The higher the managerial level, the more one relies on those lower in the hierarchy to have, use, and provide advice based on their technical knowledge and skills. Higher-level managerial tasks focus more on human relations and conceptual skills, including planning, organizing, staffing, coordinating and controlling, directing, reporting, and budgeting.

Managers need to understand the decision-making process and be able to make decisions whether problems are structured or unstructured. Their decisions may range from longer-range, strategic decisions about the nature and role of information systems in their organizations to short-range decisions affecting the day-to-day efficiencies of programming or computer operations. Managers at lower levels are more likely to address short-term problems requiring immediate decisions. Managers at higher levels are more likely to focus on longer-term issues and strategic resource allocations.

Managerial work in the information systems area is similar to managerial work in other areas. Studies (e.g., Mintzberg 1973, Ives and Olson 1981) have shown that managers conduct most of their work by interacting extensively with others rather than working alone. To a large extent, others initiate the interactions. The activities of managers are fragmented and brief. These activities have been described in various ways, some of which have already been presented. Kotter's (1982) description includes setting an agenda of goals and actions needed to reach them, building a network of cooperative relationships among people in all kinds of positions who can satisfy the emerging agenda, and getting the network to implement the agenda. One way a manager may get others to implement the agenda is to articulate and communicate a persuasive vision of the future and how to get there. To see that the agenda is being implemented, the manager may monitor how well the vision is being realized and take appropriate corrective action.

Managerial work is significantly different from other jobs in information systems, and the transition from a nonmanagerial to a managerial job is a significant one. Movement through different levels of job responsibilities, particularly into senior and lead positions (e.g., in systems analysis and programming), should provide various first-level experiences in managing people and projects. These experiences should help in assessing one's interest in moving farther along the managerial career path. Ferratt and Starke (1989) present a self-diagnostic motivational test that may also help assess one's interest in making the transition from a nonmanagerial to a managerial position.

CAREERS

A career is a series of job experiences over a significant span of time. Although some careers may consist entirely of jobs related to information systems, sequences of jobs both in and outside of information systems may define other career paths. Studies of information systems careers show no formally defined career paths. However, a number of possibilities exist; several are suggested below. (See Table 2 for a brief summary of each.) Suggestions for managing one's career are also offered.

Potential Career Paths

Just as lives go through various stages, careers go through stages. One description of these stages has been presented by Dalton et al. (1977). They describe four stages in the careers of high-performing professionals, such as engineers and accountants. Although not all information systems careers will necessarily mirror the career stages of these professionals, the activities associated with the four career stages suggest potential shifting points from one career stage to another. The activities associated with the four

TABLE 2. Career Stages and Potential Career Paths

Career Stages
  Apprentice
  Colleague
  Mentor
  Sponsor

Technology-Oriented Career Path
  One or more apprenticeships in information technology jobs.
  Formal education likely in higher paying technical jobs.

Career Path Involving Information Systems (IS) and Their Use
  One or more apprenticeships, some possibly outside of IS.
  Could enter a bridging job from inside or outside IS.
  Could move in and out of IS.
  Formal education in computer science more technology focused.
  Formal education in management information systems more oriented toward business use.

Managerial Career Path
  One or more apprenticeships in earlier jobs.
  Normal progression includes senior and lead IS jobs.
  Top IS job usually manages programming and analysis earlier.
  If IS not strategic, go beyond IS for top organizational job.

stages are those of an apprentice, a colleague, a mentor, and a sponsor. An apprentice spends time learning, a colleague works competently and independently, a mentor helps develop others while serving as an interface with outside people, and a sponsor shapes the future by initiating programs, building critical relationships, and developing key people.

The apprenticeship stage in information systems career paths is defined by various entry-level jobs and their formal education requirements. In some jobs learning may occur primarily via experience on the job. These apprenticeships are more likely for clerical and operations level jobs. Alternatively, learning may occur via a combination of formal education and experience on the job. These apprenticeships occur in technical, professional, and managerial-level jobs.

Consider these specific examples: Computer operators, data entry operators, data control clerks, and program/file librarians are jobs where an experience apprenticeship is most likely. The job of systems analyst is an example in which both formal education and experience are likely. University business school programs in MIS prepare students for jobs, such as systems analysis, that bridge the technology and user. To continue their apprenticeships, individuals with this formal education may move through a series of on-the-job apprenticeship experiences, such as application programming positions and/or entry-level systems analysis positions.

The time required to become proficient and, thus, complete the apprenticeship career stage, is lengthier for jobs requiring progression through a series of jobs with qualifiers, such as *junior* or *intermediate*, preceding the main title. (See Table 1.)

A career path may involve one or more apprenticeships, some of which may be inside and some outside the information systems arena. Three broad career paths appear likely. The first focuses on the technology of information systems; the second has a mixture of interests including, but not limited to, information systems technology; the third has a managerial orientation within and perhaps beyond the information systems arena.

Technology-oriented career paths. One type of career path is to move through one or more jobs with a technology focus, progressing through apprenticeship, colleague, and, perhaps, mentor and sponsor stages in the process. The activities in the mentor and sponsor stages suggest how personal productivity and value to an organization may be increased beyond that of a competent, independent colleague. Some individuals may desire to increase their value by moving from lower-paying clerical and operations jobs, focusing on operating computers, to higher-paying technical jobs, focusing on assuring that computers, individually and in networks, and databases are appropriately available and accessible. Career paths that include movement through clerical, operations, and technical-level jobs involve more than one apprenticeship. The higher-paying technical-level jobs are likely to require not only experience but also formal education in computer science to complete an apprenticeship career stage.

Career paths involving information systems and their use. Another type of career path is to move through one or more jobs involving information systems and their use, progressing through apprenticeship, colleague, and, perhaps, mentor and sponsor stages in the process. An apprenticeship in the job of an application programmer, systems analyst/ programmer, or systems analyst is likely to involve both formal education and experience. The formal education may be in computer science or management information systems; the former is likely to have heavier emphasis on information technology and the latter on using the technology for business applications. Completion of an apprenticeship involves progressing through junior and intermediate positions. Senior and lead positions in programming and systems analysis work involve responsibilities for the work of others, providing opportunities to serve as mentors or sponsors.

As in the technology-oriented career path, movement from one type of job into another may involve more than one apprenticeship. Some individuals may migrate through a series of information systems jobs.

They may start with a clerical or operations-level job focusing on information technology (e.g., computer operator) and move into a job that bridges the technology and the user (e.g., microcomputer user services specialist or junior application programmer). Others may migrate into information systems jobs from jobs outside the information systems field. They may begin using information technology in their work and move into a job in information systems that bridges the technology and the user. The growth of end user computing facilitates this career move. Still others may migrate out of the information systems field. They may have an information systems job at some time in their career that bridges the technology and user (e.g., serving as an application programmer to help support the marketing function) and then move on to a job in the user arena. The last possibility suggested is a career path including more than one migration into and out of jobs involving information systems and their use. For example, the application programmer mentioned above, who moved into the marketing arena, later returned to the information systems field as a systems analyst.

Managerial career paths. The third type of career path is to move through several jobs, with the later jobs in the path being managerial jobs within and, perhaps, beyond the information systems arena. To reach a managerial job requires progressing through apprenticeship, colleague, and, perhaps, mentor and sponsor stages in earlier jobs. Individuals who follow a technology-oriented career path, or a career path involving information systems and their use, may make a transition to the managerial career path by moving through senior or lead positions into manager positions.

As managers mature, they are more likely to engage in the activities of the mentor and sponsor career stages. Their value to the organization may be recognized through promotions or salary increases.

A career path with prior experience in the systems analysis and application programming area (i.e., experience that bridges the technology and user) has been more likely to lead to the top management position within the information systems arena. Individuals desiring to be the top manager in an organization should consider moving outside the information systems area at some point in their careers to gain management experience in strategically important organizational areas, particularly if the information systems area is not strategically important. In larger organizations, and those where information systems are strategically important, managerial career paths with movements into and out of the information systems area may be more likely.

Suggestions for Career Management

Given the opportunity for alternative career paths, individuals must take the responsibility for managing their own careers. Chesebrough and Davis (1983) suggest that one may follow a top-down, bottom-up, or mixed strategy for planning a career. In the top-down approach, the individual identifies a single objective, such as being a director of MIS or company president; studies what the position associated with the objective requires; and determines the activities and sequence of jobs most likely to lead to the objective. In the bottom-up approach, the individual's current position is the starting point. The individual identifies alternative next steps, and where they might lead, before making a choice. In the mixed approach, the individual identifies a few objectives and the paths that are likely to lead to them, but also looks at the options from the current position to take advantage of opportunities when they present themselves.

Managing one's career also means recognizing and taking steps to adjust, if appropriate, one's career stage and objectives. Is it time to move from being a competent, independent colleague to being a mentor? Is it time to move from a technology-oriented job to a bridging job and start an apprenticeship again? Do I need to get more formal education in the near future? Can I successfully make the transition to manager? Should I move outside information systems to gain experience in another organizational area? Is it feasible to make such a move in my current organization? Asking these kinds of questions should help in managing one's career.

CONCLUSION

As the use of information technology increases, job growth is expected in technology-oriented jobs, jobs that bridge the technology and users of information technology, and managerial jobs in information systems. (See Table 1 for various job titles.) These jobs are likely to be found not only within organizations that develop, acquire, and use information systems to support their primary purpose but also within organizations that specialize in developing, integrating, or selling information systems and consulting services.

Career paths in information systems are sequences of jobs. No fixed career paths exist in information systems. However, careers are likely to include one or more iterations involving movement from an apprenticeship to a colleague and, perhaps, to a mentor and sponsor. Moving beyond an apprenticeship stage requires experience for clerical and operations level jobs. Higher-paying technical, professional, and managerial-level positions require not only experience but also formal education. Table 3 shows the relative worth of various jobs one might consider in an information systems career.

Individuals should take responsibility for managing their own careers. They need to understand their goals, determine possible paths for reaching their goals, and take appropriate steps along their career paths. Potential career paths include a sequence of jobs focusing primarily on the technology of information systems, a sequence with some jobs focusing on information systems and their use, and a sequence involving information systems technology and managing. (See Table 2.) A particular sequence of jobs may be completely within the information systems arena, or it may involve movement in and out of information systems. The latter is more likely for individuals with career goals beyond information systems or in organizations where information technology and support are strategically important or distributed throughout the organization. For individuals with an interest in information systems, the opportunities for beginning a career in this area look promising over the next decade.

TABLE 3. Selected Information Systems Jobs and Salaries (1990) (rounded to the nearest thousand)

Jobs with a Technology Focus

Control Clerk	$20,000
Reviews and verifies data before/after programs are run	
Lead Computer Operator	25,000
Sets up computers and peripheral devices to run jobs	
Junior Systems Programmer	32,000
Works with operating system to improve performance	
Network Administrator	33,000
Optimizes telecommunications network performance	
Database Administrator	47,000
Installs/revises database management system and database structure to facilitate data access and use	

Jobs Involving Information Systems and Their Use

Junior Applications Programmer	$26,000
Writes computer programs based on specified system design to satisfy user needs	
Systems Analyst/Programmer	36,000
Identifies user requirements, designs system, and writes programs	
Senior Systems Analyst	45,000
Identifies user requirements and designs system to meet requirements	

Managerial Jobs

Computer Operations Manager	$43,000
Applications Programming Manager	52,000
Systems Analysis Manager	52,000
Database Administration Manager	53,000
Director of Data Processing/Management Information Systems	66,000
Vice President of Information Systems	85,000

Salaries Source: Pantages 1990.

References

Carlyle, R. E. 1989. What are you worth? *Datamation* 35 (19):22–30. This industry magazine publishes a yearly salary survey for various job classifications in information systems. For the 1990 survey, see Pantages (1990) reference below.

Chesebrough, P. H., and G. B. Davis. 1983. Planning a career path in information systems. *Journal of Systems Management* 34 (1):6–13.

Dalton, G. W., P. H. Thompson, and R. L. Price. 1977. The four stages of professional careers—A new look at performance by professionals. *Organizational Dynamics* 6 (1):19–42.

Ferratt, T. W., and F. A. Starke. 1989. Making the transition: Systems analysis to management. *Journal of Systems Management* 40 (4):14–17.

Ives, B., and M. H. Olson. 1981. Manager or technician? The nature of the information systems manager's job. *MIS Quarterly* 5:49–63.

Kotter, J. P. 1982. *The General Managers.* New York: Free Press.

Mawhinney, C. H., E. G. Cale, and D. R. Callaghan. 1988. Perceptions of the CIS graduate's workstyle: Undergraduate business students versus CIS faculty. In *Proceedings of the 1988 ACM SIGCPR Conference on the Management of Information Systems Personnel.* New York: Association for Computing Machinery. Contains a brief summary of studies discussing the decline in U.S. college student enrollment in computer-related fields.

Mintzberg, H. 1973. *The nature of managerial work.* New York: Harper and Row.

Pantages, A. 1990. Salaries rise 5.6% in soft market. *Datamation* 36 (21):42–48.

For Further Reading

Ahituv, N., and S. Neumann. 1990. *Principles of information systems for management.* 4th ed. Dubuque, Ia.: Wm. C. Brown. Chapter 12 classifies nonmanagerial information systems jobs into three categories rather than the two used in this article: operation-oriented, technology-oriented, and system-oriented. Alternative career paths are discussed. Chapter 13 discusses the management role in information systems. Chapter 14 discusses two other jobs: EDP auditor and security specialist.

Ginzberg, M. J., and J. J. Baroudi. 1988. MIS careers—A theoretical perspective. *Communications of the ACM* 31 (5):586–94.

Kaiser, K. M. 1983. DP Career Paths. *Datamation* 29 (12):178–88.

Robert Half Salary Survey 1990. 1989. Menlo Park, Calif.: Robert Half International Inc.

Tanniru, M. 1983. An investigation of the career path of the EDP professional. In *Proceedings of the Twentieth Annual Com-*

puter Personnel Research Conference, pp. 87–101.

United States Bureau of Labor Statistics. 1990. *Occupational outlook handbook.* 1990–1991 ed. Washington, D.C.: U.S. Department of Labor, Bureau of Labor Statistics. For various job titles, this handbook describes the nature of the work; working conditions; employment; training, other qualifications, and advancement; job outlook; earnings; related occupations; and sources of additional information.

United States Employment Service. 1977. *Dictionary of occupational titles.* 4th ed. Washington, D.C.: U.S. Government Printing Office.

United States Employment Service. 1986. *Dictionary of occupational titles.* 4th ed. Supp. Washington, D.C.: U.S. Government Printing Office. This and the previous source include job descriptions for various job titles.

Thomas W. Ferratt

CASE TOOLS

See Computer-Aided Software Engineering

CHAOS THEORY

The subject we know as chaos theory blossomed only during the 1980s of this century (Gleick 1987). For hundreds of years physicists had been studying what might be called the regularities of physical systems, from celestial mechanics to flows in fluids. What formulas could be developed and what regularities would they predict? Here was work enough to employ physicists and applied mathematicians for centuries to come.

From their inception computers have played a key role in using such formulas to simulate the behavior of these dynamical systems. Yet it was also the computer that played a key role in the emergence of a new paradigm that, to some extent, has displaced

the search for regularity in behavior by the exploration of irregularity, or chaos, in behavior.

Far from being a synonym for the irregular, however, chaos has a very precise meaning when scientists use the word. Although a certain irregularity is the hallmark of some types of chaos, "sensitivity to initial conditions" would make a better defining condition. Perhaps the experiment of Edward Lorenz, the Massachusetts Institute of Technology physicist and meteorologist who first described chaos in detail, illustrates the idea most clearly.

In the early 1960s, Lorenz decided to study weather systems on his computer. He represented the Earth's surface by a mathematical map and employed dozens of mathematical formulas to describe the interplay of temperature, pressure, and humidity in his model (Lorenz 1963). He sought regularities of behavior that would enable meteorologists to predict weather over several days, not just a few hours. If he could succeed with a model of the weather, perhaps he could succeed with the real thing.

The model was far simpler than the real thing, of course, but complicated enough that it took several hours to simulate just a few weeks of real weather. A typical run would begin when Lorenz would enter initial conditions, such as a distribution of temperatures, around his "world." He would then wait several hours while his computer weather patterns developed, record the conditions prevailing in his model at the end of the run, then begin all over again.

A meticulous observer, Lorenz one day repeated a run with what he thought were the same data he had entered initially. But, because he had copied them from a printer in which each number was shortened by a few digits, each number differed from the one he had actually used by an amount that most meteorologists would have considered insignificant. He left for a cup of coffee then returned an hour later to find that the conditions on his simulated world were already completely different from the conditions he had obtained in the previous run. This struck Lorenz as odd and just to be sure that some other blunder had not been committed, he repeated both runs several times. The initial conditions differed by what can only be called a tiny amount, yet the final results were totally different!

A dynamical system is "sensitive" to initial conditions when this type of large difference can appear between the way the system develops under two sets of initial conditions that differ by even a slight amount. The "chaos" involved has nothing to do with tornadoes, storms, or other disorderly phenomena. It concerns only the implications of this sensitivity for our ability to predict the behavior of a dynamical system. It turns out that it makes no difference how "close" the two initial conditions are to each other. They can be so close that one might need hundreds of digits of accuracy simply to express the difference between them. In other words, the two sets of initial conditions may be so similar that there is no difference in the starting numbers unless one looks several hundred digits along them. There, in the five hundredth place, say, is a two instead of a three. And in only one of the inputs! Yet this slight difference *may* lead, in a surprisingly short run, to wildly different scenarios. The word *may* is used because often it makes little or no difference that the initial conditions *do* differ slightly. In terms of the weather, you might sneeze in your backyard on a Tuesday and inadvertently cause unusually heavy rainfall over the Bay of Bengal on the following Saturday. But most of the time this would not happen.

Precision, the number of digits that a computer normally alots to its numbers, carries a cost. For very special problems several hundred digits of precision can, in fact, be used. But for large simulation models with millions of calculations on thousands of separate variables to be executed and stored in memory, such precision is out of the question. It follows that no computer will ever be able to predict the behavior of a dynamical system that is capable of chaos in the way that Lorenz's original model was. It will never be possible to emulate, let alone measure, the precision of "natural" variables to an extent that would make even 5-day prediction infallible. Lorenz was so impressed by the sensitivity of his weather simulation model that he began immediately to search for its source. By the process of

simplification so common in research, he ended with what might be called a system in a cylinder. Three differential equations described the current of air inside a hypothetical cylinder. A source of heat applied to the bottom warmed the air enough to cause a convective flow upward around the walls of the cylinder. Cooling, the air would form a descending column inside this. When he ran this much simpler model on his computer, he discovered the same kind of sensitive dependence on initial conditions. He would not even be able to predict the weather inside a cylinder!

When a physicist or mathematician wants to study a dynamical system, he or she will sometimes generate what is called a phase portrait. The variables that describe the system are treated like geographic or space coordinates. If there are two variables, a two-dimensional phase space results. If there are a hundred variables, a hundred-dimensional space must somehow be visualized. Whatever the dimension of the resulting phase space, the entire behavior of a dynamical system is summed up by the position of a single point in the space. Moreover, as the system changes over time, the point that represents it wanders through the space, producing a trajectory. Computers can often be used to graph these trajectories, giving insight into the behavior of a system. Computing trajectories through phase space often reveals the presence of an "attractor," a geometric configuration that consists of all trajectories under equilibrium conditions. No matter what conditions the dynamical system starts out under, the point that represents its behavior will wander, in time, toward the attractor and thereafter orbit within it forever.

When mathematicians examined Lorenz's equations for the cylindrical weather system and plotted the model's three variables as points in phase space, a surprising picture emerged (Figure 1). The attractor of the system consisted of innumerable trajectories woven into a two-winged configuration that we now know to be a fractal (see DATA COMPRESSION AND FRACTALS). Attractors with a fractal structure are called *strange attractors*.

A fractal is a geometric structure with a

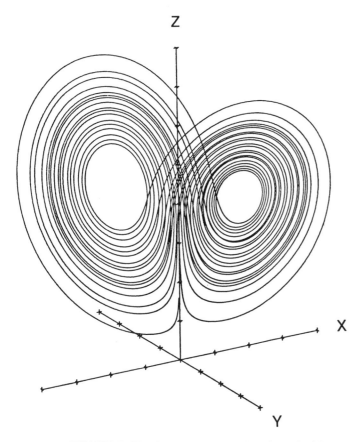

FIGURE 1. The Lorenz attractor is a fractal of lines.

fractional dimension. If enough lines are wound within the same three-dimensional space, for example, the resulting structure loses the strict one-dimensionality of the lines that compose it and may even approach a two-dimensional geometry. The actual dimension of the space might be 1.53, for example. Another feature of fractal geometry is its endless regress of detail. If we magnify any portion of the Lorenz attractor we would see a similar arrangement of lines all crowding together. In fact, the number of windings of the trajectories within the Lorenz attractor is infinite. Moreover, a line that leads to one of the wings can be arbitrarily close, in phase space, to a line that leads directly to the other wing.

In this sense, the Lorenz attractor illustrates in graphical terms just what goes on when a physical system is sensitive to initial conditions. The two aforementioned lines represent two trajectories that are very close

together. If the system were started up first on one line, then on the other, it would evolve into very different states, as represented by the widely separated "wings" of the Lorenz attractor.

The search for chaos has revealed an extraordinary variety of physical systems that exhibit it. Besides the weather, many other real-world systems display chaotic behavior: the flow of streams, the slow rise and subsidence of sand dunes, and many forms of mechanical and natural vibration, to name a few. Yet, in classifying the kinds of chaos that might arise, scientists have more to gain by studying the very simplest systems they can find. Some of these simple systems can be constructed in a laboratory but others exist only in a computer.

A double pendulum, in which a lower pendulum with its own bob is hinged from the bob of an upper one, may show behavior that a computer cannot predict, in general, more than a few minutes ahead. Physicists now study such simple systems seriously, whereas in the 1960s and 1970s such research would have been considered "unscientific." It is ironic that many of the differential equations that have been studied for decades by physicists and applied mathematicians have harbored chaos in their signs and symbols all this while: When they were simulated on a computer and the trajectories of the underlying dynamical system were mapped in phase space, strange attractors emerged.

The simplest known dynamical system that is capable of chaotic behavior is called the logistic equation. It has a loose connection with predator–prey dynamics and is so simple that it can be presented to anyone with a little high-school algebra as background. It consists of a formula involving a so-called state variable x and a parameter a. A computer is normally used to evaluate the formula by substituting the current value for x into the formula. The value that emerges becomes the new value for x and the process is repeated, or iterated. In its iterated form the equation can be presented with a left-pointing arrow instead of an equal sign:

$$x \leftarrow ax(1-x)$$

The equation is studied by fixing the value of the parameter a, then starting x off with a randomly chosen value. As new values of x are computed, they may show a trend. They may converge on a single value, namely, a one-point attractor, or on a finite set of values, a multipoint attractor. Such behavior would be called "regular" or predictable. Once such behavior begins it continues virtually forever and can easily be predicted. On the other hand, the values of x may show no tendency whatever to settle down to one or a few stationary values. It all depends on the fixed value adopted for the parameter a.

The whole story is told by a map of the logistic equation. As there is only one variable in the equation, the phase space of the system has only one dimension. It is a line on which attractors are sets of points. If the parameter a is systematically increased from a value of 2 up to 4 in small steps and if, for each parameter value, a computer plots the attractor that results, a strange-looking map develops (Figure 2). For when the attractors are stacked up, from small parameter values down to large ones, the development of one-point attractors can be traced into two-point attractors, then four-point ones, and so on. This so-called period-doubling phenomenon abruptly gives way, around a parameter value of 3.2714, to chaotic behavior. The attractor is no longer a few points. Instead it consists of an infinite number of points. It is a fractal (see Figure 2).

Even a one-dimensional phase space can contain a fractal. The dimensions of the strange attractors produced by the logistic equation all lie somewhere between zero (the dimension of a finite set of points) and one (the dimension of a line). Some of the fascination of the logistic equation lies in its ability to sum up the main elements of chaos theory in a nutshell. Some dynamical systems show no evidence of chaos whatever until certain of their inherent properties, represented by one or more parameters, change. When a fluid flows slowly over a surface, it may be regular or "laminar." But when the same fluid is forced to flow more quickly, turbulence may develop and the behavior of the fluid suddenly becomes impossible to predict.

The parameter a in the logistic equation represents an aspect or quality of the system that may change. If x is the number of predators in a given region, for example, the quantity $1-x$ will be roughly proportional to the amount of prey available to eat. When the expression $ax(1-x)$ is iterated, one may think of a month, year, or some other suitable period of time passing. The new value of x then represents the number of predators in the region after that period. The parameter a may be thought of as a "fecundity factor." At low fecundities, the predator population may alternate between two more or less fixed values. At higher fecundities, the population may swing between many values. At still higher fecundity levels, however, the predator population may take on virtually any value from one period to the next. It would not only be impossible to predict with any great reliability more than a few periods ahead; it may on occasion swing wildly in the direction of extinction. In this particular case, to the extent that the logistic equation actually represents real populations, it does not pay predators (or any consumers of limited renewable resources) to be too fecund!

The key question to be raised in the study of chaos is this: If we cannot predict the behavior of a system once it becomes chaotic, can we at least predict when chaos is about to develop? The answer is "yes" if one knows the key system parameters and can measure them accurately enough. But in most real-world systems this is impossible for all but a few, simple, manmade systems. And if the weather is chaotic anyway, as some scientists believe, there is no possibility of making completely reliable predictions more than a day or two ahead of time.

Something, however, can be done. A complex weather model for a given patch of the Earth's surface can be run for a day or two starting from conditions as they currently are. If the same conditions are varied slightly in many different ways and essentially the same pattern emerges at the end of all computer runs, we might suspect that the model's prediction is pretty secure and pass its predictions along to weather offices around the world. But if this particular sub-

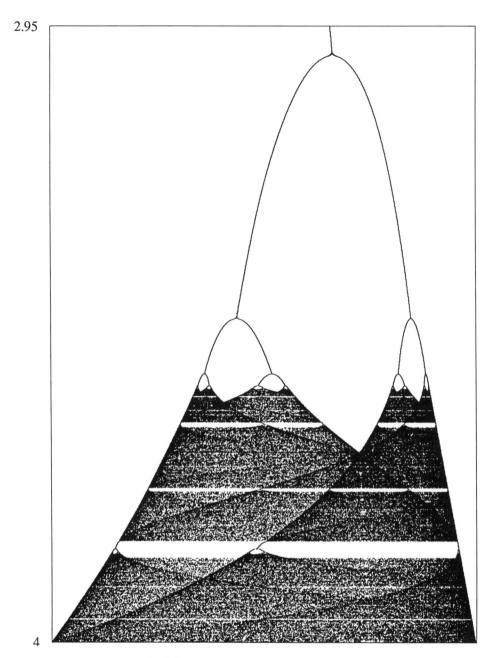

2.95

4

FIGURE 2. A map of the logistic equation is a fractal of points.

system shows sensitivity to initial conditions, if the slightly different initial conditions lead to at least one very different end result, the current weather could be called "unstable" at least in the dynamical sense, and all predictions must be hedged.

One might suspect that the same kind of sensitivity analysis could be applied to other dynamical systems where prediction has practical importance. Playing a crucial role,

computers, especially the supercomputers that are currently becoming common, will push the envelope of predictability by small but important increments into the future. Their ability to handle larger and larger amounts of data at greater speeds and accuracies will also make it possible to run many versions of the same system under slightly different initial conditions—all at the same time!

References

Gleick, J. 1987. *Chaos: Making a new science.* New York: Viking Penguin.

Lorenz, E. 1963. Deterministic nonperiodic flow. *Journal of the Atmospheric Sciences* 20:130–41.

A. K. Dewdney

CHARACTER GENERATION

See Typesetting

CHECK PROCESSING

See Banking, Computer Use in; Financial Services, Computer Use in

CHEMICAL INDUSTRY, USE OF COMPUTERS IN THE

Almost in parallel with the industrial revolution, we have had a chemical revolution. In the chemical revolution we have learned to synthesize, isolate, purify, manufacture, and use individual chemical compounds that make up the world around us and the natural chemicals that are used in our own bodies. With the chemical knowledge we have gained, we can isolate compounds so they can be used to provide fuel (gasoline and other fuels from petroleum), synthesize fibers (rubber and rayon from petroleum), create foods (beer, wine and cheese), synthesize drugs, fertilizers, and pesticides, and create cosmetics and fragrances. This chemical knowledge has recently led to the development of the biotechnology industry in which genetically altered microorganisms are used as chemical factories.

Controlling the production of these chemical compounds requires instruments that can monitor the flow of chemicals within a chemical plant, identify compounds, and

measure their amount or concentration. Computers are widely used in the chemical industry as parts of these instruments that control the production of chemicals, as well as in all phases of research and development of new chemicals, chemical processes, or chemical formulations.

Computer-controlled instruments are also used to monitor the purity and production of our food and the air and water that make up our environment. All phases of food production and commercial food preparation are monitored using computer-controlled instruments. These same instruments are used to detect the presence and concentration of toxic chemicals and monitor their removal and cleanup.

CHEMICAL PROCESS CONTROL

Computers have played a pivotal role in the advancement of chemical instrumentation, and not coincidentally the chemical industry has historically invested heavily in the development of better computers. One of the major factors leading to the rapid development of computers and electronic components was their wide application in the chemical industry. The development of the first minicomputers was catalyzed by their use in the chemical industry to monitor and control the production of chemicals and their use in chemical instrumentation. Chemical companies and computer companies formed joint projects to develop systems that could perform chemical applications. These applications required a type of computer system different from those used in business. These systems needed the ability to monitor a process and perform tasks in "real time" rather than in "batch" mode. Those early minicomputer-based process control systems have evolved into today's modern process control systems, which continue to use minicomputers but now also employ computer workstations and even personal computers.

These process control systems use cutting-edge real-time graphics coupled with the capability to monitor hundreds of real-time sensors located in the chemical plant. This information along with data from within historical databases is used to assist chemical plant engineers and operators during chemical plant production. Some process control systems are using computing techniques originally developed for artificial intelligence to increase production and product purity. These process control systems monitor not only the production of chemicals but also the equipment in the plant, ensuring that it is operating properly and is maintained on a regular schedule.

In the last decade, personal computers have found a wide array of applications in the chemical industry. Personal computer-based process control systems have been developed and personal computers are widely used as data handling systems in chemical instrumentation. Personal computers using "off-the-shelf" spreadsheet, data management, graphics, and word processing software are widely used to analyze and report the results of chemical processes and experiments.

CHEMICAL INSTRUMENTATION

Most chemical instruments used today rely heavily on computers or computer technology to perform their applications. Most modern chemical instruments would not exist were it not for the computers embedded in them. These computers are used to control the instrument, acquire data, analyze the data, and report the results.

Computer-controlled robots are used in chemical laboratories to perform repetitive operations once performed by humans. In particular, the steps required to prepare a sample for analysis are now commonly performed by a computer-controlled robot or a fluid handling instrument. These devices can take an original sample and perform any number of dilutions or additions of reagents to prepare the sample for analysis. Computer-controlled robots can be trained to perform nearly any task that has previously been done by a human. This frees humans from performing tedious repetitive tasks and it ensures better accuracy, as there is no chance of human error. Computer-controlled robots are also used to perform tasks humans dare not perform, for example, handling radioactive materials or highly toxic compounds.

COMPUTERS IN CHEMICAL INSTRUMENTS

Personal computers, computer workstations, and minicomputers are used as the basis for nearly all modern chemical instrument data systems. Just a few years ago, most chemical instrumentation did not use "off-the-shelf" computer systems. Major instrument manufacturers would develop their own computers and write their own software. These companies would even write their own operating systems and manufacture many or all of their own computer components. This strategy of course made the development time for an instrument quite long. Today, instrument manufacturers take advantage of the wide availability of computers and computer components. They can then focus on developing sensors, detectors, analyzers, and data analysis software in the development of their instruments.

A good example of the wide use of computers in chemical instruments is a liquid chromatography system. A liquid chromatograph separates a mixture of compounds into their individual components. A mixture is injected onto a column where separation occurs while the compounds are transported down the column using a constant flow of a liquid. The liquid's composition can be altered to sweep specific types of compounds more rapidly down the column. The output from the column is monitored using various types of detectors. The usual detector output is in the form of an analog signal (voltage) that is proportional to the amount or concentration of the compound currently in the detector.

Other types of chromatography are widely used by the chemical industry, including gas chromatography, ion chromatography, supercritical fluid extraction chromatography, and capillary electrophoresis. All of these types of analysis have the ability to separate a mixture of chemicals into their pure or nearly pure individual chemical compounds.

Computers play a major role in nearly

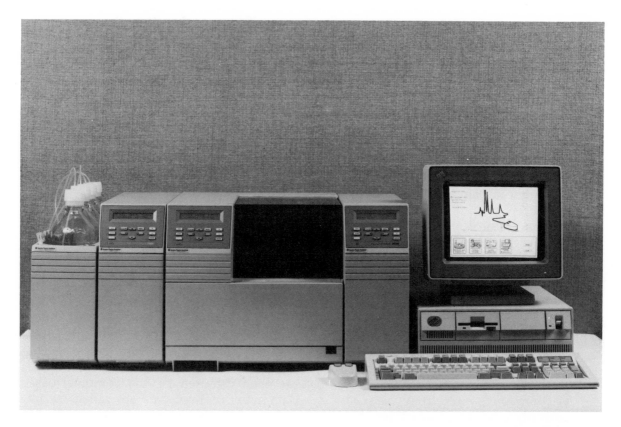

FIGURE 1. In this liquid chromatography system, the pump, autosampler, and detector are all operated from a personal computer, which stores and manipulates data and issues reports. *Courtesy Spectra Physics Analytical.*

every phase of a chromatographic instrument's operation. In each instrument there are usually a number of computers that work together to control and perform the various functions of the instrument. These computers are usually dedicated microprocessors programmed in assembly language. A main computer controls the overall operation of the instrument. This computer interacts with the user, so the user can select the parameters for the current experiment. The user selects the parameters by entering values through a keyboard or keypad. The user is prompted for input through a video screen or light-emitting diode display.

Once the experimental conditions have been entered, the controlling computer takes over operation, making the actual execution of the whole experiment totally automatic. Human interaction is not needed unless there is a major problem. Literally hundreds of individual analyses can be performed without the user even being present. Different samples to be analyzed are provided to the instrument by a module called an autosampler. Autosamplers can hold 50 or 100 different samples ready to be analyzed.

On-line monitors have also been developed. These systems can automatically acquire their samples directly from the source. For example, they can take a sample from a chemical stream or by drawing in a specific volume of air.

VALUE OF AUTOMATED ANALYSIS

By the use of automated analysis, the results of one analysis can be directly compared with the results of another analysis performed under the same conditions. Calibration and instrument performance check samples are interspersed with normal unknown samples so the performance of the analysis and instrument is monitored. When human intervention is required during an analysis, errors can result from operator error or confusion. Whenever a human is involved in an analysis, operator error cannot be eliminated. That is why automated analysis is such a valuable technique and experimental strategy.

The controlling computer within the liquid chromatography instrument can initiate the sequence of operations required to inject a sample. This includes drawing up the sample from a sample vial in the autosampler and checking to ensure that the system is ready to perform an analysis. Then, the mixture can be injected. Simultaneous with the injection, the instrument starts data acquisition. Another computer embedded in the instrument constantly monitors and controls the pumps supplying the liquid that transports the compounds down the column. The pump-controlling computer ensures that the liquid flow is precise, constant, and nearly pulse free. The pump-controlling computer, if directed by the instrument user, can also change the flow rate and the composition of the liquid during the analysis.

As compounds elute from the separation column, they are detected by one of many types of detectors. A common detector used in liquid chromatography is one that monitors the change in the absorption of specific wavelengths of ultraviolet (UV) light. The change in absorption of UV light is output as an analog voltage. As different compounds elute from the column the voltage will rise and fall, forming a peak. Liquid chromatography is both a qualitative and a quantitative analysis. The height of the peak or area under the peak is proportional to the concentration or amount of compound in the original mixture.

IDENTIFICATION USING RETENTION TIME

The amount of time a compound remains on the column under a specific set of conditions is normally constant. The time required to pass through the column, from when the mixture is injected onto the column until the compound elutes, is called the retention time. Retention time is used to identify compounds. The retention time of a compound is found by performing calibration analyses using known amounts of pure compounds analyzed under identical conditions (same

flow rate, same solvent composition, same column type, etc.). Modern computer-controlled automated instruments ensure that analytical conditions are as close to identical between runs as possible.

Detectors that can precisely identify a compound can also be used. For example, mass spectrometers are interfaced to liquid chromatographs. The mass spectrum of a compound is like a fingerprint; it can reliably identify a specific compound.

DATA ANALYSIS

Before computerized data systems were available, the output from a chromatography experiment was captured on a strip chart recorder. In a modern data analysis system the analog voltage signal from the detector is converted into a digital value using an analog-to-digital converter. The digital values are then captured by the computer-based data system. These data are called the raw data, as they have been captured directly from the instrument. The data system has software that can analyze the raw data. This software finds the retention time and areas or heights of the peaks in the data. The actual amount or concentration of the chemical compound can then be computed if calibration standards have been previously analyzed.

In a calibration standard analysis, a known amount of the pure chemical compound is analyzed. The retention time of the peak and the area or height of the peak are recorded. When calibration standards are analyzed at various amounts, a least-squares curve-fitting algorithm can be used to identify a calibration curve or line. This calibration curve or line can then be used to compute the amount of compound in the original mixture. All of these calculations are performed by the computer-based data system.

When data analysis is complete, the data system prints a report showing the results of an analysis including the peak retention times, the peak areas or heights, and the calculated amounts of the compounds analyzed in the experiment. The output of the detector is also displayed graphically. This graphical data presentation is called a chromatogram. Usually the chromatogram will have the retention times displayed above each peak along with the name of the compound assigned to the peak. The chromatogram will show the "baselines," which indicate where the areas of peaks were calculated.

REPROCESSING STORED DATA

Many chromatography data systems provide the capability to reprocess raw data stored on disk. These systems are interactive, allowing the user to change data processing parameters and view the results of the change after the raw data are reprocessed. Selected parts of the data can be viewed graphically. The user can interactively zoom in to blow up selected sections of a chromatogram. The reprocessed results can be reported just as they were during the original data processing.

OTHER CHEMICAL INSTRUMENTS

Literally hundreds of other instruments employed in the chemical industry use the same techniques described here for a liquid chromatograph. They are computer controlled. They acquire data from a calibration run on a sample or a pure, known amount of the compound or compounds of interest. Through additional calibration runs using different amounts of the pure compounds, a calibration curve or line can be generated. Then a sample can be analyzed and the amounts of the compounds of interest in the sample can be computed by using the calibration curve or line. Many older instruments that do not have a flexible data system are interfaced to a computer. The raw data or the results of the instrument analysis are sent via a data bus or communications port to a computer. Personal computers have been widely used for this type of application. The most common communications port used is the RS-232, or asynchronous communications port. Once the instrument data have been captured by the computer system, they can be analyzed and reported. Application programs written specifically for the particular type of data analysis can be written and used. Alternatively, many chemists use spreadsheet programs to perform calculations and generate reports. Spreadsheet programs have the ability to import instrument data, so the user does not have to manually enter values. Spreadsheet templates can be created. These templates can include all the calculations required to analyze a set of raw data. Once a template has been developed, the user needs only to import new raw data to have them analyzed and ready to report. Graphics programs are used to graphically display instrument data. The data can be imported into database management programs allowing the user to track data trends over time (see LABORATORY INFORMATION MANAGEMENT SYSTEMS).

CHEMICAL INSTRUMENTS IN MEDICINE

Computerized chemical instrumentation is widely used in doctors' laboratories, medical clinics, and hospitals. Instruments such as blood analyzers perform a battery of tests, determining the concentration of up to forty different compounds and ions in only a few minutes. The test methods used were originally developed as "wet chemical" tests. Now, computer-controlled instruments perform all of the various tests on small volumes of blood. Each test requires precise, computer-controlled measuring and mixing of reagent. Usually the actual measurement of the compound or ion of interest is done using a spectroscopic technique. The instrument performs all of the calibration analyses and calculates the concentration of the compound or ion and prints it on a report.

Many of the medical instruments used today were originally developed for chemical use. For example, magnetic resonance imaging (MRI) was originally developed as nuclear magnetic resonance (NMR) for chemical structure elucidation. None of these instruments would exist without the availability of powerful computers to control the instrument; acquire, analyze, and display data; and print results. These instruments use cutting-edge computer graphics technology to display three-dimensional images, and computer-generated images to diagnose disease or injury.

CHEMICAL INFORMATION

Large databases of chemical information are available on-line from various commercial companies and chemical societies. One of the largest databases, developed by the American Chemical Society, is called the *Chemical Abstracts Service*. From this database, structures of compounds that have been synthesized or isolated can be found along with the physical properties of the compound, such as molecular weight, boiling point, melting point, refractive index, and solubility in water. For many compounds, other known properties such as the compound's toxicity or medicinal use are included in the database. Reactions used to synthesize compounds are also stored in this database. The database can be searched to find compounds that fit a specific set of criteria. Research articles that describe how specific compounds were synthesized or isolated are also available on-line from the system.

Many companies, particularly chemical and pharmaceutical companies, have their own private databases to hold the results of their own internal experimentation. As the chemical and pharmaceutical industries are very competitive and the potential return on the discovery of a powerful drug or valuable chemical is so high, the information held in these private databases is extremely valuable. The application of this information has led to the development of many valuable compounds and medicines. Computer-aided drug and chemical design systems use these internal databases to focus on specific compounds as candidates to perform a particular function. Computer-aided design systems are now used by nearly all major chemical and pharmaceutical companies.

COMPUTERIZED EXPERIMENTATION

With the wide availability of computers and computer components, computerized chemical experimentation is now routinely performed. Data acquisition cards integrating analog-to-digital converters and digital input/output ports that plug directly into a computer's bus are available from a wide variety of vendors. These boards are usually supplied with software that can start data acquisition, log acquired data to disk, and even display the acquired data graphically in real time. More sophisticated software packages are also available, allowing the user to set up an experiment graphically by moving and connecting icons that represent instruments, data acquisition components, and data processing algorithms.

NEW CHEMICAL SENSOR AND INSTRUMENT DEVELOPMENT

Chemical sensors are continuously being discovered, developed, and perfected. All phases of this research and development are being aided by computer technology. Many of the components used in personal computers and consumer electronics are being integrated into new chemical sensors and instruments. For example, photodiode arrays used as components in television sets are used as components in liquid chromatography detectors, and image-capturing and display components found in television sets are being integrated into various chemical instruments. Even synthetic organic reactions are being performed on a microscale using computer-controlled robots to handle the reagents and harvest the products. There is great interest in the development of sensors and instruments to detect and quantitate large macromolecules like proteins and DNA segments, as a result of the boom in biotechnology.

Modern computer electronics has vastly improved the performance and reliability of chemical instrumentation. Modern instruments, the original models of which were used only in research laboratories by highly trained individuals, can now be routinely operated by technicians. The modern chemical laboratory is no longer filled with test tubes and distillation equipment. Very few manual "wet chemical" tests are performed. The modern chemical laboratory is filled with computers and computer-controlled instruments and sensors. These laboratory computers, many interfaced directly to instruments, are networked into other computers where chemists can view, analyze, and report the results of experiments. The modern chemist is an important participant in our information-based society.

For Further Reading

American Laboratory (International Scientific Communications). This monthly publication has many articles on computer applications in chemical instrumentation.

Analytical Chemistry "A" pages (American Chemical Society). This bimonthly publication has numerous articles on computer applications in chemistry.

Laboratory PC User, monthly newsletter of the Laboratory PC Users Group (5989 Vista Loop, San Jose, CA 95124). Provides tips on using personal computers in scientific laboratories with special emphasis on laboratory data management and instrument interfacing.

Mezei, L. 1989. *Laboratory Lotus: A complete guide to instrument interfacing.* Englewood Cliffs, N.J.: Prentice-Hall. A guide for using Lotus Symphony or 1-2-3 for instrument interfacing.

————. 1990. *Spreadsheet statistics and curve fitting for scientists and engineers.* Englewood Cliffs, N.J.: Prentice-Hall. A guide to using spreadsheet programs for performing scientific applications.

Moore, J. H., C. C. Davis, and M. A. Coplan. 1983. *Building scientific apparatus: A practical guide to design and construction.* Reading, Mass.: Addison-Wesley. A hands-on book describing techniques for building experimental apparatus. More than 140 pages are dedicated to electronics and electronic components.

Ouchi, G. I. 1987. *Personal computers for scientists: A byte at a time.* Washington, D.C.: American Chemical Society Press. An introduction to scientific personal computer applications using off-the-shelf software programs.

————. 1988. *Lotus in the lab: Spreadsheet applications for scientists and engineers.* Reading, Mass.: Addison-Wesley. On the application of Lotus 1-2-3 to scientific problems.

PC Magazine (Ziff-Davis). Published 22 times a year. This is the best source for personal computer information, including product reviews, hands-on applications, and computing trends.

Personal Computing Tools Catalog (Personal Computing Tools, 17419 Farley Road, Los Gatos, CA 95030). Published quarterly. Valuable catalog of products for scientific computing.

Ratzlaff, K. L. 1987. *Introduction to computer-assisted experimentation.* New York: Wiley. Good book on basic electronics and computerized data acquisition and control.

Glenn I. Ouchi

CHURCHES, COMPUTER USE BY

See Religion, Computer Uses in

COBOL

COBOL is an acronym for COmmon Business Oriented Language. It is a programming language used primarily in business applications. It is the dominant language in business with billions of lines of code in use.

THE HISTORY OF COBOL

The COBOL language was defined in 1960 by a committee from government, industry, and academia. The committee, called the Conference on Data Systems Languages (CODASYL), was responsible for developing COBOL-60 (named for the year in which it was developed). In later years, three subsequent versions of COBOL were developed by CODASYL: COBOL-68, COBOL-74, and COBOL-85. The versions tend to be upward compatible.

The American National Standards Institute (ANSI) adopted the CODASYL COBOL as the American COBOL standard. The Institute regularly tests different COBOL compilers for conformance with CODASYL COBOL specifications. Most COBOL compilers conform to the CODASYL and ANSI standard, and business organizations usually avoid nonstandard compilers.

COBOL was originally designed for large mainframe computers. COBOL is also available for microcomputers. Most microcomputer versions conform to COBOL standards, but some do not.

Approximately 70 percent of the installed business systems in use have been written in COBOL, and a large proportion of new development is in COBOL.

ADVANTAGES OF COBOL IN A BUSINESS ENVIRONMENT

The business computing environment has specific requirements that differentiate it from other computing environments. These center around transaction volume, portability, and maintainability. COBOL is designed for these requirements.

Transaction Volume

The business environment is characterized by the need to process a very large number of transactions. In a typical business, orders must be taken for products or services, inventories and sales accounts must be updated, deliveries must be scheduled, and bills must be sent out to customers. In contrast, a business rarely needs to perform mathematical calculations up to the twentieth decimal point. Thus, a business computer language should support programming procedures to input a large volume of information (e.g., customer orders), perform relatively simple calculations on the information (e.g., update sales), and output a large volume of information (e.g., customer bills). It need not be able to perform extremely complex mathematical calculations with high precision. Additionally, when large volumes of transactions are processed in a business, many reports are created to aid in the decision-making activities of managers. COBOL was designed for programming transaction processing and contains extensive formatting capabilities that allow programmers to specify business reports as outputs.

Portability

In addition to the need to process large volumes of transactions, the business environment requires a language that can be used with many types of hardware (e.g., from IBM mainframes to Macintosh personal computers). Such a language is said to be portable. To create a portable language, the language must be defined in the same manner for all types of hardware. To accomplish this, a standard for the language is usually required. CODASYL and ANSI serve as the standard-setting committee for COBOL, thereby ensuring portability.

Easy Maintenance

The business environment requires a programming language that is easy to use when programs are to be modified. COBOL was designed to be similar to the English language to facilitate documentation and maintenance. Sentences in COBOL can be read in much the same way as sentences in English. For example, the COBOL statement ADD STORE-1-SALES, STORE-2-SALES GIVING TOTAL-STORE-SALES is easily understood. This statement simply sets TOTAL-STORE-SALES equal to the sum of the sales for two stores. Because COBOL is so like the English language, it is often said to be self-documenting.

COBOL is also used in non-English programming environments. The standard English-like commands of COBOL are employed, but data names may be in the language of the developer.

WEAKNESSES OF COBOL

The most common criticisms leveled at the COBOL language center around its attempt to be similar to the English language and its awkward data definition requirements.

The frequently made claim that COBOL programs can be read like English prose is only partly achieved. The argument made against the use of English-like statements in COBOL is that if a person does not understand how to write a program, the English-like statements will not be sufficient to provide understanding, and if a person does understand how to write a program, English-like statements simply make the processes of writing and reading the language very time consuming. The claim that COBOL programs are self-documenting and require no comments lines within the program for clarification is also subject to challenge.

Critics of COBOL also state that the data definition sections in COBOL are awkward and time consuming. An example of this is seen in the definition of a report heading. To define a single line title for a report with eighty-character lines, the following definition is required:

```
01 REPORT-TITLE.
   05 FILLER        PIC X(20) VALUE
                    SPACES.
   05 FILLER        PIC X(14) VALUE "A
                    SALES REPORT"
   05 FILLER        PIC X(46) VALUE
                    SPACES.
```

Every one of the eighty character positions in the line must have its value defined by the title.

THE STRUCTURE OF COBOL

A COBOL program is made up of four divisions that separate different kinds of specifications within the program. The identification division gives information about the program such as its name. The environment division describes the type of hardware that the program is to run on and the files that are to be read and written. The data division defines the data used by the program. The procedure division contains the statements that instruct the computer how to perform a desired task (e.g., print a report).

An Example

Figure 1 is a very small but complete COBOL program that illustrates the language and its use. The purpose of the program is to read sales records from a file and print out a sales report. The input file that the program reads from is shown in Figure 2 and the sales report created by the program is shown in Figure 3.

Identification Division

The identification division contains the name of the program, the name of the author of the program, the date on which the program was written, and the date on which the program was last compiled (converted to machine-usable object code).

Environment Division

The environment division contains two sections. The configuration section specifies the computer on which the program is to be developed and run. In this case, the program was developed on and designed to run on an IBM personal computer. The input–output section matches file names to be used in the program with file names stored on the computer (e.g., SALES-INPUT-FILE is matched with INFILE.CBL). This improves portability by allowing a programmer to change the input and output files simply by changing the files associated with INFILE.CBL and OUTFILE.CBL rather than by changing the names SALES-INPUT-FILE and SALES-REPORT-FILE throughout the program each time a different set of files is processed or the program is run on a different computer.

Data Division

The data division is made up of two sections. The file section contains a description of the file of sales records that are to be read into the program and the file of sales report lines that are to be written out from the program. For example, within the SALES-INPUT-RECORD, the data name STORE-NAME-IN is defined to be twenty-five characters long followed by sales data (STORE-SALES-IN) that can be up to five digits long. The working-storage section defines all other data names used within the program such as REPORT-TITLE and WS-STORE-SALES-TOTAL.

Two clauses within data definition statements are used to define the length of a data name and to initiate its value at the start of the program. These are the PIC and VALUE clauses. The PIC clause defines how long the variable is in terms of digits or characters. In the example, STORE-NAME is defined as part of REPORT-DETAIL-LINE. It is defined

```
IDENTIFICATION DIVISION.
PROGRAM-ID. PRINT-SALES-REPORT.
AUTHOR.         J. SNYDER.
DATE-WRITTEN. JANUARY 1, 1991.
DATE-COMPILED. 01/01/91.

ENVIRONMENT DIVISION.

CONFIGURATION SECTION.
SOURCE-COMPUTER. IBM-PC.
OBJECT-COMPUTER. IBM-PC.

INPUT-OUTPUT SECTION.
FILE-CONTROL.
   SELECT SALES-INPUT-FILE ASSIGN TO "INFILE.CBL"
        ;ORGANIZATION IS LINE SEQUENTIAL.
   SELECT SALES-REPORT-FILE ASSIGN TO "OUTFILE.CBL"
        ;ORGANIZATION IS LINE SEQUENTIAL.

DATA DIVISION.
FILE SECTION.
FD SALES-INPUT-FILE
   LABEL RECORDS ARE STANDARD
   DATA RECORD IS SALES-INPUT-RECORD.
01 SALES-INPUT-RECORD.
   05 FILLER              PIC X(7).
   05 STORE-NAME-IN       PIC X(25).
   05 STORE-SALES-IN      PIC 999V99.
   05 FILLER              PIC X(41).

FD SALES-REPORT-FILE
   LABEL RECORDS ARE OMITTED
   DATA RECORD IS REPORT-LINE.
01 REPORT-LINE            PIC X(80).

WORKING STORAGE SECTION.

01 REPORT-TITLE.
   05 FILLER              PIC X(23) VALUE SPACES.
   05 FILLER              PIC X(14) VALUE "A SALES REPORT".
   05 FILLER              PIC X(33) VALUE SPACES.

01 REPORT-DETAIL-LINE.
   05 FILLER              PIC X(10) VALUE SPACES.
   05 STORE-NAME          PIC X(25).
   05 FILLER              PIC X(10) VALUE SPACES.
   05 STORE-SALES         PIC $Z,ZZZ.99.
   05 FILLER              PIC X(26) VALUE SPACES.

01 END-OF-FILE            PIC X(1) VALUE "N".

01 WS-STORE-SALES TOTAL   PIC 9999V99 VALUE ZERO.

PROCEDURE DIVISION.

MAIN-PROCEDURE.
   OPEN INPUT SALES-INPUT-FILE.
   OPEN OUTPUT SALES-REPORT-FILE.
```

```
WRITE REPORT-LINE FROM REPORT-TITLE.
PERFORM READ-SALES-RECORD.
PERFORM PROCESS-SALES-RECORDS UNTIL END-OF-FILE EQUAL TO "Y".
MOVE "TOTAL STORE SALES" TO STORE-NAME.
MOVE WS-STORE-SALES-TOTAL TO STORE-SALES.
WRITE REPORT-LINE FROM REPORT-DETAIL-LINE AFTER ADVANCING 1 LINE.
CLOSE SALES-INPUT-FILE
    SALES-REPORT-FILE.
STOP RUN.


PROCESS-SALES-RECORDS.
    MOVE STORE-NAME-IN TO STORE-NAME.
    MOVE STORE-SALES-IN TO STORE-SALES.
    ADD STORE-SALES-IN TO WS-STORE-SALES-TOTAL.
    WRITE REPORT-LINE FROM REPORT-DETAIL-LINE.
    PERFORM READ-SALES-RECORD.


READ-SALES-RECORD.
    READ SALES-INPUT-FILE
    AT END MOVE "Y" TO END-OF-FILE.
```

FIGURE 1 (facing page and above). Sample COBOL program.

as being twenty-five characters long with the use of the PIC X(25) clause.

In addition to specifying the length of a data name it is often desirable to initialize the value of the data name at the start of the program. In COBOL this is accomplished through the use of a VALUE clause. In the example, the data name FILLER is defined with a VALUE SPACES clause that initializes its value to spaces. Values other than spaces may be assigned using the VALUE clause as in the case of the data name END-OF-FILE that is initialized to a value of "N."

Procedure Division

The procedure division contains the instructions that tell the computer how to create the sales report. The computer executes each statement in the procedure division sequentially unless a PERFORM statement is used to tell the computer to skip to another para-graph, execute the statements in that para-graph, and return to the statement following the PERFORM statement. Beginning with the MAIN-PROCEDURE, the instructions first tell the computer to open the files to be used (i.e., make them available to the program). The next statement causes the report title to be written to the report file through the use of a WRITE verb.

A PERFORM statement then causes the computer to transfer to the paragraph called READ-SALES-RECORD. This paragraph causes the first sales record to be read into the program. When the READ-SALES-RECORD paragraph has been completed, the computer transfers back to the instructions following the PERFORM READ-SALES-RECORD statement. The computer performs the PROCESS-SALES-RECORDS paragraph until there are no more sales

STORE 1	20099
STORE 2	13268
STORE 3	65399
STORE 4	87254
STORE 5	32111
STORE 6	66868
STORE 7	24389
STORE 8	20967

FIGURE 2. Input file "INFILE.CBL."

A SALES REPORT

STORE 1	$ 200.99
STORE 2	$ 132.68
STORE 3	$ 653.99
STORE 4	$ 872.54
STORE 5	$ 321.11
STORE 6	$ 668.68
STORE 7	$ 243.89
STORE 8	$ 209.67
TOTAL STORE SALES	$3,303.55

FIGURE 3. Output file "OUTFILE.CBL."

records to process (i.e., until END-OF-FILE EQUAL TO "Y").

The first two statements in the PROCESS-SALES-RECORDS paragraph move the store name and the store sales information into data names that are to be written to the output file. The third statement performs a mathematical calculation using the ADD statement. The ADD statement takes the value of STORE-SALES-IN and adds it to the current value of WS-STORE-SALES-TOTAL. Because this paragraph is performed once for each store to be processed, WS-STORE-SALES-TOTAL will contain the total of all store sales at the completion of the program.

The PROCESS-SALES-RECORDS paragraph also contains a WRITE statement that prints out a sales report line and a PERFORM statement that causes the next sales record to be read from the sales input file. Because the PROCESS-SALES-RECORDS paragraph is performed until no more sales records are present, all sales records will be read and written.

After all sales report records are written, the computer executes the statements following the PERFORM PROCESS-SALES-RECORDS statement. These statements cause the sales total line to be written, close input and output files, and stop processing (STOP RUN).

James R. Snyder

CODING THEORY

The primary objective of a communication system is to convey an information-bearing signal from an information source to a destination over a communication channel. All communication systems are subject to noise and disturbances resulting in signal distortions. In 1948, Shannon proposed a mathematical theory of communication, called information theory, dealing with the fundamental limits on the representation and transmission of information.

Information theory is based on a probabilistic model of the communication system. Let the discrete random variable U represent the output of a source generating a symbol every signaling interval in a statistically independent manner. This discrete memoryless source (DMS) is assumed to generate symbols from a fixed finite alphabet $\{u_1, \ldots, u_K\}$ with probabilities $P(U = u_k) = p_k$, $k = 1, \ldots, K$. The amount of information gained after observing the symbol u_k is defined by the logarithmic function

$$I(u_k) = \log(1/p_k)$$

Thus, $I(u_k)$ is inversely related to the likelihood of a symbol occurrence. For a DMS, the average information per source symbol is given by

$$H(U) = \sum_{k=1}^{K} p_k \log(1/p_k)$$

This quantity is known as the entropy of the source and represents the average amount of uncertainty regarding the source. The base of the logarithm is usually taken to be 2 and the unit is called the bit. The entropy is bounded as $0 \le H(U) \le \log K$.

An important problem in communications is the efficient representation of symbols generated by a DMS. Each symbol u_k is assigned a binary code word of length l_k. For an efficient representation, it is desirable to minimize the average code word length $\bar{L}$ where

$$\bar{L} = \sum_{k=1}^{K} p_k l_k$$

Shannon's first theorem, also known as the source coding theorem, provides a fundamental limit on $\bar{L}$ in terms of the entropy of the source.

SOURCE CODING THEOREM: *Given a DMS with entropy* H(U), *the average code word length* $\bar{L}$ *for any source encoding scheme is bounded as* $\bar{L} \ge$ H(U).

Huffman code is an example of a source code where $\bar{L}$ approaches $H(U)$. Also, this code is optimum in that no other uniquely decodable code has a smaller $\bar{L}$ for a given DMS.

Let the discrete random variables X and Y represent the input and output of a communication channel. The channel is assumed to be memoryless in that any output symbol depends only on its corresponding input symbol. The discrete memoryless channel (DMC) is characterized in terms of the transition probabilities $p(y_k|x_j)$, $j = 1, \ldots, J$; $k = 1, \ldots, K$. The conditional entropy $H(X|Y)$ is defined as

$$H(X|Y) = \sum_{k=1}^{K} \sum_{j=1}^{J} p(x_j, y_k) \log[1/p(x_j|y_k)]$$

This represents the amount of uncertainty remaining about the channel input after observing the channel output. As $H(X)$ represents the uncertainty about the channel input prior to transmission, $H(X) - H(X|Y)$ gives the amount of uncertainty reduced or the amount of information transmitted over the channel. This difference is defined as the mutual information

$$I(X;Y) = H(X) - H(X|Y)$$

The channel capacity of a DMC is defined as the maximum mutual information for any signaling interval where the maximization is performed over all possible input probability distributions:

$$C = \max_{p(x_j)} I(X;Y)$$

To combat the effects of noise during transmission, the incoming data sequence from the source is encoded into a channel input sequence by introducing redundancy. At the receiver, the received sequence is decoded to reconstruct the data sequence. Shannon's second theorem, also known as the channel coding theorem or the noisy coding theorem, provides the fundamental limits on the rate at which reliable information transmission can take place over a DMC.

CHANNEL CODING THEOREM: (i) *Let a DMS with entropy* H(U) *produce a symbol every* T_s *seconds. Let a DMC have capacity* C *and be used once every* T_c *seconds. Then, if*

$$\frac{H(U)}{T_s} \leq \frac{C}{T_c},$$

there exists a coding scheme using which data transmission can take place with an arbitrarily small probability of error. (ii) *Conversely, if*

$$\frac{H(U)}{T_s} > \frac{C}{T_c},$$

it is not possible to transmit data with an arbitrarily small probability of error.

It must be emphasized that the above result only states the existence of "good" codes but does not provide methods to construct such codes. Development of efficient codes has remained an active area of research. In error-control coding, redundant symbols are added to the transmitted information at the transmitter to provide error detection and error correction capabilities at the receiver. Addition of redundancy implies increased data rate and thus an increased transmission bandwidth.

There are two main kinds of codes, namely, block codes and convolutional codes. Block codes are based on algebraic concepts. The channel encoder partitions the message sequence into blocks of length k, adds $n-k$ redundant bits in a prespecified manner, and then transmits the resulting code word of length n. This is known as an (n, k) block code and the ratio $r = k/n$ is the code rate. The $n-k$ bits are called the parity bits and provide the error detection and correction capability. As an example, consider a simple parity-check code where, for every k bits of information, we add a $(k+1)$th bit so that the total number of ones in a code word is even. This $(n, n-1)$ block code provides the capability to detect a single error. It does not have any error correction capability. Another elementary code is the $(n, 1)$ repetition code where each information bit is repeated n times. This code can correct up to $(n-1)/2$ errors. Many efficient error control codes, which attempt to approach the fundamental limits of Shannon, have been proposed in the literature. Some examples are the Hamming code, the Bose–Chaudhuri–Hocquengham (BCH) code, the Reed–Muller code, the Reed–Solomon code, and the Goppa code. These codes are used extensively in practical applications.

In block codes, the code words are generated on a block-by-block basis. It is necessary to store the incoming message bits before a block is encoded into a code word. In applications where messages arrive serially rather than in large blocks, it is sometimes desirable to encode the incoming message continuously in a serial manner. Such codes are called convolutional codes. The encoder for these codes can be viewed as a finite-state machine that consists of a finite-length shift register with specified connections to several modulo-2 adders and a muliplexer that generates the output in a serial manner. This encoding scheme exhibits memory in that a message bit entering the shift register influences a number of outgoing coded bits. The length of the shift register and the number of adders specify the memory (the constraint length) and the rate of the code, respectively. Convolutional codes are decoded using the Viterbi algorithm, which is optimum in terms of its error performance, but the computational complexity is high. Suboptimum decoding algorithms with reasonable complexity such as the class of sequential decoding algorithms are used in some applications.

Information theory provides the theoretical foundation for the fields of CRYPTOGRAPHY and data security. An important data security problem is that of privacy. A privacy system prevents the extraction of information by unauthorized persons from messages transmitted over a public channel. The source generates a plaintext or an unciphered message to be transmitted over an unsecure channel to the intended user. The goal of the cryptographic system is to prevent an unauthorized person from learning the contents of the message from the intercepted message. The transmitter operates on the message using an invertible transformation to generate the ciphertext or cryptogram. The key for deciphering is sent to the intended user on a secure channel enabling it to perform the inverse transformation. This problem is analogous to the problem of communication over noisy channels where the noise corresponds to the enciphering transformation. The role of the receiver in the cryptography problem is similar to that in the communication problem. But the goal of the enciphering operation is to introduce enough uncertainty so that the deciphering operation becomes computationally infeasible for an unauthorized user. In fact, perfect secrecy can be achieved if the probability of receiving a particular ciphertext given that a specific message enciphered under some key was sent is the same as the probability of receiving the same ciphertext given that some other message was sent enciphered under a different key. Thus, information

theory and coding techniques have had a major impact on the design of modern data security systems.

Reference

Shannon, C. E. 1948. A mathematical theory of communication. Parts 1, 2. *Bell System Technical Journal* 27:379–423, 623–56.

For Further Reading

Blahut, R. E. 1983. *Theory and practice of error control codes.* Reading, Mass.: Addison-Wesley.

———1987. *Principles and practice of information theory.* Reading, Mass.: Addison-Wesley.

Gallagher, R. G. 1968. *Information theory and reliable communication.* New York: Wiley.

Hamming, R. W. 1980. *Coding and information theory.* Englewood Cliffs, N.J.: Prentice-Hall.

IEEE Transactions on Information Theory. Journal publishing recent results in the areas of information theory and coding.

Imai, H. 1990. *Essentials of error control coding techniques.* San Diego, Calif.: Academic.

Konheim, A. G. 1981. *Cryptography: A primer.* New York: Wiley.

Lin, S., and D. J. Costello, Jr. 1983. *Error control coding: Fundamentals and applications.* Englewood Cliffs, N.J.: Prentice-Hall.

McEliece, R. J. 1977. *The theory of information theory and coding.* Reading, Mass.: Addison-Wesley.

Rao, T. R. N. 1989. *Error control coding for computer systems.* Englewood Cliffs, N.J.: Prentice-Hall.

Pramod K. Varshney

COMPILERS

A compiler is a computer program that is capable of translating programs written in one language, called the *source language*, into equivalent programs written in another language, called the *target language.* Usually, the source language is a high-level programming language such as FORTRAN or Ada, and the target language is a machine language of a particular computer. Having written a program in a programming language, the programmer submits it to a compiler for translation (or *runs it through the compiler*), before the program can be executed on a computer. This is true on the smallest of personal computers or on the largest of supercomputers.

To be able to produce a target program equivalent to the source program, the compiler must, in some limited sense, be able to *understand* the source program. Just like a natural language, a programming language is defined by its *syntax* and *semantics,* both of which must be understood by the compiler. The syntax of a language defines the rules that govern the formation of sentences in the language; the semantics of a language define *the meaning* (more appropriately, in the case of a programming language, *the effects*) of the valid sentences.

Advances in compiler construction have been accompanied and aided by advances in the understanding of programming languages and theoretical computer science. In particular, formal definition techniques of language syntax and semantics and also of machine architectures have led to a common structure for compilers, consisting of a fairly standard set of components, many of which may be generated automatically. In the next section, we examine the architecture of a typical compiler.

Compilers are used because it is more convenient for people to program a computer in a high-level programming language rather than in the low-level language that the computer is capable of executing. Compilers were invented in the early 1950s as computers were being used by more people—in those days, using machine language—who found that the programming of computers involved many extremely tedious, error-prone, and repetitive tasks that could best be done by the computers themselves. Examples of these tedious tasks are deciding on where in memory a data item should be stored and keeping track of it, or what ele-

mentary computer operations are necessary to compute the result of an arithmetic expressions such as $(3X + 4Y)^2$. Indeed, as the early computers were used primarily in computing formulas, compilers were viewed as translation aids for formulas, as can be seen from the name of one of the early languages, FORTRAN, which stands for formula translator.

Once the programmer has decided that a formula such as $(3X + 4Y)^2$ has to be evaluated, the compiler can decide where to store the variables X and Y and what machine instructions to use to accomplish the addition, multiplication, and squaring operations. Thus, built into the compiler is a knowledge of the source language (what formulas, operations, variables, etc., are valid); a knowledge of the target language, that is, the target computer (what instructions the computer is capable of executing, where and how can data be stored, how can the data be accessed, etc.); and rules for performing translations that preserve the *semantics* of the source program, that is, that the target program will produce exactly the same result as the source program, if it could be executed directly.

COMPONENTS OF A COMPILER

A compiler's job is divided into two phases that perform, respectively, analysis and synthesis. In the analysis phase, the compiler analyzes the source program to determine its semantics; in the synthesis phase, the compiler synthesizes a target program that achieves the same semantics. A typical compiler is organized according to Figure 1, in which each box represents one component of the compiler. We use the FORTRAN assignment statement

$$VOLUME = (3*X + 4*Y)**2$$

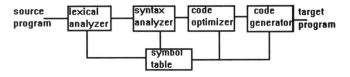

FIGURE 1. Components of a typical compiler.

to help describe the function of each compiler component. This statement says to "add 3 times X to 4 times Y, square the result, and assign it to VOLUME."

Lexical analyzer. The lexical analyzer reads the input program, character by character, and groups the characters into larger units called *tokens.* In our example assignment statement, the lexical analyzer recognizes the variable identifier VOLUME, the operation =, the symbol (, the constant 3, the operation symbol *, the variable identifier X, the constant 4, the operation symbol *, the variable identifier Y, the symbol), the operation symbol **, the constant 2, and finally an end-of-line mark. The tokens (or *lexemes,* or *lexical items*) found by the lexical analyzer are passed on to the next component. The lexical analyzer uses the lexical rules of the language, such as what characters are valid, what characters may be used in identifiers, and what length an identifier may be. Lexical analysis removes all extraneous characters such as spaces from the program.

Syntax analyzer. The syntax analyzer, or *parser,* groups the tokens found by the lexical analyzer—*parses* them—according to the syntax rules of the language. The job of the syntax analyzer is to produce a parse tree or a syntax tree, which shows the syntactic structure of the source program clearly, such as the association of operations with their operands. Syntax analysis removes all extraneous tokens such as parentheses, whose purpose is reflected in the structure of the syntax tree as produced by the syntax analyzer. A typical syntax tree for our example assignment statement is shown in Figure 2.

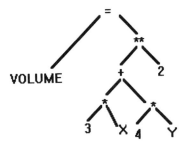

FIGURE 2. Syntax tree for the assignment statement VOLUME = (3*X + 4*Y)**2.

Code optimizer. In general, the straightforward translation of a source program into a target program is relatively easy. What makes it difficult is to generate a target program that makes efficient use of the resources of the target computer. The job of the code optimizer is to improve the efficiency of the generated program. Some optimizations are machine independent. For example, the code optimizer may change the square operation into a multiplication, which is usually much faster. Other optimizations are machine dependent. For example, if a computer has several processors, capable of performing several different operations simultaneously, the code optimizer may rearrange the order of some operations (while preserving their semantics) to make more operations available for simultaneous execution.

Code generator. Finally, after the source program has been analyzed, and the necessary optimizations have been decided, the code generator generates the target program. The code generator obviously must have intimate knowledge of the workings of the target computer. The encoding of this information for the code generator is a major design aspect of the code generator and the whole compiler.

Symbol table. During the operation of a compiler, often a piece of information is discovered that must be recorded for later use. A *symbol table* is a repository for all such information. For example, the symbol table may contain the type and address of the program variables. Each of the other components of the compiler store information in and retrieve information from the symbol table.

Another common component of a compiler is the *error analysis* component that deals with errors in the source program. On detection of an error, a compiler tries to *recover,* if possible, so that it can either find more errors in the rest of the program or generate a target program despite the presence of errors. Finding more than one error at a time helps the programmer remove them more quickly. The error analysis component of a compiler may detect lexical, syntactic, or some semantic errors in the program.

INTERPRETERS

An alternative way to execute a program on a computer is to use an *interpreter* instead of a compiler. An interpreter, rather than translating a source program into a target program, executes the source program directly and produces the results of the program. It contains a routine for each operation that may appear in the source program.

The structure of an interpreter is similar to that of a compiler except that it does not have a code generator. When processing a program, the interpreter first analyzes the program and produces a syntax tree. It then traverses the syntax tree, and as it visits each node of the tree, it calls the appropriate routine to evaluate the operation that corresponds to that node.

DEVELOPMENTS IN COMPILER WRITING

Compiler writing is one of the most developed areas of computer science. Not only has the practice of compiler writing advanced tremendously but a rich supporting theory has also been developed. In the early days, a compiler was written in an ad hoc fashion, just like any other program. Over the years, it was discovered that most compilers, even if they translate different source languages and generate target programs for different computers, performed many of the same tasks. This discovery led to the development of compiler-building components, tool kits, and tools. We have seen the most common components in the previous section. Tools exist for automatically generating, at least partially, lexical analyzers, syntax analyzers, code optimizers, and code generators.

Compiler-writing tools depend on a formal definition of the component to be generated. For example, a *parser-generator* accepts as input a formal definition of the syntax of the source language and produces a parser for that language. Thus, the development of formal definition methods for languages has been a necessary ingredient of the advances in compiler writing. Some of the tools and theories developed for compiler writing are applicable to programs other than compilers. For example, parsing techniques can be used in text formatters or database query processors and optimizers.

In general, a compiler has a model of the source language and a model of the target machine, and it performs a mapping from the former into the latter. For automatic compiler generation, it is necessary to formally define the source, the target, and the mapping. This can be done completely for simple languages and simple machines. The reason that compiler writing is not yet completely automated is that new programming languages and new computers are constantly being developed that do not fit within the existing models of the available compiler generation tools. For example, models of sequential machines do not accommodate the emerging parallel machines, which contain many functional units, capable of executing many operations, tens or hundreds, simultaneously. An important phase of a compiler for such a parallel machine involves the *scheduling* of operations to ensure the maximum utilization of all the functional units and thus the efficient execution of the source program. Compiling for parallel machines is a challenging and active area of compiler research.

As compilers constitute one of the fundamental tools necessary for the use of computers, each computer manufacturer produces compilers for its own machines. In addition, there are software companies that specialize in the building of compilers and even compiler-writing tools. Depending on the complexity of the language and the machine, the amount of optimization the compiler is capable of performing, other compiler features, and the sophistication level of the tools being used, a team of two to ten compiler writers may require one or more years to build a compiler.

For Further Reading

Aho, A. V., R. Sethi, and J. D. Ullman. 1987. *Compilers: Principles, techniques, and tools.* Reading, Mass.: Addison-Wesley.

Bauer, F. L., and J. Eickel. 1976. *Compiler construction: An advanced course.* 2nd ed.

Lecture Notes in Computer Science 21. Berlin: Springer-Verlag.

Ghezzi, C., and M. Jazayeri. 1987. *Programming language concepts.* 2nd ed. New York: Wiley.

Lewis, P. M., II, D. J. Rosenkrantz, and R. E. Stearns. 1976. *Compiler design theory.* Reading, Mass.: Addison-Wesley.

Mehdi Jazayeri

COMPLEXITY

See Algorithms

COMPUTER-AIDED DESIGN AND MANUFACTURING

Computer-aided design, abbreviated CAD, refers to the replacement of paper-and-pencil drafting with computer-based drafting systems. Computer-aided manufacturing, abbreviated CAM, refers to the use of computer systems to control the manufacture of finished products.

One perspective of CAD and CAM is that the two are distinct activities, performed by different people, often at different locations; however, the design of a product can hardly occur in isolation from the manufacturing process used to finally produce it. A mass-marketed, disposable consumer product, for example, will not be successful if designed in such a way as to require expensive manufacturing processes. In the real world it is virtually impossible to separate the design process from the manufacturing process. In Great Britain and in many areas of Europe the integration of CAD/CAM is reflected in the merger of the two abbreviations as CADAM; however, Lockheed and IBM have registered the name CADAM as a trademark in the United States to describe a particular software product, preventing its adoption as a generic term.

It is important to understand how CAD programs are different from other computer graphics programs. The most popular drawing programs are paint programs. These programs are oriented primarily toward work with bitmaps. In a bitmap system, the final display medium, which may be either the screen or a piece of paper, is represented by a specific number of dots arranged in rows and columns. Bitmaps are typically created at a specific resolution. For example, many laser printers print at 75, 150, and 300 dots per inch. When a paint program is used to represent a drawing, the drawing is permanently tied to a specific screen or print resolution. Enlarging the drawing does not increase the amount of detail in the image, only the size of the individual dots.

Computer-assisted design programs are based on maintaining a database of drawing geometry that is displayed at varying resolutions on different display screens, printers, and plotters. In a bitmapped paint program, a line is represented as a specific number of pixels, depending on the drawing resolution. A CAD program uses a vector-based representation system. Each object, or drawing entity, is represented by its mathematical description. A line, for example is represented in the geometry database by recording, at a minimum, its startpoint and endpoint. A circle is represented by recording its center and radius. Professional CAD programs additionally record attribute information about drawing entities. Attributes can include such information as the line type, the color, or the material of which the entity is constructed.

DEVELOPMENT OF COMPUTER-AIDED DESIGN

Early work on CAD began in an effort to automate the representation, revision, and validation of drawing geometry. This effort led to the development of the mainstream of CAD development. Although the productivity enhancements brought about by this first phase were significant, they ushered in a second phase of CAD programs. Now that the basic geometry of the drawing was in a computer-based format, sophisticated analysis could be performed. For example, the benefits of computerized finite element analysis as part of the design process provided an even greater economic payback to manufacturers than the original goals of verification of drawing geometry (i.e., making certain that all the lengths and angles were mathematically consistent). The third emphasis in CAD development evolved from the desire to link the manufacturing process more closely with the design process. Although numerically controlled machines had been widely adopted by the mid-1960s on the manufacturing floor, their development was independent of the rise of CAD; however, linking the computer-based drawing geometry of a CAD drawing to numerically controlled manufacturing machines was a natural method to enhance the link between the design and manufacturing processes.

DEVELOPMENT OF COMPUTER-AIDED MANUFACTURING

Computer-aided manufacturing is a natural extension of computer-aided design. In the real world, the design of a product consists not only of a product's description, but also of information related to its manufacture. Designers cannot work in a vacuum. Mass market products, for example, must be designed in such a way that they can be produced easily through low-cost manufacturing techniques.

Numerically controlled machines are the foundation of CAM. By the early 1950s, it had proved possible to construct machines that were controlled by numerical information punched onto paper tape. Unfortunately, highly skilled numerical control programmers were required to transfer the design information into tool paths and cutting speeds. Adjustments for clamp positions, cutting speed, and materials characteristics invariably had to be made after the first parts were machined using this method. As a result, the use of numerically controlled machinery was practical only for the production of large numbers of parts. It was not an efficient manufacturing technique for short runs or one-of parts.

Today's CAD programs, however, are able to produce as output geometric modeling information in a format appropriate for direct input into numerically controlled manufacturing equipment. As a result, numerically controlled equipment can be highly effective as a tool for producing not only high-volume parts runs, but short runs and individual pieces as well—and at a lower cost than manufacturing the parts with traditional techniques.

COMPUTER-AIDED DESIGN AND COMPUTER DEVELOPMENT

As computers first became viable tools in the corporate world, the mainframe computer, shared by many individuals, was the only possible choice. Computer-aided design is, by its very nature, processor intensive. As a result, early CAD initiatives were frequently scorned by corporations. Few companies were willing to have their newly acquired mainframe computer consumed by the processing demands of CAD programming. Only large corporations, such as General Motors, and technological leaders, such as Lockheed and other aerospace companies that required sophisticated structural analysis calculations be performed on their designs, could afford the capital investment required to invest seriously in CAD.

The 1970s brought the development of the minicomputer and the resultant order-of-magnitude decline in the cost of computer processor power. This development made two things possible at once. First, a minicomputer could be cost-justified exclusively on the basis of its CAD potential. Second, the lower costs of minicomputers provided a business opportunity for independent software developers to develop and market turnkey CAD programs, rather than requiring that CAD programs be developed by in-house computer programmers.

The 1980s brought the development of both the desktop personal computer and the desktop UNIX workstation. During the 1980s desktop CAD exploded. Originally divided into distinct markets, by 1990 the gap had closed between personal computers and workstations. The most powerful personal computers were now more powerful than the least powerful workstations. At that point, the purchasing decision as to which platform to implement CAD on became less dictated by search for raw power than by the total applications mix required by a designer's job.

STANDARDS

There will probably never be a single product that meets everyone's needs for CAD and manufacturing. There will always be a need to move data between one CAD program and another, between CAD programs and analysis programs, and between CAD programs and CAM programs. The competitive nature of CAD has driven each CAD system vendor to adopt its own internal representation of drawing geometry. As a result, the drawing files created by one CAD program are seldom readable by any other computer program. There are two approaches to the solution of this problem: (1) de facto industry standards and (2) standards constructed by committees of interested individuals.

The DXF (Drawing Interchange Format) file format is an excellent example of an interchange format that has become a de facto industry standard. The format was created by AutoDesk, the developer of the Auto-CAD software program, for the purpose of allowing the geometry of AutoCAD drawings to be communicated to analysis programs and CAM programs. AutoCAD's dominant position in the small-computer-based CAD market has allowed AutoDesk to be highly successful in dictating the DXF format as a standard. It is difficult for a small CAM company to compete without the ability to accept drawing geometry from the market leader.

The IGES (Initial Graphics Exchange Specification) is an effort by multiple vendors of CAD/CAM software to create a generic file interchange format. At first glance, the creation of a universal CAD geometry specification seems like a perfect solution to drawing interchange; however, the IGES specification can also be a limiting factor for CAD software vendors. For exam-

ple, the IGES specification lacks a method for describing a line that tapers in width. As a result, CAD vendors desiring to implement such a drawing primitive are limited in their ability to export their drawing geometry to an IGES file.

GRAPHICS DISPLAYS

Early CAD systems used a display subsystem based on vector technology. In such a system, the electron beam follows the line segments in the drawing. There are two advantages to such a system. First, because the path of the electron beam is entirely free-form, it can accurately represent complex graphic forms without the limitations of a fixed-grid raster-based display system. Second, such a system does not require the memory to maintain the graphics bitmap required by a raster-based display.

Raster displays are based on a bitmap where each pixel is represented by a location in the computer's memory. In the early days this was a significant disadvantage. As silicon random-access memory (RAM) chips have replaced core memories constructed of iron doughnuts hand threaded on fine wire, the cost of memory for a bitmapped graphics subsystem has become a relatively minor consideration.

One significant development that has great impact on CAD systems is the graphics coprocessor. For a CAD program to draw a line on a basic bitmap display system, the computer's central processing unit (CPU) must calculate the address of each bit position along the line and illuminate it in the correct color. More advanced display subsystems make use of graphics coprocessor chips to free the CPU from the computation of each individual pixel address. With a graphics coprocessor, the CAD program uses the computer's CPU to calculate only the starting point and ending point for the line, then passes that information on to the graphics subsystem. The graphics coprocessor then performs the low-level work of calculating the addresses of the intermediate points and storing the correct color codes at the required locations in the video memory. As a result, the CPU is immediately freed to perform other work within the CAD program.

VISUALIZATION

When paper-based drafting systems are used, for some applications, notably architecture, the artist's rendering was the most important drawing created during the development of an architect's proposal to a client. Visualizing a finished object, whether a machine part or a building, from a set of blueprints is a task that requires significant skills. These visualization skills may not be found in individuals on a board of directors, who make the final decisions on the selection of an architect for the construction of a new corporate headquarters or manufacturing facility.

Many CAD programs now contain, either as an integral part of the program or as a separate add-on package, a subsystem for the production of shaded renderings of three-dimensional drawings. One of the most important developments in visualization in recent years incorporates the original *Star Wars* technology. As Lucasfilms worked to refine the production techniques that made the movie *Star Wars* a technical masterpiece, they experimented with various computer algorithms for representing surfaces as a photorealistic shaded rendering. Eventually, they spun off a small company, Pixar, whose main product became an imaging system known as Renderman. The Renderman specification allows surfaces to be defined both in terms of realistic materials, such as wood and marble, and in terms of color and specularity. Renderman is to photorealistic rendering what Postscript is to laser printer page description. The Renderman output can be displayed on a computer screen or a film recorder, transferred to videotape, or exported to an animation program.

A carefully constructed series of renderings of a building can allow the prospective client to, in effect, tour the facility prior to the beginning of construction.

Some CAD programs allow the articulation of parts within a drawing. This process,

called kinematics, allows the designer, for example, to visualize the raising and lowering of an automotive hatchback, verifying that the rear seatback does not hit the hatchback window in the closed position or the radio antenna in the open position. Such articulated modeling can save corporations tens of thousands of dollars of modeling and cut months out of the time from initial design to final product manufacture.

VIRTUAL REALITY

Stereo photography provided an interesting parlor amusement during the early days of photography. By use of a special stereoscopic camera, a pair of images are produced of the same view from lenses spaced to approximate the view seen by a pair of eyes. A stereoscopic viewer provides each eye with an image representing a slightly different viewpoint.

Virtual reality is the computer-generated version of the same technology. Using a special headset containing a small video monitor for each eye, a graphics workstation creates an image for each eye that, when combined, produces a computer-generated stereoscopic view. Placing three-dimensional position sensors on the headset allows the workstation to generate a continuously changing view of a virtual world.

The world of virtual reality typically begins as a CAD drawing. Although the high price of such systems (a basic system is typically over $100,000) has limited their acceptance, when the technology is applied to such tasks as allowing members of a corporate board of directors to tour a proposed skyscraper, the costs may be quickly recovered through the architectural fees associated with such a structure.

Architecture is not the only potential beneficiary of such technology. Virtual reality techniques can allow dynamic three-dimensional visualization of such things as automotive interiors, the fit between machine parts, and even the interior fit of engine or transmission parts. Although the costs of a virtual reality system are high, the costs of building physical models are frequently higher. A physical model costs real dollars both in terms of the direct labor and materials costs required for its construction and in terms of the opportunity costs of the lost sales opportunities of the calendar time required to respond to changing market conditions.

MODELING

The construction of physical models has always been an important part of the design process. There are certain design elements, the spacing between a car door and the frame, two moving parts that interfere with each other in an unforeseen way, that have traditionally been dealt with through the production of physical models. Although sophisticated visualization techniques have reduced the need for physical models, and virtual reality systems promise to reduce that need even further, the building of physical models remains a costly element in the design process.

Regardless of the sophistication of our visualization systems, the ultimate method for visualizing small parts is through the construction of a physical model. Several methods have been developed for this. The oldest is the use of a numerically controlled milling machine to construct the part. The use of soft materials, such as plastics, for the construction of the model allows less costly machines to be used for the fabrication of prototype models.

A more recent method for the construction of models is through the process of photopolymerization. A merger of chemistry and photography, photopolymerization exploits the fact that certain liquid plastic polymers solidify in the presence of ultraviolet light. The first step in the construction of the model is to describe the three-dimensional entity in terms of slices, which may be as thin as 0.005 inch using today's techniques.

An ultraviolet laser scans the surface of a container of liquid polymer, hardening a thin layer of the liquid. A stage in the container lowers the hardened material into the liquid by the thickness of the slices, and another scan is made. This process is repeated until the entire object is constructed. One major

advantage of this system over a cutting tool-based system is that the technique can construct objects with hollow interiors, representing not only the exterior shape of an object, but its interior characteristics as well.

Once the layer-by-layer scanning process is completed and the object has been constructed, it is removed from the container of liquid and exposed to more ultraviolet light to allow the object to cure.

Three significant factors have, so far, limited the acceptance of this modeling technique. First, the cost of the apparatus begins at about $100,000. Several commercial systems cost several times that amount. Second, the only photosensitive polymers identified to date have the poor characteristic of shrinking during the curing process; this limits the applicability of the process. Third, today's equipment is capable of constructing parts no more than a foot across.

A related technology, selective laser sintering, uses a powder rather than liquid polymer to create the model. After each laser scan, a thin layer of powder is spread across the model in preparation for the next scan. The laser fuses the powder into a solid as it scans the model. The advantage of the powder-based system over the liquid polymer system is that more appropriate materials are available in this form. Researchers hope that in the future this method will allow the use of metal powders, allowing the creation of fully functioning metal parts rather than just plastic prototypes.

The most radical method of model construction makes use of a particle accelerator to build up a model one particle at a time. This technology, called ballistic particle manufacturing, is still in its early development stages. Although it holds promise for the future, it is not available as a commercial product today.

CONCLUSION

The acceptance of CAD/CAM software technology has exploded in concert with the advances in processor, memory, display, and disk technologies that make CAD and CAM possible. As the price/performance ratio of CAD/CAM systems continues to improve, additional applications for the technology continue to emerge. As a result, CAD/CAM promises to be a growth technology through the end of the century.

Paul L. Schlieve

COMPUTER-AIDED SOFTWARE ENGINEERING

In its broadest interpretation, the acronym CASE connotes computerized support for information systems development and maintenance. Historically, the acronym referred to computer-aided (or -assisted) software engineering. Today, some prefer the broader connotation of computer-aided *systems* engineering.

There are CASE tools that support information systems planning, systems design, construction (or code generation), and program code reengineering. Design activities include data structure modeling, process modeling, and real-time modeling, each with its own methodology. Sometimes these various functions of CASE are combined into a single integrated tool called I-CASE.

There is a dual imperative behind the use of CASE, an imperative in both *quantity* and *quality*. CASE improves quantity by assisting people to be *faster* and more productive at building information systems. CASE improves quality by assisting people to develop *better*, more reliable information systems.

FEATURES OF CASE

Several characteristics contribute to the objectives of CASE in assisting the human-intensive activities of systems development and maintenance:

- *Central repository* to capture and store *all* design specifications for a developing information system, and do it only once
- *Graphical representations* of design modeling specifications for more effective and rapid human communication
- *Reusable code and design specifications*, using parts from earlier systems or suggested starting designs from third-party vendors, building up libraries of common elements that can be reused in new systems development, rather than starting from scratch with each new development project
- *Automatic generation* of definitions and software code for the designed information system for a target computing platform
- *Management tools* for project control, access control (security), and documentation

Using comprehensive CASE tools produces several results:

- *Computerized analysis* of proposed design models and specifications
- *Application of discipline and standards* in the design and development process
- *Coordination of teamwork* across several designers and users
- *Iteration* over several revisions of a proposed design
- *Production* of graphic representations and supporting *documentation*
- *Versioning or configuration management*, as the design for a system is periodically frozen for production and delivery to the users

Does the use of CASE tools reduce systems development time? CASE technology may require additional time and effort in planning and design because of the increased discipline of a methodology and adherence to standards; however, CASE adds elements of quality and flexibility. Because iterative revision is easier, developers are better able to modify and enhance existing designs and existing systems. It also is easier to maintain, modify, and enhance information systems. The result is increased responsiveness to changing user needs and external environmental demands.

Every CASE tool embodies some system development methodology. The *engineering* in CASE connotes a disciplined, systematic, and rigorous approach. CASE tools use standardized procedures and representations for what system developers do. Consistent, standardized representations, especially in graphical models, result in clearer, more complete documentation for better human communication. A methodology applied manually can be burdensome, but with computerized support it becomes more practical.

CASE TOOLS IN THE SYSTEMS DEVELOPMENT LIFE CYCLE

Information systems pass through a life cycle: planning, design, construction, installation, operation, maintenance, and revision. Figure 1 categorizes CASE tools according to the function supported in the system development life cycle.

Front-end or upper CASE tools capture design specifications. These specifications may range from planning objectives and system requirements to detailed design models, data definitions, programming steps, and so forth. Back-end or lower CASE tools operate on generated or existing software code. A construction tool uses the information in the design database or repository to generate software code.

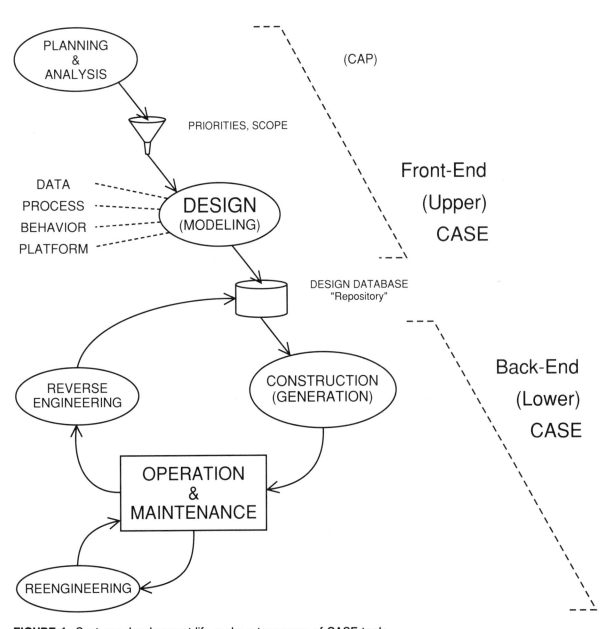

FIGURE 1. Systems development life cycle: a taxonomy of CASE tools.

Any particular CASE tool may emphasize a particular phase or function. Most CASE tools span multiple functions to some extent. For example, a back-end tool is used primarily for system construction or generation, yet, to operate standalone, it must still have some front-end mechanism for capturing design specifications. (Alternatively, it can extract such specifications from a design database prepared by some other CASE tool.)

The major functions supported by CASE tools:

1. *Planning.* Developing *global architectures* and setting *priorities* by looking at objectives, problems, opportunities, critical success factors, and other factors.
2. *Design (modeling).* Developing *models* of a system. Each system is a piece of the global architecture. Modeling may be done from differing viewpoints—data, processes, real-time control, the computer and communications platform—each using its own methodology and diagramming conventions.
3. *Construction.* Building or generating the system from a set of design specifications to run on a target computing platform.

CASE tools also support reconstruction or redevelopment functions:

4. *Reengineering.* Rebuilding and restructuring existing computer programs to make them easier to understand, maintain, and revise, thus prolonging their life.
5. *Reverse engineering.* Extracting information from existing computer programs and putting specifications into the design database to provide a starting point for enhanced systems development.

A central objective of CASE technology is to provide the systems developer with a unified and consistent working environment—a workbench. There are two approaches to achieving this objective. The first is a set of functions integrated into a single CASE tool. The second is to use multiple CASE tools as components, allowing developers to pick the tools that most closely fit their approach to design and development.

"REPOSITORY": THE DESIGN SPECIFICATION DATABASE

Front-end CASE tools capture and store information in the design database, also called a data dictionary, information system resource catalog, encyclopedia, or repository. It contains all information about the information system being designed. It includes graphic representation of models, descriptions of various types of objects in the system, and the interactions between objects in the models.

The objects described in a design database may include descriptions and specifications for planning objectives; system requirements; people and organizational units that use systems; databases (stored collections of data files); screen displays of data, menus, helps; printed output reports; control flows of operations, dialogue flows, and executable instructions (programs), sometimes with critical time sequence dependencies; and computer sites and communication links.

CASE SUPPORT FOR SYSTEM PLANNING

CASE planning tools assist in developing an organization's information system architecture. Such an architecture is a blueprint for a portfolio of information system applications. The architecture is composed of potentially four high-level views: the process architecture, the information architecture, the control architecture, and the technology architecture (see Figure 2).

A CASE tool may be designed to provide direct support for one (or more) planning methodologies. These methodologies generally involve preparing lists of planning objects and then cross-referencing them to identify interactions. The planning objects may be business functions or activities, categories of information or subject databases, organizational goals and objectives, major user groups or organizational units, key problems or opportunities, critical success factors, or key decisions. Some CASE tools dictate, others suggest, categories of planning objects—the categories of things about which information is gathered. The most common categories are business functions and databases. A cross-reference matrix of

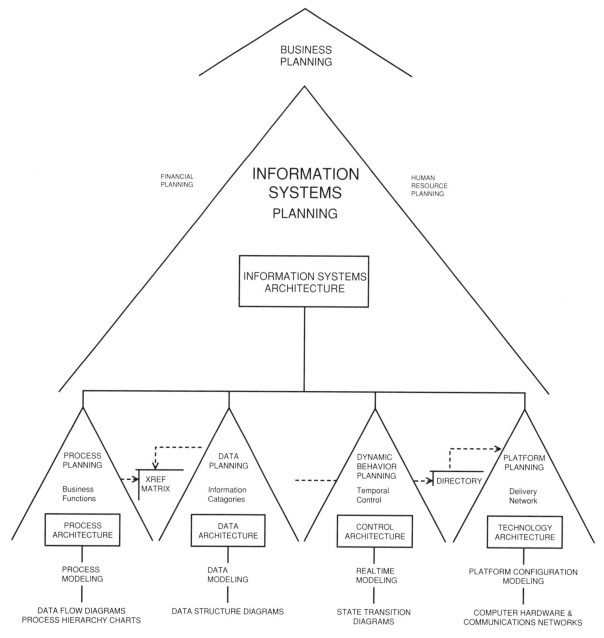

FIGURE 2. Components of an information systems architecture.

these two has been called an "information architecture." An example is shown in Figure 3.

To serve as a basis for planning and setting priorities for subsequent design and development activities, the descriptions of information categories and business functions must also indicate how well an information need of a business function is cur-

rently being satisfied, the level of quality of an information category, and the criticality of an information category to the organization. Some of this information is derived from cross-reference matrices.

An information × process matrix shows where, by whom, and how information is or will be used to support various business functions and decision-making activities.

BUSINESS FUNCTION/ENTITY TYPE USAGE MATRIX

Key: (Enter highest classification only)
C CREATE
D DELETE
U UPDATE
R READ ONLY

ENTITY TYPES	GOVERNMENT CONTRACTS	PURCHASING	RECEIVING	WAREHOUSING	LEGAL SERVICES	GENERAL ACCOUNTING	COST ACCOUNTING	ORDER PROCESSING	SHIPPING	PACKING	MATERIAL REQUIREMENTS	RELEASE PLANNING	FINITE CAPACITY SCHEDULE	FACTORY MONITORING	METHODS ENGINEERING	FACILITY MAINTENANCE	BASIC RESEARCH	PRODUCT DESIGN	SCRAP DISPOSAL	EMPLOYEE RECORDS MAIN	PAYROLL AND BENEFITS	EMPLOYEE TRAINING	SECURITY	TRANSPORTATION PLANNING	FLEET MANAGEMENT	FLEET AQUISITION	FLEET MAINTENANCE	VEHICLE DISPOSAL
SALES ORDER						R	R	C	U	U	U	R	R	R		R								R	R			
CUSTOMER								U	R	R						R									R			
CONTRACT	C															R												
SHIPMENT			C																						R			
SUPPLIER	R	R	U			R	R									R									R			
PURCHASE ORDER			R	R							R	R	R			R						R						
PRODUCT		R	R		R			R	R	R	R	R	R			R	C	R				R						
RAW MATERIAL		U	U								U					R												
CHEMICAL		U	U								U					R												
SHOP SUPPLY		C									R	R																
WORK ORDER											R	C	U	R														
WAREHOUSE			R	C																U								
BIN			U	C						R										U								
SUPPLIER INVOICE	U	C				R	U																					
LEDGER ENTRY						C	C																					
PRODUCT INVENTORY		R	U	R				U		U		R	R							U								

FIGURE 3. An ''information architecture.'' *Reprinted by permission of Texas Instruments.*

This can be depicted in a two-way table or matrix. The number of connections or the absence of connections in the matrix can provide useful information. For example, assume a matrix with information categories down the rows and business functions or processes across the columns.

- A row with no entries indicates no source or usage of that information category.
- A row with multiple sources may indicate inefficiency and inconsistent data.
- A row with many usages indicates a widely needed information category that should be given priority in the development of information systems if those data are not currently available, that is, no data sources appear in that row.
- A row with only sources may indicate that information is being produced but not being used.
- A column with no entries indicates a business activity that neither produces nor uses any information, an unlikely situation.

CASE SUPPORT FOR SYSTEMS DESIGN (MODELING)

An information system is actually a single entity, but there are different *views* of the same entity, of the same whole. Useful views focus on or emphasize some particular aspect of the whole. These views focus on processes, data, temporal behavior, and the computer systems and communications network. These views are complementary, no one being self-sufficient in describing an information system.

Process Modeling

Process planning focuses on the business functions of an organization to develop a process architecture or application systems architecture. In its simplest form, the process architecture consists of a profile of major business functions performed in an organization, how they flow in a sequence, and the information that is transferred from one to the next. The major business functions can be decomposed into detailed processes, which may be manual or automated. The performance of business functions generally translates to application systems running on one (or more) computer system. Methodologies and diagramming techniques, such as Data Flow Diagrams (DFDs) and process hierarchy charts, represent some of the detailed design products of process modeling. CASE tools are used in drawing these charts. An example is shown in Figure 4.

The processes in a typical data flow diagram can be decomposed down to the level of individual computer programs.

CASE tools support various modeling techniques to represent the flow of control and data within a computer program. One example uses action diagrams to model a computer program (see Figure 5).

Data Modeling

Data modeling tools are used to identify the categories of data that are useful to, or used in, the business functions of an organization. The designer identifies entities, objects or events, in the real world of a community

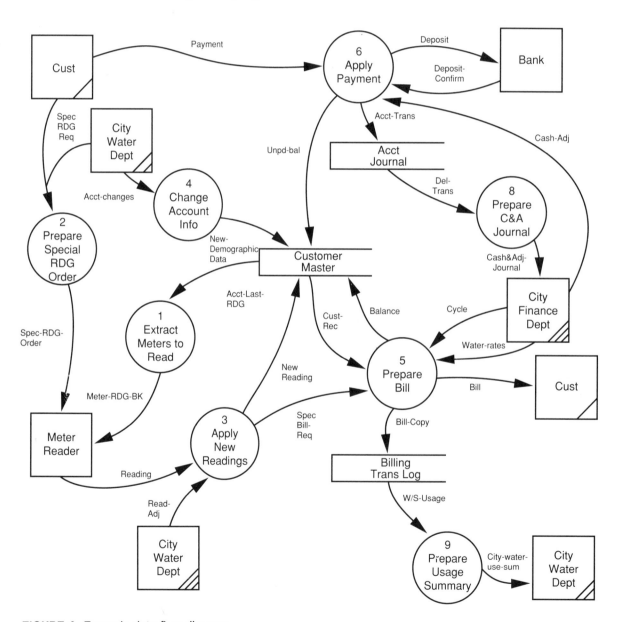

FIGURE 4. Example data flow diagram.

of users, and describes those entities, their attributes, and their interrelationships. CASE tools can support various data modeling methodologies and diagramming techniques.

An example of a data structure diagram is shown in Figure 6 (as produced in the Excelerator CASE tool from Intersolv, Inc.). This diagram highlights data entities (in an oval) and relationships (arcs between ovals) without showing any details regarding the attributes of the entities.

Behavioral Modeling

For certain types of computer-based systems, dynamic and temporal control aspects are important for the proper operation of the system in its environment. Such systems are called real-time or embedded systems. System environments requiring real-time modeling include aerospace (avionics) and defense, telecommunications, on-line transaction processing, robotics, process control, and interactive software for personal computer workstations. Several CASE tools allow a systems developer to design a system using behavioral modeling methodologies.

CASE CONSTRUCTION AND RECONSTRUCTION TOOLS

Back-end or lower CASE tools support the actual construction or implementation of systems. Some examples of these tools are those that support the generation of

- program code, in COBOL or other programming languages
- Data Definition Language (DDL) statements plus integrity constraints
- Structured Query Language (SQL) statements for database processing
- database management system definition of screens, reports, and menus, etc.
- test data

As their results are easier to measure and their objectives easier to define, back-end construction tools were the first in use (even before the acronym CASE emerged). They are generally less expensive and easier to

Process: ADD_NEW_CUSTOMER

```
ADD_NEW_CUSTOMER
IMPORTS: Entity View candidate customer
EXPORTS: Entity View newly_created customer
ENTITY ACTIONS: Entity View brand_new customer

    READ brand_new customer
            WITH name EQUAL TO candidate customer name
    WHEN not found
        CREATE brand_new customer
        SET name TO candidate customer name
        SET number USING calculate_customer_number
            WHICH IMPORTS : Entity View candidate customer
        SET street_address TO candidate customer street_address
        SET city TO candidate customer city
        SET state TO candidate customer state
        SET phone_number TO candidate customer phone_number
        SET credit_limit TO 0
        SET date_added TO CURRENT_ DATE

    MOVE brand_new customer TO newly_created customer
```

FIGURE 5. Example action diagram to model a computer program. *Reprinted by permission of Texas Instruments.*

implement in an organization, but their impacts are primarily at the construction phases of systems development, and therefore limited in the long term.

Most companies have a sizable investment in their current system base. One way to reduce the cost of maintenance is to bring the current applications up to date with the new technology in the shortest possible time; the other is to try to extend the life of the applications and therefore spread, and simplify, the conversion phase. Two types of CASE tools are useful in this transition: reengineering and reverse-engineering tools. Reengineering tools help rebuild, clean up, maintain, restructure, and prolong the life of existing programs. Reverse-engineering tools extract the essential processing logic from current systems with a view to replacing them with newly developed software.

For Further Reading

Case, A. F., Jr. 1986. *Information systems development principles of computer-aided software engineering.* Englewood Cliffs, N.J.: Prentice-Hall.

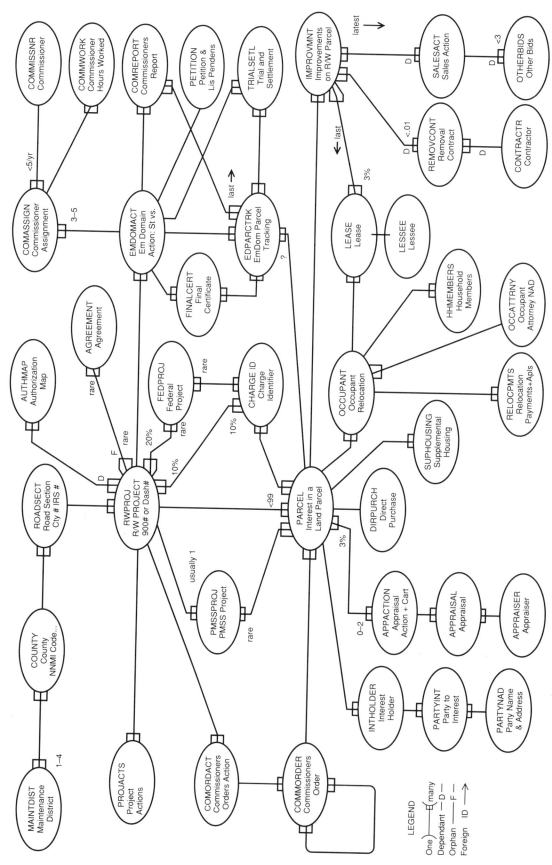

FIGURE 6. Example data structure diagram (from Excelerator), showing structure of a right-of-way database designed for a state transportation agency.

Fisher, A. S. 1988. *CASE—Using software development tools.* New York: Wiley.

Gibson, M. L. 1989. The CASE philosophy. *BYTE,* April, p. 209.

Goldberg, R. 1986. Software engineering: An emerging discipline. *IBM Systems Journal* 25(3):334–53.

Hughes, C. T., and J. D. Clark. 1990. The stages of CASE usage. *Datamation,* February 1, pp. 41–44.

Humphrey, W. S. 1989. *Managing the software process.* Reading, Mass.: Addison-Wesley.

McClure, C. 1989. The CASE experience. *BYTE,* April, p. 235.

Moad, J. 1990. The software revolution. *Datamation,* February 15, pp. 22–30.

Norman, R. J., and J. F. Nunamaker. 1988. An empirical study of information systems professionals' productivity perceptions of CASE technology. In *Proceedings of the Ninth ICIS Conference,* Minneapolis, Minn.

Olle, T. W., et al. 1991. *Information systems methodologies.* 2nd ed. Reading, Mass.: Addison-Wesley.

Rochester, J. B. 1989. Building more flexible systems. *I/S ANALYZER* 27(10).

Zachman, J. A. 1987. A framework for information systems architecture. *IBM Systems Journal* 26(3).

Gordon C. Everest

COMPUTER CENTERS

See Organizing Institutional Information Systems Infrastructure

CONSTRAINT REASONING IN MECHANICAL ENGINEERING DESIGN

Mechanical engineers often design systems by selecting mechanical components, such as motors, transmissions, and hydraulic pumps and valves, from catalogs. This routine, even boring, job seems worth automating. One approach is to treat the selection as a "constraint satisfaction" problem. The user provides to the computer program a schematic drawing showing how the components are to be connected (Figure 1), a catalog of possibilities for each component, and specifications describing, for example, the characteristics of the ice cream stirrer. The program eliminates components that either do not meet the specifications or will not work with the other choices and, finally, arrives at the best combination that will work.

Constraint satisfaction programming has a long history; the first computer-aided design (CAD) drawing system, Sutherland's Sketchpad (Vissell 1990), used constraints in the form of algebraic equations to control the picture displayed on the computer screen. This approach lost favor for 30 years, but is beginning to appear again in advanced CAD systems. Another classic application of constraint propagation determined the meaning of line drawings by examining the possible meanings of corners in the drawings (Waltz 1975). Indeed, even the spreadsheets so widely used in financial analysis can be thought of as simple constraint propagation systems.

Most efforts (e.g., Sussman and Steele 1980) to use numeric constraint propagation in design have involved simple algebraic relationships. For example, if $y=2x$ and $x=2$, the program can conclude that $y=4$; however, mechanical designers often reason about inequalities as well as equalities. For example, if we did not know the exact value of x, but did know that x was between 1 and 2 ($1 \leq x \leq 2$), we could conclude that y was between 2 and 4 ($2 \leq y \leq 4$). Some researchers have investigated the use of such constraints in reasoning about physical systems (Davis 1987), but (as we will see later) even this kind of mathematical process is not adequate to capture some very simple kinds of design reasoning. Hence, one relatively successful mechanical design program is based on a new mathematical formalism called the *labeled interval calculus.*

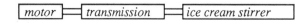

FIGURE 1. A mechanical schematic.

NEW MATHEMATICS FOR OLD PROBLEMS

People often assume that all the mathematics needed for commonplace problems was developed long ago. In fact, as artificial intelligence researchers try to program computers to perform tasks previously done by humans, they often discover new mathematical relationships and operations hiding in quite commonsense kinds of reasoning.

For example, suppose we wanted to select a motor and a mechanical transmission for an ice cream stirrer (Figure 1 again). The design uses a transmission because the motor turns too fast for the stirrer, and also because the motor produces much less torque, or twisting force, than is needed to drive the stirring blades. The transmission trades speed for torque; its output shaft turns more slowly, but with greater twisting force, than its input shaft. The "transmission ratio" r equals the speed of the input shaft divided by the speed of the output shaft. If we ignore friction in the transmission, r also equals the output shaft torque t_0 divided by the input shaft torque t_i; that is, $t_0 = rt_i$. This equation is illustrated in Figure 2; the input torque is on the vertical axis, and the ratio is on the horizontal; each curve has constant output torque.

Suppose that we have available only transmissions with ratios between 2 and 4, as shown by the vertical dashed lines. Then, if we

know something about the torque required at the output shaft, that is, the input to our ice cream stirrer, we may be able to formulate some requirements on the torques at the transmission input shaft, that is, the motor torques. Let us imagine two different cases.

In the first, suppose that we know that any torque over 8, delivered to the stirrer, is likely to damage it. That is, the output torque is restricted to the interval from 0 to 8 (assuming we never want to try to drive the stirrer backward). Looking at the diagram, we see that if the transmission ratio is at its lowest value, 2, a motor torque of 4 will provide a torque of 8 at the stirrer. Any motor torques greater than 4 will damage the stirrer for any transmission ratio between 2 and 4; hence, in our constraint satisfaction process we should eliminate motors providing more torque.

This sort of inference is just the interval constraint propagation described in the introduction. Let us now consider a second kind of inference.

Suppose that we know that depending on the conditions (say, whether the ice cream stirrer is full of room-temperature Ice Milk Lite or cold Double Dutch Chocolate), we may need torques anywhere from 0 to 8 to drive the stirrer. Then, looking at Figure 2, we see that because our maximum possible transmission ratio is 4, any motor with a maximum torque less than 2 should be eliminated. In both cases we started with the same intervals and equations, but our "inferences" produced two different results. Somehow, we used the meaning of the intervals to apply two mathematically different operations. How can we define these operations, and how can we represent the meanings of these intervals in a form the computer can understand?

Suppose we have an equation with three variables, $G(x,y,z)=0$. (We are treating the equation as a variable itself, hence using G rather than any specific equation.) Then we can define an operation called Range, which accepts the equation and two intervals, say for the variables x and y, and returns an interval for the variable z; we write $Range(G,X,Y)=Z$. We can calculate the interval Z simply by solving G for z, then plugging in the endpoints of X and Y—the maximum and minimum of the four results are the endpoints of Z. In our particular example,

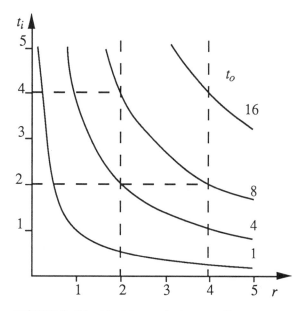

FIGURE 2. The ideal transmission equation.

$G(x,y,z)=0$ stands for $t_0-rt_i=0$; we solve for t_i to form $t_i=t_0/r$, then insert the combinations of t_0 equal to 0 or 8 and r equal to 2 or 4 to get the possible values 0,0,2,4 for t_i. Taking the minimum and the maximum, we have the interval 0 to 4 for t_i.

The second of our inferences used another operation on an equation and two intervals, called Domain. Domain is an inverse of Range, much as division is an inverse of multiplication. We could define division by saying that $x/y=z$ if and only if $yz=x$. Similarly, we can define Domain(G,X,Y) as equal to Z if and only if Range$(G,Y,Z)=X$. Domain, given the ideal torque equation and the intervals 0 to 8 for t_0 and 2 to 4 for r, returns the interval 0 to 2 for t_i. We can check this by applying Range to the intervals 0 to 2 in t_i and 2 to 4 in r; as expected, Range returns the interval 0 to 8 in t_0.

There is one more problem: How does the computer tell which operation to apply? Note that these intervals mean two different things. In both cases, the interval for r meant that r could take *only* values between 2 and 4. In the first case, similarly, the interval for t_0 meant that t_0 could take *only* values from 0 to 8. In the second case, however, the interval for t_0 meant that t_0 must take *every* value from 0 to 8. It is this difference in the meaning of the intervals that caused us to apply a different operation.

The labels *only* and *every* capture these meanings; another four labels are used in "labeled interval calculus." The computer can easily be programmed to recognize appropriate combinations of labeled intervals, apply the required operations, and form new labeled intervals. For example, in the second case above, the computer would produce an interval showing that t_i must take every value from 0 to 2.

The full labeled interval calculus involves more labels, mathematical operations, and *inference rules* that capture a variety of reasoning steps mechanical engineers might use in selecting components. It has become the basis of a program, called a *mechanical design compiler*, that accepts schematics and specifications for mechanical designs from the user and returns to the user a list of the best choices for the components from its built-in catalogs. The program has been tested successfully on a variety of mechanical and hydraulic systems.

References

Davis, E. 1987. Constraint propagation with interval labels. *Artificial Intelligence* 32.

Sussman, G., and G. Steele. 1980. Constraints—A language for expressing almost hierarchical descriptions. *Artificial Intelligence* 14.

Vissell, D. 1990. The father of computer graphics. *Byte* 15.

Waltz, D. 1975. Understanding line drawings of scenes with shadows. In R. Winston, ed. *The psychology of computer vision.* New York: McGraw-Hill.

For Further Reading

Ward, A., and W. Seering. 1989. Quantitative inference in a mechanical design compiler. In *Proceedings of the First International ASME Conference on Design Theory and Methodology, Montreal, Canada.*

Allen C. Ward

COOPERATIVE WORK SYSTEMS

Cooperative work systems are information technology–based environments that support groups of people working together toward a common objective. The cooperative work meetings may be distributed geographically and temporally as well as held in a more traditional face-to-face context. These cooperative work systems have been labeled with a variety of names, including group decision support system (GDSS), group support system, groupware, computer-supported cooperative work (CSCW), group deliberation support system, and group process support system. Each label represents a somewhat different perspective of the application domain. *Electronic meeting systems* is useful as a term to represent the different cooperative work system perspectives.

The information technology environment for cooperative work systems includes meeting rooms with computer hardware and software, audio and video technology, and electronic networks to interconnect offices and meeting rooms and provide access to a wide variety of information sources. Group tasks supported by these electronic meeting systems include communication, planning, idea generation, problem solving, issue discussion, negotiation, conflict resolution, systems analysis and design, and document preparation and sharing.

Cooperative work systems are desirable for a number of reasons. Working environments are becoming increasingly complex and team oriented (Drucker 1988). Organizations are recognizing the need to network, communicate, and generally interact with a wider variety of external stakeholders, interests, and other organizations. There is a heightened interest in teamwork as a mechanism to address organizational problems, enhance commitment, and deal with complexities beyond the scope of any individual's ability.

Cooperative work systems provide a cost-effective technological solution to assist in addressing these issues. These systems provide an extra degree of freedom in group support options that enable groups to work more effectively and efficiently in a single location or in different locations.

Group size, group proximity, and time dispersion are three especially important dimensions to classify electronic meeting system (EMS) environments (Dennis et al. 1988). Each of these dimensions is subdivided as illustrated in Figure 1 to facilitate taxonomy development and develop a sense of the cooperative work system spectrum. This taxonomy extends the work of DeSanctis and Gallupe (1985, 1987) and Johansen (1988) through consideration of group size in addition to aspects of proximity and time dispersion. Further, the proximity dimension is subdivided into three components reflective of the focus of contemporary cooperative work systems. Each of these dimensions is developed in detail and followed by sections illustrating cooperative work system characteristics.

Group size (subdivided in Figure 1 as large or small) is a relative concept, meaning different things to different people. Most of us would agree, though, that a group of three or four members is small while a group of twenty or more is large. Note, however, that a distinction can also be made between the physical size of a group and its "logical" size.

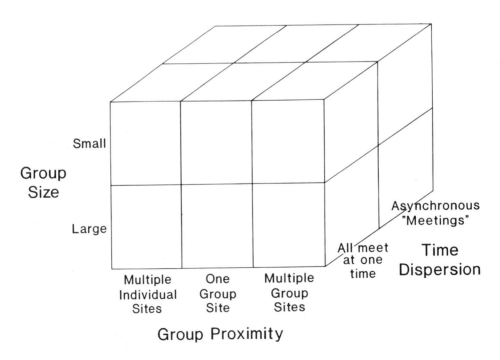

FIGURE 1. Electronic meeting system environments.

A physically large group from a common culture that has met repeatedly on a task may have a high degree of overlapping domain knowledge that results in the group being "logically" small. Conversely, a physically small multicultural group exhibits characteristics of a much larger group with multiple and often conflicting perspectives, points of view, diverse knowledge domains, and opinions. As such, it is "logically" large. For the purposes of this article, we are considering only the physical size of the group that is typically supported in each of the EMS environments discussed, and we will consider groups of size ten or less to be small and those greater than ten to be large.

Group proximity refers to a single group in the sense that all participants are addressing the same task. Not all participants need to be present in the same physical location (i.e., part of one physical group). Group proximity as illustrated in Figure 1 has three levels that describe the degree of geographic dispersion. The first, multiple individual sites, is indicative of situations in which the individual group members are working in their individual offices. The second, one group site, reflects the situation in which all members are in the same place at the same time, for example, a face-to-face environment supplemented by computer support. The third, multiple group sites, represents those situations in which members of the group meet in separate locations in subgroups that are electronically linked with a combination of audio, video, and data channels, for example, teleconferencing combined with additional computer-based support.

The time dimension recognizes that groups may meet synchronously (i.e., at the same time) or asynchronously (i.e., at different times). An important distinction between EMS environments and traditional face-to-face meetings is removal (when appropriate) of the constraint of requiring everyone to be in the same meeting room at the same time. Existing electronic mail and computer conferencing are primitive examples of this capability; however, these technologies lack much of the group dynamic that accompanies a successful meeting. Capturing the essence of a successful meeting that arises as a result of participant synergism and simultaneous exchange, under conditions where not all members are participating at the same time, is a challenge. One intermediate possibility, however, exists under conditions where a larger session can be envisioned as a linked set of subgroup sessions, each of which is conducted in a synchronous fashion, even though the overall group appears to be operating in an asynchronous mode. In this situation the focus shifts to the effective integration of information across sessions and between subgroups.

The following sections present examples of EMS environments to illustrate the application of the taxonomy presented in Figure 1. The category labels (decision room, legislative session, EMS teleconference, EMS teleconference/broadcast, local-area decision net, computer conference) are those most commonly associated with each category and can be used either synchronously (all members meeting at the same time) or asynchronously.

DECISION ROOM

Decision rooms are EMS environments intended to support small groups (typically of four to twelve) where all the participants meet in one place at one time. Such a decision room typically contains a series of networked computer workstations with software that complements face-to-face discussion, plus some form of large front screen or group feedback capability.

Each facility has its own focus and vision that to some extent dictate the functionality provided. Differences also exist among those systems that provide individual workstation support. Some software is directed primarily toward support for small homogeneous cooperative work groups; other software supports larger task forces that may have internal conflicts, strongly vested interests, private agendas, and multiple perspectives in addition to striving toward a shared objective.

The differences and distinctions between various decision room systems are blurring with time through extended software functionality and integration with additional organizational information systems. In addition to supporting groups in which all participants meet at the same time, decision rooms can be used to support asynchronous meetings. In this sense, the decision room becomes a team room. Different project teams meet at different times in the decision room to share information and build toward a common objective. The technology maintains shared files and provides shared agendas and processes.

LEGISLATIVE SESSION

A legislative session is similar to a decision room in terms of use of a single site, but differs in size and degree of audiovisual support. The larger group size supported often necessitates a more "tiered" layout of the room. Verbal communication is complemented by computer-supported interaction accompanied by additional focus on presentation support. For example, the University of Arizona room extends group support capability to up to forty-eight members using twenty-four workstations. Two large-screen projectors provide feedback to the group in conjunction with use of the software tools, as well as presentation support for a wide variety of visual sources including video tapes, videodiscs, and television channels.

Like a decision room, a legislative room can be used for situations in which not all participants are present at the same time, for example, prerecorded comments from some participants or different members wandering in and out of a longer session or a remote hookup for out-of-session review by one or two group members. In the sense that the decision room provides team room asynchronous support for project teams, the legislative room becomes an organization room as different groups use the facility asynchronously to work on a part of a larger objective.

ELECTRONIC MEETING SYSTEM TELECONFERENCE

Electronic meeting system teleconferencing facilities are useful when a small group meets at several separate group sites at the same time. Here, the decision rooms holding the various segments of the group are linked with teleconferencing support. As such, video and audio channels are used to support the face-to-face communication (both verbal and nonverbal) that would occur in the context of a meeting in a single decision room. The addition of EMS workstations for the participants is a particularly significant extension of traditional video conferencing. Existing video conferencing capabilities are too limiting and lack information integration continuity.

Software developed for use in the context of a single decision room has been successfully demonstrated to work for multiple groups in which not all participants meet at the same time. There exists a common "organizational memory" that all facilities draw from based on the accumulated contributions of numerous groups working on a particular project (Nunamaker et al. 1991).

ELECTRONIC MEETING SYSTEM TELECONFERENCE/BROADCAST

Electronic meeting systems can also be used for multiple groups meeting at the same time with a teleconference/broadcast emphasis. Systems of this type are often accompanied by audio feedback to the source, for example, questions to the presenter. Additional support is supplied for asynchronous meetings, for example, taped delay to compensate for worldwide time differences. Perhaps the best known operational examples of systems of this type are those used primarily for educational purposes, both private and public, where courses or special presentations are broadcast to large numbers of geographically distributed locations.

LOCAL-AREA DECISION NET

A local-area decision net is used to support a small group of dispersed individuals working at different sites (such as their offices). Note that a local-area decision net may be used with groups meeting at the same time or asynchronous meetings where participants are working independently. Some of these local-area decision net systems are extensions of electronic mail and calendaring support. Other local-area decision net systems tend to be oriented to shared document preparation as an extension of word processing. They combine electronic mail, word processing, conferencing, and personal utilities with a high degree of user freedom and ability to create custom applications.

Over time, local-area decision net support will increasingly be multimedia oriented, providing technology currently present in EMS teleconferencing domains and embedding it in office workstations. It provides participants with the means for sharing information in such multimedia forms as video images, voice, text, graphics, static images, and hand-drawn figures. It provides integrated support for both asynchronous interaction-based personal work and simultaneous interaction-based cooperative work.

COMPUTER CONFERENCE

In the context of the EMS, computer conferencing provides the opportunity to transmit information from a single source to a large number of recipients. Although use in this fashion is more typically asynchronous, there is nothing to prevent essentially an on-line conference in which a large group of people are simultaneously contributing to various streams of thought in a conference context.

THE FUTURE

In total, these six environments represent aspects of the broader group support arena. Each has some perspectives and features that are relevant to effectively supporting groups. The ultimate goal is to provide a system that effectively and efficiently meets the needs of groups as an integrated part of an organization's information system.

References
Dennis, A., J. George, L. Jessup, J. Nunamaker, and D. Vogel. 1988. Information technology to support electronic meetings. *MIS Quarterly* 12(4):591–624.

DeSanctis, G., and B. Gallupe. 1985. Group decision support systems: A new frontier. *Data Base*, Winter.

———. 1987. A foundation for the study of group decision support systems. *Management Science* 33(5):589–609.

Drucker, P. 1988. The coming of the new organization. *Harvard Business Review* 88(1):45–53.

Johansen, R. 1988. *Groupware: Computer support for business teams.* New York: Free Press.

Nunamaker, J., A. Dennis, J. Valacich, D. Vogel, and J. George. 1991. Electronic meetings to support group work: Theory and practice at Arizona. *Communications of the ACM*, July.

Douglas R. Vogel

COPYRIGHT LAWS

The primary purpose for establishing copyright laws is to stimulate and protect creativity. Copyright protects the form in which an idea is expressed, but not the ideas themselves. Without some form of limited protection, authors and creators would find themselves vulnerable to the theft of their materials and the loss of financial reward for their efforts. The laws, however, also recognize the needs of society to use the materials created and therefore provide authors with a limited time of protection, after which their creations enter the public domain and may be used by anyone without fear of infringement. Most foreign countries also have copyright laws, and the United States has entered into a number of international agreements, the most recent being the Berne Convention, whereby there is mutual recognition of the protection of authors' rights, no matter where the material may have been created.

The United States operated under the copyright law of 1909 until its revision in 1976. Because of the widespread development and use of many technologies not foreseen in 1909, Congress embarked on a major revision of the law, enacted on October 19, 1976, and known as the Copyright Act of 1976, or Public Law 94-553. In Section 102(a) of the new law, a much broader definition of materials eligible for copyright protection was included. This definition states that a copyrighted work is "a work of authorship fixed in any tangible medium of expression, now known or later developed, which can be perceived, reproduced, or otherwise communicated, either with the aid of a machine or device." Computer software falls under this broader definition, but several issues remained unresolved at the time of the adoption of the law regarding the actual rights the author retained and the usage rights of the owner of the software. Congress could not even come to agreement as to the definition of a computer program and what would constitute a "copy."

As a result of the difficulties in defining computer software and additional issues related to photocopying, a commission was appointed to make recommendations to Congress concerning guidelines for the protection and use of new technologies. Known as the National Commission on New Technological Uses of Copyrighted Works (CONTU), this commission submitted its final report on July 31, 1978. Its importance lay in the fact that almost all of the recommendations pertaining to computer software were incorporated into an amendment to the Copyright Act of 1976. This amendment, commonly known as the Computer Software Act of 1980, or Public Law 96-517, became law on December 12, 1980. The majority of court cases that have taken place since that time have centered on the interpretation of this amendment and the intent expressed in the CONTU report.

AUTHOR'S RIGHTS PROTECTED

Under the terms of the Copyright Act, an *author* (a broad term encompassing creators, composers, designers, artists, etc.) is granted the exclusive right to do and authorize:

1. Reproduction of his or her work
2. Preparation of a derivative work based on the copyrighted work

3. Distribution of copies of the work by public sale, by transfer of ownership, or by rental, lease, or lending
4. Performance of the work publicly
5. Display of the work publicly

The preceding protections are offered to all authors and pertain to any medium eligible for copyright protection; however, the law also contains provisions for special exemptions or privileges, some of which apply only to libraries, nonprofit agencies, educational institutions, and other specifically defined groups. When an individual or group exceeds the privileges granted and violates a right given to the author, an infringement takes place. The Copyright Act provides for statutory penalties for infringers and also makes the violator(s) liable to civil lawsuits. As such, it is important that computer users and owners of computer software become more knowledgeable of their rights and responsibilities when they acquire and use copyrighted computer software.

SOFTWARE COPYRIGHT ACT OF 1980 AND USER RIGHTS

The CONTU report recognized a need to provide a definition of computer software in order to be able to interpret eligibility for protection and to provide owners of software with rights of use that would not immediately be interpreted as copyright infringements. Such a definition was incorporated in the Software Act of 1980.

Section 117 of the Copyright Act of 1976 was amended to include the definition of a computer program as "a set of statements or instructions to be used directly in a computer in order to bring about a certain result." Congress, by adopting this definition, qualified computer programs to be registered for copyright as literary works, since such works represent reality through letters, numbers, or symbols.

In addition to the definition, the 1980 amendment to the law included two privileges for the owners of copyrighted programs by permitting the making of another copy or adaptation of the program if the following criteria are met:

1. The new copy or adaptation is created to be able to use the program in conjunction with the machine and is used in no other manner.

2. The new copy or adaptation is for archival purposes only and all archival copies are destroyed in the event that continued possession of the computer program should cease to be rightful.

3. Any copies prepared or adapted may not be leased, sold, or otherwise transferred without the authorization of the copyright owner.

The intent of the preceding, as found in the CONTU report, was to allow an individual or institutional owner of a program to modify or adapt a program to meet local needs (as long as the modification is not a major reworking of the program) and to make a copy of such program for use on his or her machine. This was recognized as necessary because of the variances between pieces of hardware that might make it impossible to use the program on a particular machine. The archival privilege was to permit the creation of a single, protection copy to be held in the event the working copy is destroyed or no longer functions; however, the law does not permit the continuing generation of more replacement copies from the archival copy or the simultaneous use of the archival copy and the original. The archival copy, therefore, cannot act as a second copy of the original. Finally, none of the copies made for either adaptation or archival purposes may be passed on to others, by sale, lease, transfer, or other means, without the permission of the copyright holder, unless the original software is being passed on at the same time.

In addition to the preceding, Congress, by its action in accepting the CONTU report and incorporating it into law, recognized that the mere loading of a program into a single computer's memory did not constitute a violation of copyright, even though, by definition, a copy was being made of the software. Loading of the software was viewed as the only means by which it could be used, and it was not believed that the copyright holder would wish to restrict its use for the purpose for which it was intended.

GUIDELINES, RECOMMENDATIONS, AND CONTINUING ISSUES

As much as the new Copyright Act of 1976 and the addendum of 1980 aided in providing guidelines for authors as well as users, they also opened the door to many questions. Could an owner place a program on a network? Could one disk be used to "boot up" several machines? Is a program that looks similar to the original, but is written in a different code, a violation of the derivative work protection? Are the built-in computer directions found in a chip inside the computer eligible for copyright protection? These questions have been answered, to one degree or another, by interpretation of the law or by court precedent. As with most laws, only those who wrote them actually know their intent and, as well written as they may be, they do not necessarily cover all possibilities. This is especially true in the area of the new technologies, which are continuing to evolve and to interact with each other.

Interpretations of the law are the result of legal opinion based on court cases in related, but not directly similar, circumstances, or on inference as to what was believed to be the intent of the law. The interpretations provide the basis for the development of guidelines that are technically not legal until an issue arises in which they may be tested in court. Even court decisions sometimes result in incomplete clarification of an issue, although they may set some precedents. As such, copyright law continues to undergo changes in interpretation and guidelines, and the user of copyrighted materials should bear in mind that change is possible.

In 1983 and again in 1987, the International Council for Computers in Education issued policy statements consisting of recommendations for educational institutions with regard to computer software. This organization appointed a committee consisting of educators, software developers, and hardware and software vendors whose charge was to address software issues not directly dealt with in the law. The committee stated that multiple machine loading of computer software (loading a computer program into multiple computers with one disk) was not considered a permissible activity and that networking of computers would require obtaining a license for placing software on the network. Even though directed toward educators, the same interpretations would apply for all users of computer programs.

The duplication of a computer chip was found to be an infringement of copyright in the *Tandy Corp. v. Personal Micro Computers, Inc.* case of 1981. The issue was not the physical chip design, but rather that the duplication of the chip also resulted in copying the directions to the computer that were found therein. In the more famous *Apple Computer, Inc. v. Franklin Computer Corp.* case of 1983, Franklin was found guilty of infringing Apple's copyrighted operating system directions to its computer, which were stored on a read-only memory chip. Franklin did not duplicate the chip, but simply copied the directions into its own chip. These cases were important in setting a legal precedent for the opinion that eligibility for copyright protection could go beyond application (end-user) software written in source code (human intelligible). Protected software could now also include directions for the machines' operation written in object code (machine readable only).

In 1986, in the case of *Broderbund Software, Inc. v. Unison World, Inc.*, Broderbund sued Unison for developing a banner-, poster-, and card-producing program that was substantially similar to its *Print Shop* program in the way it presented menus and the sequence of processes on the screen. As a result, a precedent was established for determining possible infringement of the copying or derivative work provisions of the law by reviewing the "look and feel" of the program as it appears on the screen, in addition to the object and source code.

All of the preceding court decisions were made by judges who arguably may not have had the technical background required for such decisions. As a result, there has been debate as to whether the expansion of copyright protection that has taken place is within the intent of the law. For example, a 1990 seminar sponsored by the Practising Law Institute addressed the issue of what parts of a computer program were eligible for protection in the context of the separation of ideas from expression. (Again, ideas and processes are not subject to copyright protection.) The "look and feel" issue was also raised with regard to the flow and sequence of screen displays, as some court decisions have interpreted the order in which screens are presented as copyright protected, while others argue that the sequence is a process. Other areas open to interpretation that affect owners of software are the types of materials that may be scanned or digitized, especially if the items desired are copyrighted, and the extent to which one may print out copies of what appears on a computer screen. (Single screen copying is considered permissible.)

The copyright law exists to protect the rights of the author while providing users of copyrighted materials with certain fair-use privileges. As the use of computer technology continues to expand, so must the authors' and users' knowledge of their rights and limitations according to copyright laws.

For Further Reading

Becker, G. H. 1986 (update 1988). *The copyright game resource guide.* 2nd ed. Longwood, Fla.: G. H. Becker, Consultant.

Copyright and instructional technologies: A guide to fair use and permissions procedures. 1989. Washington, D.C.: Association for Educational Communications and Technology.

Dannay, R., ed. 1990. *Current developments in copyright law.* New York: Practising Law Institute.

Final report of the National Commission on New Technological Uses of Copyrighted Works (CONTU). 1979. Washington, D.C.: Library of Congress.

General guide to the Copyright Act of 1976. 1977. Washington, D.C.: Copyright Office, Library of Congress.

General Revision of the Copyright Law, 17 U.S. Code, Public Law 94–553. Washington, D.C.: U.S. Govt. Printing Office, 1976.

General Revision of the Copyright Law, House Report 94–1476. Washington, D.C.: U.S. Govt. Printing Office, 1976.

General Revision of the Copyright Law, Senate Report 94–473. Washington, D.C.: U.S. Govt. Printing Office, 1976.

General Revision of the Copyright Law, Conference Report 94–1733. Washington, D.C.: U.S. Govt. Printing Office, 1976.

Helm, V. 1984. *Software quality and copyright: Issues in computer assisted instruction.* Washington, D.C.: Association for Educational Communications and Technology.

Johnston, D. F. 1982. *The copyright handbook.* 2nd ed. New York: R.R. Bowker.

Sherman, C. H., Sandison, and Guron. 1989. *Computer software protection law.* Washington, D.C.: BNA.

Strong, W. S. 1984. *The copyright book: A practical guide.* Cambridge, Mass.: MIT Press.

Weil, B. H., and B. F. Polansky. 1989. *Modern copyright fundamentals.* Medford, N.J.: Learned Information, Inc.

Gary Becker

COST/BENEFIT ANALYSIS OF COMPUTER USE

The methods of cost/benefit analysis (CBA) can provide an objective basis for determining the worth of making an investment in a computer system. Costs and benefits of the existing system are compared with costs and benefits of developing and operating a new system. The system being evaluated can be an entire hardware and software system or an application system.

The existing system, as discussed here, may be either a manual system (done by hand) or a computer-based system. The costs considered include hardware, software, personnel, data entry, training, and all other costs associated with developing and operating a business application system such as an accounting system or a video checkout system.

STEPS IN COST/BENEFIT ANALYSIS

The general format of CBA is illustrated in Table 1.

Step 1: Estimate the Cost of Operating the Existing System

If the current system is a computer-based system, then cost estimates can be provided by in-house computer staff, consultants, and/or people who actually use the system. Costs of operating the existing system include computer time, leased or purchased software, peripherals, disk storage, salaries of operators and programmers, salaries of data entry clerks, supplies, and other associated expenses. If a manual system is currently used, then clerical expenses associated with the task should be estimated.

Step 2: Estimate the Costs of Developing and Operating the Proposed System

The proposed system can be a new system (as in going from a manual to a computer-based system or from one computer-based system to an entirely different one) or a major modification to an existing system. In either case, there will be costs associated with developing the proposed system. These costs can include personnel expenses (often the largest cost factor), such as the time needed to write programs and for end users to define their requirements. Other costs include computer hardware, purchased software packages, consultants, communications wiring, supplies, and installation. After a system has initially been developed, it still has to be maintained over time. These costs are referred to as operating expenses and recur each year. Examples of operating expenses include annual hardware maintenance contracts; software upgrades; the costs for personnel to keep the system up and running; supplies such as computer paper, printer cartridges, tapes, and disks; and the cost for storing backup copies of important software and data off-site.

Step 3: Estimate Recurring Benefits of the Proposed System

Benefits are typically expressed in terms of tangible cost reductions and/or the time savings (personnel costs) associated with clerical work. An example of tangible cost reduction is the following: Under the existing

TABLE 1. Sample Cost/Benefit Analysis

Budget Chainsaws
System: Daily Inventory Status Report, Ver. 1
Proposal: Request for Modification

Prepared by: Dick Smith   Date: 01/06/91
Approved by: Janet Clayborn   Date: 02/19/91

	Amount
1. One-time Change Costs	
Personnel expense	
100 workdays analyst	$12,000
200 workdays programmer	16,000
60 workdays clerical	1,920
Machine hours cost	
40 CPU hours	24,500
Equipment and supplies	
Paper and office supplies	200
50 reels magnetic tape	1,250
Subtotal	55,870
2. Recurring Costs and Savings	
Clerical savings, annual, 50 workdays/month	(19,200)
Supplies	(200)
3. Intangible Costs and Savings	
Information available earlier (not quantified)	(0)
Subtotal	(19,400)
4. Payback Period	
55,870/19,400 = 2.88 or less than 3 years	
5. Return on investment over 4 years	
19,400 × 4 − 55,870 / 55,870 = 39%	

system it may cost $2.50 to produce a customer billing statement, whereas it would cost only $0.50 to produce the equivalent statement using the new proposed computer-based system, thus yielding a transaction cost savings of $2.00 per bill. The following is an example of time savings: By implementing the proposed system an organization would save 15 hours of clerical time per week at $10.00 per hour (i.e., $15 \times 10 = \$150.00$ per week) in wages and benefits, or by implementing the proposed system, this organization would avoid the costs of hiring an additional billing clerk as the business expands.

Intangible benefits (not easily quantifiable) should also be identified, even if a specific dollar amount cannot be estimated. Examples of important intangible benefits include more timely management information, reduced customer waiting time for service, better delivery schedules, reduced clerical errors, improved product design, and reduced lead time. One suggested approach for incorporating intangibles into CBA is to identify these in the CBA and then ask management this question: How much is it worth to you to reduce manufacturing lead time, or to reduce customer waiting time by 3 days? The intent here is to get management to recognize the real value of these intangibles and to perhaps assign lower and upper boundary benefits in dollar terms (i.e., managers may respond that the intangible would be worth more than $50,000 but less than $100,000).

Step 4: Calculate Payback Period
The term *payback* refers to the time needed for system benefits to equal (or "pay back") the cost of the investment. For example, in Table 1, the costs of the system ($55,870) divided by the recurring benefits of $19,400 per year means that the projected investment would presumably pay for itself in less than

3 years. This is a rough but often useful measure.

Step 5: Calculate Return on Investment

In addition to the payback technique, some organizations may elect to use return-on-investment (ROI) analysis. To calculate a rough ROI for benefits that occur evenly over the useful life, divide the average annual benefits by the average investment. Table 1 shows both payback and ROI calculations. More sophisticated techniques can also be applied.

BENEFITS OF COST/BENEFIT ANALYSIS

Major benefits and limitations of CBA are summarized in Table 2. Benefits of CBA include the following:

- It permits an objective basis for determining the worth of a computer system investment relative to other investment opportunities.
- It is calculated using standard accounting techniques for capital investments that are familiar to most executives.
- It serves as a benchmark for postimplementation audits; that is, once the computer system is actually implemented, it allows an organization to answer the question "Were the predicted benefits actually achieved within the estimated costs?"
- As managers frequently turn over, a CBA also provides some protection from criticism by new managers who ask the information services department to justify the

current level of expenditures; that is, even though absolute expenditures may have gone up, a CBA can justify these by the cumulative savings over time in affected user departments.

LIMITATIONS OF COST/BENEFIT ANALYSIS

Cost/benefit analyses for proposed systems are always projections of what the costs and benefits should be. The real question is whether the computer system, once implemented, in fact delivered what was projected within the cost guidelines. A possible discrepancy between actual and projected costs/benefits is not really a limitation of the CBA method, but rather a reminder that the projected worth of an investment does not always equal its actual worth. Also, both the risk of doing and the risk of not doing the project must also be weighed in any kind of investment analysis.

Cost/benefit analyses are most easily applied to computer systems where productivity gains are relatively easy to measure (e.g., accounting systems, order entry systems). Bottom-line payoffs become more difficult, if not infeasible, to assess where computer systems are designed primarily to support white collar managerial decision making (e.g., market analysis, sales forecasting, expert systems). In such cases, the benefits are important, but often soft (hard to measure). Using CBA does not take into account the strategic importance of the investment to the company. For example, applications such as computer integrated manufacturing (CIM) are geared toward providing soft benefits such as increased

TABLE 2. Major Benefits and Limitations of Cost/Benefit Analysis

Benefits	Limitations
Provides objective basis for assessing a computer system investment	Is an estimate versus actual costs and benefits
Uses standard accounting methods	Difficult to apply to systems designed to improve white collar decision making and productivity
Serves as benchmark for postimplementation audit	
Provides justification for current expenditure levels	Does not assess strategic business impact of a system investment

shop floor flexibility, improved quality, better responsiveness to the customer, innovative expansion of products, and reduced lead time. Although these benefits may be hard to quantify individually, collectively they can reduce operating costs and increase sales over time.

ALTERNATIVE APPROACHES TO COST/BENEFIT ANALYSIS

Given the limitations of traditional CBA, organizations have turned to alternative approaches for assessing the worth of a potential computer system investment. Three of these approaches are briefly described here: the time-savings-times-salary, work value analysis, and body count models.

Schwartz (1987) has summarized several alternatives to traditional CBA for justifying systems, notably the time-savings-times-salary (TSTS) and work value analysis (WVA) models. The TSTS model is based on projected increases in efficiency among white collar professionals as a result of implementing a proposed computer system. In this method, office professionals are asked to estimate the time they spend in specific activities. Time savings from implementation of a proposed system are then calculated and expressed in dollar salary savings. If, for example, they estimated that 10 percent of their workday was spent attempting to contact people on the phone (i.e., "playing telephone tag") and the proposed electronic mail system was projected to reduce that time to 5 percent, then the savings are figured as follows: 10 percent multiplied by a 40-hour week, multiplied by 5 percent, multiplied by an hourly salary. To illustrate,

$$0.10 \times 40 \qquad = 4 \text{ hours}$$
$$4 \text{ hours} \times 0.05 \quad = 2 \text{ hours}$$
$$2 \text{ hours} \times \$20.00 = \$40.00$$

The cost savings per week would equal $40 for each manager (or 40 × 52 weeks = $2,080 annual cost savings per manager). The flaw in the TSTS model is that it fails to distinguish between time saved on lower-value activities (e.g., clerical work) and higher-value activities (e.g., market analysis).

Work value analysis, unlike TSTS, explicitly evaluates the payoff from a computer system as it affects the effectiveness as well as efficiency gains of white collar professionals. To accomplish this, WVA explicitly distinguishes between high- and low-value managerial activities. High-value activity might be that of an accountant analyzing a company's cash flow needs or a marketing manager designing new products. On the other hand, a low-value activity might be the clerical work that is part of every professional's job. In this model, effectiveness is recognized as a shift in the professional's work profile that produces more valued activities. With wages used as a benchmark, the dollar worth of changes in work patterns can be determined analytically. For a more detailed discussion of the WVA method, see Schwartz (1987).

A third alternative to CBA is what one executive refers to as the "body count" model. To illustrate, a bank executive was told by the information services manager that the purchase of a fourth-generation language would significantly improve the productivity of bank programmers. As one way that productivity can be improved is to produce the same level of output with fewer inputs (staff resources in this case), the executive approved the purchase of the fourth-generation language with the provision that the information systems manager would reduce staff by two in exchange for the tool. (Staff members were not actually laid off; rather, it was understood that when programmers left the organization, their two positions would be eliminated.) The point here is that it would have been hard to justify the cost of a fourth-generation language (or any other programmer "productivity tool" for that matter) by using strict CBA because the benefits are often difficult or infeasible to measure.

In conclusion, a CBA can permit an objective basis for determining the worth of a proposed computer system investment, as well as yield other important benefits. Cost/benefit analysis, however, does have limitations and should be used carefully in conjunction with other methods of justifying technology expenditures.

Reference

Schwartz, P. 1987. When you're asked to cost-justify systems. *Computerworld* (In Depth section), August 3, pp. 47–52. Excellent summary of alternative approaches to cost/benefit analysis, especially for those computer systems that are oriented toward improving white collar productivity.

For Further Reading

Connell, J. J. 1986. Operating goals determine ultimate cost effectiveness of PCs. *Data Management,* September, pp. 41–43.

Lay, P. M. 1985. Beware of the cost/benefit model for information system project evaluation. *Journal of Systems Management,* June, pp. 30–35.

Lincoln, T. 1986. Evaluating the returns from information technology. *Management Accounting* 64(4):24–26.

McFarlan, W. F. 1981. Portfolio approach to information systems. *Harvard Business Review,* September–October, pp. 142–150.

Polakoff, J. C. 1990. Computer integrated manufacturing: A new look at cost justifications. *Journal of Accountancy,* March, pp. 24–29. This article describes the traditional accounting cost justification methods of payback, return on investment, net present value, and internal rate of return. It also discusses the limitations of these traditional approaches.

Singleton, J. P., E. R. McLean, and E. N. Altman. 1988. Measuring information system performance: Experience with the management by results system at Security Pacific Bank. *MIS Quarterly* 12(2):325–37.

Diane Lockwood

CRAY, SEYMOUR

Seymour Cray was born in Chippewa Falls, Wisconsin, on September 28, 1925. His father was a city engineer in Chippewa Falls. After a few years as an electrician in the army, Cray began his college education at the University of Wisconsin in Madison. He later transferred to the University of Minnesota. Cray received a bachelor's degree in electrical engineering in 1950 and a master's degree in 1951.

Cray began in the computer business working for Engineering Research Associates (ERA) and its successors, Remington Rand and Sperry Rand Corporation. Engineering Research Associates was a pioneering computer firm started in 1946 by a small group that included William NORRIS. Cray involved himself in circuit, logic, and software design, a collection of subjects that few could do all at once. He designed the ERA 1101, one of the first scientific machines. He was the main designer on the UNIVAC 1103 computer.

In 1957 Cray, along with William Norris and seven others, left Sperry Rand Corporation to start a new company, Control Data Corporation (CDC). Tremendous number-crunching capabilities are required to process scientific data. Cray was determined to build superfast and superpowerful computers to meet these needs. Cray convinced the company president, William Norris, to build such equipment. The computers could be sold to aircraft firms, universities, and the Department of Defense. Such clients did not need heavy investment in support or marketing and they could do their own programming. Cray's first project, the CDC 1604 computer, was so successful in the scientific community that CDC built a private laboratory for Cray in his hometown. The laboratory was within walking distance of Cray's house. The CDC 6600 computer followed 5 years later. This was the most powerful computer of its time. The CDC 6600 was the first computer to employ a freon cooling system, to prevent the densely packed components (the CDC 6600 had 350,000 transistors) from overheating. But it was not until the 1969 introduction of the CDC 7600, considered by many to be the first supercomputer, that Cray found his computing niche. Later, Cray designed the CDC 8600, but CDC chose not to market it.

Cray left CDC in 1972 to set up Cray Research Inc. with $500,000 in startup money from CDC. Cray insisted that the new firm would build only supercomputers and that it would build them one at a time. Cray Research had become the dominant force in supercomputers by the late 1970s.

The first CRAY-1 supercomputer made its debut in 1976 at Los Alamos National Laboratories. The CRAY-1 was unique; it was the first practical and effective example of vector processing, in which the computer works on many different parts of the problem at once. This high-speed parallel processing is meant to increase processing rates.

Three years after the debut of the CRAY-1, Cray Research announced the decision to build the CRAY-2, which was to have six to twelve times as much power as the CRAY-1. The first production model was released in 1985. It had the largest internal memory capacity of any computer—2 billion bytes—and a speed of 1.2 billion floating-point operations per second.

By early 1985, Cray was working on a follow-up to the CRAY-2, to be called the CRAY-3. This computer has an 8-billion-byte memory and is five to ten times faster than its predecessor.

Seymour Cray is the man who put the speed and the "super" into the supercomputer. Without his systems, what now takes seconds to solve would have required months, maybe even years.

For Further Reading

Slater, R. 1989. *Portraits in silicon*, pp. 195– 204. Cambridge, Mass.: MIT Press.

Donald D. Spencer

CREDIT SYSTEMS

The process of granting credit is one with which most of us are familiar. The company granting credit (retailer, bank, etc.) gathers information from the consumer on a credit application, uses that information to make a decision on the consumer's creditworthiness, and sets up an account and issues a credit card(s) if the consumer is accepted. In most large companies today, the process is almost completely automated. The information on

the application is entered into a new accounts system, which provides a recommendation within seconds.

The system checks for duplicate accounts using name and address, and requests credit reports from one or more credit bureaus. Credit bureaus compile data on a consumer's credit history from many companies and then provide that history to help a company decide whether or not to grant credit. Credit reports are sent electronically from the credit bureaus to the new accounts system, which uses the credit history information along with demographic data from the credit application to "score" the applicant.

In scoring an applicant, points are assigned for various characteristics and then summed up to determine an overall score. Points are assigned according to scoring models in the new account system. The models are developed by statistical analysis of historical data to identify the characteristics that are the best predictors of creditworthiness. Many times, characteristics in these models are intuitively obvious, such as number of bankruptcies, but often, other characteristics prove to be excellent predictors. For example, residing in a mobile home may be assigned a very high score in some models if statistics show that these people are rarely delinquent in paying their bills. If the applicant's score is sufficiently high, credit is granted. In many cases, the system then rescores the applicant according to a different model to determine how much credit to extend. Building on the previous example, the person living in the mobile home could be very likely to pay his or her bills, but might not be able to handle a high credit limit. If a decision is made to deny credit, the new accounts system will generate a letter informing the applicant according to legal guidelines. Also, the system retains all of the information about the application in the event of a question or legal challenge.

Scoring is a process used by companies to make better decisions on granting credit and thus reduce bad debt expense. The desire to reduce bad debt must be balanced against the desire to encourage credit use; thus each company must make a judgment call regarding the scoring threshold required to receive credit and how much credit to extend. The models and thresholds are also adjusted periodically to reflect economic and demographic changes.

On approval, new accounts systems produce an electronic record of the customer's account that is used to set up the customer's account on authorization and billing files or databases. A record is also sent to a card embossing machine, which encodes information such as account number, expiration date, and name in the magnetic stripe on the back of the card and embosses the account number and name on the front of the card.

The next step in the process is credit authorization and control. The authorization process has the same basic goal as the new accounts process—to enable the use of credit by consumers yet control bad debt expense at the same time. In today's most sophisticated authorization systems, purchase information is entered into an electronic cash register, also known as a point-of-sale (POS) terminal. Many POS systems are able to read data from the magnetic stripe on the credit card, not only speeding up the transaction but also providing an extra measure of security because special codes in the magnetic stripe enable a company to be certain that the card itself was used at the POS, as opposed to the account number being key entered. The POS system in the store is connected to a network that can transmit authorization requests to an authorizing system. Within seconds, the authorization system sends a response back through the network to the POS system.

The response is one of the following: approval, contingent approval, hard referral, or soft referral. The POS system immediately completes the sale transaction if it receives an approval, and captures an authorization code sent back by the authorizing system. A contingent approval means that the purchaser must satisfy a contingency before the sale is completed. Requiring the customer to show a picture identification, restricting use of the account to only the cardholder or spouse, and requiring the card user to have a purchase order are examples of contingencies. Contingencies are typically used to place restrictions on accounts based on account holder requests, or as an extra precau-

tion in the case of a high level of recent activity. A hard referral causes the sale to be canceled; credit is denied. This would occur when a card is lost or stolen or when an account is severely delinquent. A soft referral response occurs when a consumer's account is slightly delinquent or over its credit limit. The salesperson is required to call a credit authorizer to obtain approval to complete the sale. In these cases, the credit authorizer may wish to talk to the consumer prior to approving the request. Assuming the response from the consumer is satisfactory, the authorizer provides an approval code to the store salesperson, which is then entered into the POS system. The codes are used to ensure that proper authorizing procedures were followed.

Many authorizing systems use scoring models like new accounts systems. Unlike new accounts, the scoring models are based primarily on a customer's actual credit history with the company because this history is a better predictor of that customer's future credit performance. They are used to determine the authorizing response, and in some cases are used to adjust credit limits automatically.

System performance is a critical issue for authorizing systems because they frequently must handle hundreds or even thousands of requests per second. They must not only be very fast; they must also be extremely reliable. To maximize speed, the amount of data used to process an authorization request is kept to a minimum. For example, a consumer's authorization score can be periodically calculated and stored for use when a request is processed. At each request, the authorization system needs only to access the score plus other critical data, rather than access all of the history used to compute the score. To improve reliability, redundancy is often built into components of the network and of the systems. As an example, an authorization system might run on a host computer, with a similar computer designated as a standby in the event that the main host fails. Redundancy can be very expensive, but the exposure to the business when the system is down is also very great.

Another method used to reduce exposure and ensure prompt responses is use of floor limits. Point-of-sale and authorizing systems automatically approve transactions below floor limits whenever a request cannot be fully processed through the authorizing network. On-line floor limits are used when the network is up but is too busy to keep up with the volume, and off-line floor limits are used when the network, or any part of the network, is down.

When a sale has been authorized, it must subsequently be billed by the billing system. On the surface, this seems simple and straightforward: take the consumer's beginning balance, add new charges, subtract payments and credits, and bill the customer the new balance. In actuality, this process can be very complicated.

First, billing systems must deal with many legal issues. Each state has laws governing interest rates and other terms relating to financing, and billing systems must be able to support all of the laws that apply to a company's business. Some of the other terms include late fees, minimum payments, and disclosures of any changes.

In many cases, billing systems must support many different payment plans. For example, a retailer may offer terms of "no payment for 90 days" on a particular item. The system must hold a record of that sale and release it for billing at the appropriate time. Many department stores also offer special accounts with unique billing rules for items such as jewelry and furniture. The system must support all of these special rules in addition to the rules for "normal" accounts.

Support for customer service is a critical element of all billing systems. The customer must be able to call and have questions about his or her bill answered accurately and quickly. To expedite this process, reference numbers are generated for each purchase on the bill, and detailed data regarding that purchase are stored by reference number for easy retrieval. Many companies provide a voice response system for inquiries into their billing systems. Voice response devices can answer a customer phone call and determine the type of question. If the question is routine, for example, What is my balance? and What is my credit limit?, the system can

access data in the billing system and formulate a voice response without any human intervention. Nonroutine questions are forwarded to customer service personnel. In the event of an error, billing systems have the ability to make adjustments to purchases, finance charges, and other fees.

Billing systems often must bill millions of customers each month. To spread the workload, groups of customers known as *cycles* are formed. A company using ten billing cycles would bill approximately 10 percent of its customers every 3 days. Each cycle bills on the same day each month, with some variance at the end of the month for 31- and 28-day months. Each cycle has a cutoff date, also referred to as a billing date. All transactions dated prior to the billing date are billed and shown on the statement.

In addition to spreading the computer workload, cycles help smooth the mailing process. The billing statements are printed in zip code sequence and then run through a machine called an inserter, which inserts the statements into envelopes. The inserter automatically inserts all pages of a customer's statement(s) into one envelope and will optionally include advertising or disclosure information. The inserter is controlled by bar codes printed on each statement page indicating page number and the options that apply to each customer.

The account number is printed on the remittance coupon portion of the statement to ensure accurate and timely processing of payments. When a payment is received, remittance processing equipment reads the account number from the coupon and the checking account number from the customer's check. In most systems, an operator must key enter the dollar amount, but some systems have handwriting recognition capability that automates the entire process. In either case, the remittance processing equipment electronically forwards the payment data to the billing system for processing into the next set of billing cycles.

When accounts go into arrears, they are placed in the collection process. Collection systems have the unenviable task of supporting the collection of past due expense without upsetting the customers involved. Scoring is again used to facilitate this. Collection scores are similar to authorization scores in that they are based on the customer's credit history with the company. The systems use the score to determine the appropriate collection efforts as well as the timing of those efforts.

Collection efforts include *dunning*, which means notifying the customer that the account is past due. This is typically done as a message on the customer statement produced by the billing system, and is the first step in the collection process for accounts that are slightly past due and are not likely to default. As an account moves further and further in arrears, the collection effort intensifies to letters and phone calls. Accounts with a high statistical default rate are immediately assigned to more intense activities. Collection systems capture detailed history of the account during the collection process, generate and print the letters automatically for all appropriate accounts, and also automate the phone call process.

Each night, the collection system identifies the customers who should be contacted and produces a schedule for each collector. The collector then attempts to contact the customers and enters the results of the call into the system. Typical entries include "no answer," "promise to pay by xx/xx/xx," "refuses/unable to pay." These data are used to create a collection history for each account which is used by the collector to take appropriate action if another contact is needed. Some collection systems automate the process even more through autodialing. In this case, the daily collection schedule and account history are loaded into an autodialing machine. The autodialer then automatically dials the customers on the schedule. If the phone is not answered, the autodialer updates the account history accordingly. When the phone is answered, the autodialer transfers the call to a collector and displays a record of the customer's collection history on the collector's terminal or PC. Autodialing improves collectors' productivity by eliminating their need to deal with "no answer" phone calls (which account for a large percentage of calls) and by eliminating dialing on the part of the collector. As a result, an autodialer often has more than twice as many outbound phone lines as it has collectors.

In addition to all of the above automation, credit systems also provide companies with another key benefit: customer purchase history. Companies can use this information to direct their marketing and promotional activities to customers whose history indicates that they are likely buyers of particular goods or services.

In conclusion, credit systems are instrumental in virtually every aspect of retailing operations. They provide automation for the entire credit process and enable companies to manage risk associated with credit. Computer systems also make it possible to provide excellent customer service and reduce the expense of running a credit operation.

Jon K. Nordeen

CRIME AND COMPUTERS

See Ethics and Computers; Hacking; Law Enforcement, Computers in; Viruses

CRYPTOGRAPHY

Cryptography is the study of methods for secret writing. This science is one of the two main branches of *cryptology*, the other being *cryptanalysis*. Cryptography formulates procedures and algorithms for the scrambling or *encipherment* of data, usually under the control of a secret *cipher key*. Cryptanalysis, popularly called "code breaking," studies methods of recovering the original data without knowledge of the secret key(s) involved.

The realm of cryptography is vast and includes not only traditional encipherment techniques but also diverse fields such as invisible inks, the hiding of messages in works of art and music, and other techniques of disguised communications.

Before the widespread use of computers, the principal users of cryptography were diplomatic and military agencies. For these users, the desire for secrecy in communications was paramount. Nongovernmental use of cryptography began an expansion during the 1960s that is expected to continue into the foreseeable future. The growth of cryptography among civilian organizations was further accelerated by the development and marketing of microcomputers starting in the 1970s.

Computers and their associated telecommunications networks have presented cryptography with two major problems to solve. The first is protection of data files stored on disks or other electronic media from tampering, alteration, or unauthorized examination. The second is prevention of disclosure of data while in electronic transit between computer systems. In both cases, cryptography scrambles the data involved, so that even if a file is obtained by outside sources, it cannot be read or altered without a knowledge of the scrambling algorithm used and the secret key.

In the private sector, banks and financial institutions are the heaviest users of cryptography. The transfer of funds electronically, which involves the clearing of checks and the authorization of ordinary cash machine transactions, requires messages to be sent over public communications networks where they are often subject to interception. Thus, these communications generally require some form of cryptographic protection to ensure their integrity. The use of electronic mail, which is increasing every year, also mandates data scrambling, particularly when the messages sent contain sensitive or personal information.

BASIC METHODS OF CRYPTOGRAPHIC SCRAMBLING

Although modern cryptographic algorithms are often very complex, there are only three basic procedures for enciphering data: substitution, transposition, and fractionization. Through the employment of these three methods in various combinations, highly secure cryptographic algorithms can be created.

The illustrations show examples of all three cryptographic methods. In Figure 1, the secret keyword COMPUTER is used to scramble the ordinary alphabetic sequence. Below this *keyword mixed alphabet* is written another alphabet. In this example, the second alphabet is the normal A to Z alphabet, but this second alphabet could be mixed as well. Each letter of the message or *plaintext* is found in the top alphabet and replaced by the letter lying directly below it. The top alphabet is called the *plaintext alphabet* and the bottom alphabet, the *ciphertext alphabet*. Finally, the spaces between the words are eliminated to make the final ciphertext harder to solve if it is intercepted by a third party. Anyone who receives the ciphertext and knows the secret keyword can easily reconstruct the system and reverse the encipherment to *decipher* the original message. Because the plaintext letters are substituted for other letters, this method of encipherment is known as (simple) substitution.

Figure 2 shows a transposition cipher. The secret keyword VERMONT is used to derive a mixed sequence of digits from 1 to 7. This mixed sequence is obtained by numbering the letters in the keyword from left to right in the order in which they occur in the alphabet. Once the transposition digit se-

PLAINTEXT: C O M P U T E R A B D F G H I J K L N Q S V W X Y Z
CIPHERTEXT: A B C D E F G H I J K L M N O P Q R S T U V W X Y Z

PLAINTEXT: I C A M E I S A W I C O N Q U E R E D
CIPHERTEXT: O A I C G O V I W O A B S T E G H G K

CIPHER WITH WORD DIVISIONS: O AICG O VIW O ABSTEGHGK
CIPHER WITHOUT WORD DIVISIONS: OAICG OVIWO ABSTE GHGK

FIGURE 1. Simple substitution.

KEYWORD: V E R M O N T
TRANSPOSITION SEQUENCE: 7 1 5 2 4 3 6
                            I C A M E I S
                            A W I C O N Q
                            U E R E D

CIPHERTEXT: CWEMC EINEO DAIRS QIAU

FIGURE 2. Columnar transposition.

quence is derived, the plaintext is written by rows into a rectangle as shown and then copied off by columns in an order determined by the digit sequence. In transposition all of the letters of the message are present in the cipher, but in a scrambled order.

Figure 3 uses the keyword TEXAS to construct an alphabet or *Polybius square*, as it is sometimes called. The row and column coordinates of the plaintext letters are then used to translate the plaintext into digit form. In this process, each plaintext letter is represented by two digits written vertically. These two coordinates, the fractions of the plaintext letter, are then scattered by recombining them in rows as is shown.

Because data stored in computers may be thought of as being represented by strings of binary 0s and 1s, the processes of substitution, transposition, and fractionization take place on bit combinations instead of discrete letters; otherwise, the ideas and procedures involved are the same.

THE TWO TYPES OF CIPHERS

The development of electromechanical cipher machines, which began shortly after World War I, resulted in two general types of ciphering devices and algorithms: alphabet generators and key generators. Alphabet generators construct the equivalent of a table where each unit of plaintext is replaced by a ciphertext unit. A class of cipher devices called wired rotor codewheel machines were developed to perform this enciphering function. It is as if the process of simple substitution were used but a new mixed alphabet was provided to encipher every letter of the plaintext! This type of algorithm is still used in electronic cryptography, but with tables stored in the machine used to replace the rotors of the electromechanical devices. If the required tables are too many or too large, then their equivalent is generated through use of the three processes described earlier.

Key generators operate by deriving long streams of random-looking numbers or bits, called a *keystream*. The keystream is then combined with the plaintext to arrive at the ciphertext. Most modern electronic cipher machines are key generators. If you think of both the plaintext and ciphertext as represented by strings of bits, a keystream encipherment might appear as in Figure 4. The combining process used is modulo 2 addition without carry, which is implemented as an *exclusive or* (XOR) operation in all com-

POLYBIUS SQUARE: 1 2 3 4 5
                     1 T E X A S
                     2 B C D F G
                     3 H I K L M
                     4 N O P Q R
                     5 U V W Y Z

PLAINTEXT: I C A M E I S A W I C O N Q U E R E D
PLAINTEXT   3 2 1 3 1 3 1 1 5 3 2 4 4 4 5 1 4 1 2
IN DIGITS: 2 2 4 5 2 2 5 4 3 2 2 2 1 4 1 2 5 2 3

FRACTIONATED TEXT GROUPED BY ROW AND RECOMBINED:
        32 13 13 11 53 24 44 51 41 22 24 52 25 43 22 21 41 25 23
         I X X T W F Q U N C F V G P C B N G D

FINAL TEXT: IXXTW FQUNC FVGPC BNGD

FIGURE 3. Fractionization.

KEYSTREAM: 1 0 1 1 1 1 1 0 0 0 0 1 0 0 0 1 1 0 0 1 0 1 0 1 1 1
PLAINTEXT: 0 1 0 0 1 1 0 0 0 1 1 1 0 0 0 0 1 1 1 1 0 0 0 0 0 1
CIPHERTEXT: 1 1 1 1 0 0 1 0 0 1 1 0 0 0 0 1 0 1 1 0 0 1 0 1 1 0

FIGURE 4. Keystream encipherment.

puters. In XOR operations, each two bits are added modulo 2 but any carry is discarded. Therefore, the ciphertext is obtained by XORing the bits of the keystream to the plaintext. The decipherment process is essentially the same operation, XORing the keystream to the ciphertext to recover the plaintext. This method of enciphering data is attributed to the American engineer Gilbert Vernam, who proposed it around the end of World War I, long before the advent of computers.

Recently, the terms *block cipher* and *stream cipher* have come to be used in place of the older but somewhat more accurate designations *alphabet generator* and *key generator*.

REQUIREMENTS FOR A GOOD CRYPTOGRAPHIC SYSTEM

Many people can devise cryptographic systems so that a message enciphered in that system cannot be solved by anyone else. Why, then, is cryptography of such interest? The answer to this question is evident if all the conditions necessary to have a secure and practical cryptographic system are considered. First, a system that keeps a single relatively short message secret is not of much interest. In computer systems, there is a need to encipher thousands of messages and data files, often of very large size. Persons attempting to penetrate the cipher often know not only the algorithm used but much of the plaintext of the files. A system that might protect a message or two could be trivial to solve if hundreds of such messages are available for analysis. Second, the cryptographic system must resist solution if the algorithm or program used is known. The security must rest entirely in the secrecy of the key used. Any encipherment method in widespread use simply cannot be kept secret for long. Third, whatever method is used for scrambling the data must be implementable at a

suitably fast rate. Computers are fast and accurate but a very complex algorithm might prove too slow to keep up with the load of messages that need to be sent. On the other hand, if the algorithm is not complex enough, it might prove solvable. Fourth, errors that occur in the ciphertext, perhaps as a result of the noise over communications circuits or equipment malfunction, must not render the recovery of the data difficult or completely impossible. With some types of cipher systems, an error in the 10,000th character sent would require retransmission of all 10,000 characters to continue the ciphering accurately. Required properties of a cryptographic system such as rapid enciphering rates and high security often prove to be contradictory. These considerations, as well as those specific to the particular communications system being used, make the design of cryptographic systems quite difficult in practice.

CURRENT TRENDS IN CRYPTOGRAPHY

As interest in nongovernmental cryptography increased beginning in the 1970s, so did the efforts of private sector researchers and academics to formulate the principles and protocols necessary for successful application of this previously closely guarded subject. Although cryptography has been extensively studied by the world's major powers for a long time, the results of that work remain classified and unavailable for public use. Additionally, communications systems such as electronic mail, in which the users themselves may not be sharply defined, present special problems not inherent in military and diplomatic message systems. There is, for instance, the problem of developing an electronic counterpart of the ordinary written signature that is difficult to forge. Sometimes the material to be protected does not really need to be kept secret, but merely protected from unauthorized alteration. Hence, there is a problem, not of secrecy, but of authentication. Current cryptographic research attempts to develop methods for handling these and still more perplexing problems that arise with electronic storage and distribution of information that needs to be protected.

[See also: Access Control.]

For Further Reading

Basic Cryptographic Methods and History

Deavours, C. A., and L. Kruh. 1985. *Machine cryptography and modern cryptanalysis.* Norwood, Mass.: Artech House. Moderately technical but very readable account of the development, use, and failures of machine cryptography during the World War II era. Lots of pictures.

Friedman, W. F., and L. D. Callimahos. 1988. *Military cryptanalytics: Parts I and II,* 4 vols. Laguna Hills, Calif.: Aegean Park Press. Formerly classified U.S. government text. Extensive survey of the manual-substitution-type cryptographic systems that are usually encountered in practice. Problems for solution.

Kahn, D. 1969. *The codebreakers.* New York: Macmillan. This comprehensive tome, which has appeared in various editions and several foreign languages, is the starting point for anyone interested in the subject. Indispensable.

Current Work and Trends

Barker, W. 1986. *Cryptanalysis of shift-register generated stream cipher systems.* Laguna Hills, Calif.: Aegean Park Press. Very elementary account (with problems to solve) of the analysis of keystream ciphers.

Denning, D. 1982. *Cryptography and Data Security.* Reading, Mass.: Addison-Wesley. Good source of reference material on most aspects of recent research.

Hutt, A. E., S. Bosworth, and D. Hoyt, eds. 1988. *Computer security handbook.* New York: Macmillan. Cryptography discussed in the broader field of computer security.

O'Connor, L. J., and J. Seberry. 1988. *Public key cryptography: Cryptographic significance of the knapsack problem.* Laguna Hills, Ca-

lif.: Aegean Park Press. Technical but clear work on some aspects of public key methods and more general concerns in the new public key cryptography.

Rueppel, R. 1986. *Analysis and design of stream ciphers.* Berlin: Springer-Verlag. Highly technical but up-to-date study of keystream generation in the algebraic setting of Galois fields. Good, but not for beginners.

Cipher A. Deavours

CYBERNETICS AND ARTIFICIAL INTELLIGENCE

Artificial intelligence and cybernetics are not the same thing, nor is one simply about computers and the other about robots. Rather, they are separate but interconnected fields of inquiry. This article discusses the relationships between them.

Artificial intelligence (AI) uses computer technology to strive toward the goal of machine intelligence and considers implementation the most important result; cybernetics uses epistemology (the limits to how we know what we know) to understand the constraints of any medium (technological, biological, or social) and considers powerful descriptions the most important result.

The field of AI came into being when the concept of universal computation (Minsky 1967), the cultural view of the brain as a computer, and the availability of digital computing machines were combined. The field of cybernetics came into being when concepts of information, feedback, and control were generalized from specific applications (e.g., in engineering) to systems in general, including systems of living organisms, abstract intelligent processes, and language.

ORIGINS OF CYBERNETICS

The term *cybernetics* originated in 1947 when Norbert Wiener used it to name a discipline apart from, but touching on, such established disciplines as electrical engineering, mathematics, biology, neurophysiology, anthropology, and psychology. Wiener, Arturo Rosenblueth, and Julian Bigelow needed a new word to refer to their new concept, and they adapted a Greek word meaning "steersman" to invoke the rich interaction of goals, predictions, actions, feedback, and response in systems of all kinds (Wiener 1948; the term "governor" derives from the same root). Early applications in the control of physical systems (aiming artillery, designing electrical circuits, and maneuvering simple robots) clarified the fundamental roles of these concepts in engineering, but the relevance of cybernetics to social systems and the softer sciences was also clear from the start. Many researchers from the 1940s through 1960 worked solidly within the tradition of cybernetics without necessarily using the term, in fields where cybernetics clearly applied (R. Buckminster Fuller) and in others where this was not obvious (Gregory Bateson, Margaret Mead).

LIMITS TO KNOWING

In attempting to abstract concepts common to all systems, early cybernetic researchers quickly realized that "the science of observed systems" cannot be divorced from "the science of observing systems" (von Foerster 1974), because it is we who observe. The cybernetic approach is centrally concerned with the unavoidable limit of what we can know: our own subjectivity. In this way, cybernetics is aptly called "applied epistemology." At minimum, its utility is the production of useful descriptions, and, specifically, descriptions that include the observer in the description. Cybernetic descriptions of psychology, language, arts, performance, or intelligence (to name a few) may be quite different from more conventional, hard "scientific" views—although cybernetics can be rigorous too. Implementation may then follow in software and/or hardware, or in the design of social, managerial, and other classes of interpersonal systems.

ORIGINS OF ARTIFICIAL INTELLIGENCE IN CYBERNETICS

Ironically but logically, AI and cybernetics have each gone in and out of fashion and influence in the search for machine intelligence. Cybernetics started in advance of AI, but AI has dominated for the last 25 years. Recent difficulties in AI have led to renewed search for solutions that mirror the past approaches of cybernetics. Warren McCulloch and Walter Pitts were the first to propose a synthesis of neurophysiology and logic that tied the capabilities of brains to the limits of Turing computability (McCulloch and Pitts 1965). The euphoria that followed spawned the field of AI (Lettvin 1989), along with early work on computation in neural nets, or, as they were then called, perceptrons. However, the fashion of symbolic computing rose to squelch perceptron research. Only when discontent slowly grew over repeated failures to achieve machine intelligence by symbolic means within AI did interest in neural networks increase again in the late 1980s. This is not to say that current fashion in neural nets is a return to the ground covered by cybernetics. Much of the modern work in neural nets rests in the philosophical tradition of AI and not in that of cybernetics.

PHILOSOPHY OF CYBERNETICS

AI is predicated on the presumption that knowledge is a commodity that can be stored inside a machine, and that the application of such stored knowledge to the real world constitutes intelligence (Minsky 1968) (Figure 1). Only in such a "realist" view of the world can, for example, semantic networks and rule-based expert systems be a route to intelligent machines. In contrast, cybernetics has evolved from a "constructivist" view of the world (von Glasersfeld 1987) in which objectivity derives from shared agreement about meaning and information (or intelligence, for that matter) is an attribute of an interaction rather than a commodity stored in a computer (Winograd and Flores 1986). These differences are not merely semantic in

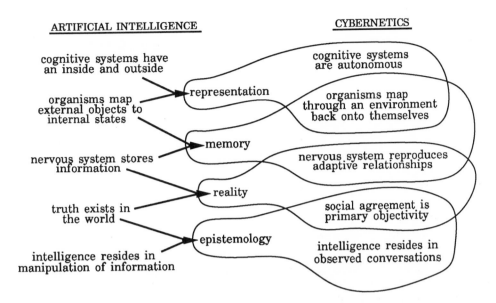

FIGURE 1. Underlying philosophical differences between artificial intelligence (AI) and cybernetics are displayed by showing how they each understand the terms in the central column. For example, the concept of "representation" is cast quite differently in the two fields. Relations on the left are causal arrows and reflect the reductionist reasoning inherent in AI's "realist" perspective of the world-as-it-is. Relations on the right are nonhierarchical and circular and reflect a "constructivist" perspective, in which the world is invented by an intelligence acting in a social tradition, rather than discovered.

character; they determine fundamentally the source and direction of research performed from a cybernetic rather than an AI perspective.

INFLUENCES

Winograd and Flores (1986) credit the influence of Humberto Maturana, a biologist who recasts the concepts of "language" and "living system" with a cybernetic eye, with shifting their opinions away from the AI perspective. They quote Maturana:

Learning is not a process of accumulation of representations of the environment; it is a continuous process of transformation of behavior through continuous change in the capacity of the nervous system to synthesize it. Recall does not depend on the indefinite retention of a structural invariant that represents an entity (an idea, image or symbol), but on the functional ability of the system to create, when certain recurrent demands are given, a behaviour that satisfies the recurrent demands or that the observer would class as a

reenacting of a previous one. (Maturana and Varela 1988)

Cybernetics has directly affected software development in intelligent training, knowledge representation, cognitive modeling, computer-supported cooperative work, and neural modeling. Useful results have been demonstrated in all these areas. Like AI, however, cybernetics has not produced recognizable solutions to the machine intelligence problem, or at least has not produced them for domains considered complex in the metrics of symbolic processing. Many beguiling artifacts have been produced with an appeal more familiar in an entertainment medium or to organic life than in a piece of software (Pask 1970). Meantime, in a repetition of history in the 1950s, the influence of cybernetics is being felt throughout the hard and soft sciences, as well as in AI. This time, however, it is the epistemological stance of cybernetics, rather than its abstraction of the concepts of information, feedback, and purpose, that is its contribution to these fields.

References

Lettvin, J. Y. 1989. Introduction to Volume 1. In R. McCulloch, ed. *W. S. McCulloch.* Vol. 1, pp. 7–20. Salinas, Calif.: Intersystems Publications.

McCulloch, W. S., and W. H. Pitts. 1965. A logical calculus of the ideas immanent in nervous activity. In W. S. McCulloch, *Embodiments of mind*, pp. 19–39. Cambridge, Mass.: MIT Press.

Maturana, H. R. 1970. Biology of cognition. Reprinted in H. R. Maturana and F. Varela. 1980. *Autopoiesis and cognition: The realization of the living*, pp. 2–62. Dordrecht: Reidel.

Maturana, H. R., and F. J. Varela. 1988. *The tree of knowledge.* Boston: New Science Library, Shambala Publications.

Minsky, M. 1967. *Computation: Finite and infinite machines.* Englewood Cliffs, N.J.: Prentice-Hall.

———, ed. 1968. *Semantic information processing.* Cambridge, Mass.: MIT Press.

Pask, G. 1970. A comment, a case history and a plan. In J. Reichardt, ed. 1971. *Cybernetics, art and ideas*, pp. 76–99. London: Studio Vista.

von Foerster, H., ed. 1974. *Cybernetics of cybernetics.* Urbana: Biological Computer Laboratory, Univ. of Illinois.

von Glasersfeld, E. 1987. *The construction of knowledge, contributions to conceptual semantics.* Seaside, Calif.: Intersystems Publications.

Wiener, N. 1948. *Cybernetics, or control and communication in the animal and the machine.* Cambridge, Mass.: The Technology Press; New York: Wiley.

Winograd, T., and F. Flores. 1986. *Understanding computers and cognition: A new foundation for design.* Norwood, N.J.: Ablex.

Paul Pangaro

CYBERNETICS AND NATURAL COMPUTING

Cybernetics, as defined in Norbert Wiener's seminal book on the subject, is the study of control and communication in animals and machines (Wiener 1948). The field prospered as a broad interdisciplinary movement in the 1950s, with connections to physiology and biological modeling, control systems, information theory, neural networks, automata theory, self-organizing systems, and incipient computer science and artificial intelligence. Recent years have seen new interdisciplinary thrusts under the guise of nonlinear science, neural computing, molecular computing, adaptability theory, evolutionary programming, and robotry that have significant roots in cybernetics.

This article focuses exclusively on those aspects of cybernetics and its modern manifestations that connect to models of biological computing and to biologically motivated approaches to computer science. The term *natural computing* is appropriate here. Digital computing was in its infancy when Wiener popularized the term *cybernetics.* With the growth of computer science a more strictly computational paradigm for understanding intelligence, control, and communication came to the fore. Computer simulation made increasing contributions to the analysis of complex systems, including the brain, the immune system, and evolutionary systems.

THE TURING AND McCULLOCH–PITTS MODELS

The Turing machine model of computation (Turing 1936) played a pivotal role in the development of natural computing, as it served both to stimulate the interface zone between computer science and biology and to separate computer science from biology. A Turing machine is a finite automaton along with a read/write head and a potentially infinite tape. The automaton can read or write symbols on the tape square that it currently accesses, and can move to neighboring squares. Turing was at least in part motivated by the image of a person (the finite automaton) working arithmetic problems on a lined notebook (the tape). The person in an initial "state of mind" reads a symbol on the tape and, depending on this state–input pair, rewrites the symbol, moves to a new position on the tape and goes into a new "state of mind." Turing argued that he could express any algorithmic process in terms of a program comprising a collection of such sequences of operations. The Turing machine formalism is one of many equivalent formulations of algorithmic processes. It attracted particular attention, however, largely because of the putative connection it established between algorithmic and psychological processes.

This connection was extended by McCulloch and Pitts (1943) to encompass neuroanatomy. McCulloch and Pitts showed that any finite automaton could be realized as a network of elements that emitted a pulse whenever the sum of excitatory and inhibitory pulses inputted to them exceeded a threshold. Such threshold elements are called formal neurons, because they capture in a highly abstracted manner the all-or-none firing behavior of biological neurons. Real neurons are very much more complicated. The significance of the McCulloch–Pitts model is that it demonstrated for the first time that any Turing-computable function could be embodied in networks of highly simplified neurons; hence they should be implementable even more efficiently in networks of more realistic neurons.

Ashby (1956) enlarged the circle of ideas by relating automaton behavior to the cybernetic principle that the steady (or homeostatic) state of the organism is maintained through negative feedback signals. He pictured the organism as a polystable system taking actions to maintain the stable state of selected variables in accordance with a program (the rules governing the state-to-state behavior of the system). This extension provided the basis for a computational concept of control, and also shifted the focus to the role of intelligent behavior in control processes.

Some investigators interpreted the work of Turing and McCulloch and Pitts as justifying the separation of artificial intelligence and cognitive psychology from brain theory. The assumption was that if neural nets implement cognitive functions as programs, the nets could be forgotten and the programs written directly (for example, in a psychologically motivated fashion) and run on programmable digital computers. This view was reinforced by Minsky and Papert's 1969 analysis of limitations in pattern recognition capabilities of single-layer perceptrons, early neuronlike computers with a definite learning algorithm (Rosenblatt 1958).

NEURAL COMPUTING

The situation has changed dramatically in recent years, with a significant return to the early objectives of using neural models of computation and self-organizing principles. This is due largely to the recognition that the computing power available to serial digital computers is insufficient to duplicate many important human capabilities. The term *connectionism* captures the main feature of most current neural computing models as the intelligence is vested in interconnected networks of simple elements. Another term is *parallel–distributed computing*, because a major objective is to use the vast underutilized switching capabilities afforded by integrated circuit technology (Rumelhart and McClelland 1986).

The difficulty, as with all parallel computation, is in communicating programs to the network. An important advance was achieved by Hopfield (1982), who showed that it is possible to assign a notational computational energy to a subclass of neural network models and to use this to structure the networks efficiently for performing computational tasks (such as optimization and pattern recognition). In recent years many learning algorithms have been developed for educating neural nets to perform a variety of functions.

MOLECULAR AND NEUROMOLECULAR COMPUTING

Molecular computers are information processing systems in which individual molecules play a critical computational role (cf. Conrad 1985, 1990). They include natural biological systems, computer models of biomolecular systems, and bona fide fabrications. Neuromolecular computers are molecular computers with a neurallike structure. They differ from neural computers in that the material substrate for the computing is all important. In the case of neuromolecular computing models, signals impinging on the external membrane of the neuron are transduced to chemical and molecular representations inside the neurons. The firing of the neuron is significantly influenced by subneuronal processing.

The shape properties of proteins and other macromolecules play a key role in biomolecular computing. Proteins are linear strings of amino acids that fold up into an intricate three-dimensional shape, in a manner that can be analogized to the spatial self-organization of a string of magnetized beads. Protein catalysts (or enzymes) recognize molecular objects in their environment on the basis of complementary shape fitting, in the fashion of a lock–key fit. Switching involves making or breaking specific covalent bonds. Change in an enzyme's shape in response to control molecules can alter its recognition and catalytic properties, and thus corresponds to another level of switching (at this level the enzyme can be analogized to a simple finite automaton). The complementary fitting of proteins can also allow them to self-organize into supermolecular mosaics, like self-assembling jigsaw puzzle pieces (see Figure 1). Some aspects of the switching behavior of macromolecular networks can be abstracted in Boolean networks. Cellular pattern recognition and neuromolecular computing models cannot be fully captured in this manner as they exploit the pattern recognition properties of proteins.

SELF-ORGANIZING SYSTEMS

From its inception cybernetics was concerned with the problem of self-organization. The distinction between self-organization and externally imposed organization is not absolute. The question has to do with how many of the rules that a system ultimately follows are supplied to it in an intentional manner. There are two broad streams of work in this area, one emphasizing nonlinear dynamics and the other adaptive algorithms. In the dynamical style local rules are specified among a network of components. The global rule, and potential computational function, emerges from the local

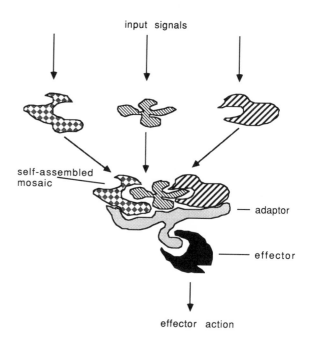

input signals

self-assembled mosaic

adaptor

effector

effector action

FIGURE 1. Schematic illustration of the manner in which shape-based interactions can mediate pattern recognition (cf. Conrad 1990). Signals arriving along different input lines at a biological cell (or device) release differently shaped macromolecules. These self-assemble into a polymacromolecular mosaic, largely on the basis of complementary shape fitting. An adaptor molecule picks out shape features of the mosaic common to some set of input patterns and links these to an effector molecule that controls output action.

interactions. Alternatively, a global description may be specified without any foreknowledge of its computational significance. Adaptive algorithms are rules for learning, often in response to reward. The two approaches are complementary, as adaptive algorithms are usually required to tune the local interactions or global parameters to obtain a useful function. Connectionist neural networks are a commonly used medium for combining the dynamic and adaptive approaches. Molecular computing provides a farther-reaching example, as the pattern recognition function of the proteins, the basic switching elements, is itself an emergent computational property.

The negative feedback principle of cybernetics is the simplest example of self-organizing dynamics. A continuous dynamical system with negative feedback will exhibit steady-state, or homeostatic, behavior if its state space contains basins of attraction, or valleys, that run uphill in all directions. The self-organization corresponds to falling back to the bottom of the valley as long as the disturbance, or perturbation, is not too great. The stabilized behavior might be much more elaborate than a simple steady state, in which case the basins of attraction would have a complex structure. Complex spatial and temporal patterns are possible (Turing 1952, Nicolis and Prigogine 1977) as is chaotic behavior that appears stochastic despite the fact that it is generated by a deterministic process (cf. Holden 1986). Such self-organizing dynamics can for the most part be elicited from cellular automata as well as from differential equations. The former are spatial arrangements of finite automata, usually chosen to be extremely simple, with neighbor–neighbor interactions. They were originally proposed by Ulam to model multicellular morphogenesis of biological systems, and were used by von Neumann (1966) in a serial mode to formulate models of abstract self-reproducing systems. The advantage of cellular automata is that they provide models of parallel computational systems (Wolfram 1986). Consequently, they illustrate how self-organizing dynamical processes can serve to bring signals together in space and time for pattern recognition, effector control, or other computational functions.

EVOLUTIONARY PROGRAMMING AND THE TRADE-OFF PRINCIPLE

Of the adaptive algorithms those that mimic the Darwinian mechanism of evolutionary search through variation, selection, and reproduction are of particular importance, because they require a minimal preexisting organization. Evolutionary programming techniques, sometimes called genetic algorithms, were proposed early in the development of computer science (Bremermann 1962, Holland 1975, Fogel et al. 1966). These techniques are applicable only to systems with malleable structure–function relations; computer code is too brittle to learn through an evolutionary mechanism. Systems with self-organizing dynamics provide a moldable substrate for evolutionary search, and in addition afford high potential computational efficiency due to the fact that multiple components and multiple interactions contribute to the computational function. The relationship between programmability, efficiency, and evolvability is summarized in a trade-off principle that captures the comparative capabilities of digital computers and organisms: *a system cannot at the same time have programmable structure–function relations, high evolutionary adaptability, and the high computational efficiencies afforded by self-organizing dynamics.* The trade-off principle (Conrad 1985) implies that biological systems operate in a computational mode that is very different from that of digital machines, and that for artificial systems to capture this mode they should embody malleable structure–function relations, either at the level of hardware or through simulation.

References

Ashby, W. R. 1956. *An introduction to cybernetics.* New York: Wiley.

Bremermann, H. J. 1962. Optimization through evolution and recombination. In Yovits, Jacobi, and Goldstein, eds. *Self-organizing systems.* Washington D.C.: Spartan Books.

Conrad, M. 1985. On design principles for a molecular computer. *Communications of the ACM* 28:464–80.

———. 1990. Molecular computing. In M. C. Yovits, ed. *Advances in computers*, vol. 31, pp. 235–324. New York: Academic Press.

Fogel, L., A. Owens, and M. Walsh. 1966. *Artificial intelligence through simulated evolution.* New York: Wiley.

Holden, A. V. 1986. *Chaos.* Manchester: Manchester University Press.

Holland, J. 1975. *Adaptation in natural and artificial systems.* Ann Arbor: University of Michigan Press.

Hopfield, J. 1982. Neural networks and physical systems with emergent collective computational abilities. *Proceedings of the National Academy of Science (USA)* 79:2554–58.

McCulloch, W. S., and W. Pitts. 1943. A logical calculus of the ideas immanent in nervous activity. *Bulletin of Mathematical Biophysics* 5:115–33.

Nicolis, G., and I. Prigogine. 1977. *Self-organization in nonequilibrium systems.* New York: Wiley–Interscience.

Rosenblatt, F. 1958. The perceptron: A probabilistic model for information storage and organization in the brain. *Psychological Review* 65:386–407.

Rumelhart, D. E., and J. L. McClelland, eds. 1986. *Parallel distributed processing: Explorations in the microstructure of cognition.* vol. 1: *Foundations;* vol. 2: *Psychological and biological models.* Cambridge, Mass.: MIT Press.

Turing, A. M. 1936. On computable numbers, with an application to the Entschei-dungsproblem. *Proceedings, London Mathematics, Society,* ser. 2–42:230–65.

———. 1952. The chemical basis of morphogenesis. *Philosophical Transactions of the Royal Society of London Series B* 237:5–72.

von Neumann, J. 1966. In A. W. Burks, ed. *The theory of self-reproducing automata.* Urbana: University of Illinois Press.

Wiener, N. 1961. *Cybernetics, or, control and communication in the animal and machine,* rev. ed. Cambridge, Mass.: MIT Press. (originally published in 1948).

Wolfram, S., ed. 1986. *Theory and applications of cellular automata.* Singapore: World Scientific.

Michael Conrad

D

DATA

The term *data* refers to the coded representations of numbers, alphabetic characters, and special characters that are input, stored, and output from computers. At input and output, data representations are in the numeric, alphabetic, and other representation used in human communication. They are entered into the computer system via devices such as a keyboard or a mouse. In the computer system, different coded representations are used. (*Data* is the plural of *datum*, so that in a strict sense it should always be used with a plural verb. In practice, however, it is very common to use *data* with a singular verb. The singular term *datum* is rarely used in the computer and data processing literature.)

The discussion of data in computerized systems can be carried on from two points of view. First, *data representation* refers to the way data values are represented in computer systems, that is, in the computer memory, on storage devices, or while transmitted by data communication facilities. Second, *data organization* refers to the way pieces of data are grouped according to application needs or considerations of processing efficiency.

DATA REPRESENTATION

Almost all computers are digital, which means that they represent data and perform operations using devices that can have two values. These two values represent binary digits usually designated as having a value of 0 or 1. (See also BINARY NUMBERING SYSTEM.) To represent data that can have more than two values, it is necessary to use groups of binary digits. Some common combinations

of groups of binary digits and their purpose are character coding, binary coding for numeric data, and binary-coded decimal coding for numeric data. In some cases, a single bit within a set may be used for coding logical data. A logical data item represents only two values, such as "true" or "false," "exists" or "does not exist," and so forth. For example, a single bit may represent whether a student has completed a course.

A character (usually termed a *byte*) consists of a set of bits that can encode any alphabetic, numeric, or special character. The most common size is 8 bits, which can encode 256 different characters (because there are 256 different combinations of 1s and 0s in a set of 8 bits). These combinations are assigned to various symbols or characters, namely, the digits, lowercase alphabetic characters, uppercase alphabetic characters, punctuation marks, and special symbols (such as ∞, $\uparrow$, α, Σ). Some combinations may be assigned to characters that cannot be printed, but can control the behavior of input and output devices (e.g., printers). There are two commonly used systems of assigning a bit string combination to a symbol: American Standard Code for Information Interchange (ASCII) and Extended Binary-Coded Decimal Interchange Code (EBCDIC).

Characters are useful for representing data that can be described as strings of symbols, especially text; however, the use of character coding to represent numeric information has several drawbacks. In particular, the amount of memory (or storage, or communication time) required is considerably more than necessary. Also, a special conversion process may be required before any calculation can be performed with the data, resulting in reduced processing efficiency.

Therefore, data that are mainly processed numerically are usually represented not on a character-by-character basis, but by use of a binary-system *numeric representation.*

In the binary system, a string of bits, each having a value of 0 or 1, is interpreted as a sum of powers of 2. For example, consider the bit string 10101. Each of its five positions is assigned a "weight," increasing from right to left as follows: the rightmost digit is assigned weight 1 (2^0), the next digit to the left is assigned 2 (2^1), the next one is assigned a weight of 4 (2^2), and so on. The whole value is now $10101_2 = 1 \times 2^4 + 0 \times 2^3 + 1 \times 2^2 + 0 \times 2 + 1 \times 1 = 21_{10}$ (the subscript "2" and "10" indicate the number system being used). As in the decimal system, binary fractions can also be represented, by assigning weights of $\frac{1}{2}$, $\frac{1}{4}$, and so forth, to the right most digits in a binary number. To show the storage efficiency obtained with the binary system, consider the number 12345. In a character representation it occupies 40 bits (5 bytes). In comparison, it can be represented in the binary system using only 14 bits, but in practice, binary numbers utilize a fixed-length set of bits (such as 16 or 32 bits). The fixed length and binary representation are very efficient for processing.

Various types of numeric representations are used to code numeric data with strings of binary digits, depending on the range of values and accuracy required. The following are the most common:

- *Integers:* Numeric data that have no fraction.
- *Fixed point:* Numeric data that have a predetermined assumed length for the fractional part of the value (as in cash registers, which allow only two positions for cents).
- *Floating point:* Numeric data composed of two parts: a value (often called a mantissa) using a fixed number of digits and an exponent to define the decimal point location, for example, 1.2345×10^6. This representation allows for a large range of values (with precision dependent on the digit length used for the value) and is widely used in scientific and engineering applications.

As there is a limited number of bits in a string of bits used for binary coding, a number represented in a computer system may have to be truncated or rounded. This may result in some inaccuracies in calculations, which are generally termed *round-off errors.* Such errors can occur even when values having a small number of decimal digits are converted into the internal binary representation of the computer system, because some decimal fractions have no exact representation in binary.

In certain types of applications (especially administrative applications such as accounting) round-off errors are unacceptable. In such applications a special type of numeric representation is used in which each decimal digit of the value is kept as a separate "unit." Such numeric representations are termed *decimal.* There are two decimal representations. In one, each digit occupies a whole byte (*character,* or *zoned decimal*). In the other, each digit occupies four bits, that is, half a byte (*packed decimal*). Although decimal representations solve the inaccuracy problem, they are less storage efficient, as 4 bits at least are used for each digit. Also, they limit considerably the range of values that can be stored in a given number of bits, but for administrative applications this is usually not a problem.

Beyond logical, character, and numeric data, other types of data can be represented. A *data type* is defined by the meaning and range of values it can accommodate and by the operations that can be applied to these data. A common example is the definition of dates as special data types. The use of specialized data types facilitates the development of applications that use nonstandard data types; however, their availability depends on the particular software being used. Some programming languages enable the user to define data types as required. These are termed *abstract data types.*

DATA ORGANIZATION

Most data in scientific or engineering applications are numeric, or may be converted to numeric data (this is the case for diagrams and for geographical data). In many applications, however, especially administrative applications, the data are usually combinations of items represented by different data types (consider, for example, an invoice containing a customer name, address, date, product codes, quantities, and price). Also, frequently, many similar groups of data are entered into the computer system, stored, processed, and reported. Hence, several "levels" of data are recognized in what is termed a *data hierarchy*.

The data hierarchy begins with the representation of a simple, one-valued fact that is termed a *field* or a *data item* (sometimes the word *attribute* is also used). A field can be logical, character string, numeric, or any other special type (e.g., date). Examples are a customer name and amount owed. In most applications, data items appear in groups (for example, the details of an employee or of a customer order). Hence, a logical *record* or a *data aggregate* is defined as a group of logically related fields. For example, in an account record made up of account number, name, and balance, the fields are related because they "belong" to the same customer. Other terms used to describe data aggregates are *segment* and *tuple*.

In administrative applications a distinction is usually made between two types of records based on their meaning. A *master* record represents information about a given entity at a given time. An example of a master record is the status of a bank account. A *transaction* record represents a change that occurred. An example of a transaction record is the data about the withdrawal or a deposit in the account.

Records, or data aggregates, may be processed one at a time; however, for efficiency reasons, they are usually stored in collections. Such a collection is called a *file* or a *dataset*. The records in a file do not have to be related, but they will usually be processed and used in the same computerized application. Finally, in certain computerized applications, records from more than one file may be processed at the same time. Several files that are usually used together may be linked so that they will appear to the application as a combined collection of various records, for example, the master accounts file and the transactions file mentioned earlier. Such a collection is termed a *database*.

For Further Reading

Binary Representation of Numeric and Character Data
Blissmer, R. H. 1989. *Introducing computers: Concepts, systems, and applications*, 1989–1990 ed., Appendix D, pp. 409–17. New York: Wiley.

Detailed Discussion of Data Representation
Dasgupta, S. 1989. *Computer architecture, a modern synthesis*. Vol. 1. *Foundations*, Sect. 4.6, pp. 121–31. New York: Wiley.
Schneider, G. M. 1985. *The principles of computer organization*, Part One, pp. 15–84. New York: Wiley.

Data Hierarchy and Data in Business Applications
Burch, J. G., and Grudnitski, G. 1986. *Information systems, theory and practice*, 4th ed., chap. 8, pp. 251–75 (especially pp. 251–56). New York: Wiley.
Senn, J. A. 1989. *Analysis and design of information systems*, 2nd ed., chap. 11 (especially pp. 530–36). New York: McGraw-Hill.

Yair Wand

DATA ACQUISITION BOARDS

Today, computer-based data acquisition is done mostly with circuit boards that plug directly into the computer's bus. These boards may be classified in major categories:

1. Boards with analog connections
2. Boards that connect to an external chassis, or "remote instruments" with high-speed proprietary parallel interfaces to the computer's bus
3. Boards that connect to industry-standard interfaces to the computer, for example, RS-232 interfaces and IEEE-488 interfaces

These boards then in turn connect to remote instruments.

The following is a list of some of these types of boards by category. The vendor name is given first, then the part number. All of these work on computers with IBM PC-XT-compatible buses, currently the most popular computer bus for data acquisition.

1. Boards with analog interfaces

   - Analog Devices—800 series
   - Burr-Brown—PCI-20000 series
   - Data Translation—DT series
   - Keithley/Metrabyte—DAS series

2. Boards with parallel interfaces to remote instruments

   - Keithley/Metrabyte Instruments—500 series
   - Scientific Solutions—Lab Master

3. Boards with industry-standard interfaces connecting to remote instruments

   - *RS-232/RS-422* interface boards, connecting to

     Analog Devices—4000 and 6000
     John Fluke Mfg. Co., Inc.—Helios
     Omega Engineering—OM-900

   - *IEEE-488* interface boards, connecting to

     Hewlett-Packard 75000 VXI Bus cardcage
     Oscilloscopes and other electronic test instrumentation from Tektronix, etc.

IMPORTANT HARDWARE CHARACTERISTICS

Some important hardware characteristics can be used to match appropriate devices with given applications. In the following paragraphs, these device characteristics are discussed in relation to the different device types presented previously.

Speed/Throughput

Data acquisition speed must be considered in relation to the desired destination as well as the duration for which this speed must be maintained. In other words, one should not ask only "how fast?" but also "to where?" and "for how long?" The consideration of

speed, destination, and duration combined is referred to as *throughput.* The possible destinations are, in order of speed (fastest first), (1) to the device, that is, inside the remote instrument or on the board; (2) to the computer's memory; (3) to the computer's disk; and (4) to the computer's cathode-ray tube (CRT, screen).

In selecting the board hardware only, items 1 and 2 above are most important. Once the data are entered into the computer's memory, the throughput to the disk and to the CRT depends more on the software and the speed of the computer than on the device. Also, item 1 applies only to devices with internal buffer memory.

In general, boards without industry-standard interfaces (categories 1 and 2) have the best throughput to the computer's memory, because they are located right on the computer's bus. The fastest boards have either (1) direct memory access (DMA), which allows the board to enter data directly into the computer's memory without involving the computer's processor, or (2) dual-ported on-board buffer memory. Boards are currently available with throughputs greater than 1 MHz to the computer's memory. Depending on the hardware design, however, the number of samples that can be gathered at this rate is typically limited to 32,768 (2^{15}) or 65,536 (2^{16}). Vendors are actively competing with each other on speed/throughput, and boards with higher speeds are constantly being introduced.

In general, the remote instruments are much slower for throughput to the computer's memory. Those with serial (RS-232) interfaces are limited to 100 to 50 readings per second by the rather slow speed of the interfaces they use to transfer data into the computer. Some of the remote instruments have internal memory, however. These can be extremely fast, even in the megahertz region, as with digital oscilloscopes; however, the data then have to be moved from the remote instrument's memory to the computer's memory at a slower rate.

It is important to consider the speed of the device under evaluation in relation to the speed of the application at hand. The Nyquist theorem states that to be able to resolve frequencies up to a certain limit, one needs to sample at twice that limit. In general, one should be more conservative than this, and use hardware that can sample several times faster. A large body of experimental work in chromatography and spectroscopy has shown that if one samples ten times as fast as the width of the peaks, this is fast enough for accurate peak integration. In general, then, the hardware should be capable of sampling at least ten times the time scale of the events of interest.

Once the throughput requirements are determined, all hardware that does not meet those requirements can be eliminated from consideration.

Channel Types

Available hardware can accommodate a wide variety of data input channel types. The most common of these follow:

- Voltage (analog) input
- Thermocouple input
- Voltage (analog) output
- Current (analog) output
- Digital input—transistor–transistor logic (TTL) or contact closure
- Digital output—TTL or relay closure
- Strain input
- Thermistor input
- Resistance input
- Counter input
- Frequency input
- Pulse output

For any given application, the types of channels required must be determined. Any hardware that does not support these channel types can be eliminated from consideration.

Number of Channels

Available board hardware varies greatly in channel capacity, from single-channel devices to devices that can handle thousands of channels. Channel capacity must be considered in relation to the number of bus slots in the computer that will be occupied. How many free slots one has depends strongly on what one is doing with the computer. In general, it is wise to use as few slots as possible with data acquisition boards, as slot space (like memory) is always at a premium. So, determine how many slots can practically be allocated to data acquisition, and then ask the hardware vendor how many channels of the appropriate types can be accommodated in these slots. The board/remote instrument combinations tend to excel in the area of channels per slot, as many of them contain their own card cages into which various boards can be placed. The RS-232 remote instruments can be regarded as occupying zero slots if the computer already has an RS-232 port on the computer's motherboard (main circuit board).

Resolution

For analog signals, a variety of converter resolutions are available. These are usually specified in converter "bits." Resolutions typically vary from 8 to 24 bits. The more resolution, the more expensive the converter. The great majority of computer applications today are nicely accommodated with 12-bit converters, as these are widely available at reasonable prices, and their resolution is sufficient for most applications. At full scale, an n–bit converter will resolve, at best (i.e., at full scale), one part in 2^n. For a 12-bit converter, 2^n is 2^{12}, or 4,096. This corresponds to 0.02 percent. At one hundredth of full scale, however, the same converter will resolve one part in 410, or only 0.2 percent. This relationship is shown graphically in Figure 1.

In considering resolution, divide the voltage range covered by the converter by 2^n to calculate the voltage resolution. A 12-bit converter spanning a range from -5 to 5 volts will resolve 10 volts/2^{12}, or 2.4 millivolts. A 24-bit converter will resolve 0.5 microvolts.

Dynamic Range

Dynamic range refers to the voltage range over which an analog converter can achieve a certain resolution. As Figure 1 shows, the percentage precision of a converter degrades seriously toward the lower voltages. Although the converter covers a range from 0 to 10 volts, it achieves 0.1 percent precision only over a 2.4-volt to 10-volt dynamic range.

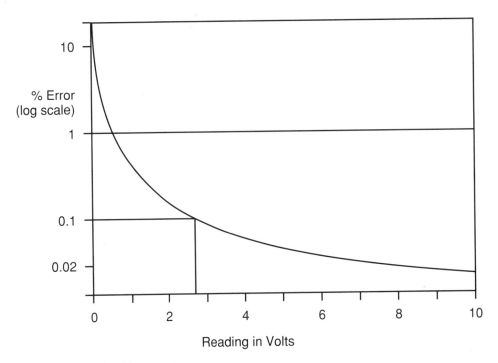

FIGURE 1. Twelve-bit converter error.

To achieve a greater dynamic range, many analog input devices have programmable gain. The gain may be either hardware or software programmable. It is much more convenient if the gain is software programmable. When reading lower voltages, amplifier gain is switched in to raise the full-scale voltage and provide additional resolution. An additional feature, autoranging, is sometimes made available to make this gain switching automatic, so that the converter is always operating with a gain that yields good precision. A typical programmable gain board offers gains of 1, 10, 100, and 500, with a full scale for the gain of 1 corresponding to 10 volts. With autoranging, this board can offer a precision of 0.25 percent over a range from 2 millivolts to 10 volts with a 12-bit converter, or 0.015 percent over the same range with a 16-bit converter.

Noise Immunity and Isolation   The resolution and dynamic range that a device can achieve may be useless if the input signal is sufficiently noisy. The most common source of noise in data acquisition is 60-Hz pickup of power line voltages. Unless extensive *shielding* is done, this noise can easily approach several hundred microvolts or more. This is especially damaging to the accuracy of thermocouple temperature measurements. A change of 1° Centigrade corresponds to about 50 microvolts for a typical thermocouple (Type J, iron–constantan at 0° Centigrade). This means that, unless it is filtered out, 250 microvolts of noise would degrade the thermocouple accuracy to ±5° Centigrade. Thermocouples are especially susceptible to this type of noise because they are difficult to shield.

Noise can be reduced either with analog low-pass filters or with integrating converters. Both of these approaches integrate the input signal for a characteristic time, which has the effect of averaging out the noise. The use of analog low-pass filters is usually referred to by vendors as *signal conditioning*. Integrating converters are speed limited (because of the necessity to average out 60-Hz noise) to 20 Hz or so. Faster converters, the successive approximation type, tend to be more susceptible to noise. This is because these converters usually incorporate a sample-and-hold circuit that samples the input for a very short time, typically a few microseconds, which does not filter out noise.

(Noise can also be reduced with digital filtering, but that is a function of the software.)

Noise immunity must be taken into account. If the application's measurements include thermocouples, or if they take place in a high-noise environment, signal conditioning or an integrating converter should be used to attain good accuracy. Most industrial plant settings are noisy environments, because there are typically many sources of AC power-related noise.

Another kind of noise is the DC potential difference that can build up between devices. It is typical in industrial settings, and is often referred to as *common mode noise,* or a *ground loop.* Some devices offer a feature called isolation to eliminate this noise problem. Isolation can either be built into the device or supplied in signal conditioning modules that are placed between the device and the signal source. Isolation is expensive, but very nicely eliminates this source of noise. For industrial and medical applications, isolation is often required for safety reasons.

Remote instruments tend to have the best noise immunity and isolation. The boards' location on the computer's bus contributes noise, as the bus is digital and operates continuously at megahertz rates. Boards tightly coupled to remote instruments are intermediate, as would be expected.

Ease of Use

Data acquisition boards and the remote instruments to which they are connected vary considerably in the degree to which they are easy to use. Most data acquisition hardware requires the user to use a pair of needlenose pliers to move around tiny jumper blocks on circuit boards. Some newer devices do not have this "feature," however. Completely jumperless boards, which are vastly easier to set up, are now available, especially with the IBM microchannel bus. The sophistication required to set up the hardware should match the level of sophistication of the user.

Interconnection Hardware

Many vendors supply only card-edge or pin-and-socket connectors to their devices, and sell separate interconnection panels that are necessary for most end-user applications. This, as well as the ease with which signals can be connected to panels, must be taken into account.

Computer and Bus Compatibility

Whether a board is compatible with a given computer is determined primarily by the bus for which the board was designed. Today, most boards are designed for and used with IBM-compatible products. Although all boards work on the lowest common denominator, 4.77-MHz Intel 8088 PCs, and most work on 6-MHz Intel 80286 PC-compatibles, some hardware works only on the AT 16-bit bus, and some does not work on the faster clock rate machines such as 8- to 16-MHz PCs. As 20-MHz and faster PCs will be introduced in the next few years, users would like to be able to transfer their data acquisition hardware to these faster machines. They should therefore steer toward PC compatibles that run the bus at the standard IBM rate, 8 MHz.

Reliability

Reliability is of undeniable importance, but it is one of those factors that is difficult to quantitate and to predict. Yet, it must be part of any board evaluation. Reliability must also relate to the application. Hardware that is to be used for critical industrial or medical monitoring or control obviously has to have extremely high reliability. For scientific experimentation, lower reliability may be tolerable.

In general, the data acquisition hardware that is available today takes advantage of the same integrated circuit advances that made state-of-the-art computers possible. In our experience, hardware failures have been rare.

One reliability matter is how the hardware will respond if it is mistreated. Also, how likely is it that the hardware will be mistreated? When students are using the equipment, some errors are part of the learning process and must be planned for. What happens if an inattentive operator connects a 110-volt line circuit across a 10-volt analog input? What happens if a lightning bolt strikes a thermocouple? Will it destroy the data acquisition hardware? Will it also destroy the computer? Both can happen.

The remote instrument approach is the best way to allow for the kind of high reliability just discussed, as the data acquisition hardware is physically and electrically separated from the computer. The board approach is the most risky, but may be entirely acceptable if the installer is careful and knowledgeable.

Price

Little needs to be said about price, except that each application has its price constraints, and each different hardware approach has a different price. Price must be weighed along with all the other factors to arrive at the best balance. In general, the boards are the least expensive, the remote instruments are the most expensive, and the proprietary board/remote instrument combinations are intermediate. This is because a remote instrument must contain its own power supply and also a communication subsystem to talk to the computer.

Software

Software is an important part of the total picture, as none of these hardware devices can be used without it. Many of the aforementioned characteristics, such as speed, throughput, channel type capability, channel number capacity, and (especially) ease of use, depend on the software as well as the hardware. This article is mainly about hardware, however.

Customer Support

It is likely that sometime in the life use of any data acquisition equipment, the manufacturer will have to be called for service or support. This important factor should not be overlooked. One good way to evaluate companies in this regard is to pose some good hard application questions to them before buying. Another method is to ask for and follow up on references.

SELECTING A DATA ACQUISITION BOARD

To match application requirements to data acquisition boards, first collect the literature on likely candidates. Then consider each of the aforementioned factors in the order of their importance to the application at hand, discarding candidates that do not meet the requirements. The list of candidates will narrow to two or three by the time this process is finished. If this is the case, consult a colleague if possible on the relative merits of the remaining candidates. Review the list one more time, rating each candidate on each factor with a score of 1 to 10, and then total the scores. The highest final score wins!

Frederick A. Putnam

DATABASE DESIGN, AUTOMATED

A database system is a collection of related records stored in a manner that makes the storage and retrieval of the data very efficient. The four well-known data models for databases are the hierarchical, network, relational, and object-oriented models.

The oldest of these models, the hierarchical model, was established out of necessity in the early 1960s without any prior formal study or definitions. Theoretically, the many-to-many relationship type between records (as when a student takes many courses and a course has many students) is not permitted in the hierarchical model. The IMS Data Base Management System (DBMS) package is the oldest and most dominant hierarchical DBMS package.

The network model is the product of the Database Task Group Committee (CODASYL 1975). Its first version appeared in 1961. This model permits all different types of connectivity: one-to-one, one-to-many, and many-to-many relationships (through the composition of two one-to-many relationships). Some network database packages are IDMS and IDMS/R of Cullinet Software, IDS of Honeywell, DMS II of Unisys, DBMS 10 and 11 of Digital Equipment, and Image of Hewlett-Packard.

The theoretical foundation for the relational database model was established by E. F. Codd in 1970 (Codd 1970). In this model, information is stored in a two-dimensional table called a relation. Each column represents a field of the record and is called an attribute. Each row of the table represents a data record of the file and is called a tuple. All the elements of the table must be simple. In other words, no element of the table can be a table on its own. The reservoir from which the values of an attribute are drawn is called the domain of that attribute. A process called normalization is used for grouping information in these tables so that duplicate values of attributes are eliminated. These tables are constructed in such a manner that

1. All the requirements of the client for whom the system is designed are satisfied.

2. The relationship between attributes within a table or between attributes of different tables or between tables themselves enables the user to add new data to the databases or to delete data from the databases or to update data without causing any anomaly (inconsistency) within a database.

Some well-known relational database packages are DB2 of IBM; Ingres of Relational Technology; Oracle of Oracle, Inc.; Unify of Unify, Inc.; dBASE of Ashton-Tate; Rdbase 5000 of Microrim; Informix of Informix Software, Inc.; and Paradox of Borland, Inc.

The object-oriented data model uses the concepts of entities and objects. An object is a representation of an entity in the database system environment. An entity has an infinite number of properties, but an object will take only a finite subset of these properties to represent the entity in the system. An object encapsulates both the data and the operations that can be performed on them. The operations are known as methods. Some examples of object-oriented database packages are Vbase Integrated Object Oriented System of Ontologic, Inc.; GEMSTONE/OPAL of Serviologic; and ORION of Micro-Electronic and Computer Technology Corporation.

In database terminology a record type means a file. In relational databases, record types are called relations, and fields are known as attributes. The record types in object-oriented databases are called objects, and the fields are called properties. In general, a file has one or more candidate keys. Each candidate key is a field or a group of fields that identifies a unique record within the file. Any of the candidate keys can be chosen as the primary key of the file; thus the primary key of a file identifies a unique record of the file. A foreign key is a field or a group of fields within a file that is the primary key of another file. The primary key is used to access a specific record from a file, and the foreign keys establish the links between different files.

A database management system (DBMS) is a software package. Its main functions are (1) to provide the facility to set up the database, (2) to retrieve and store source data (actual data in the database), (3) to retrieve and store the data about the structure of the database (data dictionary), (4) to provide the facilities to enforce security rules, (5) to back up the database, and (6) to control the concurrent transactions so that one user's environment is protected from others.

DATABASE DESIGN

Before discussing automated database design, it is essential to understand the meaning of database design and the processes involved. Basically, database design means identifying all the needed files, the fields of their records, and all candidate and foreign keys. Databases, like any other software system, have their own software design life cycle. The process involved in the design of database systems are:

1. Analysis of the required information. In this phase, like any other software system, a precise definition of the problem at hand is established from interviews and examination of the organizational documents. Also in this phase, the description of the system constraints, requirements, queries, transactions, and needed reports are expressed in short, concise sentences, usually called a dependency list (Smith 1985). Figure 1 is an example of such a dependency list.

2. Establishing the structure of the database. From the information gathered in the previous phase, the final structure of the database is established. First the logical schema is designed; then the implementation schema is created by modifying the logical schema (blueprint of the database) to comply with the data model (such as a hierarchical, network, relational, or object-oriented model) and the DBMS package that will be used. Like the blueprint of a building, which can be independent of the building site, the logical schema, which is also called the conceptual schema, is independent of the database model (hierarchical, network, relational, or object-oriented) and the computer system where the database is to be implemented. The next step is the modification of the logical schema to comply with the requirements of the data model and database package. This new final schema is the implementation schema. (We will refer to it simply as the schema.) The schema contains all record types, their fields, and the primary and foreign keys. A schema can be expressed graphically, or by having a set of tables and/or the description of the files (record types) along with attributes and different types of keys. Currently the following five

1. A university has a unique name, address, and president, and several colleges.
2. Each college has a unique name, dean, and address, and several departments.
3. Each department is identified by a unique name and headed by a department head and has several courses and a number of faculty members.
4. Each faculty member has a major specialty. A faculty member teaches several courses, and a course is taught by several faculty members.
5. Each course has a unique course name, description, and number of credit hours.
6. Each president, dean, department head, and faculty member is an employee of the university. Each employee has an employee identification number, name, salary, and address.

FIGURE 1. A dependency list.

different methods to construct schemas are popular:

1. Normalization
2. Entity and extended or enhanced entity relationship method
3. Rigorous and extended rigorous dependency diagram
4. Object-oriented method
5. A mixture of the above methods

Figure 2 is the logical schema in object-oriented notation for the database described in Figure 1. Figure 3 is the relational structure, which also contains a set of tables fully normalized, of the schema of Figure 1.

To appreciate the importance of automated database design tools, we briefly discuss the above methods:

1. Normalization. This is the method used to identify the minimum number of files (i.e., relations) needed to establish the database system along with their attributes and primary and foreign keys so it will be free from all undesirable consequences of insertion, deletion, and update operations. In database terminology the undesirable results produced as the consequences of these operations are called anomalies. For example, a deletion operation may lead to the loss of some information that was not intended to be deleted, or in the case of the update operation a change of a specific piece of information such as the salary of an employee may not be performed throughout the database if the salary of the employee appears in more than one place in the database. Thus the database will be inconsistent. The insertion anomaly means that some new information cannot be entered into the database, or at least there will be difficulties inserting it.

E. F. Codd (1970), who established the foundation for relational database systems, defined the first three normal forms in 1970. Later, two additional normal forms were defined. Fagin (1981) stopped further normalization by defining domain/key normal. He further proved that every domain/key normal form relation is free from all anomalies. Normalization is a top-down method;

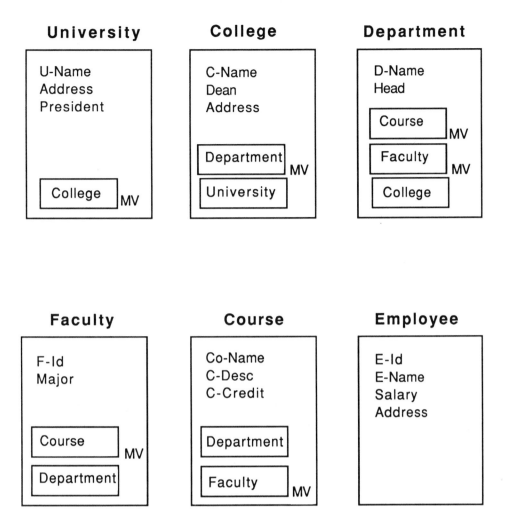

FIGURE 2. Logical schema in object-oriented notation. MV means multivalue.

the designer may start with a single relation (table). Any relation that is not in domain/key normal form is split into two or more relations, and the process continues until all the relations will be in domain/key normal form. It is not easy to express all relations in domain/key normal form. Normalization is a tedious method. The designer must remember all the normalization rules and make sure that all relations are fully normalized.

2. Entity and extended or enhanced entity relationship method. In 1974 Chen (1976) introduced the entity relationship (ER) method. This top-down method uses a rectangle to represent an entity, an ellipse for attribute, a diamond-shaped box for rela-

tionship, and doubly enclosed rectangles for weak entity. In ER a common noun in English represents an entity, and a transitive verb corresponds to a relationship type. Primary key attributes are underlined. A weak entity does not have all the elements of the primary key on its own. In other words, it cannot exist by itself alone. For example, a guest in a hotel is an entity identified by an account number, but daily charge is a weak entity that cannot exist unless there is a guest. The primary key of the weak entity daily charge is made up of two components. One is the account number, the primary key of the entity guest. The other component is the attribute, the date of the daily charge. Teorey et al. (1986) extended the entity relationship model, enhanced it, and made it

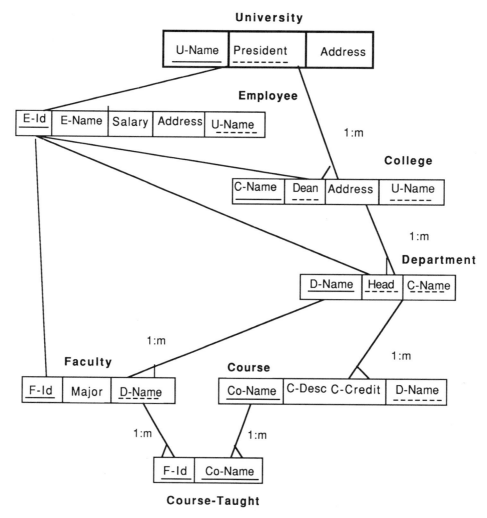

FIGURE 3. Relational diagram and implementation schema. Each rectangle is a file. Underlined items are primary keys, and items underlined with dotted lines are foreign keys.

capable of representing ternary and higher-degree relationships and exclusive and overlapping generalization concepts (generic and special entities), whether the occurrence of an entity in a relationship is mandatory or optional. Figure 4 is the schema for Figure 1 using the extended entity relationship model. Tables are extracted from the ER diagram and tested for normalization. Any table that is not fully normalized must be fully normalized.

3. Rigorous and extended rigorous dependency diagram. In 1985 Smith (1985) introduced the rigorous dependency dia-

gram to design relational database systems. This is a bottom-up method. The designer uses bubbles to enclose attributes. A bubble that contains the primary key has a single-headed arrow departing from it, or a double-headed arrow points from it to a bubble from which no arrow is departing. Single-value dependency is represented by a single-headed arrow, and multivalue dependency is represented by a double-headed arrow. No attribute should appear more than once on the diagram.

In 1989 Khailany (Khailany and Khorshid 1990) extended the rigorous dependency diagram, made it capable of repre-

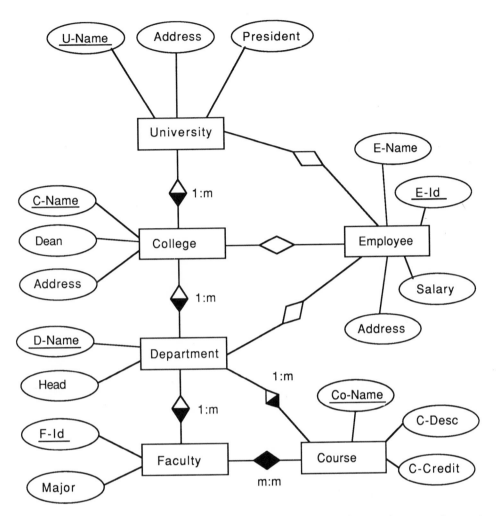

FIGURE 4. Extended entity relationship model. Each rectangle contains an entity, and each ellipse contains an attribute.

senting class and subclass entities and ternary or *n*-ary relationships between entities, and developed notation to represent whether the existence of an entity in a relationship is optional or mandatory. This method guarantees that the tables that will be extracted according to the above rules will be fully normalized. Figure 5 is the rigorous dependency diagram schema of Figure 1.

4. Object-oriented method. In this method, objects are enclosed in rectangles. The property (attribute) of an object can be simple, or it can be an object of its own. A simple object contains only simple properties. An associated object contains at least one multivalue simple property or a multi-

value of a group of simple properties. In a complex object at least one of its properties is an object. An associated object has its own key that exists on its own and represents the relationships between or among two or more objects by containing them and by being contained in those objects. An aggregation object is a class or a superclass of objects. The object diagram will be converted to a relational diagram, and from the relational diagram tables are extracted.

Automated Database Design Tools
Ideally an automatic database design tool should be capable of performing the following tasks:

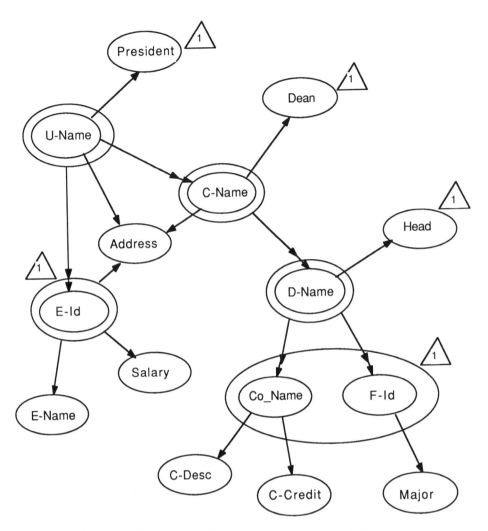

FIGURE 5. Rigorous dependency diagram. The number 1 within a triangle means different names for the same attribute, E-Id.

1. Creates the final schema from the information gathered in the information requirement and analysis phase, the first phase of database design that identifies all needed files, their attributes, and their keys.

2. Converts the structure of the previous step to comply with the requirements of the specific database model of the designer's choice. The final schema has to be the best possible schema and free from all anomalies.

3. Generates the code required to install the structure of step 2 (this process is usually called physical database design) on the computer, using the data definition language of the database package for the data model chosen in step 1.

4. Generates computer programs using the data manipulation language (of the same database package of the previous step) to produce the required reports and to make the system able to perform all the transactions that were identified in the first phase, the information requirements and analysis phase.

For a manually designed database, the hardest tasks are those performed in steps 1 and 2. To perform these tasks one must have a complicated technical background and expertise in designing database systems. Not every programmer or systems analyst can perform the tasks of step 1 and 2. All the software packages that help design some parts of the database and that are currently available require the user to have some technical background.

Currently there are several software packages available to help design database systems. Most of these packages guarantee the generated tables to be only in third normal form. In the remainder of this article we highlight and describe the capability of four systems. The simplest of these is Rapid Expert Automatic Database Design (READD), created by Khailany of Rapidinfo Computer Systems. This package concerns only the design of schema for relational databases. However, it guarantees that all tables will be fully normalized—that is, they will be in domain/key normal form.

The other three software packages—ER Designer of Chen & Associates, Inc.; Application Development Workbench of KnowledgeWare, Inc.; and Holland Systems of Holland Management, Inc.—are more complicated and complete; nevertheless, all three packages guarantee that the relation will be in third normal form only.

ER-Designer generates tables in third normal form. Using the entity relationship method, it generates schema for a number of DBMS packages; produces entity relationship diagrams from schema (reverse engineering); and generates a data flow diagram, a systems analysis tool, to design systems. Like ER-Designer, both Application Development Workbench and Holland Systems provide the user with capabilities for planning, analysis, construction, and automatic code generation of information systems.

Following is a brief description of these computer-aided software engineering tools:

Rapid Expert Automatic Database Design (READD)

This interactive system asks the user to input the information listed in the dependency list. More precisely, it asks the user to type in the names of the reports, transactions, and the fields that are associated with these transactions and reports. After feeding the names of all the reports and transactions, the system creates a number of temporary entities called tables and asks the user to identify candidate keys, the primary key, and foreign keys for each table. The user can invoke a help menu for the meaning of these terms and keys. Then the system takes one entity at a time and asks the user to identify the relationship between the primary key and other attributes in the entity, or between the attributes of the entity under consideration and other entities, and the relationships between or among different entities. Some highlights of this product are:

1. The system uses a combination of all the database design methods.

2. The final tables are fully normalized—that is, all the tables are in domain/key normal form.

3. The user can start with a single report or transaction. This will generate a temporary table. Then the system leads the user to full design of the database, satisfying the requirements outlined in the dependency list.

4. The set of generated tables can be printed or stored on disk.

5. The user can modify the design. New tables or attributes can be added to the set of tables that have been previously stored. Note that adding a single attribute or a table to a currently fully normalized set of tables may require complete redesign, which is taken care of by the system automatically.

6. The system provides a help menu, which makes a person with very little technical background able to use the system.

7. The final table contains the name of each table, its attributes, candidate keys, primary key, foreign keys, the names of the tables, and alias names for the foreign keys.

ER Designer

This computer-aided software engineering (CASE) tool is a product of Chen & Associates, Inc. This system is a systems analysis and database design tool that consists of the following nine modules:

1. Data flow diagram designer. Generates a data flow diagram using Yourdon and Demarco or Gain and Sarson notations.

2. ER Designer. Creates multilevel ER diagrams with integrity and consistency checking.

3. Data dictionary and report generator.

4. Normalizer. Guarantees that any ER diagram or relational tables are in third normal form.

5. Schema generator. Generates schema for any of the following DBMS packages:

Mini/Micro DBMS

dBASE	HP/IMAGE	Progress
Db_VISTA	Informix	Sybase
DEC/rdb	Ingress	ZIM
DG/SQL	Oracle	

Mainframe DBMS

ADABAS	IDMS/R	NOMAD
DATACOM/DB	IMS	Oracle
DB2	Ingres	SQL/DS
FOCUS	Model 204	UNISYS/RDMS

6. DDS-Link. Creates files for any of the following commercial data dictionaries: Brownstone, CA/IDD, DEC/CDD/Plus, IBM DB/DC, MSP, and UNISYS/DDS.

7. Reverse engineering. Converts an existing DBMS application of any of the following to an ER diagram: CAT/DATA-COM, DB2, HP/MPE, IMS, Informix, Model 204, MSP, Oracle, PRESENT.DF MULTI-LEVEL DBAM, PRESENT.DBF ISAM FILES, and RDB.

8. AutoDraw. Creates an ER diagram from English-like textual inputs.

9. Case-Link. Establishes interface to other case vendors.

Application Development Workbench

This CASE tool is the product of KnowledgeWare, Inc. It includes subsystems called workstation tools for planning, analysis, construction, and automatic code generation of information systems. The Application Development Workbench (ADW) stores all the knowledge about a given application in a subsystem called Encyclopedia, which is the key integrating factor for all tools in the ADW. The ADW provides planning, analysis, design, and construction tools as personal computer–based tools. For mainframe-based tools, ADW provides application generation, tools for Encyclopedia management, and an import/export subsystem.

1. Planning workstation. This automated tool is used to manage and analyze planning data. This subsystem provides a set of integrating diagrams, including a decomposition diagram, entity relationship diagram, association matrices (tables), and property matrices for analyzing knowledge about the system to be designed.

2. Analysis workstation. This subsystem determines what processes and data are necessary to meet end user needs and identifies the relationship between these data and processes. To achieve these goals, the subsystem uses a set of integrated diagrams, including decomposition diagrams, data flow diagrams, entity relationship diagrams, and minispec action diagrams.

3. Design workstation. This component of the system provides tools for process and data design by helping the user capture knowledge about program structure, procedural logic, data structure, databases, file structure, report layouts, and screen layouts.

4. Construction generator. This subsystem has two components: a code generator and a micro action diagrammer. This module is the back-end tool for processing information that has been collected in the Encyclopedia via the above front-end tools. Its main purpose is automatically to generate the COBOL programming source code, database definitions, data access routines, screen maps, and system documentation.

KnowledgeWare's Cross System Product Enablement Facility provides the user with the capability to develop applications utilizing IBM Cross System Product. The types of database structures that can be defined for Cross System Product include DB2, DL1, VSAMN, QSAM, and ISAM. In addition, the system provides the database diagrammer with relational and hierarchical databases that can be used to generate the database definitions for associated Cross System Product applications. The Construction Work Station makes it easy for the user to create DB2 applications. The data manipulation language is SQL for the database package. DB2 is automatically generated to give relational database access.

Holland Systems

This CASE tool has three main components: proplanner, prodeveloper, and promanager. The proplanner component is the front end of the system and has four components: business planning, data planning, application planning, and technology planning. The prodeveloper has database design, database construction, application design, application construction, and database implementation subsystems. The components of the promanager subsystem are task planning, resource allocation, and resource and result tracking. The proplanner provides the user with capabilities to identify organizational priorities, organizational objectives, project dependencies, scheduling, monitoring activities, required information for business actions, and overall view of current and future data, and it documents the existing technology components and the guidelines for transition to a new technology architecture.

The prodeveloper enables the user to design logical and physical databases and to normalize data elements from an entity relationship model to produce a logical data model, and it produces a functional design specification that describes inputs, outputs, interfaces, and processing and data components for application systems. Also, the prodeveloper provides the user with the ability to generate code, install new systems, and test modules.

The promanager subsystem produces Gant charts to plan and control projects, provides the user with resource spreadsheets for staffing projects, performs critical-path calculations to control projects, and uses dependency diagrams to analyze dependency relationships between activities.

[See also Database Management; Query Processing in Databases.]

References

Chen, P. P. 1976. The entity relationship model—Toward a unified view of data. *ACM Transactions on Database Systems* 1(1): 9–36.

CODASYL. 1975. *Database Task Group report 1971.* New York: Association for Computing Machinery.

Codd, E. F. 1970. A relational model of data for large shared data banks. *Communications of the ACM* 13(6):377–87.

Fagin, R. 1981. A normal form for relational databases that is based on domains and keys. *Transactions on Database Systems* 6(3):387–415.

Khailany, A., and W. Khorshid. 1990. Comparison between extended rigorous diagram and extended entity relationship models. *Proceedings of 1990 International Academy of Management and Marketing Conference,* vol. II, pp. 149–58.

Smith, H. 1985. Database design: Composing fully normalized tables from a rigorous dependency diagram. *Communications of the ACM* 28(8):826–38.

Teorey, T., D. Yang, and J. Fry. 1986. A logical design methodology for relational databases using the extended entity-relationship model. *ACM Computing Surveys* 18(2):197–222.

For Further Reading

Chen & Associates, Inc. 1989. *ER Designer user manual.*

Codd, E. F. 1979. Extending the relational model to capture more meaning. *ACM Transactions on Database Systems* 4(4):397–434.

Date, C. 1986. *An introduction to database systems,* vol. I, 4th ed. Reading, Mass.: Addison-Wesley.

Elmasri, R., and B. Shamkant. 1989. *Navathe fundamentals of database systems.* Menlo Park, Calif.: Benjamin-Cummings.

Holland Systems, Inc. 1990. *Holland Systems user manual.*

Khailany, A. 1989. An expert .system for automatic relational database systems (ERDS). *Proceedings of the Tenth European Conference on Operational Research,* Belgrade, Yugoslavia, pp. 26–27.

KnowledgeWare, Inc. *APW user manual.*

Kroenke, D., and K. Dolan. 1988. *Database processing.* 3rd ed. Chicago: Science Research Associates.

Teorey, J. T. 1990. *Database modeling and design—The entity-relationship approach.* San Mateo, Calif.: Morgan Kaufmann.

Welzer, T., I. Rozman, and J. Gyorkos. 1989. Automated normalization tool. *Microprocessing and Microprogramming* 25(1):375–80.

Asad Khailany

DATABASE MANAGEMENT

As mass storage prices fall and computers are used extensively throughout businesses and other organizations, vast amounts of valuable information are piling up in electronic repositories. Finding ways to organize this information and to allow convenient access to it is steadily becoming more important. The emergence of advanced concepts based on artificial intelligence will make the storage and management of such vast amounts of information even more critical.

Software developers have come up with a variety of database management systems, which accept, organize, store, and retrieve information quickly and efficiently. A *database* is a collection of related data that contains information about an enterprise such as a university or an airline. *Data* include facts and figures that can be represented as numbers, text strings, images, or voices stored in files on disk or other media. A *database management system* (DBMS) is a set of programs (a software package) that allows accessing and/or modification of the database. A major goal of the DBMS is to allow the user to deal with the data in abstract terms, rather than as the computer stores the data.

Before databases were introduced, users had to write programs to manipulate data stored in files (conventional file systems environment). Database management systems differ from the conventional file systems as follows.

Data dependence.   File systems exhibit data dependence, whereas a DBMS exhibits data independence. That is, changes in the organization of physical data and/or storage device parameters are absorbed by the DBMS and, therefore, do not affect the user of the database. If data were stored in a conventional file, changes in the record length, for example, would affect the program that manipulates (or uses) those data.

Data redundancy.   In file systems, data may be duplicated. For example, the address of a customer may appear in a file representing the data for orders received and in a file representing orders shipped. An objective of a DBMS is to avoid this type of redundancy by placing common information in a single file and then, as users request the information, applying a certain set of operations on stored data to obtain the necessary information.

Inconsistency.   In file systems, there is no technique for checking whether various copies of data are consistent. For example, if the customer address changes, then the user might change that address in the order-received file and not in the order-shipped file; the customer address therefore becomes inconsistent. It is the responsibility of the programmer to manipulate the data so that they are consistent; if he or she fails to do so, the program may produce incorrect results. In DBMSs, the database is always in a consistent state because changes to one piece of data are automatically absorbed throughout the entire system. Note that in databases, for efficiency purposes, the data might be duplicated; however, this redundancy is controlled.

Lack of data integrity.   Constraints may be imposed on certain data. For example, a customer can charge a sum greater than her or his allowed credit limit. In file systems, it is the responsibility of the user to determine if information entered violates the specific constraints imposed, in this case, a credit limit. In DBMSs, however, constraints can be handled automatically. If the data entered into the system violate the constraints, the system rejects the data and/or warns the user about them.

Lack of security. In conventional file systems, the unit of access is a file. Therefore, the user can access all the information in a file or none of it. In DBMSs, however, the user can view only a portion of the data. For example, a travel agent in an airline reservation system is allowed to check seat reservation and flight status, but not the salary of the airline employees.

What we have described so far demonstrates the usefulness of the DBMS as compared with the conventional file system; however, one has to realize that a DBMS may become large and very complex, requiring special hardware for support. Therefore, the implementation of a DBMS may become costly.

USERS OF A DATABASE MANAGEMENT SYSTEM

Three different types of user interact with a DBMS: application programmers, naive users, and database administrators.

Application programmers are computer professionals who interact with the DBMS through *data manipulation language* (DML) calls that are embedded in a program written in a host language such as COBOL or C. These programs are commonly referred to as *application programs*. Application programmers are frequently users of the DBMS.

Naive users use the DBMS less frequently than the application programmers, and they do not need to know the details of the system. These are casual users of the system, such as bank tellers. Their main interaction with the system is through the application programs written by the application programmers.

The *data administrator* has central responsibility for the data. The data administrator decides what data should be stored in the database initially and establishes policies for maintaining and dealing with those data once they have been stored. An example of such a policy would be one that dictates who can perform what operations on what data in what circumstances. The data administrator is a manager and not a technical person.

Database administrators are rare users of the system. Some of the tasks of a database administrator are to grant access authorization to various users, to create the original description of the database and make subsequent changes to it, to make backup copies of the database, and to repair damage to the database resulting from hardware or software failures or misuse. The description of the original database and subsequent changes to it is accomplished using a *data definition language* (DDL). The DDL is not used for obtaining and/or modifying the actual data. Manipulation of the database is done through the DML or query language.

COMPONENTS OF A DATABASE MANAGEMENT SYSTEM

Database management systems consist of five major components: file manager, database manager, query processor, data manipulation language precompiler, and data definition language compiler.

The *file manager* is responsible for physical storage of data on disk or any other physical media. The *database manager* provides the interface between the low-level data stored in the database and the application programs and queries submitted to the system. A database manager is responsible for integrity, security enforcement, concurrency control, backup, recovery, and interaction with the file manager.

The *query processor* translates statements in a query language into low-level instructions that the database manager understands. In addition, the query processor attempts to transform a user's request into an equivalent, but more efficient form, thus finding a good strategy for executing the query.

A *data manipulation language precompiler* converts DML statements embedded in an application program to normal procedure calls in the host language. A *data definition language compiler* converts DDL statements to a set of tables containing information about data (metadata). This table is referred to as a *data dictionary* (catalog). A data dictionary, in addition to storing information about the structure of the database, stores information such as authorization for a given table or different access methods available.

DATA MODELS

The overall design of the database is called the *database schema*. There are three different types of schemas in the database, and these are partitioned according to the levels of abstraction. At the highest level we have multiple *external schemas*, which correspond to different perceptions of the data in the database. Sometimes in the literature an external schema is referred to as a *subschema*. At the intermediate level we have the conceptual level, sometimes referred to as the *conceptual schema* or simply *schema*. The conceptual level is the view of the database as a whole by the community. The conceptual schema describes the logical relationship between data items, together with integrity constraints. At the lowest level of abstraction we have the *physical* or *internal schema*. The internal level deals with the physical organization of the database. The DBMS software is responsible for mapping between these three types of schema.

To describe the structure of a database, a *data model* is created and is administered by a database administrator. A data model is a collection of conceptual tools for describing data, data relationships, data semantics, and data constraints. A database designer can choose among several data models, such as

the relational data model and the network data model.

RELATIONAL DATA MODEL

A *relational database* consists of a collection of *relations* (or *tables*), each of which is assigned a unique name. In this model, data are represented as a table, with each horizontal row representing a *tuple* or a *record* and each vertical column representing an *attribute* or *field* of the tuple. Because rows are required to be nonredundant within a relation, each row can be identified uniquely by a subset of its attributes. Such a set of attributes is called the *key* of a relation. The minimum-sized set of attributes that uniquely identifies tuples of a relation is referred to as the *primary key*. A relation may have many primary keys, and one such primary key is selected by the database administrator as the *candidate key*.

Figure 1 shows a simplified relational database for a university that maintains information about the faculty and departments. This database contains three relations: Faculty, Department, and Faculty–Department. The Faculty relation can be thought of as a relationship among such attributes as "Faculty Name" (FN), "Faculty ID" (FID), "Faculty Home Telephone Number" (FTEL), and "Faculty Title" (FTIT). The Department relation contains the attributes "Department Name" (DN), "Department Location" (DLC), "Number of Faculty in the Department" (NFAC), and "Department Budget" (DB). We need also a third relation to link information about the faculty and the department in which they work. This is represented by the relation Faculty–Department in Figure 1. This relation contains the attributes FID, DN, and the number of years in which a faculty member has worked in a department (NYRS).

The *degree* of a relation is defined by the number of attributes in it. For example, the Faculty relation in Figure 1 is of degree 4. The *size* of a relation is the number of records in that relation. For example, the Department relation is of size 3. The primary key for the Faculty relation is FID; for the Department relation DN; and for the Faculty–Depart-

Faculty	*FN*	*FID*	*FTEL*	*FTIT*
	Jones	123	577-1232	Assistant Professor
	Smith	234	456-1765	Professor
	Hayes	345	876-2435	Lecturer
	Smith	456	675-9008	Professor

Department	*DN*		*DLC*	*NFAC*	*DB*
	Computer Science		State Hall	2	$10,000
	Chemistry		Science Bldg.	1	$15,000
	Physics		Science Bldg.	1	$14,000

Faculty-Department	*FID*	*DN*	*NYRS*
	456	Computer Science	3
	234	Computer Science	5
	345	Physics	8
	123	Chemistry	2

FIGURE 1. A simplified relational database for a university.

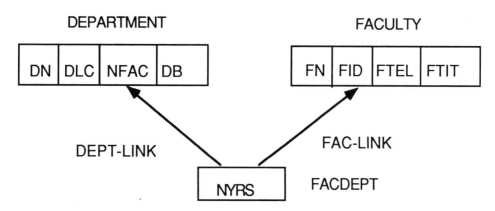

FIGURE 2. A simple network structure for the university database.

ment relation, the combination of attributes FID and DN.

NETWORK DATA MODEL

Much of today's awareness of the concepts of the database can be credited to the work of CODASYL (Conference on Data Systems Languages) and its committees. CODASYL's first project was to develop specifications for a common business-oriented language, given the acronym COBOL. In 1966 CODASYL started a new task force, called the Data Base Task Group (DBTG), to extend COBOL for handling databases. The basic underlying data model in 1969 reports by the DBTG is a network data model.

The *network data model* is the data model of a network DBMS. The network data model can be described, in the graph theoretic sense, as a graph having no cycles, with a collection of record types (as the nodes of the graph) connected by a set of links (as the edges of the graph). In this model, the links are built into the design of the database, and the program must follow the established paths to find information. A record type or simply a record represents an entity, which is a collection of fields, each of which contains only one data value. Figure 2 shows an example of a network diagram for the university database given in Figure 1. In this figure, we have three record types, namely, FACULTY, DEPARTMENT, and FACDEPT. Figure 3 shows the sample database corresponding to the network diagram in Figure 2.

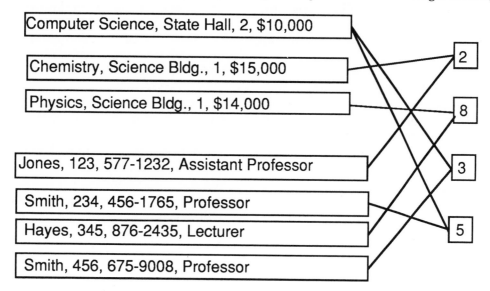

FIGURE 3. A sample database for the network structure in Figure 2.

[*See also* Data; Database Design, Automated.]

For Further Reading

Date, C. J. 1990. *An introduction to database systems*, 5th ed., vol. I. Reading, Mass.: Addison-Wesley.

Elmasri, R., and S. Navathe. 1989. *Fundamentals of database systems*. Redwood City, Calif.: Benjamin Cummings.

Korth, H., and A. Silberchatz. 1986. *Database system concepts*. New York: McGraw-Hill.

Ozkarhan, E. 1990. *Database management, concepts, design and practice*. Englewood Cliffs, N.J.: Prentice-Hall.

Ullman, J. D. 1989. *Principles of databases and knowledge-base systems*, vol. I. Rockville, Md.: Computer Science Press.

Farshad Fotouhi

DATABASE PROGRAMMING

Over the years, programming languages have increasingly isolated the user from the inner workings of the computer and its operating system; database programming partially isolates the programmer from the details of data management by applying appropriate rules to the data handling, thus partially automating that part of the programming task.

Databases are large, usually complex lists of facts and information; they usually contain regular arrangements of text and numbers, but modern databases, especially on personal computers, can contain video images (still or moving), sounds, large bodies of text, or combinations of all these elements.

Many types of data fit best into databases; today, most telephone directories, library card catalogs, airline flight guides, and bibliographic references are kept in database forms, as are conventional databases containing accounting information, mailing lists, and the like.

Although you can still get many reference works in paper, or "hard copy," locating the data in a large volume requires elaborate indices, which are both tedious and expensive to prepare and keep up-to-date. A database on a computer, on the other hand, can easily be re-indexed whenever the underlying data are changed; in fact, this tedious and complex task is automatically handled by the database management system whenever the data in the database are changed.

The craft of data management dates back to Aristotle, the Greek philosopher, and the scheme of interlocking knowledge classifications he expounded in his *Physica*. Automated data storage and retrieval first appeared in the 1880s when the Jacquard loom was developed; the loom could weave intricate patterns under the control of programs recorded on punched cards. The use of punched cards as a general-purpose data storage medium was further developed by Herman Hollerith. His card-sorting device, a precursor to the modern report generator, was used in the 1890 census.

Over the years, data storage has come a long way, from the Hollerith cards to magnetic tape (with the data usually still in Hollerith's format) to massive modern databases stored on disk. Many modern databases are huge and complex, but the data input and inquiry programs make it relatively simple to use the data in them without a great deal of computer knowledge. When you call an airline's reservations agent, a special type of report generator tells the agent what seats are available on what flights and at what prices (see also AIRLINE RESERVATION SYSTEMS).

In discussing database programming, it can be helpful to distinguish between the database management system (DBMS) and the database programming language (DBPL). The DBMS performs the task of manipulating the data under the control of the DBPL. In many cases, however, the DBMS and the DBPL are integrated, and presented to the user or programmer as a command line or prompt at which one can type various commands to manipulate the chosen data.

The permissable commands include both ad hoc commands, like LIST ALL

WHERE STATE IS GEORGIA, and the ability to run programs written in the command language or DBPL. In these and many other cases, it is difficult to draw the exact dividing line between the DBMS and the DBPL, so in the discussion that follows just remember that DBMS is the side that is more computer oriented, and DBPL is on the side more oriented to the human operator.

Using a DBPL, or a DBMS add-on to a conventional language, usually provides a number of benefits to both the software developer and the eventual user of the application. The developer saves both time and money, in most cases, because licensing the DBPL is quicker and less expensive than designing and writing one from scratch. The end user benefits because the data are in a standard format, and many DBPLs have accessory programs, such as report generators, that can be used directly on the data.

TYPES OF DATABASES

There are four types of databases.

Hierarchical Database

Every set of facts belongs to a larger category. The biological classification system (kingdom, phylum, class, order, family, genus, species) places living things in a hierarchical database.

Relational Database

A relational database is a rows-and-columns, or tabular, approach to the organization of facts. A typical list of animals, with their names in a column down the left margin of the page and various animal characteristics (habitat, range, diet) assigned to the other columns, is a relational database.

Multiple-File Relational Database

A multiple-file relational database is a linked group of relational databases used where the data are too complex for a single file. In a public library book catalog and circulation system, for example, there might be separate, but linked, databases for book publishers, the books they publish, the books the library owns, the subjects those books cover, the library's patrons, the location of the books, and their circulation status.

Unstructured or Full-Text Database

Unlike the other database forms, full-text databases have very little organization beyond the indexing of key words. Many newspapers' entire noncommercial contents are available in full-text databases, as are magazines, wire service reports, scholarly and professional research papers, press releases, and other forms of information. Some of these databases use the HYPERTEXT concept, where words in one article are linked to other articles; if this encyclopedia entry were linked that way, you could select the word *hypertext* in the body of the text, see a complete article explaining that concept, and then return to this discussion on report generators.

Although the exact nomenclature differs, databases can generally be thought of as being divided into records (the rows in the relational model above), with each record divided into fields (the columns in the relational model). Of course, something like a full-text database may have very long records (a complete magazine article, perhaps) that contain only one field: the whole record.

DATABASE ORGANIZATION

Most database organization schemes include three parts.

Data Dictionary

The data dictionary contains the names of the various data fields, along with information on the size and type of data they contain. In a simple mailing list database, the data dictionary may include only the field names, their data types, and their lengths. In more complex databases, the data dictionary may include definitions of the relationships between the various fields, as well as data processing rules and other information.

Index Files

There may be one or more index files, each containing key values and information on the location of the associated records in the data file. In a mailing list, there might be separate index files for last names, states, and zip codes, with each index entry having a "pointer" to a record in the data file.

Data File

The heart of the system, the data file contains the data itself, in the layout defined by the data dictionary and in the order described by the index files. In our simple mailing list example, the data fields might contain first names, last names, street addresses, cities, states, and zip codes, and each group of fields is combined into a record describing one person or organization. Of course, multifile databases may have numerous data files that are linked, through indices or other means, to provide the complete data required for a particular task.

Some DBMSs maintain each of these classes of files as separate files, some combine them into one file, and still others combine them in various ways. dBASE II and its descendents, for example, combine the data dictionary, the data, and the index in a single file, but allow the programmer to create temporary or permanent external indices as well. Naturally, although programmers may have some level of interest in the way the DBMS organizes the parts of the database, they can rarely do very much about it, as the DBMS itself takes care of it as part of its data management task. That is, in fact, the point of using a DBPL: you do not have to delve into the details of the data management.

All DBMS data management tasks can be broken down into three classes of activities:

1. *Addition.* Add a new record to the database. The DBMS handles the details of inserting or appending the record, and modifies the indices to reflect the new contents of the database.

2. *Deletion.* Remove a record from the database. The DBMS handles the details of removing the record, and modifies the indices to reflect the new contents of the database. Most modern DBMSs maintain a list of the locations of deleted records, so the "hole" in the file can be reused when another record is subsequently added. Some older DBMSs require periodic reorganization to accomplish this.

3. *Modification.* Change the contents of the database. The amount of work the DBMS must do to accomplish this varies widely, depending on the length of the modified data record and its key values. If all the records in the database are of the same length, the DBMS can put the changed record back where it came from, but if the data field is now a different length, and the DBMS allows variable-length records, it is usually treated as an addition of a new record and a deletion of the old one. In any case, if any of the key values have changed, the DBMS updates the indices.

A combination of operations, particularly in a multifile database, can be considered a transaction, and some DBMSs have a facility to ensure that all parts of the transaction have been successfully completed before returning control to the program or the operator. This type of DBMS will reverse the successful parts of the transaction automatically if any part of the transaction fails. This feature is sometimes called "automatic transaction recovery," and can be very important in multifile databases because it prevents the various files from showing different values for the same data.

For instance, at a credit bureau it is likely that all the debtor database files would be organized by social security number, as any individual's social security number is unlikely to change. If, however, someone's social security number does change, all the records containing, and indexed by, that number must be changed. The operator who keys in the new number is probably unaware that he or she is changing multiple files in a single transaction, as the DBMS puts the information from several files on the screen at one time. Suppose one of the social security number changes fails because of a hardware error. The accuracy and uniformity of the data is better preserved if the entire transaction is rejected, rather than the changes applied only to some of the files.

If the DBMS does not provide automatic transaction recovery, and the level of programming allows it, it can sometimes be programmed into the application itself; however, as the thrust of DBPL development is toward less and less detailed programming, this may not be possible with all DBPLs.

CLASSES OF DATABASE MANAGEMENT SCHEMES

Self-Contained Database Management Schemes

The self-contained DBMS includes a complete DBPL, with facilities not only for data record handling, but for data input screen construction, numerical computation, and other general programming tasks. In fact, the DBPL has largely replaced general-purpose computer languages like BASIC and Pascal for systems whose main purpose is data file manipulation. Most commercially available, microcomputer-based, general accounting systems, Peachtree Software's for instance, are still written largely in BASIC, but most special-purpose systems designed and developed for specific customers are probably written in dBASE II, its derivatives, or similar languages. Many self-contained DBMSs are available in both single-user and multiuser/network versions.

Link-in Database Management Schemes

Link-in DBMSs are designed to be used with conventional programming languages such as BASIC, Pascal, and C. They are called "linked-in modules" or "link libraries" because they are added to the main program during the compilation process, as part of the linkage step that makes the program runnable. In general, the link library DBMS becomes an extension of the programming language in use, and is treated as a function, subroutine, procedure, or subprogram. This type of DBMS allows programmers to write the user-visible parts of the program, like the screen presentation and data processing tasks, in a language they already know and understand, but gives them sophisticated file handling capabilities without requiring that they write the necessary routines themselves.

In addition, some link library DBMSs allow existing software, already developed in conventional languages, to be enhanced with additional file handling capabilities, and the ability of many link library DBMSs to handle multiuser file access allows programmers to add multiuser or networking capabilities to their programs without requiring complete redevelopment.

Btrieve is a leading link library DBMS; it is published by Novell.

Server Database Management Schemes

Server DBMSs constitute a growing class of DBMSs characterized by multiuser and networking powers. Server DBMSs typically run on a network's file server, rather than on the workstations. This DBMS "engine" accepts data transaction requests over the network, and sends the required data back by the same path. Of course, appropriate software must be running on the workstation in question, and the workstation software can be either a standalone DBMS or a conventional program into which a special module was linked when it was written. Novell's Btrieve is also available as a DBMS server.

ADD-ONS/ACCESSORIES

Many DBPL packages include various accessories. In other cases, add-ons that work with the DBMS are available from other vendors.

Report Generators

A special type of database programming, a report generator is a program designed to assist the user in extracting from a database the information sought and in putting it in the format desired. Report generators generally allow the user to specify three characteristics of the data he or she wishes to see: the selection, that is, those qualities that qualify a record for inclusion in a report; sort order, which specifies the order in which the selected records should be listed in the report; and the presentation format, which specifies how the report should look, what fields should be totaled, where page breaks should occur, and other specifics. Some report generators can be used to create data files, rather than hard-copy reports, so that data can be easily transferred to other computers without being reentered.

Most report generators can be used for both permanent reports, those that are a part of regular data processing for the database concerned, and ad hoc reports, "spur of the moment reports" for special situations, simulations, and modeling.

Screen Generators

As a very large proportion of a commercial programmer's time is spent writing the "front end" of a program, anything that saves time in this regard is a boon to programmer productivity. With a screen generator, the display screens that make up a program's front end can be prototyped without the programmer having to write a program code. Then the prototype screens are processed by a special program that generates the program necessary to produce the screens. In some cases, the programmer or designer can specify the derivations and processing rules for the data on the screen, and the processor will generate the code for that, too.

Computer-Aided Software Engineering Tools

Computer-aided software engineering (CASE) is an emerging field that uses a system of computer programs to guide a program designer in the creation of complex software systems. The designer specifies data flows, processing rules, screen designs, logical dependencies, and other parameters, and the CASE software analyzes the results for consistency. CASE tools generally produce flow charts, data layouts, and other programming specifications, but some also produce the necessary program code for the application.

Application Generators

Long billed as the ultimate development tool, application generators seek to combine a screen generator, a DBMS, and some CASE influences to produce ready-to-compile application code in a variety of languages. Compared by some to a machine that takes the idea of breakfast as input, deduces the existence of eggs, and produces omelettes as the output, CASE tool application generators available on mainframes are actually capable of writing the complete code for complex applications. It is only a matter of time until such development tools become available for the microcomputer.

Other Link Libraries

Used most frequently with the link-in DBMS, and particularly in the popular C language, linked-in modules can perform the same management for serial communications, screen handling, printer management, and network communications that the DBMS does for data file handling. Some standalone DBMSs can use these add-ons, too, if they are available in the appropriate formats, and, of course, applications in a server DBMS can use them as well.

SUMMARY

As you can see, the possible combinations of database type, DBMS type, transaction, and other data handling details and the possible inclusion of various tools and add-ons make database programming a fascinating field.

The future direction of DBPL developments is pretty clear. With CASE tools and application generators leading the way, and with an admixture of artificial intelligence, it is likely that the past progression of computer languages from the concrete to the increasingly abstract will prevail. It has often been said that computers do not do what you want them to, they do what you tell them to do. In the future it will be easier to tell them what you want.

For Further Reading

Shuster, H. L., and R. D. Dillion. 1988. *The financial manager's guide to microsoftware.* New York: Wiley.

Walter, R. 1991. *The secret guide to computers,* 14th ed. Somerville, Mass.: Russ Walter Publications.

Hergert, D. 1985. *dBASE III, the Microsoft desktop dictionary and cross-reference guide.* Bellevue, Wash.: Microsoft Press.

Sheldon T. Hall

DATABASES

[*Database management systems were originally developed in a business environment for the efficient storage and retrieval of information. Currently, however, the field is undergoing much ferment as its scope widens to a larger user community as well as to other types of information besides standard record–oriented business data. The article* Database Management *gives a general introduction to the field, whereas* Query Processing in Databases *explains the efficiencies that database systems achieve in the retrieval of information.* Database Programming *by Sheldon C. Hall explains how database access can be accomplished by means of various sorts of command languages as well as programming languages. The manner in which multiple databases are becoming integrated and distributed over computer networks is covered in the article* Distributed and Heterogeneous Databases. *Finally, many of the new generation of database management systems that are being designed for such tasks as the administration of temporal data, geographical data, rule–based data, and objects are discussed in* Nonstandard Database Systems.]

DATABASES, ON-LINE

Since the beginning of the Industrial Revolution the need for, coherent information—data sorted and ordered to provide meaning to the user—about companies and products, populations and processes, has been ever increasing. Traditionally, this need has been filled by book publishers, some of which specialize in providing certain sorts of information in the form of printed and bound directories, catalogs, indexes, and encyclopedias such as this one, and by libraries dedicated to organizing books, dissertations, and articles on a myriad of subjects for easy retrieval.

Because it became possible to quickly and easily connect widely separated computers to each other via modems, the 1970s saw the beginning of what has become a very large and very rapidly growing interactive information retrieval industry in the United States. On-line databases, mounted on computers and scattered from coast to coast, can be searched from nearly anywhere by remote control, and the needed information can be delivered in seconds to a researcher who may never know just where the information is physically located.

A vast web of interconnections, held together by telephone wire, satellite transmissions, fiberoptic networks, packet-switching systems, and money, stretches across North America and even reaches Europe, Japan, Australia, in short, every continent and most islands of the world.

The richness and variety of information contained in that network is incredibly beyond what any one library of printed works could contain, much less organize for retrieval. In fact, it could be said that the real wealth lies not in the sheer volume of information but in the ease of access to it. Rather than spending days, weeks, even months in a search for prior knowledge, a scientific researcher can sit at a keyboard and, with a well-designed search strategy, discover who has written what, where primary sources can be found, what paths are dead ends, which are promising, and even who is following what new path. Or perhaps the researcher is interested only in the batting averages of the St. Louis Cardinals for the past 5 years; or average rainfall in the month of May in Guatemala; or opinion on the President's handling of the China question.

All that and much, much more is available on-line, in databases accessible by anyone with a phone line, a computer, and a modem. A researcher can electronically ransack a database clear across the country or right next door, or both, and with a single computer-generated phone call can sometimes discover literally hundreds of articles that contain some part of the information sought or, even better, the single reference available that might otherwise never be found.

HISTORY

The total mass of information available in the United States, scattered across the continent and therefore weakly organized, had already become unmanageably large by the time the electronic computer was invented. Although some recognized almost immediately that these new machines would have a profound effect on information management and dissemination, fulfillment of the promise had to await the development of adequate storage and retrieval devices.

Equipment

In the 1960s, useful but still slow devices became available with the reel-to-reel magnetic storage tape deck. Then, in 1973, IBM introduced the Winchester hard (or fixed)-disk drive. Magnetic storage of information on rapidly rotating disks made true random access to data possible. These devices rapidly replaced the old, slow, and bulky punch-card storage systems. Rapid strides in communications technology allowed widely separated computers to "talk" with one another, to transmit data electronically through ordinary telephone lines.

The First On-Line Database

In the early 1960s Lockheed Corporation, a major defense contractor, found itself awash in technical papers and reports generated for and by the U.S. government. The task of organization combined with the need for various far-flung units of the corporation to have swift access to the data prompted the development of what was probably the first true on-line database, brought up for internal use in 1965. It used reel-to-reel technolo-

gy; was, compared with modern databases, quite slow; and could be accessed only through the corporate computer network. As slow as it was, it did not take long for other corporations to notice the advantages in speed and accuracy Lockheed had gained. Some began to organize other database systems while Lockheed recognized the profit potential and opened theirs, newly named DIALOG and with a total of six databases, in 1972 to anyone who wished to pay for access.

The Scene Today

The number of on-line databases is now literally in the hundreds and subjects cover nearly every facet of human activity: sports, medicine, law, transportation, and more. The most avid, if not the first, nontechnical users of on-line databases are probably lawyers. The LEXIS system now allows a lawyer to practice law without the expense of acquiring and maintaining a library. Discovery of legal precedent is swift, sure, accurate, and voluminous.

OVERVIEW OF DATABASE SYSTEMS

An on-line database is one large file mounted on a host computer that can be accessed remotely. The terminology dates back to the days of reel-to-reel drives. Information was mounted by physically loading the reel containing it onto the drive mechanism. Because of the expense of drive units, the early systems kept technicians busy mounting and unmounting reel after reel. Those systems have all been replaced by rows and rows of quietly humming hard-disk drives that provide nearly immediate access the moment a request is received.

A successful search request results in a "hit," which can be displayed in a number of ways depending on the system in use. Often, the system simply tells the user how many hits were found and asks whether the user wishes to retrieve any or all of the data.

Where the Information Comes from

Information providers develop and maintain the individual databases, which are packaged and marketed by vendors usually called information systems. Often, some of the databases are developed and maintained by the information system operator but others are provided by outside concerns on a royalty basis. Sometimes, the database is mounted directly on the information system's own computers. Other times it is mounted on a distant machine. Some are exclusive to one information system; others are offered by several systems.

Flow of Information

The host computer handles the search instructions and routes the information found to the correct user. Each host can handle information requests from a number of users limited only by the number of modems connected to the host.

Gateways

Because there are so many of them, the requested database is often not mounted on the first host accessed. When that occurs, the host connects itself to another host, sometimes in the next cabinet, often clear across the country, and becomes a "gateway." The first host passes the search request to the new host. The data are found and passed to the first host, then to the user.

Interconnections

The transfer of data is carried over high-speed packet-switching networks such as TYMENET and TELENET, independent of the telephone system. In fact, most on-line access, even from home computers, is made through these or similar systems. A remote user's computer, through a modem, dials the number of an "access node," usually in the local telephone exchange. The node is a collection of modems and small computers that automatically—after passwords are exchanged—connects the user's computer to a host through the network.

In recent years, the packet-switching web has become so extensive that virtually no locality in the United States is overlooked. Meaningful research can be conducted on-line with just a local phone call from nearly anywhere. What this means or will mean to universities and colleges, the traditional repositories of knowledge, remains to be seen but many are convinced that the changes will be significant. Already, several universities have become information providers to various information services and derive income from the activity.

KINDS OF INFORMATION TO BE FOUND

Nearly all sorts of information are available now in on-line databases. Many of them are U.S. government data files, including technical papers, census data, industrial production and sales data, and import/export data, placed on-line royalty free. Other sources include commercial information-gathering firms, such as Dun & Bradstreet and Dow-Jones, for financial and business data, or Wilson and National Register Publishing, for directories of publications or businesses.

Practically all of the "standard reference works" usually found on a library reference table are available on-line. Among them are *Marquis' Who's Who* in its various editions, *Books in Print*, and the *Reader's Guide to Periodical Literature*. The full text of dozens of regional newspapers is carried on the VU/Text service, with search software specifically for searching newspaper data. Various financial services are available from Standard & Poor on-line, along with Dun & Bradstreet products and databases from Dow-Jones, including the full text of the *Wall Street Journal*. An information service called NewsNet carries the full text of literally hundreds of newsletters, some available nowhere else, covering nearly every imaginable field. This brief summary has truly only scratched the surface. At least one database, however, indexes the databases available on-line. The Cuadra directory (officially, *Directory of Online Databases)* is available through EasyNet and, thus, on CompuServe and Western Union.

Kinds of Databases

Databases come in three main varieties. Each presents its information differently. First, and briefest, is the bibliographic database.

This contains only the sort of citation usually found in the bibliography of a scholarly book or article, combined with a series of "key words." The bibliographic database can be both the most difficult sort of database to search and the least accurate, as the results of a search are sharply affected by the skill of the editor who draws up the list of key words for each citation. Often, a bibliographic database offers "off-line" reprints of articles cited. These are usually mailed quickly at fairly low cost, around $3 to $5 or more, depending on length.

The second kind of database is the somewhat easier to use "abstract" database, which contains condensations of articles. These usually allow wider scope to the searcher because each word of each abstract is tested against the search criteria. Once again, the skill of the abstracter is a factor. Abstracts are always accompanied by full bibliographic information. Off-line reprints of the full text are usually available but because the abstract frequently contains the needed information, the researcher may not need to see the actual article.

The third sort of database is "full-text." Many newspapers are available in full text, as are many magazines, newsletters, catalogs, directories, and encyclopedias. It has become increasingly easy for publishers to offer their wares on-line as nearly all published material now routinely goes through a computer system, for typesetting if nothing else. The accumulated files are merely passed on to the information service as they become available. Most of the full-text professional and technical journal databases return bibliographic and abstract citations and allow optional on-line or off-line delivery of the full text.

SEARCHING FOR INFORMATION

Most on-line services require the searcher to know which database is most likely to carry the needed information. This can lead to a good deal of wasted time and money if the searcher guesses wrongly. All the services publish manuals that, ideally, describe in detail each of the databases offered on that service; however, because things change

very rapidly on-line, even the best of these manuals can only guide, not lead. So, some "slippage," as you might call it, is inevitable.

Deciding which database to search is easiest when the subject is technical or scholarly as each topic tends to be isolated into its own databases. For general information, the field is wide open; finding the proper database can be more a matter of luck than of skill. One strategy that seems to work very well is the same you might employ in a conventional library: Search an index database, such as the *Reader's Guide*, first, then search the databases that contain the full text of the publications cited.

Search Protocols

Each information system has its own search protocol or "language" which must be learned before any efficient use of the database system is possible. Some are extremely powerful, such as the search language for the DIALOG system; others are less flexible but simpler to use. Each contains its own maddening idiosyncrasies. Nearly all information systems have also implemented user-oriented interactive systems, which include menus and help screens. As handy as these can be, they are also very costly in connect time. So most systems also operate in "command mode," which requires that the user understand how the system works. To that end, each host service publishes an operating manual that should (but does not always) contain a description of each database on the host system, the search language, special features, and so on. Many of these manuals run to several hundred pages and are extremely detailed and quite well written and organized. Others, regrettably, are less complete. Even though the price for an operating manual can run as high as $75, it is very nearly an essential investment for any but the most casual of users.

Searching Across Databases

Some help has become available from a new, fourth, level of the database industry, however. The new kind of service might be called a translation and interconnection platform. Telebase Systems has developed a "super-gateway" service called EasyNet to tie many information systems together under a single search protocol and allow the user to be ignorant of which database might contain a given sort of information. The costs are, understandably, somewhat higher than might be encountered by accessing each database individually but the learning curve is remarkably short and shallow. EasyNet is marketed under several names, including IQuest on CompuServe and InfoMaster on Western Union.

EasyNet connects more than 800 databases from twelve host services (including Dialog, NewsNet, VU/Text, and Questel), though not every database from every host is available. The user can access individual databases directly or by use of a menu system that allows a narrowing of focus based on the information desired. During the "narrowing" process only normal connect time charges apply, but because it is interactive, and therefore slow, charges can mount rapidly. To help ease the burden, EasyNet allows an alternative, called SmartSCAN, that accepts search criteria and quickly reviews all associated databases. The resulting menu shows the number of articles found in each database that can then be reviewed at standard EasyNet search charges. The cost for each SmartSCAN search is usually $5 but, to encourage use of the system, special low prices are frequently offered.

EasyNet is not the only information provider with the ability to help a user choose the proper database but, at the moment at least, it has the easiest and quickest method of doing so. EasyNet accesses a large number of general information databases, any of which might or might not contain desired information. This is a very good way to discover, at low cost, where desired information can be found.

CONSTRUCTING SEARCH CRITERIA

Even though each information service has its own search protocol, all have certain things in common. Each accepts one or more key words, most accept Boolean operators, and most accept a "wildcard" character. So, even though syntax varies, a searcher can con-

struct a valid search "template" using any system of logical operators and expressions desired.

Planning a Search

For example, to find a recent magazine article on the president of XYZ Company or Corporation, a searcher might use this as a template: *Find 'XYZ Co*' and 'President' and yeardate <= '1990'*, where items in single quotes are key words, an asterisk is a wild card, and operators appear without punctuation.

This exact expression does not work directly but, by referring to the information services' operating manual, one can design a valid expression off-line based on the template. This sort of planning is crucial to successful on-line searching. Without it, a user can flounder through the data aimlessly, leaving the information service unable to deliver a useful product while still absorbing large amounts of the user's money.

Search Precision

One major problem, which can only be lessened but never overcome by experience in searching databases, is that of framing the search expression. Frequently a searcher leaves the search expression too "loose," resulting in several useless hits. The opposite problem occurs when the expression is too tight: A database may respond with no hits at all even though it contains a wealth of information on the desired topic.

The following example illustrates the problem. Using EasyNet, a search for *'Oil' and 'Wyoming'* will produce numerous hits scattered over several databases. Once the "detailed" search is made, most of the citations prove to concern oil production and exploration in the Wyoming Valley area of Pennsylvania, which will do little for the searcher who needs information concerning the oil business in the State of Wyoming. But, if the search expression reads *'Wyoming' and 'Oil' not 'Pennsylvania'*, the expression will prove to be too tight, because a good deal of oil in the state of Wyoming comes from formations called Pennsylvania Sands. Researchers in other fields will almost inevitably find similar situations. The only solution to the problem seems to be to keep the search expressions loose enough to rake up some "garbage" along with the nuggets of information desired.

The problem of search precision is especially acute in bibliographic databases. These are by nature limited to searches by specific key words; there is no access to the text of a citation. When the data are entered, an editor must decide which key words most nearly fit the citation. This is often a subjective opinion and may not match the searcher's needs. The key words for a given bibliographic database are drawn from an official list, often several thousand in number, called the *thesaurus* for that database. The information system's operating manual should contain the thesaurus for each available bibliographic database.

COSTS TO THE USER

An information service charges fees for access and search services that generally run in the range of $30 an hour for government databases to as high as $300 an hour for certain commercial, specialized information collections. These charges are usually "connect time" fees and accrue as long as a user is connected to a host, whether or not an actual search is taking place. Some services charge only connect time, which can vary depending on the database in use; others charge a combination of connect time and hit fees; still others offer a mixed bag, billing some of their databases according to connect time only, some by connect time plus hits. Occasionally, a database may carry a charge for the number of characters transmitted. Often, the only way to know what the charges are and how they are calculated for a given database is to read, carefully, the operation manual published by each individual information service.

The savings to the researcher in time and effort, when compared with the "old" methods of reviewing literature, are immense. Previously, a researcher might hire an assistant to handle the library chores or would be forced to do the "donkey work" personally. Either way, time and money were

spent lavishly. With easy access to on-line databases, search sessions are very fast, allowing more creativity to enter into the search process. Newly opened paths of inquiry can be followed; new connections between disparate facts can be discovered because the time and drudgery involved are no longer factors.

SUMMARY

For many years, critics of the academic and scientific community have charged that each discipline was becoming too insular, too self-involved. Subdisciplines arose that eventually found themselves almost completely out of contact with the parent subject. Much of this segregation is due, say the critics, to the vast amount of material published in every scientific and technical discipline. A student or practitioner is forced to narrow reading to only those journals that provide insight into the chosen subject.

Now, anyone can have the world's vastest library on a desk top. Cross-connections between disciplines are laughably easy to find. Just enter a key word or two and let the electronic librarian dig through the magnetic stacks. Cross-fertilization between disciplines has already occurred because of on-line databases; more is likely.

As costs come down—as they traditionally have done since the inception of the computer revolution—electronic databases will become more specialized, as have hand-held calculators, and have broader uses. Very soon, for example, television listings may be interactively available through a cable TV channel. You will ask your TV "What's on tonight?" and it will be able to tell you. The same channel may allow you to read reviews of books, then retrieve the full text for you to read on the TV screen, if that is your desire.

All that is intriguing, even benign, but the on-line database system can become a monster. As more transactions take place with computers as media, as when a credit card is "swiped" through a terminal box, larger volumes of data are accumulated about each person. These data are in databases. Access to most of the data is restricted but even so, canny searchers are, this moment, gathering this snippet and that—about your buying habits, your credit, the car you drive, your income—compiling them and offering the data for sale to the highest bidder, on-line.

INFORMATION SERVICES

Listed here are some of the major database vendors. Many of them can also be accessed through CompuServe, GEnie, or another on-line gateway, but for the serious searcher, direct connection is probably the best strategy. In each case, a customer service number is listed. These information services will be pleased to provide you with promotional and descriptive material, so do not hesitate to call.

- Bechtel Information Services
  15740 Shady Grove Road
  Gaithersburg, MD 20877
  (301) 258-3231
    Contractor for U.S. Securities & Exchange Commission. Lists financial records for thousands of U.S. and international companies.
- BRS Information Technologies
  1200 Route 7
  Latham, NY 12110
  (800) 227-5277
    Focused especially on the medical and social science areas.
    BRS/SEARCH. BRS's full product. Access to all databases. Complete search language. No off-hours discount.
    BRS/After Dark. A lower-cost, off-hours service with fewer available databases.
    BRS/BRKTHRU. Menu-driven. Most BRS/SEARCH databases. After-hours discounts. Probably best BRS service for PC users.
- Congressional Information Services, Inc.
  4520 East-West Highway
  Bethesda, MD 20814
  (301) 654-1550
    Indexes the millions of pages produced each year by the U.S. Congress, government agencies, and organizations. Includes full text of the *Federal Register.*

- DIALOG Information Service, Inc.
  3460 Hillview Avenue
  Palo Alto, CA 94304
  (800) 858-3810
    Largest and most complete information system but also somewhat more costly than other systems. DIALOG claims, however, to have consistently faster response times, which lowers the overall cost. Connect rate varies widely depending on the database in use.
    DIALOG Business Connection. A subset of DIALOG, available at a flat hourly rate, regardless of database used.
    The Knowledge Index. An off-hours, low-cost subset of DIALOG. Contains perhaps a tenth of the full set of databases. Flat hourly rate includes telecommunications charges.
- Dow Jones News/Retrieval Service
  P.O. Box 300
  Princeton, NJ 08540
  (800) 257-5114
    Source for current financial market information. Also known for quality and accuracy of information. Full text of the day's *Wall Street Journal* is on-line by 6 AM. Can be accessed through CompuServe or directly. Various discount plans are available.
- LEXIS/NEXIS
  Mead Data Central
  9393 Springboro Pike
  P.O. Box 933
  Dayton, OH 45401
  (800) 227-4908
    The premier full-text provider. Commands are idiosyncratic and charges can mount up rapidly but coverage of periodicals and newspapers is unparalleled. Began as a legal library service. Can search across databases. NEXIS is the periodical and newspaper service; LEXIS is the legal library service.
- NewsNet, Inc.
  945 Haverford Road
  Bryn Mawr, PA 19010
  (800) 345-1301
    Electronic vendor of trade, industry, and professional newsletters, many of which sell for $100 to $500 per year in print form. Very easy to use interface.

Allows easy searches across databases. Includes access to TRW credit reports.

- ORBIT Search Service
  SDC Information Services
  2500 Colorado Avenue
  Santa Monica, CA 90405
  (800) 456–7248

    Primarily a bibliographic service, especially strong on technical matters. Some databases are "closed," requiring permission for entry. Charges vary widely depending on database. Display and off-line reprint charges apply.

- VU/Text Information Services, Inc.
  1211 Chestnut Street
  Philadelphia, PA 19107
  (800) 258–8080

    Began as an in-house automated clipping file (a "morgue" in newspaper jargon) and grew to include full text from several dozen regional newspapers. Software is specifically designed for newspaper search and retrieval. Manual is a must.

- Wilson Line
  H. W. Wilson Company
  950 University Avenue
  Bronx, NY 10452
  800-367-6770

    Source for the "standard library references: *Reader's Guide, Book Review Digest,* and so on. The manual is a must. Allows searches across databases.

For Further Reading

A great many books have been written about databases. Many of them are highly useful. Those listed are either widely available or have special merit or both.

Felknor, B. L. 1988. *How to look things up and find things out.* New York: Quill/William Morrow. Not directly concerned with on-line databases but still a very good primer on research technique and sources. Does cover electronic databases in passing. Should be used in conjunction with Glossbrenner. Index.

Glossbrenner, A. 1987. *How to look it up online.* New York: St. Martin's Press. Essential work for the beginning on-line searcher. Contains history as well as detailed advice for saving money on-line. Many details are outdated, particularly prices, but the essential information is well presented and quite necessary. Good index.

Lancaster, F. W., and E. G. Fayon. 1973. *Information retrieval on-line.* Los Angeles: Melville Publishing. Discusses vocabulary control and searching techniques, especially for bibliographic databases. Index, references.

Mathies, M. L., and P. G. Watson. 1973. *Computer based reference service.* Chicago: American Library Association. Development of an early data-retrieval system. Discusses how and why certain standards were adopted. Index, bibliography.

Meethan, R. 1970. *Information retrieval: The essential technology.* Garden City, N.Y.: Doubleday. Begins at the beginning with data bits. Some technology discussed is obsolete, but basic knowledge is presented clearly and well. Index, reading list.

National Academy of Sciences. 1972. *Databanks in a free society: Computers, recordkeeping and privacy.* New York: Quadrangle Books. Discussion of ethics of databases. Makes predictions, some of which cut close to the mark of current practice. Index, footnotes.

Nees, D., Jr. 1986. *Fast facts online: Search strategies for finding business information.* Homewood, Ill.: Dow Jones–Irwin. Includes an excellent section on search strategy as well as detailed descriptions of many databases and information services. Somewhat outdated, but the general principles are still valid. Bibliography, glossary, index.

Rohm, C. E. T., Jr., and W. T. Stewart, Jr. 1988. *Essentials of information systems.* Santa Cruz, Calif.: Mitchell Publishing. Textbook. Excellent overview of computers, peripherals, and applications. Has detailed chapter on workings of databases in general. Good illustrations. Detailed, outline-style table of contents, glossary, index.

Sharp, J. R. 1965. *Some fundamentals of information retrieval.* New York: London House & Maxwell. Mainly of historical interest;

the very beginnings of large databases. Index, references.

Walter Hawn

DATA COMPRESSION AND FRACTALS

Storage of digitized data, especially visual data gathered via surveillance satellites or reconnaissance crafts, requires an enormous amount of memory. We therefore need a mechanism to "compress" the information while preserving the essential details. The level of clarity needed is specified by the user. Information theoretic approaches exploit the redundancy present to compress the data. Such techniques are used for instance in facsimile (fax) transmission. For example we may use run length coding, where long strings of ones or zeros are represented by the type (zero or one) and the length of the string. This and similar techniques, like pulse code modulation and differential pulse code modulation, do not achieve a high degree of compression, but can be implemented in real time; however, if the requirement is for a compression that is many orders of magnitude better, we have to look for some basic feature (or features) of the picture that can be stored and the original scene must be reconstructed from this with use of some reconstruction rule. For example, a chess board may be specified as having black and white squares of a certain dimension, and the rule of reconstruction is that there are sixty-four squares and the colors alternate. The processes of analysis (to extract the features) and synthesis (reconstruction) may require a lot of time. One such technique makes use of the so-called fractals and can offer compression ratios as high as 1,000:1 or even higher sometimes.

Historically, the work of mathematicians such as Cantor, Peano, and von Koch among others has pioneered the study of fractals. Their work resulted in the production of the so-called "monster curves," curves made up of smaller segments of the same shape as the larger one. This property of "self-similarity" is the key to the fractal technique. The most

significant work in defining the fractal is due to Mendelbrot. Another important contributor to the use of fractals (especially data compression) is Michael Barnsley.

WHAT ARE FRACTALS?

According to Euclidean geometry any line that is drawn on a paper and that does not cross itself is assigned a dimension of 1, regardless of whether it is a straight line or a curve that goes all over the plane. Some mathematicians, however, felt that this was not the right way of looking at things, and argued that if the same line were to fill the entire plane of the paper its dimension should be 2 rather than 1 and that curves ought to be assigned dimensions whose value is between 1 and 2. As Euclidean geometry has no such provision, a new dimension (whose value can be between 1 and 2) called the Hausdorff–Besicovitch (HB) dimension is assigned to a curve. Formally specified, a fractal is any curve whose HB dimension is larger than its Euclidean dimension and has the self-similarity property.

GENERATION OF FRACTALS

The Initiator–Generator Method
The starting point is a polygon, which is called the *initiator* (a straight line is also a polygon). Each side of this initiator is then replaced by a curve called the *generator*. The generator is a connected set of straight lines between the beginning and the end of the original side of the polygon. The newly formed figure is another polygon. The sides of this newly formed figure are again replaced by the generator. Note that in the second step, each line is smaller and so the segments of the generator will also be smaller. This process of replacement is carried on endlessly.

Consider, for example, the generator that is an equilateral triangle ABC as shown in Figure 1. This is replaced by the generator *abcde*, such that segments *ab* and *de* are equal to one third of the side of triangle ABC. Segments *bc* and *cd* are equal to the length *bd*. If the number of segments = N (4 in this

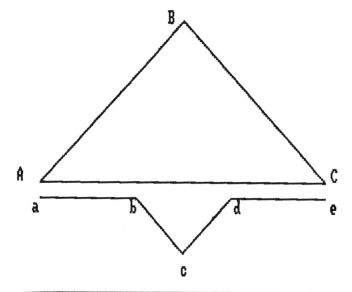

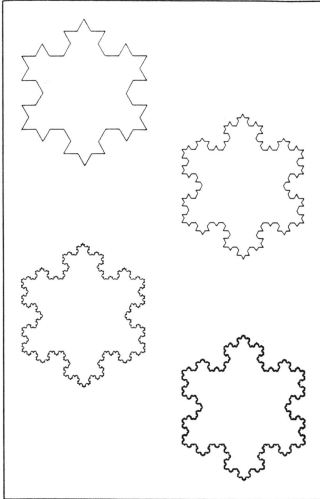

FIGURE 1. (a) Example of an initiator and a generator. **(b)** Von Koch snowflakes after (a) is modified two, three, four, and six times.

case, i.e., *ab, bc, cd,* and *de*), and the generator divides the side of the original polygon into *K* segments (*K* = 3 in this example), then the fractal dimension of such a curve is defined as

$$D = \log (N)/\log(K)$$

For this example

$$D = \log(4)/\log(3) = 1.2618$$

The algorithm, if carried out successively, results in the curves that appear in Figure 1b. These are known as von Koch snowflakes. Thus, the snowflake can be characterized by its initiator, generator and the rule of generation, and the number of steps in the process.

The Integrated Function Systems Method of Generation

This method of generating a fractal curve was devised by Barnsley. This uses a set of transformations on each point of an initiator, which may be just a point. Every point (*x,y*) in the two-dimensional plane is subject to rotation and translation using the rule

$$\begin{bmatrix} x(n) \\ y(n) \end{bmatrix} = \begin{bmatrix} a & b \\ c & d \end{bmatrix} \begin{bmatrix} x(n-1) \\ y(n-1) \end{bmatrix} + \begin{bmatrix} e \\ f \end{bmatrix}$$

where [*x(n)*, *y(n)*] is the new position of the point and [*x(n−1)*, *y(n−1)*] is the previous position. The values of *a, b, c,* and *d* must be chosen such that the resulting magnitude scaling will not let *x(n)* and *y(n)* become unbounded. Any figure to which we apply this type of transformation will be reduced in size, rotated, and moved to a different location. The integrated function systems (IFS) algorithm itself is of two types: the deterministic algorithm and the nondeterministic algorithm.

THE DETERMINISTIC INTEGRATED FUNCTION SYSTEMS ALGORITHM

The transformation (also called affine transformation) is applied repeatedly to a polygon. Consider the rectangle *ABCD* shown in Figure 2a. The four corners have coordinates *D* (0,0), *C* (8,0), *B* (8,16), and *A* (0,16). The

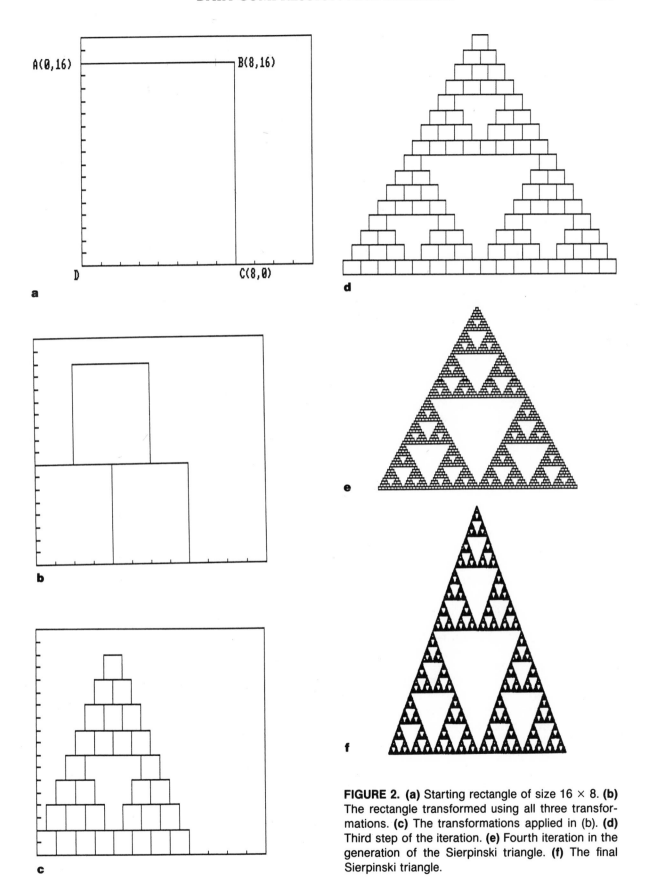

FIGURE 2. **(a)** Starting rectangle of size 16 × 8. **(b)** The rectangle transformed using all three transformations. **(c)** The transformations applied in (b). **(d)** Third step of the iteration. **(e)** Fourth iteration in the generation of the Sierpinski triangle. **(f)** The final Sierpinski triangle.

Table 1

a	b	c	d	e	f
0.5	0.0	0.0	0.5	0	0
0.5	0.0	0.0	0.5	4	0
0.5	0.0	0.0	0.5	2	8

affine transformations shown in Table 1 are applied to each point of the rectangle, resulting in Figure 2b. (In this example we need apply them only to the four corners.)

Application of the same three transformations to the points of the new figure gives us Figure 2c. Repeated application of the algorithm results in the shapes shown in Figures 2d and 2e. The final shape, after the algorithm is applied a large number of times, is the Sierpinski triangle (Figure 2f). Figure 3 is a simple program in BASIC that performs this algorithm.

THE NONDETERMINISTIC VERSION OF THE INTEGRATED FUNCTION SYSTEMS OR THE CHAOS ALGORITHM

Referring to the example of generating the Sierpinski triangle, the three affine transformations indicated in Table 1 may be used in such a way that each transformation is selected at random. A probability is associated with each of the transformations. At each step, one of the transformations is selected based on a random number that is picked in

```
10 SCREEN 2
20 PRINT" input the number of iterations to be performed (up to 6)"
30 INPUT N
40 CLS
50 WINDOW (−5,−5) − (20,20)
60 DIM X(3000),Y(3000)
70 X(1)=0
80 X(2)=8
90 X(3)=8
100 X(4)=0
110 Y(1)=0
120 Y(2)=0
130 Y(3)=16
140 Y(4)=16
150 FOR K = 1 TO N
160   FOR J = 1 TO 4*3^(K−1)
170     X(J)=X(J)*.5
180     Y(J)=.5*Y(J)
190   NEXT J
200   FOR J = (4*3^(K−1)) + 1 TO 8*(3^(K−1))
210     X(J)=X(J−4*3^(K−1)) + 4
220     Y(J)=Y(J−4*3^(K−1))
230   NEXT J
240   FOR J = 8*(3^(K−1)) + 1 TO 4*(3^(K))
250     X(J)=X(J−8*3^(K−1)) +2
260     Y(J)=Y(J−8*3^(K−1)) + 8
270   NEXT J
280 NEXT K
290 FOR J = 1 TO (4*3^(N))−3 STEP 4
300     LINE (X(J ),Y(J)) − (X(J + 1),Y(J + 1))
310     LINE (X(J + 1),Y(J + 1))−(X(J + 2),Y(J + 2))
320     LINE (X(J + 2),Y(J + 2))−(X(J + 3),Y(J + 3))
330     LINE (X(J + 3),Y(J + 3))−(X(J ), Y(J))
340 NEXT J
```

FIGURE 3. A program that performs the Sierpinski triangle iteration up to six levels.

Table 2

a	b	c	d	e	f	Probability
0.5	0.0	0.0	0.5	0	0	1/6
0.5	0.0	0.0	0.5	4	0	1/3
0.5	0.0	0.0	0.5	2	8	1/2

that step. This procedure is carried out a large number of times. Table 2 indicates a possible rule for generating the Sierpinski triangle.

USE OF FRACTALS IN DATA COMPRESSION

With knowledge of the starting polygon and the set of transformations, it is easy to generate the pretty-looking pictures. But for data compression, we need the reverse algorithm. That is, given a picture, what will be the transformations and the corresponding initiators? A given picture has to be broken up into various segments, each segment is to be treated as a separate fractal, and an IFS has to be obtained. The segmentation of the picture and the IFS finding is not a trivial problem. For example, if we consider a scene with a few trees, the sky with some cloud pattern, and the ground, we may segment the picture into three parts: the clouds, the trees, and the ground. An IFS algorithm may be developed for each segment and stored. The original picture may be reconstructed from the IFS algorithm for each segment. The amount of compression that can be achieved is dependent on the picture itself. The book by Barnsley (1988) and the papers authored by Barnsley and his colleagues (1985, 1988) address the relevant issues involved as to how a scene has to be segmented and how the IFS for each segment may be extracted. Barnsley's text has an accompanying design handbook that guides the reader through the various steps of the IFS code generation, and also has a library of fractals. The code for the program is already in compiled form, and familiarity with a language is not required. The book by Stevens (1989), however, requires the user to be familiar with the C language and is more flexible, because it lets the user write new programs or modify existing ones.

References

Barnsley, M. F. 1988. *Fractals everywhere.* Boston: Academic Press. Provides a formal treatment of fractal geometry. Easy to read, but is mathematical in content. Provides a good set of references.

———— 1989. *The desktop fractal design system.* San Diego, Calif.: Academic Press. This program package is very helpful in gaining an understanding of the basics of fractals. The programs are available for both IBM and Macintosh personal computers.

Barnsley, M. F., and S. Demko. 1985. Iterated function systems and the global construction of fractals. *Proceedings of the Royal Society, Series A* 399:243–75.

Barnsley, M. F., and A. D. Sloan. 1988. A better way to compress images. *Byte,* January, pp. 215–23. Easily understood article on the use of fractals. No background is needed.

Stevens, R. T. 1989. *Fractal programming in C.* Redwood City, Calif.: M&T Books. A collection of programs in the C language. For anyone who wants to have fun.

For Further Reading

Demko, S., L. Hodges, and B. Naylor. 1985. Construction of fractal objects with iterated function systems. *SIGGRAPH '85* 19(3):271–78.

Mandelbrot, B. 1983. *The fractal geometry of nature.* New York: Freeman. A very good reference for the study of fractals.

Zaropette, G. 1988. Applied fractals. *IEEE Spectrum* 25:29–31. Short description of the use of fractals in data compression. Aimed at a very general audience.

C. V. Chakravarthy

DATA ENTRY

Data entry is the process of transforming data from a non-computer-usable form into a computer-usable form. This definition encompasses the processes of preparing data to be transformed, the hardware that transforms the data, and the people that control the processing. By this definition the use of almost any input device constitutes data entry. The process of data entry involves more than just this transformation; the new form of the data must be verified against the original data to ensure accuracy. Historically data entry was considered a people-intensive operation; however, a number of devices have automated much of this work.

Several devices were used for the purpose of data entry during the early years of computing. Perhaps the earliest data entry was performed by setting switches on the console of such machines as the Whirlwind. The *binary* values, 0 and 1, used for the representation of numbers inside the computer, were easily represented on the console by a two-position switch. The switches were grouped in sets of six or eight. An individual switch represented a single bit in the number represented by the group of switches. The machine operator converted numeric values from their base ten representation into a base two representation. The resulting string of zeros and ones were used to configure the switches on the console, for example,

$$35_{10} = 00100011_2 = \text{OFF OFF ON OFF OFF}$$
$$\text{OFF ON ON}$$

The accuracy of this translation process was the sole responsibility of the person preparing the data. Data were verified by repeating the calculations and by double-checking the switch settings. Most of this early work was mathematical calculations that could be checked against estimates prepared by hand.

Data entry was soon also performed by using a keyboard. The keyboard might be attached directly to the computer, in which case it was part of the *system console,* or it might be part of a punching machine. The punching machine was intended to create a reusable form of input. A paper tape machine punched a pattern of holes in a 1-inch-wide continuous strip of paper. A paper tape reader was then used to transform the holes into electrical impulses that represented the pattern of punches.

The *card punch* machine, or *keypunch,* represented data in columns on individual cards (see Figure 1). Data entered into this medium took more storage space than the same information entered onto paper tape but individual values could be modified, by replacing the card that held the piece of data, without repunching the entire set of data. Each column had ten punch positions numbered zero through nine to represent any single digit of a number. A column also had two additional punch positions for *zone punches.* A punch in the topmost row, termed the 12 zone, combined with a punch in rows 1 to 9 represented one of the letters A to I. The next punch area, the 11 zone, plus a punch in a numeric row represented one of the letters J to R. A punch in the zero digit row combined with a punch in rows 1–9 represented the letters S to Z. Special characters required three punches; for example, a 12 zone, a numeric 6, and a numeric 8 represented a plus symbol (Prince and Nyman 1977).

Information represented by the cards was then read by a card reader attached to a computing system. Photoelectric cells were used to sense the presence or absence of punches, the binary paradigm again. The mechanical reading of the cards was fast by human standards but slow by standards of electronic data transfer rates. Cards that were folded, spindled, or mutilated caused errors and jams in the card reader. Both the punched tape and punched cards moved the translation of data values from the user to a machine. The keypunch operator pressed the "A" key and did not have to consider the

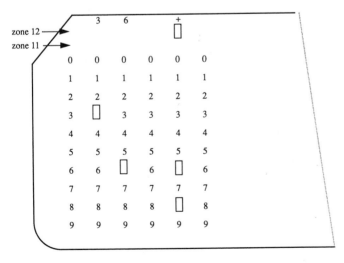

FIGURE 1

combination of punches the machine cut into the card.

The keypunch was modified, because of the relatively slow speed of the mechanical punchers and readers, to place the data directly on magnetic tape or disk. The keyboard was teamed with a cathode-ray tube (CRT) display device to form an input/output (I/O) station. Several of these I/O stations, sometimes referred to as terminals, could be connected to one computer. The computer used for this purpose was often a small, slow machine that was used to prepare data for use by a large, fast system (Figure 2). The difference in speed between the two systems was often so great that several smaller computers served as feeders into the larger central system. The software used for data entry echoed each keypress from the keyboard onto the screen. The mechanical punching and repunching of the heavy paper card were eliminated, thereby saving trees and time. The echo of each keypress allowed the operator to see and correct mistakes much more easily than with the keypunch. The use of the magnetic format improved the reliability of the reading process and speeded up the process as well.

Reviewing the evolution of data entry, the techniques have changed to allow more natural and reliable input. The conversion from our natural modes of base ten numerals and alphabetic characters to the computer's internal binary representation has been moved from the responsibility of the user to the responsibility of the computer system. Intermediate steps, such as preparing cards, have been eliminated to save time and to reduce the possibilities of error.

Two other types of data entry were also used during this time and continue to be used: magnetic ink character recognition (MICR) and optical character recognition (OCR) (Awad 1973). Banks use forms for deposit slips and checks that have characters printed with special ink in a distinctive typeface, or font. These characters can be read from the face of the form by machines that can use the information to sort and group all the forms for one account. Optical character recognition has advanced rapidly. The number of fonts that can be recognized has increased and the reliability of the equip-

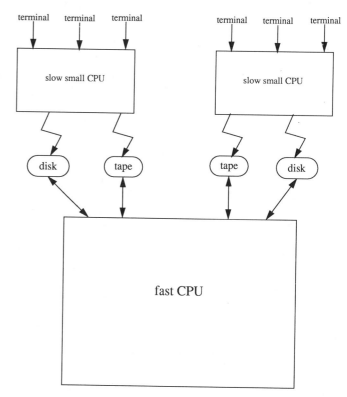

FIGURE 2

ment has improved. Machines equivalent to copying machines can read entire pages of text and translate the printed information into computer-usable form. In this form, it may be made available for editing or it may serve as input into a voice output system to provide an automated reader for sightless people.

The process of data entry includes not only the initial conversion of data from one form to another but also the *validation* of the data. When data were prepared using a keypunch machine, the prepared cards were processed by a second machine, termed a *verifier*, before being fed into the computer. During the verify operation, an operator typed the same data that had originally been used to punch the card. The verifier read the data punched into the card and compared the data with what was being typed at the moment. If a difference was found, the verifier signaled the operator to stop and check the particular column. If errors were found, the card was repunched with the correct data.

Validation remains an important part of data entry today. The echoed display on an

I/O station allows the user to be certain that the keys he or she meant to press are the keys that were read. Scanning devices often make two passes over information and compare the two sets of data to identify discrepancies between the two. Applications use a variety of techniques for validation. Word processors have spell checkers. The spell checker performs two validation functions. The spell checker does not check that the key read is the one the user intended to press. It checks that a group of letters entered form a legitimate word. This procedure will locate many cases of incorrect key presses such as *helol* when *hello* was the intended sequence. It will not identify mistakes such as *sin* when *son* was the intended sequence because both are valid words.

Data entry was a specialized operation using personnel dedicated to that function. Large typing pools of keypunch operators prepared data such as bill payments or insurance policy purchases for processing by the computer. This activity required the efforts of several people. In addition to the person operating the keypunch machine, a second person checked the typing of the first person and a third person operated the card reader or mounted the magnetic tape on the computer system. Data entry also required a person to collect the data. Insurance salesmen might record information on the purchase of a policy by filling out a special form that required each alphabetic character to be placed in a separate block.

Data entry is no longer as specialized nor as personnel intensive as described above. Data entry has been moved out to the users of the systems. Grocery clerks, engineers, and teachers all perform data entry functions. They are responsible for collecting, entering, and validating data such as bar codes on merchandise, dimensions of parts in a design, or grades. They use hardware and software that require little or no special training to operate. The same insurance agent mentioned previously now carries a laptop computer into the client's home and enters information directly into that portable computer.

Data entry equipment has been specialized to the areas to which it is applied. Checkout counters at grocery stores have laser vision systems that read the universal product code (UPC) on each item being purchased. These systems transform the BAR CODE on a package to an identification number that is used to uniquely identify the manufacturer, type of item, package size, and ultimately the price. Even telephones support the data entry process. Callers may push buttons to make selections that control the operation of computer programs at the other end of the connection. Data such as credit card numbers and catalog item numbers can also be entered using the keypad on the telephone instrument.

The grocery checkout example illustrates the concept of scanning as a data entry operation. In the scanning process a scan beam sweeps a designated area searching for particular data such as ink on a printed page or radioactive isotopes in blood vessels. Based on photocopying technology page scanners detect ink on a piece of paper and translate the density of the ink into binary information. If the page contains text, character recognition algorithms are employed to turn that binary information into alphabetic characters. Medical imaging devices have replaced x-ray machines for much medical diagnostic work. Techniques such as nuclear magnetic resonance (NMR) capture information in a digital form rather than on a piece of film. This information is stored in a computer-usable form and can be manipulated by the physician to provide three-dimensional views of sections of the patient's body.

Sensing devices measure temperature, pressure, and flow in many industrial processes. Each device transforms the data into a digital format that serves as data input into a process control software system. Radar systems transform radar waves into computer-usable data that serve as input to air traffic control systems.

Techniques for data entry are being adapted to the natural routines of the system users. The mouse is perhaps the most widely used input device after the keyboard. The user can "point" with the mouse by positioning the on-screen cursor and then press one of the buttons that are part of the mouse. Graphic design programs allow artists to choose cursor types that correspond to the

FIGURE 3. The image of the user's hand displayed on the monitor is generated from data transmitted by the DataGlove. *Courtesy VPL Research Inc.*

References

Awad, E. M. 1973. *Automatic data processing.* Englewood Cliffs, N.J.: Prentice-Hall.

Prince, L. J., and D. F. Nyman. 1977. Introduction to computers and computer programming. Englewood Cliffs, N.J.: Prentice-Hall.

Stewart, D. 1991. Through the looking glass into an artificial world—via computer. *Smithsonian* 21(10):36–45.

Wilson, M., and A. Conway. 1991. Enhanced interaction styles for user interfaces. *IEEE Computer Graphics and Applications,* March, pp. 79–90.

John D. McGregor

types of brushes that they would have used. The "brush" is moved by manipulating the mouse. Touch screens, which allow the user to place a finger on the display screen to make a selection, provide the illusion of "virtual" push buttons. These buttons can be changed as easily as modifying the program. The DataGlove used by NASA provides a very natural data entry device that allows the user to move his or her hand normally and have these movements translated into data for the computing system. The gloves are integrated with sensors that can detect the movement of any joint of any finger. This physical movement is translated into data that can be used to model the movement of a hand. The wearer can point, hold up a certain number of fingers, or hold the hand up in a "stop" motion. Each of these movements is correctly modeled by the glove (Stewart 1991; Wilson and Conway 1991).

Data entry has undergone vast changes since rooms of keypunch operators translated handwritten data onto punch cards. At home data entry is performed on microwave ovens, and in offices keyboards and mice attached to personal computers are used to translate thoughts and movements into computer-usable data. Machines of many types translate physical data such as temperature and movement into computer-usable data. Devices, such as the DataGlove, now being developed will make the data entry process even more natural and more a part of our everyday lives.

DATA MODELING, LOGICAL

Effective information systems development depends on (1) accurately representing the data and processing requirements of the application area, (2) validating those requirements with end users, and (3) transforming the data requirements into a database schema and the processing requirements into computer programs (in the target database management system [DBMS]/programming language environment).

Logical data modeling is a process by which the data requirements of an application area are represented. A *data modeling formalism* defines a set of constructs used in the representation. The product of logical data modeling is a *logical data model.*

A logical data model represents the "things" that are a part of the application (e.g., customers, inventory items, orders), their characteristics (e.g., customers are identified by customer number and are described by customer name, credit limit, etc.), and their interrelationships (e.g., each order must be associated with a single customer). Such a representation can be validated by end users to ensure accuracy of the data requirements.

A logical data model does not specify the physical storage of the data. It provides a precise data representation that must be implemented in a DBMS/programming language environment. The process of developing a DBMS schema from a logical data model is termed *physical database design.*

The goal of logical data modeling (also termed *logical database design*) is to accurately and completely represent the data requirements. The goal of physical database design is to implement a database that efficiently meets those requirements.

Numerous data modeling formalisms have been proposed: the entity-relationship (ER) model, the logical data structure model, the semantic data model, and the object relationship model. Such formalisms have come to be termed *semantic* data models to differentiate them from *traditional* data models (hierarchic, network, and relational) used by commercial DBMSs to represent the database schema. For comparisons of the most popular semantic data models, see Hull and King (1987) and Peckham and Maryanski (1988). Chen (1976) provides an overview of the entity-relationship model.

The traditional data models focus on the storage description of data, that is, implemented file structures and access paths. Semantic data models focus on the meaning of the data (its *semantics*); that is, they represent "things" in the world, their descriptions, and their logical associations.

This article describes logical data modeling and the process of transforming a logical data model into a traditional data model. The next section introduces basic data modeling constructs. A simple graphic notation is introduced. This is followed by a section that discusses techniques for developing data models and presents criteria by which to evaluate them. The final section illustrates how to transform a logical data model into each of the traditional DBMS schemas.

BASIC DATA MODELING CONSTRUCTS

Four basic constructs are common among data modeling formalisms: entity, attribute, relationship, and identifier. These are first defined and then illustrated in an example data model (Figure 1).

Definitions

An *entity* is a category or grouping of objects (people, things, events) or roles of objects (e.g., customer, employee) each sharing a common set of characteristics or *descriptors.* The individual members of the category are termed *entity instances* (e.g., the employee with employee number 12314, the customer with customer number 5958). Some formalisms refer to the category as an *entity type* and the instances as *entities.* The important consideration is to distinguish the category or type from its instances.

Two kinds of descriptors are distinguished: attribute descriptors and relationship descriptors. An *attribute descriptor* (or just *attribute*) is a single-valued characteristic of each member of an entity (multivalued attributes are not allowed).

A *relationship descriptor* characterizes an association between two (not necessarily distinct) entities (only *binary* relationships are allowed). Each relationship has two relationship descriptors, one for each direction of the relationship. That is, each entity in a relationship both describes and is described by the other. A relationship instance characterizes the association between two entity instances (one instance of each of the two related entities).

A relationship descriptor is characterized by its *minimum and maximum degrees* (the smallest and largest number of instances of the describing entity that can be associated with one instance of the described entity). Only one descriptor of a relationship may have a maximum degree that is greater than one (many-to-many relationships are not permitted).

If the minimum degree of a relationship descriptor is one or greater, then the described entity is said to be dependent on the describing entity. That is, an instance of the described entity cannot exist without an associated instance of the describing entity. This type of dependency is often termed a *referential integrity constraint*, because an instance of the "referred-to" entity must exist. If the minimum degree is zero, then the described entity is said to be *independent* of the describing entity (it can exist without an associated instance of the describing entity).

Each entity has at least one set of attribute and relationship descriptors, the entity's *identifier*, whose values uniquely distinguish its instances. An entity may have alternative identifiers. Given the value of an entity's identifier, there is at most one corresponding instance of that entity in the domain of interest. Employee number 12314, for example, identifies one specific employee just as customer number 5958 identifies one specific customer.

Often identifiers are *artificial* in the sense that an identifying attribute is created for the entity and values are assigned to the instances (employee number and customer number are examples of artificial identifiers). The reason is that often there is not a set of "natural" attributes that are guaranteed to uniquely distinguish all instances of an entity (e.g., there may be several employees with the same name or even the same name and address).

An Example Data Model

Figure 1 is a graphic representation of a data model. There are four entities: DEPARTMENT, EMPLOYEE, ASSIGNMENT, and PROJECT. These are each represented by an oval enclosing the name of the entity. Attributes are connected to entities by arcs. Attributes must be uniquely named within an entity; however, the entity name may be used to qualify attribute names where neces-

sary. As an attribute of DEPARTMENT, "budget" is more precisely named "budget-of-DEPARTMENT"; as an attribute of PROJECT it is "budget-of-PROJECT."

Relationships are represented by arcs connecting pairs of entities. Two types of relationships are permitted: one-to-many relationships (represented by an arc with a "chicken foot" on the many side of the relationship) and one-to-one relationships (represented by an arc with no chicken feet). The chicken foot notation visually portrays the minimum and maximum degrees of the two descriptors of a relationship. The chicken foot represents a minimum degree of zero or one and a maximum degree greater than one. The lack of a chicken foot represents a minimum degree of zero or one and a maximum degree of one.

Specifying a minimum degree of zero *or* one is not very precise. It fails to represent possible dependencies between the related entities. To address this issue, some data modeling formalisms annotate each end of a relationship with its minimum and maximum degrees. Other formalisms use a special symbol (such as a "D") on the relationship arc to represent dependency. Still other formalisms visualize dependency by having the relationship arc touch the entity if the mini-

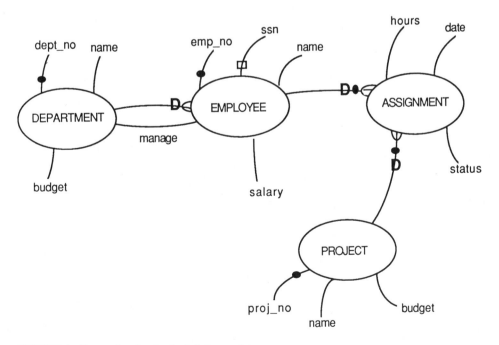

FIGURE 1. Example of a logical data model.

mum degree is one and leave a gap between the end of the relationship arc and the entity if the minimum degree is zero.

In Figure 1, there are two relationships between EMPLOYEE and DEPARTMENT. The first (unlabeled arc) is the association of employees with the departments to which they administratively report. Each employee reports to one department; however, a department may have many employees report to it (a one-to-many relationship). The "D" on this relationship next to EMPLOYEE specifies a minimum degree of 1. Each employee instance must be associated with a department instance (EMPLOYEE is dependent on DEPARTMENT along the "administrative-reporting" relationship). The lack of a "D" on the DEPARTMENT side specifies that a department can exist without having any employees that report to it (DEPARTMENT is independent of EMPLOYEE).

The second relationship between EMPLOYEE and DEPARTMENT (labeled MANAGE) associates a department with the employee who manages it. A department has one manager; similarly, an employee can manage at most one department (a one-to-one relationship). The lack of any "D" symbols on either side of this relationship specifies that not all employees are managers and that a department may be without any manager (presumably the lack of a manager is temporary).

As discussed earlier, many-to-many relationships are not directly supported. They are represented by creating an "intersection" entity. Although this may seem somewhat artificial, our experience suggests that such "relationships" often have attributes (and hence technically qualify as entities by the aforementioned definition). More importantly, such entities are often a major focus of the information system. Frequently they represent "events" occurring at a point in time (or having some time duration) about which information must be maintained.

In Figure 1, ASSIGNMENT is an intersection entity representing the many-to-many relationship between EMPLOYEE and PROJECT (one employee can be assigned to many projects and one project can have many employees assigned to it). It represents the event of assigning an employee to a project. This event is described by the date of assignment, the status of the employee, and the number of hours the employee worked on that assignment.

Finally, identifiers are denoted by a special symbol on each arc that composes the identifier. The dot on the arc "emp_no" indicates, for example, that each EMPLOYEE instance is identified by "emp_no." The box on the arc "ssn" indicates that employees are also identified by "ssn" (Social Security number). Each entity must have at least one identifier.

Intersection entities typically have an identifier that contains one or more of their relationships. The intersection entity ASSIGNMENT is identified by the combination of EMPLOYEE and PROJECT. This fact implies that an ASSIGNMENT is dependent on both EMPLOYEE and PROJECT (note the "D" symbols on the ASSIGNMENT side of both relationships), as an ASSIGNMENT instance cannot exist without corresponding EMPLOYEE and PROJECT instances. Neither EMPLOYEE nor PROJECT is dependent on ASSIGNMENT.

Many data modeling formalisms directly support multivalued attributes, ternary (and higher-order) relationships, and many-to-many relationships. Several data modeling formalisms also allow relationships to have attributes. These constructs can all be represented by an intersection entity. Hence they are not included in the formalism described earlier.

Generalization

A common criticism of early data modeling formalisms was the lack of an abstraction capability. Process modeling was based on the concept of functional decomposition, that is, breaking a complex process down into simpler ones. Data models, on the other hand, tended to be relatively "flat." Each entity was defined as a set of nonoverlapping instances. This made it difficult to model certain types of data adequately.

Consider, for example, the way in which managers are represented in Figure 1. A manager *is* an EMPLOYEE, but a special kind of EMPLOYEE, one with a special function in the organization and perhaps having characteristics different from those of other employees. The fact that the "manage" relationship between EMPLOYEE and DEPARTMENT has a minimum degree of zero indicates that there is some heterogeneity among the instances of EMPLOYEE. This heterogeneity forces application programs and database accesses to treat some employees differently from others. The data model does not adequately represent the domain of interest.

Smith and Smith (1977) introduced *generalization* as a mechanism by which to increase the fidelity of data models to the domain of interest. Generalization allows the instances of different entities to overlap and provides a means for defining the nature of that overlap.

A more accurate representation of managers and employees and their association with departments uses generalization as shown in Figure 2. EMPLOYEE is a generalization or *supertype* of MANAGER. Conversely MANAGER is a specialization or *subtype* of EMPLOYEE. This is indicated by the arrow from MANAGER to EMPLOYEE. Generalization is a special case of a one-to-one relationship, termed an *ISA* ("is a") relationship. Each manager ISA employee, but not all employees are managers. Generalization makes it clear that the "manage" relationship applies to only a subset of employees.

As each manager ISA employee, each instance of MANAGER has a corresponding instance of EMPLOYEE. Thus, all attributes of EMPLOYEE apply to all instances of MANAGER. It is said that MANAGER *inherits* all properties (descriptors) from EMPLOYEE. This so-called property inheritance is fundamental to the object-oriented data models. Korson and McGregor (1990) provide an overview of this formalism.

Often a subtype such as MANAGER will have its own set of descriptors that do not apply to the supertype. Managers, for example, might have attributes such as parking space number or credit card number that are not applicable to any other employees. In Figure 2, MANAGER has a relationship descriptor, "department managed," that does not apply to other employees.

Whenever there is an entity with a relationship descriptor whose minimum degree is zero or whenever there are attributes that

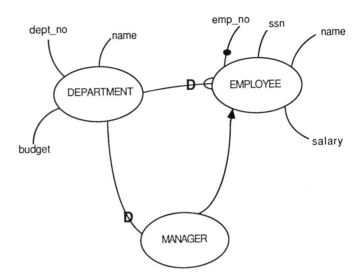

FIGURE 2. MANAGER as a subtype of EMPLOYEE.

do not apply to all instances of an entity, generalization can be used to decompose that entity into one or more subtypes. When generalization is used in this way, the data model increases its fidelity to the domain of interest.

The earlier example illustrated the case where a subtype is completely contained in a single supertype, a generalization hierarchy. It is also possible for subtypes of a supertype to overlap, for entities to be subtypes of more than one supertype, and for "subtypes" to contain instances that are not members of the supertype (a *generalization lattice*).

TECHNIQUES FOR BUILDING A DATA MODEL

Data modeling is part of an overall process of developing a system representation. Numerous techniques have been proposed; however, the process remains highly subjective. The key tasks are (1) identification of the major entities (with supertypes and subtypes), (2) establishment of relationships, (3) determination of attributes and identifiers, and (4) documentation of dependencies. The developed data model must be cross-validated with other representations of the information system such as process and behavior representations.

A key approach to modeling the data content of an existing system is an analysis of documents including transactions and reports. As mentioned earlier, it is extremely common for an organization to create artificial identifiers for important entities. These identifiers appear on reports or transaction documents as <entity> Number (or No. or num) or as some other obvious designator of an entity. To analyze a document, each heading on the document is examined and classified as representing (1) an entity (its identifier), (2) an attribute, or (3) calculated data. This determination is done by an analyst in conjunction with the end users.

Consider the invoice document illustrated in Figure 3. A scan of that document reveals 21 headings: Invoice Number, Invoice Date, Customer Number, Bill to Address, Customer PO, Terms, FOB Point, Line Number, Product Number, Product Description, Unit of Sale, Quantity Ordered, Quantity Shipped, Quantity Backordered, Unit Price, Discount, Extension, Order Gross, Tax, Freight, and Order Net. That fact that these are on the same document indicates that there is some association among these vari-

Sample Company, Inc.
111 Any Street
Anytown, USA

Bill To:
  Customer Number: 0361

Local Grocery Store
132 Local Street
Localtown, USA

	INVOICE	
Number	Date	
157289	10/02/90	

Customer PO: 3291
Terms: Net 30
FOB Point: Anytown

Line No.	Product Number	Product Description	Unit of Sale	Quantity			Unit Price	Discount	Extension
				Order	Ship	Backord			
1	2157	Cheerios	Carton	40	40	0	50.00	5%	1900.00
2	2283	Oat Rings	Each	300	200	100	2.00	0%	400.00
3	0579	Corn Flakes	Carton	30	30	0	40.00	10%	1080.00

Order Gross   4380.00
Tax at 6%   262.80
Freight   50.00
Order Net   4692.80

FIGURE 3. Example of an invoice document.

ous items. They represent descriptors of related entities.

To develop a data model from this document, first, categorize the headings into one of three classes: entity identifier, attribute, or calculated value. This process is somewhat subjective, but given the definition of an entity as any "thing" about which information must be maintained, the following are initially classified as entity identifiers: Invoice Number, Customer Number, and Product Number. Tax, Order Gross, and Order Net are classified as calculated values. All others are classified as attributes. For each entity identifier, the entity is named: Invoice Number identifies Invoice, Customer Number identifies Customer, and Product Number identifies Product.

Second, establish relationships. It is obvious that Customer relates to Invoice. The relevant questions are "How many Customers are responsible for a single Invoice?" (answer: one) and "Can a single Customer be responsible for more than one Invoice?" (answer: yes). In this way a one-to-many relationship is established between Customer and Invoice (represented by the chicken foot on the Invoice side of the relationship in Figure 4). Similarly establish a many-to-many relationship between Invoice and Product. At this time, minimum and maximum degrees should be specified for each relationship descriptor.

The many-to-many relationship between Invoice and Product needs clarification. It indicates that one Invoice contains many Products (this is obvious) and that the *same* Product can be on many Invoices.

How can the *same* product be on more than one Invoice? This assumes that what is meant by the *same* Product is not the same physical instance of the product, but the same *type* of product, having a single Product Number, the instances of which are completely interchangeable. After all, the customer is being invoiced for some *quantity* of this *same* product. In Figure 3, for example, "Cheerios" is Product Number 2157, sold in units of cartons. Local Grocery Store is being invoiced for 40 cartons of this *same* product. Presumably 40 more cartons of the *same* product could be shipped (and invoiced) to a

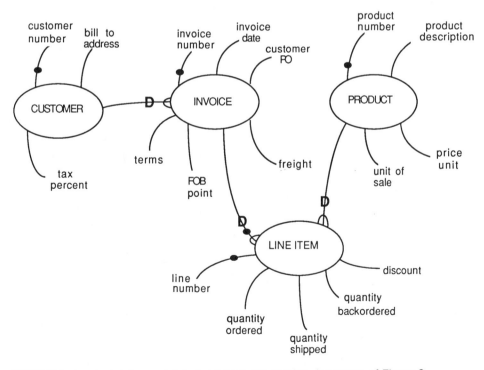

FIGURE 4. Logical data model derived from the invoice document of Figure 3.

different Customer; hence the many-to-many relationship.

As many-to-many relationships are not permitted in this formalism, an intersection entity must be created between Invoice and Product. The intersection entity is related many-to-one to each of the entities in the many-to-many relationship (chicken feet on the intersection entity). An obvious name for the intersection entity is *Line Item*, because, in common business terminology, a line item on an invoice represents a single product on the invoice. Each Line Item is identified by the combination of the Invoice to which it relates and the Line Number (as illustrated in Figure 4 by the dots on the arcs representing these relationships).

Third, determine the attributes needed to calculate the calculated values (e.g., Customer Tax Percent is needed to calculate Tax) and associate each attribute with the appropriate entity. If there is not an entity that is uniquely described by an attribute, then there is a missing entity.

Finally, review the model to identify subtypes. If a relationship applies to some but not all instances of the related entities (that is, the minimum degree of one of the relationship descriptors is zero), then subtypes exist in at least one of the entities (i.e., the subtype participates in the relationship and the supertype does not).

Similarly, if an attribute applies to some but not all instances of an entity, then subtypes exist for the entity (i.e., the subtype has the additional attributes). The value of explicitly recognizing subtypes depends on the degree of heterogeneity among the subtypes. The purpose of the data model is to communicate the meaning of the data. If the introduction of subtypes confuses rather than clarifies, they should not be introduced.

In the data model of Figure 4, some Customers may not have any outstanding Invoices (Customer is not dependent on Invoice). Thus there are two subtypes of Customer: those with Invoices and those without Invoices. If this is the only distinction for subtyping, it is probably not worthwhile explicitly recognizing the subtypes. If, on the other hand, Customers with Invoices have additional attributes or are viewed different-

ly from Customers without Invoices, then the subtype should be created.

The quality of the data model is ensured by the way in which it is constructed. The construction described earlier is based on the principle of *normal forms* originally proposed by Codd (1971) and extended by numerous others (Date [1986] provides a nice overview). Each attribute is associated with an entity *only* if that attribute directly describes that entity with a single value. In the normal forms terminology, the assignment of attribute to entities in this way ensures that each attribute is "fully functionally dependent" on the identifier of the entity.

Similarly, disallowing many-to-many relationships ensures that each relationship corresponds to a functional dependency. The identifier of the entity on the "one" side is "fully functionally dependent" on the identifier of the entity on the "many" side. Thus, the resultant data model is "well formed" in the sense that it can be directly transformed into a relational schema in "third normal form."

There are structural rules for evaluating a data model:

1. Each entity must be uniquely named and identified.

2. Attributes are associated with entities (not relationships), and each entity must have one and only one value for each of its attributes (otherwise an additional entity must be created).

3. Relationships associate a pair of entities or associate an entity with itself (only binary relationships are allowed but relationships can be recursive).

4. Many-to-many relationships are not allowed (an intersection entity with two one-to-many relationships must be created).

5. Subtypes are identified when the minimum degree of a relationship descriptor is zero or when an attribute does not apply to all instances of an entity; these subtypes are explicitly recognized when there is a "significant" difference among the subtypes (e.g., they have multiple attributes or relationships).

TRANSFORMING A LOGICAL DATA MODEL INTO A DATABASE MANAGEMENT SCHEMA

Three traditional data models are used to represent database schemas in commercial DBMSs: hierarchic, network, and relational. To implement a database for a given logical data model, that data model must be transformed into a schema in the appropriate traditional data model.

There are numerous efficiency issues related to transforming a data model into a database schema. These are discussed briefly here; however, a "quick and dirty" approach simply maps entities into files (hierarchic segments, network record types, or relational tables) such that all of the attributes of an entity are in the same file.

The remaining problem is how to represent relationships (file interconnections). In the hierarchic model, where only one-to-many, parent-to-child relationships can be represented, this can be problematic. If an entity has more than one relationship descriptor with maximum degree greater than one, it has two "parents." The designer must choose one of the parents to be specified in the database schema and designate the other as a "logical parent." In Figure 4, for example, Line Item has two parents: Order and Product. A hierarchic schema can designate *either* Order *or* Product as the parent of Line Item, but cannot designate both. These two options for a hierarchic schema are shown in Figure 5a.

In the network model a relationship is represented by a *set*. A set represents the connection between two record types. Each relationship in the data model becomes a set in the database schema. The entity (record type) on the "one" side of the relation is designated as the *owner* of the set and that on the "many" side is designated as a *member* of the set. As illustrated in Figure 5b, Line Item is a member of the set "order line" whose owner is Order *and* a member of the set "product ordered" whose owner is Product.

In the relational model all interconnections among files are represented by data values. In this case, data elements (columns in the tables termed *foreign keys*) must be created to represent relationships. For a one-to-many relationship a column is created in the entity (table) on the "many" side for each attribute in the identifier of the entity on the "one" side. As illustrated in Figure 5c, the Line Item table has two "extra" columns: Invoice Number (representing the relationship with Order) and Product Number (representing the relationship with Product). A one-to-one relationship may be represented in the table corresponding to either entity in the relationship.

This type of direct transformation from a data model into a database schema may be inefficient for database processing. Decisions related to efficiency of implementation are part of physical database design.

There are numerous physical database design possibilities. The following are illustrative. For efficiency reasons, an entity may be split, with subsets of its attributes being assigned to different files. Alternatively, entities may be combined yielding (1) files with repeating groups of data elements, if the entity on the "many" side is stored together with the entity on the "one" side (e.g., storing Line Items in the Order file), or (2) redundantly stored data, if the entity on the "one" side is stored together with the entity on the "many" side (e.g., repeating the Order data in each Line Item). Specific attributes may be redundantly stored with related entities (e.g., Product Description may be redundantly stored with Line Item to avoid access to the Product file for certain reporting activities).

SUMMARY

Logical data modeling is a process by which the logical or "natural" data structure of a domain of interest is represented using a predefined set of constructs. The set of constructs is termed a *data modeling formalism.* The product of data modeling is a logical data model.

References

Chen, P. 1976. The entity-relationship model—Toward a unified view of data. *ACM Transactions on Database Systems* 1(1):9–36.

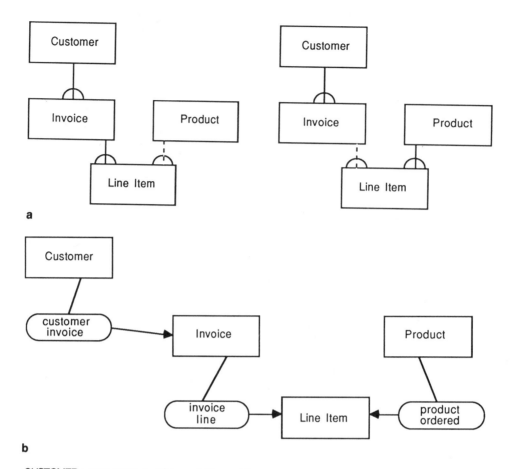

CUSTOMER(<u>customer-number,</u> bill-to-address, tax-percent)

INVOICE (<u>invoice-number,</u> customer-number, invoice-date, customer-PO, terms, FOB-point, freight)

PRODUCT (<u>product-number,</u> product description, unit of sale, unit-price)

LINE ITEM (<u>invoice-number, line-number,</u> product-number, quantity-ordered, quantity-shipped, quantity-backordered, discount)

c

FIGURE 5. Possible schemas for the logical data model of Figure 4: (a) two possible hierarchic schemas (dashed lines represent logical parents); (b) a network schema (arrows point from set owner to set member); (c) relational schema (identifiers are underlined).

Codd, E. F. 1971. Normalized database structure: A brief tutorial. In *Proceedings of the ACM SIGFIDET Workshop on Data Description, Access and Control,* pp. 1–17. New York: ACM.

Date, C. J. 1986. *An introduction to database systems,* Vol. 1, 4th ed. Reading, Mass.: Addison-Wesley.

Hull, R., and R. King. 1987. Semantic database modelling: Survey, applications, and research issues. *ACM Computing Surveys* 19(3):201–60.

Korson, T., and J. D. McGregor. 1990. Understanding object-oriented: A unifying paradigm. *Communications of the ACM* 33(9):40–60.

Peckham, J., and F. Maryanski. 1988. Semantic data models. *ACM Computing Surveys* 20(3):153–89.

Smith, J., and D. Smith. 1977. Database

abstractions: Aggregation and generalization. *ACM Transactions on Database Systems* 2(2):105–33.

Salvatore T. March

DATA PREPARATION

See Data Entry

DATA SECURITY

See Access Control; Coding Theory; Security, Information Systems; Viruses

DATA STRUCTURES

Consider the problem of organizing a large box of paper slips, each containing either the name, the address, or the phone number of a person or business in Manhattan, into a phone book. Without some method of structuring these data, the task is overwhelming. How do you remember which phone number goes with which name? How do you arrange all the names in alphabetical order? Given a name, how do you check for its phone number? How do you insert a new telephone customer's information into the list?

The problem is that unstructured data usually have no meaning. The box of numbers must be organized before it can yield useful information. *Data structures* are ways of arranging data so that, when stored in a computer, the individual data items are readily accessible.

For a programmer to define data structures, a programming language must provide two things, atomic data and data constructor operators. *Atomic* data are the elementary forms that cannot be broken up into smaller parts. In Pascal, for example, integers, reals, Booleans, and characters are the kinds of atomic data. *Constructor* operators form compound data objects from more primitive data. Array, record, and pointer constructors are familiar to most programmers.

ELEMENTARY DATA STRUCTURES

Primary computer memory is almost always organized as a linear array, a sequence of numbered locations each of which can be accessed through its number or address. The simplest data structures are those that are arranged similarly, allowing the implementer to use the memory organization to structure the data.

Arrays

A *one-dimensional array* is a sequence of data objects and corresponds to the mathematical notion of a vector. With each element of an array is associated a position or *index* that uniquely identifies the element in the array. In C, an array with n elements must be indexed by the integers $0, \ldots, n-1$. FORTRAN gives much more freedom in indexing, allowing the use of any *interval*, a block of n consecutive integers $m, \ldots, m+n-1$. Pascal allows noninteger indices as long as they are consecutive members of an ordinal data type. Most programming languages require all the members of an array to have the same type.

An *n-dimensional array* is a collection of data objects, each of which has n indices. A two-dimensional array corresponds to the mathematical notion of a matrix. The following Pascal declaration specifies a two-dimensional array containing 200 elements of type real:

`var twodim = array[1..4, 1..50] of real;`

Each element of twodim is uniquely specified by a pair of indices, the first in the interval $1, \ldots, 4$ and the second in the interval $1, \ldots, 50$.

Although it is not necessary, array elements are normally stored in consecutive memory locations, allowing efficient calculation of the address of each element through a *mapping function*. For example, if the memory address of the first element of a one-dimensional array is m, then the address of element i is $m+i-1$. Addresses for multidimensional arrays can be similarly calculated. This property makes an array a good choice for storing data lists when the number of elements is known in advance.

Because of their correspondence with vectors and matrices, arrays are also extensively used in mathematical and scientific calculations.

Records

A *record*, like an array, is a sequence of data objects. Record elements, called *fields*, may have different types and are accessed through a field name, rather than through an index. Records are used extensively in such database applications as personnel records and inventory control. Figure 1 shows the structure of a record for a phone book. A Pascal declaration for such a record is

```
type phoneentry =
   record
      name : array[1..20] of char;
      address : array[1..20] of char;
      number : integer
   end;
```

DYNAMIC DATA STRUCTURES

Arrays and records are often called *static* data structures because their structure never changes. The value of an element can change, but the element itself can never be deleted from the structure. Neither can a new element be added to the structure. In contrast, *dynamic* data structures are change-able, growing and diminishing as new elements are added and old elements deleted.

Lists

The simplest dynamic data structure is the *list* (or *linked list*). A list is essentially a sequence. As in arrays, the list elements are ordered, but unlike in arrays, individual elements do not have indices by which they can be accessed. Because of this lack of a simple means to access elements, operations on lists can be more cumbersome than on arrays; however, the flexibility in structuring data provided by lists more than makes up for this problem.

As list elements do not have indices, with each element must be associated a *pointer* (sometimes called a *reference*) to its successor in the list. In languages like C and Pascal, these pointers must be manipulated explicitly by the programmer. In other languages like LISP, pointers are implicit and handled by the system.

The standard way of visualizing lists and related structures is called *box–and–pointer* notation. Figure 2a shows a linked list L of names. Each list element is represented by a box containing two cells. The first cell contains the data value (the name) and the second cell contains a pointer linking the box to the next list element. A special pointer *nil*, which points to an empty list, is used to terminate the list.

In Pascal, lists are usually implemented using records:

```
type box = record
              datavalue : datatype;
              link : ↑ box
           end;
     list = ↑ box;
```

In manipulating lists, the programmer must manipulate both the data and link fields. For example, inserting the new name *ellen* into the list L after the element p (see Figure 2b) requires the following sequence of Pascal instructions: (1) temp := p ↑ .link; (2) new(p ↑ .link); (3) p ↑ .link ↑ .datavalue := "ellen"; (4) p ↑ .link ↑ .link := temp. Similar-

name	address	telephone number

FIGURE 1

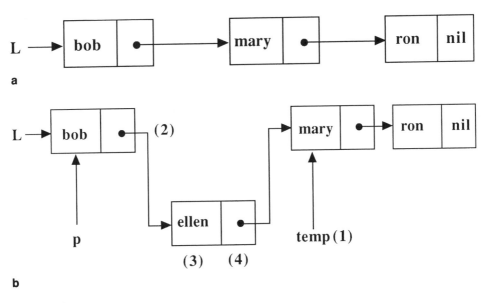

FIGURE 2

ly, deleting the element following p from the list is done with the instruction $p \uparrow .link :=$ $p \uparrow .link \uparrow .link.$

Variations on Lists

Lists are used to implement many important data structures, such as stacks, queues, trees, and graphs.

A *stack* is a list in which insertions and deletions occur only at one end, called the top of the stack. The other end is called the bottom. As a stack has the property that the last element to be put on the stack is the first one to be removed, a stack is sometimes called a LIFO (last-in first-out) or LIFO list. Stacks are used extensively in computer science for implementing recursion, translating languages, evaluating arithmetic expressions, editing texts, and many other applications.

A *queue* is a list in which deletions occur only at one end, called the front of the queue, and insertions occur only at the other end, called the rear of the queue. In a queue, the first element to be added to the queue is also the first one to be deleted, so a queue is sometimes called a FIFO (first-in first-out) or FIFO list. Queues are used for scheduling in operating systems and simulations, as well as many other applications.

Trees

A *tree* is a generalized form of a list in which an element can have more than one successor. The elements of the tree are generally called *nodes* and the links, *branches*. If the node p is a successor of the node q, then p is called a *child* of q and q is called the *parent* of p. For a data structure to be called a tree, two conditions must be satisfied. First, there must be exactly one node, called the *root*, that is not the child of any other node in the tree. Second, no node may be the child of two different parent nodes.

A tree node that has no children is called a *leaf*; the other nodes are called *interior* nodes. A node p is a *descendant* of a node q if p is a child of q or if p is a descendant of a child of q. If the node p is a child of the node q, then all other children of q are called the *siblings* of p. Siblings are normally ordered from left to right.

If p is a node of a tree T, then p together with all its descendants form another tree, called the *subtree* of T rooted at p. The *depth* of a node in a tree is the length of the path from that node to the root. The *height* of a tree is equal to the depth of the leaf whose depth is largest.

In Pascal, tree nodes are usually implemented as records. Figure 3 shows a tree representation of the expression $x(3y+5)$.

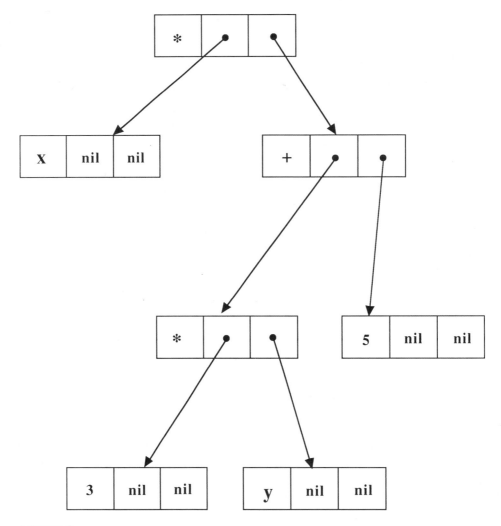

FIGURE 3

Each node has a data field plus two link fields:

```
type node = record
              datavalue : datatype;
              leftchild : ↑node;
              rightchild : ↑node;
            end;
      tree = ↑node;
```

Besides inserting and deleting nodes in a tree and changing data values at nodes, the most common operation on trees is a *traversal*, visiting all the nodes of the tree in some order. There are three standard methods for traversing a tree. In a *preorder* traversal, each node is visited before any of its children are considered. In a *postorder* traversal, each node is visited after all of its children have been visited. In an *inorder* traversal, each node is visited after its leftmost child has been visited but before any of its other children are visited.

Which method is used depends on the application. For example, consider evaluating the expression $x(3y+5)$ in Figure 3 when $x=2$ and $y=7$. Our strategy might be to traverse the tree, calculating at each node the value of the subexpression represented by the subtree rooted at that node. In that case, before we can calculate a value for an interior node, we must already have the values for each of its children. Therefore, we would want to perform a postorder traversal.

As another example, to calculate the depth of each node in a tree, we would perform a preorder traversal, because to know the depth of a node we must already know the depth of its parent. Therefore, a parent must be visited before its children.

Binary Trees

A *binary tree* is a tree in which each node has at most two children. The tree in Figure 3 is a binary tree. When a node has only one child, that child must be distinguished as a *left* child or a *right* child. Probably the most common use of binary trees is for dynamic data storage. For example, suppose that a very long list of names is being generated by some process. A running record of how many times each name has appeared must be kept. An efficient data structure for the problem is a binary tree in which each node has the following structure:

```
type binarynode = record
                    name : nametype;
                    count : integer;
                    leftchild : ↑binarynode;
                    rightchild : ↑binarynode
                  end;
     binarytree = ↑binarynode;
```

The first name produced is inserted into the root of the tree with a count of 1. As each name is generated, it is compared with the name at the root. If they are the same, then the count field is incremented. If the new name comes before the root name in dictionary order, then the search descends to the root's left child; if the new name comes after the root name in dictionary order, then the search descends to the root's right child. If at any point there is no child to which to descend, then the new name is not in the tree and a new node containing it must be inserted into the tree at that place.

A binary tree is said to be *balanced* if, for each node in the tree, the numbers of nodes in its left and right subtrees differ by at most one. The above binary search process is very efficient if the tree being searched is approximately balanced; however, if an already sorted sequence of names like "ann," "bob," "carl," "donna," "ellen" is produced by the generating process, then the resulting tree is very unbalanced. Several variations on the binary tree have been suggested that automatically produce an approximately balanced tree. These include *AVL trees, 2–3 trees,* and *B-trees.*

Graphs

A *graph* consists of a set of vertices and a set of edges, where each edge joins a single pair of vertices. In *directed* graphs, each edge has a direction, pointing from one of its vertices to the other. In *undirected* graphs, the edges have no direction.

Graphs have many applications. They can be used to represent a network of cities and highways, a network of computers, or an electronic circuit. Directed graphs model the flow of control in a computer system or the priority relationships among a set of actions.

Many graph applications involve repeated traversals of the graph in which each node must be visited. In this case, one efficient way is first to identify a *spanning tree* for the graph, a tree whose links are edges of the graph and whose nodes are all the vertices of the graph. A tree traversal algorithm can then be used to visit all the nodes of the graph. Figure 4 shows a graph and one of its spanning trees.

Sets

A *set* is an unordered collection of data objects, corresponding to the mathematical notion of a set. Sets are used mainly for categorizing data. A typical set operation involves examining the elements of a list one by one, classifying each of them by assigning it to a set.

In mathematics, sets may contain any sorts of objects and may even be infinite. It is very difficult to capture these properties in a set data structure, so most programming languages restrict sets in some way. In Pascal, for example, the elements of a set must be taken from the members of some ordinal data type.

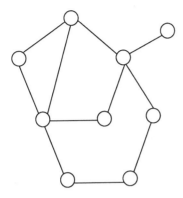
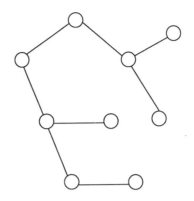

FIGURE 4

For Further Reading

The classic books on data structures and algorithms for manipulating them are the two volumes by Knuth and the book by Aho, Hopcroft, and Ullman. The new book by Lewis and Denenberg provides an excellent introduction to this area, as well as good references for advanced topics. Another good, comprehensive source is the book by Gonnet and Baeza-Yates, as is the one by Standish. An early survey of the mathematical theory behind data structures was the essay by Hoare, which remains still a very readable introduction to the topic.

Aho, A. V., J. E. Hopcroft, and J. D. Ullman. 1983. *Data structures and algorithms.* Reading, Mass.: Addison-Wesley.

Gonnet, G. H., and R. Baeza-Yates. 1991. *Handbook of data structures and algorithms in Pascal and C.* 2nd ed. Reading, Mass.: Addison-Wesley.

Hoare, C. A. R. 1972. Notes on data structuring. In O.-J. Dahl, E. W. Dijkstra, and C. A. R. Hoare, eds. *Structured programming.* New York: Academic Press.

Knuth, D. E. 1973. *The art of computer programming,* Vol. 1: *Fundamental algorithms.* 2nd ed. Reading, Mass.: Addison-Wesley.

———. 1973. *The art of computer programming,* Vol. III: *Sorting and searching.* Reading, Mass.: Addison-Wesley.

Lewis, H. R., and L. Denenberg. 1991. *Data structures and their algorithms.* New York: Harper Collins.

Standish, T. A. 1980. *Data structure techniques.* Reading, Mass.: Addison-Wesley.

Tom Jacob

DEBUGGING

See Software Engineering

DECISION MAKING

Our intuitive notions of decision making center on the act of choice. One makes a decision by choosing from a set of alternatives. More broadly, decision making is the thinking one does in determining how to act. This thinking can also be termed *problem solving.* There are different kinds of decision problems, reflecting underlying task characteristics and the knowledge available to the decision maker. Problem differences are largely responsible for the different conceptualizations of decision making to be found in decision research. Problem differences also drive variations in decision aids, the means by which computers and other interventions are applied in support of decision making.

CONCEPTUAL FRAMEWORK

Decision making can be characterized in a variety of ways. For instance, considering the nature of the decision maker, researchers often distinguish between individual, group, and organizational decision making. For the purposes of this article, four species of decision making will be identified, based primarily on task differences. Rather than an exhaustive set of possibilities, these categories organize decision-making research so as to highlight the actual and potential applications of computers. The categories are listed in increasing order of task difficulty and ill-structuredness.

Rule-based decision making Rule-based decision making encompasses situations in which the appropriate choice is prespecified for every possible circumstance. The decision maker's task is to determine which circumstances apply, identify the related rule, and implement the indicated course of action.

Model-based decision making The model-based approach involves the construction of a formal model intended to represent decision-relevant realities. Manipulation of the model allows one to identify preferred, and sometimes optimal, courses of action.

Classical decision theory Decision theory prescribes how to make preference-maximizing choices in situations where alternatives are usually known, preferences may be unclear, and the outcomes that follow from a choice may be known with varying degrees of certainty.

Decision processes In ill-structured situations, decision making is best studied and understood as a psychological process. Decision problems pose various demands (e.g., defining the problem), which humans respond to with their basic mental capacities and acquired knowledge.

RULE-BASED DECISION MAKING

In this, the most elementary kind of decision making, the selection of an action is determined entirely by the current system state or condition. Choice is driven by circumstance. It is assumed that all possible situations or system states can be characterized in terms of a limited set of attributes; that alternative courses of action are all known; and that a set of rules specifies, for each possible situation, the action(s) to be taken when it pertains. Decision making becomes a matter of determining which situation holds and which

rule(s) consequently applies, and then acting as directed. In classificatory decision making, a variation of this approach, rules effectively define categories of situations. The decision maker determines the kind of situation at hand, and selects the action appropriate for that category. Research on medical decision making indicates that physicians employ a taxonomy of disease categories in diagnosing and prescribing for patients.

Although often simple, rule-based decision making can challenge the capabilities of unaided humans. Many Americans, for instance, invariably get lost while working through Internal Revenue Service rules for preparing their tax returns. Situation descriptions can be complex, both because of the number of attributes involved and because of the conjunctive ("you are married *and* filing a joint return") and disjunctive ("the income is interest *or* dividends") relationships among those attributes. The most effective way of aiding such decision making is through the use of lucid representations. Diagrams or other depictions can make all situation–action pairings explicit in an organized and compact manner. Decision tables and trees are the most widely used representational formats. In addition to their application for general decision making, these representations have been used in the systems analysis and design process. Much of a computer's processing can be thought of as choice behavior in which the next processing step depends on a potentially complex combination of conditions. Decision tables and trees provide an easily understood representation of the structure of such situations, facilitating the translation of this structure into program logic.

The decision table in Figure 1 concerns the activities of ABC Company, a mail order firm that periodically develops mailing lists for its catalogs and mailers. Mailing decisions are based on information about ABC's current customers (e.g., past purchasing activity, current balance outstanding). ABC has also acquired a list of XYZ Company's customers, from which it will select promising candidates for a mailing. In a decision table, the conditions are listed as rows at the top of the table, and the action alternatives are listed as rows at the bottom. Each condition

CONDITIONS/ COURSES OF ACTION	DECISION RULES							
	1	2	3	4	5	6	7	8
ABC Customer?	Y	Y	Y	Y	Y	Y	N	N
ABC Activity > 100 ?	Y	Y	Y	N	N	N	–	–
ABC Balance Outstanding?	N	Y	Y	N	Y	Y	–	–
Age > 60 Days?	–	N	Y	–	N	Y	–	–
XYZ Customer?	–	–	–	–	–	–	Y	Y
XYZ Activity > 100 ?	–	–	–	–	–	–	Y	N
Send Catalogue	X						X	
Send Mailer		X		X				
No Current Mailing			X		X	X		X
Delete From File							X	X

FIGURE 1. Decision table.

row includes a stub, on the left-hand side, that describes the relevant condition, and a set of entries, on the right-hand side, that specifies the condition's possible values. Entries can be restricted to three values, as in Figure 1: yes (Y) if the condition must apply; no (N) if the condition must not apply; and indifferent (—) if the condition is irrelevant. Alternatively, entries can assume other sets of prespecified values. For instance, entries for the ABC Balance Outstanding? condition might have been assigned values of 0, 1–25, and >25 if these criteria were deemed significant. Each action row also consists of a left-hand side stub and a right-hand side set of entries. An action entry's value is marked, as with an "X," when the related action is called for. Or actions can be sequenced, the positive entry being a sequence number rather than a mark, when a specific order of actions is required. Each column of a decision table expresses a decision rule, a pairing of defined conditions with the appropriate response(s). The set of decision rules should cover all possible combinations of conditions, it being important to include an "else" rule for combinations that are not explicitly represented. The theory and practice of this representational format have been developed most fully in the systems analysis literature (cf. London 1972, Pollack et al. 1971).

Decision trees, the other decision model used in systems design, are representationally equivalent to tables but rarely as compact. Less effective than tables at representing

complex condition–action pairs, trees are suited to the depiction of action sequences. Consequently, they are the standard model for decision theory, and will be described more fully in that context. Decision trees have never been widely employed in systems development, and the use of decision tables also seems to be in decline. Compared with other schemes for representing program logic (e.g., flowcharts), tables have the advantages of being compact, easily understood, and amenable to fairly rigorous completeness and validity checks. On the other hand, table size is subject to combinatorial explosion, each new condition potentially doubling the number of rules. Increases in table size undermine the aforementioned advantages.

Although graphic representations can be used to aid rule-based decision making, such tasks are often susceptible to complete mechanization, computers effectively replacing human decision makers. Traditional computer programs routinely incorporate this type of decision making. Moreover, many large artificial intelligence (AI) programs, mostly expert systems, are built around a database of productions, "if–then" rules, or condition–action pairs instructing the system to perform certain actions when specified conditions apply. The performance of such programs in medical diagnosis, chemical analysis, and other applications demonstrates the expressiveness and power of decision rules. But although computers can handle even the most complex rule-based decision tasks, many problems fail to satisfy the assumptions and requirements of the rule-based approach. Decision situations cannot always be defined in terms of a specified set of characteristics; all possible courses of action are not always known; and there may be no condition–action rules prescribing choices for each circumstance.

MODEL-BASED DECISION MAKING

Beginning in the 1940s, a family of emergent disciplines, notably operations research (OR) and management science (MS), proposed a scientific methodology for decision making and problem solving in real-world domains. These fields quickly generated theoretical advances in queueing theory, linear and dynamic programming, and inventory theory, which enabled significant improvements in applied problem solving. Operations research/management science methodology is essentially one of mathematical modeling. Model-based decision making centers on the development of a representation or model of a decision situation. It is assumed that important structural aspects of the situation are captured in the model's mathematical expressions. Once the problem has been modeled, the model itself can be manipulated or even solved: one can determine, for given values of input variables, the values of output variables generated by the model. If the model captures all key characteristics of the situation, then it is reasonable to regard its output or solution as information pertaining to, perhaps even the solution of, the original decision problem.

Operations research/management science research has developed an array of models applicable to a variety of decision situations. There are simulation models, Markov models, and network models, as well as linear, nonlinear, integer, and dynamic programming models. Other kinds of models derive from queueing theory, game theory, and inventory theory. The latter is the source of the well-known economic order quantity result (Hillier and Lieberman 1974):

$$Q^* = \sqrt{\frac{2AD}{h}} \qquad (1)$$

This model prescribes the optimal number (Q^*) of items to order or produce for inventory, in light of a known product demand per period (D), a known setup or reorder cost per order (A), and a known inventory carrying cost per unit per period (h). The model is derived analytically from equations describing basic inventory dynamics and cost relationships. It is applicable when inventory shortages are not allowed. Thus, if a firm sells 3,000 widgets per year, has a reorder cost of $100 per order, and an annual unit carrying cost of $20, a decision maker, using (1), would compute a reorder quantity of 173

widgets. This solution could be accepted as the proper reorder quantity, or it could be judgmentally adjusted to reflect factors not included in the model.

Computers play an integral role in model-based decision making. Most mathematical models of real-world problems are too large to be solved manually, and so computers are used for this purpose. Indeed, much OR/MS research is concerned with finding more efficient computational procedures or algorithms for solving standard models. Commercial software packages providing easy-to-use implementations of particular modeling techniques are widely available. Related packages help in the selection of a modeling or statistical analysis method. Though broader in scope, decision support systems (DSSs) were initially developed as aids in model-based decision making, and most current DSSs still exhibit these modeling origins.

Some have argued that because any decision situation can be modeled, the only real limitation on model-based decision making is the availability of computational power for solving or manipulating models. This argument fails to recognize that not all models are valid representations of their target situations, and that the effectiveness of the modeling approach is critically dependent on model validity. Model-based decision making is restricted to situations having structures compatible with known mathematical representations. This domain of application has never been precisely defined; however, the past quarter century of OR/MS research has witnessed few innovations (i.e., new modeling techniques applicable to previously unmodelable problems) comparable to those produced in the field's early years. So there is reason to believe that many important decision problems are simply not amenable to model-based decision making.

CLASSICAL DECISION THEORY

Classical decision theory differs from rule- and model-based decision making in that it places the decision maker on center stage. It regards the decision maker's preferences as the ultimate criteria of choice and as unknowns that must be determined. It also looks to the decision maker for knowledge about alternative–outcome relationships, the consequences of making particular choices. Such knowledge is assumed by and embedded in the rules and models of the other approaches. Individuals routinely confront situations in which they must choose from among a set of alternatives. Each alternative can lead to one or more possible outcomes (i.e., future states). Based on knowledge of these, a rational decision maker will choose the alternative that maximizes his or her expected preference satisfaction or utility. The simplest situation—decision making under certainty—involves alternatives having known outcomes. As with a grocery-shopping consumer, one gets what one selects, the challenge being to choose the alternative that is truly most preferred. In more complicated situations, selection of an alternative can lead to various outcomes, depending on intervening states or events. Each intervening event or contingency, like the dice rolls in a game of chance, has multiple possible outcomes, providing various degrees of preference satisfaction. When all the contingencies in a decision problem involve known, objective probabilities, the situation is one of decision making under risk. When one or more contingencies cannot be fully and objectively quantified in this way, it is a

situation of decision making under uncertainty.

The classical model of decision making can be depicted with decision table or decision tree representations (Figure 2). Consider the case of a person who wants to invest $1,000 in one of three ways—stocks, bonds, or gold—where the investment payoff depends on the state of the economy during the one-year term of the investment. The box or choice node at the left center of Figure 2 originates the three alternatives. Each leads to a chance node, a circle depicting the contingent economic state. Economic conditions can be up (U), steady (S), or down (D), with unspecified probabilities summing to one at each node. Each investment alternative–economic condition path leads to an outcome, the final dollar value of the investment under the assumed economic conditions. Thus, an initial $1,000 investment in stock will be worth $2,000 if the economy is up, but only $500 if it is down. When probabilities are added to the tree, the worth of each alternative can be computed as the sum of its ultimate outcomes multiplied by their respective probabilities. For instance, if $P(U)$ = .3, $P(S)$ = .4, and $P(D)$ = .3, the expected value of an investment in stock is $1,150 [(.3 × 2,000) + (.4 × 1,000) + (.3 × 500)], that of bonds is $1,100, and that of gold is $1,000. Consequently, a profit-maximizing individual would invest in stock.

This simple model of decision making can be elaborated to encompass various complexities. First, one can often acquire information bearing on decision outcomes (e.g., an economic forecast). This new decision problem—whether or not to buy the information—can be modeled as an extension of the original decision tree. Second, because humans are concerned with maximizing preferences rather than wealth per se, outcomes should be expressed in terms of utility, a purer measure of value. The development of expected utility theory by Von Neumann and Morgenstern (1947) enabled the assessment of individual utility curves over risky outcomes, allowing decision problems to be represented with utilities as outcome values. Third, decision problems commonly involve outcomes that are valued in

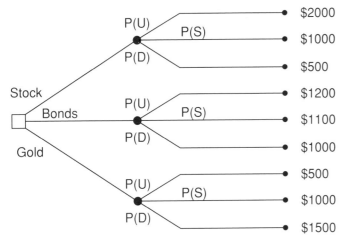

FIGURE 2. Decision tree.

more than one way. For instance, in buying a house, price is one factor, along with size, location, and appearance. The best outcome is that which scores highest in a complex weighing and combining process. Decision theorists developed multiattribute utility theory for determining the most preferred of a set of multivalued alternatives (Keeney and Raiffa 1976). Finally, decision situations often involve contingencies for which there are no known objective probabilities. The uncertainty about economic conditions in Figure 2 could hardly have been quantified with objective probabilities. Rather, one might have asked a panel of economic forecasters for their predictions, consolidating these into numerical estimates. The fourth development in classical decision theory employs this strategy. When objective probabilities are lacking, subjective probabilities—degrees of belief—are assessed from knowledgeable parties.

Interest in applying decision theory to real-world problems led to the development of decision analysis (Raiffa 1968). Decision analysts have devised techniques for structuring problems (i.e., representing them as decision trees), identifying relevant values and assessing preferences, and eliciting subjective probabilities. Decision analysis is a computationally intensive procedure, and computers have been heavily employed in its support. Decision analysis software is used to construct and revise decision trees; to compute outcome values from the weighted sums of their partial utilities; to translate networks of conditional probabilities into probabilities for final outcomes; to calculate the value of information that could be acquired; and to analyze the sensitivity of suggested decisions to variations in assigned probability and outcome values.

Classical decision theory has limitations. Despite its focus on the individual decision maker, the theory's psychological account is both weak and incomplete. Empirical research has demonstrated that people do not really make decisions in the way proposed by the theory. Decision theory also ignores certain common demands of decision-making tasks, notably the identification of alternatives. Subjective probabilities are

regarded as effective representations of individual knowledge, but the theory provides no explanation of how these numbers could achieve this status or of how elicitation practices can make them more substantive. The theory's prescriptive generality can also be questioned. Not all decision making hinges on individual preferences, and when relevant knowledge is effectively captured in rules and models, those other strategies are more effective. Nor is all decision making (in the broad sense) centered on choice among alternatives. When solutions are designed rather than selected, the decision theoretic perspective has little relevance.

DECISION PROCESSES

Decision process research has been motivated both by the inadequacies of decision theory and by the growth of cognitive science research on human thinking. The work of Simon (1976) is of central importance in each respect. Simon regarded humans as "boundedly rational," subject to severe limitations of knowledge and cognitive capacity. As a result, decision makers "satisfice," choose the first acceptable alternative, rather than determine the preference-maximizing option. Decision making, broadly conceived, is action-oriented thought, and is virtually indistinguishable from problem solving, a topic of long-standing interest to psychologists. Many problems cannot be adequately represented with decision trees, mathematical models, or rules. The decision making done in response to ill-structured problems must be studied as a cognitive process.

There are several distinguishable, but overlapping, varieties of decision process research. Behavioral decision theory, for instance, accepts the decision theoretic claim that decision making is essentially a judgmental process. Among other things, behavioral decision theorists have concluded that human judgment involves mental heuristics that can lead to biased, inaccurate probability assessments (Kahneman et al. 1982). In contrast, cognitive accounts of decision making employ a broader repertoire of mental contents and activities. Humans are able to acquire knowledge by perceiving, attending to, and categorizing relevant stimuli. This knowledge is stored in memory as a network or in integrated schematic structures. Thinking involves the mental representation of knowledge and transformations of these representations. In addition to making judgments, people can reason or make inferences; they can creatively imagine possibilities; and they can understand the meaning of information. Low-level cognitive activities can be combined into higher-level decision-making strategies, another target of decision process research. Scientists have found that humans use such weak methods as "generate and test," in which alternatives are repeatedly produced and tried until an acceptable solution is found; or "means–ends analysis," in which large tasks or ends are successively decomposed into smaller tasks or means that can be readily solved.

Most commonly, decision processes are described as a set of functions or phases performed in the course of moving from identification of a problem to implementation of a course of action. Such accounts are often represented by flow models or box diagrams. A model's components (e.g., problem definition, alternative generation) are functions that arguably must be performed if an appropriate course of action is to be taken. The simplest and most influential model was proposed by Simon (1960). Consisting of three phases—Intelligence, Design, and Choice—it is compatible with the decision theoretic framework, which it encompasses under Choice. Others reconcile the two approaches by proposing that decision making, as classically conceived, is preceded by a front–end problem formulation process.

As the breadth of the decision process perspective suggests, this approach accommodates a variety of computer-based interventions. Management information systems support decision processes by providing the information on which effective decision making depends. In recent years, decision support systems have become increasingly oriented toward aiding human decision processes. Decision support systems have given rise to the development of group deci-

sion support systems (GDSSs), designed to support the communication, meeting management, and deliberative needs of decision-making groups. Many DSSs and GDSSs include facilities for supporting problem definition, idea generation, alternative evaluation, and other functional demands of decision making. In addition to improving our theoretical understanding of decision making and other high-level mental processes, AI research has improved practical decision making, notably through the development of expert systems that replace humans or serve as intelligent assistants to skilled professionals. And there is a plethora of software serving specific functional demands of decision making. For instance, one's definition or mental representation of an ill-structured problem can be depicted as a cognitive map, computers having been used to construct and draw inferences from such maps.

The limitations of the decision process perspective reflect its descriptive orientation. The thinking that people do in trying to solve a problem may not be especially interesting or effective, particularly if important structural features of the problem situation have been overlooked. Decision process research has often been inadequately sensitive to the characteristics of decision tasks. This approach also suffers from the lack of a strong conceptualization of higher mental processes, a weakness that cognitive science promises eventually to overcome.

CONCLUSIONS

The practical importance of decision making explains the variety of efforts made to improve it through decision aids, computer-based and otherwise. What are the challenges and opportunities for future decision-aiding research? First, there is a need to more rigorously assess the effectiveness of decision aids. As is suggested by the vast number of untested problem-solving techniques, it is far easier to develop an intervention than it is to validate its effectiveness in actual applications. Second, the most promising paths to improved decision making seem to lead through a deeper understanding of problems and the decision-making process. Scientists must develop more substantive ways of characterizing decision situations so that task-appropriate interventions can be applied. Given a richer and more coherent account of human thinking, decision scientists will be able to design tools that are better matched to user needs. Finally, there is an opportunity to broaden the use of artificial intelligence and expert system technology into applications traditionally addressed by decision support systems, management information systems, and other interventions. Decision making is truly an information-intensive or knowledge-intensive activity, and there are significant opportunities for improving it through the application of computer technology.

References

Hillier, F. S., and G. J. Lieberman. 1974. *Operations research.* 2nd ed. San Francisco: Holden-Day.

Kahneman, D., P. Slovic, and A. Tversky. 1982. *Judgment under uncertainty: Heuristics and biases.* London/New York: Cambridge University Press.

Keeney, R. L., and H. Raiffa. 1976. *Decisions with multiple objectives: Preferences and value tradeoffs.* New York: Wiley.

London, K. R. 1972. *Decision tables.* Princeton, N.J.: Auerbach.

Pollack, S. L., H. T. Hicks, and W. J. Harrison. 1971. *Decision tables: Theory and practice.* New York: Wiley.

Raiffa, H. 1968. *Decision analysis.* Reading, Mass.: Addison-Wesley.

Simon, H. A. 1960. *The new science of management decision.* New York: Harper & Row.

————. 1976. *Administrative behavior.* 3rd ed. Glencoe, Ill.: Free Press.

Von Neumann, J., and O. Morgenstern. 1947. *Theory of games and economic behavior.* Princeton, N.J.: Princeton University Press.

Gerald Smith

DECISION MODELS

See Queueing Theory

DECISION SUPPORT SYSTEMS

Decision support systems (DSSs) are computer-based information systems that have as their primary purpose the support of decision makers in their decision-making processes. Consider the following example:

> Dispatchers in the Alabama Division of the Southern Railway make their dispatching decisions with the help of an on-line optimal route planning system. The minicomputer-based system helps the dispatcher minimize delay time by identifying the best points along the line's more than 800 miles of track for trains to meet and pass. The system continually accepts data about actual train positions, and updates its recommendations to reflect changing conditions. The dispatcher, though continuously consulting the system, remains in complete control, and can override any of its suggestions. (Sauder and Westerman 1983)

In this case, the computer-based system, the DSS, is an integral part of the decision-making process. There is real interaction between person and machine, and the system is involved throughout the decision process.

Decision support systems are "computer-based information system[s] used to support decision-making activities in situations where it is not possible or not desirable to have an automated system perform the entire decision process" (Ginzberg and Stohr 1982). This definition highlights several critical aspects of DSSs. First, they are computer-based systems. The scope and complexity of the situations to which DSSs are applicable necessitate computer-based support. Second, they are systems to support decision making. Decision support systems cannot replace a human decision maker; they only provide support to that person. This is because, third, DSSs are applicable only to decisions where human judgment is necessary. There are complex decision situations where the process can be completely automated and the person eliminated (e.g., process control in many chemical plants). The systems that perform this automation are not, however, DSSs.

HISTORY OF DECISION SUPPORT SYSTEMS

Gorry and Scott Morton (1971) identified DSSs as the systems needed to address a class of problems, unstructured decisions, that had until then been largely ignored by system developers. They suggested that computer-based systems could be developed to address these unstructured decision problems, but that they would require design approaches and people different from those appropriate for traditional computer-based systems.

Throughout the 1970s, DSS activity was generally limited to the large organizations (including universities) that could afford the expensive mainframe software packages and the professional staff needed for DSS development. Much of the focus in universities at that time was on the methodology for DSS development. In parallel with the efforts in the United States, some DSS development activity was occurring in Europe (especially at the University of Grenoble, France) during this period.

Interest in DSSs increased substantially by the late 1970s, coincident with the development of spreadsheet software and affordable personal computers. The introduction by IBM of the personal computer (PC) in 1981 marked the start of widespread DSS development in organizations of all sizes. Throughout the 1980s there was growth in the level of commercial DSS activity. Many organizations set up DSS departments or assigned staff within business functional areas (e.g., marketing, finance) to develop DSS. A large number of software and services vendors developed offerings to support DSS activity. At least one annual conference for DSS practitioners emerged, the DSS-8x Conference sponsored by The Institute of Management Sciences. As the field grew, several offshoots arose. Executive support systems

and group decision support systems emerged as active areas of interest for DSS practitioners and academics in the late 1980s.

DECISION SUPPORT SYSTEMS IN CONTEXT

Decision support systems developed from earlier activity in the information systems field, but they have their roots in several other fields as well. Computer science, management science, and organizational behavior are all important contributors, and an understanding of DSSs requires an understanding of how DSSs have been influenced by these other areas.

Much of the DSS technology base comes from computer science. All of the basic hardware, software, and design tools employed for DSS development are shared with other types of computer-based information systems. Database and human–computer interface technologies are central to DSS development and arise from more general work in the computer science field. Decision support systems have often been at the forefront of the *application* of new information technologies, but these technologies have almost never been developed specifically for DSSs.

Management science/operations research (MS/OR) has also played a key role in the development of DSS. Since World War II, MS/OR has been concerned with the application of formal mathematical models to real-world problems. The application of models is also central to DSSs. The MS/OR field focused on the model itself, and paid little attention to the interfaces with the model user and with data sources. Decision support systems have adopted much of this work in modeling, and added mechanisms for integrating models with data and delivering the package to a user.

The field of organizational behavior has contributed a perspective to the DSS field that differentiates it from other technical fields, for example, computer science and MS/OR. Most other technical fields make assumptions about people, their abilities, and their behavior that are not realistic. These assumptions, often implicit, include

(1) having limitless time for and computational capacity in decision-making situations, and (2) being able to unambiguously rank decision alternatives. Given these assumptions, an individual can always identify the *best* alternative in a decision situation. Organizational behavior theorists recognize that these assumptions are seldom valid, that people in fact have limited time, calculating ability, and sensitivity to differences among alternatives. Hence, they adopt a variety of compensating strategies and tactics to enable them to cope with complex problems. The decision support system field, unlike some other technical fields, accepts this more realistic view of people and their behavior, and aims at providing systems that will work within these boundaries.

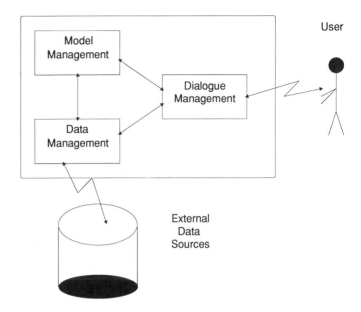

FIGURE 1. Decision support system structure.

STRUCTURE OF DECISION SUPPORT SYSTEMS

Decision support systems are composed *physically* of program modules that together accomplish the system's purpose; however, these systems can be viewed *conceptually* as composed of three functional components: (1) a facility for managing data, (2) a facility for managing models, and (3) a facility for managing user dialogues. The structure of a DSS composed of these three components is illustrated in Figure 1.

All DSSs must provide for dialogue with their users. The dialogue management component must establish and maintain communication with the user, enabling the user to access the other components of the DSS. The three capabilities needed to do this are (1) control of the "look and feel" of the interaction (the syntax), (2) translation of the physical interaction (e.g., keystrokes, mouse clicks) into messages that have meaning within the context of the decision problem (the semantics), and (3) interfacing of the dialogue with the data and model management capabilities.

Retrieval of data is the most elementary service a DSS can provide, and all other more advanced services require data retrieval as a base. Consequently, managing data is a critical function for a DSS. The data manage-

ment component must provide for capturing data items, storing them, and making them available for manipulation by other components of the DSS. This generally requires the provision of (1) a database, (2) a database management system to provide high-level access to the database, (3) a data dictionary that maintains data definitions and other information about the data, (4) a facility for interpreting data requests and determining how to fulfill them, and (5) a mechanism for accessing external data sources.

Most DSSs provide services beyond the simple retrieval of data. All of these advanced services are based on the application of a formal model. Thus, the management of models is also a critical capability for DSS. The model management component should provide for developing, storing, inspecting, manipulating, and running models. A facility to provide these capabilities would likely include (1) a model base for storing models or model segments, (2) an editing facility for building and changing models, (3) an execution control facility to ensure that models and model segments are properly linked and that they are executed in the proper order, and (4) interfaces to the data management and dialogue management facilities.

As shown in Figure 1, dialogue management, data management, and model management are connected to one another. Dialogue management provides the connection between the DSS and its user, and data management connects the DSS to external data sources. This is the generic structure for a DSS; however, not all of these connections, nor even all of the components, are present in every system. Different DSSs play different roles in supporting decision-making processes. The system's specific role determines the extent to which each functional component is necessary and how the components should be linked together.

WHERE CAN DECISION SUPPORT SYSTEMS SUCCEED?

The definition of DSS provided earlier indicates that DSSs have limited applicability; that is, not every situation requiring computer-based support is appropriate for a DSS. Ultimately, the role of any DSS is to support decision making. There are, however, many ways that such support can be provided. The support role provided by a DSS can be defined in terms of (1) the range of decisions supported, that is, a single, well-defined decision or a collection of related decisions; (2) the level of support, that is, the extent of data-based versus model-based support; and (3) the decision process supported. The range of decisions and the level of support require little explanation. The process supported deserves greater attention.

At least three decision-related processes can be supported by DSS: cognitive enhancement, learning facilitation, and support of communication and coordination. Cognitive enhancement is improvement of an individual's information processing capability through the provision of tools that enable more information to be processed or enable the information to be processed more quickly, more accurately, or better. Tools to support recall, calculation, and presentation all aim to enhance cognitive processing.

Learning facilitation refers to the support of learning about a decision-making situation, either by an individual or by an organization. Provision of a new framework for a decision and provision of tools for the long-

term storage of data describing a decision process are ways to facilitate learning. Often, as much learning takes place during the DSS development process as during the subsequent use of the system.

Support of communication and coordination is relevant only in multiperson decision situations. In such situations, both those where multiple individuals must *jointly* reach a decision and those where multiple decision makers must make *separate, but comparable* decisions, a DSS can provide the common "meeting ground" for all participants. The DSS can serve as a communication channel, a repository for data and models, or a sequencer of events in the decision process.

Decision support systems are appropriate in situations where the types of process support outlined here are needed. One other characteristic of the situation is, however, critical. That characteristic is complexity. Unless the decision situation is complex, for example, has a large number of variables or alternatives, ambiguity about objectives, or conflict among participants or objectives, a DSS is not appropriate. Without complexity, the cost of developing and using a DSS, including the cost of learning to use it, will exceed the perceived benefits, and the DSS will not be successful.

APPROACHES TO DESIGN AND DEVELOPMENT OF DECISION SUPPORT SYSTEMS

Traditional system design and development methods rely on observation of an existing system as central to determing the requirements for the new system. Decision support systems seldom replace existing systems. Rather, in most cases they represent attempts to systematize activity where no formal system previously existed. Consequently, an existing system cannot be used as a template for design of the new system, and substantial uncertainty about system requirements often exists. Frequently, this uncertainty cannot be resolved until after the DSS users have had an opportunity to use the system to support their decision-making process. The experience of using the system often points to new requirements for the system. For many DSSs, then, design and development must be an iterative process. At each iteration, a set of requirements are derived, a new version of the system is built on the basis of these requirements, the new system version is used, and the experience of using the system leads to a new understanding of the problem and points out shortcomings of the system.

A key issue in DSS design is how the requirements statement can be derived. Three widely accepted approaches to DSS requirements specification have been suggested (see Ginzberg and Ariav 1986): the linguistic approach, the ROMC approach, and decision research.

The linguistic approach (Keen and Gambino 1983) focuses on the dialogue between the DSS and the user, defining what the user says and sees. By working with a "good user," one knowledgeable about the problem and curious about the application of information technology to that problem, the system "verbs" (i.e., the actions the system may take) are identified and implemented as system functions. Other system aspects, for example, data and models, are developed as needed after the dialogue shell has been developed.

The ROMC approach (representations, operations, memory aids, and control) takes a broader cut, and defines the system objects (representations) and actions (operations) as well as the supporting tools (memory aids and control devices) the user needs to weave them into a useful system (Sprague and Carlson 1982). The ROMC approach is unique among DSS design methods, as it explicitly avoids any attempt to specify what the decision process should look like. Rather, it aims to provide a set of components that the user is free to string together to support whatever process he or she finds appropriate.

Decision research (Stabell 1983) is perhaps the most formal of the DSS design approaches. It requires that a normative model of the decision-making process, that is, a model identifying how that decision *should be* made, be built. The normative process model is then compared with a descriptive model, that is, a model of how the decision *is being* made. The differences between these two process models become the basis for specifying what the DSS should do.

Each of these approaches to analyzing DSS requirements can be applied at any iteration of the development process.

BUILDING BLOCKS FOR DECISION SUPPORT SYSTEMS

Computers of all sizes, from micros to mainframes, have the power and capacity to serve as the host platform for DSSs, and these systems are now built on the platform most appropriate to the system's purpose. A DSS to support a single decision maker in an isolated task may reside on a standalone microcomputer; however, a DSS to support the coordinated planning efforts of a senior management team would more likely be developed on a mainframe computer providing shared access to the entire user group.

General-purpose programming languages still provide the greatest flexibility for developing DSSs. Such languages, however, do not provide powerful development facilities, and there are now many software packages designed specifically for DSS development that provide both significant power and adequate flexibility. These software packages range from single-function (i.e., dialogue, data, or model management) DSS tools to DSS generators and generalized DSSs, which incorporate all three functional components in a single package [see Ariav and Ginzberg (1985) for a more thorough discussion of DSS software resources]. Both mainframe and microcomputer versions of these types of software packages are readily available to the DSS developer.

EMERGING DIRECTIONS

Three important current directions for DSS evolution are (1) the development of a group problem-solving focus, (2) the support of users at a higher organizational level, and (3) the incorporation of artificial intelligence technology.

Most early DSSs were designed to support individual problem solvers. Even those systems supporting multiple users, supported them as isolated individuals, not as interacting members of a problem-solving team. Recent DSS efforts have focused on developing group decision support systems to support the problem-solving and decision-making activities of several individuals who *must* interact to complete their task. This requires different capabilities in both the hardware and software than are required for individual support, and is an active area of current research and development (see COOPERATIVE WORK SYSTEMS).

Another area of DSS evolution is the type of user being supported. Most DSSs have been used by middle-level managers and staff support personnel. Senior executives have rarely been the direct, hands-on users of these systems. This is beginning to change, and EXECUTIVE INFORMATION SYSTEMS, DSSs tailored to the needs and working habits of top-level managers, are springing up in many organizations. Much remains to be learned, however, about how to make these systems effective tools for senior executives.

Finally, DSSs are beginning to utilize the technologies of artificial intelligence, particularly that of expert systems (see KNOWLEDGE BASES AND EXPERT SYSTEMS). Many possible uses of these technologies within DSSs have been suggested, and much effort will be required to determine how this can best be done (see Turban and Watkins 1986).

References

Ariav, G., and M. J. Ginzberg. 1985. DSS design: A systemic view of decision support. *Communications of the ACM* 28(10): 10–1052. Employs systems theory as a framework for DSS.

Ginzberg, M. J., and G. Ariav. 1986. Methodologies for DSS analysis and design: A contingency approach to their application. *Proceedings of 7th International Conference on Information Systems*, pp. 46–56.

Ginzberg, M. J., and E. A. Stohr. 1982. Decision support systems: Issues and perspectives. In M. J. Ginzberg, W. R. Reitman, and E. A. Stohr, eds. *Decision support systems*, pp. 9–31. Amsterdam: North-Holland.

Gorry, G. A., and M. S. Scott Morton. 1971. A framework for management information systems. *Sloan Management Review* 13(1): 55–70. The seminal article in the DSS field.

Keen, P. G. W., and T. J. Gambino. 1983. Building a decision support system: The mythical man-month revisited. In J. L. Bennett, ed. *Building decision support systems*, pp. 133–72. Reading, Mass.: Addison-Wesley.

Sauder, R. L., and W. M. Westerman. 1983. Computer aided train dispatching: Decision support through optimization. *Interfaces* 13(6):24–37.

Sprague, R. H., and E. D. Carlson. 1982. *Building effective decision support systems.* Englewood Cliffs, N.J.: Prentice-Hall.

Stabell, C. B. 1983. A decision-oriented approach to building DSS. In J. L. Bennett, ed. *Building decision support systems*, pp. 221–60. Reading, Mass.: Addison-Wesley.

Turban, E., and P. R. Watkins. 1986. Integrating expert systems and decision support systems. *MIS Quarterly* 10(2):121–36.

For Further Reading

Alter, S. 1980. *Decision support systems: Current practices and continuing challenges.* Reading, Mass.: Addison-Wesley. Includes eight extensive case descriptions of large-scale DSSs developed in the early 1970s.

Keen, P. G. W., and M. S. Scott Morton. 1978. *Decision support systems: An organizational perspective.* Reading, Mass.: Addison-Wesley. The most comprehensive treatment of the behavioral aspects of DSSs available.

Michael J. Ginzberg

DECISION TABLES

See Pattern Recognition

DESIGN

See Hardware: Computer Design

DESKTOP PUBLISHING

DEFINITION AND HISTORY

A working definition of desktop publishing might be the efforts of individuals to communicate their ideas, in print, from their personal desktops. The first practitioners were ancient scribes and, later, monks working to preserve knowledge in their cloistered monasteries. They held complete control of the visual appearance of their documents within the grasp of their hands on their pens. They could select any letter form for the text, choose a size and color to fit their own ideas, and create any picture they felt was needed.

With the development of printing using movable type, control of page appearance and selection of type fell to the print shop. Authors delivered their manuscripts to the printer who selected the typeface, size, line length, and line spacing for the publication. Page margins, borders, columns, and paper selection were also decided by the printers.

The development of the typewriter represented an opportunity for authors to regain control of the appearance of the page. The typewriter was a personalized application of the letter press to the desktop environment, and was advertised as a substitute for ordinary printing for those in remote areas. It also developed as the medium of choice for office administrators to communicate with their staff and other businesses. Writers followed the lead of Mark Twain in using the typewriter as a creative tool, completing the establishment of the typewriter as the first desktop publishing machine.

Introduced in the 1930s, the offset lithographic press generally replaced the letter press by 1950. Offset printing, and electrostatic printing developed by Xerox, allowed the desktop author to publish anything that could be photographed.

About this same time, typesetting was changing from Linotype and hot metal to photographic type and the so-called "cold"-type technology. As computers became more available, engineers devised ways for the computer to control the positioning of the type negatives and the exposure of the photographic film and paper in the typesetting machines. Eventually, the computer directly controlled the light source, eliminating the type negatives and leading to digital typesetting.

The computer joined the typewriter in 1964 with the introduction of the IBM magnetic-tape Selectric typewriter. This was the beginning of what is now called electronic word processing, and was an important expansion of the power of desktop abilities. Now, only the corrections needed to be retyped, not the entire document, thus eliminating a major source of errors. Computers eventually replaced the typewriter, controlling the saving and printing of the document.

By the early 1980s, personal computers and special-purpose word processing computers had replaced typewriters in many applications. Prominent among these machines was the IBM PC-XT and its imitators. Another personal computer, the Apple Macintosh, was introduced in January 1984, and had a profound impact on desktop publishing.

Except for the fact that corrections could be made on a screen before printing, these first personal computers were more of an enhancement of the typewriter than anything else, suffering the same limitations of the typewriter: impact printing character-by-character and limited fonts and font sizes. The Macintosh offered the addition of graphics, but was tied to a dot-matrix printer to provide them. A year later, in January 1985, Apple introduced the LaserWriter and the desktop publishing scene changed completely. The Apple LaserWriter used PostScript, a page description language developed by Adobe Systems, to control the way the image was generated within the printer. This enabled the LaserWriter to print almost any image the Macintosh could produce.

The IBM PC-AT with an EGA- or VGA-type graphics board, coupled with the Hewlett-Packard (HP) Laser Jet printer, arrived at about the same time, but this combination was much more limited, especially in its first versions. Text and graphics could not be printed at the same time, and the type fonts were limited to hardware cartridges that had to be plugged into the printer.

The term *desktop publishing* was first coined by Paul Brainerd, president and founder of Aldus, at a board meeting in October 1984. He first used the term in public at the Fall Comdex show that same year. Brainerd identified three criteria for his original definition: (1) personal computer- and laser-based technology, (2) nondedicated systems, and (3) single-user orientation (Saffo 1989). This definition served Aldus and Apple well, for it crystallized the market concept and gave direction to the newly emerging technology. The persistent thread through all of this, however, is the focus on the individual as publisher.

The hardware that Brainerd described was the Macintosh computer coupled to the LaserWriter (Figure 1). The computer was a general-purpose computer with an easily learned operating system and a high-resolution screen display. The printer had a resolution intermediate between the 72-dot-per-inch (dpi) pin printers and the 1,000- to 2,000-dot resolution of the digital typesetters, and came with a built-in basic complement of PostScript typefaces. At 300 dpi, the LaserWriter could produce type images that rivaled those of the expensive typesetters, at least to the untrained eye.

The factor that made this combination so potent was the software. Aldus released its PageMaker page composition package in July 1985. This program enabled the user to import word processing documents, which could then be formatted into type much more simply than the code-driven typesetters. In addition, the program allowed the importation of graphics from a variety of different graphics programs. Once the graphic was visible on the screen, it could be sized, cropped, and moved into position in the document. The result was an easy-to-use machine that produced crisp pages that could serve as camera-ready originals for quick printing or photocopying (Figure 2).

Time reported in 1986 that publishing is now "economically feasible for every man." The computer has taken publishing technology full circle, from the pen in the hand of the author to the computer in the hand of the author. From this beginning, modern desktop publishing has grown in many directions and developed many additional abilities.

EARLY DEVELOPMENT OF COMPUTER DESKTOP PUBLISHING

The market impact of the Macintosh/ LaserWriter/PageMaker package was dramatic; 50,000 units were sold the first year. Users of word processors or code-driven

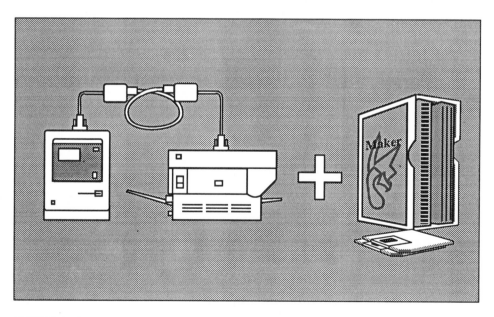

FIGURE 1. Basic setup for desktop publishing, including a computer, a laser printer, and page composition software.

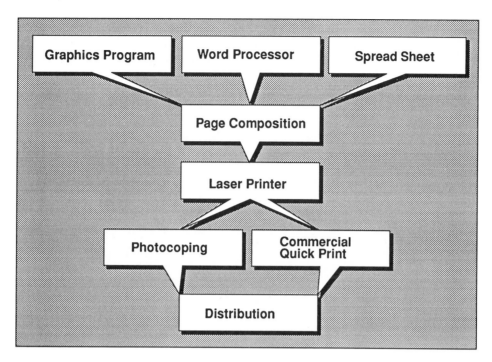

FIGURE 2. Example of a production process chart for computer desktop publishing.

Glossary: Terms Used in Desktop Publishing

Desktop publishing (DTP)	Designing, editing, and laying out a publication electronically, using a personal computer, word processing, graphics, and page layout software
Imagesetter	An output device for pages produced on desktop publishing systems; usually able to provide a positive photoprint or negative (film) image as final output to be supplied for printing
Prepress link	Hardware/software configuration that provides the ability to connect a personal computer or workstation to high-end color separation equipment
Raster image process (RIP)	Hardware or software that translates the DTP language into the language of the imagesetter
Resolution	Number of dots in a given area; resolution on a printer refers to the number of dots printed per square inch; resolution on a scanner refers to the number of dots saved for a given area of the scanned piece of art
Scanner	Hardware device that reads information from a photograph or other graphic, converting it into a bit-map graphic
Spread	Photographic thickening of type characters or other printing detail that will provide a color or tint overlap and allow for slight misregister in printing
Trap	Overlap allowed for two colors to print on the same sheet; used to compensate for misregister and to avoid white space between colors

Source: Impressions, Summer 1991, p. 4. Reproduced with permission from S. Rosenthal & Co.

typesetters had resigned themselves to the loss of visual control in favor of the increased efficiency. This equipment was much more efficient than older systems, but the appearance of the final document was never certain until it was printed. The Macintosh desktop publishing system introduced the concept of "what you see is what you get," or WYSIWYG. In other words, the user was able to compose not only the words, but the visual appearance of the document on the screen, and be reasonably assured that it would come out the way it appeared on the screen. Users of electronic word processors discovered that they could now have their cake and eat it too. No wonder the initial response was strong.

The potential buyer was presented with two choices: the more visually capable Macintosh/LaserWriter/PageMaker package or the stolid IBM/VGA card/HP Laser Jet/Lotus/WordPerfect package. Those who could make an independent choice frequently chose Macintosh. Many, however, had to bow to corporate compatibility with the huge number of existing IBM systems already installed.

Four basic software programs were used in desktop publishing during the first years: word processors, spreadsheets, graphics, and page composition programs.

Word processors handled the tasks needed to quickly write and edit text, and had the basic typewriter kinds of formatting control over margins, tabs, and line spacing. The documents produced might have many pages, but the point at which copy jumped from one page to another was not always obvious. Page numbers, footnotes, headers, and footers were available, but exactly how they would appear could be determined only by printing the document.

Spreadsheets handled numbers, formulas, and large blocks of data. They also provided some basic charts and graphs that derived from the data. Spreadsheet programs could generate report documents, but only the most rudimentary control was provided for the layout of the document. Again, screen displays and printed results were not necessarily the same.

Graphics programs allowed the cre-

ation of drawings, charts, graphs, diagrams, or any other visual the author might envision. There were two different approaches to these programs, called "paint" and "draw."

Paint programs map out the entire surface of a single letter-size sheet and divide it into a matrix of seventy-two picture elements (pixels) per inch, which was the screen and dot-matrix printer resolution. This map was often referred to as a bit map. The art was created by using the tools provided on screen to turn on or turn off each pixel. The resulting image was just the final pattern of on and off pixels in the map of the page. The valued features of these programs were their ease of use and the rich patterns possible.

Draw programs treat the page as an almost infinite grid on which the coordinates and characteristics of objects are recorded. Page size can be adjusted and a large drawing can be accommodated by tiling the image over several pages like a mosaic. Object characteristics include such features as line width and pattern, object fill pattern, location on the page, size, position above or below adjacent objects, and whether or not the outline of the object is angular or smoothed. Draw programs were easier to edit because the various pieces of the image retained their identity instead of being lost in the bit-map pattern. These programs produced cleaner and more precise images at the loss of the wide variety of patterns inherent in paint programs. The resolution of the images that these programs produced was limited by the resolution of the selected printer, rather than fixed by the nature of the program.

Page composition programs differed from the other programs by being designed to create documents composed of material principally originated in other programs rather than to create a complete document using a single program. The major abilities of these programs include the following:

- Ability to read many different file formats so the contents of those files can be incorporated into the active document
- Tools for sizing and cropping images imported from graphics programs
- Very basic word processing tools

- Very basic drawing tools
- Specialized text handling tools for controlling the arrangement of text
- Reasonably complete type handling tools
- Ability to insert or delete pages in a document
- Ability to see facing pages

The function of the program was to produce documents composed of completely designed discrete pages with linked text and with finished graphic images in place.

The quality of type produced by the new systems was no competition to typesetters for fine-quality printing, but there was a world of lesser typesetting jobs that could be satisfied by the desktop systems. The new systems also used plain paper, whereas the typesetters used photographic processes with their associated chemicals and plumbing concerns. This made the systems even more desirable to small shops and individuals.

Office communications almost immediately took on the appearance of commercially printed material. Frequently desktop systems were installed as replacements for word processors to be operated by the same staff. This worked as long as the character of the jobs remained the same, but that is often not the way it happened. As office administrators became aware of the system's capability, they began to ask their staff to produce more and more ambitious projects. Some office personnel were happy to extend themselves into more creative areas, and rose to the occasion. Others were already working at their visual limits and produced the more forgettable examples of business communications of the 1980s. Corporations and other users began to realize that something more than new equipment was needed if they wanted good design in their desktop publications.

Designers and artists took to the Macintosh at once and found that they could accomplish at home, in half the time, what they were doing at work. At first they smuggled their personal computers into their studios, but as supervisors saw the advantages to be gained, the Macintosh became a permanent feature in the art rooms of newspapers and the studios of advertising agencies.

As time passed, developers produced other devices that improved the power of desktop systems. Image scanners that converted photographs and hand drawings into digital data the computer could store and manipulate enabled graphic images other than those created in a graphics program to be included in a document. These new images took up large blocks of memory space both in the computer and on the storage disk. The storage problem was solved by the development of affordable memory expansion boards and hard disk drives in the range 40 to 60 megabytes (a megabyte is equal to a million characters or keystrokes).

Designers still had a problem with the 300-dpi resolution of the laser printer. It was acceptable for page proofing and low-quality typesetting, but they wanted access to higher-resolution printers. Linotype Corporation solved this deficiency when they introduced a PostScript-reading interpreter for their Linotron L-100 and L-300 series digital typesetters. The typesetters became imagesetters with 1,250 and 2,540-dpi resolutions, respectively. Now no apologies were needed for the type produced on the desktop systems, when printed on a Linotron. The Linotron also allowed designers to create designs with bleeds—images that extend beyond the trimmed edge of the page—which they could not do on a laser printer.

Software developers were also at work. Manhattan Graphics came out with a page composition program called Ready-Set-Go!, and later the Quark Company came out with Quark Express. Both of these programs contained search and replace features as well as a spelling checker, features that Aldus resisted including in PageMaker. Adobe came out with the first PostScript graphics program, called Illustrator, that promised smooth lines and control unavailable in older programs. Aldus followed with Freehand, also a PostScript graphics program, which allowed the user to create images using the mouse in a free drawing mode similar to that employed in other drawing programs.

While Macintosh users worked with PageMaker, IBM users were having to do their desktop work without the benefit of an easy-to-use page composition program. Xy-Write, Interleaf, and Ventura Publisher were very powerful tools, but were complex programs, difficult for a beginner to use. These programs had been converted to use on the personal computer from larger programs designed to run on mainframe or minicomputers and retained many of the code protocols of the larger machines. In 1988 Aldus bridged the gap between the IBM and Macintosh systems by releasing version 3.0 of PageMaker for the IBM. It worked within the Windows environment developed by Microsoft for the PC. File-sharing software even allowed PageMaker documents created in one environment to be used by PageMaker in the other. Finally, the IBM had an easy-to-use page composition program.

IMPACT OF DESKTOP TECHNOLOGY ON PUBLISHING

No sooner had desktop publishing developed a niche in the publishing business than computer technology and user demand began to expand the uses and application of existing systems well beyond the realm of the individual desktop. Personal computers had taken over the abilities of many of the dedicated, standalone workstations that had been used in publishing. Because they were also cheaper to purchase they quickly replaced the more limited, dedicated machines. Being general-purpose machines, personal computers could help out in any other computer function, such as balancing the books and keeping track of inventory. This made them very popular with small operations, where multiple functions meant real economy.

When used in place of a dedicated workstation, the personal computer was usually hooked into a communications network where many users contributed toward the completion of several documents at a time. Many different printers, hard drives, and other devices (peripherals) were also connected so they could be accessed by any of the computers on the network. These networks were referred to as local-area networks (LANs). Large-scale use of desktop systems in such environments to produce

high-quality or large-volume publications was clearly beyond the definition of desktop publishing. In fact Jonathan Seybold and others began to call these applications "computer publishing," dropping the desktop appellation. Others have begun to call this use of personal computers in commercial publishing midrange printing. By whatever name it comes to be known, it will not be desktop publishing.

This is not to say that desktop publishing had ceased to exist, only that there was beginning to be a division in the use of the personal computer in publishing. The machines released in the late 1980s and early 1990s possessed many refinements and more abilities than the first models. Apple came out with the Macintosh II series of open-architecture machines (easy insertion of additional boards and accessories without professional installation), and IBM introduced its PS/2 series of office machines. Both systems offered color in the screen display, and in the software's ability to manipulate color images for placement in documents. Thus, it was natural for commercial publishers to seek the economy and power represented by the more advanced desktop publishing systems. Large-scale commercial use, however, is beyond the scope of desktop publishing.

Desktop applications remain in the advertising, design, public relations, newsletter, and magazine businesses. Magazines, with the notable exceptions of the well-known national circulation consumer magazines, are usually small operations employing two to twelve employees. Many advertising, public relations, and design firms are of similar size. Add to this all the small business, community, religious, neighborhood, club, and public service organizations, and the scope of real desktop publications becomes more defined. Even quick-print/copying services are providing pay-as-you-go desktop facilities and services. For the small user who needs high-quality output, service bureaus now offer imagesetter printout to paper or film for a fee. Simply bring in your hard disk, plug it into their system (or, in some cases, telecommunicate the file via a modem over telephone lines), and print out your work.

Even within this more restricted meaning, the powers and abilities of the emerging systems have expanded greatly. Desktop image scanners can handle 128 shades of gray or even color. Computers treat these images as low-resolution images; the high-resolution images come from the commercial drum scanners, such as those manufactured by Hell, SciTex, or Crossfield. This is important to desktop users because stock photo houses may be making their image files available via modem to agencies, designers, or other users who wish to place them in their publications. These images will take even more memory to store and handle, but the cost of a megabyte of computer memory is well below $100. Hard disk drives now come in two varieties: (1) two- and three-platter units that range to 120 megabytes, and (2) drives with removable hard disk cartridges that each hold from 40 to 60 megabytes. Other storage devices include compact optical disks. Some of these are write once, read many times, meaning you cannot erase them; others are erasable and can be used somewhat like an ordinary hard disk that uses a magnetic medium. The difference is that erasable compact optical disks hold 600 and more megabytes of information per disk. These drives are in the range from $3,000 to $5,000 and are considered affordable for the user making money with desktop publishing.

Laser printers had long been a problem for commercial artists and designers because of the limitation to letter or legal paper, with the last quarter inch around the edge unavailable for printing. Seymour (1990) reported on the availability of large (11 × 17-inch) laser printers with 600-dpi resolution. These could be used to print posters or full sheets of camera-ready artwork for reproduction. They even had a Small Computer System Interface (SCSI) port for a hard disk so that large files of downloadable fonts could be stored in the printer.

Software manufacturers have provided a wide range of application programs that enable users to do many of the tasks that were available only through special service bureaus a short time ago. Color correction of photographic images, digital photo retouching, image integration within the page composition program, as well as color separation and proofing, are now available.

Advertising agencies and design and public relations firms can now produce video programs with computer animation from their desktop in addition to the traditional printed materials.

Still, no matter how wonderful the system, the quality of the finished product remains closely tied to the skills and creativity of the operator.

FUTURE PROSPECTS

The lack of compatibility between the various computers from different manufacturers is a major issue concerning desktop publishing that is yet to be resolved. Software manufacturers have had a difficult time writing programs that would operate on more than one computer system without severely limiting the capability or speed of the resulting program. Many developers have said that programmers should not have to be concerned about system configurations when writing their programs. System compatibility issues may be reconciled with the close ties developing between Apple and IBM. Compatibility between programs has always been a feature of Macintosh software. IBM software compatibility has not fared as well. With closer collaboration, computer hardware and software may become much more internally compatible.

A larger number of computers using the same parts means a larger production run on computer components and reduced price. In the past this has usually led to smaller, faster, more powerful machines with more sophisticated software, and is likely to remain so in the future as well.

Another development that will affect desktop publishing will be the increasing use of networks and large text, art, and photographic databases. These will give the desktop publisher access to information resources previously available only to large publishing houses. The newer faster machines will make the use of these resources possible.

Today's computer bulletin boards are small examples of electronic publishing. With the advent of national networks that give the desktop publisher access to a national audience, some aspects of desktop publishing will develop into true electronic publishing, where the document may achieve a physical existence only if the end user chooses to print it.

[*See also:* Typesetting.]

References

Saffo, P. 1989. Publishing moves beyond the desktop. *Personal Computing* 13(2):67–72.

Seymour, J. 1990. New large-sheet printers destined to be a big hit. *PC Week,* July 30, p. 15.

For Further Reading

Abrams, M. E., and R. L. Norvelle. 1987. *Learning computer graphics,* published under a grant from the American Newspaper Publishers Association Foundation, pp. 1, 18, 24, 26, 33–41.

Anderson, K. 1989/1990. Page-layout packages boost text handling. *PC Week,* December 25, 1989/January 1, 1990, p. 63.

Berk, E., and J. Devlin. 1989. Page-layout software divides to conquer niches. *PC Week,* September 18, pp. 95, 97.

Burger, R. E. 1989. Desktop color publishing. *NCGA '89 Conference Proceedings,* April 17–20, Vol. III, pp. 135–42.

Byrne, C. 1989. A designer's guide to the computerized studio, or—how to stop worrying and start exploiting the tools of desktop publishing. *NCGA '89 Conference Proceedings,* April 17–20, Vol. III, pp. 143–53.

Diehl, S., and H. Eglowstein. 1990. Is the typesetter obsolete? *Byte* 15(10):152–68.

Hibbard, J. L. 1990. Document processing by computer: Some generic models. *Technical Communication* 37(1):13.

Kalmbach, J. 1988. Reconceiving the page: A short history of desktop publishing. *Technical Communication* 35(4):277–81.

Leeke, J. 1988. Companies have designs on protecting their image. *PC Week,* June 14, pp. 50, 51.

Lewallen, D. 1989. Page-layout software: Smooth integration is the key. *PC Week,* July 17, pp. 42, 43.

Machover, C. 1989. Future hardware directions. *NCGA '89 Conference Proceedings,* April 17–20, Vol. I, pp. 285–91.

Manes, S. 1988. Desktop publishing: Can you justify it? *PC Magazine,* November 29, pp. 85, 86.

Marcus, A. 1989. Standards provide publication consistency. *NCGA '89 Conference Proceedings,* April 17–20, Vol. III, pp. 170–71.

Matazzoni, J. 1990. Prepress progress report. *Macworld* 7(10):168–75.

Rizzo, J., and MacUser Labs Staff. 1990. Maximum movable megabytes: Erasable optical disks. *MacUser* 6(11):102–30.

Taylor, S. 1991. Electronic color scanning in a desktop environment. *Publisher's Weekly,* January 18, pp. 35, 36.

Treadway, R. 1989. Separating form from function in future interface management technologies. *NCGA '89 Conference Proceedings,* April 17–20, Vol. II, pp. 239–47.

Van Name, M. L., and B. Catchings. 1990. Entry level packages offer users versatility in laying out a page. *PC Week,* June 4, pp. 129, 132.

Verhoeven, D. L. 1989. Future directions in graphics software tools. *NCGA '89 Conference Proceedings,* April 17–20, Vol. II, pp. 289–95.

Wallia, C. J. 1989. Technology reviews, laser printers: Editor's choice. *Technical Communication* 36(3):250.

Ronald L. Norvelle

DIJKSTRA, EDSGER W.

Edsger W. Dijkstra was born in the Netherlands in 1930. He entered the programming profession in 1952, programmed computers for 3 years, and then decided to help make programming a respectable discipline in the years to come. He was aware that automatic computers were here to stay.

Dijkstra worked in theoretical physics, algorithm design, compiler construction, process synchronization, operating system design, programming language semantics, programming methodology, and mathematical methodology in general, such as the design of adequate notations and the exploitation of proof theory to guide the design of streamlined formal arguments.

The working vocabulary of programmers everywhere is studded with words originated or forcefully promulgated by Dijkstra: display, semaphore, deadly embrace, go-toless programming, structured programming.

Dijkstra has had a strong influence on programming. He has introduced a special style: his approach to programming as a high, intellectual challenge; his eloquent insistence and practical demonstration that programs should be composed correctly, not just debugged into correctness; and his illuminating perception of problems at the foundations of program design.

He has published many papers, both technical and reflective, among which are especially to be noted his already classic papers on cooperating sequential processes, his indictment of the go-to statement, and his philosophical addresses at the IFIP Congresses in 1962 and 1965. An influential series of letters by Dijkstra were published on the art of composing programs.

Dijkstra was presented the 1972 Association for Computing Machinery (ACM) Turing Award in recognition of his outstanding contributions to the programming field. The Turing Award, the Association's highest recognition of technical contributions to the computing community, honors Alan M. TURING, the English mathematician who defined the computer prototype Turing machine and helped break German ciphers during World War II. In his Turing lecture at the 1972 ACM Annual Conference, Dijkstra remarked: "We shall do a much better programming job, provided that we approach the task with a full appreciation of its tremendous difficulty, provided that we respect the intrinsic limitations of the human mind and approach the task as very humble programmers."

As of 1991, Dijkstra occupied the Schlumberger Centennial Chair in Computer Science and was a professor of mathematics, both at the University of Texas at Austin.

For Further Reading
Dijkstra, E. 1972. The humble programmer. *Communications of the ACM* 15(10):859–66.

Donald D. Spencer

DIRECT SCREEN MANIPULATION

Computer operations often involve selecting, creating, or manipulating items on a screen. These kinds of tasks can be performed quickly with a pointing or drawing device such as a mouse, a touch screen, or a digitizing tablet.

HISTORICAL EVOLUTION

Symbolic Interaction
The development of time sharing during the mid-1960s created the need for an easy way to enter a program and communicate with it while the program was executing. The keyboard of a teletypewriter became popular for symbolic interaction: people typed instructions to the computer in much the same way they would write a list of instructions for a human assistant. Paper printing teletypewriters eventually gave way to video display terminals (VDTs) as the norm for human–computer interaction. On these devices, the keyboard remained the principal form of input from a person to the machine. Output appeared on the computer terminal's screen.

Iconic Interaction
As computers became less costly and microcomputers began to proliferate throughout the work force, potential users sought ways to become proficient more quickly at causing results to appear on a computer screen. Devices were needed that would allow a person to point to a selection on the screen, as a person who does not know the (symbolic) language of a foreign country might point to items in a coffee shop to order a meal. Many direct screen manipulation devices

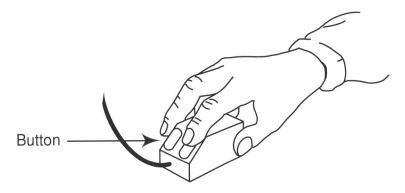

FIGURE 1. A typical mouse.

have been created to allow a computer user to point to the desired action or move the object of interaction on a screen. Specific examples of these devices are discussed in the following sections.

POINTING DEVICES

Mouse

The computer mouse is an input mechanism that bears some resemblance to the animal. It is "a hand-operated pointing device that senses movements as it is dragged across a flat surface and conveys this information to the computer" (Anderson and Sullivan 1988, p. G13). A mouse is commonly used to work with graphical images, but it can also be used to aid traditional keyboard operations such as changing the position of the text cursor on a screen. A mouse usually contains one to three buttons that are clicked when the user wants the computer to take notice of the cursor's current position. An example of a mouse is shown in Figure 1.

A mechanical mouse contains a ball on its underside that rolls on a surface as the mouse is moved. As shown in Figure 2, two small wheels inside the mouse touch the ball and spin as the ball rolls. These wheels are connected to devices that use infrared light shining through slits in a rotating disk to measure the distance moved. Mounting each wheel perpendicular to the other (and to the desk surface) provides two sets of coordinates that indicate movement in an x, y

plane. Thus, physical movement of the mouse can be directly translated into cursor movement along the x and y axes on a computer screen.

Nonmechanical mice exist as well. One common type is the optical mouse, which has no rolling ball or spinning wheels, but slides over a special pad ruled with alternating dark and light lines to form a grid. Two light-emitting diodes (LEDs) send beams from the bottom of the mouse at an angle so that corresponding optical sensors count the reflected pulses of light as the mouse is moved. Usually the dark lines on the pad running in one direction are black, and the dark lines running in the other direction are

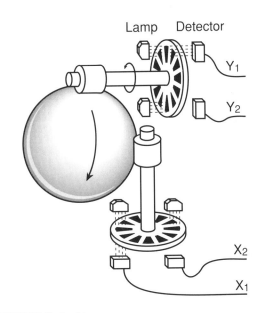

FIGURE 2. Inside a mouse.

blue; one LED emits red light, which is absorbed by the blue lines, and the other LED emits infrared light, which is absorbed by the black lines. Thus the (nonabsorbed) reflections are translated into cursor movements in the x and y directions (Van Name and Catchings 1989).

Cordless mice are beginning to appear that do away with the inconvenience of a connecting cable (Bobker 1990). Indeed, wireless, hands-free mice have provided computer input alternatives for the physically challenged for many years. Two products in the latter category are The Headmaster, by Prentke Romich, which uses ultrasound signals emitted from a headset to determine desired changes in cursor location; a puff tube performs the function of a mouse click. The Freewheel Pointer, by Pointer Systems, Inc., determines the user's head position by bouncing infrared light off a small, lightweight mirror on the user's forehead. Both devices allow users to make selections from images of keyboards displayed on a screen (Berliss and Borden 1989). (See also DIS-ABLED, TECHNOLOGY FOR THE.)

The major advantages of using a mouse, compared with cursor control keys on a traditional keyboard, are the mouse's speed of repositioning and its more natural (user-friendly) way of enabling a computer user to point to a particular position on the screen. The major advantages of a mouse over other types of pointing devices are its accuracy and proven efficiency (Anderson and Sullivan 1988). One disadvantage of a mouse is that it requires clear desktop space to be used effectively.

Trackball

A trackball is essentially a mechanical mouse turned upside down so that the input device remains stationary and hand movement is used to roll the ball. As with a mouse, cursor movement on the screen corresponds to the direction of physical hand movement. Advantages of a trackball are similar to those of a mouse, but trackballs save desk space because the user does not have to move the entire device (Wallace 1990). One disadvantage of a trackball is that long, continuous cursor movements are more difficult than with a mouse because the user must periodically reposition his or her hand on the ball to make it rotate a full revolution.

Trackballs are common in environments where a mouse would be useful but working space is expected to be cramped. For example, the Macintosh portable computer comes with a trackball built into the system. Trackballs are also used with computers designed for use in K–12 education (e.g., Unisys Icon), because of the perceived need to have as few as possible movable peripheral components attached to a student workstation.

Other Mouse-Type Devices

Touchpads are input devices quite similar to a trackball, except that they contain no rolling ball. For example, MicroTouch's UnMouse is a "pressure sensitive, stationary touchpad with a function button" (Gillooly 1989), and Sirius Industries Inc's Motionless Mouse "is controlled by tilting instead of pushing or dragging" (Gillooly 1989).

One of the newest mouse-type devices is the IsoPoint Control, "a pencil-type roller bar located just below the space bar on the keyboard" (Bethoney 1990). Rolling the bar up or down or sliding it from left or right produces corresponding cursor movements on the screen. Pressing the roller bar serves the same function as clicking a button on a mouse. Using the device is reported to be more time consuming than using a mouse or trackball, but it saves space and allows a person's hands to remain on the keyboard (Bethoney 1990, Brownstein 1990). The most popular use of the IsoPoint Control is in laptop computers.

Touch Screen

Several pointing devices exist that enable a screen to become the input as well as the output device for a computer system. Some screens sense the touch of a human finger; others require a special pen or stylus to activate a command displayed on the screen. Three methods for making screens touch sensitive are described in *Microcomputers: Software and Applications* (Curtin and Porter 1986):

1. *Infrared screens* surround the screen with LEDs and photodetector cells, producing a grid. A touch breaks some of the vertical and horizontal beams, and the computer calculates the position of the touch.
2. *Pressure-sensitive screens* use two sheets of slightly separated Mylar embedded with rows of wires running horizontally on one sheet and vertically on the other. When pressure is applied to the screen, the two sheets touch at the pressure point, closing the circuit for the crossing wires and enabling calculation of the screen position.
3. *Capacitive screens* sense a change in electrical field at the point where the screen is touched by a finger or stylus.

A light pen can be used for many of the same applications as a touch screen; however, the light pen's mode of operation is reversed, in that a sensor in the pen determines where it is pointing by tracking the video screen refresh activity (which occurs thirty times per second) as it passes under the pen (Gruman and Needleman 1990). A button on the light pen serves the same selection and movement functions as the button(s) on a mouse.

A sonic pen uses reflected or emitted sound to determine where the pen is pointing on the screen. It is sometimes possible to hear a sonic pen crackle (Sullivan et al. 1988).

The major advantage of a touch screen as an input device is that it requires little user training compared with a keyboard or a mouse. One disadvantage of a touch screen is that a computer user's arm tends to tire more quickly. Touch screens are very popular for applications where people are standing and/or require only brief interactions with the computer system. For example, touch screens are commonly used in videotex systems at shopping mall directories to aid prospective buyers in quickly locating specific products or types of stores.

DRAWING DEVICES

Digitizing Tablets

Although the keyboard is a practical text entry device, and the mouse and touch screen are effective for pointing, none of these input mechanisms are particularly effective for drawing an image on a computer screen. In fact, using a mouse for tracing or freehand drawing has been likened to "drawing with a bar of soap" (Johnson 1990). Digitizing tablets (also called graphics tablets) help overcome these difficulties.

Digitizing is "the process of converting positions on a plane (Cartesian x and y coordinates) into digital values that can be used by an application like computer-aided design (CAD), illustration, and paint programs" (Rosch 1989). A digitizing tablet is an input device, resembling a paper drawing tablet, on which a pen (stylus) or other device is used to draw or trace an image for computer entry.

One distinctive feature of a digitizing tablet is that positions on the tablet usually indicate absolute locations. If one points a pen to a certain location on a tablet and later returns to that point, the cursor will also return to the same point as it previously occupied on the screen. By contrast, when a mouse is returned to the same point it physically occupied on a desk, the cursor seldom returns to the same point on the screen. This is because the degree of rotation of the ball within the mouse has usually changed. The fixed frame of reference of the tablet is helpful for such tasks as image tracing and free-form drawing, where connecting lines originate from several different points.

Below the surface of most digitizing tablets lies an electromagnetic matrix formed from a radio antenna with conductive traces spaced about 0.1 inch apart. A radio transmitter in the drawing pen sends out brief pulses, which, when the tip position switch or pen's button is clicked, are used by the tablet to compute the stylus coordinates based on the signal it receives across several grid wires. This method of detection allows digitizing tablets to function properly even if several pages of paper separate the pen's stylus from the tablet surface (Johnson 1990).

Modern digitizing tablets have greatly improved capabilities over earlier models, especially in the areas of features that make them easier for use by artists. For example, the Watcom SD-420L has a wireless pen with a pressure-sensitive tip that works much like a normal drawing pen. Pressing harder on this tool makes the digitized line on the screen appear wider (Johnson 1990).

Puck

A puck (also called a tablet cursor or cross-hair mouse) is a mouselike device designed for digitizing a printed image. It has a small magnifying glass with cross hairs that make it especially useful for digitizing pictorial data with fine resolution. Pucks are reported to be more accurate but less convenient to use than mice (Rosch 1989). Common applications for pucks are digitizing maps, blueprints, and medical images.

COMBINATION DEVICES

Several devices have appeared on the market that incorporate both pointing and drawing tools. One is Calcomp's Wiz, which has a digitizing tablet and pen as its basis, but also comes with a puck attached to the tablet. In addition, the company also offers template overlays for the tablet that allow the pen to be used to point to alternative selections much as one might use a touch screen. The Wiz can also be switched from absolute to relative mode, which allows the tablet and puck (or pen) to be used like a mouse. These features are all incorporated into a unit that has a footprint about the size of a normal mouse pad (work area) and lists for less than $300 as of 1990 (Johnson 1990).

An example that goes one step further is the GriDPad portable computer. This notebook-sized machine has no keyboard, relying instead on an electronic glass data surface and an electronic pen that functions much like a mouse. A graphic keyboard representation can be called up and pointed to whenever traditional keyboard-style input is desired. Built-in character recognition algorithms also enable data to be entered by writing (printing) characters on the data en-

try surface. The GriDPad is billed as being as convenient to carry and use as a clipboard, opening up the world of automation to delivery persons, police staff, survey takers, or anyone who needs to enter data from a standing or walking position (Gruman and Needleman 1990).

FUTURE PROSPECTS

Many of the pointing and drawing devices discussed above have been enhanced to allow three-dimensional as well as two-dimensional input. For example, the Elographics Company has used surface acoustic-wave (SAW) technology to add a z axis to its touch-screen product line (Sullivan 1989). This allows users to elicit additional or more rapid responses by applying more pressure to the touch screen. The stylus of Mira's Hyperspace modeling system can be waved through space like a sparkler or used to trace the edges of a cube, and the three-dimensional representation will be logged in the machine (Countryman 1989).

Even more advanced input devices are already in production and appear destined to become widely used. Perhaps the most unique is the DataGlove, developed jointly by NASA and VPL Research, Inc. (see Figure 3). The DataGlove is "a sensor-lined Lycra glove that converts hand gestures and positions into computer-readable form, enabling the wearer to interact with simulated environments and control the action" (NASA 1990). It "allows the computer user to handle

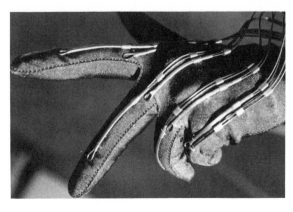

FIGURE 3. The DataGlove. *Courtesy VPL Research, Inc.*

on-screen images as if they are real three-dimensional objects" (NASA 1990).

The DataGlove can be used to replace a mouse or similar input device for controlling conventional computer screens. For example, Mattel Inc. is already distributing a licensed version of the glove as an accessory for Nintendo video games. Nintendo players can use hand motions to throw a ball or battle a villain; however, NASA's primary interest is in using the glove for "the brave new world of virtual reality (VR), where you can be anything and anywhere you want to be—given the right software program" (NASA 1990). Already this technology is being used for Department of Defense flight simulations and a commercial VPL product called Reality Built for Two (RB2), where the primary user input devices are the Data-Glove and a Polhemus magnetic head-tracking device attached to three-dimensional goggles with stereoscopic color and three-dimensional sound. According to Ann Lasko, director of product design at VPL, the DataGlove "provides a natural, intuitive way to interact with your computer" (NASA 1990, p. 11).

Most who have studied the field of human–computer interaction might agree with Ms. Lasko's appraisal. For example, Alan Kay, one of the developers of the icon-based pointing interface while at Xerox PARC, was strongly influenced by psychologist Jerome Bruner's thoughts on human modes of achieving understanding (Kay 1988, 1990). Bruner (1966) proposed that children initially understand things in terms of actions and reactions within their physical environment; he called this enactive representation of knowledge. Somewhat older children learn to think at the iconic level, where a picture of an object can substitute for the real thing. Still later, humans come to translate experience into language and can use arbitrary characters for symbolic representation.

Kay's guide for the development of pointing input devices was the desire to move human–computer interaction away from typing symbols, the most difficult level for humans to learn, to the more easily mastered level of iconic representation. Most

agree that this endeavor has been successful. The next logical step is to move human–computer input down still another level, to enactive (sometimes called kinesthetic) representation, such as is found in a virtual reality. New developments in direct screen manipulation seem certain to emerge from this area.

References

Berliss, J., and P. Borden. 1989. Building a better mouse.

Bethoney, H. 1990. Outbound's Mac Laptop: Smallest and lightest yet. *PC Week* 7(14):19+.

Bobker, S. 1990. The cordless mouse: Build a better mouse for the same price—with no wire attached. *MacUser* 6(2):88.

Brownstein, M. 1990. For the mouse-shy user, alternatives abound: Pointing devices. *InfoWorld* 12(9):27.

Bruner, J. S. 1966. *Toward a theory of instruction.* Cambridge, Mass.: Harvard University Press.

Countryman, K. 1989. Mice in space. *MacUser* 5(10):131.

Curtin, D. P., and L. R. Porter. 1986. *Microcomputers: Software and applications.* Englewood Cliffs, N.J.: Prentice-Hall.

Gillooly, B. 1989. New faces for the mouse. *Computer Reseller News,* December 11, 1989, No. 345, p. 71+.

Gruman, G., and R. Needleman. 1990. Graphical interfaces spur the development of alternative input devices. *InfoWorld* 12(17):72.

Johnson, T. E. 1990. Closer to that pen-and-paper feel. *MacWeek* 4(16):45(4).

Kay, A. 1988. Keynote address to the EDUCOM Annual Conference, Washington, D.C., October 25–28, 1988.

———. 1990. *Point of view is worth 80 IQ points: The user interface as an amplifier of human endeavor.* Keynote Address to the Fifth World Conference on Computers in Education, Sydney, Australia, July 9–13, 1990. Abstract in McDougall and Dowling, eds. *Computers in education,* p.4. Amsterdam: North-Holland/Elsevier.

NASA. 1990. Computerized reality comes of age. *NASA Technical Briefs* 6(8):10(3).

Rosch, W. L. 1989. Digitizing tablets: Pointing the way to easier input. *PC Magazine* 8(20):227+.

Sullivan, D. R., T. G. Lewis, and C. R. Cook. 1988. *Computing today: Microcomputer concepts and applications*, 2nd ed. Boston: Houghton Mifflin.

Sullivan, K. B. 1989. Advances in touchscreens attract new users. *PC Week* 6(38):97.

Van Name, M. L., and B. Catchings. 1989. Mighty mice. *PC-Computing* 2(12):248+.

Wallace, P. 1990. Expert mouse. *PC-Computing* 3(6):133.

For Further Reading

Apple Computer, Inc. 1985. *Inside Macintosh,* vol. III. Reading, Mass.: Addison-Wesley.

Kliewer, B. D. 1990. More than upside-down mice. *Byte* 15(5):175+.

Silverstone, S. 1990. Mouse input options multiply. *MacWeek* 4(21):51+.

Winship, S. 1990. Trackballs. *PC Week* 7(18):113.

Gerald Knezek

DISABLED, TECHNOLOGY FOR THE

The development of assistive/adaptive/augmentative technologies for use by the disabled is a new field that computer technology has helped bring into existence. On November 29, 1975, President Ford signed the Education for All Handicapped Children Act, Public Law 94-142. The law included provisions to ensure that all disabled children have a free and appropriate public education, to ensure that the rights of disabled children and their parents are protected, and to assist state and local education agencies in providing this education. In 1990, Public Law 94-142 was amended by Public Law 99-457. References to assistive/adaptive technologies were included for the first time and defined as "any item, piece of equipment or product system, whether acquired commercially off the shelf, modified, or customized, that is used to increase, maintain, or improve functional capabilities of individuals with disabilities" (Section 101[g]).

Manual systems were previously used by disabled persons who needed alternatives to reading, writing, or verbal communication. Manual systems, such as American Sign Language and Braille, are still in use, but have limitations. For example, a deaf person using American Sign Language must find another communication partner who knows signing. Furthermore, American Sign Language cannot be used to talk over the telephone. It is through assistive technologies that written and spoken communication has recently become widely available to disabled individuals. This unprecedented revolution is gaining momentum as new devices are invented.

DISABLING CONDITIONS

There are many different types and degrees of physical impairment. There is, correspondingly, an increasingly diverse number of adaptative/assistive/augmentative devices available, and the challenge is to find the best device for a person with mental and/or physical disabilities.

MULTIDISCIPLINARY TEAM

A team of practitioners should be assembled to determine the proper hardware and software solutions for a disabled user. It is imperative that the individual be evaluated by a multidisciplinary team of specialists including, as appropriate, the teacher(s), the parent(s), an occupational therapist, a physical therapist, a speech clinician, and a technology specialist. It cannot be stressed enough that the opinion(s) of the user must also be considered when selecting an adaptive device. If the disabled person is not satisfied with the selection of a device, effective use of the computer will not occur. It is also important to note that as the user's needs, environment, and motor, cognitive, and perceptual skills will change over time, the access method and the technology used should be reevaluated on a regular basis. The team needs to consider the following types of conditions while conducting the evaluation:

- Ease of use: How much energy does the individual need to use the selected method?
- Stability of movement to activate device: Does the use of a device cause any side effects such as uncontrollable movement or poor positioning?
- Exhaustion: How long can the individual maintain use of the device?
- Placement of the device: Is the placement convenient? Does it reduce stress and exhaustion?
- Range of motion: Can the user easily and comfortably reach the device?
- Ability to depress the device: Can the user target and hit the device?
- Control to release the device: Can the user release the device in timely fashion to prevent accidental or false input? For example, if a user strikes the letter "w" on the keyboard, can the finger be removed from the key before the rapid repeat function causes several w's to appear on the screen?
- Visual acuity to identify the device as a target: Is the device large enough and positioned correctly so that the user can see it?
- Mental ability to make an intelligent choice: Does the user understand the relationship between the device and the result-

ing input that appears on the computer screen?

HEARING IMPAIRED

People with hearing impairments do not need adaptations to the technologies as much as they need appropriate selection of software that builds vocabulary and promotes language development. An exception to this rule is the use of the telephone. Telecommunication devices for the deaf (TDDs) convert telephone signals into written output that can be read by a deaf person. These devices can be interfaced with computers to provide multiple options in originating and receiving "telephone" conversations.

INPUT/PROCESS/OUTPUT

A computer has a basic data flow pattern: input/process/output. *Input* into the computer is usually done through the keyboard. The computer *processes* the information, then displays the *output* either on a monitor or on hard copy produced by a printer. The input and output methods are the two areas that are most often adapted for a handicapped user. In general, persons with physical impairments require adaptations to the input method. Persons with visual and speech impairments require adaptations to the output method (Table 1).

TABLE 1.

Input Methods	Output Methods
Common input devices	Common output devices
Keyboard	Monitor
Adapted input devices	Printer
Keyboard membrane	Adapted output devices
Pointing device	Braille printer
Joystick/mouse	Speech synthesizer
Touch-sensitive tablet or screen	Large-screen monitor or software to enlarge
Adaptive Firmware Card	image on screen
Scanning	Telecommunication devices for the deaf
Expanded keyboard	
Voice recognition systems	
Light sensor device	
Augmentative communication aids	
Telecommunication devices for the deaf	

INPUT ADAPTATIONS

The computer input method by direct selection is the most challenging to adapt. Direct selection is any technique where the individual directly points to the various choices presented by a computer program. Direct selection, through the keyboard, is the standard means used to get information into a computer. The computer keyboard is the easiest way to make a direct selection, but a joystick, a touch-sensitive tablet, or a mouse serves the same purpose.

Most computer keyboards are identical to typewriter keyboards, except they have the addition of special keys such as *break*, *reset*, and *control*. The standard keyboard can be used by most disabled individuals and, when possible, the standard keyboard should be used, because it remains the most efficient way of interacting with a computer. When a standard keyboard is not acceptable, adaptations or modifications need to be made.

Keyboard Modifications

A number of simple adaptations can make the use of the keyboard easier for individuals with mental or physical impairments. Simplifying the "mixed up" letters on the keyboard can be done with color coding. Examples of color-coding techniques include painting or sticking small, colored dots or stickers on selected keys.

Several commercial products, including protective membranes, templates, and mechanical latches, are available to adapt a keyboard. A protective membrane is made of soft plastic that is molded to fit tightly over a keyboard to protect it from liquids. This protection allows use of the keyboard by people who have drooling problems.

A template can be custom designed for a specific model of keyboard, to restrict access and limit stimuli. Templates are generally made of hard, clear plastic and are installed on a keyboard with Velcro. Holes are drilled through the plastic to correspond to the positions of the keys on the keyboard. Templates are used when the user has uncontrollable, spastic movements that result in frequent, accidental input. Custom templates can be ordered so that only selected keys are exposed. Custom templates help not only the physically disabled, but also assist individuals who are easily distracted or confused by the keyboard.

Mechanical latches lock down, and can be added to a template to help a user access multikey functions. For example, a warm boot requires the user to strike three keys simultaneously. To accomplish this, a person who types with one finger can press down and lock two latches positioned over two of the keys and then strike the third key with a finger.

A mouse or joystick can also be used as an alternative input method; however, both peripherals require consistent visual motor coordination. Joysticks serve a different purpose when they are adapted to function as a switch.

Software Solutions

Many computer manufacturers have begun to acknowledge the difficulties experienced by physically impaired computer users, and have built options into the DOS or read-only memory (ROM). Through a menu of options, the user can control selected features of the computer. For example, the rapid-repeat function causes many users with physical impairments to have "false hits" or accidental input. When the rapid-repeat function is turned off, the user can depress a key for any length of time and still have only one character accepted as input by the computer.

A number of software programs have also been designed to help control computer functions. These programs, as well as the adapted DOS and ROM, can turn off the rapid-repeat function, enlarge screen text, or allow the user to create *macros* for faster input or to execute a multiple-key function.

Touch-Sensitive Tablets

Disabled users often have difficulty with the size of the keys on a keyboard or with the limited amount of space between the keys. Many of the touch-sensitive tablets address this problem. Touch-sensitive tablets are software-specific devices that vary in the sensitivity of the surface, in size, and in the manner to which they are connected to the computer.

The Muppet Keyboard (Sunburst) and the Power Pad (Dunamis) are two software-specific touch tablets that can be used as alternative keyboards. Both devices require the use of specific software programmed to interact with the tablet. The Muppet Keyboard is a colorful, plastic tablet with the keys arranged in alphabetical order. The Power Pad has a larger touch-sensitive surface (Figure 1). There is software available to customize the Power Pad for speech output. The surface of the Power Pad can also be divided into different-size contact points to serve as an alternative keyboard.

Touch-sensitive screens are similar in concept to the touch-sensitive tablets. The screens allow the user to make input at the same point where the information is displayed. This can be particularly helpful to mentally disabled users who demonstrate difficulty understanding the relationship between keyboard input and the data displayed on the screen. The Touch Window (Edmark) is a separate peripheral device that has additional versatility, because it can be used in three ways: as a touch-sensitive screen, as a graphics tablet, or as an overlay to give animation to a book. In each case, specific software must control the device.

Transparent Access

The Adaptive Firmware Card, also referred to as the AFC (Don Johnston), provides powerful direct selection alternatives. The AFC is an external interface box connected to an integrated circuit board plugged into a slot in an Apple computer. Variations of the AFC are available for other computers, but the Adaptive Firmware Card provided the

initial standard for transparent, optional computer access for the handicapped.

Transparent access means that the AFC works at the hardware level to intercept alternative input methods and send them to the computer as if they were standard keyboard input. This capability means that a switch scan, an expanded keyboard, a mini-keyboard, or Morse Code can be used to input information into a computer. Because the AFC operates at the hardware level, a disabled person can control any software program using an alternative input method.

Expanded Keyboards and Minikeyboards

The expanded keyboard is used by persons with physical impairments, visual impairments, developmental delays, or other learning disabilities. One example of an expanded keyboard is the Unicorn (Unicorn Engineering), which plugs into the AFC interface box. The Unicorn is a membrane keyboard made of sturdy acrylic. It features 128 large, touch-sensitive, user-definable keys. The Unicorn can be programmed to interface with the Echo Speech Synthesizer (Street Electronics) for speech output. Overlays for the Unicorn can be programmed in 1-, 2-, or 3-inch or larger squares, to accommodate the needs of the user. It can also be programmed to accept delayed input, so that users can drag their hands over the surface of the board without causing accidental activation.

Minikeyboards have capabilities similar to those of expanded keyboards. The difference is in their size. Minikeyboards are used by people who have fine motor control in their hands, but have limited range of motion.

Switches

Hundreds of commercial switches are available for disabled users. Switches interface with the AFC to provide computer input through scanning or Morse Code.

In the scanning mode, a switch is hit to start a scan array. A scan array is a series of choices on one line of the computer screen. A cursor moves through the choices. As the cursor progresses, the user hits the switch again to make a selection. A second type of

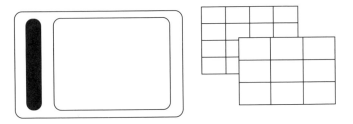

FIGURE 1. The Power Pad with overlays.

scan requires the user to hit a switch to make the cursor move. When the desired input is highlighted, the user leaves the cursor in place for a specified time (about 1.5 seconds) and the input is automatically registered.

Scanning is the slowest input method, unless it is combined with other features such as word prediction. A simplified, alphabetical scan is demonstrated in Figure 2. The user must wait until the desired letter appears in the scan. Calculate the number of seconds it would take to type "hello" if the cursor highlights each letter for one second.

Switches can also be used to send standard Morse Code signals to the computer. The AFC translates the Morse Code into letters, numbers, characters, or commands that are read by any application software. Morse Code can be generated with either a single or a dual switch. A single switch produces a constant tone and requires exact timing and precise motor control. The user must correctly time the duration of the dit (short) and dah (long) signal. In the dual-switch mode, the AFC controls the length of signal (dit or dah) received by the computer. If a disabled person must use a switch to control the computer, Morse Code input should be considered. It is faster than scanning, but requires that the user have the cognitive ability to learn the code. A short sample of the code is printed in Figure 3.

Optical Pointers

Optical pointers use a beam of light to interact with software that overlays an application program. Optical pointers are frequently attached to the head of the computer user. Slight, rotating movements of the head control the direction of the light beam. When the light rests on a specific character for a set period (about 1.5 seconds or more), the character is "typed" into the application program.

Voice Recognition

Computer access can be very laborious for quadriplegics or severely disabled individuals. Voice recognition is an important option for these users. Current voice recognition software can be trained to "learn" the speech

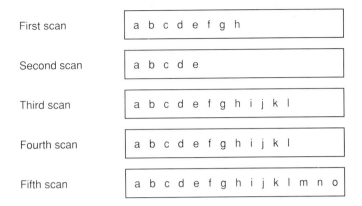

FIGURE 2. A simplified, alphabetical scan.

patterns of an individual. Clear enunciation of words is not as important as consistent utterances. If the user says "Sta" to mean "start," the system can learn the pattern. After training the voice recognition software, a user can control most application programs.

Word Prediction

Some of the voice recognition programs also have word prediction capabilities. Word prediction uses a word processor with edit and print capabilities. In addition, it features a word prediction box that appears in the corner of the screen. In some programs, the word prediction box is coupled with a scan alphabet that can be controlled by a joystick or switch. Word prediction software can either predict the next most logical word or provide a dictionary of words that begin with the same letter(s) the user has started to type.

Figure 4 is a diagram simulating a word prediction screen. The user can select num-

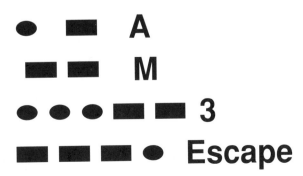

FIGURE 3. Short sample of Morse Code.

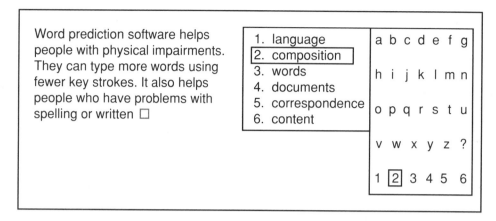

FIGURE 4. A diagram simulating a word prediction screen.

ber 2, "composition," and the word will be pulled into the word processing document. This saves ten key strokes needed to type the word.

OUTPUT DEVICES

The most common output devices for a computer are the monitor and the printer, but synthesized or digitized speech output is becoming increasingly common. Many computers have speech output built into their processing unit, but the speech capability must be accessed through a software application program.

Speech synthesizers were originally peripheral devices added to a computer system. They can still be purchased as an integrated circuit board with a speech box that must be installed into a computer. Speech synthesizers tend to have robotic speech, and can be difficult to understand. The synthesized speech is produced a letter or a word at a time, making the connected discourse sound artificial. The advantages of using synthesized speech are an unlimited vocabulary and the efficient storage of text (i.e., a lot can be stored on a disk). Speech synthesizers are software specific.

Blind computer users require speech output to operate a computer. Other people, with poor reading skills or visual impairments, also benefit from this technology.

The popularity of speech output has led to the development of digitized speech, which involves the coding of prerecorded speech into a series of digits that can be read by a decoding card and translated into sounds that approximate the human voice. Digitized speech has better quality but also takes up more computer memory, resulting in a limited vocabulary.

Large Text

Visually impaired computer users may require enlargement of the image on the screen. The standard text generated by computers is 10 or 12 pitch, which may be too small for some people to see. The text can be enlarged through hardware or software options. The easiest adaptation is to hold a magnifying glass to the screen when reading text. A large-screen monitor or television can also be interfaced with most computers. The larger screen automatically enlarges the images generated by the software. Some software application programs have options that allow the user to select the size of the text generated on the screen. Other software programs have a specific utility function that magnifies the text image of standard application software.

Braille Printers

Blind users who have learned Braille can print data stored in computers, on a Braille printer. Some models of Braille printers produce Braille print only. Others print the English below the Braille, so that sighted individuals can also read the document.

AUGMENTATIVE COMMUNICATION

Augmentative technology is a category by itself. Augmentative communication aids operate as self-contained systems. The term *augmentative* refers to a communication system for a nonspeaking person. Graphic communication systems let nonverbal people express their feelings, needs, and ideas by pointing to various contact points on a communication display. The term *graphic communication system* refers to the use of pictures, symbols, and words on the display. Most communication systems were originally manual boards, but in the last 10 years, an increasing number of electronic communication systems have been developed. Manual boards are still needed as a backup system or supplement to the electronic device.

The problem of verbal communication is compounded when the loss of speech is caused by a physical impairment that affects control of the upper limbs, including the ability to point a finger. The input method must then be adapted to make communication possible.

Augmentative communication systems need to be lightweight, portable, and easy to carry. The systems can be mounted on wheelchairs.

Augmentative electronic systems vary tremendously in cost and capabilities. Most have rechargeable batteries, making them portable communication aids, and many can be programmed so that a personalized vocabulary and specific learning experiences (e.g., a trip to the zoo) can be entered into the device. The more sophisticated electronic communication devices can be interfaced with computers so that they can control software application programs.

Augmentative electronic systems may have several output methods built into the device. These include speech output, a built-in printer, and a small liquid crystal diode display. The voice output qualities have improved dramatically and some devices now offer the option of selecting from variations of a male, female, or child's voice.

The contact points for electronic augmentative devices vary in size. Whenever possible, the user should use direct selection to make choices on the touch-sensitive surface. If a finger cannot be used, then various pointing apparatus, including head pointers, can be tried.

Some augmentative devices have light-sensitive models, and can take direct selection input from an optical head pointer. In the direct selection mode, the disabled person uses an optical pointer to direct a light beam to the exact selection desired.

Light-sensitive models can also use a scan mode. In the scan mode, the device scans the rows until a selection is made by hitting a switch. Then, the device scans the columns one at a time until a second activation is made.

In the system illustrated in Figure 5, the third row is lit. If a switch is activated, each column in row 3 lights up one at a time, until the switch is hit again to indicate the desired choice.

MODULAR APPROACH

Increasingly, disabled people are learning ways to integrate different electronic devices to expand their opportunities. The possibilities of assistive device integration are endless. Using a device as a "module" that can be interfaced with different technologies in different settings maximizes the use of the equipment and reduces cost. One example of an assistive device integration project is outlined here.

A systems operator for a telecommunication network uses an optical scanner to scan a school science assignment into a word processor on an IBM computer. The scanned document is saved as an ASCII or text file, and is transferred by a telecommunication program to the network's computer where it is stored in the electronic mail section. It is assigned to the mailbox of a blind student. That evening, the blind student plugs his or her Braille 'n Speak (Blazie Engineering) into a Tandy computer, so that it will serve as a speech synthesizer while he or she reads the telecommunication mail. The student retrieves the science assignment, logs off the telecommunication program, and pulls up a word processor to complete the assignment. The blind student then saves the document to the Braille 'n Speak, which now serves as a

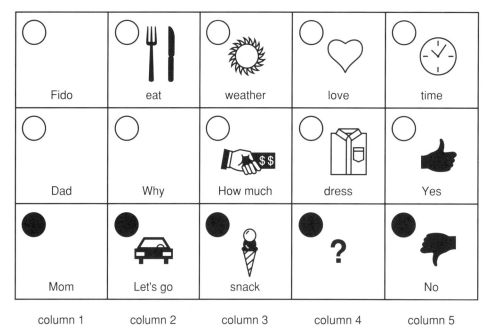

column 1   column 2   column 3   column 4   column 5

FIGURE 5. Communication board. This board is only a sample. It is not an authentic communication system.

data storage device. The next day at school, the student plugs the Braille 'n Speak into an Apple computer system that has Braille conversion software and both a Braille and dot matrix printer. The student first uses the Braille conversion program to print the document in Braille so that he or she has a copy to take to class. Then, the student uses the software options to print the document on the dot matrix printer. The second copy will be given to his or her science teacher. The student saves the assignment on the Braille 'n Speak, so that he or she can make corrections or revisions while in class.

CONCLUSION

A major frustration experienced by disabled people is that they are not able to explore, manipulate, and play with their environment. The result may be less constructive stimulation to the person's brain, resulting in a more passive, dependent attitude. The disabled person learns to be helpless. Disabled people expect that the important events in their lives do not depend on their own responses. They stop trying to control events in their lives. The challenge of the adaptive/

assistive/augmentative technologies is to provide the users with a means to interact with and control their environment. Users must be taught that their own responses, through computer-aided adaptive technologies, can make things happen in their lives.

For Further Reading

Adaptive Firmware Card operator's manual and application guide, System Software 4.0. 1989. Wauconda, Ill.: Don Johnston Developmental Equipment, Inc. Excellent step-by-step guide on all the application options available through the Adaptive Firmware Card.

Aids and Appliances Review, published quarterly by the Carroll Center for the Blind, 770 Centre Street, Newton, Mass. 02158.

Apple Computer resources in special education and rehabilitation. Cupertino, Calif.: Apple Computer, Inc., Office of Special Education Programs. Excellent listing of software, hardware, publications, and networks.

Bleck, E. E., ed. 1982. *Physically handicapped children: A medical atlas for teachers.* New York: Grune & Stratton. Concise information on various types of disabling conditions.

Burkhart, L. J. 1985. *Homemade battery powered toys and educational devices for severely handicapped children*. College Park, Md.: Linda J. Burkhart.

———. 1985. *More homemade battery devices for severely handicapped children with suggested activities*. College Park, Md.: Linda J. Burkhart.

———. 1989. *Using computers and speech synthesis to facilitate communication interaction with young and/or severely handicapped children*. Wauconda, Ill.: Don Johnston Developmental Equipment, Inc.

Charlebois-Marois, C. 1985. *Everybody's technology: A sharing of ideas in augmentative communication*. Montreal: Charlecoms.

Clinton, J. S. 1987. *Instructional technology adaptive/assistive devices*. ERIC Document Reproduction No. ED 320 546. Provides details on evaluating handicapped individuals for devices and on installing and using various devices.

———. 1989. *Morse code activity packet*. ERIC Document Reproduction No. ED 321 462.

Closing the Gap, bimonthly newspaper. Available from Closing the Gap, P.O. Box 68, Henderson, Minn. 56044.

Computer equipment and aids for the blind and visually impaired. 1985. New York: CCVI Publishing.

Directory of services and specialized equipment for the physically impaired. 1982. Kingston, N.Y.: IBM.

Funding devices and services in augmentative and alternative communication. Wall chart available from Prentke Romich Company, 1022 Heyl Road, Wooster, Ohio 44691.

Goossens, C., and S. Crain. 1986. *Augmentative communication assessment resource*. Birmingham: Sparks Center for Developmental and Learning Disorders, University of Alabama.

Levin, J., and L. Scherfenberg. 1987. *Selection and use of simple technology in home, school, work, and community settings*. Wauconda, Ill.: Don Johnston.

Project ACTT, College of Education, 27 Horrabin Hall, Western Illinois University, Macomb, Ill. 61455. Products include software and hardprint.

*Selecting an augmentative communication de-*vice. Wall chart available from Prentke Romich Company, 1022 Heyl Road, Wooster, Ohio 44691.

Trace Research and Development Center, University of Wisconsin-Madison, 314 Waisman Center, 1500 Highland Avenue, Madison, Wisc. 53706. Publications include *The rehabilitation aids resource book: Telecommunication, monitoring and environmental controls* and *Communication Outlook*, a quarterly newsletter.

Wise, R. 1989. *Can't wait to communicate*. Wauconda, Ill.: Don Johnston.

Wright, C., and M. Nomura. 1985. *From toys to computers: Access for the physically disabled child*. Available from Christine Wright, P.O. Box 700242, San Jose, Calif. 95170.

Products Manufacturers

Apple Corporation
contact local area educational representative or contact
Apple Computer Corporation
Office of Special Education Programs
20525 Mariani Ave, MS 36M
Cupertino, Calif. 95014

Blazie Engineering
3660 Mill Green Road
Street, Md. 21154

Don Johnston
1000 North Rand Road, Bldg. 115
P.O. Box 639
Wauconda, Ill. 60084

Dunamis, Inc.
3620 Highway 317
Suwanee, Ga. 30174

Edmark
P.O. Box 3903
Bellevue, Wash. 98009-3903

IBM
contact local area educational representative or contact:
IBM National Support Center for Persons with Disabilities
P.O. Box 2150
Atlanta, Ga. 30055
1–800–IBM–2133

Prentke Romich Company
1022 Heyl Road
Wooster, Ohio 44691

Street Electronics
6420 Via Real
Carpinteria, Calif. 93013

Sunburst
    39 Washington Avenue
    Pleasantville, N.Y. 10570-9971
TASH, Inc.
    70 Gibson Drive, Unit 12
    Markham, Ontario, Canada L3R4C2
Unicorn Engineering Company
    5221 Central Avenue
    Richmond, Calif. 94804
Words+, Inc.
    P.O. Box 1229
    Lancaster, Calif. 93534
Zygo Industries, Inc.
    P.O. Box 1008
    Portland, Ore. 97207

Janeen Clinton

DISTRIBUTED COMPUTING

Distributed computing entails performing a computation over a network of computers. In a typical distributed computation, a problem is decomposed into several smaller subproblems and these subproblems are sent over a communication network to individual computers, which then solve/compute these problems simultaneously. Availability of low-cost yet very fast processors and advances in computer communications technology have triggered considerable interest in distributed computing systems and have made distributed computing a viable means of problem solving and information processing. A distributed computing system consists of a collection of geographically dispersed autonomous computers (henceforth also referred to as *sites*), which are connected by a communication network. The sites can send messages to each other over the communication network.

Enslow (1978) has characterized a distributed computing system as possessing five features:

1. A *multiplicity* of general-purpose hardware and software resources: There are multiple instances of computers each of which contains its own central processing unit (CPU) and memory.
2. A *physical distribution* of the resources:

The resources are geographically apart and interact with each other over a communication network.
3. A *high-level operating system:* This manages and controls the distributed resources.
4. *System transparency:* A user perceives the entire system as a single "virtual machine" rather than as a collection of independent computers.
5. *Cooperative autonomy:* Even though the computers are autonomous, they interact and cooperate with each other.

MESSAGE PASSING

Sites of a distributed computing system do not have a globally shared memory. Therefore, they cannot communicate to each other via shared variables. The sites have direct access only to their private local memories and all the communication among the sites is done only by message passing. A site requests a service from another site or exchanges some information with some other site by sending an appropriate message to that site. Transfer of a message from one site to another site is handled by the communication network.

There are two models of communication among sites: blocking and nonblocking. In the blocking model, the sender process of a message is blocked (i.e., it cannot execute further instructions until the message has been delivered to the intended receiver site). In the nonblocking model, the sender process of a message is not blocked (i.e., it starts executing further instructions even though the message has not yet been delivered to the intended receiver site). The nonblocking model provides higher flexibility because the computation and transfer of messages can proceed concurrently; however, it makes programming and debugging very difficult because of time-dependent errors.

MOTIVATIONS FOR
DISTRIBUTED COMPUTING

A distributed computing system offers several advantages over a single mainframe computer:

1. *Resource sharing:* As a site can request a service from another site by sending an appropriate request to it over the communication network, the hardware and software resources can be shared among sites. For example, a printer at a site can be shared among a set of sites. Likewise, a compiler, a text processor, or a database at a site can be shared among several sites.

2. *Enhanced performance:* A distributed computing system is capable of providing better response time and system throughput, because a task can be broken into several subtasks that can be executed in parallel at different sites.

3. *Higher reliability and availability:* A distributed computing system provides higher reliability and availability because a few components of the system can fail without interrupting the user access to other parts of the system.

4. *Modular expandability:* Distributed computing systems are amenable to modular expansion as the demand grows because new hardware and software resources can be easily added without replacing the existing resources.

PARALLEL VERSUS DISTRIBUTED COMPUTING

Parallel computing involves decomposing a task into several smaller subtasks and executing these subtasks in parallel on several computers. Demarcation between parallel computing and distributed computing has been a much-debated issue because both involve performing computations in parallel, multiple computers, and some form of communication; however, they have several features distinguishing them from each other.

Figures 1a and 1b respectively show typical parallel and distributed computing systems. In distributed computing systems, there is no shared memory; each processor has its private memory. Thus, processors can interact and exchange information only by passing messages. In parallel computing systems, processors share a common memory; a processor can access any memory module

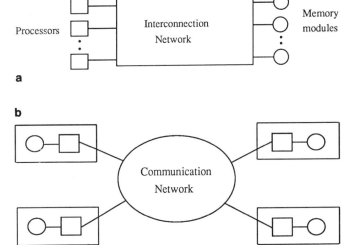

FIGURE 1. (a) A typical parallel system. (b) A typical distributed system.

via the interconnection network. Therefore, processors can communicate via shared variables in parallel computing systems. There is no global physical clock in a distributed computing system. In parallel systems, a global physical clock can be implemented using the shared memory. Intersite communication delays are generally much larger in a distributed computing system. A distributed computing system is loosely coupled because computers are autonomous, generally physically far apart, and often slow in communication. On the other hand, a parallel computing system is tightly coupled because computers are under the control of a single operating system resident in the shared memory, are closer to each other physically, and have very fast communication among them.

DISTRIBUTED OPERATING SYSTEMS

A distributed operating system is a layer of software over the network of computers, which makes the system appear to its users as a single powerful computer (Tanenbaum and van Renesse 1985). Geographic locations of the computers and the communication network are transparent to the users. A user simply submits his job/command to the distributed operating system through his or her local computer. The distributed operating system performs distributed execution of the job (i.e., it decomposes the job into subjobs, sends the subjobs to other computers using the communication network, collects results, and then hands over the results to the user). A user does not know on which computers his or her job was executed, on what computers the files needed for execution were stored, and how the communication and synchronization among different subjobs were carried out.

The design of a distributed operating system faces several challenging problems, such as interprocess communication, process synchronization, deadlocks, naming and addressing, security and protection, reliability and crash recovery, fault tolerance, distributed file system, and resource management. Note that most of these problems are encountered in the design of a single mainframe operating system. A single mainframe computer has a global memory (hence, the state of the processing is completely and accurately known). Therefore, these problems are well understood and their efficient solutions exist for a single mainframe operating system. In distributed computing systems, however, these problems take on new dimensions and their solutions become a magnitude higher in complexity. This is because as a result of the lack of a global memory and unpredictable message delays, it is practically impossible for a site to collect up-to-date information about the global state of the distributed computing system (LeLann 1981). Therefore, a fundamental problem in the design of a distributed operating system is the determination of efficient techniques to implement decentralized systemwide control where a site does not know the current and complete status of the global state.

Concurrent Programming

In concurrent programming, several program modules are concurrently active, as opposed to sequential programming, which has a single locus of control. A concurrent programming language provides high-level constructs for specification of processes and interaction among the processes. The inter-

action among processes can be through shared variables or by message passing. Shared variable–based programming languages are not suitable for programming a distributed computing system because of the lack of a shared memory. Instead, message-based programming languages are more natural for programming distributed computing systems because they can exploit the message-passing capability of a distributed computing system.

Remote procedure call is a useful paradigm for interaction between modules of a distributed program (Birrell and Nelson 1984). In the execution of a remote procedure call, the calling module is suspended, parameters are passed across the network to the callee module, the callee module is executed, results are passed back to the calling module across the network, and then execution of the calling modules resumes.

A distributed program consists of several program modules dispersed over the various sites of a distributed computing system such that these modules interact with each other via remote procedure call. A concurrent programming language for distributed computing systems must enable programmers to build distributed programs with modules running on several sites. It must therefore support concurrency, data abstraction, and remote procedure call. Argus is an example of a concurrent programming language for implementing distributed programs (Liskov 1982). Argus includes facilities for declaration and manipulation of abstract data types. It has a built-in mechanism for concurrency control to regulate concurrent access to shared objects. The basic module of Argus is called a "guardian" and is a collection of processes at a site. A guardian maintains and controls access to resources. Therefore, a typical distributed program in Argus has several guardians spread over a set of sites. Two guardians interact with each other using remote procedure call.

CASE STUDIES

Over the last decade, several research projects aimed at experimental distributed computing systems have been launched at several universities and research laboratories.

Locus

The Locus distributed operating system was designed and implemented at the University of California at Los Angeles in the early 1980s (Walker et al. 1983). It was implemented on a collection of DEC's Vax computers connected by an Ethernet. Locus provides a UNIX-like distributed programming environment to its users. It provides system-wide file naming and replicates files for enhanced performance and fault tolerance. Locus provides a transaction mechanism to users for execution of their requests. It guarantees atomic behavior of transactions by using a "shadow page" technique. That is, all changes by a transaction are first made on a tentative storage and are finally written into actual files only after the transaction has been completely executed.

The V System

The V distributed system was developed at Stanford University as a part of a research project to explore issues in distributed systems (Cheriton 1988). The V distributed operating system is designed for a cluster of workstations connected by a high-speed communication network. A small operating system kernel, called *V-kernel*, implements the basic protocols, run-time libraries, and services that provide a software backplane on which the rest of the system can be built in a transparent manner. Each computer of the system executes an identical copy of the kernel, and kernels at all the sites cooperate to provide a single system view at the process level. A distributed service can be implemented using the basic functions provided by the V-kernel.

The file system in the V system is a traditional UNIX-like hierarchical system. The naming scheme of the V system permits the assignment of symbolic names to addressable entities. The V system provides practically no support for fault tolerance and failure recovery because it is intended primarily for interactive applications (i.e., users are supposed to retry if the system fails).

The Amoeba System

The Amoeba distributed operating system was developed at the Free University at Amsterdam in the Netherlands (Mullender et al. 1990). Amoeba hardware consists of four components: workstations, pool processors, specialized servers, and gateways. The workstations execute tasks that require fast interactive response (e.g., editor, window control). The pool processor is a group of processors that can be dynamically allocated to tasks and provide most of the number-crunching capability. Specialized servers perform dedicated chores such as directory service and database management. The gateways are used to link several Amoeba systems over wide-area networks.

The Amoeba is an object-based system; that is, resources are treated as objects on which well-defined operations can be performed by the users. Naming and protection are achieved by using capabilities. A capability contains the systemwide unique name of an object. The objects can be assigned symbolic names, and a directory service is maintained to map symbolic names to their capabilities. Amoeba has a UNIX emulation facility, which consists of a library of UNIX system calls and allows users to execute UNIX programs on Amoeba.

References

Birrell, A. D., and B. J. Nelson. 1984. Implementing remote procedure calls. *ACM Transactions on Computer Systems*, February, pp. 39–59.

Cheriton, D. R. 1988. The V distributed system. *Communications of the ACM*, March, pp. 314–33.

Enslow, P. H. 1978. What is a 'distributed' data processing system? *IEEE Computer*, January, pp. 13–21.

LeLann, G. 1981. Motivation, objective, and characteristics of distributed systems. In Lampson et al., eds. *Distributed systems—Architecture and implementation*, pp. 1–9. Berlin: Springer-Verlag.

Liskov, B. 1982. On linguistic support for distributed programs. *IEEE Transactions on Software Engineering,* May, pp. 203–10.

Mullender, S. P., et al. 1990. Amoeba: A distributed operating system for the 1990s. *IEEE Computer,* May, pp. 44–53.

Tanenbaum, A., and R. van Renesse. 1985. Distributed operating systems. *ACM Computing Surveys,* December, pp. 419–70.

Walker, B., et al. 1983. The Locus distributed operating system. In *Proceedings of the 9th ACM Symposium on Operating Systems Principles,* October, pp. 49–70.

Mukesh Singhal

DISTRIBUTED AND HETEROGENEOUS DATABASE MANAGEMENT SYSTEMS

This article presents the concepts fundamental to distributed and heterogeneous databases, followed by a brief survey of several systems that have been built or are under development in universities and industrial research laboratories.

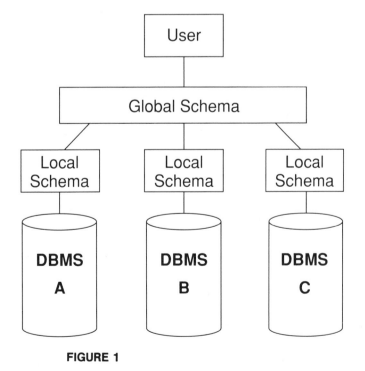

FIGURE 1

WHAT IS A DISTRIBUTED DATABASE MANAGEMENT SYSTEM?

A *distributed system* consists of a collection of sites (or nodes) connected via a communication link. If the sites cooperate to provide users a database management system (DBMS), then the distributed system is a *distributed database management system* (DDBMS). Such systems offer several advantages over centralized database management systems including increased performance, reliability, and availability. The degree of sophistication of a DDBMS depends on the degree of distribution transparency the system provides to the users.

Because there were many obstacles to be overcome, most of the effort in the late 1970s and early 1980s was devoted to the *homogeneous* DDBMS. The following assumptions characterized such systems (see Figure 1):

- DBMSs at different sites belong to the same family, typically relational.

- There is a single global conceptual database that is physically distributed (using either vertical or horizontal fragmentations of relations).

- There is a directory (or a catalog) at each site containing all location information.

- All sites fully cooperate with each other to provide integrated access to data, even if this means that a site must give up control over its local data.

Under these assumptions, the distributed databases can behave as a single integrated database. A DDBMS can provide distribution transparency to the users. The users do not have to determine what data are located where; the system takes the responsibility of mapping the user query into one or more subqueries to the databases at different sites.

The early research prototypes such as SDD-1, R*, Distributed Ingres, Porel, and Sirius-Delta followed this approach (see Ceri and Pelagatti 1984, for example). Because of these successful efforts, numerous commercial products have begun to appear in the marketplace.

In spite of this success, the problem of integrating data within an organization and across organizations has proved extremely difficult, if not impossible. There are two reasons for this.

1. Many organizations already have a collection of independent databases (or even file systems) (see Figure 2). They found that it is not possible to derive a global conceptual schema from the various local schemas because of the complexity of the task. One way to integrate all the data is to replace the old system with an entirely new system. This alternative is not only dangerous but very costly as well. Consequently, organizations that currently face a situation similar to the one shown in Figure 2 wish to move toward integration of data slowly.

2. Database technology is rapidly evolving with the ever-increasing demand for constructing large, complex information systems encompassing different application areas such as office systems, computer-aided design systems, database management systems, knowledge bases, temporal databases, and, in general, the management of multimedia information (voice, text, images, graphics, audio, etc.).

In view of these trends, recently database researchers have begun focusing on *heterogeneous* databases (sometimes also known as *federated* databases or *multidatabases*). Although heterogeneous databases are also DDBMSs, most of the time when we say "distributed databases," we mean homogeneous distributed databases.

WHAT IS A HETEROGENEOUS DATABASE MANAGEMENT SYSTEM?

According to the Webster's New World Dictionary, the word *heterogeneous* is defined as "differing or opposite in structure, quality, etc.; dissimilar; incongruous; foreign" or "composed of unlike elements or parts; varied; miscellaneous." In the context of databases, a heterogeneous system is a collection of independent, cooperating databases. Its goal is to integrate the previously existing database components and provide access to the data in a transparent manner. The problem of making heterogeneous databases be-

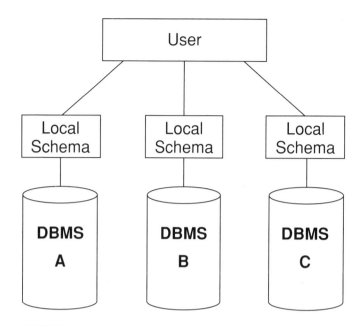

FIGURE 2

have like a single integrated database is often called *interoperability*.

The heterogeneous databases share the following characteristics:

- There exist a number of sites, each site containing an independent database management system. Each site is capable of functioning autonomously, and from time to time these sites cooperate to provide integrated access to data.

- Although the various sites cooperate among themselves, each site is autonomous and makes all decisions affecting its local database.

- There may not exist a global schema to provide integrated knowledge of the contents of the component databases.

A heterogeneous database differs from a homogeneous database in that the component databases in a heterogeneous database are autonomous and they may not share a data model or use the same database management systems.

RESEARCH PROTOTYPES

Several systems are under development in universities and industrial research laboratories. Some of these are listed below. We refer the reader to Reiner (1990) for a brief description of several of these systems.

System	Organization
DAVID	Goddard Space Flight Center, NASA
INTERBASE	University of Southern California
CISL	Massachusetts Institute of Technology
MDAS	Concordia University
HD-DBMS	University of California, Los Angeles
Client/Server Model	Sybase
INGRES Gateways	Ingres Corporation
DataLens	Lotus Development Corporation

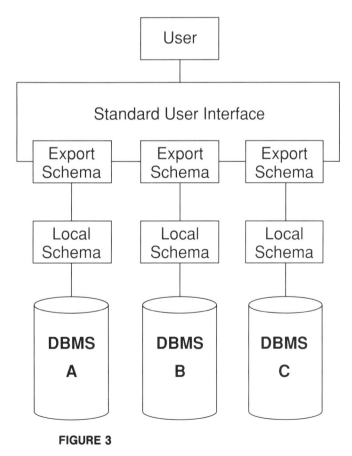

FIGURE 3

Most of these systems have taken one of the following two approaches.

Canonical form. The objective of the first approach is to determine if a canonical form can represent data items and structures across multiple databases. (One can attempt to define a common schema for each pair of databases, but this would be very inefficient.) This standard form must support the association of similar data across database boundaries despite differences in structure and content.

Multi-database approach. The second approach recognizes that the choice of a heterogeneous database over an integrated one seems to imply that the component databases are unable to support a true global schema. Thus one must assume that the heterogeneous database system will lack a global schema and is instead composed of a federation of local database schemas. One method of federating schemas is to use multiple *export* schemas (see Figure 3). Each database devises an *export schema*, which is available to user queries and user transactions. The export schema provides a simple way for people to determine what data are available and where to find them. These export schemas are maintained by the local nodes. Next, these systems provide a data manipulation language for accessing the different data collections. For example, Litwin and Abdellatif (1987) have proposed a *multi-database manipulation language* (MML). The fundamental difference between the MML and a standard data manipulation language is that the MML allows users to specify component databases explicitly in their queries.

RESEARCH ISSUES

Several difficult issues must be resolved to provide proper user support in a heterogeneous environment. Some of these are listed next.

Data and Program Translation
The first issue concerns the association of data and programs across independent data-

bases. Its objective is to determine if a standard form can represent information across multiple databases. This standard form must support the association of similar data across database boundaries despite differences in structure and content. The problem is difficult in a heterogeneous system as databases may partially or fully overlap or be mutually exclusive in their data coverage and information structure.

Incompleteness and Inconsistency

A basic assumption in distributed databases has been that there is complete agreement among the different databases. This assumption no longer holds in a heterogeneous environment where data are drawn from two or more autonomous databases with varying degree of completeness and correctness. We need techniques to deal with elimination of redundant data across the databases and the resolution of conflicting values for these data elements.

Transaction Management

The fundamental purpose of a database management system is to execute transactions. A transaction is a sequence of operations on one or more database objects. A transaction is atomic in the sense that either all its actions are performed in entirety or none of the actions are visible in the system. Although transaction management is very well understood in a homogeneous environment, it poses many fundamental difficulties when we move into a heterogeneous environment. This problem is especially made difficult if the sites in a federation insist on local autonomy. Standard techniques such as two-phase commit, which is used to ensure atomicity of transactions in a distributed environment, are no longer applicable.

References

Ceri, S., and G. Pelagatti. 1984. *Distributed database: Principles and systems.* New York: McGraw-Hill.
Litwin, W., and A. Abdellatif. 1987. An overview of multi-database manipulation language MDSL. *Proceedings of the IEEE* 75(5):621–32.
Reiner, D. S., ed. 1990. Special issue on database connectivity. *Bulletin of the IEEE Computer Society Technical Committee on Data Engineering* 13(2).

Sushil Jajodia

DOCUMENTATION

The purposes of documentation are to communicate specifications and designs among those developing an application and to record the final results for use by those making subsequent changes, corrections, and enhancements. Documentation is for human use, and so its organization and format must fit the needs of human communications. There are many approaches to and methods of documentation.

LEVELS OF DOCUMENTATION

Figure 1 shows the three stages in the applications development process. Each stage has associated with it forms of documentation. A system model describes the application and a program model describes the program.

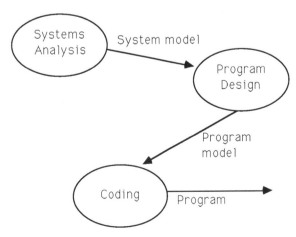

FIGURE 1. Generalized system development life cycle.

FIGURE 2. Entities.

DOCUMENTATION OF SYSTEMS ANALYSIS

Systems analysis is the process of understanding the nature of information systems, the requirements for changes, and how the changes can be synthesized with the existing system to produce a solution to meet user needs. Two aspects of a system may be documented at this stage: data and process.

Data Documentation by Data Modeling

Data documentation is the result of data modeling (see DATA MODELING, LOGICAL). The basic high-level notation used in modern systems analysis for data modeling is the *entity–relationship diagram*. There are several closely related notations in use; this article uses one called Bachman diagrams (Martin and McClure 1985).

An *entity* is something in the real world about which we store data. It is documented by a box inside of which is the name of the entity (Figure 2).

Entities have various *relationships*, often named by putting the name next to the graphical depiction. Figure 3 illustrates the types of relationships that are of interest. Figure 4 shows how entities and relationships are combined into an entity–relationship diagram. This example is highly simplified; real-world systems have dozens or hundreds of entities.

After describing entities and their relationships in systems analysis, additional details are added in program design by documentation of the properties of the objects in the real world. This is commonly done using data dictionaries (to be described under Documentation of Program Design).

Process Structure Documentation

Process approaches to systems analysis, such as the Yourdon data flow diagramming approaches (DeMarco 1979, Gane and Sarson 1979, Powers et al. 1984), have been used since the mid-1970s. These approaches are often referred to as "structured analysis." A specification consists of data flow diagrams. These are supplemented in program design by a data dictionary and pseudocode.

A data flow diagram describes the processes that transform data and the data flows between them. The basic element of such a diagram is the "data flow," represented as an arrow (Figure 5).

The other major element in a data flow diagram is the process (Figure 6). The process transforms a data flow. The name of the

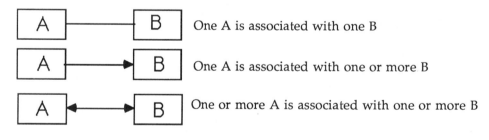

FIGURE 3. Relationships.

FIGURE 4. Entity–relationship diagram.

FIGURE 5. Data flow.

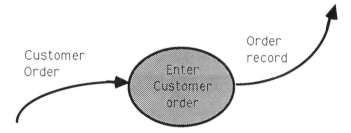

FIGURE 6. Process.

process is a verb–object expression that describes the action performed on the data.

Additional elements in the model of the system are "sources" and "sinks." A *source* is a source of data flows that come from outside the boundaries of the system under study. A *sink* is a consumer of data flows from outside the current system. Both are represented by boxes. In Figure 7, *Customer* is both a source and a sink.

Sometimes data flows are not used directly by other bubbles, but are stored for later use in a "data store." The symbol for a data store (Figure 8) is a pair of lines with the name of the data store between them.

DOCUMENTATION OF PROGRAM DESIGN

Program design documentation consists of detailed descriptions of data elements, of program structure, and of process logic.

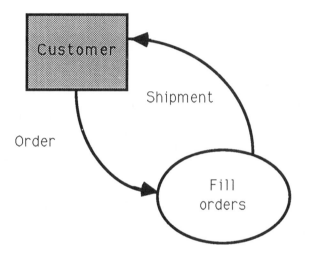

FIGURE 7. Sources and sinks.

Data Element Documentation
To document data elements, it is desirable to use a notation that is independent of the programming language. The most common notation is the data dictionary. Data dictionaries, as illustrated in Figure 9, are alphabetical listings of the data elements that make up records. Data dictionaries are organized alphabetically because they serve as a reference for all of the data defined by the analyst or designer. Data dictionaries are useful for data definition at all stages of system design.

Program Structure Documentation
Program structure means the selection and organization of modules in a program design. A module has a *function* and a *name*,

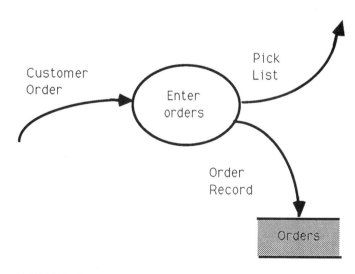

FIGURE 8. Data store.

ADDRESS	=	NUMBER + STREET + CITY + [STATE | PROVINCE] + ZIP-CODE
CITY	=	*Post Office Designation — e.g. "Fairbanks", not "College"*
LAST-NAME	=	*Family name*
NUMBER	=	*Leave blank if Post Office Box*
PROVINCE	=	*Spelled out*
STATE	=	*Two letter abbreviation*
STREET	=	*Include entire PO Box Number here*
ZIP-CODE	=	*5 digit US; 6 character Canada*

FIGURE 9. Data dictionary.

uses *input* data from the rest of the system, and may produce *output* data used elsewhere in the system. Typical documentation for program structure is a structure chart.

A structure chart is a hierarchical (tree) diagram composed of modules. Figure 10 shows a simple example with three modules. Note that the direction of the arrows rather than their position to the right or the left determines input versus output. Note also that the ellipses in Figure 10 are not part of the structure chart notation, but are added to

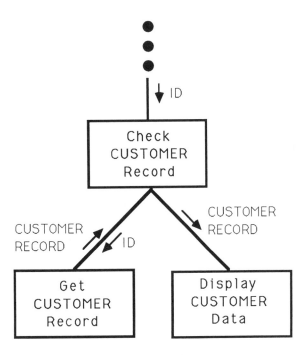

FIGURE 10. Simple structure chart.

the figure to indicate that the structure chart is incomplete.

Process Logic Documentation

Process logic is the step-by-step series of operations that the program carries out. There are three common notations for representing program-level process logic: flowcharts, pseudocode, and action diagrams.

Flowcharts were developed during the 1950s as aids to documenting the structure of programs written in second-generation (assembly) languages. Because they were developed to represent primitive assembly-language control structures, flowcharts are not as suited to modern programming languages. Figure 11 shows a program in flowchart form.

Pseudocode is a highly structured form of English with rules such as the following:

- All sentences are imperative.
- All nouns are from the data dictionary.
- All control structures (specification of conditions under which something is to be done) are specified in a standard fashion.

Figure 12 shows our example. There is no standard for the control structure representation—most authors suggest using the notation from the language Pascal. Pseudocode is probably the most widely used nota-

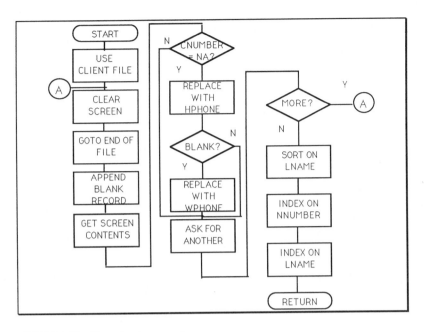

FIGURE 11. Flowchart example.

tion in practice. Its major disadvantage is that it is nongraphical.

Action diagrams as illustrated in Figure 13 are pseudocode with a simple graphical overlay. They preserve the advantages of pseudocode and add the advantages of pattern recognition.

Program Code Documentation

Computer program instructions are an important part of application documentation. If written in a high-level language, the instructions are an essential form of communication with information systems personnel, especially those who will have to modify the

```
use CLIENT datafile
DO FOREVER.
    clear screen
    goto end of file
    append blank record
    get screen contents
     IF CNUMBER="NA"
    THEN replace CNUMBER with HPHONE
         IF HPHONE is BLANK
           THEN replace CNUMBER with WPHONE
         ENDIF
    ENDIF
    ask for another customer? (YES or NO)
    IF NO
     THEN   sort file on LNAME
            index on CNUMBER
            index on LNAME
    ENDIF
     BREAK
ENDDO
RETURN
```

FIGURE 12. Pseudocode example.

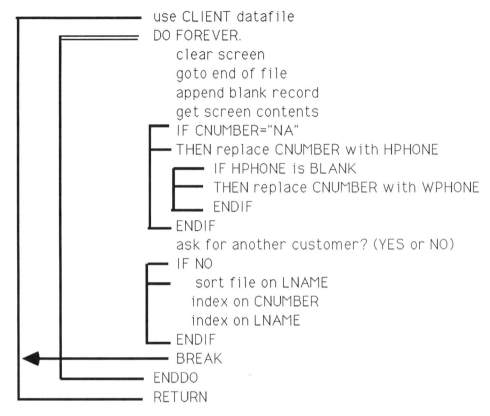

```
        use CLIENT datafile
        DO FOREVER.
            clear screen
            goto end of file
            append blank record
            get screen contents
            IF CNUMBER="NA"
            THEN replace CNUMBER with HPHONE
                IF HPHONE is BLANK
                THEN replace CNUMBER with WPHONE
                ENDIF
            ENDIF
            ask for another customer? (YES or NO)
            IF NO
                sort file on LNAME
                index on CNUMBER
                index on LNAME
            ENDIF
            BREAK
        ENDDO
        RETURN
```

FIGURE 13. Action diagram example.

system. These instructions are best maintained using a source-code management system to ensure that the latest version of each part of the program can be found. Such systems are found in library software and some system software.

References

Demarco, T. 1979. *Structured analysis and system specification.* Englewood Cliffs, N.J.: Prentice-Hall.

Gane, C., and T. Sarson. 1979. *Structured systems analysis: Tools and techniques.* Englewood Cliffs, N.J.: Prentice-Hall.

Martin, J., and C. McClure. 1985. *Diagramming techniques for analysts and programmers.* Englewood Cliffs, N.J.: Prentice-Hall.

Powers, M., D. Adams, and H. Mills. 1984. *Computer information systems development: Analysis and design.* Cincinnati: South-Western.

For Further Reading

Cameron, J. 1986. An overview of JSD. *IEEE Transactions on Software Engineering* 21(2):222–40.

———. 1989. *The Jackson approach to software development.* 2nd ed. Washington, D.C.: IEEE Computer Society Press.

Jackson, M. 1975. *Principles of program design.* London: Academic Press.

King, D. *Creating effective software: Computer program design using the Jackson methodology.* New York: Yourdon Press.

Lehman, J. 1991. *Systems design in the fourth generation: Object-based development using DBASE.* New York: Wiley.

Orr, K. 1977. *Structured systems development.* New York: Yourdon Press.

Shlaer, S., and S. Mellor. 1988. *Object oriented systems analysis.* New York: Yourdon Press.

Warnier, J. 1981. *Logical construction of systems.* New York: Van Nostrand Reinhold.

John A. Lehman

DOCUMENT IMAGE PROCESSING

See Electronic Document Image Processing
and Management

DOS

See Microcomputers (Personal Computers);
Operating Systems

DOT-MATRIX PRINTERS

See Printing Technologies

DRUG INFORMATION

See Pharmacy Practice, Use of
Computers in

EBCDIC

See Binary Numbering System

ECKERT, J. PRESPER

J. Presper Eckert was born on April 9, 1919, the only child of prosperous Philadelphia parents. Eckert had a stimulating childhood peopled with such figures as Douglas Fairbanks, Sr., Charlie Chaplin, and President Warren Harding, and punctuated with world travel totaling 125,000 miles by the age of 12. The Hollywood stars were colleagues in John Presper Eckert, Sr.'s World War I bond drive efforts and the travel included the elder Eckert's business and vacation trips.

In 1937, Eckert graduated from the William Penn Charter School, the oldest private boys' school in the United States. He breezed through his regular courses and took on 2 years of college math, as well. Eckert received a bachelor of science degree in electrical engineering from the University of Pennsylvania's Moore School of Electrical Engineering in 1941. After graduation, he stayed at the university to teach, do research, and pursue graduate studies.

It was in Eckert's role as lab instructor, at age 22, that he met 34-year-old John MAUCHLY. During an 8-week government-paid defense course in electronics, Eckert and Mauchly discussed what they both wanted to do—build a computer. Two years later, Eckert received his master's degree in electrical engineering and the two joined forces to begin work on their first computer. In Mauchly, Eckert had found a mind that

complemented his almost perfectly, and did so for many years. It was a team like Rodgers and Hammerstein or Gilbert and Sullivan, a perfect blend of complementary talents that time after time produced compelling works that would eventually enchant millions.

Both were already interested in the possibilities of automatic computation when World War II turned possibilities into urgent needs. In 1942, the Ballistic Research Laboratory of the U.S. Army Ordnance Department was assigned the job of recomputing firing and bombing tables for the springier ground of Africa and for proposed gun/projectile combinations, rockets, missiles, and other strategic arms.

In 1942, Eckert and Mauchly submitted a proposal to the U.S. Army describing an electronic computer, which resulted in a contract from the Army's Ordnance Department to build the machine. Eckert, the only full-time person on the project, served as project manager. Mauchly, who was teaching full-time, found himself consultant to a team of fifty people (at its largest) assigned to build the computer. Begun in April 1943, on Eckert's twenty-fourth birthday, ENIAC was completed more than 200,000 people-hours later, 3 years after it was started. ENIAC, which stands for Electronics Numerical Integrator and Computer, was unveiled in formal dedication ceremonies on February 16, 1946. Flawlessly, it completed its first problem: a highly secret numerical simulation for the yet-untested hydrogen bomb. This exercise, which would have taken existing calculating machines 40 hours, took ENIAC 20 seconds.

The ENIAC was literally a giant. It contained more than 17,000 vacuum tubes, weighed 30 tons, and occupied a room the size of an average three-bedroom home. It was capable of performing 5,000 additions per second. This was considerably faster than any existing device or any machine that was even under development elsewhere. ENIAC functioned until October 2, 1955, when it was dismantled and part of it was sent to the Smithsonian Institution in Washington, D.C., where it became part of an exhibit on computing.

During the course of development work on ENIAC, Eckert and Mauchly and their associates recognized many deficiencies in this device. In 1944, the Moore School obtained a supplement to the ENIAC contract for the development of the Electronic Discrete Variable Automatic Computer (EDVAC). This computer was to be a stored-program computer with a 1,000-word capacity that would use mercury delay lines for storing data. During the next 18 months, Eckert and Mauchly and their associates completed ENIAC and began development of EDVAC. John von Neumann became a consultant to the Moore School and assisted the staff in formalizing the stored-program concept for this computer.

Eckert and Mauchly left the University of Pennsylvania in 1947 to form their own company, the Eckert–Mauchly Computer Corporation, where they developed the Binary Automatic Computer (BINAC) in 1949. BINAC was the first computer to be programmed by internally stored instructions (EDVAC would not be completed until 1952).

BINAC was never more to Eckert and Mauchly than a steppingstone to their next computer—UNIVAC I. The two men believed in the commercial potential of computers. By the fall of 1949, the Eckert–Mauchly firm was in financial difficulties. A year later the company was sold to Remington Rand. In 1951, UNIVAC I was delivered to the Bureau of the Census. UNIVAC I was the world's first general-purpose commercial computer able to handle a wide variety of applications.

Both Eckert and Mauchly had become employees of the Remington Rand Corporation (which later became Sperry Rand Corporation and then Unisys Corporation). After almost two decades of working together, the Eckert–Mauchly team split up in 1959 and Eckert went on to become the director of the Univac Division. In 1955, he was named vice-president and director of research at Univac. Eight years later, Eckert was appointed vice-president and technical advisor for computer systems at Sperry. Eckert received an honorary degree of doctor of science in engineering from the University of Pennsylvania in 1964. Between 1948 and 1966 Eckert received eighty-five patents, mostly for electronic inventions. In 1969, Eckert was awarded the National Science Foundation's National Medal of Science, the nation's highest award for distinguished achievement in science, mathematics, and engineering.

For Further Reading

Wulforst, H. 1982. *Breakthrough to the computer age.* New York: Charles Scribner's Sons.

Donald D. Spencer

EDI

See Electronic Data Interchange

EDUCATION, COMPUTERS IN

As computers were gaining a reputation as "efficiency experts" in offices of the 1950s, the public was beginning to worry about the efficiency of its educational system. With the sudden appearance of Sputnik in a startled American sky, that worry grew to a fear. Postwar schools were seeing record numbers of students. How would each learn the new and complex array of skills that would keep our society competitive in the coming Age of Technology? To many people in education and the fledgling computer industry, the answer seemed to lie in the same computer capabilities that were making office work more efficient and that were rapidly becoming a pervasive presence in our culture.

Some 30 years later, computers are in common use in schools across the country although not, perhaps, in ways some of the early planners envisioned. Richard Atkinson, one of the pioneers in instructional applications and later director of the National Science Foundation, wrote in 1978 that "by 1990, the cost of computer-assisted instruction will be so cheap and its applications so broad that it will be viewed as an educational necessity" (p. 60). In 1991, a *Time* magazine article declared that educational computing is a "revolution that fizzled" and that "computers have not lived up to their promise to transform America's struggling schools" (p. 48). A true picture of the impact of computers in education lies somewhere between these two perspectives and can best be viewed in light of a history of use that began in the late 1950s as an attempt to mechanize teaching methods and continues today in a variety of forms far removed from this early goal.

HISTORY OF COMPUTERS IN EDUCATION

Today's educators often tend to think of the history of educational computing as beginning with the introduction of microcomputers in about 1978. And, indeed, this was a pivotal point in the field. But the first educational use of computers seems to have been nearly three decades prior to that, in 1950 (see Milestones chart, Table 1), with a computer-driven flight simulator used to train pilots at MIT (Lockard et al. 1990). The first attempt to use computers with schoolchil-

dren was in 1959, when the IBM team of Rath, Anderson, and Brainerd reported a program to teach binary arithmetic to New York elementary-school students via a "typewriter inquiry station" connected to an IBM 650 computer. Over the years there has been a steadily increasing and fairly low-profile use of computers to support school and college administrative functions (Bozeman and Raucher 1991), but it is the classroom application of computers that has seen the most dynamic and problematic growth. The period from 1960 to 1980 was shaped by time-sharing activities offered by universities and especially by three major instructional computing projects, all of which were developed on and driven by large-scale mainframe or minicomputer systems. The 1980s were a time of such intense interest in and purchase of standalone microcomputers for schools that it came to be known as the "Microcomputer Revolution" in education. In the 1990s microcomputer use is still widespread, but schools may be witnessing a resurgence of interest in centralized systems.

The Pre-Microcomputer Era

The IBM 650 was the beginning of IBM's large-scale effort over the next 15 years to develop special-purpose instructional computers and software and implement them in universities and schools around the country. Stanford University was a major partner in this effort, and Atkinson and Wilson (1969)

TABLE 1. Milestones and Trends in the History of Educational Computing

1950	MIT scientists train pilots with a computer-driven flight simulator
1959	IBM develops first CAI program to teach binary arithmetic to schoolchildren
1960	CDC and University of Illinois begin PLATO development
	First CAI authoring system (Coursewriter) developed
1963	Stanford project begins to develop CAI for elementary-level reading and mathematics
1964	BASIC developed at Dartmouth
1966	IBM 1500 systems installed at Stanford and other sites around the country;
	Philadelphia and Kansas City school systems adopt CAI into instructional programs
1967	CCC formed
1968	Logo introduced into education by Papert at MIT
1974	TICCIT marketed by Mitre Corporation
1977	Commodore Pet, Apple II, and Radio Shack TRS-80 are developed; grass-roots micro computer movement in schools begins
1980s	MECC and book publishers begin to produce computer software (courseware); computer literacy movement begins
1990s	Computers used as basis of multimedia learning stations

document two parallel efforts at Stanford by about 1967. One was the IBM 1500 system, which they described in the following way: ". . . an IBM 1800 Central Processing Unit with bulk storage maintained on tape and . . . disks, a station controller and peripheral devices. . . . The student terminal interface consists of a cathode ray tube, a typewriter keyboard, a light pen, . . . an image projector with a capacity of 1000 frames which may be randomly accessed under computer control, and a set of earphones and microphone. Audio messages may be played to the student from a bank of audio-tape playing and recording devices" (p. 6). This was a tutorial system with a "rich branching structure" and was used to teach reading and mathematics to Brentwood Elementary School students in East Palo Alto. The other Stanford development effort was on a Digital Equipment Corporation PDP-1, which had a simpler hardware configuration and which was used for more instructionally simple drill and practice activities in mathematics and reading. In 1967 the latter was used as the basis of an instructional system marketed by a new company, Computer Curriculum Corporation (CCC). By 1978 CCC had thousands of terminals installed in public schools around the country (Suppes and Macken 1978). Until IBM stopped supporting the 1500 system (c. 1975), it was also used in some twenty-five universities and school districts, including Philadelphia and Kansas City, which by 1966 had made computer-assisted instruction (CAI) an integral part of their instructional programs.

At almost the same time as IBM and Stanford began their work, a team at Control Data Corporation also began to develop another computer system dedicated to instruction: Programmed Logic for Automatic Teaching Operations (PLATO). The PLATO system used a different technology for its screen display—the plasma panel—and concentrated on full-scale tutorial courses as well as a variety of single-skill lessons.

Instructional software—or *courseware*, as it came to be called—was developed for all of these systems using special authoring languages that contained commands especially designed for displaying text-and-graphics frames of instruction and judging students' responses to questions. One early authoring language for the IBM systems was Coursewriter; the PLATO language was TUTOR.

From 1975 until about 1980, the CCC and PLATO systems dominated CAI use in the field. Schools accessed PLATO software and services primarily through universities tied into the CDC or University of Illinois systems. Another large-scale effort at this time involved Time-Shared Interactive Computer Controlled Information Television (TICCIT), which added color television to the computer learning station and which was developed at Brigham Young University on an IBM 1800 system and marketed by the Mitre Corporation. Some large systems were also developed to manage student information and make it easier to individualize instruction, the so-called computer-managed instruction (CMI) systems known as Program for Learning in Accordance with Needs (PLAN), developed by the American Institute for Research, and Individually Prescribed Instruction (IPI) at the University of Pittsburgh.

Dr. Patrick Suppes, Stanford professor and founder of CCC, is often referred to as the "Grandfather of CAI" for his pioneering work in the early days of instructional computing. But many other prominent people of the era made significant contributions. These include William Uttal, Harvey Long, Edwin Adams, and Ralph Grubb at IBM; William C. Norris at CDC; Max Jerman, Richard Atkinson, and H. A. Wilson at Stanford; John Hirschbuhl of the University of Akron; Don Bitzer at the University of Illinois; Lawrence Stolurow at Harvard University; Duncan Hansen at Florida State University; Harold Mitzel and Keith Hall at Pennsylvania State University; Michael Allen at Ohio State University; Karl Zinn at the University of Michigan; Victor Bunderson and Dexter Fletcher at Brigham Young University; Robert Glaser at the University of Pittsburgh; and Sylvia Charp in the Philadelphia School District.

Although CAI and CMI systems had high-profile use in those early days, they were by no means the only computer use for instruction. In the 1960s and 1970s some twenty-two large universities around the country established computer centers with time-sharing systems that public schools in the area would access through terminals (Hunter et al. 1975). Schools mainly taught programming with these resources, but also shared programs and utilities among themselves. While not as highly publicized as the industry-driven CAI/CMI systems, these time-sharing activities thrived and became a popular resource for teachers and students, especially in urban areas immediately surrounding university centers.

The Microcomputer Era and Beyond

The first microcomputers (Commodore Pets, Tandy/Radio Shack TRS-80s, and Apples) entered schools in 1977, and by 1980 the focus of instructional computing had shifted from large, centralized systems to small, standalone ones. The microcomputer movement differed dramatically from the earlier instructional computing efforts in several major ways. First, microcomputers were brought into schools by teachers and students rather than by computer companies and universities; it was a "grass-roots" movement. Second, software for microcomputers came not from professors and programmers at university R&D centers but from small companies and development centers, from teachers themselves, and later from book publishers. Educators now had more individual control over computers and the software to run them. Previously they were dependent on whoever was in charge of running the mainframe computer to allow them access. Now they could buy software and use it at their convenience. (Microcomputer software was initially sold and used on cassettes and cartridges and later on 5¼-inch "floppy disks.") But the most significant difference was in the nature and scope of the role computer technology would play in education.

An emerging curriculum focus in the 1980s was problem solving, research, and critical thinking skills that could be used in any content area. The first microcomputer programs seemed to be shadows of the tutorials, drills, and simulations from earlier days. But in the hands of creative educators, microcomputer products quickly branched out to other forms of instruction that could support these new skill areas. Educators and others began to explore new ways of applying microcomputer capabilities to instructional problems. A language called LOGO had been developed in the 1960s by a team at Bolt, Beranek, and Newman, Inc., and had been introduced into education by MIT professor Seymour Papert in 1968. When microcomputer use became widespread, a Logo "culture" sprang up, nurtured by Papert through his writings and work with schools (Papert 1980). Logo and its derivatives became the focal point for the new curriculum emphasis on problem solving and had a profound influence on shaping perceptions of how computers should be used for instruction.

Teachers found that their major problem in the early days of microcomputer use was locating good-quality courseware. Several major projects arose to help meet these needs. The Minnesota Educational Computing Consortium (later Corporation) (MECC) received funding from companies and the federal government, developed an array of programs, and for a time became the single largest provider of software in the field. The MicroSIFT project at the Northwest Regional Educational Lab in Portland, Oregon, and the Educational Products Information Exchange (EPIE) were projects to evaluate courseware and publish listings for teachers. As with the older mainframe and minicomputer systems, software development for microcomputers was also made easier with authoring systems such as GENIS, PILOT, SuperPILOT, and PASS. Later, HyperCard became a prominent authoring tool. (See also AUTHORING LANGUAGES, SYSTEMS, and ENVIRONMENTS.)

More widespread access to computers also made it possible to address an instructional need that had been suggested some years before and only partially addressed through university time-sharing systems in the premicrocomputer days: the need for *computer literacy* or skills in using the computer (Molnar 1978; Luehrmann and Peckham 1984). Computer skills began to appear in the curricula of school systems around the country.

In the 1990s, microcomputers are still the dominant form of computer technology in schools but are also beginning to be used in multimedia learning stations that are, in some ways, reminiscent of the IBM 1500 "student terminal interfaces." CCC systems are still in use along with other systems that have even more extensive curricula; all these systems are now called *integrated learning systems* (ILSs). (See also "ILS: Its New Role in Schools" 1990.) There are about 2.7 million computers in schools, or about one for every sixteen students (*Time* 1991). However, as recent demographic studies have shown, these computers are unevenly dispersed (Becker 1986), and the ratio is much greater in some areas, especially those with high populations of lower-income and minority students. The role of the computer, which began as a way to mechanize instruction, is now a multifaceted one and is the subject of both continuing optimism and controversy.

CURRENT USES OF COMPUTERS IN EDUCATION

When people think of computers in education, many envision children in front of keyboards and screens. But computers have actually developed equally important dual roles, supporting functions in both the classroom and the school or college office. The computer's role in administrative support has been the more straightforward one, mirroring the way that technology has been used to streamline operations in business offices across the country. Few schools or colleges do not use computers in some clerical or record-keeping capacity; larger educational organizations computerize nearly all their operations, from mailing labels to staff payroll. The computer's instructional support role has been more problematic and controversial, reflecting fundamental disagreements among educators about the goals and methods of education. However, both aspects of educational systems have changed dramatically as a result of computer use. Thus educational applications are described here in terms of the computer's two differing but equally important roles: administrative and instructional.

Administrative Uses

Administrative applications may be thought of in the general categories described in Charp et al. (1982). Systems are in common use to accomplish all of the following:

1. Student applications. Student scheduling, report cards, grade and transcript information, attendance, student demographic and health records, district test scoring and reporting, tuition and fee statements

2. Personnel applications. Payroll, personnel records, staff assignments, teacher certification records, health records, tax information and reporting

3. Financial applications. Budget/accounting, food service, accounts receivable/payable, general ledger, purchase order generation, salary schedule analysis

4. Facilities and equipment. Room locations, capacities, and utilization; equipment, furniture, and supplies inventories; maintenance scheduling; energy control

5. Research and planning applications. Budget forecasting, bus routing, statistical analysis, test item analysis, project planning and evaluation

6. Office applications. Filing, word processing, mailing lists, and labels

7. Library and media center applications. Bibliographic information retrieval, circulation, cataloging, purchasing

In school districts some of these functions (e.g., food service) are handled at the school level. Others (e.g., personnel records) are typically managed at the district level. Computerization of some administrative functions has only recently come into common use. These include telephone registration, in which a computer system includes a voice component and students can drop and add college courses by calling up and responding to verbal prompts; and attendance monitoring systems, which automatically dial home telephone numbers to inform parents that their children are not in school.

Instructional Uses

Disagreements about the computer's appropriate instructional use seem to be reflected in differences of opinion among authorities as to the labels and categories that should be used to describe types of instructional applications. Consequently, the lack of standard terms makes discussing and resolving questions about the computer's role even more difficult. Since there are more than one or two recognized, authoritative sources of information, attempts to create clearer, more all-encompassing categories have resulted in more ambiguous terms. So the problem continues.

In the pre-microcomputer era of the 1960s and 1970s, when computer uses were limited in number and type, instructional applications were classified as CAI or CMI (Suppes and Macken 1978). CAI described applications wherein students received some kind of direct instruction via a computer screen or teletype device. Drill and practice; tutorial; and, later, simulation programs fell under this heading. CMI programs helped the teacher keep track of student progress by skill objective, either through testing on the computer and subsequent processing and reporting of results, or simply through processing results of tests taken on paper and entered into the computer (Baker 1978).

When microcomputers were introduced, the field began to proliferate with other types of instructional tools that either supported instruction or supported the teacher's efforts to prepare or deliver instruction; the "terminology wars" began. In 1980 Robert P. Taylor introduced the framework he called "tutor, tool, and tutee": the three modes of using computers in instruction. The *tutor* mode was any application in which the computer had been preprogrammed to present information to students as an authoritative source—much like the teacher. The *tool* mode was any application that had some practical, time-saving utility programmed into it, such as word processing or statistical programs. The *tutee* mode referred to situations where the student "taught" the computer by programming it. Taylor identified the latter use as the most powerful one in terms of its potential to change instructional practices.

Taylor's framework served to clarify general roles for the computer and, for a while, the terms came into common use in the field. However, the framework left the reader with the task of identifying and placing specific applications under each heading and also failed to take into consideration such items as the nonprogramming aspects of computer literacy and new resources that blurred the lines between the modes.

The following categories of instructional applications should be viewed within this historical perspective. Some authors still use the general terms CAI and CMI (Bullogh and Beatty 1991), or derivative terms such as computer-based instruction or computer-based learning, which they view as more all-inclusive. Others still use the schema suggested by Taylor in 1980 (Lockard et al. 1990). Still others have created other terms to encompass all the newer types of products. For example, Troutman et al. (1988) replace the term CAI with two other terms: computer-directed instruction, under which they place tutorials, authoring systems, and simulations; and computer-enhanced instruction, under which they describe computer resources used to create teaching and learning aids. Under CMI they describe updated versions of how to carry out the traditional progress-tracking functions, and also list other teacher aids. They combine direct instructional uses and teacher support uses of word processors, databases, and spreadsheets under another section, called "tools." Since selecting any of these categorization schemes would be strictly a matter of personal preference, the description that follows will offer a largely label-free summary of current uses of computers related to instruction in terms of the functions they serve in the classroom.

Computers as a topic of instruction: Computer literacy and computer science education.
Teaching students about how computers work and how to program them began in the early 1960s at both the school and college levels (Seidel et al. 1982). Much of the early instruction at the precollege level focused on programming in commonly used languages of the time (e.g., BASIC and FORTRAN); the intent was to prepare a limited number of students to enter college computer science

programs. These courses were the bases for today's advanced placement programs in computer science through which students may obtain college credit for programming courses while still in high school. Computer science is a large and important curriculum at the college and university level, training professionals in areas ranging from data processing to computer engineering and design.

However, in the early 1970s another, more egalitarian kind of computer education emerged in public schools: the computer literacy movement. The term "computer literacy" is usually credited to Arthur Luehrmann, who says he coined it in the 1960s while at Dartmouth College (Luehrmann 1972). In his view, the coming Information Age would make knowing how to use a computer as essential as knowing how to read and write. While hundreds of computer literacy resources and publications are now available, and school districts across the country include computer literacy skills in some way in their curriculum, the movement continues to be marked by disagreement and controversy. Experts and educators alike debate issues ranging from the definition of computer literacy to the skills that should be included to how the skills should be taught. In an attempt to settle some of these issues, the National Science Foundation and the Human Resources Research Organization cosponsored a conference of experts in the field in 1980. While much valuable information was summarized (Seidel et al. 1982), there was little agreement on any of the issues; even a definition remained elusive. Luehrmann (see Luehrmann and Peckham 1984) maintains his original view that computer literacy should be "being able to tell the computer what you want it to do" (p. x)—that is, programming and tool uses. But other experts pointed out that technological developments will result in uses of computers that require no programming knowledge but may require other skills such as troubleshooting ability based on knowing how a computer works. Other computer-related knowledge may be necessary to make citizens able to purchase computer resources to meet their needs and to react knowledgeably to issues related to privacy and ethics (e.g., government use of databases on U.S. citizens).

Even in the absence of firm guidelines, many education organizations proceeded to develop curricula and teach computer skills at various grade levels (Hunter 1983; Bitter and Camuse 1988). Some states such as Florida have even experimented with making computer literacy part of required basic skills along with reading and writing. The trend toward offering separate computer literacy courses seems to be subsiding, but computer education of some kind will probably continue to take place in the context of other content areas.

Computers as instructional delivery systems: Tutorial, drill, and simulation uses. The first instructional uses of computers as tutors, "electronic worksheets," and simulating systems are still very much in evidence in schools. The purpose of all these products is to teach via computer concepts that are normally taught by human teachers.

1. *Tutorials* are, perhaps, the least frequently used products. Their intent is to carry out instruction in much the same sequence as a teacher would by giving verbal explanations, asking questions, giving examples and illustrations, providing practice with feedback, and, depending on the student's input, directing the student to cover information again or go on to new information. Lockard et al. (1990) describe two kinds of tutorials: linear and branching. Linear tutorials present the same information in the same sequence to all students. Branching tutorials may give a different instructional sequence to each student, depending on their responses to questions interspersed through the material. In classroom use, tutorials are intended to introduce new topics or let students cover the same material already seen in another medium.

2. *Drill and practice* programs, sometimes referred to simply as "drills," still represent the single most common use of computers in instruction. They do not introduce new information but give the student practice on or review of previously covered concepts or facts. Typically the screen presents a problem to be solved (e.g., an arithmetic problem), the student enters an answer, and the program responds with some feedback and/or by showing yet another item. Drills may be very simple "flash-card"-type programs, which offer yes/no feedback, or may give extensive corrective feedback based on the student's answer. In the classroom, drills take the place of flash cards or work sheets.

3. *Simulations* differ from the other two products in that they are usually less structured in terms of what the student must do to learn from them. They are products designed to model some real or imaginary system, but in most cases there are specific skills students are to learn from them. Since students may not only have to learn what the simulation is "teaching" but also how best to use the program, simulations are considered more complex forms of instruction than drills and tutorials. Lockard et al. (1990) describe several different kinds of simulations. Some, such as flight simulators or medical diagnostic programs, call for students to learn how to do something correctly in light of changing factors or environments. Others let students learn rules or procedures by role-playing—for example, playing the role of a storekeeper in a store or a teacher facing various situations in a school. Still others allow students to become experimenters, changing the factors and observing the results in such areas as population growth or genetic experiments. In classrooms, simulations help students learn through models what they cannot do in real situations because of unavailable materials, or because too much expense, time, or danger is involved.

Computers as learning aids for students: Computer-assisted guidance, problem-solving aids, and tools. Other types of instructional products have been developed to meet various needs. For example, *computer-assisted guidance* systems (Sampson and Reardon 1990) were developed to help students find information on jobs of potential interest to them as careers and to match their personal

characteristics with the requirements of various career areas. These began as large-scale systems on mainframe computers and were later available on microcomputers and networks. When educators began to emphasize the importance of so-called problem-solving skills in the 1980s, computer products began to appear to support this instructional trend. Some educators say that technology actually helped shape the trend. In any case, there are a variety of products whose common purpose is to get students to think and solve problems rather than learn specific information or skills. Such products frequently offer the most innovative and creative formats of any instructional software, and many have simulationlike characteristics. For example, a program might let students try to manufacture products by operating machines in a certain order or might be designed to improve memory and study skills by letting students wander through an imaginary land meeting and overcoming obstacles.

Another group of products originated in the business office as clerical assistants and migrated to the classroom as instructional tools. These include word processing, spreadsheets, and databases. Most student uses of word processing and spreadsheets are fairly straightforward; they help with the typing and calculation tasks that are an inherent part of learning many skills. For example, word processing is rapidly becoming a standard tool in writing classes, where it allows students to make corrections rapidly without having to retype entire papers and to check compositions for spelling and grammar. More capable word processing systems may also help students structure their writing assignments. Predesigned spreadsheet templates are often used when simple arithmetic tasks could interfere with learning higher-level concepts such as amortization of loans. Students are sometimes encouraged to design their own spreadsheets to learn skills such as budget preparation. Uses of databases are more complicated. Students may be asked to create a database to learn how information is summarized, stored, and retrieved. Or they may learn researching skills by perusing prepared databases on a topic such as animals or American presidents. In short, databases are often used as unstructured problem-solving tools for which the teacher and student must determine appropriate instructional goals and activities.

The lines among the instructional computing products described here are not always clear-cut. For example, another type of software product—the instructional game—can overlay drills, simulations, or problem-solving programs with a set of game rules to increase students' motivation to use them. Or a program may simulate an environment such as a store in which the student must figure out the best strategies to solve purchasing problems. The sheer variety and number of different resources that have arrived on the school scene in the past 10 years make it easy to see why current instructional computing applications cannot fit neatly into a few standard categories.

Special mention must be made of a product that began as a programming language and has emerged as a problem-solving tool in widespread use in schools: Logo. As described above, Logo has had a significant impact on shaping the direction of computer use in education. Simonson and Thompson (1990, p. 289) describe Logo as "an expandable learning experience, applicable across the curriculum." Other authors pay similar homage to it as a versatile tool to help teach both problem-solving skills and content skills. Logo derivatives are also in common use in schools. These include Logowriter, a word processor; and LEGO TC Logo, a tool for programming machines built from Lego pieces.

Computers as support tools for teachers: Productivity and management resources. Some of the same products used by students to aid in their learning are also used by teachers to help them do paperwork or preparation tasks more efficiently. Teachers use word processors to do any work that requires typing (e.g., letters, lesson plans), and spreadsheets for anything that requires calculations or preparation of information in neat rows and columns (e.g., grades, school budgets, attendance lists). Databases are also used, albeit less frequently, as teacher filing systems (e.g.,

for classroom inventory and student records).

Using a computer system to track progress (CMI), one of the earliest teacher uses of computers, is still in evidence in most of the forms described by Baker (1978). Designed to assess student mastery of learning objectives and help teachers match instruction to each student's needs, these systems yield reports that summarize test data in various ways and identify specific areas of strength and weakness in terms of objectives to be learned. Management systems may function as:

1. Part of a computer learning system that collects data as students go through the instruction
2. A computerized testing system that students use after learning from other media; or
3. A data analysis system that processes students' test data entered from scanned sheets or by hand

There are also a myriad other computer support tools detailed by Lockard et al. (1990), which include the following:

1. Graphics programs. Assist in preparing and presenting classroom materials
2. Classroom desktop publishing. Help teach writing and document preparation skills (e.g., newsletters)
3. Test generators. Help teachers generate tests from stored banks of test items
4. Worksheet and puzzle generators. Provide printed exercises for homework or seatwork from stored banks of items
5. Readability analyses. Automate known readability formulas and calculate the reading level of textbooks and storybooks
6. Gradebooks. Special purpose packages used instead of spreadsheets to let teachers store and calculate grades
7. Statistical packages. Summarize and analyze data from research and classroom work and do statistical tests (e.g., t-tests and analysis of variance) on them

Other computer resources and activities. Newer uses of computers are constantly emerging. Some that are gaining in popularity include:

1. Telecommunications. Computers are connected to telephone lines to allow students and teachers access to on-line databases on topics ranging from education to current news, and let schools link with other schools to exchange information and engage in joint learning projects. Computer conferencing is gaining in popularity as a means of decreasing the inherent isolation of teachers by putting them in contact with each other and with useful information sources. Networks such as the Apple Computer company's Applelink have made this kind of contact more practical.

2. Uses with videodiscs and compact-disk read-only memory (CD-ROM). Computers can also be used in conjunction with other technologies to help structure lessons or make it easier to locate information on a disk. When a computer is used in this way, it makes the technology interactive.

IMPACT ON EDUCATION AND EDUCATIONAL METHODS

The sheer number of administrative and instructional products in use in school systems and colleges is evidence of the profound impact computers have had on all aspects and levels of education. As is the case in other areas of modern society ranging from business operations to space travel, computer technology has changed fundamentally and permanently the very nature of educational processes. In larger school systems and postsecondary institutions, computers have so optimized administrative operations that more time and energy can be dedicated to the central goal of educating students. Having up-to-date information on students also makes it easier and faster to make informed instructional decisions.

However, capturing and summarizing the computer's contribution to improved instruction and, consequently, better student learning have been more difficult and controversial. There are also continuing arguments about possible negative effects of computers on students and what must be done to make sure computer technology solves, rather than creates, educational problems. One may look at concerns about impact from three perspectives: past research findings, problems and issues related to instructional uses, and potential for future impact.

Research Findings

Research studies on the effects of computer applications on student attitudes and achievement began at the same time as the first systems went into use in schools. The first instructional systems from IBM and CDC were fairly well evaluated, but federal cutbacks in education funding in the 1970s caused a decrease in research efforts, and attempts to track the effects on various skills and types of students became fragmented and unsystematic. Early reviews of research (Jamison et al. 1974) offered the tentative conclusion that CAI was apparently an effective supplement to traditional methods (usually as drill and practice) and could be used "in some situations" to improve achievement. The reviewers expressed a concern that was to be repeated by many later reviewers (Roblyer et al. 1988): Studies in the area were so few and so flawed or lacking in data that it was difficult to draw any reliable conclusions across studies. Even improved statistical methods of summarizing study data (meta-analysis methods) helped only slightly. The larger problem was that there were so few studies on a given line of interest (e.g., Logo effects on problem-solving ability) that reported required data and that were not too methodologically flawed to be included in the review. Adding to these problems is the inherent difficulty of studying phenomena as complex and hard to measure as teaching and learning. Research that seeks to isolate and measure the unique impact of computers is rarely replicable because environmental factors bear so heavily on how effective the technology can be.

The lack of consistent, reliable findings does not seem to have halted the flow of computers into schools. Apparently the tentative finding from most reviews that computers are at least as effective as other methods in most subject areas, along with some positive evaluations of individual projects in schools, has been sufficient rationale for continuing their use.

Problems and Issues

Lack of firm research evidence to guide the course of computer use in instruction is a concern to many educators, but most also acknowledge that implementation issues are just as important in shaping the impact computers can have on education.

Costs and equity. In the early days of educational computing, when mainframe computers were the primary delivery system, costs of computer services were the major problem. High costs meant that only limited numbers of schools could get the benefits offered by this technology. Later, with the coming of low-cost microcomputers, the technology equity issue seemed to have been addressed. But Molnar (1978) pointed out that equity problems were just beginning. If one agrees with the assumptions that computer literacy is a required basic skill and that access to computer resources (at least as efficiency tools) will also help students learn, then those students with access to computers will surge ahead of others without it. Molnar predicted what later demographic studies showed (Becker 1986): School districts with wealthier populations would have microcomputers in greater numbers than those populated by lower-income families, and wealthier students would also have more home computers. Whether this inequity will bring about the "great crisis in education" Molnar warned of remains to be seen.

Software quality and sources. In the early years of microcomputer use, other problems were added. There was much discussion about evaluating the quality of instructional software and who should provide it (i.e., teachers vs. computer companies). Book publishers and an array of new software development companies became the primary sources of instructional software (courseware), although educators still disagree on what constitutes good-quality material. This lack of agreement has made it difficult for software providers to create products that support and further sound instructional practices.

Teacher training, access, and integration. Teacher training has been and remains a primary need. Computer capabilities continue to expand and outstrip teacher abilities to implement them. Software companies and innovators in the field are constantly discovering newer, more creative ways to use computers to enhance learning, but many teachers are still grappling with basic issues, such as how to get access to a computer for support tasks and where to integrate existing software into various curriculum areas.

Computer role in instruction: Three controversies. Another controversy overshadows all of the other major concerns about computer use: What is the most appropriate instructional role for this technology? There are at least three interrelated lines of debate, all of which have been going on for some time and any of which could shape the resolution of issues such as software quality, teacher training, and appropriate integration strategies. One is a disagreement between those who believe the computer should be used primarily as a tool and as a vehicle to become "computer literate" or "technologically literate" and those who feel the computer should also be used to teach content such as mathematics and language skills. A second controversy was generated by Papert's much-quoted book *Mindstorms* (1980), which proposes a new vision for education, a much less structured learning environment that lets students use computers to create "microworlds" for learning how to think and solve problems. Sloan (1985) and others have expressed strong reservations about this new vision. They are concerned that these computer-based "microworlds" will be cold, impoverished places in which to learn. One author opines, "What kind of a culture are we developing if we have to meet its most powerful ideas through machines rather than people?" (Sloan 1985, p. 16). A related area of controversy focuses on whether computer-driven systems can or should be used to replace teachers to any degree. Mechanizing instruction, the reason computer systems were introduced into classrooms in the 1950s, still seems a goal for those who see current teacher-based delivery systems as too inconsistent in quality and too expensive (Norris 1977). Others warn against thinking of the computer (even in conjunction with other technologies such as videodiscs) as a deus ex machina, observing that even artificial intelligence (AI) applications hold no promise for shaping learning environments capable of replacing human teachers.

Unanswered Questions

The computer's instructional role is still evolving, and resolution to any of these debates does not seem imminent. To date, computers have not replaced teachers—either in school district budgets or in classrooms—to any extent. Whenever computer-based "microworlds" or any other computer-based learning methods are introduced, they seem to be add-ons to more traditional kinds of learning activities. The current trend toward using integrated learning systems (ILS) seems to be an effort to replace some teacher functions, but no teacher layoffs have been linked to this trend and no decreases in education budgets for teacher salaries have been identified. Meanwhile, lack of agreement on directions for computer use is probably a reflection of more fundamental disagreements about how to restructure an educational system sorely in need of improvement (National Commission on Excellence in Education 1983). If the current role of computers in schools changes, it would most likely be as part of a major change in the educational system itself (Smith 1991). Traditionally, about 80 percent of total education budgets has been directed toward personnel salaries, and educators continue to be viewed as underpaid. The other 20 percent is used for running the school plant and must allow for increasing costs of fuel and other essential resources. Thus far, the "Microcomputer Revolution" has been financed primarily from private sources such as grants from agencies and businesses and allocations from state and federal governments (e.g., Chapter II funds for underachieving students). To address current and future demands on our educational system, some fundamental questions must be answered:

1. How can educational opportunities provided by computers and other technology be made more equitable to students of all types and income levels?
2. Should computer use in education become more centralized (i.e., increased use of ILS-type resources) to allow more control over software quality and make implementation more cost-effective?
3. Can computer technology play a major role in helping restructure our failing educational system? If so, what should that role be?
4. Since there are no large, displaceable costs in the education budget, and since the costs of both teacher salaries and technology are increasing, can or should any major teacher functions be replaced by computers as a way to defray the costs? (Smith 1991). What impact would this kind of change have on the overall quality and nature of students' education?

Impact in the Future

As writers such as Atkinson (1978) demonstrated, it is difficult to make predictions about the potential impact of a technology and an application area that are both changing so rapidly. There seems little doubt that computers will continue to play an increasingly greater role in administrative applications. On the instructional side, some trends, at least in the short term, seem evident and are seen in such prediction papers as a major study and report done by the U.S. Office of Technology Assessment (1988):

1. Computers in multimedia environments. Most computers in schools and colleges are standalone microcomputers, but many educators are impressed by the power of combining visual technologies such as compact-disk read-only memory (CD-ROM) and videodiscs with the interactive capability of the computer (Van Horn 1991). The use of interactive videodiscs and CD-ROM as the bases of multimedia learning stations seems to be increasing.

2. Computer networking. To optimize computer resources, expedite communications, and allow teachers and students easier access to software, many schools are beginning to link up microcomputers within schools via networks. This makes it possible for software and services to be centralized, much as they were in the beginning days of educational computing, but now more locally controlled.

3. Telecommunications. The use of computers as links to the world of information is increasing. More and more students and teachers are using computers as communications stations to access databases and contact people in other locations.

4. Home as an extension of school. Less documented but still possible is the increased use of computers as home telecommunications terminals and intelligent tutoring systems (ITS), taking the place of learning traditionally done in schools and supporting the trend toward home education. (See also HOME, COMPUTERS IN THE.)

5. Integrated learning systems. Many school systems, especially larger ones, faced with growing numbers of students, decreasing scores in basic skills, and higher teacher salaries, are turning to ILSs. These systems usually combine tutorial, drill, and management functions to create self-contained packages that teach a variety of basic and higher-level skills. ILS use is increasing; whether their use will replace teachers remains to be seen.

Since our educational system is continually under fire for having unclear goals, it is not surprising that precise measures of the computer's impact on achieving those goals remain elusive. Technology has been and will continue to be a substantial force for change. If American education goes through the long-awaited reform and restructuring predicted for it, computer technology will be both a catalyst and a means for bringing about that change.

References

Atkinson, R. C. 1978. Where will CAI be in 1990? *Educational Technology* 18(4):60–63.

Atkinson, R. C., and H. A. Wilson. 1969. *Computer-assisted instruction: A book of readings.* New York: Academic Press.

Baker, F. B. 1978. *Computer-managed instruction: Theory and practice.* Englewood Cliffs, N.J.: Educational Technology Publications.

Becker, H. J. 1986. *Instructional uses of computers: Reports from the 1985 survey.* Baltimore: The Center for Social Organization of Schools, Johns Hopkins University.

Bitter, G. G., and R. A. Camuse. 1988. *Using a computer in the classroom.* Englewood Cliffs, N.J.: Prentice-Hall.

Bozeman, W. C., and S. M. Raucher. 1991. Application of computer technology to educational administration in the United States. *Journal of Research on Computing in Education* 24(1):62–77.

Bullogh, R. V., and L. F. Beatty. 1991. *Classroom applications of microcomputers.* New York: Macmillan.

Charp, S., W. C. Bozeman, H. Altschuler, R. D'Orazio, and D. W. Spuck. 1982. *Layman's guide to the use of computers in education.* Washington, D.C.: The Association for Educational Data Systems.

Hunter, B. 1983. *My students use computers: Learning activities for computer literacy.* Reston, Va.: Reston.

Hunter, B., C. S. Kastner, M. L. Rubin, and R. J. Seidel. 1975. *Learning alternatives in U.S. education: Where student and computer meet.* Englewood Cliffs, N.J.: Educational Technology Publications.

ILS: Its new role in schools. 1990. *Electronic Learning* 10(1):22–24, 31–32.

Jamison, D., P. Suppes, and S. Wells. 1974. The effectiveness of alternative instructional media: A survey. *Review of Educational Research* 44(1):1–67.

Lockard, J., P. D. Abrams, and W. A. Many. 1990. *Microcomputers for education.* Glenview, Ill.: Scott, Foresman/Little, Brown Higher Education.

Luehrmann, A. 1972. Should the computer teach the student or vice versa? *Proceedings of the 1972 AFIPS Spring Joint Conference,* vol. 40.

Luehrmann, A., and H. Peckham. 1984. *Computer literacy survival kit.* New York: McGraw-Hill.

Molnar, A. 1978. The next great crisis in American education: Computer literacy. *T. H. E. Journal* 5(4):35–38.

National Commission on Excellence in Education. 1983. *A nation at risk.* Washington, D.C.: U.S. Department of Education.

Norris, W. C. 1977. Via technology to a new era in education. *Phi Delta Kappan* 58(6): 451–59.

Office of Technology Assessment, U.S. Congress. 1988. *Power on! New tools for teaching and learning.* Washington, D.C.: U.S. Government Printing Office.

Papert, S. 1980. *Mindstorms: Children, computers, and powerful ideas.* New York: Basic Books.

Roblyer, M. D., W. H. Castine, and F. J. King. 1988. *Assessing the impact of computer-based instruction: A review of recent research.* New York: The Haworth Press.

Sampson, J. P., and R. C. Reardon, eds. 1990. A thematic issue on evaluating computer-assisted career guidance systems. *Journal of Career Development* 17(2):79–149.

Seidel, R. J., R. E. Anderson, and B. Hunter. 1982. *Computer literacy: Issues and directions for 1985.* New York: Academic Press.

Simonson, M. R., and A. Thompson. 1990. *Educational computing foundations.* Columbus, Ohio: Merrill.

Sloan, D. 1985. *The computer in education in critical perspective.* New York: Teachers College Press.

Smith, R. 1991. Restructuring American education through technology: Three alternative scenarios. *ISTE Update* 3(8):1–2.

Suppes, P., and E. Macken. 1978. The historical path from research and development to operational use of CAI. *Educational Technology* 18(4):9–12.

Taylor, R. P. 1980. *The computer in the school: Tutor, tools, and tutee.* New York: Teachers College Press.

Time. 1991. The revolution that fizzled. 137(20):48–49.

Troutman, A., J. White, and F. Breit. 1988. *The micro goes to school: Instructional applications of microcomputer technology.* Pacific Grove, Calif.: Brooks-Cole.

Van Horn, R. 1991. *Advanced technology in education.* Pacific Grove, Calif.: Brooks-Cole.

For Further Reading

Alessi, S. M., and S. R. Trollip. 1985. *Computer-based instruction: Methods and development.* Englewood Cliffs, N.J.: Prentice-Hall.

Committee on Science and Technology, U.S. House of Representatives. 1978. *Computers and the learning society report.* Washington, D.C.: U.S. Government Printing Office.

Flake, J., C. E. McClintock, and S. Turner. 1990. *Fundamentals of computer education.* Belmont, Calif.: Wadsworth.

Niemiec, R. P., and H. J. Walberg. 1989. From teaching machines to microcomputers: Some milestones in the history of computer-based instruction. *The Journal of Research on Computing in Education* 21:263–76.

Office of Technology Assessment, U.S. Congress. 1989. *Linking for learning: A new course for education.* Washington, D.C.: U.S. Government Printing Office.

Roblyer, M. D. 1988. Fundamental problems and principles of designing effective courseware. In D. Jonassen, ed. *Instructional designs for microcomputer courseware.* Hillsdale, N.J.: Lawrence Erlbaum Associates.

Wall Street Journal. 1985. Schools keep buying computers, but pupils may not benefit much. April 17:1, 23.

M. D. Roblyer

ELECTRONIC DATA INTERCHANGE

Electronic data interchange (EDI) is defined as the intercompany, computer-to-computer exchange of standard business documents in standard formats. Through EDI, such common business forms as invoices, bills of lading, and purchase orders are transformed to a standard data format and electronically transferred between trading partners. Companies using EDI transfer business documents from the computer of one company to the computer of the other over a telecommunications network, instead of the more common method of sending paper documents back and forth (Figure 1). Among the many

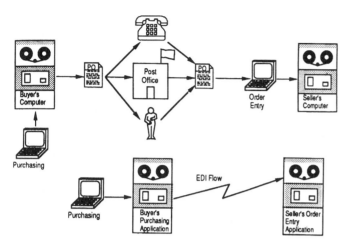

FIGURE 1. Electronic data interchange versus traditional methods. *Reprinted with permission from Emmelhainz 1990.*

benefits EDI offers to companies are decreased costs, increased reliability and accuracy, and better customer service.

Electronic data interchange was first implemented in the early 1970s by the U.S. rail industry, with shipping and trucking following soon thereafter. The growth of EDI systems has been very rapid. In some industries, EDI capability has become a requirement if a company wishes to do business. The U.S. automobile industry is a good example. The "big three" manufacturers (General Motors, Ford, and Chrysler) expect their parts suppliers to be able to support the entire procurement cycle from purchase order to payment using EDI.

For EDI to work, trading partners must agree on the format of records to be exchanged. Initially, such standard formats were agreed on between individual companies. Later, industry standards were established, followed by national and international standards, which are still in an evolutionary state. Software packages are available to translate from the record format used internally by one trading partner to the format expected by the other. Value-added networks often provide such translation software in addition to network services to enable disparate trading partners to implement an EDI relationship with little or no concern over technical issues.

Electronic data interchange is one subset of a category of information systems most commonly called interorganizational systems. A benefit from EDI (possibly more significant than cost and time savings) is the development of close working relationships by trading partners.

HOW ELECTRONIC DATA INTERCHANGE WORKS

Most companies have automated much of the work required to prepare routine business documents. For example, purchase orders may be printed as a by-product of a company's inventory control system. All of the purchase orders prepared in a day are then inserted in envelopes and mailed to supplier companies. When the supplier company receives an incoming purchase order, a data entry clerk enters data from the purchase order into the supplier company's computer system for order processing, shipment, and billing. When the items ordered are shipped, the supplier company's computer system prepares all necessary shipping documents, which accompany the goods, and prints an invoice for mailing to the ordering company. The ordering company enters data from the accompanying shipping document into its inventory control computer system, enters data from the invoice into its accounts payable computer system, and, later, prints a check that is inserted into an envelope for mailing to the supplier company in payment for the goods received. There are time delays required for clerical processing and the mail, and there exists an opportunity for errors at many steps in the process, particularly in the data entry steps.

Electronic data interchange permits this entire process to take place by substituting computer-to-computer transmission of the standard business documents, thus bypassing both the data entry steps at each company and the postal service. Electronic data interchange systems are faster, more accurate and less costly than the method of intercompany communication they replace.

There are two types of services provided to EDI trading partners by third-party companies that make the adoption of EDI less of a burden than it would otherwise be: value-added networks and translation software.

Value-Added Networks

A value-added network (VAN) is an independent company that makes it easier for trading partners to send EDI transactions to each other over telecommunications lines. Rather than establishing telecommunications links with each trading partner directly, companies using EDI send their EDI transactions for all trading partners to a VAN. The VAN separates the EDI transactions by company and "inserts" them in the proper "electronic mailbox" maintained for each trading partner company. Once or twice each day, for example, XYZ Company will instruct its computer to dial the VAN's computer. All pending EDI transactions will be transmitted to the VAN for later distribution to the company's trading partners, and all EDI transactions waiting in the company's electronic mailbox will be extracted and sent to XYZ Company's computer. The added convenience of not having to establish direct links with each trading partner often justifies the cost of using a VAN.

Translation Software

Trading partners must agree on the specific format of each EDI transaction. The sequence, length, and permissible contents of each data field in the purchase order, for example, must be defined so that the trading partner's computer will be able to interpret what it has received. Therefore, the computer record for a purchase order as prepared by a company must be translated into the format individual trading partners expect. In some cases the format is simply one agreed on between two trading partners; in others, it is an industry standard. More and more often, however, one of the standard formats such as ANSI X.12 or EDIFACT (see next section) is used. Translation software accomplishes any required translations, thereby eliminating the need for trading partners to write custom translation programs.

STANDARDS

Document content standards for EDI transactions establish the format and context of data used in specific business documents. Most U.S. companies adhere to a set of standards known as ANSI X.12, developed and promulgated by the American National Standards Institute (ANSI). Internationally, the EDIFACT (EDI for Administration, Commerce, and Trade) standard is more important and has the support of the United Nations. (EDIFACT is sometimes labeled UN/EDIFACT.) There are strong efforts underway to reconcile ANSI X.12 with EDIFACT, thus establishing a single worldwide EDI standard. For some time, however, ANSI X.12 will remain important in North America and EDIFACT will be more important in Europe and in international trade generally. The Customs Cooperation Council, an organization of 104 national customs services including the U.S. customs service, is developing EDI standards for customs documents within the EDIFACT standard.

Electronic data interchange is easier to implement between trading partners if there is a single standard for their EDI transactions on which they can quickly agree. Until there is a single worldwide standard, however, translations between different formats can be accomplished using the translation software referred to earlier.

IMPACT ON HOW BUSINESS IS CONDUCTED

Individual companies using EDI can expect to achieve the benefits of speed, accuracy, and lower cost. In addition, EDI is changing the way companies do business in more important ways. The speed and accuracy of EDI permit companies to adopt more efficient business processes. In addition, EDI use promotes closer cooperation with a smaller number of trading partners. This process, called "partnering," is one in which a company reduces the number of suppliers it deals with for a particular part or commodity to a few and forms much closer relationships with those that remain, facilitated by EDI. Production schedules of suppliers are more closely tied to those of their customers in a "just-in-time" (JIT) inventory management environment, for example. Manufacturers ask their parts suppliers to adopt the same computer-aided design technology so that information on new parts specifications can be exchanged on a computer-to-computer basis.

Thus, many of the long-term benefits accruing to users of EDI are likely to arise from information systems developed in cooperation by two or more trading partners. Just as transaction processing systems have provided the data that make strategic information systems possible in the single-company environment, EDI is expected to provide the foundation for the strategic information systems that will be built in the interorganizational systems environment.

For Further Reading

Davis, H. 1988. *Electronic data interchange and corporate trade payments.* Morristown, N.J.: Financial Executives Research Foundation.

Emmelhainz, M. A. 1990. *Electronic data interchange: A total management guide.* New York: Van Nostrand Reinhold.

Sokol, P. K. 1989. *EDI: The competitive edge.* New York: Intertext Publications/McGraw-Hill.

Donald J. McCubbrey

ELECTRONIC DOCUMENT IMAGE PROCESSING AND MANAGEMENT

An electronic document image processing system is a computer-based system that converts the contents of paper documents to digitized images that can be viewed at a computer workstation. These digitized images can be held and manipulated in the memory of the computer, stored on magnetic or optical disk storage media, transmitted over networks and telephone lines, and converted back to a paper image by a laser printer.

An electronic document image processing system includes a scanner to convert a paper image to a digitized image, a computer with sufficient memory and monitor graphics capability to hold and present the digitized image, a magnetic or optical media drive to store images for processing and retrieval, and a laser printer. Additional hardware components may include network interfaces, erasable optical drives, optical jukeboxes, digitizing cameras, and other output devices such as plotters. Figure 1 illustrates an example system.

ELECTRONIC DOCUMENT IMAGE PROCESSING

In the typical business document image processing system, documents that enter the system are read by the scanner. Operation of

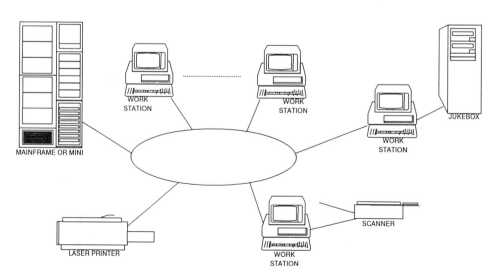

FIGURE 1. Example of an image processing management system.

the scanner is a clerical function that is performed as soon as possible after receipt of the documents by mail or other delivery service. The scanner converts the figures on paper to a sequence of binary codes representing the presence or absence of ink while the scanner moves horizontally across the paper image. Dots of the image are also called *pixels* or *picture elements.* The left-to-right top-to-bottom coded image is called a *rasterized image.* Typically, the binary coded image is displayed on a computer workstation monitor for review. An operator at the workstation can accept the image as an accurate image of the paper document or can rescan the document with adjustments to scanner settings. Adjusting the scanner is similar to adjusting a paper copier for different levels of darkness.

Upon operator acceptance, the image is given a unique identification code by the system and is stored in image storage. Computer indexes are prepared so that images can be located and retrieved. It is very common to have two or more different processes running on the workstation at the same time; for instance, the image reading process, image storage process, and indexing process may be operating concurrently.

When a document is scanned, the image consists of codes for thousands of tiny dark or light dots. As most documents will have relatively large amounts of white space codes, it is possible to reduce the number of coded spaces by replacing sequences of similar spaces with a unique code indicating the type and number of codes replaced. This is known as compression and is important in reducing storage requirements. Decompression reverses this process. Compression and decompression may be done in the workstation's memory or by an interface device attached to the workstation. Different image processing hardware configurations and topologies allocate the compression and decompression tasks between the user station and other computer units in the configuration differently. There is no standard configuration because most systems are customized for particular applications, but there are two general rules for systems. All systems compress image files before storing them and decompress the images before displaying

retrieved images, and the compression and decompression are done as close as possible to the display station to limit traffic on communication links.

Some workstations and scanners have optical character recognition (OCR) capabilities to identify characters and words from the coded images. This capability allows the system to index a text document by keywords, or from specific fields in a form document, without operator intervention.

Compressed images are stored on a random-access medium, magnetic or optical, for retrieval. Magnetic media disk drives offer faster retrieval of document images but are more expensive per megabyte of capacity than optical drives, and they have much less total capacity per drive. Optical drives have larger storage capacities (from hundreds of megabytes to gigabytes per drive) but have longer access times for images. Document images, even though they are compressed, require significant storage space. A typical document page, depending on the type of document and effect of compression, may require between 12,000 and 50,000 bytes of storage. This means that a gigabyte (approximately a billion bytes) of storage can store about 20,000 to 80,000 pages. Documents with much detail require scanning at higher resolution rates and significantly more storage space per page.

Applications determine the mix of magnetic storage and optical storage. A low-volume system used for archiving images that are not retrieved for immediate on-line access may use only optical disk storage. A customer service department may use magnetic media to store an image of a customer's letter while it is being processed by the department and then archive the document on optical storage until the next communication from the customer, at which time the system can bring the original image back to magnetic media. A transaction-based system, such as order entry, may use the scanned document image for data entry of information into an order database on magnetic media. After processing, the image may be archived on optical media.

The scheduling of retrievals to fit the application is a very important system efficiency design. Documents may be stored as single images or may be organized into "folders" containing several related documents. This allows the terminal operator to browse the folder quickly and allows the system to fetch the entire folder with a single request rather than waiting for a request by the operator for each page.

The following examples illustrate how document images are used in organizations:

- *Data entry:* A document may be retrieved and used as a data entry original (perhaps with the use of OCR to fill some data fields, reducing the keystrokes required of the data entry operator).

- *Customer service:* A document letter image may be retrieved by an operator in customer service, who attaches a note to the document in either image or computer text form and forwards the document image to a customer service representative, who may resolve the customer complaint, write a letter that will be attached to the image, and schedule both for printing and mail delivery.

- *Distributing copies:* A document image may be received via electronic mail by a manager, who decides that the document should be relayed to several subordinates. He or she sends a unique identifier of the document image via electronic mail so that as they each read their electronic mail the image management system will supply them with copies of the document image. Once an image is in the system, an unlimited number of copies of the image can be viewed at any one time. If an image is replaced by another, all subsequent copies will be the updated document image.

- *Distributing forms:* Paper forms needed by clients or customers of the organization can be stored as images. In response to a written, phone, or in-person request, the workstation operator retrieves the required forms and prints them. Generating forms this way reduces the amount of paper being stored by the organization, rids the organization of the task of searching through files or stacks of paper to find the required forms, and allows the organization to make modifications to forms and have the modifications in effect from a

particular date without having new forms printed and using up or discarding the old forms.

The laser printer is the final component of the typical image processing system. Any document scanned into the electronic image management system can be reproduced in paper form by the laser printer attached to the system. For the very few systems that have color images, there are several ways to reproduce color images: color laser printing, color photographs, and slides.

IMAGE PROCESSING EQUIPMENT

Scanners

Scanners come in several forms. The most popular scanner type for document image processing systems is the sheet feeder scanner. The sheet feeder scanner scans by moving a single sheet at a time through the scanner. There is a wide range of document throughput capacities for this type of scanner, and autofeed capability is available to assist the operator. Another form of scanner used for image input is the flatbed scanner, which uses a platform or table similar to a copier. A document is placed on a glass table and the scanner either moves the table over a scanning bar or moves the bar under the document. This is an excellent scanner for documents that are not in single sheet form. Of the many scanner types available, several combine the flatbed and sheet feeding capabilities. Handheld scanners, with a [3- to 4-inch scanning width, are used to input text or graphics for desktop publishing, but can be used for document image processing.

Image processing scanners have different levels of resolution and adjustable sensitivity. Most documents are scanned at a resolution level of 150 or 200 dots per inch, with more detailed images or master forms scanned at a resolution level of 300 dots per inch. Both lesser and greater resolution levels are available, depending on the application and laser printer capability. Also, for better graphic images, scanners are available that interpret the dots in a range of gray levels, which allows shading and other features of documents to be retained by the image system.

Computers

Image processing can be installed on almost any computing system. Mainframes, minicomputers, and personal workstations all have image processing systems available. The requirements follow:

- Computer monitors with graphics capability equal to or surpassing the Video Graphics Array (VGA) standard for personal computers

- Computer memory sufficient to hold the image processing program, an image, and any index or database programs linking the image (This requirement is very application specific. There are image compression and decompression coprocessors available as hardware options to speed this part of the image process.)

- Magnetic media to store system programs and folders of images (The amount is application specific. If a system is designed for rapid access and processing of images, it may store all images on magnetic media. Typically, there is a mix of magnetic and optical disk storage in an image processing system.)

Optical Storage

Optical storage systems have several advantages over magnetic storage systems. Optical storage systems cost much less per megabyte of storage than magnetic media storage systems. Optical storage is more reliable than magnetic media. The use of laser light and an optical system allows the reading and writing head to be ten times more distant from the media than it is for magnetic media. This distance and the plastic or glass covering of optical disks reduce the hazard of "head crashes," the most frequent cause of data loss in computing systems. Finally, the capacity of optical disks is much higher, up to hundreds of times the capacity of the equivalent-size magnetic disk.

Three types of optical media are used for storage of documents for image processing: (1) WORM, (2) rewritable or erasable, and (3) CD-ROM. WORM, or write-once-read-many optical technology, is the most popular for document image processing. WORM is excellent for archiving document images. The disks and drives are designed to allow the system to write to any area on the disk only one time, after which the data can only be read.

Erasable optical technology allows reuse of areas of the disk as if it were a magnetic medium. Erasable technology has the reliability and capacity of optical technology and the reusability of magnetic media. The erasable option requires additional protection procedures to protect valuable data.

CD-ROM, or compact-disk read-only memory media, is the technology for publishing retrieval-only applications. CD-ROM has a very large capacity and disk readers are inexpensive. For document image processing, drawbacks are the need to mass produce the disks to make them cost effective, the inability to write any additional information to the disk, and the slow access time because of the error detection and correction scheme required to compensate for manufacturing errors.

Optical jukeboxes are used for applications involving many disks. Optical media disks are stored in slots in the jukebox, retrieved by a mechanical device, and placed on a drive to be written or read by the computer system. The optical jukebox may have a number of drives and the drives may be of different types. The optical jukebox allows a large amount of optical storage to be accessed on-line, but there is a time delay of up to 10 seconds for access to a file on a disk. This is still a small amount of time compared with the time required to retrieve documents on microfilm or in a paper filing system and then to refile the documents.

EFFECTS OF DOCUMENT IMAGE MANAGEMENT SYSTEMS

An image processing system results in a large reduction of the amount of paper handled in the organization. Less storage space is required (a 12-inch optical disk will hold the equivalent of approximately 25 drawers of files). There is reduced need for clerical workers and equipment to retrieve paper files, and a reduction of missing files. Implicit in these benefits is a reduced cost for processing documents.

Additional organizational benefits include elimination of the need to refile microfilm and paper documents, which reduces the likelihood of misfiling and losing important documents. Image processing systems also aid in directing the flow of documents, or work flow, through the organization, and the system can maintain an audit trail for the documents. Documents can be linked with computer databases and files already in use in the organization and can be indexed in a number of ways.

For the users of documents, benefits include increased productivity from having documents available for immediate access at the user's workstation; the ability to share a document image with others; the ability to work concurrently with others on a document, without having to create additional copies; and the ability to mail any document electronically. Users wishing to reference documents by key words in the documents can have that ability with the incorporation of OCR into the system.

For documents that are archived to meet legal requirements, there is some concern that document images may not meet the requirements. A response to this conjecture has been that electronic images meet the best-available-evidence rule if the original has been destroyed. If litigation is expected, there are some options: retain all originals, probably off-site; be prepared to prove image integrity and security with expert witnesses; and be very careful with the use of rewritable or erasable media.

The first document image systems required custom design and integration. The cost limited the application to very high volume transaction-oriented applications. Decreases in the cost of the technologies used in systems, the appearance of system integrators with image processing experience, and experience in the workplace all indicate that document image processing is

an important technology for business systems.

[*See also:* Image Processing.]

For Further Reading

Held, G. 1987. *Data compression.* New York: Wiley. This is a recommended book on a fascinating subject. Included are programs to let the reader experiment with the subject.

McConnell, K., et al. 1989. *FAX: Digital facsimile technology and applications.* Norwood, Mass.: Artech House. There is a strong relationship between document image processing and facsimile. This reference is an excellent overview of the technology and communication standards.

Ranade, S., and J. Ng. 1990. *Systems integration for write-once optical storage.* Westport, Conn.: Meckler.

Saffady, W. 1987. *Optical storage technology 1987.* Westport, Conn.: Meckler. The author issues periodic reviews of this technology.

Stallings, W. 1990. *Business data communications.* New York: Macmillan.

Storer, J. 1988. *Data compression.* Rockville, Md.: Computer Science Press. An academic treatment of a very interesting subject.

Journals

The field of data communications, of which document image processing is an integral part, is evolving rapidly. Single text references are quickly out of date. I recommend that the reader review the more recent issues of the following journals for additional information on the topic.

Computer Communications. London/Stoneham, Mass.: Butterworth-Heinemann Ltd.

IEEE Journal on Selected Areas in Communications. New York: Institute of Electrical and Electronic Engineers.

IEEE NETWORK. New York: Institute of Electrical and Electronic Engineers.

Andrew Jansma

ELECTRONIC FUNDS TRANSFER

See Financial Services Computer Use in

ELECTRONIC MAIL

Electronic mail, sometimes called e-mail, is a communication tool that enables the noninteractive transmission of text, data, graphics, or audio messages between a sender and a designated recipient. The transport of such electronic objects can be between people, between people and computer software applications, or between applications only.

As the name implies, electronic mail is modeled after the mail services provided by the post office. Instead of being written and physically delivered by the postal service, messages are typed or scanned into an electronic mail system, addressed to a unique "mailbox," and then transmitted electronically.

The term *electronic mail* was first used to describe a messaging system developed for use on computers. Since then, the term has been used to depict a variety of different technologies and has become more generalized as a descriptive phrase.

Since its birth in the 1970s, electronic mail has grown into a worldwide, multibillion dollar business. Approximately 3 billion electronic mail messages were exchanged in 1988, and the volume is expected to grow to 16 billion in 1992 and 60 billion by the year 2000. Multinational corporations use it to manage their international sales forces and distribution services. University researchers around the world are linked together through a variety of electronic mail networks. Members of the White House, the Cabinet, and the Pentagon routinely use electronic mail for fast, efficient communication. Even students in different countries are using it to participate in long-distance learning projects with each other.

Electronic mail systems may be composed of one or a combination of several different technologies. Such systems can be implemented by means of computer-based messaging, telex, teletex, voice mail, and videotex. (For another related technology, see FAX.)

COMPUTER-BASED MESSAGING SYSTEMS

The "electronic mailbox" was invented in the early 1970s by researchers working for the U.S. Department of Defense under the Advanced Research Projects Agency Network (ARPANET). Software was written that allowed users of a computer to exchange messages among themselves. The computer program set up a unique mailbox for each user and provided all the tools needed to compose, send, receive, and file messages.

Computer-based messaging evolved into the comprehensive electronic mail systems of today. These programs have been written for almost every kind of computer, from mainframes to microcomputers. Even though computer-based messaging systems (CBMSs) differ widely as to capabilities, features, and ease of use, most share certain basic features. The software, for instance, is typically built around a word processor or text editor so messages, letters, and documents can be typed. Once the correspondence is drafted, it can then be sent to other users of the mail system by addressing it to their personal mailbox. When the intended recipient logs into the computer, the system gives notification that new mail is waiting.

The electronic mail system retains information on all correspondence such as the dates and times letters have been read, when they were sent, and from whom. Notification is also given when new mail has arrived. Any mail in a mailbox can be viewed by directing the system to display it on the monitor. It can then be deleted or saved as a file in a separate "file cabinet." Carbon copies, distribution lists, directories, calendars, interactive messaging, and notification of phone messages are a few of the services offered.

The newest generation of CBMSs provides several advanced features. Previously, electronic mail was limited to transmissions of textual information only. Now, binary (nontext) files may be sent as attachments to an electronic mail message. It becomes quite easy, therefore, to send graphics files, digitized images, and executable programs through the mail. Some vendors are also working to integrate their electronic mail products with other programs such as database software, libraries, and archival services. In these cases, a person might, for instance, send a mail message to a personnel database asking for information on staff positions. The database application would process the request and return a response by electronic mail.

Early computer-based messaging systems were computer specific and could not exchange mail with systems running on other computers. Now it is possible for any number of dissimilar mail systems running on a variety of different computers to exchange mail. Unfortunately, electronic mail connectivity grew up in the absence of any international standards of communication, leaving incompatibilities and gaps in service between mail systems. In an effort to enable comprehensive communications services, a major attempt is being made to provide international standards and protocols. In 1984, the Consulting Committee for International Telephone and Telegraph (CCITT) approved the X.400 Message Handling Facility. This standard has received broad support and holds great promise for the widespread interconnection of electronic mail systems.

TELEX AND TWX

Telex evolved from the telegram, which was itself developed over a hundred years ago and remains the earliest example of an electronic mail system. Since the 1930s, telex has proved to be the most enduring electronic messaging system for text, with about 1.2 million terminals around the world.

Also known as a teletypewriting system, telex is an international teleprinting service based on the transmission of textual information. There are two forms of telex that use different protocols, telex I and telex II; telex II is also known as TWX (teletypewriter exchange). International telex service lines link teletypewriters together, and messages typed on one machine are immediately transferred to another where they are printed. Depending on the equipment, information can also be kept on disk or magnetic tape for later transmission.

Current systems have been updated to provide store-and-forward features, distribution lists, and computer-controlled switching. Telex centers can also now be reached using teletypewriters, advanced terminals, computers, and telephones. Mail "gateways" are also available that allow the exchange of mail between computer-based messaging systems and telex terminals.

TELETEX

Teletex is relatively new and should not be confused with telex. The teletex recommendations were laid down in 1980, and thus far, the systems are used primarily in Europe, particularly in West Germany, Sweden, and the United Kingdom.

Teletex services can operate on current communications networks that support the teletex communication protocol. These networks support a mix of terminal types including full-capacity word processors, multifunction workstations, electronic typewriters, and dumb terminals. A variety of text processors, therefore, can be accommodated through this technology and used to transmit textual information from one site to another.

VOICE MAIL

The first voice mail system was purchased and installed by the 3M Company in 1980. As the name implies, voice mail systems transmit the human voice, or any audio input, in much the same way as other technologies transmit data, text, or graphics. Typically, these systems use a computer to handle telephone calls over a local PBX (private branch exchange). The telephone, then, becomes a "terminal" for inputting and receiving information.

In many ways, voice mail functions like a sophisticated telephone answering machine. A phone call is answered with prerecorded instructions, and at the tone, the caller can leave a verbal message. The sound is converted into digital signals for storage on the disk drive of a computer. Later, the recipient can retrieve the message by phoning the system, dialing in an access code, and checking a personal voice mailbox. The stored signals are then reconverted to a verbal output and played back to the recipient over the phone.

Features of voice mail allow one to listen to a caller, make a reply, and cancel, delete, replay, or send messages. Stored messages can be played back as many times as desired. Multiple copies can also be made easily and sent to other people on the system. One can also integrate voice mail with computer-based messaging systems by using a voice synthesizer to read a textual electronic mail message over the telephone.

VIDEOTEX

Only recently have videotex systems been developed that fall into the category of electronic mail technologies. The CCITT recommendations treat it as an interactive rather than a store-and-forward medium, but current developments in videotex usage with computers allow the classification of these systems to fall under the definition of electronic mail.

When the technology first became popularized in the 1970s, the most common use of videotex was to transfer pages of information from a central site to a television over phone lines, coaxial cable, or standard television broadcasts. The viewer simply selected a television channel to view listings of products, announcements, news, schedules, activities, and other information.

Interactive videotex systems have since been developed that carry text, voice, and video signals to the consumer and accept responses to the information viewed on the screen through the use of additional equipment, such as a keypad or keyboard. Services are provided such as banking, shopping, or the booking of travel reservations. Again, though, these types of videotex systems lack the store-and-forward features of electronic mail.

In the 1980s, videotex software was developed to run on computers. In such cases, a computer can be used to access memos, reports, manuals, weather reports, sales data, or any other textual information interactively. Some systems also handle graphics and digitized images. System subscribers can add their own information for public viewing.

The technology is rapidly evolving beyond even these capabilities. Videotex is being integrated into electronic mail systems so that selected text can be easily copied into an electronic mail message. Other advancements allow the user to send commands to a videotex system through electronic mail messaging. The videotex system processes the query and transmits the requested information to the appropriate mailbox. Because the transport of electronic objects in this case is between a person and a software application, this usage conforms to the definition of an electronic mail technology.

[*See also:* Fax; Videotex.]

For Further Reading

Alter, A. E. 1989. The long hello. *CIO: The Magazine for Information Executives* 2(12): 47–59.

Cross, T. B., and M. B. Raizman. 1986. *Networking: An electronic mail handbook.* London: Scott, Foresman.

Gabriel, M. R. 1989. *A guide to the literature of electronic publishing: CD-ROM, desktop publishing, and electronic mail.* Greenwich, Conn.: JAI Press.

Mortensen, E. 1989. Electronic mail is one of many different technologies. *The Office,* August, pp. 24–37.

Neither rain, nor sleet, nor computer glitches. *Business Week,* 8 May 1989, p. 135.

Parfett, M. C. 1985. *Teletex: A practical evaluation guide.* Manchester: NCC Publications.

Pyne, A. M. 1988. Future developments in electronic messaging. In *Electronic message systems 88.* London: Blenheim Online Publications.

Stidd, J. 1988. The coming impact of electronic mail. In *Enterprise conference proceedings.* Dearborn, Mich.: Society of Manufacturing Engineers.

Vallee, J. 1984. *Computer message systems.* New York: McGraw-Hill.

Vervest, P. H. M. 1986. *Innovation in electronic mail.* Amsterdam: Elsevier Science.

James R. Neill

END USER COMPUTING

Traditionally, people who work with computers have been divided into two categories: computer professionals, for whom computer work comprises the core of their work responsibilities; and *end users,* for whom the computer is merely a tool in achieving their functional work in marketing, finance, and other corporate functions. They were originally called end users because they were the final or "end" users of computer systems developed by computer professionals. Given this distinction, end user computing can be defined as any computing work done primarily by end users under their own control.

While end user computing can be defined very simply, it is an evolving concept. This article discusses end user computing in terms of its historical evolution, beginning with its early days and discussing how it is likely to change in the future.

An important theme in this history is the idea of end user control. In the early days of computing, end users had little control over the computing process. Computer professionals were treated as experts to whom users should defer. But as end users grew in expertise, and as computers became cheaper and easier to use, end users began to exercise more and more control over their computing environment. Today, end user computing is far larger than information systems professional computing, and end user control has become pervasive in corporations.

A second, related theme is the relative roles of end users and end user departments, on the one hand, and the corporate information systems (IS) group, a staff group created to manage and support corporate information technology, on the other hand.

The third major theme will be the importance of *power users*—people who work in functional departments such as marketing and finance and have functional jobs in those areas but who also have considerably more computer knowledge than the average worker.

ERA 1: EXPERT DEVELOPMENT USING THE TRADITIONAL SYSTEMS DEVELOPMENT LIFE CYCLE

In the early days of computers, the complexity of programming meant that the experts in the IS group had to create all new applications. End users did what these programs required of them in terms of input. This was an era of high central control of computing by computer professionals.

Because application development was complex and prone to error, a disciplined development process was created. This was known as the SYSTEMS DEVELOPMENT LIFE CYCLE (SDLC). The SDLC consists of a number of steps, to be performed in order, with each step completed before the next is begun. In general, the idea is to be sure you know what you are going to do before jumping into the details of application development.

Early steps in the SDLC are controlled by a *systems analyst,* who is skilled at analyzing and developing procedures.

After requirements have been clearly laid out and the entire system has been defined, the work of developing the required software is done by a programmer. The programmer develops and tests the required programs. The systems analyst manages the implementation of systems, including required training.

The role of end users in a traditional SDLC is to provide complete and correct requirements and then wait for the implementation of the system.

ERA 2: END USER DEVELOPMENT

During the 1960s and 1970s, computers became somewhat easier to program as simpler programming languages, such as BASIC, emerged and as interactive time-sharing began to replace batch processing. In addition, many users had relatively simple needs that did not require the skills needed to develop large applications such as payroll systems. Finally, there was so much work to be done that the IS group was badly overloaded. The backlog of work waiting to be done averaged two or three years, so end users were faced with long waits even if they could get their jobs approved.

The first end users to take matters into their own hands were scientists and engineers. By the late 1960s, many technical academic programs began to teach FORTRAN programming, and by the mid-1970s, it was common to see technologists writing their own programs.

By the late 1970s, managers too began to develop some of their applications. While some managers learned BASIC and other "third-generation" programming languages, most managerial end users were using simpler "fourth-generation" programming tools that allowed them to do with reasonable ease such limited but important things as generate reports from corporate data files and even develop simple record-keeping applications. Although not many managers actually used such tools, the phenomenon was sufficiently pronounced for IS specialists to take notice. The term *end user computing* was born.

Because tools for application development were extremely complex during the 1970s, corporations generally saw a need to provide assistance to end users and to provide some degree of control over end-user computer use. Typically, a specialized unit was developed inside the IS group. This was the *information center.*

The information center has three main functions. The first is to manage the technological infrastructure, that is, hardware, software, and communications. Generally, the information center maintains a list of "supported" products. Other products either are forbidden or are allowed only with the understanding that they will not be supported. The information center helps users specify purchases, often makes the purchase itself, installs hardware, software, and communications, and fixes technical problems.

The second function of the information center is support. The information center generally provides general tool training, consulting on individual end user projects, and

hotline support to answer user questions if they get into trouble.

The third function of the information center is control. Often, the information center requires users to justify individual purchases, although how to evaluate these justifications is a matter of considerable debate. A few information centers also audit computer uses and specific applications to make sure that general principles of good practice are being followed.

ERA 3: THE PERSONAL COMPUTER ERA

Note that end user computing initially meant something very specific, namely end user development of programmed applications. This was because application development was the only way to use computers without central corporate application development specialists. But this limitation changed rapidly in the 1980s, as personal computers increased in number and made available to end users a way of using computers that did not involve programming at all.

This new way of using computers was typified by word processing and spreadsheet analysis—the dominant uses of personal computing in business. Both are called applications, but this is a new use for the term. Instead of writing specific programmed applications for individual tasks, users bought an "application package" to handle a wide variety of writing or modeling tasks.

Developing models with a spreadsheet program is much simpler than developing a programmed application. Although these packages include embedded programming languages, such as the Lotus 1-2-3 macro language, only advanced users usually learn to use them.

With use greatly simplified, end user computer use exploded. At the start of the 1980s, few managers and professionals used computers; but by the start of the 1990s, a large majority of managers were using computers as an integral part of their daily work. By every measure, end user computing is now far larger than the traditional centrally developed information system applications.

The SDLC process is not usually applied in the development of end user systems, such as spreadsheet models for evaluating purchases. First, these systems are much smaller, so that the traditional SDLC process is not required. In addition, the SDLC requires that the problem be understood before any actual development begins; but managers and professionals often face poorly understood problems and use modeling, writing, and other computer work to help them understand the problem.

Therefore, for end user computing, a different development approach is usually used. This is *iterative* development, in which an initial model or document draft is built on the basis of initial understanding of the problem. This initial draft or model is carefully tested for errors and used to help get a better understanding of the problem. This leads to another iteration of conceptualization, development, and testing, culminating in a better application. Several of these disciplined iterations may be necessary to develop a model, document, database application, graphics image, or other output.

End users must also perform a number of ongoing tasks that were handled by computer professionals for large systems. They must back up their own data and programs, protect their equipment and data against theft and other threats, and plan their future requirements.

During much of the 1980s, end user computing focused on individual uses. But a great deal of end user computing is a departmental matter, not just an individual matter. Planning must be done for entire departments, and procedures implemented to share applications and to retain the value in end user systems when the developers leave the position. As an example, one marketing department staff member may develop a spreadsheet tool or other application for another member of that department; it needs to be of high quality. When someone leaves the department, his or her data files, models, and other files must be "handed off" for others to use and maintain.

GROUP PRODUCTIVITY TOOLS

By 1990, more than 80 percent of office workers used computers on a regular basis.

Information exchange among computer users is a major problem. Many organizations have responded to these needs by installing personal computer networks.

The networking environment presents new challenges. First, one networking professional is needed for approximately every twenty-five network users. In addition, training in data communications technology is required for both users and support personnel.

A new family of applications has emerged, known as *group productivity tools* to distinguish them from traditional personal productivity tools such as spreadsheet analysis tools on personal computers. (See also COOPERATIVE WORK SYSTEMS.)

One of the new applications is electronic mail, which may be viewed as an "unstructured" group productivity tool, because it does not impose a specific way of working on people. Another set of groupware tools supports group decision making and group writing. These tools require the work to be done in a certain way. New tools are likely to be "structurable" to allow users to structure their own work processes.

PROFESSIONAL DEVELOPMENT FOR NONDATA APPLICATIONS

The distinction between management information systems and end user computing has often been viewed as a dichotomy. Management information system applications are large, involved structured data files and are centrally developed; end user applications are seen as small, involve many types of information, and are developed by users. However, there are many important applications that do not involve procedural data processing but are too large for end users to develop themselves.

One example is the executive information system (EIS). As the name suggests, these systems are defined for individual executives or for groups of executives. An EIS typically appears to the user as a menu-based system that gives access to information from many sources inside and outside the corporation. The information may consist of several corporate databases as well as external news services and external financial services. Putting together such systems is very difficult—far beyond the abilities of typical end users. As a result, corporations need to develop EIS development and maintenance teams to create them and keep them going.

Another example is decision support systems (DSS). Whereas an EIS focuses on bringing together information from a wide variety of sources, a DSS marshals resources to support a specific decision, such as whether to purchase a competitor. This normally requires three things: specific data, specific analytical models, and a user interface to present information graphically and to tie everything together. In practice, the model working with the data will present the potential value of the purchase given certain assumptions, such as purchase price. The user varies these assumptions to assess whether the purchase is justified under a wide variety of conditions. The DSS supports the decision maker by carrying out calculations, which is a difficult task for users, while leaving the tasks of varying assumptions and making the final decision to the human user.

[*See also* Decision Support Systems; Executive Information Systems.]

For Further Reading

Carr, H. H. 1988. *Managing end user computing.* Englewood Cliffs, N. J.: Prentice-Hall.

Kaiser, K. M., and H. J. Oppelland. 1990. *Desktop information technology.* Amsterdam: North-Holland.

Nelson, R. R. 1989. *End-user computing: Concepts, issues, and applications.* New York: Wiley.

Panko, R. R. 1988. *End user computing: Management, applications, and technology.* New York: Wiley.

Raymond R. Panko

ENGINEERING

[*Computers play a vital role in all phases of engineering. The articles listed here give an insight into this role from the initial design phase through the final implementation phase.* Constraint Satisfaction in Mechanical Engineering Design *discusses a state-of-the-art approach in which computers are being used in the design phase;* Artificial Intelligence in Engineering Design *elucidates the ways in which the techniques of artificial intelligence can be used in this area; and* Solid Modeling and Finite Element Analysis *discusses the ways in which computers support the design of components in the automotive industry.* Manufacturing Engineering *shows how computers are used to manage the entire manufacturing process. Finally,* Robotics *covers this very important productivity-enhancing, multidisciplinary field.*]

EQUITY ISSUES AND COMPUTERS

By the year 2000, about 85 percent of new workers will be minorities, women, and immigrants. Changing needs in the work force require more workers prepared to handle technical jobs, and the nation requires a population that is scientifically, mathematically, and computer literate. The untapped potential of women, minorities, and the disabled could help meet these needs. The National Science Board report on *Educating Americans for the 21st Century* (1983) said it well: "By 1995, the Nation must provide, for all its youth, a level of mathematics, science and technology education that is the finest in the world, without sacrificing the American birthright of personal choice, equity and opportunity" (p. v). Computers and so-called "high-technology" now permeate virtually every work environment, from auto parts stores and fast food restaurants to savings banks and insurance offices, yet for large numbers of students the supply of appropriate role models, facilities, and instruction is lacking.

CURRENT STATUS OF EQUITY PROBLEMS

In our nation's schools, the number of computers being installed has been growing steadily since the early 1980s. The average computer:student ratio is 1:16. Yet access to computers and technology continues to be skewed, limiting access for many students both to knowledge and skills and to future employment opportunities. In 1986, the National Assessment of Educational Progress conducted a nationwide computer examination and survey of student attitudes. The results of the assessment were summarized in the 1988 report on computer competence. Key findings included significant differences based on race, ethnicity, and gender:

> There are clear racial/ethnic differences in computer competence, favoring White students over Black and Hispanic students. These differences are present even between students who have comparable levels of experience. But the differences are accentuated by greater experience with computers among White students. (Martinez and Mead 1988, p. 6)

Whites scored higher than African-American and Hispanic students in assessments of computer competence at all grade levels tested (3, 5, 8, and 11). The greatest competence was found among those who both had computers at home and were studying computers in school. The largest group of students in this category was white males. In all three computer experience categories asked about in the survey—use, instruction, and home access—whites were shown to have an advantage and achieve higher competence scores (Martinez and Mead 1988). Males scored higher in computer competence than females across all grade levels tested. Here again, access is the issue, in that boys were slightly more likely than girls to have used a computer, and, especially in the upper grades, boys were more likely than girls to have access to a computer at home (Martinez and Mead 1988).

Gender Differences

Although girls may have the same access to computers in a given school, they tend not to be involved with computers unless it is required. They opt out of advanced classes and extracurricular activities that use computers (Fredman 1990). The Computer Equity Training Project at the Women's Action Alliance, New York, has identified a number of subtle factors, listed here, that keep girls away from computers:

Why Girls Opt Out of Computing:

1. The chicken and the egg pattern: Girls consider computers unfeminine because they see mostly boys using them.
2. Girls stay out of the computer room because their girlfriends aren't there—an important social dynamic.
3. Schools often make computers available for optional use on a first-come, first-served basis, and boys, in their enthusiasm for the machines, aggressively capture the opportunities.
4. Most girls find Logo an interesting computer language, but most schools teach BASIC.
5. One student to each computer—the usual school arrangement—doesn't meet girls' needs for social interaction. (Sanders 1985, cited in Fredman 1990, p. 1)

Reasons for girls' negative perceptions of computers include the fact that computers are often associated with mathematics, and girls have learned to avoid math. Computer games have traditionally involved attacking various "enemies" with large arsenals of "weapons" or with martial arts, activities most girls have not been encouraged to embrace. Role models for girls are also lacking of women using computers either on advertising or in television and movies (Fredman 1990).

Racial Inequities

Inequities also exist in the access to computers among and within schools with different minority student populations. An example of such inequitable access can be seen in Table 1, which shows the prerequisites for a basic computer programming course in the six high schools in a medium-sized school district in a large southeastern state. In this district there are six different sets of prerequisites for the same basic computer programming course at each of that district's six high schools. It is obvious that minority students in this district do not have the same access to computers as their white peers.

These data reveal several problems. First, decisions with impact on equity are being made at the school level with little or

TABLE 1. Course Prerequisites for Basic Computer Programming in One School District

School	Minority Student Enrollment	Requirements for Basic Computer Programming Course
A	15%	No prerequisite
B	35%	Algebra 1 with grade of C
C	38%	Algebra 1 with grade of C
D	51%	Geometry corequisite
E	53%	Geometry honors prerequisite; Algebra 2 corequisite
F	97%	Course not offered

no knowledge of district policies or of practices at other schools. Second, although it may appear to be a conscious conspiracy, it is not that. Rather it is the result of differential expectations that are based on stereotypes and misconceptions about the motivation, abilities, and behaviors of certain groups of students. Third, it may be that the course in computer programming is not offered at the minority school because that school does not have the computers or the staff available to teach the course.

"Differently Abled" Students

Computers have the capacity to allow physically and developmentally different students to compete on an equal footing with so-called normal students. As Fredman (1990) put it in a recent International Society for Technology in Education publication, "For students with physical and developmental handicaps, using the computer unlocks their potential. It is an enabling tool—allowing them to function as other students function without the barriers that their handicaps impose" (p. 47). Yet these students are often prevented from having access to computers because the computers are housed in laboratories that are not wheelchair accessible or because they cannot communicate with the computer using a traditional keyboard. Special input devices and speech synthesizers have been developed to remediate this situation, but teachers, counselors, and parents often lack the information to make this equipment available. (See DISABLED, TECHNOLOGY FOR THE.) Computers can allow developmentally or behaviorally different stu-

dents to circumvent problems with memory, perception, or communication so that they can spend their energy on learning rather than laborious calculations or writing (Fredman 1990). Too often, however, these students are not allowed the "privilege" of using the computer lab, or they are limited to remedial drill and practice applications.

Unrealized Potential of Computers

Computers in schools can provide motivation, improve attitude, and increase student learning. They can also provide nonbiased and patient feedback and individualized instruction for both basic skills and higher-order cognitive activities. Yet computers are being used more for remediation and drill-and-practice activities than for enhancement and strengthening of higher-order skills, especially with traditionally underachieving students. This limits the potential for creative involvement with technology for these students, increases the "technology gap," and may turn students off to computers (Astrein and Steinberg 1985). The underutilization of challenging computer software is amplified by the lack of teacher preparation for using computers. In a recent summary of research on mathematics learning, for example, the following conclusions were made:

> Computers have an abundance of exciting math applications—in geometry, simulations, and equation solving, for instance—that most schools have not begun to tap . . . Many teachers lack the skills to implement more advanced computer applications. They may also be insecure about their own computer literacy. In the haste to acquire microcomputers and be on the cutting edge, many

school districts skimped on teacher training and support services. (Kober 1991, p. 35)

The issue of teacher preparation is well recognized, but is only slowly being addressed in a systematic manner. In 1989, the National Education Association's *Special Committee on Educational Technology Report* recommended that "all schools should develop and implement a plan to install a computer with adequate software on the desk of each teacher by 1991" (p. 6). The goal is far from being reached, even in the most progressive states.

In the results of their survey, the Wirthlin Group (1989) reported that 32 percent of the teachers polled *do not* use computers for instruction, even though they teach in districts where computers are used in other classes. Another 2 percent, or 58,000 teachers, do not use computers *and* computers are not used in their districts for instruction. Thirty-eight percent of the teachers polled said that inadequate training or experience among teachers was one of the greatest obstacles to more effective use of computers for instruction. Next to the lack of resources, it was the second most frequently cited obstacle to more effective use of computers. Computer access by minority children is particularly limited by these conditions because teachers in financially strapped inner cities and rural areas, communities that often have large minority populations, are most affected by these obstacles.

SOLVING EQUITY PROBLEMS

When confronting the problem of equity and access to computers and technology, strategies can be applied at several levels: at the state level, the district level, in the school, and in the classroom.

State-Level Strategies

There are at least three roles that education leaders and policy makers can take to close the gap in participation and achievement for underrepresented students using computers. One role is to provide accountability by documenting the institutional and systemic obstacles, such as the prerequisite disparity cited earlier, that prevent certain groups of students from being successfully involved with technology. Another role is to provide assistance and support to schools through incentives and grant programs. A third role is to identify and promote effective practices that address the needs of these groups of students.

Accountability   A primary role for the state is in the area of accountability, that is, documenting the indicators of disproportionate participation. The comparison among schools documented earlier is an example of the work that can be done at the state or district level to highlight inequitable situations that may otherwise go unnoticed. These discriminatory policies are a symptom of the stereotypes and misconceptions that people have about who can "do" computers and technology. To help people recognize the obstacles to participation and achievement that their misconceptions create, the state can continue to collect, analyze, and publicize data of this type. Then, efforts can begin to remove the obstacles and achieve the goals that have been established for all students to be successful in the application and use of technology. For example, the state of Florida now has the capability to monitor course enrollment at the secondary level by race, gender, and limited English proficiency. This capability will be used to publicize school-by-school data about *which* students are taking which courses. Because of Florida's common course numbering system and curriculum frameworks, the content of a given course is standard across the state, so it is easy to identify systematic differences in the content students with different demographic characteristics are experiencing.

Incentives and priority funding   Another avenue for the state to address equity goals is by tying funding for grants and entitlements to district attention to the needs of underrepresented students. For example, one state's $7 million Instructional Technology Challenge Grant program gave priority funding to districts that focused their grant proposals on increasing the access and involvement of female, minority, and disabled students. Existing programs can also be refocused on integrating technology. Staff development workshops can be reorganized to use technology as an integral part of any subject area training. In one school district, a state entitlement for elementary teacher enhancement training in mathematics and science was used to instruct teachers in the use of LEGO TC Logo, a program that interfaces the computer with the popular toy to teach physics and geometry. This activity was featured at a state conference as an exemplary use of state funds, and other districts were encouraged to replicate the workshops.

Collaboration among universities, community colleges, and school districts can also be encouraged through targeted state-level funding to restructure teacher preparation programs to produce teachers better prepared to use computers at both the elementary level and the secondary level. Federal programs such as the Eisenhower Mathematics and Science Program can be directed toward this effort.

Funding incentives send the clear message to schools, parents, and communities that addressing the needs of underrepresented students is priority. These incentives encourage schools to keep the issues of equity and access prominent in every educational improvement activity they undertake.

Innovative programs The national school restructuring movement is also an avenue for improving student access to computers. Restructuring often helps students of varied backgrounds to improve learning and achievement. Project CHILD (Computers Helping Instruction and Learning Development) is a technology-based restructuring project in Florida at the elementary-school level. The program has been developed over the past 2 years, and this year six demonstration schools will be established. One of the schools in Miami is 100 percent nonwhite (largely African-American and Hispanic). Students work with computers and direct their own learning; teachers teach in specialty areas in teams that continue for 3 years with the same students. The sense of community developed with the team of teachers over 3 years and the capability for students to progress at individual rates have been found to increase student achievement. This type of

learning environment may be more successful for female and minority students because of the ongoing support and the opportunity for consistent and frequent use of technology.

Another statewide restructuring effort in Florida, called the Blueprint for Career Preparation, calls for the infusion of career preparation, including technology education, in all subject areas. Schools are linked from kindergarten through postsecondary school so that students continue to follow the *Blueprint* as they move through the educational system. The study of science and technology begins in elementary school with an applied, integrated curriculum. Computers are used as both tools for and subjects of instruction. Middle-school students study technical literacy and develop career plans that tell them the academic and computer knowledge they need to succeed in their chosen careers. All the participating schools make an effort to integrate technology into their instruction.

Enrichment The state can fund activities such as computer contests and summer camps that are offered throughout the country at schools, community colleges, universities, and science museums. Many summer camps are targeted to disadvantaged students who pay a minimal fee or attend free. Camp themes range from an astronaut's camp, which emulates the physical and computer training that astronauts experience, to a COAST (Consortium of Adolescent Science Teams) camp, which involves high-potential minority middle-school students in three different locations collecting marine data and then using computers and modems to exchange their findings.

Recognition Recognizing outstanding programs in computer education is another approach that states can take to ensure access and achievement for all students. Awards and publications featuring successful programs can reinforce ongoing efforts and encourage new activities and programs. Federal recognition programs such as the U.S. Department of Education's National Diffusion Network provide information and contacts so that interested schools and districts can replicate successful projects. States and school districts have developed similar recognition programs. Examples of outstanding local programs that have been recognized include Chapter 1 HOTS (Higher Order Thinking Skills), which builds basic skills through creative challenges using the computer; Computer Buddies, which pairs gifted and educable, mentally disabled elementary school students; and the Computer Resource Center at the Florida School for the Deaf and Blind, which allows hearing- and vision-impaired students to communicate electronically with each other and with other students around the state.

Local and District Efforts

Schools and school districts are implementing many approaches to increase the involvement of all students with the use of technology. Many of these strategies involve partnerships with businesses or higher education institutions that contribute equipment and expertise.

Business and community partnerships One successful approach is to develop magnet schools in schools or neighborhoods where students have traditionally had little access to enrichment programs and state-of-the-art technology. A large inner-city middle school near an IBM office was able to obtain computers donated for a magnet "school within a school." Another successful strategy combines the use of technology, cooperative learning, and interdisciplinary curricula. The use of technology and cooperative learning has been successful with at-risk students at a middle school funded with a grant from Apple Equal Time. Students use HyperCard software on their Macintosh computers to teach each other about science and social studies as well as to keep their course work organized.

Research indicates that the context of learning about and using computers directly affects the involvement of female and minority students. Planning learning in contexts that are meaningful to them, for example, work applications or home, family, and community, produced positive responses and involvement. Involving parents, community members, businesses, universities, government, and other out-of-school resources and settings also contributed to maintaining a meaningful context (Cole and Griffin 1987).

Staff development One way to address the technological education needs of minorities and women is to educate teachers, parents, and other school personnel to increase their expectations and support of traditionally marginalized groups (Cole and Griffin 1987). There are several areas to be addressed in staff development programs. First, the conception that "If there is quality instruction, it will meet the needs of traditionally underrepresented groups," must be replaced by the notion that "If instruction is designed to meet the needs of underrepresented students, it will be good for all students." Strategies that are effective for girls and minorities, such as cooperative learning, applied problem solving, and use of meaningful context, as mentioned earlier, have been shown to increase learning for all students.

Second, teachers need assistance with changing the status expectations of students for one another in heterogeneous groups (Malcolm et al. 1984). Research with gender differences in science learning discovered that even when girls had developed confidence in their abilities, boys' expectations of them limited the girls' successful participation and learning in hands-on activities. Cooperative groups need to define students' roles so that each student has the opportunity to contribute to the accomplishment of learning tasks and to acquire the respect of her or his peers.

Third, counselors need to be made aware of their biases and ensure that they actively counsel traditionally underrepresented students into technical and higher-level courses and activities. Equity offices have uncovered many instances of female and African-American children with borderline test scores and grades being counseled out of advanced math and computer courses while their white male peers in the same category are given a chance to pursue those courses.

Fourth, school administrators must ensure access to computers for differently abled students by rearranging computers in labs and classrooms, if necessary. Federal programs, including the Education for the Handicapped Act, have made millions of dollars in funds available for technology in special education, so parents, teachers, and administrators need to locate and take advantage of the resources available in each state under this program. Most important, principals need to work with school districts and states to make sure that teachers have what they need to meet the computer requirements of all their students.

Student recruitment There is a misconception that the inclusion of minority, female, and disabled students in advanced courses and enrichment activities means that standards must be lowered. All minority students are not in need of remediation, and all students who require remediation are not minorities. Schools can change entrance requirements for special and gifted programs to include alternative criteria to test scores, such as portfolios and parent recommendations, so that a wider variety of students have an opportunity to participate. Talented minority, female, and disabled students should be aggressively sought out and recruited for activities involving creative applications of computers, such as computer clubs, contests, and summer camps.

Intervention programs The characteristics of effective intervention programs have been identified in several reports that have reviewed and identified successful programs (Clewell et al. 1987, Cole and Griffin 1987, Malcolm et al. 1984, McBay 1986). The findings are summarized here:

1. Successful intervention programs balance academics, attitudes, and motivation. Motivated students who have a positive attitude but no academic skills have no more success than those who have the skills but are afraid or unsure whether or how to use them. Programs for female students often focus on attitudinal rather than instructional activities. Although this is an important area, the knowledge deficits that exist as a result of early unfavorable attitudes must be compensated for as well. Programs for minorities, on the oth-

er hand, often address academic achievement without enough attention to motivational factors such as expanded career opportunities.

2. Successful programs have long-term investments both by participants and by sponsors. Students are involved more than one year. Funding and resources are integrated from many sources to reduce costs and ensure investment in success from a broad range of people.

3. Successful programs are staffed by members of target groups. Obviously, there is a shortage of such individuals, so alternatives are needed, such as visits to and from appropriate role models in the community or videotapes of these individuals at work.

4. Successful intervention programs emphasize contexts for learning that are meaningful to the target students, including "real-world" application and careers.

Model intervention programs include SECME (Southeast Consortium for Minorities in Engineering) and Girls', Inc. Operation SMART (Science, Math and Relevant Technology), both of which involve business and community partnerships and are available to schools and districts nationwide.

Classroom Teaching Strategies

In addition to intervention programs, teachers can implement strategies in their classrooms with the varying degrees of support necessary. Some can be implemented with little or no additional training, and some require additional physical, logistical, and educational resources.

Using the computer as a tool Computers can be an integral part of daily activity in any classroom. Whether the computer is used to collect scientific data on a spreadsheet, write and illustrate poetry, access a database for a research project, explore a foreign country through a simulation, or review basic mathematics skills, both teachers and students must be given the skills and opportunity to use the computer as a tool for learning. Software applications such as spreadsheets and graphs, science data probes, computer network activities, and simulations are available and being used successfully around the country. Staff development for teachers and the placement of computers in classrooms rather than in specialized labs are necessary to implement this strategy.

Focusing on higher-order skills Higher-order skills can be emphasized even at beginning levels. Basic skills are most effectively learned through higher-order thinking activities. Learning hierarchically detaches and "turns off" students, especially those from already disadvantaged groups. The gap between low and high achievers is increased by restricting low achievers to role learning (Resnick 1987). Programs such as HOTS, mentioned earlier under Recognition, are being used successfully to engage so-called remedial students in higher-level computer activities.

Problem solving A problem-solving approach gives students a purpose for learning and for using computers, and research has shown that successful computer learning is need driven. If the creative use of computers continues to be restricted to advanced students, minority and female students may develop a skewed perception of the potential of the technology. Using computers for remediation, although novel at first, over time reinforces negative attitudes toward the medium as well as the content. The potential for computers to inspire new interest in learning is lost if drill-and-practice is the sole experience students are given.

Cooperative grouping Classrooms and curricula can be organized around activity-centered, heterogeneous, cooperative groups—not ability tracking. Students can learn from one another as they use computers to solve problems. Cooperative grouping makes learning time more effective and increases higher-order thinking. This approach requires appropriate activities and evaluation schemes that enhance interaction and reduce status differences. Specific grouping plans and activities have been developed at various research centers, for example, Johns Hopkins University in Baltimore. Their models and

others are being widely used in staff development workshops around the country.

Networking Electronic computer networks can link minority students and teachers across the country and can allow interaction between minority students in this country and students of the same ethnic background in another country where they may not be the minority. Electronic communication via computers allows an exchange of ideas and feelings that can empower students to be active learners and can motivate students to stay involved with technology by showing a broader purpose for its use. *National Geographic*'s Kids Network is a national curriculum project that links students electronically working on projects to collect data about the environment.

Computer authoring Perhaps the most interesting recent development in computer applications is hypermedia. This type of software allows teachers and students to author their own computer-based interactive instructional programs, complete with graphics, sound, and the ability to interface with other media such as compact-disk read-only memory and videodiscs. This can allow minority, female, and disabled students to develop materials that are appropriate and meaningful for their own learning. The experience of producing specialized new programs as well as the products themselves both increase the computing power of these groups of students and address their specific educational needs.

CONCLUSION

Computers have the potential to solve many educational equity issues as well as to exacerbate them. The resources are available—funding, hardware, software, and staff development—but setting priorities for their expenditure and distribution will make the difference. Educational leaders, school boards, district supervisors, and teachers must make decisions that promote access to quality, computer-enhanced education for all students.

Unknown reference

References

Astrein, B., and A. Steinberg. 1985. *Computers, equity and urban schools.* Cambridge, Mass.: Educational Technology Center, Harvard University.

Clewell, B. C., M. E. Thorpe, and B. T. Anderson. 1987. *Intervention programs in math, science and computer science for minority and female students in grades four through eight.* Princeton, N.J.: Educational Testing Service.

Cole, M., and P. Griffin. 1987. *Contextual factors in education: Improving science and mathematics education for minorities and women.* Madison: Wisconsin Center for Education Research.

Educating Americans for the 21st Century. 1983. Washington, D.C.: National Science Board Commission on Precollege Education in Mathematics, Science and Technology.

Fredman, A. 1990. *Yes, I can: Action projects to resolve equity issues in educational computing.* Eugene, Oreg.: International Society for Technology in Education.

Kober, N. 1991. *EdTalk: What we know about mathematics teaching and learning.* Washington, D.C.: Council for Educational Development Research.

Malcolm, S. M., M. Aldrich, P. Q. Hall, P. Boyulware, and V. Stern. 1984. *Equity and excellence: Compatible goals.* Washington, D.C.: Office of Opportunities in Science, AAAS.

Martinez, M. E., and N. A. Mead. 1988. *Computer competence: The first national assessment.* Princeton, N.J.: Educational Testing Service.

McBay, S. M. 1986. *Increasing the number and quality of minority science and mathematics teachers: Task Force on Teaching as a Profession.* New York: Carnegie Forum on Education and the Economy.

National Education Association. 1989. *Special Committee on Educational Technology Report.* Washington, D.C.: National Education Association.

Resnick, L. B. 1987. *Education and learning to think.* Washington, D.C.: National Academy Press.

Sanders, J. S. 1985. Here's how you can help girls take greater advantage of school computers. *American School Board Journal*, April, pp. 37–38.

Wirthlin Group. 1989. *The computer report card: How teachers grade computers in the classroom. A nationwide survey of precollegiate teachers.* McLean, Va.: Wirthlin Group.

For Further Reading

Crist-Whitzel, J. 1985. *Computers for all children: A literature review of equity issues of computer utilization.* San Francisco, Calif.: Far West Laboratory for Educational Research and Development.

Office of Technology Assessment, U.S. Congress. 1988. *Power on! New tools for teaching and learning.* Washington, D.C.: U.S. Government Printing Office.

Sanders, J. S., and A. Stone. 1986. *The neuter computer: Computers for girls and boys.* New York: Neal-Schuman.

Stasz, C., R. J. Shavelson, and C. Stasz. 1986. *Teachers as role models: Are there gender differences in microcomputer-based mathematics and science instruction?* Santa Monica, Calif.: Rand Corp.

Pamela Engler

ERGONOMICS

According to the *World Book Dictionary*, 1989, ergonomics is "the study of the relationship between individuals and their work or working environment, especially with regard to fitting jobs to the needs and abilities of workers." Other definitions include that of Pheasant (1986), who states that "Ergonomics is the application of scientific information about human beings (and scientific methods of acquiring such information) to the problems of design." Still other authors refer to the central focus, the objectives, and the central approach of human factors (McCormick and Sanders 1982). Although there are numerous definitions, they all include references to the basic elements—humans, equipment, environments, and the interactions between them. Regardless of the exact definition quoted, the goal is always the same—to make improvements in all aspects of the relationship and the interaction. Experience has shown that ignoring ergonomic considerations can result in increased absenteeism, reduced productivity, injuries or strains, increased probability of errors, and a lower quality of work.

HISTORY

According to Schmidtke (1980), the term *ergonomics* was first applied in 1857 by the Polish scientist W. Jastrzebowski; however, other sources credit K. F. H. Murrell, a British ergonomist, with coining the term in 1949 when he combined two Greek words, *ergon* meaning "work" and *nomos* meaning "law," to create the term *ergonomics* (Pulat 1985). At that same time in the United States, the terms *human factors, human factors engineering,* and *human engineering* were being used to describe a scientific discipline with the same focus as ergonomics. Presently, the terms are used interchangeably on both sides of the Atlantic.

The increased interest in ergonomics during the last four decades was the result of problems that occurred with the technology during World War II that evidenced the lack of human factors engineering in the design. After the end of the war, as technology was advancing rapidly on the industrial front, especially in the areas of air traffic control and national defense, more attention was being focused on the ergonomic issues.

Although industrial applications will always be of prime concern, the presence of computers in nearly every segment of daily life has led to an exponential growth in the applications of ergonomic principles. The ever-increasing number of nontechnical computer users is some measure of the success of this work.

To be able to continue to make improvements, the relationships and the interactions between human beings and their work environment must be reviewed and examined regularly. It is the job of human factors engineers or ergonomists to do just that, and to report the findings and apply that information to new designs.

COGNITIVE ISSUES

One of the most important areas in the field of ergonomics or human factors is that of cognitive psychology or human information processing. It seems only natural that a designer should know everything possible about the way humans process information if the match between the human users and the computer systems is to be a good one. It has been noted that user interface design really came into being when designers realized that a better understanding of how human minds worked would completely shift the interface model (Kay 1990).

In dealing with the topic of how humans process information, many capacities and limitations must be considered. It is important to consider how humans take in information, how they store it, and how they manipulate it. Designers must learn about visual perception and how this relates to information printed on a computer screen. They must also have a knowledge of the other sensory inputs, for example, hearing and touch, and how humans process these inputs. A knowledge of how the human memory functions is imperative to being able to design systems that do not create overloads on the part of the users.

Another important concept in design is that of the cognitive style of the user, which refers to the thought processes and patterns used by individuals (Carland and Carland 1990). Because of the vast differences in the ways people think and respond to stimuli, designers would like to be able to configure computer systems to meet the cognitive style needs of each user.

PHYSICAL FACTORS

Anthropometry

An important area in the field of ergonomics is that of anthropometry, the branch of anthropology concerned with measuring the human body. It deals with the sizes, shapes, weights, strengths, and other physiological characteristics of human beings. There are two basic types of anthropometric measurements: structural (static) and functional (dynamic). Structural measurements are taken when the body is in a number of standard, stationary positions; functional measurements represent compound measurements of the body in common movement positions. There are a number of sources from which data that have been compiled for males and females, both adults and children, from all over the world can be obtained. One source, for example, contains tables that list thirty-six different static body dimensions including overall stature, shoulder height, hip height, sitting height, sitting shoulder height, thigh thickness (the vertical distance from the seat surface to the top of the uncompressed thigh at its thickest point), knee height, hip breadth, elbow–fingertip length, hand length, hand breadth, and elbow span. In addition, the tables contain these static body dimension measurements for the 5th, 50th, and 95th percentiles along with the standard deviations for both men and women in nine different countries, and for British children from age 2 through age 18 (Pheasant 1986). And these tables are only a small sampling of the data that have been collected by various researchers.

Of particular interest to ergonomists is how these measurements relate to designing computer systems for humans. The purpose of collecting and indexing all of this information is to be able to assist designers who typically design for the 5th to 95th percentile range, that is, the middle 90 percent of the population. In situations where greater accuracy is needed, they design for the 1st to 99th percentile range, that is, the middle 98 percent of the population. This effectively means that the 1 percent on either end will be unable to use the equipment because it is impossible to accommodate the extremes in human diversity without endangering the majority in the middle.

Workstation Design

With regard to the design of a computer workstation, for an adult user to be comfortably seated, the thighs should be approximately horizontal with the lower legs verti-

cal. Based on the anthropometric data for adults, this implies that the workstation chair should be adjustable from 38.0 to 53.5 cm above the floor. In addition, for maximum writing comfort, the desk surface should be at or a little (5.5 cm) above the user's elbow height (Grandjean 1982). The information contained in the anthropometric tables indicates that the desk height should be 72.0 ± 1 cm. For typing comfort, the upper arms should hang vertically with the forearms horizontal, and the home row of the keyboard should be at the user's elbow height. Consequently, unless desktops and keyboards are very thin, it is almost impossible for about 50 percent of the population to attain the recommended typing posture.

According to the majority opinion, the use of a video display terminal (VDT) requires the same desk and chair configuration so as to provide the user with the recommended typing posture (Cakir et al. 1980); however, besides the furniture heights, there are other human factors considerations relating to the keyboard and the screen placement. Ideally, these two should be physically distinct components so that the user can position both optimally. The ideal zone for the location of the VDT screen extends from the horizontal line of sight downward about 30 degrees, but the optimal area is somewhere at about 15 degrees down from the horizontal line of sight. The keyboard should be raked at 5 to 15 degrees to the horizontal and the keys should be about 1.3 centimeters square, with about 2 centimeters of space between the center of any two keys (Pheasant 1986).

Theoretically, if the chair, desk, keyboard, and VDT screen were all adjustable, the user could decide on the optimal settings for each; however, more often than not, users in laboratory settings will simply use the equipment the way it was set by the previous user, rather than making any adjustments.

INTERACTION DEVICES

Once the workstation design has been selected, there are still many human factors issues to resolve. One issue deals with the types of devices used to interact with the software. The choice as to which device to use depends largely on the application being undertaken and on the user.

Keyboards

The primary interaction device is the keyboard. This device is ideally suited for applications that require a great deal of free-form text entry. Although human factors research indicates that the Dvorak keyboard arrangement allows for greater typing speed, the QWERTY keyboard continues to be the industry standard. While the use of a keyboard for selecting items from a menu is slower than pointing and clicking, it is still a very popular general-purpose interaction device.

Touch-Sensitive Devices

Another category of interaction device is the touch-sensitive device. These are display devices, usually panels or screens, that allow the user to make a selection or designate a location on the display by touching that location or item with either a stylus or a finger. Human factors studies indicate that they are best when used for coarse pointing, such as pointing to the store you would like to go to next on a map in a shopping mall, and when the amount of interaction on the part of the user is very small.

Pointing Devices

Pointing devices used for human–computer interaction may be classified as either direct or indirect. An example of a direct pointing device is the light pen, which allows users to point, draw, move the cursor, and select items from a menu. A light pen is ergonomically suited only to tasks where very little computer–human interaction is required. This is because of the arm fatigue that can result from holding a light pen for an extended period.

Although the most popular of the indirect pointing devices is the mouse, that was not always the case. When it was first introduced, many people objected to its design (Berliss and Borden 1989). The mouse is well suited for tasks that require frequent and moderately precise cursor movement, and it has the advantage of allowing the user's hand to rest on the table so that the fatigue factor is almost eliminated. Although many ergonomic studies indicate that the mouse is a very popular pointing device, it is not without disadvantages. It requires a significant amount of eye–hand coordination, takes up a good deal of space on the desktop, and has a cord that trails behind it.

Alternative indirect pointing interaction devices include the trackball, joystick, and graphics tablet. Each of these devices has both advantages and disadvantages, and human factors researchers will continue to study the best device for the tasks at hand.

INTERACTION TECHNIQUES

The continuing growth in both the quantity and the quality of human factors or ergonomic research is due in part to the fact that now a significant number of computing systems are being used by people who are not computer professionals. That is, the majority of the people who use computers at work or at home were educated in some profession other than computer science. Therefore, the techniques used to enter information into and receive a response from the computer must be geared toward this new population of user. Many techniques are currently being used for human–computer interaction; some of the most common are command languages, menu systems, graphical user interfaces that employ direct manipulation, natural language, and form fill-in (Shneiderman 1986). The language that must be used to communicate with the computer, the messages the systems use to relay information back to the user, and the user manuals and documentation are all being redesigned to meet the changing needs. Part of the job of human factors or ergonomics researchers is to determine what the needs are and how best to meet them.

Command Languages

One of the most common ways to interact with a computer is by using a command language. This approach has been recommended for computer applications that have a large number of functions or for experienced computer users (Reid 1985). Command languages may consist of single commands, which may be very concise with a simple syntax or very complex. One example of a command language is Disk Operating System (DOS) for many personal computers. When the computer is booted initially, a prompt such as A> appears on the screen and the system waits for a DOS command to be entered. The user might type a command such as

Copy A:Unit.* B:/V

which means to copy all files from the diskette in drive A that are named "Unit," regardless of their file extensions, to the diskette in drive B. The "/V" tells the system to verify that every file that is copied is an exact duplicate of the original. Some problems with command languages are that they take time to learn, they may be difficult to use if they are not used often, and they require an exact syntax, that is, the punctuation, spelling, and spacing of the command must adhere to strict guidelines. Also, it is often very difficult to recover from an error. One advantage of using a command language is that it is immediate, which means that the system responds to the user's instruction as soon as the control passes from the user, usually by pressing the RETURN key. Other advantages are that command languages are faster than most other forms of interaction, and that they allow the user to build complex commands, which save time. Some of the human factors issues relating to the use of command languages include determining the most appropriate hierarchy and structure for the commands; deciding whether commands should be abbreviated and, if so, what guidelines should be used for abbreviating; and investigating the merits of using symbols and/or keywords in commands.

Menu Selection

Another dialog design technique involves the use of menu selection. Menus in computer software are analogous to those for selecting food items in restaurants. The choices are listed in some logical order and the user need only select the desired item using some interaction device such as a keyboard or a mouse. This interaction style is particularly appropriate for novice users because of the ease of use. On the other hand, they do not always appeal to more experienced computer users because they are generally much slower than some of the other techniques, for example, command languages. Human factors research in this area deals with topics such as the number of items on a menu (breadth) as compared with the number of menus (depth), menu selection techniques, and the arrangement of items on a menu.

Graphical User Interfaces

One of the more exciting interface techniques is the graphical user interface. This consists of a visual representation of the tasks and the tools with which to accomplish the tasks. The user can then use one of a variety of interface devices to manipulate the objects on the screen to achieve a particular goal. One of the most common examples of computer software that uses a graphical interface is a video game. From a human factors standpoint, graphical user interfaces are popular because they are very easy to learn, use, and explore. On the other hand, users may have to purchase some additional computer hardware, such as a mouse, to manipulate the objects on the screen.

Natural Language

Although an unrestricted natural language interface would be easy for even the most naive computer user to learn, it has proven to be one of the most difficult to perfect from the perspective of the computer hardware. A natural language interface implies that the user would be able to enter free-form requests and responses and the computer system would be able to deal with then. Because the English language is so complex, with multiple meanings for the same word and numerous other quirks, it will be many years before computers will be able to process unlimited interactive natural language dialogue (Michaelis et al. 1980).

Form Fill-In

Sometimes called "fill in the blanks," form fill-in involves exactly what the name implies. The computer screen display contains field labels followed by blank spaces that the user is to fill. This is an extremely uncomplicated dialogue mechanism that requires very little training and that simplifies the process of entering data into the system. The only disadvantage is that it may be slower than most other methods of data entry.

References

Berliss, J., and P. Borden. 1989. Building a better mouse. *MacUser* 5(10):124–26.

Cakir, A., D. Hart, and T. Stewart. 1980. *The VDT manual.* New York: Wiley.

Carland, J. C., and J. W. Carland. 1990. Cognitive styles and the education of computer information students. *Journal of Research on Computing in Education* 23(1):114–26.

Grandjean, E. 1982. *Fitting the task to the man: An ergonomic approach.* London: Taylor and Francis.

Kay, A. 1990. User interface: A personal view. In B. Laurel, ed. *The art of human computer interface design.* Reading, Mass.: Addison-Wesley.

McCormick, E., and M. Sanders. 1982. *Human factors in engineering and design.* New York: McGraw-Hill.

Michaelis, P., M. Miller, and J. Hendler. 1980. Artificial intelligence and human factors engineering: A necessary synergism in the interface of the future. In A. Badre and B. Shneiderman, eds. *Directions in human/computer interaction.* Norwood, N.J.: Ablex.

Pheasant, S. 1986. *Bodyspace: Anthropometry, ergonomics and design.* London: Taylor and Francis.

Pulat, B. 1985. Introduction. In D. Alexander and B. Pulat, eds. *Industrial ergonomics: A practitioner's guide.* Norcross, Ga.: Industrial Engineering and Management Press.

Reid, P. 1985. Work station design, activities and display techniques. In A. Monk, ed. *Fundamentals of human–computer interaction.* Orlando, Fla.: Academic Press.

Schmidtke, H. 1980. Ergonomic design principles of alphanumeric displays. In E. Grandjean and E. Vigliani, eds. *Ergonomic aspects of video display terminals.* London: Taylor and Francis.

Shneiderman, B. 1986. *Designing the user interface: Strategies for effective human–computer interaction.* Reading, Mass.: Addison-Wesley.

Cathleen A. Norris

ETHICS AND COMPUTERS

Ethical use of computers emerged as a major concern of the computer community in the 1980s. Many articles appeared in professional journals and addressed computer ethics as a whole, or addressed specific ethics questions. Professional computer societies updated their professional ethics standards, and began to establish new committees or boards to deal with issues related to ethics.

Why was there such a sudden surge of interest in computer ethics? The answer lies in several recent well-publicized incidents that brought the issue of computer ethics into the spotlight. The reason for the publicity surrounding these incidents is the ever-increasing presence of computers in our lives. Today, when a person receives a paycheck, makes a phone call, is billed for a car repair, or applies for credit, computers perform the tasks. Appliances, cars, and other everyday devices are increasingly controlled by computers, which are assuming an ever larger share of the decisions originally made by the users. For example, cars of the future will have a computer on board that will perform the "pumping" of the brakes to avoid skidding. Hence, decisions critical for the safety and life of the drivers will be entrusted to computers. Television sets, microwave ovens, washing machines, telephones, and other devices contain computer chips controlling the function of the device.

At first, computers were accepted with very little hesitation. As a new phenomenon, computers were greeted with fascination and a naive belief in their usefulness. But recently, it has become apparent that computer technology also has a potential for harm.

Neumann (1989–1991) reported numerous incidents that showed clearly and convincingly that computer technology can be annoying or even dangerous if improperly used. Some mishaps were not intended and came as an unpleasant surprise to both the victims and the creators of computerized systems; other incidents raised serious questions about the conduct of the people involved.

Ethical issues can arise during both the development and the use of computer systems. The very nature of software and information makes the emergence of the problems probable. Ethical problems of both development and use, as well as what is being done to address these problems, are described here.

ETHICAL DESIGN OF COMPUTER SYSTEMS

The function of a computerized system is usually implemented by the software of the system. It is, therefore, the software engineer who makes the most important decisions, and it is the software engineer's ethics that affect these decisions. To explain the circumstances in which the decisions are made, let us look at the characteristic properties of software and information stored in computers.

Software Characteristics as Sources of Problems

Some of the most important software characteristics were summarized by Brooks (1987), who called them "essential difficulties of software." They present a difficulty to both the developer and the user, and they cannot be overcome by any additional advance in technology.

Software systems are among the most *complex* artifacts ever created by humans. They may consist of thousands of interconnected parts interacting in complex ways.

Another essential software difficulty is the *invisibility* of software. Invisibility complicates the understanding of software and communications about software. Often, the only facts known about a program are the facts that the programmer is willing to tell.

Then there is *changeability*. Change in software is very easy, because it requires only a couple of key strokes; changes in other engineering systems are much more difficult. There is the danger that some changes will be made in a rush, without proper thought, or that unauthorized changes will be made.

Then there is *conformity* of software. Because of its easy changeability, and because it determines the functionality of the system, software very often must conform to requirements and interfaces that may be very complex. For example, tax preparation programs must conform to all the laws and rulings related to the tax code on the federal and state levels. These programs must also conform to the operating system and hardware configuration. If a change in any of these interfaces occurs, the software must also change.

An additional property, not listed by Brooks, is *discontinuity* of software. Every engineering system must allow for a little imprecision, because perfection is impossible for humans to achieve. This imprecision in software always has an unpredictable impact on the function, which can range from negligible to catastrophic. An accurate means of predicting what will happen with this imprecision is lacking.

Finally, there is *ease of copying*. The cost of reproduction of software and information is practically negligible. The cost is incurred during the creation of software or the collection of information.

Each of these difficulties or properties would be of considerable concern in any system. Software has the cumulative effect of all. This is the reason why software creation is such a difficult and unpredictable art. Moreover, these difficulties may hide unethical conduct.

Ethical Issues Related to Software Design

Because of invisibility and complexity, it is difficult to distinguish good from shoddy work. It is difficult to determine whether the system is robust enough to cover all possible situations, whether it has been adequately tested, and whether it will be easy to maintain.

The invisibility, complexity, and

changeability of software can hide additional processing that could be inserted into programs against the will of the owners or users of the software. The most dramatic examples are computer viruses and time bombs. (See VIRUS.)

Because of the differences between software and other artifacts, according to one school of thought, a completely new ethics has to be developed. Followers of this school believe that the cumulative effect of the new features of software means that the old ethics no longer applies. At closer look, however, it is obvious that, in spite of these novel properties of software, the responsibilities of software engineers are the traditional human responsibilities. It is the human being who is involved in all phases, from creation of the technology to the impact of its use. The software engineer makes decisions that affect other people, and must accept the responsibility for these decisions. These are exactly the issues studied by ethics throughout its history. The discipline of ethics as described in Fagothey (1967) and Finnis (1983) provides a suitable foundation for the specific codes of conduct of programmers.

ETHICAL USE OF COMPUTER SYSTEMS

Ethical issues of design are not the only ethical issues involved with computers. There is the whole area of computer use. Perhaps the most dramatic issue in this respect is that of computer crime.

Computer Crime

Crimes are substantial and deliberate threats to the rights of others, like theft, fraud, sabotage, and vandalism. Because of the complexity, invisibility, and changeability of software, software systems are especially vulnerable to crimes. Crimes are not only easily committed, but also easily disguised. They can be committed by an unethical insider or by an outsider who breaks into a system. The outsider who illegally breaks into a system is often called a hacker.

Neumann (1989–1991) collected many stories of computer crimes. Here is a sampling:

- A bank engineer in London, England, is being investigated by police for unauthorized withdrawals from cash machines. It is alleged that he gained the customer's codes while servicing the machines.
- Travel agents in Woodland Hills, California, defrauded American Airlines of frequent-flyer tickets totaling $1.3 million. The agents used the airline reservation system, where they created fictitious accounts with miles flown by legitimate passengers not enrolled in the frequent-flyer program.
- A computer hacker in Ascot Gardens, Enfield, England, was convicted on four counts of property damage. He broke into a computer system, deleted and added files, inserted messages, and changed passwords of existing users.
- Two Staten Island, New York, youths were arrested on charges of invading the computer system of a Massachusetts firm and causing a damage amounting to $2.4 million.

These and other stories illustrate the growing problem of computer crime. Computer crime is becoming a great concern for the courts and the public. We can expect the enactment of laws that address specific issues of computer crime, as well as the reinterpretation of existing laws regarding computer crime.

Privacy and Confidentiality

The privacy/confidentiality of information is an important consequence of a person's fundamental freedom, which is a right within natural law (Fagothey 1967). An individual must have an opportunity to review information, correct all inaccuracies, and decide whether the information is being used for an acceptable purpose. If not, the individual must have a right to withdraw the information from the database, as do consumers who do not want their phone numbers to appear in the phone book.

The importance of privacy/confidentiality has been recognized as such in the medical community (Greenawalt 1978). The Hippocratic Oath contains a clause related to the confidentiality and privacy of medical data: "What I may see or hear in course of treatment or even outside of the treatment in regard to the life of men, which on no account one must spread abroad, I will keep to myself holding such things shameful to be spoken about." The amended Declaration of Geneva (1978) states: "I will respect the secrets which are confided in me, even after the patient has died."

According to Greenawalt (1978), informational confidentiality/privacy is lost when the information is diverted toward an audience different than the one for which it was intended. Examples of such situations are a friend who betrays a confidence and a person who copies a physician's files without the patient's permission. The same situation can arise with computer files, because the information is very easy to copy and, therefore, can be easily used for a purpose different than for which it was collected.

The recent state of informational confidentiality/privacy is investigated and summarized by Rothfeder et al. (1989). They describe the ways credit information is collected and redistributed. Three large organizations, called credit bureaus, collect this information. There are also a large number of smaller organizations that collect, repackage, or resell consumer information. The information collected includes mortgage payments, credit card payments and balances, incomes, family histories, driving records, and Social Security numbers. Although some nominal precautions in information distribution are observed, Rothfeder et al. illustrate how easy it is to obtain an information on just about everybody. The information is collected without the consumer's direct knowledge, and is distributed to many parties without the consumer's consent.

Recently, a problem of great concern in the community was created when a software company developed a disk with names, addresses, shopping habits, and likely incomes for approximately eighty million U.S. households. The company intended to market the disk to a broad audience for a modest price, and hence to make it accessible to many individuals. Although the company offered an option to withdraw names from the disk, many feared that the option was inadequate and not known to the people listed on the disk. Nevertheless, the company was swamped by mail and phone calls from people who wanted their names withdrawn. Many justifiably feared the possibility of nuisance mail and phone calls, and perhaps even becoming a crime target. Based on the outcry, the company canceled the project.

Security of Information

As larger amounts of information have been gathered, and as the information in computers has become increasingly vital and sensitive, the security of the information has emerged as another leading concern. Security of information comprises two components: securing the information from loss, and preventing unauthorized access or copying of the information.

Information can be lost because of a natural disaster, technology failure, negligence, and other causes. The loss of information may be a devastating blow to the organization using it. Lists of customers, important process formulas, documentation, and other kinds of information are today stored in computers. Companies increasingly rely on this information, and protect it against loss by storing copies on safe media and in safe places. To avoid sabotage, the companies limit access to computers. Access is limited through various passwords and access controls.

Unauthorized access to information can occur through negligence. Neumann (1989–1991) reports many examples, two of which are repeated here.

- A broken computer with a disk containing confidential files was accidentally sold. The confidential files belonged to a federal prosecutor and contained the names of protected witnesses, informants, and others.

- The Air Force accidentally placed 1,200 surplus data tapes on sale. The tapes contained secret information on such topics as aircraft tests and vehicles. The information was not erased before the sale.

Security of information becomes a big issue when computers are interconnected into networks. Although networks usually take great care to avoid unauthorized access, there are hackers who can penetrate the security arrangements and move from one computer to another through a combination of techniques. In this way, they gain access to the resources and information in the interconnected computers. The need to secure that information against unauthorized copying was dramatically proved by Stoll (1988), who described a repeated attack on a computer system in the Lawrence Berkeley Laboratory. The attack was aimed at information related to national security. An intricate path of telephone and computer networks was used to conduct the attacks, and targets included government computers and defense contractors' computers. The intruder always took precautions not to be discovered, remaining on the system only a few minutes and attacking through different networks using different identifiers. Through careful monitoring, Stoll was able to trace the attack to Germany, where finally the perpetrator was arrested by the German police.

The "Internet worm" also belongs to the category of information security, because it used the vulnerabilities of the computer networks. It was a program created by a graduate student at Cornell University, and it attacked computers of the Internet computer network. According to Spafford (1989), it propagated through the mail system from one installation to another, using a simple algorithm to guess passwords. When it successfully attacked a computer, it multiplied, and the copies of the worm attacked the next installation. In the end, it brought the whole Internet to a halt. Although it did not read or destroy any data, it contained a mechanism of password cracking and several other mechanisms for penetration of network security.

SOME ATTEMPTS TO ADDRESS ETHICS ISSUES

Ethics issues of both software professionals and general users are being addressed in a variety of ways. Here we list some recent developments.

Ethical Codes for Software Developers

It became increasingly clear that the community of software engineers needs to accept a universal code of ethics that would both direct the members in their professional activities and protect them when there were no ethics violations. There were, however, several obstacles.

The first obstacle is the fact that software engineering has not been constituted as a profession. Anybody can write computer programs; there are no admission (and expulsion) procedures for professionals. In this respect, software engineering differs from medicine, law, and many engineering disciplines. The desirability of "professionalizing the discipline" was being debated by the community, with both pros and cons being voiced. In the current situation, where the software engineering community is only loosely constituted, it is very difficult to create a unified code of ethics.

On the national level, there are several associations, each developing its own code of ethics and its own boards and committees. The largest ones are the Association for Computing Machinery and the Computer Society of IEEE. McFarland (1991) proposed, to the IEEE Computer Society Standards Committee, the establishment of a board that would deal with ethical standards. The board would advise software engineers about their rights and responsibilities, and protect them when their activities caused unintended harm, similar to other professions.

On the issue of information privacy/confidentiality, the Council of the Association for Computing Machinery (ACM) urged Association members to observe the privacy guidelines of the ACM Code of Professional Conduct. Excerpts from the code are reprinted by White (1991), and they state:

> An ACM member should consider health, privacy, and general welfare of the public in the performance of the member's work.
>
> An ACM member, whenever dealing with data concerning individuals, shall always consider the principle of the individual's privacy and seek the following: to minimize the data collected; to limit authorized access to the data; to provide proper security for the data; to determine the required retention period of the data; and to ensure proper disposal of the data.

In response to the Internet worm, the National Science Foundation published an Ethical Network Use Statement, which deplores unethical behavior that purposefully or through negligence "destroys the integrity of computer-based information" and "compromises the privacy of the users" (Farber 1989).

An important issue is education in computer ethics, which should be offered to students in software engineering and computer science. Professional ethics should be introduced into software engineering and computer science curricula, so that the next generation of software engineers is aware of their moral responsibilities. Similar attempts are being made to introduce ethics into the curricula of other professions.

Legislative Efforts

Currently under consideration is the strengthening of the Privacy Act of 1974 in the U.S. Congress. According to Galen and Rothfeder (1989), the act bars federal agencies from allowing information they collect to be used for a different purpose. Over time, however, numerous loopholes in the act have been discovered that allow large-scale diversion of information. Galen and Rothfeder briefly summarize all major privacy/confidentiality laws and all major loopholes that are weakening the effectiveness of these laws. It is obvious that the public has to be educated in this area, and additional legislative initiatives are needed.

[See also: Social Impacts of Computing.]

References

Brooks, F. 1987. No silver bullet. *IEEE Computer*, April, pp. 10–19.

Declaration of Geneva. 1978. In W. T. Reich, ed. *Encyclopedia of bioethics*, p. 1749. New York: Free Press.

Fagothey, A. 1967. *Right and reason.* 4th ed. St. Louis, Mo.: Mosby.

Farber, D. J. 1989. Statement of ethics. *Communications of ACM* 32(6):688.

Finnis, J. 1983. *Fundamentals of ethics.* Washington, D.C.: Georgetown University Press.

Galen, M., and J. Rothfeder. 1989. The right to privacy: There's more loophole than law. *Business Week*, September 4, p. 77.

Greenawalt, K. 1978. Privacy. In W. T. Reich, ed. *Encyclopedia of bioethics*, pp. 1356–64. New York: Free Press.

McFarland, M. C. 1991. Ethics and the safety of computer systems. *IEEE Computer*, February, pp. 71–82.

Neumann, P. G. 1989–1991. Risks to the public in computers and related systems. Bimonthly column in *Software Engineering Notes*.

Oath of Hippocrates. In W. T. Reich, ed. *Encyclopedia of bioethics*, p. 1731. New York: Free Press.

Rothfeder, J., et al. 1989. Is nothing private? *Business Week*, September 4, pp. 74–82.

Spafford, E. H. 1989. Crisis and aftermath. *Communications of ACM* 32(6):678–87.

Stoll, C. 1988. Stalking the wily hacker. *Communications of ACM* 31(5):484–97.

White, J. R. 1991. Privacy. *Communications of ACM* 34(4):11–12.

Vaclav Rajlich

EXECUTIVE INFORMATION SYSTEMS

A 1989 article in *Fortune* magazine discussed the growing interest in executive information systems (Main 1989). The title proclaimed: "At Last, Software CEOs Can Use."

Until recently, the idea of an executive routinely using a computer seemed very remote. Although a small number of executives, often with engineering or technical backgrounds, were eager to use a computer system, the majority did not want to invest the time and effort to learn complicated software packages that did not really help them manage their business. "Why do I need a computer," they argued, "when my secretary handles all my mail, types my letters, and keeps my calendar, and I have staff who can spend time tracking down and analyzing data? If I take over these activities I am taking time away from the things that I need to do."

This skepticism has been replaced by increasing enthusiasm, however, as a grow-

TABLE 1. EIS Multiuser Software Market: Revenues of U.S. Vendors, Percentage Growth by Geographic Market, 1984–1992

Market	1984	1985	1986	1987	1988	1989	1990	1991	1992
Worldwide revenues ($M)	1.0	5.0	12.0	22.0	32.0	50.0	70.0	91.0	115.0
% Growth		400.0	140.0	83.3	45.4	56.2	40.4	30.0	26.4
U.S. revenues ($M)	1.0	4.8	11.4	20.5	30.0	45.0	61.0	78.0	97.0
% Growth		380.0	137.5	79.8	46.3	50.0	35.5	27.9	24.4
International revenues ($M)	0.0	0.2	0.6	1.5	2.0	5.0	9.0	13.0	18.0
% Growth		—	200.0	150.0	33.3	150.0	80.0	44.4	38.5

Source: International Data Corporation (1988).

ing number of top managers are introduced to a new breed of computer system that has been specially designed to help senior managers to their work. Called an executive information system (EIS) or an executive support system (ESS), this software is designed to enable managers to quickly access and communicate both internal and external information needed to run the business at the touch of a button. These systems are not designed as standalone packages for use by individual executives. Instead, they function as an integrated approach to managing corporate information that can be shared with the management team in an easy-to-use, flexible, and personalized way. In a 1988 study of the market for EISs, International Data Corporation (IDC) was careful to distinguish between "multiuser" information-based EISs and standalone computer software (e.g., spreadsheets, word processing, electronic mail) that just happened to be used by a senior manager. Their analysis indicates that revenues from the sale of multiuser, information-based EIS software increased from a mere $1 million in 1984 to $32 million in 1988. They predicted that revenues would top $100 million in 1991 and continue to grow (IDC 1988) (see Tables 1–3).

WHAT IS AN EXECUTIVE INFORMATION SYSTEM?

An EIS is a computer-based system that enables senior managers to access a common, shared source of internal and external information that has been summarized in easy-to-access graphical displays. These displays can be developed and customized to meet the changing information needs of individual executives, but, because the displays are created using information from a common information store, the system helps promote a shared view of the organization.

Most successful EISs are developed as one component of an integrated management support system that extends the use of the system beyond the senior management team to functional, divisional, and operational managers and their staff, and extends the functionality of the system to include other management support applications (e.g., electronic mail, spreadsheet packages, program management systems, electronic calendars, and word processing). The degree of integration among these various management support applications determines how easy it is for a manager to communicate information throughout the organization and to move from one component of the

TABLE 2. EIS Multiuser Software Market: Revenues and Market Share of Leading U.S. Vendors, 1987

Vendor	Product	Worldwide Revenues ($M)	% Total
Comshare	Commander EIS	11.5	52.3
Pilot Executive	Pilot EIS	8.0	36.4
Other		2.5	11.3
Total		22.0	100.0

Source: International Data Corporation (1988).

TABLE 3. EIS Multiuser Software Market: Units of Installed Inventory (II) of Leading U.S. Vendors by Geographic Market, 1987

Vendor	Product	Worldwide II	% Total	U.S. II	International II	Average Number of Users/Site
Comshare	Commander EIS	120	42.1	105	15	47
Pilot Executive	Pilot EIS	115	40.4	99	16	19
Other		50	17.5	45	5	—
Total		285	100.0	249	36	

Source: International Data Corporation (1988).

system to another. For example, many vendor EIS products allow a manager to move from viewing an information display in the EIS portion of the system to the electronic mail application with the touch of a button. In some cases, the display can be automatically attached to an electronic mail message and sent to another manager or analyst for review or action. Another click of the button allows the manager to return to the same place within the EIS to continue viewing information. The systems are typically designed so that different managers and their staff can choose the information displays and management support tools that they need to run their area of the business, thus developing a "personal management support workstation."

The design of an EIS that functions as a component of an integrated management support system is presented in Figure 1. Data are drawn from a wide variety of on-line external and internal data sources into a common *information management component* where they are aggregated, analyzed, and stored. Although these data are often drawn from existing transaction processing systems and are quantitative in nature, qualitative information can also be entered into the system as text-based reports, briefings, and

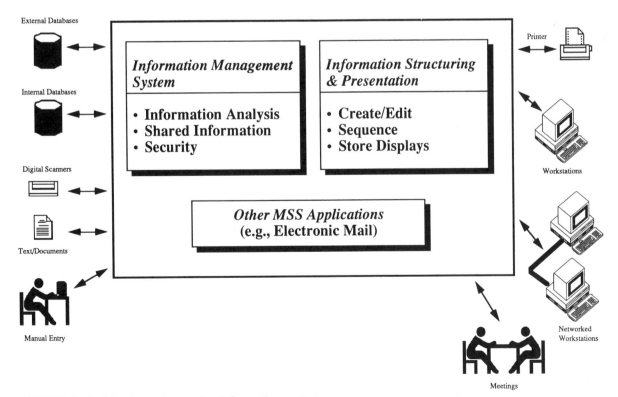

FIGURE 1. Architecture of executive information systems.

other documents prepared using standard word processing packages or "scanned" using digital scanners. In addition, qualitative comments can be added to information displays by analysts, staff, or the managers themselves. System features that ensure security, integrity, and reliability of both the system and the information contained within it are important parts of the information management component. The information management component is often implemented using a combination of a relational database management system (e.g., DB2, Oracle) and a fourth-generation modeling language (e.g., System W, IFPS).

Once information has been analyzed and stored in the information management component of the system, special software is used to create, sequence, and store graphical displays of information, and to provide users with easy access to that information in a very flexible way. This *information structuring and presentation* component is often responsible for turning a general-purpose management support system into an EIS for use by senior executives. Three major levels of functionality can be provided in the information structuring and presentation component (see Figure 2). At the most basic level, graphical displays can be accessed in a manner similar to a paper-based briefing book. Displays are stored as categories of information that often include organization unit (e.g., strategic business unit or function, such as marketing), product/project, or time (e.g., daily, weekly, monthly). Access to the information is sequential within categories. Many organizations have also adopted elaborate cross-referencing mechanisms to allow executives

to move from one category of information to another at the touch of a button. The second level of functionality enables the system to highlight critical information that falls outside exception boundaries set by the executives and provides a mechanism for executives to obtain additional detail on specific areas of interest. Most organizations have adopted a "traffic light" pattern for exception reporting, with green indicating that the information is within accepted limits, yellow indicating a marginal condition, and red indicating that the information is outside of the accepted limits and requires management attention. By clicking on a number or category of information the executive can then view more detailed information. This associative approach to viewing information is often called "drill down." Finally, many EISs provide executives with the ability to access information directly from the database through very easy-to-use, ad hoc, graphical database query mechanisms. As mentioned earlier, the EIS is often integrated with other management support system applications based on the needs of the organization and individual users.

EXECUTIVE INFORMATION SYSTEMS IN ORGANIZATIONS—AN EXAMPLE

Frito-Lay Inc.'s EIS provides an excellent example of an EIS that functions as a component of an integrated management support system within an organization (Applegate 1989). In the late 1980s, Frito-Lay developed an integrated management support system, called the Frito-Lay Decision Support System, to deliver more timely and consistent

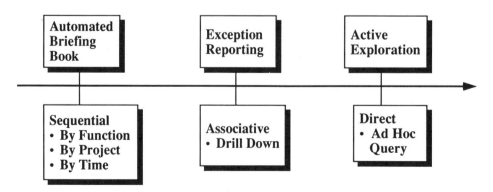

FIGURE 2. Executive support systems: a functional overview.

information to all levels of management. Data on all aspects of the business were accessed from a wide variety of internal transaction processing systems. The internal operating data were integrated with external competitive data purchased from third-party information suppliers and were stored in a central "data warehouse," a relational database that maintained business information by region, product, channel of distribution, and time. The central data warehouse established a common set of business measures that could be used by managers at all levels of the organization.

Graphical information displays were created using a vendor-supplied EIS package that allowed the managers to access information they needed to make decisions and run their area of the business. By the end of 1989, three different management support applications had been developed. The EIS delivered information to the top 200 executives in the organization; the Sales Decision Support System delivered information to sales division managers in the field; and the market analysis and profitability reporting system delivered information to executives, corporate marketing managers, and field sales managers. (Additional management support applications were in progress for manufacturing, logistics, and purchasing managers.) These three applications were also integrated with a number of other management support tools that could be used by managers, analysts, and staff at all levels of the company (e.g., electronic mail, electronic spreadsheet packages, financial modeling packages, and market analysis packages).

IMPACT OF EXECUTIVE INFORMATION SYSTEMS ON ORGANIZATIONS

Why are more and more executives turning to EISs to help them manage their companies in the 1990s? The 1980s were a turbulent decade marked by rapid environmental, organizational, and technological change. Successful management amid such turbulence requires continuous organizational and strategic adjustments and refinement. Basic assumptions that underlie strategic decisions must be challenged continuously and revised to incorporate new information and perspectives. The ability to assess a situation quickly and implement strategic decisions in an increasingly uncertain world has become a critical success factor. Finally, the ability to build organizational capacity for flexibility and change must be transferred throughout the organization.

Stalk (1988) summarized this perspective when he proposed that time would be the next great source of competitive advantage in organizations. But as companies attempt to drastically reduce product development times, production cycles, and other aspects of key business processes, many fail to recognize that time also serves as an important management tool, allowing managers and their staffs to carefully locate and sift through information before making a decision and then to communicate those decisions throughout the organization. In today's global and dynamic marketplace, however, speed counts and the traditional approaches to information access and communication simply will not work. Dramatic shortening of product development times, production cycles, and other components of critical business operations without simultaneous streamlining of management processes and the information systems used to support them can lead to dysfunction. Attempting to compete on the basis of time requires the simultaneous streamlining and "time synchronization" of both business and management processes. This increases the need for everyone to learn more about the dynamics of the business and how decisions made in one part of the organization influence the organization as a whole. All of this requires a new way of managing information access and flow within organizations.

Figure 3 summarizes the traditional approach to information access in organizations (see Huber and McDaniel 1986 for a similar discussion of the cost of information). In most hierarchically structured organizations, detailed information about competitors, customers, and internal organizational capabilities resides largely at the bottom of an organization, "where the action is." These line managers and employees, being knowledgeable only about the dynamics of their specific part of the business, tend to make decisions that are locally optimal. Con-

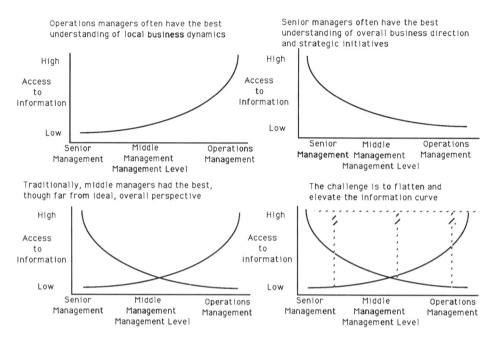

FIGURE 3. The information challenge.

versely, access to information on corporationwide policies and perspective, strategic direction, and the dynamics of the business as a whole usually resides at the top of the organization. As a result, decisions made at the top often consider corporationwide initiatives and strategic direction but may not reflect an in-depth understanding of the business.

To minimize the problem of inadequate access to information, most large, complex organizations delegate decision-making and management responsibilities to the middle of the organization, where access to both business-specific and corporationwide policy information, though not "ideal," is considered "optimal." However, critical information from both the top and bottom of the organization is often lost. In addition, the time it takes to pass information to middle managers seriously hampers the speed with which the organization can operate.

As the pace of competition increases and the environment becomes more dynamic, many companies are recognizing that they can no longer afford slow-response management systems. The solution adopted by many of them is to "cut out the middle," forcing the top and bottom of the organization closer together. To avoid organization

dysfunction, this action must be accompanied by flattening and elevating the information access curve. This does not mean that everyone in the organization receives all information, which would result in information overload. Rather, it implies the adoption of integrated management support systems designed to provide flexible, focused, and timely information that enable decision makers at all levels of the organization to make informed decisions. An EIS is a critical component of the integrated management support system.

By solving the problem of poor information access, trade-off decisions concerning where to locate accountability for decision making and control can be based on business issues rather than on who can gain access to needed information. For example, in dynamic and uncertain environments, where speed and in-depth understanding of the marketplace are critical, decision making and authority can be pushed down to front-line managers along with the necessary corporate perspective and policy information. By the same token, top management can develop a more in-depth and timely understanding of the dynamics of the business and external environment, improving decisions regarding strategic direction, control, and management of corporationwide policy initiatives. And middle managers can gain access to the information needed to coordinate, innovate, and manage change in dynamic and fast-paced environments.

An EIS that functions as one component of an integrated management support system can provide a critical tool for managers attempting to manage and control a "fast-cycle organization" (Bower and Hout 1988). But, even among those reporting the greatest benefits, implementation of an EIS is not without its problems (Rockart and DeLong 1988). Issues that must be addressed during EIS implementation are summarized in Table 4.

TABLE 4. EIS Implementation Issues

Top management vision for the organization and the role of technology in accomplishing the vision are clearly understood at all levels of the organization.

The system is tightly aligned with the organizational strategy and provides the "time-valued" information needed to accomplish that strategy.

Increased top management understanding of the business (centralized control and decision making) is balanced with increased responsibility and authority of line managers (decentralized control and decision making).

Role of middle managers, staff, and information providers is clearly understood and is consistent with technology-based management process.

Top management leadership maintains a balance between active direction and support/facilitation. Broad strategic goals and direction are clearly formulated and consistently applied. Top management remains committed throughout the project.

Centralized staff group is given overall responsibility for design, implementation, and long-term management of the system. Manager of the group (1) understands the business and top management's vision for future business and technology alignment; (2) has experience providing information to top management and understands the time value for information in the business; (3) understands how to access, integrate, and analyze internal and external data sources; (4) understands how technology can be used to accomplish organizational objectives, but is not necessarily a technologist by training; (5) has the respect and trust of the top, middle, and line managers and key information providers; and (6) is skilled at managing organizational change. Implementation team consists of business information analysts, technical specialists, and organization development specialists who can assist in building computer-based models, in accessing and storing relevant data, and in supporting changes in management processes.

Changes in roles, influence, and power relationships among top, middle, and line managers and staff have been identified and managed.

Careful attention is paid to the continued alignment of the system with evolving corporate strategies, structures, and management processes, and the control of the evolution and spread of the system throughout the organization.

Data ownership and access issues have been appropriately addressed.

System fits well with managers' individual goals and work styles, and is flexible enough to allow each manager to personally customize his or her workstation.

Technology appropriate to the requirements of the system is selected, and competent technical personnel are used to develop the system.

Critical data are available and consistent across organizational and interoganizational boundaries, and data integrity and security are ensured.

The system is easy to use and does not require extensive training or skill development.

Competent technical and information analysis support is readily available, and is perceived as helpful by managers.

Training and access to the system are provided to key administrative staff and secretaries prior to delivery of management workstation.

SUMMARY

Although the appropriateness and value of computer use by senior executives continue to be controversial topics, a growing number of executives are finding that an EIS can be a powerful tool for helping to manage their companies through the turbulent 1990s. Analysis of EISs that have been evaluated as highly successful reveals that the system was implemented as one component of an integrated management support system designed to support managers at all levels of the company—not as an isolated, standalone system for use by individual executives. In addition, the management support system was a critical tool to enable streamlining and redesign of management processes to support more effective management in turbulent business environments. Despite their potential benefits, implementation of these systems is extremely costly and is fraught with technological and organizational challenges that must be addressed if the organization is going to realize the potential benefits.

References

Applegate, L. M. 1989. *Frito-Lay, Inc.: A strategic transition* (C). Boston: Harvard Business School Case Services.

Bower, J. L., and T. M. Hout. 1988. Fast-cycle capability for competitive power. *Harvard Business Review*, Nov.–Dec., pp. 110–18.

Huber, G., and R. McDaniel. 1986.The decision-making paradigm of organizational design. *Management Science* 32(5):572–89.

International Data Corporation (IDC). 1988. *Decision support and executive information systems: Markets and trends.* Nov. International Data Corporation.

Main, J. 1989. At last, software CEOs can use. *Fortune,* Mar. 13, pp. 77–83.

Rockart, J. F., and D. W. DeLong. 1988. *Executive support systems: The emergence of top management computer use.* New York: Dow Jones Irwin.

Stalk, G. 1988. Time—The next source of competitive advantage. *Harvard Business Review*, July–Aug., pp. 41–51.

Lynda M. Applegate

EXPERT DATABASES

See Knowledge Bases and Expert Systems; Nonstandard Databases

EXPERT SYSTEMS

See Knowledge Bases and Expert Systems

FARMING, COMPUTER USE IN

Nearly all farms in the United States remain family owned and operated. Most started out small but are growing into increasingly large and complex business operations. The days of the farm record-keeping system consisting of a clip on the visor of the pickup truck are gone. Farmers today are relying more and more on the power of the computer.

Farmers have been relatively slow to purchase computers. Studies have shown that only a small percentage of farmers and ranchers own computers. At first, computer manufacturers tried to sell or lease large computers to farmers and ranchers. Some large farm operators purchased computers, but most agricultural producers could not justify the cost. Later, the introduction of personal computers made computer technology available at a price nearly all farmers could justify, but lack of appropriate software slowed adoption. Another reason farmers hesitated was lack of knowledge and training. They tended to feel more comfortable operating tractors than computers.

Although reluctant to purchase or lease computers, farmers did understand the value of computers and did make use of them. A wide variety of computer services were and still are available free or for a small fee to farmers. Land-grant universities make available computerized record-keeping and tax preparation services for farmers. Rural banks provide financial statement preparation and decision-making services. Farm organizations and industry associations offer specialized record keeping and decision information to farmers.

The barriers to the on-farm use of computers are being eliminated. With upgrades, a low-cost personal computer can be configured to handle the computing needs of even a large farm or ranch for less than the purchase price of a plow or a planter. There are many software programs now available developed for specific agricultural applications. Computer-literate sons and daughters trained in high school or college are returning to farms and ranches.

A farm or ranch can make use of some of the same software that other business firms use. For example, word-processing programs are used for correspondence and report writing. Spreadsheet programs are used for record keeping and generating information useful in decision making.

However, there are needs for specific information unique to agriculture. These needs can be grouped into three areas: accounting and decision making, physical production records and control, and marketing. Farm accounting programs are designed to keep track of expenses and revenues to determine income tax liabilities; to prepare financial records such as balance sheets, income statements, and cash flow statements to satisfy the requirements of agricultural lenders; and to generate information needed to make managerial decisions. These programs also enable farmers to keep track of valuable information on long-lived assets such as land and equipment. Specific applications include analyzing land and equipment purchases and leases as well as calculating depreciation schedules.

Farming can be thought of as a biological manufacturing operation. Inputs, including land, seed, fertilizer, and sunlight, are combined to produce output in the form of grain, livestock, milk, fruit, and vegetables. Some aspects of the manufacturing operation, such as weather, are largely beyond the farmer's control. But farmers seek more control over production to make it more efficient. Computers are increasingly being used in farming to monitor and control the production process. Examples include the use of computers for close control of the temperature, humidity, and lighting in livestock living quarters, and to monitor soil moisture and control the application of irrigation water.

Computers are also used to record and analyze physical production data. It is not uncommon for a farmer to have many fields scattered over a wide geographic area, and several landlords, each with a different leasing arrangement. Information is needed on fertilizer use, number and types of tillage operations, timing, kind, and rates of pesticide applications, and fuel usage and yields. Livestock producers use computers to keep track of vital data for individual animals. The information is used to make nutritional, breeding, and culling decisions. In the dairy industry, some dairymen have implanted miniaturized transmitters in each cow. When an individual animal enters the milking stall, the computer releases an amount of feed calculated to optimize the cow's milk output on the basis of production characteristics and the prices of feed and milk.

Farmers have become skilled managers of the biological production processes; however, in recent years most have discovered greater profit potential in improved marketing than in improved tillage practices or improved livestock husbandry. Computer linkages provide access to up-to-date market reports and prices. Charting programs help farmers comprehend complex price movements at a glance. Market planning programs are used to decide which crops to plant, to calculate the profitability of storage versus immediate sale, to formulate hedging strategies, and to time commodity and livestock sales.

Some farmers are taking advantage of direct electronic marketing programs. The farmer offers his product for sale—hogs, for example—by entering information about his hogs into his on-farm computer. Interested buyers, located in their own offices in distant cities, can make bids on the lot of hogs through their computers. The farmer can accept the best bid and arrangements can be made to ship the hogs.

Computers will play an even greater role in production agriculture in the future. Farms will continue to get larger and operations will become even more complex as technology advances. Farmers will need to become even better business managers as financial and marketing decisions play a more critical role in success. The monitoring and control capabilities of computers may be required to utilize new technology, including biotechnology.

In order to remain competitive in the world marketplace, participants in the food production industries will need to work hand in hand. Farmers will need to work more closely with input suppliers, commodity processors, and food manufacturers. Business arrangements will include contractual and informal partnerships, with the farmer's computer linked to supplier and buyer as they exchange physical production, financial, and marketing information.

References

Levins, R. A., and W. C. Walden. 1984. *Agricultural computer programming.* Englewood Cliffs, N.J.: Prentice-Hall.

Sonka, S. T. 1983. *Computers in farming.* New York: McGraw-Hill.

Woolverton, M. W. 1986. *Computer concepts for agribusiness.* New York: AVI.

Michael W. Woolverton

FAX

A *fax* (short for *facsimile*) transmission is a fixed image—graphics, text, or a combination of the two—that can be quickly sent short or long distances via telephone, radio, or submarine cable.

Initially developed in the United States in the late 1800s, fax technology was further developed by the Japanese as a better alternative to telex. Just as personal computer assembly kits were available in the 1970s, fax machines could also be put together from similar kits in the 1940s. The advent of digital electronics made mass production of small, cheaper, easier-to-operate units possible in the 1980s; by the end of the decade, a business or consumer could buy a fully featured fax machine for less than $1,000.

HOW DOES FAX WORK?

The common fax machine found in home or business scans the document to be sent and converts it into an electronic format that can be sent over ordinary telephone lines. This scanning process breaks the material down into its elementary sequential parts; it is viewed by a photosensor (phototube, photodiode, or phototransistor) through an optical system in which the lens forms an image on an aperture plate, and a direct recording is created. (The output created is an electrical breakdown of the picture.)

After the material is transmitted, it is restored to its original graphic representation through one of a variety of methods, and stored or printed at the receiving end. Though it was rarely done in the early 1990s, it is possible to transmit color documents.

STANDARDS ARE CRUCIAL

The adherence to a standard by electronics companies worldwide allows the sending of faxes anywhere in the world, except in those countries where nonvoice or encoded signals are not allowed. The Consultative Committee for International Telegraph and Telephone (CCITT) has thus far defined four group standards. Group 1—the earliest type of fax—signified machines that could transmit at 6 minutes per page.

Electronic scanning opened the door for Group 2 machines, which could send a page in 2–4 minutes. Group 3 machines, those most commonly found in the late 1980s, send at 15–20 seconds per page. Group 4 does not operate on a dial-up system, but is reserved for four-wire integrated services

FIGURE 1. The Panasonic KX-F90 fax machine. *Courtesy Panasonic Company.*

digital networks (ISDNs). These groups are generally downward-compatible.

DIFFERENT PAPERS CAN BE USED

Though the popularity of plain-paper fax machines began to grow in the early 1990s, the norm up until then had been thermal (heat-sensitive) or electrostatic paper. Both types of paper required images to be burned in. Very early facsimile machines had used a light-sensitive, or photographic, system, which required wet-process developing.

Early high-end business applications of facsimile technology included newspapers printed in cities far from their originating sites; waybills transmitted by railroad companies; and cloud cover photos sent from satellites.

WIDESPREAD USE DEVELOPED

As fax machines came down in price in the 1980s, all kinds of facsimiles crisscrossed the world. Businesspeople and consumers faxed documents instantly for a fraction of what overnight mail would have cost. A one-page letter sent from a commercial fax station cost about $5, as opposed to about $10 for overnight mail; a fax machine owner could send the same transmission for pennies. A subscriber to an *online news and information service* could generally send a one-page document for about $1; incoming faxes, though, could not be received through such a system.

Fax phone numbers became as standard as voice phone numbers on business cards and stationery. Fax directories appeared on library shelves. "Do you have a fax" gradually evolved into "What is your fax number?"

FEATURES VARIED

An alternative to dedicated fax machines appeared in the late 1980s: *fax boards* for personal computers. These boards carried an onboard processor that allowed the user to send and receive files in the background while working on other applications. No dedicated phone line was necessary.

Features of the late-twentieth-century machines varied greatly; in 1990, prices ranged from less than $1,000 to $10,000. The units were designed to maintain the highest possible operating speed with the fewest possible transmission errors. Resolution capabilities of fax machines varied in accordance with price; one writer in 1988 considered a resolution of 200×200 as ideal.

The lowest-priced fax machines did little more than accept the sheet-fed faxes and transmit them. But the bigger the price tag, the more sophisticated the range of features; businesses that sent and received faxes required many of these.

Relay broadcasting allowed the user to send several faxes, which would be programmed to be sent on to other locations when they reached their original destinations. A fax machine could do *polling*, checking with other fax machines to see if there were documents waiting to be transmitted to it. An automatic document feeder would allow the operator to load a stack of several documents that the machine would transmit unattended. *Delayed transmissions* were sent automatically at preprogrammed times. Confidential mailboxes and password protection made it possible for documents to be pulled from memory only by the intended recipient.

In the early 1990s, combination fax machine/copiers, as well as fax machines that could operate as page scanners and laser printers, began to appear. Some manufacturers were developing interfaces that would make it possible to join a personal computer with these sophisticated multifunction machines.

Thus as the decade began, facsimile transmission, which began as a simple, standalone method of transmitting documents quickly, was, in some configurations, becoming a feature of several divergent electronic tools. While it may still be a viable means of text and graphics transmission for years to come, its popularity has somewhat dimmed, too, as a result of the increasing use of electronic mail on personal computers.

[*See also:* Electronic Mail.]

Kathy Yakal

FINANCIAL SERVICES, COMPUTER USE IN

You might not be able to recognize it when you walk into your local bank to cash a check, but the U.S. banking industry is one of the largest single consumers of information technology (IT) in the world. The services you see are just the tip of an iceberg composed of many financial services. These include services that are offered on a local, national, and international basis and services that are offered to wealthy individuals, large manufacturing corporations, savings and loans and other banks, investment management firms and brokerage houses, real estate companies, the federal government and the military, as well as many other small and medium-sized business.

According to one recent estimate, expenditures on IT reached nearly $12 billion in 1988 in commercial banking, tripling the annual expenditures made in 1980. Citibank, one of the largest banks in the world, is known to invest upward of $1 billion each year in IT. Add to these expenditures the money spent by other financial services industry firms—not just commercial banks, but also investment banks, securities firms, and insurance companies—and the picture that emerges is one of an industry that is as "high-tech" as any in the nation.

This article takes you behind the scenes to examine a variety of important areas in which retail and commercial banks, and investment banks and brokerage firms, deploy IT. It will help you to understand where in the financial services industry information systems play the most important roles. Many firms invest in IT with the idea of obtaining competitive advantage in their primary market. But more often investing in IT is a "hook up or lose out" proposition: banks that do not invest effectively in IT to support their core business areas are unable to compete effectively.

The high level of IT investments among financial services firms prompts the curious observer to ask a number of basic questions:

1. What are the core applications and core business areas to which IT is applied?
2. What kinds of systems and technologies are deployed?
3. How do these systems support a bank or brokerage firm's business?

CORE APPLICATIONS

The core requirements for IT in banking cover areas of automation that are common across almost all businesses. Without them, a bank would be unable to open its doors to its customers each day. Some of the most basic ones are described next.

General ledger applications. General ledger applications maintain historical and current account records for customers and an extensive base of customer information. They also create a bank's "books" for quarterly and annual financial statements and auditing purposes. General ledger automation requires high-powered mainframe computers working with large databases of customer and transaction information.

Office automation. Office automation is one of the largest areas of computer expenditures. This category includes personal computers; microcomputer software for spreadsheets, word processors, and database management; laser printers and fax machines; and local area networks for departmental computers. Office automation reduces the cost of administering services to a bank's customers in the context of everyday office work.

Interoffice communication. In the banking industry, it is important to have the capability to maintain continuous communication links among branches, regardless of whether they are located in different parts of a city or in different corners of the globe. This enables a bank to maintain effective financial controls, as well as to deliver a broad range of high-quality services.

Now let us extend our survey of the core areas of IT investment to consider several business areas in two segments of the industry: retail and commercial banking, and investment banking and brokerage.

Retail and Commercial Banking

A number of different kinds of banks operate in the United States. These include savings and loan institutions, which concentrate mainly on retail customers, and commercial banks, which offer services to both retail and corporate customers. Their power to offer different kinds of services is strictly controlled under U.S. banking law, but when it comes to day-to-day operations, both have similar requirements for automation to support their core businesses. Some of the key applications include the following.

Electronic funds transfer.   Most banks offer electronic funds transfer (EFT) services to their customers to move money around the country or around the world, wherever it is needed most.

Check processing.   Check processing is among the most basic services offered by banks. It requires systems that can process checks rapidly, read important data on checks, and pass data to the general ledger system to provide timely updates to customer accounts.

Corporate treasury management services.   Just as retail customers require monthly account statements to enable them to reconcile their checks, large corporations need to track multiple accounts at banks where they maintain the largest borrowing relationships. During the 1980s, this business became largely automated, enabling corporate treasurers to obtain up-to-the-minute readings of funds transferred into their accounts, as well as the overall cash position of the firm.

Credit systems.   Credit systems track small loans to individuals for housing and automobile purchases, as well as large loans to corporations for plant and equipment purchases, import and export financing, or funding for their day-to-day cash requirements. Credit systems screen potential borrowers for their creditworthiness, and thus play an important role in bank lending decisions.

Brokerage Firms and the Securities Industry

Investment banks and brokerage firms provide corporate and retail investment management services most closely associated with the securities industry. Investment banks operate on behalf of large corporations, assisting in the issuance of corporate stocks and bonds and providing money market trading and specialized consulting services to help corporations minimize their financing costs. Brokerage firms provide a similar set of services to corporate clients; however, they tend to specialize in offering services for individuals who wish to participate as investors in the stock and bond markets.

Investment banks and brokerage firms also require general ledger, office automation, and interoffice communication technologies; however, firms in this industry are especially well known for investing in computer hardware and software applications that enable them to make sense of a changing market, and to rapidly implement investment decisions that earn money for their clients. The areas of automation that are specific to investment banks and brokerage houses include the following.

Portfolio management systems.   Specialized applications of IT are used when a brokerage firm performs investment management functions for corporate, municipal, and government pension fund clients. Portfolio management services require computer hardware, financial modeling software, and databases of investment market information that can be updated almost instantaneously.

Trading systems and analytics.   An example of "ultrahigh-tech" automation occurs within the money and financial market trading operations of investment banks and brokerage firms. Trading platform technologies enable traders to obtain, synthesize, and act on information about financial instruments they trade. Trading automation also provides a mechanism by which customer orders are effected as instructions to trade a financial instrument. It is often linked to other systems to enable customer accounts and the firm's inventory of securities and investment positions to be updated. "Analytics" consist of specially designed computer software packages that analyze large amounts of data, and solve a financial optimization model to determine whether to buy or sell a financial instrument at a given time. (See also TRADING, COMPUTER USE IN.)

Real-time links to financial markets. Highspeed data connections to the New York and American stock exchanges, as well as other domestic stock and commodity exchanges, are also required in this industry. They have two purposes: to enable information about changing market prices to flow into a firm, and to enable the firm to send "buy" or "sell" orders to its representatives in the marketplace. Without them, a brokerage firm or investment bank would be unable to carry out the majority of its business.

In the sections that follow, some of these core applications of IT are examined in greater detail.

ELECTRONIC FUNDS TRANSFER SYSTEMS

Electronic funds transfer systems form the spine of the retail and commercial banking system. On the retail level, automated teller machines (ATMs) provide banking customers with a variety of account query, cash withdrawal and deposit, and bill paying services available on a nearly 24-hour basis. Some of these services, for example the ability to withdraw cash from a checking or savings account, are available across the United States through ATMs that are connected to national networks. The financial services industry also provides nationwide credit services through well-known credit cards such as VISA, MasterCard, and American Express. A more recent development is direct "debit" (or reduction in funds) to an account when that customer makes a retail purchase. A similar level of comprehensive servicing is available for corporations and banks, and if anything, it is even more well developed and comprehensively used than retail EFT systems.

Servicing for Corporations and Individuals on a Domestic and Worldwide Basis

How does EFT work? Here are some examples that involve two large corporations. We examine what happens when both corporations have accounts at the same bank; the corporations' banks are leading money center banks in New York City; the corporations and their banks are located in different areas of the United States; or the corporations are located in different countries. This will enable us to identify some organizations that form the domestic and international infrastructure of EFT services.

First, imagine that there are two corporations: Corporation 1 wants to send money to Corporation 2. If both corporations have an account at the same bank (A), then the funds are transferred electronically on the books of Bank A. (See Case 1 in Figure 1.) Next, suppose that the corporations have different banks. The process begins when a second bank, Bank B, receives an EFT message from Bank A. The message will contain information in a standardized format, including the amount of money being transferred, the name of the corporation that should receive the money, the name of the corporation that requested that the money be sent, the reason the money is being sent, the date and time, and a money transfer sequence number that can be used for tracking purposes. With this information, Bank B can move the correct amount of money into Corporation 2's account.

This EFT process often occurs on behalf of some of the largest American corporations that have accounts at the largest New York City "money center banks," such as Citibank, Chase Manhattan, Bankers Trust, Chemical Bank, Manufacturers Hanover Trust, and the Bank of New York. When the funds transfer occurs among banks in this group, the Clearing House Interbank Payments System (CHIPS) is used. CHIPS is a private EFT clearinghouse that operates on behalf of its membership. (See Case 2 in Figure 1.)

When EFTs are made on behalf of American banks that are not members of CHIPS, then the normal mechanism is to use

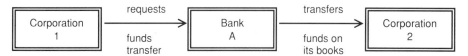

Case 1: Book transfer of funds: occurs when bank A holds accounts of both corporations.

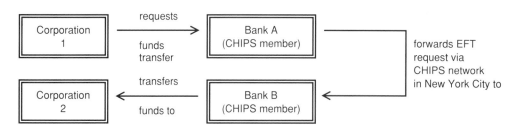

Case 2: C H I P S EFT: occurs when both corporations' banks are located in New York City and belong to C H I P S.

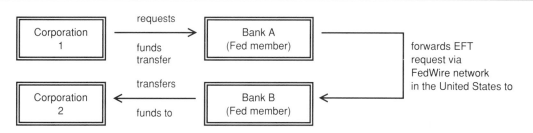

Case 3: FedWire EFT: occurs when corporations located in different parts of the United States are represented by banks that are members of the Federal Reserve Banking System.

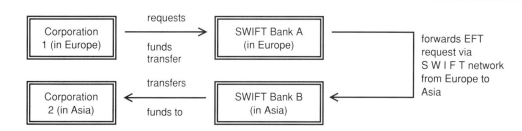

Case 4: S W I F T EFT: occurs when corporations operate in different countries and are represented by large international banks that are members of S W I F T.

FIGURE 1. How electronic funds transfer works.

the Federal Reserve Bank's dedicated funds transfer telecommunication network, the FedWire. It connects all American banks that pay to use the Federal Reserve Bank's check processing and clearing system and money transfer capabilities. When funds transfers are made on behalf of individuals, the scenario is no different. (See Case 3 in Figure 1.)

Such arrangements can also be extended to funds transfers between corporations in different countries. In this instance, imagine that Corporation 1 is a small Asian electronics firm that exports its products to a European buyer, Corporation 2. Each company is likely to have an account with a bank from its own country. In this case, the means used to effect an EFT is SWIFT, an acronym for the Society for Worldwide Interbank Financial Telecommunication. Its membership comprises large international commercial banks from many foreign countries. (See Case 4 in Figure 1.)

Retail Electronic Funds Transfer

Automated teller machines. A much more familiar EFT technology is the ATM. An ATM is a terminal connected via telephone or dedicated telecommunication lines to larger computer systems that identify a user's account on the basis of data stored in a magnetic strip on the back of a plastic ATM card. When a customer uses an ATM, it normally takes no more than 30 seconds for such verification to be made. This enables the user to withdraw cash, transfer money between accounts, or perform other banking transactions.

Although ATMs have been available since about 1975, the banks have been so successful in promoting this technology that retail banking customers can hardly do without it. Bank customers benefit because access to their money is available around the clock. They can obtain cash when they are traveling in other cities or states, and are able to conduct their financial affairs privately. But ATMs also provide benefits to the banks. It is cheaper for them to operate ATMs than branches, and ATMs also substitute for more expensive human tellers.

Automated teller machine transaction processing requires a specialized user terminal. The terminal must store and enable the withdrawal of cash, provide information on a customer's account via a screen or on a paper receipt, and be firmly protected against abuse or tampering. Behind the scenes at the bank, a high-volume, "fault-tolerant" processing capability is needed to handle incoming transactions and pass messages back to customers at ATMs. (Fault tolerance implies that transactions from multiple ATMs will continue to be processed if a connection is lost with any one of them.) Normally this is handled with minicomputers that are dedicated to processing ATM transactions. Later,

information related to all ATM transactions must be passed to the bank's general ledger system so that all accounts can be updated, and so that the bank can track the net inflow or outflow of cash.

Shared electronic banking networks. In the 1970s, the predominant form of ATM services was in small "proprietary networks" owned by individual banks in key markets around the country. A proprietary network enables a bank's customers to use any of its ATMs, but not those belonging to other banks. By the early 1980s bankers began to realize that this form of organization was not the most efficient for a number of reasons. First, a bank's customers tend to cluster in the locale of the head office of the bank. This imposes natural geographic limits on a bank's location of ATMs. A decision to locate an ATM outside the primary trade area of the bank would result in very low levels of use. Second, where competing banks' primary markets overlapped, bankers recognized the potential for "overcapacity" in electronic banking services. Taken together, these factors prompted banks to consider sharing their electronic banking facilities.

The result was the emergence of regional "shared ATM networks" in major U.S. metropolitan areas. By sharing electronic banking facilities and ATMs, banks spread the costs of providing services and expanded their servicing reach. Sharing also opened up the possibility for some banks to specialize in providing shared network services to other banks and for other banks to purchase those services.

In shared networks, there is normally a bank or organization that provides the services of a "switch." When a user attempts to withdraw cash from an ATM, the bank's computer system checks to see if the user is a customer. If the user is verified as a customer, then processing of the customer's request will continue. If the user is not a customer, the bank's computer will pass on the information obtained about the user's bank and account number to the "switching bank." The switching bank (often an owner or co-owner of the regional ATM network) operates a computerized database to determine whether the user's bank is a member of the shared network. If it is, then the transaction is passed back to the computer of the bank where the user is a customer, and if money is available in the customer's account, very shortly a message will be sent to the ATM instructing it to deliver cash for withdrawal.

Although regional sharing is very effective, it also has limitations. For example, people who travel out-of-state or beyond the region covered by a shared ATM network have cash withdrawal and account servicing needs that cannot be answered by regional shared networks. When bankers realized that demand existed for electronic banking services based on sharing at a national level, they were quick to organize "national shared ATM networks," comprising the major regional shared ATM networks.

Today, the Cirrus and Plus national networks exist side-by-side. But there is growing interest in "universal sharing" in place of the current "duality." With two national shared networks, there is duplication of effort and overcapacity; however, this present situation cannot be explained in terms of costs or economics alone. Each of the national networks is allied with a credit card firm, and many keen observers of the financial services industry are wondering how the networks will evolve, and whether bank customers in the future will be carrying just one plastic card that combines both ATM and credit card capabilities.

Point-of-sale debit and credit card systems. Another important EFT service is point-of-sale (POS) debit and credit cards. Point-of-sale debit cards are used by customers who make retail purchases; money is directly deducted from the customers' bank accounts and passed to the account of the merchant who made the sale. Unlike ATM cards, POS debit does not provide for cash withdrawals. Instead, POS debit is truly "cashless": a bank adjusts its accounts to reflect funds "debited" (deposited) to the seller's account and "credited" to (withdrawn from) the buyer's account.

Point-of-sale debit is used in retailing, for instance, by oil companies that deploy specialized gasoline pumps enabling a customer with a debit card to pay by "swiping"

it through the pump. The appropriate amount of money is deducted from the customer's account and passed directly to the oil company's account. Point-of-sale debit is highly favored among retailers as debit card transactions are "riskless": no credit is offered, and so there is no risk that a borrower does not repay. Point-of-sale debit also provides a useful audit trail for the purchaser and the merchant.

A credit card involves a decision by the institution offering it to an individual to extend a line of credit. This credit can be drawn down, but not exceeded, as a credit card user (actually a borrower) makes purchases on credit. The credit card business is also very high-tech. Each time a credit card transaction occurs, the seller "swipes" it through a specialized credit card reader terminal. This terminal passes a message along a phone line back to the bank that offers the credit card or the credit card company, to obtain confirmation that credit exists for the consumer to make the purchase. When that authorization has been obtained, the seller receives a confirmation receipt, transferring all risk of future loss to the credit card company or bank.

The volume of credit card purchases that are made each day is huge. As a result, the credit card business requires massive telecommunication, database storage, and transaction processing capabilities, making it more complex and technologically demanding than POS debit. In addition, credit cards require month-end-statement mailing to credit card customers, and a processing operation must be able to handle the large volume of monthly credit card bill payments, account adjustments, bad debt tracking, and so on.

But the central concern is really credit quality: without firm controls on who gets credit cards and how much credit is extended, banks suffer significant exposure to losses. The most sophisticated banks employ DECISION SUPPORT SYSTEMS (DSSs) and expert systems (ESs) (see KNOWLEDGE BASES AND EXPERT SYSTEMS) that assist in assigning credit limits based on a customer's credit history and monthly bill-paying performance. Expert systems in this area consist of specialized software that represents the knowledge of expert lenders; they are helpful in simulating human credit decisions, and often substitute for it. For example, daily television advertisements remind consumers that it is possible to get "special credit increases" in emergency situations. The power of DSS and ES technology makes this possible.

CHECK PROCESSING, CORPORATE TREASURY MANAGEMENT, AND CREDIT AUTOMATION

Check processing is perhaps the highest-volume operational service currently provided by the American banking industry. Although many keen-sighted industry observers predicted the demise of the paper check sometime during the latter part of the 1980s, the fact is that paper checks are still with us and are likely to remain for a number of years longer.

At the retail level, banks perform check processing on behalf of individual customers who deposit their paychecks and pay rent to their landlords or other recurring bills. At the commercial level, banks also perform processing services for corporate customers who receive checks as a primary means of bill payment. The basic requirements for check processing for retail and corporate customers are similar. Corporations, however, require far more information about processed checks, because corporations perform "treasury management," a set of procedures and policies for minimizing a firm's financing costs. As processed checks are a ready source of operating funds or "working capital," corporations do everything they can to have checks received processed quickly so they can be turned into cash.

Check Processing Automation

All checks carry predefined numbers that indicate the bank where the owner of the check has an account and the account number; the numbers are read by means of a technology called magnetic ink character recognition (MICR). When a check is deposited, a process begins that potentially can involve a number of institutions. The simplest check processing transaction occurs when the check is deposited at the bank where the writer of the check has an account. A check "drawn on" this bank can be turned into cash in one step. The check processing operation of the bank "encodes" it with the dollar amount that the writer of the check indicated on the face of the check. This enables the check to be processed through a large, computerized check reader/processor, which captures information about the dollar amount of the check and the bank that it is drawn on.

The computerized check reader/processor also is responsible for capturing images of processed checks on microfilm as they are processed. These images act as an audit trail for signature and document verification in the event of check fraud. More importantly, the reader/processor acts as a computer to determine when the "value" of a check as withdrawable cash should be assigned to a customer's account. It also passes messages back to the bank general ledger systems indicating which accounts will receive money.

Check processing operations become more complicated when a check is not drawn on the same bank where it is deposited. These are called "out-of-town" checks. An out-of-town check must be "cleared" back to the bank it was drawn on, a process involving the Federal Reserve Bank as an intermediary. Clearing gives the bank holding the account of the writer of the check a chance to determine whether that account has money in it and whether the signature on the check matches that of the owner of the account. Although check clearing via the Federal Reserve Bank involves the physical movement of paper, a significant amount of computerization is required to track checks.

When banks submit checks for clearing, the depositors of the checks do not obtain cash immediately. (Almost everyone has had the frustrating experience of trying to turn an out-of-town check into cash, and then being forced to wait as much as a week's time to get it.) In fact, cash for out-of-town checks becomes withdrawable for retail customers according to a predetermined Federal Reserve Bank "schedule," which must be represented in a bank's customer account and check processing software. This gives all parties to a check processing transaction the opportunity to ensure that no fraud is involved. It also ensures that customers receive cash in a timely fashion, and that the bank minimizes its risk of paying out money on fraudulent checks.

Computer-Based Treasury Management Services Related to Check Processing

Although the clearing process affects retail banking customers who deposit checks, it is more important to corporate treasurers who send many checks for clearing. To visualize what happens, consider a large metropolitan power and light utility company with several million customers. Each month when customers pay their heat and light bills, a huge volume of checks is sent by mail to the utility company. The sooner the utility company can obtain the cash represented by the checks the better, because even a one-day deposit of $10 or $20 million will earn a considerable amount of interest for the utility. More importantly, if the utility does not have this cash, it may have to borrow it at even higher cost.

As a result, commercial banks have developed "treasury management" services that are aimed at reducing "check float" for their corporate customers. Check float represents the value of money that is unavailable to the recipient of a check when it is in the mail or being cleared through the Federal Reserve check processing system. "Lock box" services are one example. A lock box is a large post office box to which bill payers are supposed to send their check payments. A bank that operates a lock box will send employees to the post office several times each day to pick up checks so they enter the clearing process at the earliest possible time. This reduces float and increases usable cash for a corporation.

Banks that offer lock boxes and other treasury services that speed the "collection" of checks also provide a significant amount of data about the checks that are processed. This information is reported using specialized microcomputer-based software and phone lines that link the treasurer directly to the bank's computers.

Treasury management encompasses a broad range of services. For example, banks offer highly sophisticated cash balance management software that integrates bank automation with that at the disposal of the corporate treasurer. One good example is payroll automation. Corporations pay their employees on a periodic basis, and must maintain records on employees, their wage rates or salaries, and deductions that are required for taxes, medical insurance, and so on. Automated payroll services enable a corporation to deliver a specially formatted magnetic tape to a bank. The bank processes the tape on its own computers with the result that paper payroll checks are generated or direct electronic deposits are made to the appropriate accounts. In some cases, the transfer of data related to the payroll is accomplished computer-to-computer.

Information technology also allows a treasurer to mobilize all funds that a firm has on deposit in bank accounts. This is accomplished by using software that is specialized to the task of consolidating money from all company accounts and performing computer-based analysis of where cash is required and, if there is a cash surplus, where it should be invested. A corporate treasurer is also able to effect low-cost, high-speed electronic transfers from a terminal placed at the company by a bank. This terminal can provide information on all of the corporation's bank accounts. It is also used to resolve operating problems, monitor cash balances, obtain notification of the receipt of large-dollar-value EFTs, and examine the details of check processing or funds transfer transactions.

Credit Evaluation and Loan Tracking Automation

Credit card, mortgage, and other retail lending activities require the support of large databases of historical information on borrowers, the performance of businesses in the local economy and the housing market, changing interest rates, and other factors. This information is used to gauge the likelihood that a loan, once made, will be repaid by the borrower. It also helps the bank to set interest rates on loans to different classes of borrowers that are commensurate with the different levels of risk involved.

Retail lending, especially for mortgages and auto loans, often involves a decision that can be automated. The requirements are a database containing all data that are relevant to a lending decision, and a software-based decision support model that can evaluate the creditworthiness of the potential borrower. The reason that it is possible to automate such lending decisions is that banks work with large populations of borrowers and a great many lending decisions. Thus, all they need to do is to be effective in predicting creditworthiness "on average." If the bank is unable to predict creditworthiness well, then the bank's bad debts will rise, potentially threatening its financial stability.

Credit automation is also necessary to track cumulative "lending exposure," the total of all loans made to corporate and retail customers. Knowing its exposure in aggregate and to specific customers enables a bank's managers to determine how much additional money the bank has to lend at any point in time, to accurately report its loans on its balance sheet to auditors and the Federal Reserve Bank, and to take steps to correct problems that arise when companies or individuals default.

Computers also are used to track many accounting aspects of commercial and retail loans. For example, a bank needs to send installment loan billings, to track interest on loans, to examine the characteristics of borrowers who default on loans, and to support attempts to collect on loans in default. Each of these tasks requires reliable and up-to-date information.

FINANCIAL INFORMATION TECHNOLOGIES IN INVESTMENT BANKING AND BROKERAGE OPERATIONS

The 1980s witnessed significant industry-wide advances in the use of portfolio management and investment and trading technologies, as well as trading strategies that involved the application of complex mathematical and analytical models. Such terms as *program trading* and *Wall Street analytics* have emerged and are representative of the influence that IT has had on the way that this industry operates. In fact, one of the most interesting and controversial issues discussed today is whether such well-known markets as the New York and American stock exchanges should become entirely "electronic markets," where there is little, if any, human intervention in the process of trading securities.

Real-Time Links to Financial Markets

Investment banks and brokerage firms spend a lot of money to keep track of changing markets. In-house, this requires hardware and software to capture, process, and make sense of huge amounts of data on market transactions and prices so that traders can make a profit. The most basic source of "real-time," up-to-the-second information is the "stock ticker" of the New York Stock Exchange, which offers information about securities trades and prices. This is made available to New York Stock Exchange members, and other parties who are willing to purchase it, via an electronic link that is established between a firm and the market.

There are many other sources of data on financial markets too. Some are available on a real-time basis, although others like "Compustat" report historical information on the performance of many companies. When data are delivered in the form of preformatted television screens, we call them video data feeds. However, recent advances in technology have enabled a new generation of data feeds to emerge that are based on *digital data.* Digital data enables the user to capture information about the market and import it to a spreadsheet or a database for use in a decision model. (See Table 1 for additional details. Also see TRADING, COMPUTER USE IN.)

Digital data and specially formatted "value-added" market information products are an important advance because they enable traders to use analytic models that incorporate data about the market as it exists, at the moment a profitable trading opportunity is discovered. When a firm is unable to obtain and analyze this kind of data cost-

TABLE 1. Characteristics and Uses of Video and Digital Market Data

Type of Market Data	Characteristics of Market Data	Uses of Market Data Feed in Trading Operations
Video data	Data are delivered in screen format. Contents of screens cannot be decomposed into their separate elements. Video data feed vendors offer special formats for different purposes.	The primary use of video data is to "track" a market indicator. Video feeds are delivered via dedicated terminals whose purpose is to highlight changes that occur in the market. Some video feeds deliver the results of analysis that is conducted on the "quote vendor's" computers.
Digital data	Data are delivered in "digital" format, not screens. Digital data can be built into screens, based on the specific needs of a user. This format makes the data importable to analytic models.	The primary use of digital data is in analytic models to support trading and investment decisions. Digital data also enable traders to work with programs that act as "alarms" when a specific market indicator changes.

effectively, it loses the competitive edge necessary to function effectively on behalf of its clients.

Investment and Portfolio Management Systems

Investment banks and brokerage firms employ IT to support their core business function: investment and portfolio management. The problem that must be solved is how to maximize the client's earnings or returns on the financial assets in the portfolio while minimizing risk of loss. (A basic tenet in modern finance is that the greater the expected returns, the greater the investor's exposure to risk.)

Carrying out this analysis requires the investment manager to determine how current asset prices, prior market trends, and expectations about future interest rates interact with the characteristics of the financial instruments included in a portfolio. Stocks, for example, may carry an annual or quarterly dividend; however, the size of the dividend and whether it will be paid are uncertain. But the primary determinant of their value may be the market at large. As a result, an investment manager needs the power that IT can provide to make the best possible

assessment of how the market is likely to change.

A second example is predicting the value of bonds. Unlike stocks, bonds include a series of predetermined "coupon payments" representing some percentage of the "face value" of the bond (usually denominated in thousand-dollar units) when it matures. The investor obtains the face value of a bond at maturity, sometimes ten or twenty years later. In the meantime, investment managers need to calculate their value, and determine whether the cash flows associated with the coupon payments and face value of the bond sell at a bargain or premium today.

The most famous example of the application of computer power to investment management is known as *program trading*. Program trading involves the use of specialized computer software that analyzes the current price of an aggregate "index" of securities traded on the market, and then compares that price with the prices of the securities that the index comprises. When the price of the index exceeds the sum of the prices of the stocks that constitute it, a short-lived opportunity will exist to purchase the underlying stocks and resell them at a profit as the basket constituting the index.

This is known as an "arbitrage" opportunity, and the more specific term applied to this strategy by Wall Street professionals is *index arbitrage*. Information technology provides a crucial link in scanning the marketplace for such arbitrage opportunities and then enabling automated "buy/sell" transactions to be effected, locking in profit for the firm. Without program trading software, such opportunities would be hard to detect and act on.

Another area that has benefited from advances in IT is mortgage-backed securities (MBS) portfolio management. An MBS is a special kind of security that is backed by a portfolio of mortgages or housing loans. Borrowers have the option to refinance at a lower interest rate during the life of a mortgage, and the bank expects that some borrowers will default. Mortgage-backed securities are highly sensitive to interest rates, as this is what often causes borrowers to refinance or default, and thus MBSs involve many uncertain cash flows over time. The only way that MBS portfolios can be managed effectively is through the application of extremely powerful computer technology combined with specialized application software that formalizes a "financial optimization model" that "understands" how to perform MBS valuation. We next consider some ways that computers are used to perform financial analysis.

Money and Financial Market Trading Technologies and Wall Street Analytics

During the 1970s, significant progress was made in the application of sophisticated mathematical modeling techniques to financial management problems. These included matching a corporation's balance sheet assets and liabilities, and performing many kinds of cash and risk management modeling. However, solving these models was out of reach for realistic-sized applications: sufficient computing power was not available at a reasonable price.

During the 1980s the situation changed abruptly. Computing power available to traders and portfolio managers increased by several orders of magnitude, for example, in the form of personal computers with Intel 386 and 486 class microprocessors and higher-powered engineering workstations. Even more complex financial optimization problems became solvable in real time when extraordinary computer power was applied. The result was the emergence of "Wall Street analytics." For example, in the MBS portfolio management problem discussed above, one solution involves using a supercomputer that incorporates many powerful microprocessors designed to operate in parallel.

Today, computer-based analytics are routinely applied by investment banking and brokerage professionals who have a sound knowledge of three areas: information systems, finance, and mathematical modeling. For this reason, these people may be referred to as "technology triathletes," representing the exceptional levels of knowledge that they bring to the firms that employ them. Wall Street trading technology experts continue to be among the highest paid members of the information systems profession, and this indicates the extent to which their contributions influence investment bank and brokerage firm profits.

[*See also:* Banking, Computer Use in.]

For Further Reading

Bank systems + technology (journal). New York: Gralla. Useful source of up-to-date articles on applications of IT in banking.

Carter, C., and J. Catlett. 1987. Assessing credit card applications using machine learning. *IEEE Expert* 2:71–79. Discusses a novel, high-technology approach to credit card application screening.

Clemons, E. K. 1991. Evaluation of strategic investments in information technology. *Communications of the ACM* 34(1):22–36. Discusses strategic investment in IT in general, illustrated with several short cases about investments in financial ITs.

Clemons, E. K., and M. Row. 1988. The Merrill Lynch Cash Management Account Financial Service: A case study in strategic information systems. In *Proceedings of the Twenty-first Annual Hawaii International Conference on System Sciences*, vol. 4, pp. 131–39. Case study of a classic example of the use of IT for competitive advantage in the financial services industry.

Faki, A. 1983. Regulation of electronic funds transfer. *Communications of the ACM* 26(2):112–18. Offers insight into the social welfare implications of electronic funds transfer.

Felgran, S. D. 1984. Shared ATM networks: Market structure and public policy. *New England Economic Review,* Jan.–Feb., pp. 23–38. Discusses the implications of shared ATM networks for bank competition and impacts on the pricing and quality of bank products.

———. 1985. From ATM to POS networks: Branching, access and pricing. *New England Economic Review,* May–June, pp. 44–61. Examines the emergence of point-of-sale debit networks.

Felgran, S. D., and R. E. Ferguson. 1986. The evolution of retail EFT networks. *New England Economic Review,* July–Aug. Reviews the rationale for and development of various forms of shared ATM network organization.

Gifford, D., and A. Spector. 1985. The Cirrus banking network. *Communications of the ACM* 28(8):798–807. Discusses the development, computer architecture, and performance characteristics of one of the first national shared ATM networks.

Glaser, P. F. 1988. Using technology for competitive advantage: The ATM experience at Citicorp. In B. R. Guile and J. B. Quinn, eds. *Managing innovation: Cases from the service industries,* pp. 108–14. Washington, D.C.: National Academy Press. Reports on Citibank's strategic use of electronic banking technology to obtain additional retail banking market share in the New York City area in the early 1980s.

Humphrey, D., ed. 1990. *The U.S. payment system: Efficiency, risk and the role of the federal reserve,* Boston: Kluwer. Proceedings of a Federal Reserve Bank conference on the issues associated with the regulation of electronic payments in the United States and Canada.

Leinweber, D. 1988a. Intelligent trading systems. In W. Wagner, ed. *Complete guide to securities transactions.* New York: Wiley. Discusses computer-based approaches to pattern recognition and decision support for financial and money market trading.

———. 1988b. Knowledge-based systems for financial applications. *IEEE Expert* 3: 18–31. Reviews some potential applications of expert systems for financial services firms.

Lipis, A. H., T. R. Marschall, and J. H. Linker. 1985. *Electronic banking.* New York: Wiley. Overview of all forms of electronic banking.

Lucas, H. C., Jr., and R. A. Schwartz. 1989. *The challenge of information technology for the securities markets: Liquidity, volatility and global trading.* Homewood, Ill.: Dow Jones-Irwin. Provides multiple theoretical perspectives on the architecture of electronic markets for securities and commodities, and reviews the events surrounding "Black Monday," October 19, 1987, when the stock market crashed.

Miller, R. M. 1990. *Computer-aided financial analysis.* New York: Addison-Wesley. A textbook that provides an increasingly sophisticated treatment of computer-based financial models, from simple spreadsheets for capital budgeting to "knowledge-based" expert systems approaches to the solution of more complex financial modeling problems.

Mookerjee, A., and J. Cash. 1990. *Global wholesale electronic banking.* London: Graham and Trotman. In contrast to other references that focus on retail electronic funds transfer, this book is entirely devoted to corporate use of electronic banking services and to international banking competitiveness.

Platt, R. B., ed. 1986. *Controlling interest rate risk: New techniques and applications for money management.* New York: Wiley. A useful reference to obtain an understanding of concepts from modern financial theory that are represented in Wall Street computer-based analytics.

Star, S. 1987. TRADER: A knowledge-based system for trading in markets. In J. L. Roos, ed. *Economics and artificial intelligence.* Oxford: Pergamon Press. Another example of expert system technology, but applied to market trading.

Steiner, T. D., and D. B. Teixeira. 1990.

Technology in banking: Creating value and destroying profits. Homewood, Ill.: Dow Jones-Irwin. Discusses some of the major application areas of IT in banking, and provides perspective on how IT is used by senior managers in banking in the quest for competitive advantage.

Wall Street Computer Review (journal). New York: Gralla. If you want to know about how IT is applied in portfolio management and money market trading, this is where you should start.

Robert J. Kauffman

FLYING

See Aviation, Computers in

FORTH

FORTH (as it was originally called; the language is now generally spelled with only an initial capital letter as Forth) was developed over several years in the late 1960s by Charles H. Moore. As with the genesis of many of today's computer languages, Forth was created because Moore wanted capabilities that the languages then in common use did not provide. At the time Forth was under development, Moore was working with an IBM 1130, which was called a "third-generation computer." Because the new language he had invented seemed so much more powerful, Moore thought of it as a "fourth-generation computer language," and would have named it accordingly except that the IBM 1130 allowed only five-character names.

Forth is somewhat different from other high-level programming languages. According to those who are familiar with it, Forth programs execute faster than those written in most other languages, and Forth applications require less memory. The syntax of Forth is similar to that of LISP. As programs written in Forth are fast, very compact, and transportable, and because there are versions of Forth available for virtually every mini- and microcomputer, using Forth gives the programmer a broad range of options for the finished product. Forth is used in many applications for which speed is critical (such as interpretation of data from process control sensors and instruments in manufacturing) and in those for which small code size is useful, such as arcade games, robotics, and artificial intelligence programs.

Forth is a bit more difficult to master than other high-level languages, but once its structure and syntax are understood, Forth makes it easy to create small, fast, highly efficient programs. And Forth is more than just a programming language; it includes an assembler, interpreter, and compiler, so the programmer need not follow the usual time-consuming steps of writing code with an editor, leaving the editor, loading the compiler, compiling the code, and so forth. This feature is a great time saver for the programmer, and makes repetitive program testing very easy.

Forth begins with a set of several hundred predefined commands called *words.* This standard set of commands was decided on by a committee in 1983, and has thus become known as the FORTH-83 Standard (one of the few instances in which the language's name is still spelled in capital letters). But this set of predefined words is only the foundation; the most notable feature of Forth is its extensibility. The programmer can add new words or modify the built-in ones at any time, and the language can be expanded to meet the demands of any particular application. Each new word can be defined in terms of other words almost indefinitely.

As new words are created and defined, Forth enters them into a dictionary, which is what Forth calls *compiling.* (Compiling generally means the translation of high-level language into machine code, but in Forth the term also refers specifically to entering new words in the dictionary.) On most systems, typing WORDS followed by a [return] will display all the words in the dictionary, in the order they were defined in, followed by their locations in memory.

Forth was designed to store data on disks rather than keeping it in random-access memory (RAM), and nearly all present-day Forth systems use disk memory. Forth stores data on disk in units of 1,024 characters (one kilobyte) called *blocks*. When used for source text, each block is arranged in 16 lines of 64 characters each. By convention, the first line of a source-text block (line 0) is reserved for a brief description of the purpose of the block. The rest of the block is used for definitions. Forth uses Reverse Polish Notation both for definitions and for calculations, another feature that many programmers will need some time to adjust to. (Programmers sometimes joke that Forth is a language used backward think to like who those by.) A programmer accustomed to using BASIC (for example) who wanted to look at a particular line would type LIST 10. A programmer using Forth who wanted to look at a particular block would type 10 LIST.

Forth programming involves a stepping-stone approach. Each part of the program is broken up into smaller steps, and a word defined for each small step. These smaller words are then combined to make other words, and so on, until just one word represents many steps. The Forth programmer can quickly test each new word over and over until it works correctly, simply by defining the word, loading the block that defines the word, and running it to see the results. Thus, by the time the most complex words are constructed, the code can be virtually bug free.

A thorough overview of Forth programming is beyond the scope of this article, but any of the books listed here will give the beginning Forth programmer a good foundation. Forth in and of itself is not a complex language. Each word is clearly defined and the concepts involved are not difficult to understand. But with the tremendous flexibility allowed by extensibility, using Forth requires the programmer to have a clear perception of each program's design and purpose. Forth is rather like a collection of small, simple kitchen tools that allow a chef to create culinary masterpieces.

SAMPLE PROGRAM

The following short program in Forth is the "Sieve of Eratosthenes," which calculates and prints out prime numbers.

```
0    // Sieve of Eratosthenes
1    decimal
2    8190 constant size
3    0 variable flags      size allot
4    : do-prime
5       flags size 1 fill
6       161 3 0 fill
7       0     size 0
8          do   flags i + c@
9             if i dup + 3 + dup i +
10               begin dup size <
11                  while 0 over flags + c!
12                     over + repeat
13                  2 drop 1+ then
14          loop
15       " primes =" ;
```

Going line by line, here is what the program does.

0. Gives the name of the program, "Sieve of Eratosthenes."

1. Tells Forth to give the answers in decimal, rather than hexadecimal or octal, notation.

2. Defines a constant called "size" and gives it a value of 8190.

3. Defines a variable called "flags" and sets its size to zero.

4. The colon indicates that this is the beginning of the definition of a word. The indented lines that follow will continue the definition.

5. Here we have the variable "flags" again, and the program is told to begin with whatever value "flags" has (set to zero in line 3) and begin to increment its size by a value of 1.

6. Starting at a value of 161, increment three bytes with the value of zero.

7, 8. Taken together, these lines start off at zero and loop through "flags," resetting the index pointers and fetching new values for "flags."

9. This tells the program to compare the value on the top of the stack to the value in memory. If they are the same, the program adds 3 and compares again.

10, 11. The "begin" in line 10 combined with the "while" in line 11 starts an indefinite loop that duplicates the top stack item, compares its value with the value in memory, moves another value to the top of the stack, and adds to it, continuing to compare the values and store them.

12. Keep on going as many times as it takes.

13. This line says "Discard the top pair of numbers, add one to the next one, and keep comparing."

14. This is the end of the loop.

15. Print "primes =" on the screen, followed by the values determined by the program. The semicolon ends the definition of the word.

For Further Reading

Armstrong, M. 1985. *Learning Forth: A self-teaching guide.* New York: Wiley.

Brodie, L. 1984. *Thinking Forth.* Englewood Cliffs, N.J.: Prentice-Hall.

Brodie, L. 1987. *Starting Forth.* Englewood Cliffs, N.J.: Prentice-Hall.

Dr. Dobbs' Journal Editors. 1987. *Dr. Dobbs' toolbook of Forth,* vol. 2 (book and disk). Redwood City, Calif.: M&T Publications.

Kelly, M. G. 1986. *FORTH, a text and reference.* Englewood Cliffs, N.J.: Prentice-Hall.

Tracy, M. 1989. *Mastering FORTH.* New York: Brady.

Marte Brengle

FORTRAN

FORTRAN was the first popular and commercially available higher-level computer language. Widely used by scientists and engineers, the language derives its name from FORmula TRANslation, which plainly shows its mathematical roots, primarily from algebra and algebraic notation.

Prior to the introduction of FORTRAN, programming a computer in machine language was a laborious process. Only large, rather primitive mainframes such as the IBM 704 were in existence, and the programmer had to have extensive knowledge of the internal architecture of each individual type of computer to know how to program it. Though these assembly languages offered efficient and speedy usage of the central processing unit (CPU), simple mathematical operators such as + (addition) and − (subtraction) were absent in these lower-level languages. The idea of quick processing speeds for numerical computations was extremely attractive to scientists and engineers, who before had reduced data by hand. The need for a programming language that would work on many different kinds of computers and be understandable to and easy to use for people who were not computer technicians gave rise to FORTRAN.

The FORTRAN project began on IBM computers in the 1950s. It was a "card-oriented" language, as most input for these early computers was accomplished via punched cards. A programmer would first use a flowchart to outline the loops and operations of a program, and then would write the corresponding FORTRAN code on a FORTRAN coding form, which aided in keypunching the parts of the statement in the correct columns on the cards. Each command statement of a program was typed, in a very specific way, on one keypunch card on a keypunch machine. The first statement of the program was contained on the first card, the second statement on the second card, and so on. The whole stack of cards was fed by a computer operator into a card reader attached to the computer. Many programmers never actually touched the computer itself, but only a keypunch machine used to create the set of program cards! The fact that FORTRAN was originally a card-oriented language has influenced it through the years, and has governed such aspects as placement of line numbers in the first five spaces of a line. Today's computers, from personal computers to minicomputers to mainframes, possess sophisticated text editors that allow a programmer on-line access for direct storage and editing of programs. This means direct compilation of a source program by the programmer's own hand.

As FORTRAN is a compiled language, programming in FORTRAN requires that a source program be created first using an ASCII text editor (i.e., a program designed for the editing of text in the American Standard Code for Information Interchange, or ASCII, format). At this point, the computer is unable to execute the instructions contained in the source program. Then, by use of a FORTRAN compiler or translator, the source program is translated into machine language and an executable program, the object program. During the translation from source to object code, the computer automatically reviews the program diagnostically, and notifies the programmer of any errors. This is typically called the "debugging" phase of the programming process, in which the FORTRAN programmer notes any errors, returns to the source program to correct them, then recompiles the program until successful.

Developed from 1954 to the late 1950s by John Backus, FORTRAN has evolved over time, with improvements being continually made. FORTRAN I was introduced by IBM in 1956, but the first widely available version of FORTRAN was FORTRAN II, which was introduced in 1958. FORTRAN II allowed for independent compilation of subroutines, which allowed programmers to establish large libraries of commonly used subroutines.

Originally, there was no set standard for FORTRAN, and the version recognized by one FORTRAN compiler might be very different from that recognized by another. To remedy this, the American National Standards Institute (ANSI) gave a definition of FORTRAN in 1966 and encouraged all manufacturers to conform to this standard. Thus FORTRAN IV, introduced in 1962, was standardized by the American National Standards Institute in the document ANSI X3.9-1966, which lends the name FORTRAN 66 to this version. This standardization gave FORTRAN portability from one computer to another. A new standard was adopted with ANSI X3.9-1978, commonly called FORTRAN 77, which had many improvements when compared with FORTRAN 66, most notably inclusion of modern structured programming ideas, specifically the IF–ELSE–ENDIF statements that allow *block* structuring. FORTRAN 77 also introduced more complex input and output statements, particularly for file handling, and the ability to process character-string data. Many important concepts in higher-level programming languages originated with FORTRAN, including statements, variables, expressions, iterative and conditional statements, and formatted input and output.

FORTRAN is composed of four main types of instructions: arithmetic statements, control statements, nonexecutable statements, and input/output statements. Arithmetic statements are composed of equations and other arithmetic operations. Control statements control the actions of the computer as it executes the program. Input/output statements allow input or output of data or instructions, including user interaction. Nonexecutable statements usually provide information, but do not require computer action, and include the COMMENT and DIMENSION statements. The only data structure in FORTRAN is the array, a programming concept introduced by FORTRAN, which is directly patterned after the mathematician's matrix, commonly used in scientific calculations such as vectors.

The new FORTRAN standard, previously referred to as FORTRAN 8x, as it was formulated in the 1980s, is now called FORTRAN 90. This new standard incorporates such features as array operations, pointers, user-defined data types, and a new source form that provides easier input by the programmer. Also included is the labeling of some FORTRAN 77 features as obsolescent, which gives the language a means to evolve, although FORTRAN 77 is included as a complete subset of FORTRAN 90 with no deletions of command statements. This third standardization of FORTRAN is being accomplished by the work of the X3J3 committee, which had originally planned to have the new standard ready by 1982. X3J3 is made up of forty-five representatives of academia, hardware and software vendors, and users, and is accredited by ANSI.

For Further Reading

Didday, R., and R. Page. 1984. *FORTRAN for humans.* 4th ed. St. Paul, Minn.: West.

Metcalf, M., and J. Reid. 1990. *FORTRAN 90 explained.* Oxford: Oxford University Press.

Loretta McKibben

FRACTALS

See Chaos Theory;
Data Compression and Fractals

FUNCTIONAL LANGUAGES

See Programming Language Design

G

GAMES, COMPUTER

In 1972, a young engineer named Nolan Bushnell designed a computerized version of table tennis. To play the game, players used on-screen electronic paddles to serve and volley the small ball across the net. Bushnell called the game "Pong," installed a test version in a nearby tavern in Sunnyvale, California, and watched as it became an immediate hit.

Pong's popularity launched the computer game industry and spawned hundreds of imitators. The colorful screen displays, powered by microprocessors, captured the public's imagination. These games also had important implications for personal computing, and advances in game technology have been used in a variety of applications.

The public had seen nothing like video games before. Pinball, the mechanical forerunner to the video game, paled in comparison. Its only challenge was to navigate the silver ball through a static maze of pathways. But video games provided the illusion of a real opponent. The on-screen landscapes shimmered with motion and were fraught with peril for the unskilled. They challenged players to devise game strategies, master use of the joystick and buttons, and rise through succeeding levels of complexity. They tested players' reflexes and dexterity and gave them an opportunity to take on a variety of imaginary roles: rescuer, adventurer, leader, navigator, warrior.

Hundreds of millions of dollars in quarters were dropped into machines over the next few years. Computer-based video games lined the walls of pinball arcades across the country, and then spread further to airline terminals, shopping malls, restaurants, and movie theater lobbies.

The repertoire of electronic beeps and other sound effects lured adults as well as children. Businessmen in suits with briefcases at their sides were often found at the machines. Players found a raft of games from which to choose. "Space Invaders" featured approaching enemies that moved with increasing speed, and safety shelters that disappeared as the game progressed. "Pac-Man" gobbled up dots as he worked his way through a maze. "Asteroids" players fended off approaching UFOs and colliding celestial bodies, all the while trying to avoid shooting down friendlier space beings.

In 1975, retail stores began selling versions that could be played at home by connecting a game box to a television. The games were issued on cartridges that players inserted into the game boxes. Their popularity soared even higher, and Atari, the company Bushnell founded, sold 13 million games in 3 years.

The games' popularity fueled the fledgling personal computer market. The early personal computers of the 1970s were more sophisticated than the game boxes that connected to televisions, but there was no commercial software to run on them, and they were built with extremely limited memory. Their most common applications were for games, which were still at a primitive level. The first computer games were entirely text-based programs. For example, a game might challenge the player to guess where an item was hidden, and the player and the computer would progress through a series of questions and answers until the player correctly identified the hiding place.

In the early 1980s, IBM introduced its color graphics adapter, a board that could be inserted into an expansion slot and thus allow IBM and IBM-compatible computers to

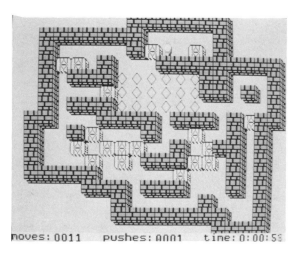

moves: 0011   pushes: 0001   time: 0:00:53

FIGURE 1. A screen from SokoBan, an early computer game. *Photo courtesy Spectrum Holobyte, Alameda, Calif.*

display graphics in a modest array of colors. Inspired by the sophistication of video games, software programmers rose to the challenge of bringing the same level of quality to the personal computer. They pushed the computers' rudimentary technology to its outer limits and devised imaginative and complex games of space travel, combat, fantasy, and jungle adventures.

Microsoft Corporation's "Flight Simulator" was a ground-breaking computer game that featured graphics and animation that far outstripped those of other games. Players faced the cockpit of a jet aircraft and, manning the controls with the joystick and buttons, guided the aircraft through its simulated takeoff, cruise, and descent.

At the height of their popularity, video games were surrounded by a swirl of controversy. Parents and educators worried about the long hours youths spent playing the games and the games' hold over youngsters' attention. Opponents claimed the games were empty entertainment and argued that they offered no learning benefits or even intellectual stimulation. Indeed, the legions of adult players supported this theory by explaining that they turned to the games for relaxation, not mental challenge.

Opponents also voiced concern about the games' themes, which they criticized as aggressive, often violent, and sexist. Many featured warring worlds, and they "armed" players with "weapons" used to destroy opposing forces. Planets and foreign worlds were blown up in elaborate on-screen explosions. Opponents also noted the sexism of the video game culture. Game devotees were largely boys and men. On screen, the characters were mostly male. Female characters tended to be relegated to playing minor, dependent roles. The packages and advertisements frequently depicted women as curvaceous damsels in distress.

The controversy developed into a furor, with the U.S. Surgeon General going on record as opposed to the games. One Massachusetts town banned the games from public places. There was widespread concern that the games were depleting young peoples' thinking processes as well as their wallets.

But the games also had their defenders. Some researchers argued that video games did indeed offer an educational component. Like chess, video games required mastery of a set of moves. High-scoring players learned from experience how a series of plays would affect the outcome. They developed scoring strategies and worked to "outguess" the machine. In addition, the machines gave the players an incentive: they asked the highest-scoring players to log their initials on a list of top players.

Not all of the games focused on death and destruction. Some were designed to develop in players a specific set of values. "Donkey Kong," a popular game, required the player to pursue the tricky rescue of another character from the clutches of a mighty gorilla. Another game, "Frogger," required the players, as an on-screen frog, to dodge a series of hazards as they hopped across a busy intersection. Simulated sports games instilled the concept of teamwork. On-screen versions of baseball, football, and basketball demanded shrewd use of team members, and some even came with a playbook.

Computer and video games were also applauded as introductory lessons in computer use. Youngsters who played them developed a feel for how computers worked, how the machines could be programmed for specific purposes like games. They learned that the games relied on an internal set of

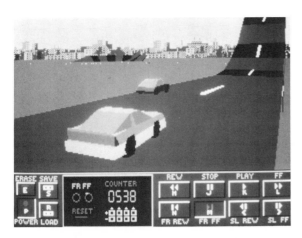

FIGURE 2. A screen from Stunt Driver, a later game with more sophisticated graphics and action. *Photo courtesy Spectrum Holobyte, Alameda, Calif.*

chips and instructions. Researchers agreed that video games could be useful in acclimating youngsters to computers.

Despite opponents' fears that video games would inflict permanent damage on children, the game craze had run its course by the mid-1980s. The video game remained popular, but the novelty had worn off, and video game playing had become routine.

The 32-bit microprocessor inside many personal computers today provides the foundation for more elaborate, colorful game scenarios. Advancements in animation have given on-screen movements a much smoother, realistic appearance. In addition, more sophisticated monitors offer crisper screen resolution and sharper, more varied colors.

Computer games are serious business; they are credited with important advancements in business computing. Game designers' achievements in color, animation, and role playing helped develop the field of personal computer-based simulations, for example. Branches of the armed services have licensed use of game technologies to provide combat simulation exercises for pilots and soldiers.

For Further Reading

Loftus, G. R., and E. F. Loftus. 1983. *Mind at play: The psychology of video games.* New York: Basic Books.

Malone, M. S. 1985. *The big score: The billion dollar story of Silicon Valley.* Garden City, N.Y.: Doubleday.

Tomczyk, M. S. 1984. *The home computer wars: An insider's account of Commodore and Jack Tramiel.* Greensboro, N.C.: Compute! Publications Inc.

Turkle, S. 1984. *The second self: Computers and the human spirit.* New York: Simon and Schuster.

Deborah Asbrand

GATES, WILLIAM H. (BILL)

William H. Gates was born in Seattle, Washington, on October 28, 1955. His father is a prominent lawyer and his mother has served on numerous corporate, charitable, and civil boards. He taught himself programming at age 13, having taken up computer studies in 1967 as a seventh-grader at the private Lakeside School in Seattle. Gates and a ninth-grader named Paul Allen were enthralled about using the school's time-shared computer. Gates and Allen's enthusiasm has not waned since. In the late 1960s, Gates and some other Seattle teenagers would ride their bicycles each afternoon to the Computer Center Corporation office, where they searched for errors in the programs being run on the Center's computer. They eventually went on the firm's payroll. Throughout their high school years, Gates and Allen worked as programming consultants.

TRW, a large software firm in Vancouver, Washington, offered Gates and Allen $20,000 a year, each, to work in a software development group. Gates took a year-long leave from high school during his senior year to go to work for TRW. When work diminished, he entered Harvard University. He was planning to stay away from computers. Allen went to work as a systems programmer for Honeywell, near Boston.

Gates entered Harvard in the fall of 1973. Allen happened to be strolling through Harvard Square one day when he noticed the

January issue of *Popular Electronics* on a news stand. Allen bought a copy and went on to visit Gates. The Altair microcomputer, based on the Intel 8080 chip, made by an Albuquerque, New Mexico, firm called MITS, and selling for $350, appeared on the cover. Here was the first truly cheap computer! To anyone who knew computers then, it was instantly clear that the Altair required, more than anything else, a BASIC interpreter, to permit users to write programs in a high-level language rather than in machine code. Allen proposed to Gates that the two try to write a BASIC interpreter for the Altair. Gates and Allen phoned Edward Roberts, the MITS founder who had built the Altair, with an offer to write a BASIC interpreter for the Altair. Roberts was interested, and the pair started working. Allen and Gates spent February and March of 1975 working in Gates' small dormitory room at Harvard. Allen flew out to Albuquerque to demonstrate the interpreter. Roberts bought it and Gates and Allen had created an industry standard, one that would hold the field for the next 6 years.

Allen promptly became MITS's software director. Gates dropped out of Harvard at the end of his sophomore year in 1975 and went to work as a freelance software writer. It was then that Gates and Allen formed Microsoft Corporation. Within 18 months, the two had made a few hundred thousand dollars for their new firm. They were writing programs for Apple Computer, Inc. and Commodore. During the first year, Gates and Allen expanded BASIC so that it would run on other microcomputers.

In 1980, IBM asked Gates to design the operating system for their new machine, what would become the incredibly popular IBM PC. In early 1981, Gates delivered the operating system that would control the IBM PC. Microsoft Disk Operating System (MS-DOS) very quickly became the major operating system for personal computers in the United States. Over two million copies of MS-DOS had been sold as of the spring of 1984.

Other companies turned to Gates as well. Apple Computer, Inc. asked him to develop software for the Macintosh computer. He helped design the Radio Shack Model 100. Beginning in the mid-1980s, Microsoft Corporation started developing applications software, including Microsoft Word, for word processing; Microsoft Works, for business applications; and Flight Simulator, which permits someone to sit at a computer and simulate the piloting of a plane.

In 1982, Gates dreamed of a piece of software, called Windows, that he hoped would push his company to the top of the personal computer software industry. The product was developed, and on April 2, 1987, IBM chose Windows as a key piece of software for their new generation of personal computers—IBM PS/2. Windows is built into the operating system—the software that controls a computer's basic functions and runs applications software such as spreadsheets, word processors, and database managers. Windows, which uses graphics similar to those of Apple Computer's Macintosh computer, makes IBM PCs much easier to use by simplifying the commands needed to operate them.

Microsoft Corporation has set standards for the software industry in languages, operating systems, and application software. Gates has provided the vision for the company's new product ideas and technologies.

For Further Reading

Lammers, S. 1986. *Programmers at work,* pp. 71–90. Redmond, Wash.: Microsoft Press.

Moody, F. 1991. Mr. Software. *New York Times Magazine,* 25 August 1991, pp. 26+.

Reflections. 1988. Manhasset, N.Y.: CMP Publications.

Donald D. Spencer

GENETIC ALGORITHMS

See Machine Learning

GEOGRAPHIC INFORMATION SYSTEMS

A geographic information system is a set of methods for using computers to store, compile, analyze, and report information with spatial characteristics. The definition of geographic information systems (GISs) is controversial and difficult because of the wide range of software and hardware vendors that purport to include GIS products in their product line. Common among these systems is the paper map as the main output format. A stricter definition has been proposed as follows: A GIS is any information management system that can

- "Collect, store, and retrieve information based on its spatial location;
- Identify locations within a targeted environment that meet specific criteria;
- Explore relationships among data sets within that environment;
- Analyze the related data spatially as an aid to making decisions about that environment;
- Facilitate selecting and passing data to application-specific analytical models capable of assessing the impact of alternatives on the chosen environment; and
- Display the selected environment both graphically and numerically either before or after analysis." (*GIS Forum* 1988)

Geographic information systems were first conceived in the early 1960s as a special application of database management techniques whereby georeferenced data stored in a computerized format could be displayed in a graphical format. In other words, an attempt was made to draw a map from a database of information. The first attempts to create a GIS were limited to mainframe hardware and custom-written software routines that were cumbersome at best and required full-time technical staff to run. Since the advent of inexpensive, powerful microcomputers, more commercial GIS software has become available. Hundreds of GIS packages have entered the market since 1985, making the prospect of desktop mapping a reality.

An information system has four components: input, manipulation, output, and feedback.

INPUT

A major division in data entry and GIS packages overall centers around the way data are stored for a given map. The GIS packages are based either on grid cells (rasters) or on lines/points (vectors), although the distinction is being blurred with new techniques for converting the two. The strength of a raster GIS is its analytical capability. Raster-based routines are simpler to develop because a raster-based map is a more simplified version of reality than a vector-based map. A vector GIS generally produces higher-quality graphics.

Data entry for GIS is most often accomplished by using a digitizing tablet or a scanner to record the X and Y coordinates of an object electronically. The objects being digitized are usually in the form of a paper (base) map that has a scale and a map projection (e.g., Universal Transmercator [UTM], state planar, or latitude/longitude). Although not a requirement, a standard projection does allow comparison of the data with other digitized maps that use the same projection (or can be electronically converted to the same projection). This has become especially important, as many digitized datasets are available commercially or from government sources and acquiring existing datasets can reduce the most expensive part of GIS development, data entry.

During the data entry process, attributes are recorded for each object on the base map. For instance, a polygon on the map may have recorded a vegetative cover type, sales figures, elevation, political district, or any other type of information that may be of interest. The type of data recorded for a digitized map defines the map's subject matter or theme. The topology, or positional relationship of an object on the map to other objects on the map, is often recorded to support various types of analyses, such as route optimization and juxtaposition studies. Other types of

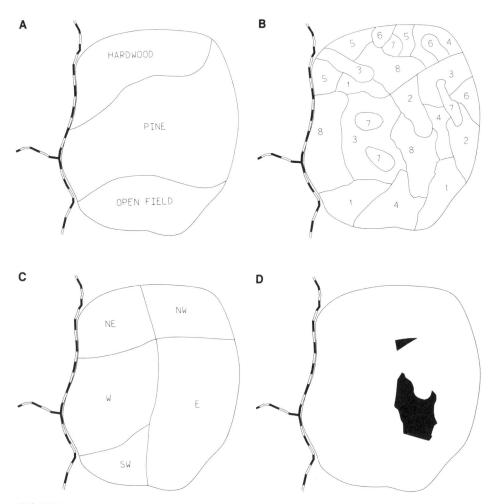

FIGURE 1. Maps of a generic study area. Three layers (soils, vegetation, and aspect) are combined to produce a map of areas that have a pine cover type, an east aspect, and soil type 8. **(a)** Vegetative cover type map of study area. **(b)** Soil type map of study area. **(c)** Slope aspect map of study area. **(d)** Overlay map of study area where pine cover type, east aspect, and soil type 8 overlap.

objects recorded for a map include point locations and map titles.

MANIPULATION

Most of the manipulation of the data once they have been entered is handled by the database management software. The most common type of manipulation is overlaying maps of various themes, by first making sure that they will be handled at the same scale and projection and then combining the two maps to form a new map that shows the interactions of the themes. For instance, a map of areas where a certain tree species is found may be combined with a map of soil types. A statistical routine may then be run to show whether one of the soil types is preferred by a given species over all the others. With this knowledge, a new map could be produced that showed where that tree species probably occurs. As another example, a government agency wants to find the best route for a new road from city A to city B. Maps of topography, soils, housing, existing roads, hydrology, and other themes can be combined and weighted. An optimization routine could be run to find the best route from city A to city B based on the weighted data in the combined map.

OUTPUT

The GIS output can take the form of graphic output (e.g., screen or paper displays of maps) or tabular output (e.g., printed lists of polygon attributes that meet a certain criteria). The primary reason for using a GIS is the visual format for reporting. Geographic datasets are complex and large by their very nature. Patterns within the data are of great interest, and pattern recognition is one of the areas where humans still excel in comparison with computers.

FEEDBACK

The human element in a GIS is probably the least understood component and also the component that most often causes failure of the GIS. The human component is also responsible for the most critical part of a functioning GIS, feedback. A given output has no meaning without the interpretation of the operator. If the operator does not constantly review, criticize, and change the system to make it more useful, obsolescence will overtake the system almost immediately. Development of a GIS assumes adequately trained and committed personnel. This applies to one-person desktop mapping applications as well as 100-person GIS application centers.

The most important implication of GIS technology is the ability to combine information from traditionally isolated disciplines and analyze it using a common data element, geographic location. Combinations of environmental, economic, governmental, and infrastructural datasets are being used to address questions and analyze options that would not even have existed 30 years ago. Increasingly, this combination of datasets results in a dialogue among professionals in a climate of informed decision making rather than conflict.

Reference

GIS Forum. 1988. GIS recognized as valuable tool for decision makers. *GIS Forum.* Spring, Tex.: Hanigan Group, THG Publishing. Premiere Issue, p. 6. An excellent source of current information on the GIS community.

For Further Reading

Bailey, R. G. 1988. Problems with using overlay mapping for planning and their implications for geographic information systems. *Environmental Management* 12(1): 11–17.

Clarke, K. C. 1986. Recent trends in geographic information systems research. *Geo-Processing* 3:1–15.

Maguire, J. 1989. *Computers in geography.* New York: Wiley.

Jefferson L. Waldon

GEOLOGY, COMPUTERS IN

Geology (from *ge*, which means "Earth," and *logos*, which means "discourse") is the science of the Earth, or the systematic study of the processes, materials, environments, and history of our planet. This science focuses on the morphology of the Earth, or the shape and evolution of its surface, which experiences continual change; the regolith of the Earth, or the loose materials on the surface; the bedrock, or the continuous solid rock that underlies the regolith; and the tectonic plates atop which the continents and oceans ride, continually pressing against and modifying one another. The major disciplines of geology include geophysics, geochemistry, geodesy, and cartography. In the years since the invention of the computer, geologists have found many ways to use computers in studying the geological processes of our planet Earth, as well as the solid surfaces of other planets and satellites of our solar system.

DATA ACQUISITION, REDUCTION AND ANALYSIS

Like scientists of other genres, geologists use the scientific method: a hypothesis is formulated; then an experiment is formulated and performed and a set of data is obtained; finally, the data are analyzed to either prove or disprove the original hypothesis. From this work a general theory might be postulated if the results warrant it. Geology was traditionally an observational science, in which the experimental phase involved gathering data from a specific geological site. Today, however, geologists also experiment in the laboratory, setting up processes that mimic those found in the field. Computers are used extensively in both observational and experimental geology.

One key way that geologists use computers is in data acquisition. Data about a specific geological process or experiment are gathered in a multitude of ways: a scientist studying the effects of the wind on sand grains would need a computer attached to equipment that measures wind speed and direction; a scientist who builds an experiment to study the deformational effects of pressure on rocks would need a different set of data, including readings of temperature and pressure; and a volcanologist, who specializes in volcanoes, may place many sensors that detect ground movement in key places around a volcano. In each of these instances, an interface of sensors and analog-to-digital converters are required to translate the information into a digital format. The software is usually designed to acquire the data at specific time intervals, to give the processes involved a meaning over time.

Once acquired, the data must be reduced into a meaningful format. Only then will the data reveal trends and patterns. Data reduction is a complex and time-consuming venture, often requiring custom software to transform the raw data into a more useful, condensed form. This often necessitates adjusting, smoothing, scaling, compacting, and ordering of the data. From the reduced data the geologist draws scientific conclusions and supports or denies any original hypotheses and theories through complex scientific analysis. The volcanologist may note, for example, an excessive amount of movement in the Earth's crust, possibly indicating movement of magma beneath the surface, sometimes a sign of an impending eruption.

Many geologists use graphical means to display information about their results, such as specialized graphs and charts to show rock-type abundances, the various chemical elements found in a particular type of rock, or other pertinent data.

TOPOLOGICAL MAPPING

Computer graphical capabilities developed since the mid-1970s contribute to the digitizing of many geological maps. In this process, a digitizer mechanism is used to translate elevation or other data from a map into a computer database. This allows for easy storage, retrieval, and modifications of maps and other topological data.

COMPUTER MODELING

Over the past several decades, geologists have begun to use the more powerful graphical and computational capacities of computers to create computer models of geological processes. Given specific parameters of, say, a volcano's lava, including its viscosity and flow rate, a computer model of an erupting volcano can simulate the real eruption, also allowing the scientist to modify elements such as wind speed and direction. By observing the volcano created, volcanologists can learn much about real-life situations in which the lava may have cooled thousands of years ago. Computer models and simulations of geological processes are currently being created to study shear stresses of geological landforms, plate tectonics and the movement of the major continental plates across our planet, and even the interaction of the atmosphere with the geological processes of our planet. These computer models would not have been possible without the computing power of today's superconducting computers and powerful mainframes.

REMOTE SENSING AND IMAGE PROCESSING

The computer-intensive fields of remote sensing and image processing have made very significant contributions to the understanding of the Earth's geology, as well as the geology of other planets and satellites in our solar system. Remote sensing involves the study of the interaction of electromagnetic radiation with materials on the surface of the Earth; image processing is the manipulation, storage, and retrieval of remote sensing images by computer. Through the years, images taken of the Earth's surface for geological study have progressed from crude photographs, both black and white and color, to sophisticated computer-based images that cover the electromagnetic spectrum, rather than only visible light. This allows geologists not only to discern geologic features, but to determine the composition and even temperature of the same features, as different substances exhibit varying signatures in the radiation they emit.

Originally, the first photos of the Earth from high altitudes (160 to 320 kilometers) were obtained by small automatic cameras on unmanned sounding rockets, launched after World War II from the White Sands Missile Range in New Mexico. Though the quality of these photos was not up to current standards, geologists were able to interpret a number of geologic features in the 1960s. Then, during the testing phase for the Mercury manned space project, NASA launched an unmanned satellite in Earth orbit that shot several hundred color photographs of the western Sahara. Astronauts who flew in the Gemini missions in 1965 and 1966 took photographs of the Earth with hand-held 70-millimeter cameras through the spacecraft windows, and produced 1,100 photographs that were usable for geology, geography, or oceanography.

The Apollo missions in the late 1960s carried astronauts to the Moon, and also orbited the Earth many times. The Apollo 9 mission included the SO-65 experiment, which was designed to obtain the first orbital multispectral photographs. This experiment was the predecessor to the Skylab mission, the first dedicated to Earth observations, which provided thousands of images of the Earth and showed the importance of obtaining high-resolution images of the Earth from space.

Perhaps the most important images of the Earth have been taken by an unmanned series of satellites, the Landsats. Landsats 1, 2, and 3 were launched in 1972, 1975, and 1978, respectively. These early Landsats carried multispectral scanners and return-beam vidicon technology. All of these satellites have now ceased operation, but only after providing hundreds of thousands of images of the Earth for scientific study. A second generation of Landsats, much more complex than their predecessors, were launched in 1982 and 1984. They included a device called the Thematic Mapper (TM) that provided images with improved spatial resolution, an extended spectral range, and additional spectral bands, so that a wider range of light wavelengths could be studied. The most important difference between the images produced by Landsat and the photos taken by astronauts is their digital format, which allows them to be processed by computer. Images are taken by charge-coupled device technology, then transmitted to Earth stations via microwave.

Radar technology, or the detection and ranging of radio waves, which operate in the radio and microwave bands of the electromagnetic spectrum, gives geologists and other scientists an important view of the Earth. Radar is considered an active remote sensing system because it provides its own source of energy. That is, radar illuminates the terrain being studied with electromagnetic energy, detects the energy that returns, and records it as an image. The advantages of radar systems are that they operate regardless of lighting conditions, are largely independent of the weather, and can see through most clouds. Originally, specially equipped aircraft operated the radar systems; however, *NASA* launched three Earth-orbiting satellite radar systems: Seasat, designed to map ocean surface roughness, current patterns, and sea ice conditions, and two radar systems flown on Space Shuttle missions (SIR-A and SIR-B, where SIR denotes shuttle imaging radar). Though Seasat was designed to study the ocean, it has provided valuable images of geologic formations, as well.

In studying the Earth, remote sensing images from space can aid in exploration of nonrenewable resources, such as minerals and fossil fuels, and provide valuable information about the environment, including the atmosphere, the continent, and the sea floor, as well as provide analyses of land use and land cover. Large-scale geologic phenomena, not as apparent on the Earth's surface, are sometimes more easily studied using space-based images.

The likelihood of the occurrence of natural hazards is another area of study to which image processing from space can contribute. By analyzing information on active fault zones, for example, geologists can help predict areas in which major earthquakes are likely to occur, as earthquakes occur in areas known to have unrelieved fault stresses. Volcanoes may be analyzed from space-based images, to help identify those that have the potential for eruption.

PLANETARY GEOLOGY

With the advent of complex computer technology and space travel, a new field of geology was formed: planetary geology. Studies of the other planets of the solar system were limited until the 1960s to wavering telescope images from Earth-based telescopes, always subject to the whims of an interfering atmosphere. Planetary geology is the study of the origin, evolution, and distribution of the matter that forms the planets, including the Earth, natural satellites, comets, and asteroids.

The Moon, our Earth's satellite, was the first extraterrestrial planet body to be extensively studied with remote sensing techniques, as well as by physical examination of actual samples of the surface brought back to Earth by the Apollo astronauts. Beginning in 1964, the Ranger and Surveyor series of space probes sent back detailed pictures of the Moon.

Since these initial explorations of the Moon, space probes have been sent to every planet in our solar system save Pluto. The United States, which is still unsurpassed in digital image processing and remote sensing technology, has sent the Voyager spacecraft to Jupiter and Saturn, giant gas planets with satellites that possess surfaces of geologic interest, as well as to Uranus and Neptune. Radar mappers from both the Soviet Union and the United States have penetrated the thick clouds of sulfuric acid on Venus, a "sister" planet to the Earth similar in size

and composition, whose atmosphere somehow went horribly askew with an uncontrollable greenhouse effect. The Viking landers on Mars have sent back breathtaking views of a sunset on that distant planet, forever changing it into a *place* that humans might one day set foot on.

From all these geological images of other planets, geologists have formulated many theories about planetary evolution, types, and formation. This information is important as these planets formed at the same time as our Earth. A new science of comparative planetology has emerged from the study of our Earth and the other planets as a "family" of planetary bodies.

One thing is certain: without computers we would have a very limited view of the geological processes of our own planet and the other components of our solar system.

For Further Reading
Greeley, R. 1985. *Planetary landscapes.* London: Allen & Unwin.
Sabins, F. F., Jr. 1987. *Remote sensing, principles and interpretation.* 2nd ed. New York: Freeman.

Loretta McKibben

GOVERNMENT, COMPUTER USES IN

Computers were first introduced into the federal governmdent in the 1950s to help tabulate the U.S. Census, and their use has increased steadily ever since. Indeed, computer use has expanded both vertically among the federal, state, and local levels of government in the federal system, and horizontally among the legislative, executive, and judicial branches at each level of government.

The initial impetus for computer use in government was largely to achieve cost savings and administrative efficiency. This led to the application of computers to the record-keeping and mass processing functions of government; however, the computer's potential for improving decision making by government officials and service delivery to citizens has spurred computer use far beyond these initial applications. Today, computers are also used for public safety and surveillance, decision and policy support, management and operations, and communication with citizens.

As computer use expanded and computer applications broadened, the results of government computerization also have become more apparent. For the most part, computer use has produced positive results not only for the government as a whole, but also for individual workers and for the citizen clients of government; however, some problems and policy issues also have emerged. Critical problems have arisen in the implementation of large computer systems. And, even when implemented successfully, some of these systems have raised issues about the trade-offs between the government's need to know and the individual's right to privacy.

This article explores each of the foregoing topics: the extent of computer use, the purposes of computer use, the results of computer use, and issues of computer use in government.

EXTENT OF COMPUTER USE IN GOVERNMENT

The federal system of government is organized into three operating levels: the federal level, the state level, and the local level. All three levels of government collect revenues from the populace and provide services in return. Computers are now an integral part of revenue collection and service provision at all levels. As government invests more resources in computers and becomes more dependent on computer-based functions, the management of computer hardware, software, and staff resources, known as information resource management, is becoming an important and distinct management function.

Federal Government

Computers are highly visible as tools of government, with federal agency budgets for information technology exceeding $25 billion in 1989. All three branches of the federal government—executive, legislative, and judicial—use computers to some extent.

The executive branch is the most heavily computerized branch of government as a result of its extensive revenue-collection and service-provision functions. Each major executive department and agency has its own computerized systems, some of which are shared with other agencies. The executive branch uses the computer's data processing and telecommunication features to operate national information systems to serve broad interest areas, including finance and banking, postal services, criminal justice, military and civil defense, and air traffic regulation. Examples include the National Crime Information Center operated by the Federal Bureau of Investigation, the air traffic control system operated by the Federal Aviation Administration, and the Federal Reserve System's electronic funds transfer network (FEDWIRE).

The legislative branch (Congress) is the second largest computer user in the federal government. Whereas computer use in the executive branch is focused around large-scale systems that serve major departments and agencies, computer use in the legislative branch centers around the 535 senators and congresspersons individually elected to represent the interests of their constituents. The political nature of the legislative branch shapes its computer use to emphasize information search and retrieval, official vote and attendance recording for members, and constituency communication. Information search and retrieval are required for elected officials to access data relevant to the thousands of topics addressed annually. Informed decisions require data on the socioeconomic, policy, and political implications of legislation. Legislatures enhance communication with their constituents to better understand constituent needs and opinions, and to better disseminate the results and justifications for their actions.

The judicial branch is the smallest branch of the federal government, and the smallest computer user. Until recently, computer use in the courts was minimal and decentralized, each court using computing for budgeting, scheduling, and case management according to preference. Since 1989, the Administrative Office of the Courts has invested heavily in equipment, software, and training, and has announced plans for a data communications network (JURIST) and a central financial system. In addition, a number of electronic docketing and case management applications are being implemented throughout the judiciary.

State Government

Over the past decade, the federal government has delegated increasing responsibility for revenue collection and service provision to the fifty state governments. At the same time, state governments have faced popular opposition to increased taxation. State governments accommodated their new responsibilities by increasing the use of computers for administration and program management. All state governments now maintain at least one mainframe computer installation to support basic administrative functions. Most states operate several additional installations dedicated to critical government functions

such as taxation, finance, public safety, human services, and transportation.

According to a recent survey, patterns of computing use in state governments vary according to different political directives, management styles, and available resources (Caudle and Marchand 1989). Despite variance, computing applications typically focus on budget monitoring, central administrative control, and the delivery of government services. Most states have already automated administrative systems, with current efforts focused on service delivery applications. State governments are attempting to leverage their investments through cooperative development projects such as interstate telecommunications networks, to increase service delivery, and intrastate information and systems sharing in functional areas like social services. State governments are actively working to integrate multiple information technologies (e.g., data processing, telecommunications, office systems, and voice communications). State resources and responsibilities drive computer use, so larger states generally have more comprehensive information systems than do smaller states.

Local Government

Surveys of local governments conducted over 10 years' time through the University of California, Irvine (Kraemer et al. 1986), show that the pattern of computer adoption follows an S-curve pattern frequently found in the spread of technical innovations: gradual introduction by a few users, followed by a period of rapid implementation by most organizations, and eventual implementation by the remaining few (see Figure 1). The rates of adoption differ according to city size, however. Large cities (population over 100,000) adopted computing over a 30-year period; a few early users in the 1950s, most cities adopting computing in the 1960s, and the remainder automating in the 1970s. Medium-size cities (population 50,000 to 100,000) followed a similar adoption pattern. Their period of adoption came 5 years behind large cities but took only 20 years to complete. Computer use in small cities (under 50,000 population) lagged behind medi-

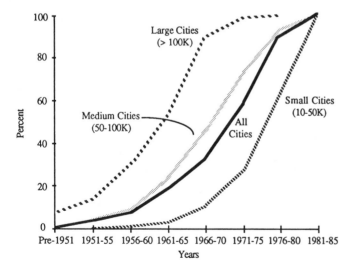

FIGURE 1. Computing adoption in cities over time. Curves are based only on cities reporting computing use and providing year of initial adoption (*N*=355). Each curve represents cumulative percentage of cities using computing, as a percentage of the total number of cities presently using computing in that cohort, at each specified time frame.

um cities by 10 years, although the rate of adoption is even more accelerated—most small cities adopted computing within 10 years.

Over 90 percent of all local governments with computers (over 10,000 population) use them in finance/accounting, and 75 percent use them in police operations. Computer use in other functional areas emphasizes financial concerns such as revenue generation and collection, cost control, and productivity improvements. Local governments with populations larger than 25,000 operate at least one minicomputer or mainframe computer. Larger cities (over 50,000 population) have additional minicomputers or mainframe computers dedicated to high-use departments, such as finance and administration, public safety, public works, and libraries. Smaller local governments (under 25,000) are using microcomputers to support specific functions such as accounting, personnel, and assessments.

In a pattern characteristic of all cities early in their adoption of computer usage, most small cities operate their computing installations as department subunits that also provide general computing support throughout city government. Larger cities moved beyond this arrangement to independent computer departments providing a broad range of general services; however, larger cities are also implementing additional subunit installations to provide special capabilities to particular departments, such as police dispatching, library circulation, and public works project modeling.

PURPOSE OF COMPUTER USE IN GOVERNMENT

The purposes of computer use in government are many and varied, but are illustrated by the following examples.

Record Keeping and Mass Processing

All government agencies are involved in record keeping and mass processing of some sort, and certain government agencies are the official repositories for records on individuals, property, funds, and organizations (e.g., businesses). For example, the Social Security Administration in the federal government is the largest and most experienced user of information systems for record keeping and mass processing in the entire government. Computerized databases track the collection of revenue from all employers and workers; monitor the distribution of checks to millions of beneficiaries; establish the eligibility of beneficiaries under retirement, disability, or survivor criteria; and modify the above functions in response to policy or legislated mandates. Social Security's databases contain over 200 million records, or one on nearly every man, woman, and child in the entire United States.

The Internal Revenue Service also uses computers to monitor the collection of revenue from employers and employees and to verify income, ensure tax law compliance, and calculate amounts owed or due. State tax agencies operate similar systems and can compare records in the federal and state systems for the same purposes. The Social Security number identifies an individual within both the federal and state tax systems, and in the Social Security system.

Public Safety and Surveillance

All levels of government are involved in maintaining public order and protecting the lives and property of citizens. To this end, federal, state, and local governments operate law enforcement agencies. Although each agency has carefully circumscribed geographic and legal jurisdictions, virtually all can cooperate and share information via computer communications linkages. The Federal Bureau of Investigation operates the National Crime Information Center (NCIC), a communications and data-retrieval system for tracking criminal activity and perpetrators. The Law Enforcement Assistance Administration, within the Department of Justice, funded state and local government efforts to gain access to the NCIC. The result is a national communication network through which law enforcement officers nationwide receive virtually instantaneous radio reports from NCIC on personal identification, criminal records, and motor vehicle registration status. Many police departments have mobile video terminals in patrol cars, which allow officers to input queries with greater accuracy and receive more extensive information displayed in print and graphic form.

Decision and Policy Support

Government agencies are large users of computerized data to inform and provide support for decisions and public policies. Often, the data are in the form of large databases or "databanks" such as are collected through the decennial population census. Such data are stored and analyzed through computers to help determine the need for programs to help the elderly, the poor, families, or any other social group of interest to policymakers and their constituents. Increasingly too, the data used come from computerized models that attempt to apply sophisticated analytic tools to complex decisions about economic or social programs. There are many computer models of the U.S. economy, and key government agencies responsible for economic forecasting tend to rely on several models to increase the accuracy of their forecasts.

For example, the Data Resources Incorporated (DRI) model is a national econometric model—a model of the economy's larger features (e.g., money supplies, interest rates, national debt levels). Properly developed macroeconomic models help forecast the probable economic conditions of the near future, and simulate the effects of possible economic policy changes. The DRI model is the most widely used macroeconomic modeling service in the U.S. government.

Similarly, computer models are also used in the social sphere. The Transfer Income Model (TRIM) and its counterpart the MicroAnalysis of Transfers to Households (MATH) model are both microsimulation models designed to analyze the effects of welfare programs on individuals and households. Microsimulation is a mathematical technique for modeling the behavior of individuals (such as households or firms) within a larger system. The approach uses data collected through surveys on the

characteristics (e.g., household income, household size) of a representative sample of individual units, along with simplified methods of behavior, to simulate the population's likely participation in some activity (such as childbearing, tax liability, or enrollment in social programs such as Food Stamps). TRIM is used primarily by the Department of Health and Human Services; MATH is used by numerous federal agencies, including the Department of Labor and Department of Agriculture.

Administration and Management

The staple of almost all government computerization efforts is the administrative and management applications of computers ranging from systems for budgeting and accounting, to personnel and payroll, to revenue collection and treasury management, to performance monitoring and managerial control. These systems exist at all levels and in all branches of the government and are essential to the day-to-day operations of the government. They are often referred to as "business" applications both because they share features with similar systems in business and because they focus on internal operations rather than service delivery. Such applications are traditionally the first automated in governments, both because of their value to the organization and because of the extensive technical support developed for similar systems in the private sector.

Communication with Citizens

Although computerization has been least applied to this area of government, its potential is great not only for government's communication with citizens but for citizens' communication with government and with one another. Members of Congress use office automation to communicate with constituents, both to broadcast messages through newsletters and to respond to their constituents' mail. City governments have set up 24-hour city halls based on voice mail where individual citizens can send messages to city officials and receive responses from them. And, at least one government has set up a network that permits citizens to communicate with one another as well as with city hall. Santa Monica's Public Information Network provides citizens with access to information about events in city government—an electronic bulletin board; electronic mail facilities for sending and receiving mail from government officials; and computer conferencing facilities for engaging in dialogue with other citizens and government officials about community issues such as rent control, AIDS treatment, care for the elderly, and latchkey children. Citizens can gain access to the network through computers in their homes, offices, shopping centers, and public facilities such as city hall, libraries, community centers, and neighborhood centers.

RESULTS OF COMPUTER USE IN GOVERNMENT

It is difficult to characterize the results of computing in simple terms. In general, the results of computing use are positive. The use of computers in automated systems speeds the transfer of information, accurately records actions and amounts, and supports an increasingly diverse inventory of computer-based applications; however, the results of computer use are marginal and indirect, and are realized only after a significant period. In fact, the computer's biggest impact may be the enormous share of public resources channeled into computer equipment, staff, and installations. Estimating this expenditure is difficult because it includes all social, economic, and national defense uses.

The benefits of computerization in government are difficult to discern because the primary task of the past three decades was developing automated systems for existing functions. Computerizing tax and land records, automating payroll and personnel, digitizing blueprints and maps, and transmitting crime information are all essential but hardly novel functions. These unglamorous applications may have saved the flow of government operation from eventual "information gridlock," but an averted catastrophe is tantamount to no catastrophe at all. The public will probably not recognize the value of information systems until innovative applications become accessible. Advances in

graphics, artificial intelligence, and interactive media will eventually generate novel computer applications worthy of notice and appreciation.

In the meantime, despite significant investment, the rapid and extensive computerization of government operations has not appreciably changed government operations, although operations have been made more efficient and are now largely dependent on their computer-based systems. Information is collected faster and in greater detail but generally in support of traditional government functions. Computerization has not, as some hoped and others feared, dramatically changed governmental functions. Moreover, potential benefits from a computer-based function, such as modeling for rational and impartial decisions and policy making, are sometimes mitigated by the contending factions with partisan views that participate in model development.

The benefits of computerization are not very visible because computers affect government functions at the margin. For example, information systems that replicate manual tasks save personnel time, but these savings are typically realized through gradual attrition rather than immediate work force reductions. Further, savings are sometimes offset by new costs generated through computer-related jobs and service jobs for new government functions made possible by computer use.

Computer use will probably gain little additional recognition, because new computer systems are becoming more complex. Increasing their complexity lengthens both the development and implementation stages. As a result, systems may not meet the high expectations established for them, or may meet a need that has changed in the interim. Moreover, new systems are typically oversold to marshall support for the projects and justify budgeted costs, which may then be exceeded during implementation. For example, Government Accounting Office reports for the past decade show that the history of executive branch computerization is replete with examples of poorly conceived systems, frequent implementation failures, and extraordinary cost overruns. Setting and accepting realistic goals would help solve these problems and enhance benefits from government computerization efforts.

ISSUES OF COMPUTER USE IN GOVERNMENT

Computer use in government raises both procedural and policy issues. In terms of procedural issues, a series of reports by the Office of Technology Assessment identified five areas where interventions would improve computing use in large federal government organizations: (1) strategic planning practices—incorporating long-term objectives for systems and developing applications from the end user's perspective; (2) information reporting standards—increasing the amount of information available for sharing and improving the quality of data collected for reporting; (3) innovation dissemination—using information technology as a vehicle for sharing knowledge about innovative developments within and between organizations to reduce replication of efforts; (4) procurement procedures and feedback—streamlining the process of acquiring computers to increase compatibility and establish prices, while applying the lessons gained through experience to acquisition decisions; and (5) information resources management—exercising collective oversight of all related technologies, including computers, telecommunications, and office automation.

These five areas for intervention illustrate the complexity of computer-based operations on the scale and scope of the federal government. Following the same pattern for the progressive diffusion of technological innovations described earlier, smaller federal agencies, state governments, and eventually all local governments will eventually face issues in the same areas.

The basic policy issue surrounding computer use in government concerns the sensitivity of the federal system to technological change. Four major nexuses of the federal system are susceptible to change via computer-based technology:

1. Interactions between, and the relative power among, the branches of the federal government—legislative, executive, and judicial—in the context of their performance of their duties and roles in governmental affairs: One fundamental principle of the U.S. government is to check and balance the central power of the national government by dividing it into three essentially equal, independent, and sometimes competing branches. The differential rate of computerization among the three branches, however, has the potential to undermine the checks and balances, by providing substantive, procedural, functional, or symbolic advantage to one or more branches.

2. Interactions between and relative power among the national government and other state and local governments in the federated system: The development of national information systems such as those in criminal justice and the growing linkage of federal–state–local information systems, such as employment, tax, and welfare systems, increase the role of the national government with potential to delocalize control over state and local policies and programs.

3. Interactions and relative power distribution between "government" and the "people": The increased sharing of computer-based information on individuals and groups, within society by all branches of government, has the potential to increase government oversight and thereby diminish individual freedoms. The issue is one of government's need for broader access to expanding information stores versus the citizen's right to privacy.

4. Functions of the political process that result in the election and appointment of officeholders: The expanding use of computer technology in political activity, including political party management, fund raising, public opinion monitoring, and direct-mail campaigning, has the potential to change the balance of power among various factions in the political system, with ensuing consequences for the current system of government.

These four nexus of the federal system bear monitoring, but may not warrant new policy directives. The federal system's checks and balances have the capacity to counterbalance potential threats posed by computerized information systems, but these systems and their use require continued vigilance.

SUMMARY

Computers in government have already delivered unprecedented, and largely unheralded, gains in administrative efficiency and service provision. They may soon improve government communication with citizens as well. The trends for technology diffusion point to continued computerization at all levels of government. In exchange for the efficiencies provided by automation, government must zealously safeguard the rights of citizens while accommodating the freedom of access to public information.

References

Caudle, S. L., and D. A. Marchand. 1989. *Managing information resources: New directions in state government.* Syracuse, N.Y.: School of Information Studies.

Kraemer, K. L., J. L. King, D. E. Dunkle, and J. P. Lane. 1986. Trends in municipal information systems 1975–1985. *Baseline Data Report* 18(2). Washington, D.C.: International City Management Association.

For Further Reading

Administrative Office of the U.S. Courts. 1990. Court automation funding and training move ahead. *The Third Branch* 22(9):6.

———. 1990. Office automation users group holds first meeting. *The Third Branch* 22(12):6.

———. 1990. *1990 Report of the director: Activities of the administrative office.* Washington, D.C.: Administrative Office of the U.S. Courts.

Kraemer, K. L. 1987. The American Constitution and the administrative state. *Public Administration Review* 47(1):93–105.

Kraemer, K. L., S. Dickhoven, S. Fallows-Tierney, and J. L. King. 1987. *DATAWARS: The politics of modeling in federal policy making.* New York: Columbia University Press.

Frantzich, S. E. 1982. *Computers in Congress—The politics of information,* vol. 4. *Managing information: A series of books in organization studies and decision-making,* A. Wildavsky, series ed. Beverly Hills, Calif.: Sage.

U.S. Congress, Office of Technology Assessment. 1981. *Computer-based national information systems: Technology & public policy issues.* Washington, D.C.: U.S. Government Printing Office. OTA-CIT-146, September.

———. 1985. *Information technology and R&D: Critical trends and issues.* Washington, D.C.: U.S. Government Printing Office. OTA-CIT-268, February.

———. 1985. *Automation of America's offices.* Washington, D.C.: U.S. Government Printing Office. OTA-CIT-287, December.

———. 1986. *Electronic record systems and individual privacy: Federal government information technology.* Washington, D.C.: U.S. Government Printing Office. OTA-CIT-296, June.

———. 1986. *The Social Security Administration and information technology—Special report.* Washington, D.C.: U.S. Government Printing Office, OTA-CIT-311, October.

Kenneth L. Kraemer

GRAPHICS

See Animation, Computer; Arts, Computers in the; Presentation Graphics

GROUP DECISION SUPPORT SYSTEMS

See Cooperative Work Systems

GROUPWARE

See Cooperative Work Systems

H

HACKING

The term *hacking* in the 1980s became a buzzword in the media. It was taken to be derogatory and, by misuse and overuse, was attached to any form of socially nonacceptable computing activity outside of polite society. Within this context "hackers" were assumed to be the fringe society of the computing fraternity, characterized mainly as "youngsters" who did not know any better and who had obtained access to a technology with which they terrorized the world of communications and computing. To be tagged a hacker was to be portrayed as a near-criminal. These connotations contrast with the use of the term in the 1950s and 1960s when hackers were at least to be tolerated for their potential, though not necessarily displayed in public. In many ways the early use of the term held a connotation similar to that of the word *boffin* during World War II. A boffin was a backroom activist who, when left to his or her own devices, could produce some wonderful inventions. Such scientists as Edison (inventor of the electric light bulb and the phonograph), Fleming (penicillin), Barnes-Wallis (the bouncing bomb and swept-wing aircraft), Watson-Watt (radar), and possibly even Babbage (the difference and analytical engines) might have been honored to be identified as hackers. Only in more recent times has there been confusion between the terms *hacker, petty criminal,* and possibly *nerd.*

THE TERM: ITS ORIGINS AND DEVELOPMENT

hack (hak), *n.* 1. a horse for hire. 2. an old, worn-out horse. 3. a literary drudge. 4. a coach for hire. 5. a taxicab. *adj.* 1. employed as a hack. 2. trite. *v.t.* to chop or cut roughly. *v.i.* 1. to make rough cuts. 2. to give harsh dry coughs. *n.* 1. a tool for hacking. 2. a gash or notch. 3. a harsh, dry cough. - **hack'er.** *n.* - **hack'ing,** *adj.* (*Webster's New World Dictionary,* 1967)

Hacking as a methodology to achieve some particular goal implies working at something by experimentation or empirical means, learning about the process under review or development by ad hoc mechanisms. This may have originated from its meaning "*v.t.* to chop or cut roughly. *v.i.* to make rough cuts," as in the process of empirical development where numerous different routes are explored in a search for the most effective approach to a solution, possibly without a prearranged ordering of search or a methodology for evaluation. To chance on a solution by "hacking through a problem" is often as educational as structured learning, and thus it is not unreasonable to approach a problem in a field that is devoid of structure and methodology by "hacking." In hacking a computer, the enhancement of the system is an end in itself; applications of that system do not count. In the same manner, hacking has no life cycle and no specific end goal; an improvement is in itself an achievement, but not necessarily a reason for further activity. Although hacking has generally been countersociety it is not necessarily antisociety. In fact, the result of hacking is a "hack" and the beauty of a hack can be realized only if its beauty can be shared with others; the private hack is nonexistent.

THE EARLY YEARS

Until the mid-1960s computing, programming, and computer science had very little

425

structure and many of the advances in the field were achieved through ad hoc methods. Hacking as a methodology matched the "freethinking" style of life of this period, and although there was an air of formalism among many professionals, in fact the basic methodology of computation was to repeat what had been successful up to that point. Hacking merely changed the focus to concentrate on what might be done, not what had been done. Hacking was (is) a form of development in which there were (are) no rules, only intelligent and intuitive exploration. Only as a structure was imposed on the field and acceptable methodologies for achieving a result were recognized did the art of hacking fall into disrepute; the hackers of the 1960s were the "flower children" of the computing world. The resurrection of the term in the 1980s implied a lack of connection to the reality and rationality of industrial computing.

Hacking is dependent on "free" access to computers; it grew up where such access was available in an unsupervised, nonregulated, nonconforming, interactive, hands-on environment (as at the Massachusetts Institute of Technology [MIT] or the University of California, Berkeley) and eventually in the environment of personal computers.

The People

Throughout the early years of computing, following the development of the ENIAC, access to computing systems was highly restricted. To use such a system required the existence of a formal problem and commonly a formal application for the award of processing time in a process similar to that involved in applying for a research grant. Thus there was very little opportunity for solving a problem by empirical means; problems and solutions were well planned in advance, and priorities of need scheduled the accessibility of the machine. Perhaps the only persons who had such opportunities for experimentation were those who constructed or managed the machines, and they generally knew enough about the systems to have no need to

experiment. Hacking had to wait until there was much freer access to computing power for those whose interests were not specific enough to write a proposal and who were attracted to the machines for the sheer enjoyment of exploration.

The first opportunities for unfettered access to computing facilities occurred at MIT in the late 1950s when Lincoln Laboratories loaned the TX-0 computer to the Research Laboratory of Electronics (RLE). Although a strong bureaucracy controlled access to the IBM 704 computer in the Computation Center run by Philip Morse, Jack Dennis, who "controlled" the TX-0, provided unrestrained access once the needs of formal research activities were satisfied. This generally meant that the available time was in the "graveyard shift"; however, this did not matter to the aficionados of what we might recognize as the first "personal computer." They merely altered their circadian rhythms to accommodate this minor shortcoming. The TX-0 was originally designed by Lincoln Laboratories as a hands-on controller for a much larger system under development, and thus its style of use was different from that of the IBM 704 and the batch processing mode of operation. The TX-0 soon fell under the spell of, and cast its own web over, the first hacker community. From this environment grew a plethora of proficiencies built-in to the skills of the hacker community. Perhaps we shall never tally all the technological concepts that originated in this environment, but by all accounts it was a very fertile bed. Primary in the collection of products must be the whole field of computer games. "Star Wars" existed on the PDP-1 computer years before the Ping-Pong paddle was introduced to family television and twenty years before there was a personal computer. The technology and theory of game playing never crossed the minds of hackers; yet their products were legends. Early script writing was developed for the TX-0, and the Computer Museum (Boston) still shows the cowboy film that resulted from this effort. In both instances such developments would not have had a high priority on a closed-shop system.

The Benefits of Hacking

With respect to the problems of testing programs, Conway and Gries (1975) suggested that this was a fertile ground to demonstrate the usefulness of the "most depraved minds"! Thus a benefit to the computer community is the free-wheeling exploration of systems by the benign hacker. Freedom and control may be incompatible attributes of such an environment, but it is clear that the tasks of program or system usage in a productive setting are not amenable to the recognition and acceptance of bugs and errors. On the other hand, the challenge of testing may be a logical outlet for hacking inclinations in the makeup of a programmer. In several cases systems have been purposely exposed to hackers to test their security and their robustness. In 1989 LeeMah DataCom Security Corporation challenged hackers to retrieve a secret message hidden in a computer in Atlanta (Irwin 1990). After the potential intruders were given a phone number and password, they were asked to retrieve a hidden message in the system. The prize was to be an 8-day, 7-night, all-expenses paid trip for two to St. Moritz or Tahiti. In a 7-day period, with the rate of calls starting at 100 calls per hour on the first day, 7,476 attempts to access the critical message were attempted. Not one attempt succeeded. The company claimed to have "proven that a system . . . will effectively meet the needs of dial-up access systems" and users "need not accept arduous, user-hostile telecommunications security plans." The challenge was repeated in 1990 with two sites, with the same basic startup information, but with the challenge period extended to two weeks. Once again the system resisted intrusion. John Tuomy stated that "the problem with all the coverage of successful hacker break-ins is that some people might get the impression that these hackers are invincible, or that the FBI arrests of some of them will act as a deterrent. The fact is that the government couldn't possibly arrest all the hackers out there, and certainly not guarantee the safety of the nation's computers. We believe strongly that computer crime can be prevented, but that businesses have to do it themselves."

The Psychology of Hacking and Programming

There is a certain allure to computing that is difficult to replicate in other environments. In many respects computing is always "real" rather than merely an example or model, though there is always the hope for more power and greater facilities to do bigger and better hacks. Whereas in other endeavors the development of a project such as a hot-rod car or a trip to Hawaii costs real dollars, computing costs nothing; it is a utility. Driving a hot rod on a dirt strip is also fraught with real physical danger, whereas hot rodding a computer is safe. The computer does not hit back even when the worst of effects are programmed.

Even the nonhacker and the nonprogrammer are affected by the computer. With the advent of electronic mail systems, the change in personality that comes from a nonevasive form of communication can easily be recognized (Shapiro and Anderson 1985). Persons who are puppydogs in face-to-face communication become wolves when they do not have to look into the eyes of the receiver and are not threatened physically by their textual combatant. Levy (1984) suggests that there is a "code of ethics" for hacking that, though not pasted on the walls, is in the air:

> Access to Computers—and anything which might teach you something about the way the world works—should be unlimited and total. Always yield to the Hands-On Imperative!
>
> All information should be free.
>
> Mistrust authority—Promote decentralization.
>
> Hackers should be judged by their hacking, not bogus criteria such as degrees, age, race, or position.
>
> You can create art and beauty on a computer.
>
> Computers can change your life for the better.

Hacking, whether benign or felonious, is associated with learning and exploration. Although there are older hackers, they grew up from the hacking covens of youngsters interested in exploring and exploiting the new ethereal world of electronic tripping. But as with so many other new technologies, amateur capabilities and the sharing of findings soon outgrow the normal and the useful; to find an area in which to make a mark requires an excursion into not-so-acceptable domains.

Communications and Accessible Computing

The early 1960s at MIT was the period when Fernando Corbató and his colleagues took on themselves the development of an interactive time-sharing system that would provide personal computing to the university community while at the same time using all the available machine cycles. John McCarthy had realized that it was essential that a machine be used to its utmost, and that although batch processing solved the administrative problem of utilization, the downside of the solution was extremely long turnaround times for individual programs. His solution was to have several programs ready for execution, so that while one program was waiting for a delaying factor (such as human input), another program could use the available machine cycles. In his memorandum to Philip Morse he used the example of the TX-0 to reinforce his arguments about how computing really should be accomplished; however, he did not realize that in the creation of such a system the bureaucracy of the batch operating system would be carried over in the form of log-in identifiers and passwords. The hacker community was continually frustrated by the bureaucracy that accompanied the use of the Compatible Time-Sharing System (CTSS) and the systems within Project MAC. The TX-0 had always been operated without a log-on identification or password; files were in public storage, unrestrained by protective systems. Persons could roam through these files at will and were free to make changes and updates to files left there by others. On the premise that *you can always make things better* programs would be debugged overnight,

have new features added, or be incorporated into other programs freely.

CTSS discouraged hacking. Add to this the fact that it was run on a two-million-dollar IBM machine that the hackers thought was much inferior to their PDP-6, and you had one loser system. No one was asking the hackers to use CTSS, but it was there, and sometimes you just have to do some hacking on what's available. When a hacker would try to use it, and a message would come on-screen saying that you couldn't log on without the proper password, he would be compelled to retaliate. Because to hackers, passwords were even more odious than locked doors. What could be worse than someone telling you that you weren't authorized to use his computer?

As it turned out, the hackers learned the CTSS system so well that they could circumvent the password requirements. Once they were on the system, they would rub it in a bit by leaving messages to the administrators, high-tech equivalents of "Kilroy Was Here."

The *Incompatible Time-Sharing System* (ITS): The title was particularly ironic because, in terms of friendliness to other systems and programs, ITS was much more compatible than CTSS. True to the hacker ethic, ITS could easily be linked to other things—that way it could be infinitely extended so users could probe the world more effectively. As in any time-sharing system, several users would be able to run programs on ITS at the same time. But on ITS, one user could also run several programs at once. ITS also allowed considerable use of the displays, and had what was for the time a very advanced system of editing that used the full screen.

There was an even more striking embodiment of the hacker ethic within ITS. Unlike almost any other time-sharing system, ITS did not use passwords. It was designed, in fact, to allow hackers maximum access to any user's file. The old practice of having paper tapes in a drawer, a collective program library where you'd have people use and improve your programs, was embedded in ITS; each user could open a set of personal files, stored on a disk. The open architecture of ITS encouraged users to look through these files, see what neat hacks other people were working on, look for bugs in the programs, and fix them. If you wanted a routine to calculate sine functions, for instance, you might look in [the] files and find [a] ten-instruction sine hack. You could go through the programs of the master hackers, looking for ideas, admiring the code. The idea was that computer programs belonged not to individuals, but to the world of users. (Levy 1984)

Of this period, self-confessed hacker Guy Steele (Steele et al. 1983) said: "Despite stories you have read about the antisocial nerds glued permanently to display screens, totally addicted to the computer, hackers have (human) friends too. Often these friendships are formed and maintained through the computer." This era reached its intended goal of providing interactive computing through the technology of time sharing. It also created the marriage between computers and communications systems, which opened a whole new field to exploration.

THE 1980s

The 1970s was a period of intense but limited activity by small groups of hackers. One such group was the Homebrew Club in the California Bay area, centered somewhat on Berkeley and concentrating on hardware systems, in contrast to the earlier hacking activities on the East Coast that had been related primarily to software. From this group came a number of innovations including a number of primordial personal computers: Lee Felsenstein and the Sol, and the 6502-based Apple I from Steve Jobs and Steve Wozniak. Previously Wozniak had developed a "blue box" to access phone systems, but he legitimized his activities by turning to the development of the Apple I board. Cap'n Crunch (John Draper, who took the pseudonym Cap'n Crunch from the cereal when he found that the plastic whistle enclosed as a premium activated the operator controls of the phone system) had earlier engineered a blue box based on the tones necessary to activate the Bell Telephone system, as published in various magazines to advertise the new tonal system. Draper added a few tones including one that accessed the operator routines and thus provided an easy entrance into the toll call network. From this community grew not only the need for personal computing but the answer to the demand. They also inadvertently opened up a Pando-

ra's box of accessibility when they connected the microcomputer to the telephone system through a modem. And so we moved into the 1980s with the personal computer now in homes and bedrooms. No longer was computing restricted to the privileged or canny few who had access to teletypes and who could access mainframe computers. Even the smallest computer costing as little as $100 could be coupled to the family TV and a modem to provide an electronic tripping medium for the new breed of hackers. And this new breed did not build on the knowledge of the advances made by their predecessors; they had the equipment, they had the urge, and, most times, unbeknownst to their parents, they acquired the knowledge to travel the world without leaving the privacy of their bedrooms. No one provided a code of ethics for their wanderings because their teachers were not sufficiently knowledgeable of the potential of this combination of computer and modem, and their parents had no adolescent experiences of their own on which to build an expectation of the outreach of the offspring. What was (and is) needed was a computer education package that would include moral and ethical scenarios like those found in high school courses in driver education and sex education.

As the owner of a personal computer extends his or her knowledge of the system there are several paths that can lead to further awareness and to further exploration: to install or develop new software packages or to explore other people's packages. Given the limited resources of a teenager, the former is not easy unless currency can be exchanged for other possessions. Bulletin boards were an early development for communication between personal-computer users, but by their very nature they insisted on the possession of an environment that permitted a wider latitude of exploration than just a bulletin board. These boards also became (and still are) the repositories of software packages, many of them donated to the public domain by their developers. In other cases proprietary or copyrighted packages were available for some small cost, either the provision of some other unique piece of software or, in other cases, an identification such as a credit card number. Though the board promised not to charge the card for any software, the card number did get used in other nefarious ways without the owner's prior knowledge; in many cases, of course, the card number belonged to the parent of the provider. Bulletin boards were the obvious places to store the necessary hacking information for the uninitiated to make their first tours of the computer world. Boards have been found to contain the telephone numbers of local (and not so local) computer systems, and information on the means of constructing blue boxes (and their modem equivalent) and other noncomputational gadgets such as Molotov cocktails and Mace guns. Other boards have contained credit card numbers (which are of limited usefulness once the cards have been reported as missing), credit card authorization information, and merchant identification codes. Of course, not all bulletin boards are provided for perverse purposes, but the question must be asked: What does a board operator get out of supplying this service? The operation of a board can use up a great deal of computing power, a dedicated telephone, and ample storage. Like the TX-0, most bulletin boards have an open storage system or, at the very least, provide supervisory access to files by the owner. The owner thus collects information and products as they pass through the board; that is his payoff.

Authors have categorized hackers of the 1980s to classify the intrusive form of their attack or the rationale for their entry into a system. Parker (1983) suggested that they could be classified into three groups based on their actions while accessing a system:

- **Benign:** the hacker whose intentions are purely educational
- **Unsavory:** the intruder whose intentions are not necessarily malicious but whose very presence can be negative
- **Malicious:** the intruder whose primary intention is to cause the system to crash or to wreck havoc in its operation

Landreth (1985) countered that they could best be categorized by their activities:

- **Novice:** the user whose first steps into the world of electronic tripping are tentative and exploratory and whose intentions are merely to emulate those who she or he believes have gone before
- **Student:** the visitor who has a fair knowledge of the means of access and whose new intentions are to learn more about the system under scrutiny without changing anything or leaving anything behind
- **Tourist:** the hacker who, having discovered all there is to be known about his or her local systems, decides to visit similar systems worldwide
- **Crasher:** the hacker whose challenge is to defeat a system by bringing it to its knees
- **Thief:** the system intruder whose intentions are to retrieve from the systems that can be accessed data and programs that can be put to personal use (including providing the stolen information to others)

Viruses, Worms, and Other Infections

In the beginning the tools of hackers were ingenuity and intuition, which, when combined with a detailed knowledge of the system being hacked, resulted in systems that did special and new things in a better and more responsive manner through software enhancements. Later, the Homebrew Club and their contemporaries achieved the same results through the development of hardware devices. With the introduction of the personal computer and modems, new tools were available and new techniques of hacking were necessary. The results were also different; now hacks could be inserted into systems a thousand miles away, though it would be very disappointing not to be around when the hack was activated. Just as in the days of CTSS, the first task was to overcome the basic security system by locating an available log-in identification and the corresponding password. Two basic approaches to identification are possible: (1) to understand the basic mechanism for assigning/selecting identifications, or (2) to find the system backdoor access that is generally provided to allow a supervisor to access the system after crashes or when it is otherwise locked. With the advent of wide-area networks and the need to send electronic mail to users, log-in identification has become much more predictable: last name, first name and first initial, first initial and last name, initials, and so on. Even when the actual identifier is different, many systems provide an alias that is equally predictable. Similarly passwords, without some special mechanism for generation, are predictable if one has a knowledge of the user: children's names, dogs' names, special interests, and so on. Landreth (1985) provided an appendix in his book that listed the manufacturer-installed identifications and passwords that were delivered with each machine. He pointed out that in many cases users did not change these "open doors" because either they were unaware of their availability or they were frightened that if these access keys were to be changed they might forget them and thus be denied entrance at a later time. More direct methods can be used in direct contact with the user of an account to be attacked. In what Parker (1983) termed "shoulder surfing," some attackers have learned the techniques of reading a user's keystrokes and obtaining the password by this means even though it is not printed on the terminal screen. This technique is particularly simple in observing the keystrokes on a number pad such as is used with an automatic teller machine.

Quite commonly banks assign personal identification numbers (PINs) that have a pattern—up and down one line (8255), the corners (7931), or some other pattern that is easier to remember than the number itself. This considerably eases the task of the shoulder surfer.

In 1984 the FBI reported that the average embezzlement netted the perpetrator $15,000, but the means for the computer-knowledgeable embezzler is simpler than that for the person who has to work in the open. Hiding behind the anonymity of a programmer, the embezzler can now alter the program to suit his or her needs (e.g., collecting the fractions of cents not assigned to an account in interest calculations) or make minor, but accumulative, modifications to the input (and corresponding output) data, termed *data diddling*. This attack methodology, which would probably be considered contrary to the hacker ethic and thus not be used by the true hacker, is much more common as a technique of embezzlement by an employee of (say) a bank or a financial agency who does not necessarily have a background in programming. An example would be the introduction of a bogus bank account through which funds are transferred long enough before assignment to the true account to accrue small amounts of interest. Very few account holders actually check their interest credits to the penny; interest after all is "free," and the interest rate changes quarterly so it is difficult for the average person to verify these account entries regularly. In social service agencies, dead beneficiaries have been kept on the books and the checks diverted to another address where they can be collected by the data diddler. One of the most insidious forms of system attack is sabotage by legitimate users, possibly disgruntled employees of the system owner, or previous employees who were discharged under a cloud. In some cases this might well be initially perpetrated as a safeguard against later unsatisfactory actions by the owner. For example, in a number of cases a piece of code has been inserted into the payroll program so that if the identification of the employee is not in the database, the system will crash! In one case examined by the present writer, this piece of code was installed as a set of data in a COBOL program that were thought to be taxation constants by other investigators of the apparently flawed hardware system. Procedures of this form are termed *logic bombs*, as they are triggered by a logical condition. Similarly, an alternative action, such as the *otherwise* of a select statement, might be filled with an unsavory procedure, thus forming a trap door through which the program may fall.

Hackers seeking to access a system can use a variety of methodologies depending on the capabilities (or weaknesses) of the system under attack. It is not unusual for multiuser systems to provide a mechanism by which legitimate users who own several accounts may move from one to another readily, thus obviating the need to exit the system before accessing the new account. In most systems this requires the use of a new password, but this password is not always subjected to the same revision policies as primary passwords. Alternatively, a user can access the data of another account by linking to that account. Thus, a hacker piggybacks on a legitimate and commonly a guest account, and thereby sidesteps into another domain. Of course, the common method of gaining access is to impersonate the legitimate user through the use of her or his identification and password.

The hackers Landreth classified as "crashers" employ numerous methods, not all of which necessitate actual access to the system code. In other methods, the actual characteristics of the system are used to make it useless to other users. For example, an interactive system that permits the instantiation of multitasking is liable to attack through the overloading of the system by nonsense, infinite, cycle (or storage) grabbing routines. Such a system will slowly grind to a standstill. In the case of the Internet virus of 1988 (ACM 1989), the communications network was slowly overloaded until it was unable to carry legitimate messages. In late 1988 a "Christmas tree" package almost brought the BITNET (*Because It's Time NETwork*) to its knees. In this case victims would find the following message on their screens: "Enter Merry Christmas." When this command was typed in, a Christmas tree was displayed on the screen with the appropriate season greetings. At the same time, however, the package sent itself in a mail message to all the names in the victim's mail distribution file! The network quickly filled with messages, but fortunately the package could be identified by potential victims and thwarted.

Virus, like *hacker,* has become a byword in recent years. Viruses and hackers seem to go together. As contrasted with logic bombs and trap doors, viruses have the basic characteristic that they replicate in certain circumstances and thus are said to "infect" other software items. In addition to replicating itself, a virus may be designed to perpetrate some mischief as a bomb or a worm. On the other hand, a virus may do nothing more than replicate itself. The minuteness of simple viruses means that they can be embedded in other systems quite easily; any differences in file size may be attributed to version differences. A common technique is to embed a virus within a commonly used system and to modify the initial load module to link to the virus before starting up the application. Because viruses attach to word processors or spreadsheets the likelihood of initiation of a virus is greatly increased. Viruses can be introduced into a system by a variety of doors. A system connected to a network is liable to entry through electronic mail, through linkage to other infected systems, and through the use of bulletin boards to download software. Viruses can also be carried in on diskettes that have been used in infected systems. Attractive software packages, commonly obtained illicitly to circumvent copyrights or protective locks, serve as "Trojan horses" and carry with them the virus. One particularly obnoxious form of virus is the "worm," which has the characteristic of eating its way (by destroying data and programs) through the storage system of a computer. Antidotes to viruses have been constructed for many of the well-known versions, and a new industry has been created to build virus detectives, immunization procedures, and antidotes. There are virtues associated with obtaining software and data through well-known, legitimate sources!

The Internet Virus

On November 2, 1988 the Internet system, which interconnects the majority of computer networks in the United States, was the victim of a virus that was later to be found to have originated at Cornell University in the account of Robert Morris (ACM 1989). The virus, dubbed a worm by some, not only replicated itself throughout the network by multiply infecting single systems but took advantage of some well-known flaws in the recent version of Unix running on Sun 3 systems and Vax computers. The basic vehicle for operation was the *finger* utility, which is provided to permit a user to locate another user on the system and possibly (depending on the amount of data captured by the system administrator) other information such as phone number and address. Fundamentally the virus used the lack of memory protection on an input buffer to modify a portion of the operating system to access user passwords and therefrom delivered a complex (but relatively small) virus that collected system files from remote machines.

The effects were twofold. On the one hand, there was an almost immediate and devastating decline in the operability of the network and numerous machines attached to it. On the other hand, the incident immediately raised the visibility of the need for action on system security, for an improved legalistic approach to computer crime, and for an awareness on the part of everyone of the consequences of and their responsibility for their actions in this nonthreatening world of computers and communications.

THE PROSPECTS AND COUNTERMEASURES

In discussing hackers and their activities, we have perhaps overlooked the ultimate instance of their trade—the computer criminal. Clearly, the computer is a tool that can be used in an illegitimate manner as can almost any other tool in our modern repertoire. Although much of the alleged activity of hackers has come under scrutiny in the legislatures, there is still a line between the hacker and the criminal. This line may hinge on intent and purpose, and although it is not clear that hackers accrue a great deal of financial benefit by their actions, the impact on the owner of a (hardware or software) system is not that different. Consider the disparity between the hacker ethic that information should be free and the right to privacy of individuals whose records are stored in a data bank. Fundamentally, system owners must rely on three elements that provide them protection:

- **Computer security:** technical means by which the system is protected by layers of security through which control of communication is verified and by which data and software are checked for safety and cleanliness

- **Computer law:** enactment of a series of punitive measures that precisely define illegitimate activities with respect to computer systems usage, and installation of an enforcement mechanism by which infringements of the law are detected and prosecuted

- **Computer ethics:** introduction of studies of ethical behavior into our educational system, in the same manner in which ethical (and moral) behavior is taught in sex and driver education courses.

References

ACM (Association for Computing Machinery). 1989. "The worm story," a collection of papers and reports. *Communications of the ACM* 32(6): 677–703.

Conway, R., and D. Gries. 1975. *An introduction to programming: A structured approach using PL/1 and PL/C.* 2nd ed. Cambridge, Mass.: Winthrop.

Landreth, B. 1985. *Out of the inner circle: A hacker's guide to computer security.* Bellevue, Wash.: Microsoft Press.

Levy, S. 1984. *Hackers: Heroes of the computer revolution.* Garden City, N.Y.: Anchor Press/Doubleday.

Parker, D. 1983. *Fighting computer crime.* New York: Scribners.

Shapiro, N. Z., and R. H. Anderson. 1985. *Toward an ethics and etiquette for electronic mail.* Rep. No. R-3283-NSF/RC. Santa Monica, Calif.: Rand Corp.

Steele, G. L., Jr., et al. 1983. *The hacker's dictionary.* New York: Harper & Row.

For Further Reading

Gemignani, M. 1989. Viruses and criminal law. *Communications of the ACM* 32(6):669–71.

Lee, J. A. N., R. Steier, and G. Segal. 1986. Positive alternatives: A report of an ACM panel on hacking. *Communications of the ACM* 29(4):297–99.

Parker, D. 1976. *Crime by computer.* New York: Scribners.

Parker, D., and J. F. Maxfield. 1985. *The nature and extent of electronic computer intrusion.* Workshop on Protection of Computer Systems and Software. Washington, D.C.: National Science Foundation.

Perry, T. S., and P. Wallich. 1984. Can computer crime be stopped? *IEEE Spectrum,* May, pp. 34–45.

Samuelson, P. 1989. Can hackers be sued for damages caused by computer viruses? *Communications of the ACM* 32(6):666–69.

J. A. N. Lee

HANDICAPPED

See Disabled, Technology for the

HARDWARE

[*This composite article comprises the following sections:*
  Computer Design
  Memory Design
  Screen Design
  Hardware Interfaces
  Computer Systems
  Computer Architecture

Although the nature of computation has been studied since the 1930s by numerous logicians, mathematicians, and computer scientists and has been sufficiently understood apart from the actual computational engine that carries out the computations, it is fair to say that without the physical piece of hardware we now know as the computer, the field of computers and computer science would not have made the impact that it has. A computational engine can be implemented in many ways, even hydraulically, but it is the speed of the electronic implementation that has changed the world in the last generation.

The original concept for a stored–program computer was developed in the 1940s by John VON NEUMANN. *In this approach, the program is stored in memory along with the necessary data. Thus program and data are interchangeable and a program can even modify itself, which is exactly how much early programming was accomplished. Along with this concept, however, came some baggage that influenced the development of the computer for many years. This baggage is called the von Neumann architecture and is commonly referred to today as the von Neumann bottleneck. The terms refer to the standard sequential architecture of the fetch–execute cycle in which a single instruction is fetched from memory and then executed. Since that time, many other architectures and implementations of a more parallel nature have been devised, including* SUPERCOMPUTERS, *dataflow processors, and multiprocessor machines such as the Connection Machine and those exhibiting the hypercube architecture.*

At a very basic level, all computers consist of three types of components: central processing unit components, memory components, and input/output components. The central processing unit, or CPU, is the focus of Computer Design, *below. This section elucidates the principles of CPU design that must be accomplished no matter what the underlying machine architecture.* Memory Design *covers similar information with respect to the memory components of a computer. Most input/output in current computers occurs through a screen of some type. A description of how this is accomplished, as well as some information regarding the design of program interfaces for human/computer interaction, is given in* Screen Design. *Computers are usually only one component of an overall system, whether that system is a computer network or a piece of military hardware. How communication between the computer and the other system components is carried out is described in* Hardware Interfaces. Computer Systems *also addresses computers as being one component of a system, but at a higher level than that of the circuitry. Finally,* Computer Architecture *addresses the concept of general computer architectures, discussing the makeup of a computer from a much higher level than the preceding sections. This section characterizes the various architectures that numerous researchers have devised over the years.*]

Computer Design

The design of computer hardware is critically impacted by the interplay of market forces and the enabling technologies. Market factors would, for example, identify the range of target applications, performance requirements, a set of relevant benchmarks, the ability of the user to optimize the computer performance, competitor pricing, and the price range for the computer. Two examples of the enabling technologies that are important for computer hardware design are the technology used for implementing the processing unit and that used for implementing the memory system. The choice of the processor implementation technology, in turn, specifies parameters such as the clock frequencies that can be used, the very-large-scale integration (VLSI) chip area available for the processor, and the associated interface hardware. Memory access time and the size of the primary memory to be supported also impact the computer design. Specifically, the number of addressable locations determines the number of addressing lines required. An analysis of the market and technology factors leads to specification of the instruction set, the word size for internal data representation, the word size for external data transfer, memory addressing requirements, input/output requirements, and desired clock frequency.

The instruction set chosen for the computer is an important input to the computer hardware design. This specification provides details regarding the type of operations that need to be performed, the instruction format(s) used, and the addressing modes adopted. Further, during development of the instruction set, a variety of architectural issues are treated and decided. These include the specification of the size and number of user accessible registers, other registers required for internal management of the computer, the interrupt processing approach to be used, and the input/output processing system.

Once the computer architectural decisions have been made the computer hardware design process begins. To be specific, a computer is usually treated as consisting of three major parts: central processing unit (CPU), main (primary) memory, and input/output processing system. This section focuses on the design of the CPU.

The CPU incorporates the computational and control capability of the computer system and is itself divided into various components. It is often convenient to visualize the CPU as a graph, in which the vertices correspond to the processing and storage elements and the edges correspond to the interconnections. With this viewpoint in mind, it is helpful to treat the overall design process as consisting of detailed design of (1) the data processing components of the CPU, (2) the interconnections between the components, and (3) the control system used to properly sequence and synchronize CPU operations.

DATA PROCESSING COMPONENTS OF THE CENTRAL PROCESSING UNIT

The data processing components of the CPU are of two types: storage elements and computational elements. Storage elements are built using sequential circuits, and the computational elements are designed based on combinational logic. The storage elements are configured using flip-flops, which are the basic building blocks for sequential circuits and are used to store the state of the system. In computers a collection of flip-flops, usually referred to as a register, is often used to temporarily store the results of computation. The functions performed by the CPU's registers are varied. Some of these functions are parallel load, serial input or output, incrementing of the contents of the register, left or right shifting of the register contents. Each additional register function requires additional hardware, and consequently all registers do not perform all the possible functions. The functions performed by each register are determined by the instruction set. For example, if one of the instructions involves incrementing of register A, then register A would have the increment operation built into it. On the other hand, there are registers for which there is no explicit incrementing instruction, but the role of that register requires repeated incrementing. It is then advantageous to build the increment function into that register. The program counter (or instruction pointer) and the stack pointer are two registers of this type. The latter requires both incrementing and decrementing operations.

The computational components of the CPU perform the arithmetic and logical operations required. A unit that performs such operations is referred to as the arithmetic and logical unit (ALU). On the basis of performance requirements, a CPU may have one or more ALUs. The choice of the primitive operations included in the ALU is made on the basis of the instruction set and the performance requirements for the operations included in the instruction set. Some of the arithmetic operations included in the ALU are addition, subtraction, multiplication, and division. For scientific applications, floating point operations are generally provided. The implementation strategy is determined by the performance requirements of the computer. The traditional approach to the design of a binary adder is, for example, to use the ripple-through-carry approach. The difficulty with this approach is that the propagation delay is large and increases linearly with the number of adder stages. The number of adder stages depends on the number of bits in the data word length. To reduce the overall delay other schemes, such as carry lookahead adder (CLA), are used. These schemes require additional hardware, but reduce the overall propagation delay. In CLA, for example, the propagation delay increases as a logarithm of the number of stages in the adder. For addition of multiple vectors, as occurs in performing multiplication, carry-save adders (CSAs) are used. In support of scientific applications, the use of vector processors is common. Such processors often use a pipeline architecture to overlap the processing. The logical operations performed by the ALU are based on Boolean operations. In addition to the elementary *AND, OR, COMPLEMENT,* and *SHIFT* operations, the more complex *EXCLUSIVE-OR* and *COINCIDENCE* operations may be included in the ALU.

INTERCONNECTIONS BETWEEN THE COMPONENTS

An important part of CPU design is determining the interconnections between the components of the CPU. The underlying requirements for this choice are ease of use, cost of implementation, and performance needs. For example, to achieve high throughput the interconnection system should be able to support simultaneous communication between all the components of the CPU. Such a completely connected system requires a large number of interconnections and is expensive to implement. An alternate strategy is to use a bus structure to communicate between the components of the CPU. This has the disadvantage that conflict resolution hardware has to schedule the use of the bus and ensure that only one message is available on the bus at any one time. Further, a single bus will permit data transfer between only one pair of components. The situation of two or more components trying to transmit simultaneously on the same bus is referred to as bus contention. To enhance the throughput of the CPU, multiple internal bus systems have been used.

To avoid bus contention special control components are required. The two devices used for this purpose are multiplexers and decoders. Both of these are combinational circuits. A multiplexer is like a switch. Depending on a chosen set of control conditions, the input on one of $M (= 2^n)$ data input lines is transferred to the output. To perform the selection function, n control lines are required. A decoder is a device with n inputs and M outputs. Depending on the input combination exactly one of the decoder outputs is a logical "1."

To illustrate the application of a combination of multiplexer and decoder for purposes of conflict-free data transmission, consider the approach used in Figure 1. A data transfer using the interconnection system can be characterized as

$$\text{destination register} \leftarrow \text{source register} \quad (1)$$

To achieve this data transfer the address of the source register is fed to the selection lines

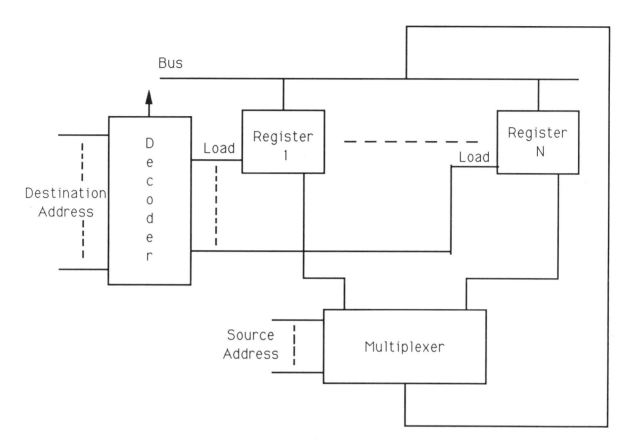

FIGURE 1. Data transfer using a bus.

of the multiplexer, and the destination register address is fed to the decoder. The multiplexer transfers the contents of the source register onto the bus, and the decoder selects the destination register. Each output of the decoder controls the load operation of a distinct register, and consequently exactly one register is designated as the destination of the data on the bus.

One approach to determining the optimal connection pattern among the CPU components is based on the use of a register transfer language (RTL). An RTL is used to represent the hardware operations and is also useful in the design of the control system of the CPU. Typically, a specific RTL statement characterizes operations like that in Equation 1. As RTLs characterize the hardware operations, they are often referred to as computer hardware description languages. An RTL is characterized by a set of symbols and microoperations. The symbols

refer to the registers involved, and the microoperations are the primitive operations that are implemented in hardware. Consequently, each instruction in the instruction set is composed of a sequence of microoperations. In other words, corresponding to each instruction is a register transfer sequence that must be executed each time that instruction is executed.

Each RTL statement consists of two parts: the control part and the data transfer part. Typically an RTL statement has the form

Control: Data Transfer

where Equation 1 is an example of data transfer. Each RTL statements indicates the data transfer(s) that occurs when the control conditions are satisfied. The data transfer part of the RTL is useful for the design of the interconnections, and the control part helps in the design of the control system.

To determine the interconnection requirements, each instruction is transformed into its equivalent RTL representation. The data transfer part of these statements identifies the data paths that must exist between the components of the CPU. Further, specification of the control and timing signals indicates the time available (number of clock cycles) to accomplish the data transfer. At this stage, whether a direct connection is required or a bus connection is adequate needs to be determined. This approach leads to identification of the interconnection requirements within the CPU.

CENTRAL PROCESSING UNIT CONTROL SECTION

The CPU control section performs the role of the coordinator between the different components of the CPU. It generates a sequence of control signals that are used to initiate the data transfers in the CPU. The user program specifies the sequence and instructions executed. The CPU control section generates the control signal sequence to execute the corresponding microoperations in the proper sequence.

Processing an instruction requires that a number of steps be undertaken, and these steps together constitute an instruction. For ease of design of the control section, the instruction cycle is generally divided into the following phases: instruction fetch (IF), instruction decode (ID), computation of the effective address (AE), and instruction execution (IE). An additional level of complexity is added because of the possibility of hardware interrupts. This generally requires another phase—interrupt handling (IH). After completion of the IE phase, the CPU determines if an interrupt is pending, and in the case of a pending interrupt the IH phase is implemented. After processing of the interrupt, the execution of the regular instruction cycle (IF–ID–AE–IE) is resumed.

The IF, ID, and AE phases are common for all instructions; this leads to a simplification of the RTL representing the CPU and also to a simpler control section design. In the IF phase, the address in the program counter is used to read the next instruction from the main memory. In the ID phase, the instruction is divided into its parts depending on the instruction format used in the instruction set, and the operation code (opcode) in the instruction is examined to determine the AE and IE phases. Special timing signals are used in the control section to synchronize the microoperation execution within each phase.

The control section can be implemented using two approaches: hardwired control and microprogrammed control. In the hardwire-based control unit the control signals are generated through the use of logic gates and flip-flops. In the microprogrammed system the microoperations corresponding to each instruction are stored in a read-only memory (ROM), and when a new instruction is identified in the ID phase, the appropriate microoperations, in the correct sequence, are extracted from the ROM. This sequence of microoperations is referred to as a microprogram. The hardwired design is less flexible than the microprogrammed approach, yet it generally leads to higher performance.

For Further Reading

Baer, J. L. 1980. *Computer systems architecture.* Potomac, Md.: Computer Science Press.

Mano, M. M. 1982. *Computer system architecture.* Englewood Cliffs, N.J.: Prentice Hall.

Shiva, S. J. 1991. *Computer design and architecture.* New York: HarperCollins.

Stone, H. S. 1990. *High–performance computer architecture.* Reading, Mass.: Addison Wesley.

———, ed. 1980. *Introduction to computer architecture.* Chicago: Science Research Associates.

Arun K. Sood

Memory Design

The overall performance of a computer system is affected by the performance and design of the computer memory. Memory performs two basic operations: *reading* data from a memory location, and *writing* data to a memory location. The former operation does not lead to a change in the memory contents; the latter does change the memory contents. The discussion of memory design issues is treated in three parts. First, the parameters used to evaluate and specify computer memories are discussed; next the different types of memory and the overall organization of the memories in a hierarchical storage structure is treated; and finally, approaches for improving memory performance are presented.

MEMORY PARAMETERS

Several parameters are used to specify a memory. Some of the more important design parameters are capacity of the memory, size of the memory word, speed of the memory, and cost of the memory.

Capacity is a measure of the total volume of data that can be stored in the memory, and is expressed in bits, bytes, or words. It is common to use prefixes like kilo-, mega-, and giga- to denote measures in 2^{10}, 2^{20}, and 2^{30} units, respectively. These prefixes are motivated by the observation that 2^{10}, 2^{20}, and 2^{30} are approximately equal to a thousand, a million, and a billion, respectively. For example, 1 megabyte corresponds to 2^{20} bytes, or 2^{23} bits (assuming an 8-bit byte).

The size of the memory word is a measure of the least number of data elements (bits) that are accessed or changed in one memory operation. Although the memory capacity is a measure of data volume, the size of the memory word provides an indication of the memory organization. Knowledge of memory capacity and memory word size provides a direct measure of the addressable memory locations. For example, 8-megabit memories with memory words of 8 bits, 16 bits, and 64 bits each would have 2^{20}, 2^{19}, and 2^{17} addressable locations, respectively. As each location requires an address, the numbers of addressing lines required in each case would be 20, 19, and 17. It is emphasized that as the granularity of the access is reduced, the number of addressable locations increases.

The speed of the memory is measured in terms of the access time and the data transfer rate. The memory access time is the time taken to read from or write into a memory location after the address of the data element is provided to the memory. The interval between two successive accesses to the memory is referred to as the memory cycle time. Typically, the access time is smaller than the cycle time. In some cases a read operation must be followed by a write operation to restore the contents of the memory location.

The data transfer rate is the volume of data that can be read out of the memory in a fixed unit of time. This parameter is specified in bits (or bytes) per second. The data transfer rate is the ratio of the number of bits accessed in a single memory access to the memory access time.

The cost of memory is specified in terms of cost per bit. By use of this parameter it is possible to compare the cost effectiveness of different types of memory.

TYPES OF MEMORY

Each computer is equipped with different types of memory. Random-access memory (RAM) is very common in computer systems. In RAM, the time taken to access any memory location is the same; that is, the access time is independent of the physical address specified. Sequential access memory (SAM) is used in computer systems for archival storage because of the low cost of such systems. Some special-purpose computers include content addressable memory (CAM). Whereas RAM accesses the contents of memory location on the basis of the address of the location, CAM accesses a memory location on the basis of the contents of that location. CAM is being used in environments that require rapid data retrieval, where the data themselves are an indicator of the location address. As RAM and SAM are much more common than CAM, the rest of this section focuses on the application of the memories accessed by location.

An overview of the organization of memory with capacity M ($= 2^n$) locations with m bits per location is given in Figure 1. The address of the location to be accessed is

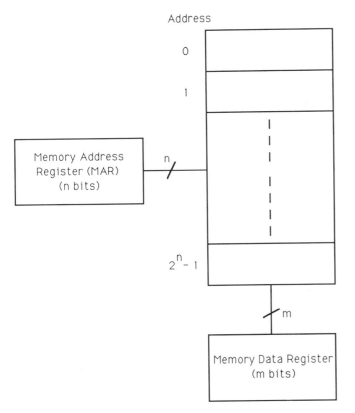

FIGURE 1. Memory organization.

loaded into the memory address register (MAR). After the access time elapses, the data at the addressed location are transferred to the memory data register (MDR).

To aid the design of the memory system it is common to categorize memories based on the performance and cost of the memory. In the context of modern technology, memories can be classified into four categories:

1. *CPU registers:* All CPUs have some user-accessible registers that provide for temporary storage of data. This is a RAM. These registers are located on the same chip as the CPU, and for this reason capacity is limited, memory access is fast, and cost per bit is high.

2. *Main (primary) memory:* This RAM is the bulk of the on-line memory available in the computer system. Usually, metal oxide semiconductor (MOS) technology is used for implementing this memory. The cost per bit is much lower than in the CPU registers and reasonably large (few megabytes to hundreds of megabytes) memory capacity is common. There are two types of MOS memory: dynamic RAM (DRAM) and static RAM (SRAM). In DRAM each location of the memory must be refreshed at regular intervals; SRAM does not require this refreshing, but the chip area per bit is higher for SRAM than for DRAM. Most of the primary memory space is occupied by read–write memory; however, often read-only memory is used to store information that may not be overwritten. Read-only memory (ROM) requires special devices to program. Some kinds of ROM have to be programmed at the manufacturing site; others can be programmed in laboratory settings or user environments.

3. *Cache memory:* Cache memory is used to bridge the gap between the CPU registers and the main memory. Cache memory is an order of magnitude faster and more expensive than main memory. Cache sizes vary from 4 to 128 kilobytes. Cache memory is implemented using bipolar SRAM semiconductor technology.

4. *Secondary memory:* Secondary memory has much lower access times than all the preceding memories, and the cost per bit is much lower. There are two types of secondary memory: direct-access storage devices (DASDs) and sequential-access devices (SADs). Disk drives are examples of a DASD and tape drives are examples of an SAD. In the former, the read–write transducers can be positioned according to the address of the data. The time taken to position the transducers is called the seek time and is of the order of tens of milliseconds. In floppy disk drives the seek time is hundreds of milliseconds. In an SAD the transducer is fixed and the media must be scanned sequentially to find the addressed data element.

It is the objective of memory design to achieve the largest amount of accessible memory at the least cost with the lowest memory access time. Toward this end computer systems use a combination of the four types of memory, by organizing them in a hierarchical fashion. The features of these four memories are summarized in Figure 2, which highlights the hierarchical nature of the memory organization. The basic principle behind this organization is the locality of reference. This principle emphasizes that access to contiguous memory locations is more frequent than access to locations that are far apart. The secondary memory stores the infrequently used data, and a block of data is transferred into the primary memory as needed. If a data element outside this block is required, then the block in the primary memory is exchanged for another block in the secondary memory. This process is called swapping. Depending on the user program being executed, a segment of the data in the main memory is transferred to the cache. Again, swapping is used to keep the most currently used data in the cache. In this way the CPU finds the data it requires usually available in the cache memory, and thus the memory speed approaches the cache speeds. Of course, events like branching lead to more swapping requirements, slowing the speed below the cache speed.

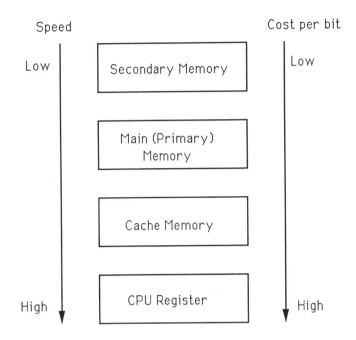

FIGURE 2. Memory hierarchy.

HIGH-PERFORMANCE MEMORY

To achieve higher throughputs several approaches have been adopted. The use of large amounts of high-speed cache memory is one approach to improve memory performance. Some modern computers use two or more levels of cache to maximize throughput. Another approach organizes the main memory into memory banks. Each bank has contiguous memory locations, and all the banks together span the entire memory address space. Then by addressing the memory appropriately, it is possible to overlap the memory access times for each of the memory banks. This suggests that if the memory bus cycle time is equal to memory bank access time divided by the number of banks, then slower-speed memory chips can be used and yet provide high data transfer rates. Of course, this requires that consecutive accesses must be made to different memory banks. Clearly, if the instructions and data were stored in different banks, then there would

be an improvement in the system throughput.

Another way to enhance memory performance is to use interleaved memory. Once again the memory is divided into banks, but now the consecutive memory locations are assigned to distinct banks. Again, by proper choice of the address allocations an overlap in memory access times can be exploited. Such approaches are common in high-performance scientific computers, like array processors. For example, distributing an array across memory banks and accessing the array elements in sequential order would reduce the number of bank conflicts and increase memory throughput.

In the last two decades the price/performance characteristics of memories have been improving rapidly. Recent developments in semiconductor technology and optical and magnetic disk technologies suggest that price/performance and reliability characteristics will continue to improve.

For Further Reading

Baer, J. L. 1980. *Computer systems architecture.* Potomac, Md.: Computer Science Press.

Mano, M. M. 1982. *Computer system architecture.* Englewood Cliffs, N.J.: Prentice Hall.

Shiva, S. J. 1991. *Computer design and architecture.* New York: HarperCollins.

Stone, H. S. 1990. *High-performance computer architecture.* Reading, Mass.: Addison Wesley.

———, ed. 1980. *Introduction to computer architecture.* Chicago: Science Research Associates.

Arun K. Sood

Screen Design

The principal means by which a computer communicates with a user is by the information presented on the computer screen. Consequently, the design of the computer screen is extremely important. Screen design is the result of the interaction of two factors, the technology available to represent information and the capacity of the user to comprehend it. Each of these aspects has two components. The technology is composed of the hardware that presents the information and the software that controls what information is presented, whereas the user is subject to physiological factors of perception and psychological factors of information processing. As a rough characterization, the hardware corresponds to the physiological factors and the software corresponds to the psychological factors.

Originally, computers were controlled by switches that input the contents of registers and output sequences of lights that represented the resulting contents of the registers. Transforming the binary light representation of the register contents into an interpretable number is a difficult task, not surprisingly, and the responsibility for that task was quickly transferred to the hardware, resulting in "nixie" lights that took the number and represented it in glowing lights. Shortly thereafter, it became desirable to represent the output of a sequence of operations and to retain a copy of the output. Similarly, input moved from switches to buttons and then to keyboard input. The result-ing input/output combination was the teletype.

The teletype was the result of more than just an advance in hardware. Primitive operating systems allowed a modicum of output control, so that the interaction with the computer could be in a control language that was a step removed from specifying the actual binary contents of the registers. Of course, these teletypes were slow, noisy, and not interactive. Further, the output could not be erased, so the teletype would have to back up and type over wrong material on the same line or retype the line. For a variety of tasks, the memory load required to remember where you were in a particular file was overwhelming. Finally, all the paper generated while editing a file, debugging programs, and doing other tasks necessary for but not part of generating a final output was a major source of waste. With increases in technology, however, a new solution became available.

The technology that provided the television also made possible a form of output that could be used for all the intermediate tasks associated with computers, but without generating the paper. There were two major benefits to using the cathode-ray tube (CRT), the technology on which a television screen is based. First, final paper output could be directed to a printer that was faster and produced more legible output than the teletype. Second, these "glass teletype" devices were faster and were essentially silent. Not surprisingly, with the advent of the CRT the teletype was quickly replaced.

The switch from the teletype to the CRT was originally only a change in the capability of hardware. For a while, the output on the CRT was in essentially the same form as the output from a teletype. The computer placed one line directly under the last until the bottom line on the screen was full, and then "scrolled" or rolled the top line off the screen to put in a new line. As the capabilities of computers became more sophisticated, computer users started demanding that the load of file manipulation be transferred to the computer. The software side of screen design was beginning to play a role.

Essentially, the screens used today are

not all that different from the "glass teletype." Though some screens have only added the capability to place characters anywhere on the screen, the real change, aside from the introduction of color, is the ability to turn on and off individual points of light on the screen. This technique is called *bit-mapped* graphics, as a one-to-one correspondence is maintained between memory locations and the points of light on the screen. That is, one bit, either on or off, will determine whether the corresponding tiny picture element, or *pixel*, is on or off on the screen (in a simple system). The characters that used to be sent to hardware that painted the characters on the screen are now created by software that creates each character by turning on and off the pixels on the screen. By these means, the software can change the way the characters look (the *font*) or their size (*point size*). Similarly, graphics can also be created this way, painting pictures and drawing diagrams by turning off and on the individual pixels. Screens can now use pictures to represent commands, programs, files, and more. Though some systems have only the capability of displaying whole characters, not creating them individually out of pixels, the rest of the discussion addresses those screens with bit-map capabilities. Most of the discussion is also applicable to character display screens as well.

HARDWARE: THE PHYSIOLOGICAL FACTORS

The major criterion in selecting among the options available for creating a screen is how many pixels the budget will support. This varies, of course, depending on whether you want color; whether you need the screen to be portable, or rugged; whether you need it to use low amounts of power, to be read under less than optimal conditions, to be able to change quickly; whether it will be used for large groups of people; how much information you need to present at a time; how detailed a resolution you need; and a variety of other factors. These factors determine the technology you use and how it is implemented. Although you would prefer to have the best of all of the above, the cost

quickly becomes prohibitive, and the issue then becomes one of what you are willing to trade off to obtain a satisfactory and affordable solution.

Dimensions

As was just suggested, there are many dimensions along which screen displays can vary. The primary consideration, however, is the screen capacity: how much information a screen can contain. Three factors interact to determine the screen capacity: how big the screen is, usually measured in diagonal inches; how many pixels wide and high the screen is; and the number of pixels per unit area, or screen *resolution*, typically measured in dots per inch (dpi). Two of these criteria are enough to specify the third. For example, the screen of the Macintosh computer is 9 inches and measures 512 × 342 pixels, which translates to about 68 dpi. Larger screens with the same amount of pixels will have fewer dots per inch or less resolution, which means a coarser picture. Larger screens with more pixels but the same dots per inch can represent more information at the same resolution. And larger screens with a higher resolution will have to contain more pixels.

Obviously, the bigger the screen and the higher the resolution, the better. In general, the more information available for display at a time, the easier it is to use the screen display most effectively. The trade-off is, of course, the cost. Bigger screens cost more, as does higher resolution. Screens run from as small as 5 inches to as large as 21 inches. Prototypes of larger screens are being investigated. Similarly, dimensions from 512 × 342 to 1024 × 1024 are common, as are pixel densities from 60 to 96 dpi.

Another decision is whether or not you need to have color capability. The cheaper option is to have a *monochrome* (one color) screen. The familiar version of this is black and white; however, the choices can also be black and orange, black and green, or other combinations. The color depends on what *phosphor* is used. Televisions and computer "monitors" (a CRT in a box) operate by electron beams scanning across the screen activating pixels, formed from phosphorous compounds that glow when struck by the beam. Control circuitry determines whether the beam is broad or narrow as the beam passes a certain pixel, determining whether the pixel is on or off. Against the black background, these pixels produce light and represent information. Some people find one color combination more pleasant than others. For many purposes, a monochrome screen is quite sufficient.

Color is a desirable option, however. The human visual system can easily discriminate between colors in conditions of sufficient light. Thus, color is not only appealing but can serve some important informational needs. Unfortunately, for many purposes color is an expensive luxury. A monochrome screen with the same resolution as a color screen can be one third the cost. This is because color screens require three phosphors for every pixel—one red, one green, and one blue—which, when activated together, produce the resultant color of that pixel. The more accurate (and costly) forms of these screens, called *RGB* (red green blue) screens, use three separate electron beams, one for each color.

Cathode-ray tube technology is the oldest but not the only way to represent information on the screen. Newer technologies, most based on the liquid crystal diode (LCD), like those used in most new calculators and digital watches, have a number of advantages over the CRT for information display, and some drawbacks. These screens are composed of semiconductor compounds that, when activated by a small electric potential, block light from a reflective background. A matrix of these diodes represents the pixels, and hardware addresses the pixels individually.

Incidentally, there are other computer technologies available for screen displays that have not yet come into general use, such as the gas plasma and the electroluminescent (EL) displays. These technologies, as yet, either are fairly expensive or do not offer any benefit over the existing technologies. As technology advances, other display technologies will need to be evaluated by the same criteria that are used here to evaluate the CRT and LCD screens.

One advantage to LCD technology is the weight. LCD displays are extremely light compared with computer monitors. This is the predominant reason why LCD screens are the screens found on most portable computers. Although screens with weights less than 1 pound can be created using LCD technology, a CRT typically weighs several pounds. Another reason to use LCD technology is power requirements. Liquid crystal diode displays can run on microcurrents at very low voltages, resulting in low power usage, but a CRT requires high voltages and has a relatively high power consumption. The hardware necessary to provide the required power also becomes a factor in the weight requirements of a screen technology. Lightweight semiconductor chips are enough to drive an LCD screen; the power coils for a monitor may add 10 pounds or more. Yet another reason to consider LCD-based screens is ruggedness. The fragility of the glass-enclosed vacuum required for a CRT is a detriment when compared with the relative ruggedness of the semiconductor construction of a LCD screen.

Another factor to consider is the speed with which the electron beam completely scans across the screen or how fast the LCD display can be updated. This is the *refresh rate,* or the frequency (measured in cycles per second, or hertz, abbreviated Hz) with which every pixel is told to stay on, stay off, or change state. The human visual system can perceive changes as fast as 50 to 75 Hz (depending on luminance). Too slow a refresh rate and the screen will appear to flicker or lag while the information is being updated. For example, you may have noticed the difference in smoothness between home movies and ones you see in the theater. As long as the refresh rate is fast enough, there is not a problem; however, the faster the refresh rate, the more expensive the screen. Most CRT devices can update information at a rate sufficient for all but the most intensive applications, but LCD technologies can be slow.

The major problem with LCD technology in contrast to CRT technology is the legibility of the screen under less than ideal viewing conditions. The human visual system is greatly facilitated in the information-gathering process by a high contrast between the on and off states of the screen. A CRT will provide its own light from the glowing phosphors, but LCD technology requires either ambient light to reflect or an included "backlight" that produces the same effect. Both the reflection and backlighting are also highly dependent on the angle from which they are viewed. Further, even under ideal conditions, the quality of an LCD screen is less than that of a comparable CRT screen. Finally, LCD screens are more difficult to manufacture. Liquid crystal diode displays with more than 640 × 480 pixels have low manufacturing yields. These factors make the CRT still the most prevalent choice for all but portable conditions.

Reality

Computer screens have some concomitant hazards that any screen designer must be aware of. Some of these are specific to the technology and some are general to the task of reading computer screens.

The most prevalent problem, one currently restricted to the CRT, is the problem of radiation. Though there is conflicting evidence about the importance of radiation as a health hazard, caution is advised. There seems to be more concern over the possible effects of low-frequency electromagnetic radiation than ever before. Anyone who spends long periods at a computer needs to be concerned and informed.

Another problem associated with computer screens is eye strain. As detailed as computer screens can get, reading a computer screen can eventually cause severe eyestrain. One problem with the CRT is that the focus at the edges of the screen can often be fuzzy, and can cause eyes to work harder. The problems with the angle of viewing for LCD screens also can strain eyes. A standard recommendation is for any regular user of computers to take a break every so often and do something else for a while. Prolonged viewing leads to the greatest risks. The discrimination ability of the human visual system also suggests that eye strain is minimized by the choice of a point size and a font that are large enough and clear enough to be easily read.

In general, however, the screen decisions available to a computer buyer, as opposed to a computer designer, are already made. The choice between a CRT and an LCD-based screen will be determined by whether the computer is a portable or not. Portables typically use LCD technologies, and any other format uses a CRT. In the case of a CRT, a choice about color has to be made. After that, the decision becomes one of how much screen capacity can affordably be purchased.

SOFTWARE: THE PSYCHOLOGICAL FACTORS

The second aspect to consider, after the actual hardware that composes the screen, is the software that controls what is presented on the screen. Software screen design began at the stage where the users became dissatisfied with the simple transition from the teletype to the CRT. Users began to ask for a representational scheme that more naturally reflected the way the user thought about the task. As the majority of computer use at the time was editing programs to be run, users wanted a way to present programs on the screen the way they thought about them on paper. The first result of this was the screen-oriented editor, a major conceptual improvement over the line-oriented editor. The obvious benefits of screen design were quickly applied to other tasks. For instance, users realized that editors would work for other writing tasks than programming. The screen-oriented editor, mimicking how people write and erase on a piece of paper, began the field now known as word processing. Eventually, a realization grew that there needed to be a science of screen design. The underlying factor in screen design, as seen from the editing example, was the way the user viewed the task. This suggested the importance of considering how users thought, in general.

The important criterion for screen design is how the information is processed once it has been perceived by the eye. The beginning point in understanding how the user thinks is the human information processing system, a model of the mind that characterizes the way users interpret the world. This model provides constraints on what constitutes good screen design. The technical study of how to build computers for people is human factors engineering or human ergonomics, and the study of how to make computers and screen displays understandable to the human information processing system is known variously as human–computer interaction, user-centered system design, or cognitive engineering.

The Human Information Processing System

In simple terms, the human information processing system is composed of three separate storage areas and a number of processes that transfer information between these stores. Each of these stores has particular characteristics, and the processes have certain limitations (see Figure 1).

Information from the eyes is first stored in the sensory register, which can hold a large amount of information but quickly decays (in under 1 second). Typically, however, the information on the screen does not change until some action is taken by the user, so the capacity and duration of the sensory register are only a minor concern. One particular feature of the sensory register is that certain configurations of elements in a visual display are automatically considered as a group rather than separate elements. For instance, items separated a half-inch from each other in a vertical list will be considered

as a unit in relation to another, similar vertical list 1 inch or more from the first. This is but one of the grouping possibilities that exist. Another phenomenon associated with the sensory register is that changing information is easily detectable. Thus, a change in information in the area of peripheral vision may draw attention to the altered area. A final characteristic of importance is the ability of users to recognize familiar patterns easily and to recognize deviations from those familiar patterns easily.

From the sensory register, information that is the current subject of attention is transferred to short-term memory (STM). Attention is limited, so only a small proportion of the available information is processed. For example, you cannot simultaneously watch two television programs at once; you must switch between them to follow the stories. Attention can also be caught by changes to features mentioned above, such as movement and pattern changes.

Short-term memory, unlike the sensory store, has only a limited capacity. Only about five things brought in (or recalled from the next storage area) can be considered at a time. Effort is required to maintain the existence of these things in mind by a process known as rehearsal, active repetition of the items to be remembered. For example, to remember the seven digits of a phone number you must repeat the number while you go from the phone book to the telephone. If something interrupts your repetition (such

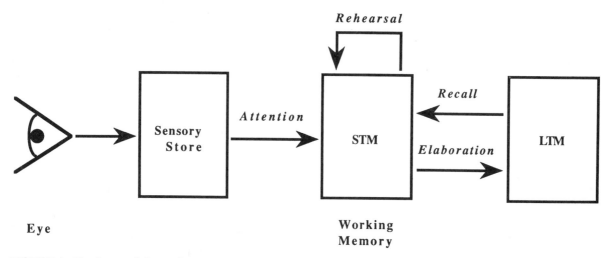

FIGURE 1. The human information processing system.

as a mischievous friend who starts reciting other numbers), you may lose the number and have to return to the phone book.

Despite the name, short-term memory has a duration longer than that of the sensory register, but earns its name by comparison with the next storage area, long-term memory (LTM). Though short-term memory has a capacity of minutes, long-term memory has a duration effectively limited only by the lifetime of the user. Information is transferred from short-term memory to long-term memory by *elaboration* of the information. Elaboration consists of connecting the information to information already stored in long-term memory. Simply repeating a phone number, for example, does not guarantee that you will be able to recall that number the next time you need it. A far better strategy is to link the number to some other information you already possess. Similarly, an easy way to choose a secret four-digit code for an automatic teller system is to choose a number already meaningful to you.

Information in long-term memory is not available to be used until it is recalled and placed into short-term memory (which is consequently also known as working memory). Sometimes this process does not succeed (for example, trying to remember someone's name that you are sure you know, but cannot seem to get when you need it). Careful manipulation of the conditions under which you learn something new, the way you elaborate the information by associating it with something already known, can greatly affect how likely you are to remember it.

Another result of the difficulty of correctly accessing information in LTM is that it takes a long time to correctly structure and learn complicated systems. The establishment of the links between the components of the system and preexisting knowledge is a detailed and time-consuming process. Consider the difficulty in learning a new language. The time to learn both the new words and the meanings associated with those words, even to a minimal communicational fluency, is a process that takes time on the order of weeks.

On the other hand, however, once complex systems are learned, their performance can often be far superior to that offered by simpler methods that provide visual clues to the system operation. Information that is frequently used is better memorized than re-created or obtained again. For example, when you need to know the meaning of a red light at a traffic intersection, it is better to remember than to re-create the origin of that usage or to look it up in a book.

Information Implications

This characterization of the human information processing system has some very specific suggestions for how information should be presented on the screen. Screen design guidelines are a direct result of the limits established by the capacities of users. These guidelines lead to systems that are easier to learn, easier to understand, easier to use, easier to return to, and generally more "user friendly" than systems that do not take careful consideration of human processing limits.

System *interfaces*, the way a user interacts with a system, started out being what are typically known as "command language" systems, where the user remembers the commands with which to control the computer (see Figure 2). This is fine for users who use the computer frequently and regularly exercise their knowledge of the commands, but for infrequently used commands, for occasional users, and for users who moved between computer systems frequently, this system was less than optimal. For these users, a new system was devised. *Menu* systems provide a list (or menu) of commands that are currently available or relevant (see Figure 3). These choices are displayed on the screen and prompt the user how to specify the appropriate one. Menu systems support the knowledge limitations of the user's information processing system by providing clues to operation. Though users who frequently interact with the same system still can choose to use command language systems, menu systems became the preferred choice of other users.

Much of the first screen display research came about when it became evident that all menus were not created equal. There are systematic principles, derived from the human information processing system model,

```
setenv PAGER page

alias cp 'cp -i \!*'
alias rm 'rm -i \!*'
alias mv 'mv -i \!*'
alias bye 'date;  logout'
alias p 'ps -au | page'
alias q 'logout'
alias l 'page \!*'
alias u 'uptime'
alias j 'jobs'
alias cd 'cd \!*; lf'
alias cn 'rn -c'
alias rn 'rn -e -m'

alias w 'w | page'
alias d 'date'
exit
csh> u
  4:23pm  up 1 day, 13:55,  52 users,  load average: 6.25, 4.74, 4.17
csh> j
csh> date
Fri May 24 16:23:46 EDT 1991
csh> ▮
```

FIGURE 2. A command line interface.

that stipulate how character-based displays can be optimized for ease of use. For example, menus are much easier to read if they are spaced apart, aligned vertically, organized hierarchically, and there are not too many options available at one time. This was the beginning of the human factors field. Many guidelines from this research are also applicable to graphic displays.

With the transition from character-based displays to bit-mapped graphic screens, the menu choices could be made more easily recognizable by providing pictorial representations (icons) of the options. Coherent graphical representations are what are known as graphic user interfaces (GUI). Another problem that character-based systems had was that the output available from a printer was capable of much finer detail than the screen display could indicate. The advent of bit-mapped representations allowed users to see on the screen a more detailed approximation of how the final output was going to appear. This led to what-

```
 PITTCAT: PITT ONLINE CATALOG                                    L211
    PITTCAT can be used to find BIBLIOGRAPHIC, CALL NUMBER, and LOCATION
    information for materials held by University of Pittsburgh Libraries.
 *****************************************************************************
 PITTCAT commands may be entered in upper or lower case letters.
 You can start an author, title, subject or keyword search from any screen.
 To correct mistakes, BACKSPACE to the error or use the HOME key to start over.
 If you need assistance, ask a library staff member.
 *****************************************************************************
 TYPES OF PITTCAT SEARCHES:                       COMMANDS
 - FOR INTRODUCTORY SCREEN FOR AUTHOR searches:   Type A
                              TITLE searches:     Type T
             SUBJECT searches (not HPIC or MEDICAL):  Type S
             MEDICAL SUBJECT HEADING searches:    Type SM
                HPIC SUBJECT HEADING searches:    Type SW
                       KEYWORD searches:          Type K

 - FOR USERS ALREADY FAMILIAR WITH PITTCAT:       Type T= A= S= SM= SW= or K=
   (To start a search from any screen)            followed by a search term
                                                  (title, author, subject
                                                   or keyword)

 Type NEWS for news concerning PITTCAT
 Type N for another introductory screen
 Type COMMAND and press RETURN ▮
```

FIGURE 3. A menu system interface.

you-see-is-what-you-get (WYSIWYG) screen representations that created the basis for the desktop publishing industry.

These screen design principles suggest potential trade-offs in system design. If a system is easy to learn, in that it relies on well-known information presented on the screen to facilitate pattern recognition, it will often do so at the expense of making it more limited in power. For example, one technique to make computers easy to learn is by using a familiar situation as a metaphor. These interfaces operate on the "direct manipulation" principle of operating on the objects of interest directly rather than through an intervening language. One case of this is the so-called desktop metaphor where the computer screen is made to look like a desk (see Figure 4). Files are stored in file folders, discarded files are put into a trash can, and files to be printed are dropped into a receptacle that is represented by a little printer. Although this is easy to learn, drawing on knowledge the user already possesses about how to conduct business in an office, complicated actions may be difficult or complicated to express. If you wanted to make a printout of a file in this hypothetical desktop system, you would have to find the file, say a folder labeled "fileX," in one of your file drawers (filedrawer1) on the desktop, drop the file into a copier that is on your desktop, wait until the copy comes out, store the original in the file drawer again, and drop the copy in the printer. On the other hand, with a command language system you might simply type the command "PR filedrawer1.fileX." A copy is automatically made and sent to the printer. Though it takes some time to learn the commands that do what you want, once you have put in the initial effort, you reap the benefit in terms of power. Similarly, if a system is easy to use by just pointing to familiar things on the screen with an input device, as this hypothetical system is, the cost is the loss of the speed made possible by a concise set of commands that can quickly be typed in and executed.

These trade-offs need to be considered in decisions about software for screen design. The task that is to be performed by the user should be the deciding criterion in design decisions. If the task is going to be one the user must frequently perform, and speed is a priority, then having a system that depends on the user's memory is probably a good choice. If, on the other hand, the task is one that may be relatively infrequently per-

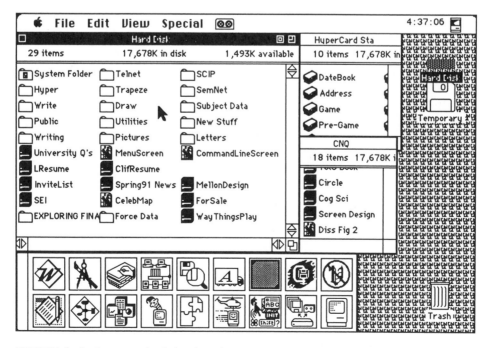

FIGURE 4. A direct manipulation interface.

formed, then using easily distinguishable representations that facilitate understanding is a good rationale.

In many ways, the principles that determine good screen design follow the same principles that underlie good graphic design. The way in which screens differ, of course, is in their dynamic quality. The fact that computer processing and feedback from the user can change the information that needs to be displayed means that a new dimension has been added to the principles of good design.

There are many implications for screen design that can be derived from the simple characterization of the human information processing system presented. Many more can be obtained from a more robust and accurate model of how users think. The point is that there are reasons to decide how information should be presented that go beyond mere intuition. These factors must be considered and analyzed to yield a good design.

Screen design has two aspects, the hardware available and the software needs. Both of these aspects must be evaluated by considering the user. Unfortunately, screen design is still an art, not a science. It is hoped that will change in the future.

For Further Reading

Baecker, R. M., and W. A. S. Buxton, eds. 1987. *Readings in human–computer interaction: A multidisciplinary approach.* Los Altos, Calif.: Morgan Kaufmann. Good overview chapters and seminal readings. Very comprehensive.

Brown, C. M. 1988. *Human computer interface design guidelines.* Norwood, N.J.: Ablex. A simple introduction to screen and graphic design.

Bullinger, H. J., and R. Gunzenhauser. 1988. *Software ergonomics: Advances and applications.* Chichester, England: Ellis Horwood. Contains a concise chapter on information design for screens.

Carroll, J. M. 1990. *Designing interaction: Psychology at the human–computer interface.* London: Cambridge University Press. A collection of articles on the importance of understanding the human information

processing system when designing interfaces.

Dumas, J. S. 1988. *Designing user interfaces for software.* Englewood Cliffs, N.J.: Prentice-Hall. A simple guide to character-based screen design.

Helander, M. 1988. *Handbook of human–computer interaction.* New York: Elsevier Science. Highly recommended as a guide to human factors in computer interaction.

Laurel, B. 1990. *The art of the human computer interface.* Reading, Mass.: Addison-Wesley. Compendium of innovative ideas on all aspects of computer interfaces.

Monk, A. 1984. *Fundamentals of human computer interaction.* New York/Orlando, Fla.: Academic Press. Several good chapters on the human vision system and the human information processing system.

Norman, D. A., and S. W. Draper. 1986. *User centered system design.* Hillsdale, N.J.: Lawrence Erlbaum Associates. Contains pioneering work on cognitive engineering and direct-manipulation interfaces as well as an introduction to other perspectives in user–system interaction.

Smarte, G., and N. M. Baran. 1988. Face to face. *Byte* 13(9):243–52. Contains a survey of screen display technologies.

Clark Quinn

Hardware Interfaces

Computers communicate with peripheral devices and with other computers through various types of hardware interfaces. Although there are many different types of interfaces, most share the following common elements: (1) a data transfer method, (2) interface circuitry, (3) interface driver software, (4) a data transfer protocol.

DATA TRANSFER METHODS

The two principal methods of transferring data are known as "serial" and "parallel." A serial interface transfers data one bit at a time. If the data to be transferred are organized into bytes, words, or other longer data structures, they are broken down into a "series" of bits, hence the name "serial"

FIGURE 1. Serial interface.

interface. The serial interface concept is shown in Figure 1.

The primary advantage of a serial interface is that only a few wires are required to transfer data between two devices. Serial interfaces also lend themselves to radio, telephone, and fiberoptic transmission of data for the same reason. The most significant disadvantage of serial interfaces is the relatively slow speed of transmission, as data are transferred only one bit at a time. Serial interfaces also frequently require complex circuitry to break the data up into bits for transmission and reassemble the received data into bytes or words.

Serial communications are categorized as either *full duplex* or *half duplex*. A full duplex interface can transmit and receive data at the same time. A half duplex interface does not have this capability and must stop transmitting to receive data.

Parallel interfaces transfer data more than one bit at a time. Common parallel interfaces use eight, sixteen, and even thirty-two lines to transfer data and are usually designed to match the internal bus structures of the two devices being connected. The

parallel interface concept is shown in Figure 2.

The principal advantage of a parallel interface is that high data transfer rates are possible as multiple bits are transferred at the same time. Interface circuitry is usually simplified because the parallel interface structure may be designed to match the architecture of the computer data bus (e.g., 8-bit bytes). The most significant disadvantage of the parallel interface method is the large number of wires or lines required to connect two devices.

INTERFACE CIRCUITRY

All hardware interfaces include electronic circuits with varying levels of sophistication. The complexity of these circuits is related to the capabilities of the interface driver software. Some computers use software to perform data formatting, error checking, and handshaking and therefore have very simple interface circuitry. This approach is used when lower hardware costs and increased flexibility are important design issues. The

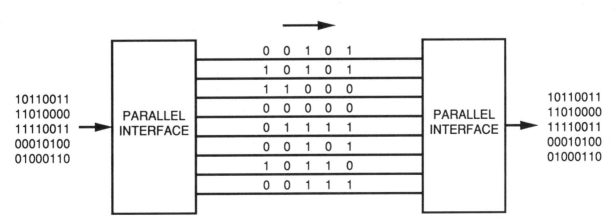

FIGURE 2. Parallel interface.

modern trend in interface circuitry, however, is toward large and very large scale integrated circuits (LSICs and VLSICs) which perform complicated formatting, error checking, and other functions on a single chip. This approach relieves the computer of these tasks and simplifies the interface driver software. Another advantage of the LSIC/VSLIC approach is that interfaces may be easily standardized, as a data transfer protocol may be "built in" to an integrated circuit.

INTERFACE DRIVER SOFTWARE

The software required to operate a hardware interface is known as an interface driver or, more commonly, a device driver. Device drivers contain instructions specific to a particular interface circuit and are usually written in assembly or other low-level machine language. Most device drivers are part of the operating system for the computer in which the interface is installed. For example, the Apple Macintosh System file contains "DRVR" resources (code segments) to operate the serial ports, parallel small computer systems interface (SCSI) port, disk drives, and other hardware devices. The software contained in these resources may be used by any application program. The device driver handles all the particulars of operating the hardware interface and thus application programs need not be concerned with the low-level details of a particular piece of hardware.

DATA TRANSFER PROTOCOLS

Data transfer protocols are the specific formats and timing criteria with which data are transferred. The following items are commonly specified by a protocol.

Data transfer rate. For serial interfaces, data transfer rate is usually specified in bits per second, or by a related measure known as baud rate (after an early Teletype protocol known as the Baudot code). For parallel interfaces, the transfer rate is defined in bytes or words per second depending on the structure of the interface.

Data formats. The format of each data transmission is defined. For serial interfaces, the number of start bits, word size, number of stop bits, and format of error checking bits is specified. For parallel interfaces, the word size is usually determined by the hardware, but the meaning of any special-purpose interface lines is also specified.

Handshaking. Hardware interfaces must provide a means for controlling the flow of data. Peripheral devices must be able to signal the host computer when the device is ready and able to send and receive data. This process is called *handshaking* and may be accomplished by either hardware or software methods. Interfaces that use hardware handshaking have dedicated interface lines to signal when data are available for transmission and when data may be received. Interfaces that use software handshaking use special codes embedded in the data to signal the same information.

INTERFACE STANDARDS

Many different standard hardware interfaces have been developed to allow devices manufactured by different companies to communicate with one another. In the late 1970s when the first mass-produced personal computers became available, few hardware interface standards existed. The process of interfacing a printer and a computer from different manufacturers required a knowledge of both electronics and assembly language programming. The computer industry soon realized the advantages of standard interfaces and began to conform to standards developed by the Electronic Industry Association (EIA) and other professional groups. Modern computers and peripheral devices are easily connected because most conform closely to published interface standards. These standards have varying levels of detail, but may include the following elements.

Electrical signal characteristics. The voltages used on the data transfer lines and their interpretations as ones and zeroes are defined.

Interface mechanical characteristics. The size of the connecting plugs and sockets and the arrangement of pins are defined.

Functional description of signals. The purpose and sense of each interface line are defined.

The RS-232C Serial Interface

The most common serial interface for connecting computers to modems and terminals is RS-232C. This standard was developed by the EIA and is fully titled, "Interface Between Data Terminal Equipment and Data Circuit-Terminating Equipment Employing Serial Binary Interface." RS-232C was originally designed to connect computer terminals (known as data terminal equipment, or DTE) to modems (data communications equipment, or DCE), and includes many signals for modem control, telephone ring sensing, and carrier signal detection. The RS-232C signals are listed in Table 1.

The full RS-232C standard includes twenty signals, but in practice only a small subset of these are required to connect a printer to a computer. The simplest RS-232C interface is shown in Figure 3.

The designations DTE and DCE are somewhat arbitrary for modern computer equipment. Rather than describing the type of equipment, these designations are used only to indicate the direction of signal flow on the various lines. RS-232C signals are named with respect to the DTE; for example, transmitted data means data transmitted from the DTE to the DCE. If the RS-232C port on a computer is wired as DTE, the user knows that pin 2 is the data output line and

TABLE 1. RS-232C Signals

PIN	Code	Signal	Source
1	AA	Protective ground	
2	BA	Transmitted data (TXD)	DTE
3	BB	Received data (RXD)	DCE
4	CA	Request to send (RTS)	DTE
5	CB	Clear to send (CTS)	DCE
6	CC	Data set ready (DSR)	DCE
7	AB	Signal ground	
8	CF	Carrier detect (CD)	DCE
12	SCF	Secondary carrier detect	DCE
13	SCB	Secondary clear to send	DCE
14	SBA	Secondary transmitted data	DTE
15	DB	Transmit clock	DCE
16	SBB	Secondary received data	DCE
17	DD	Receiver clock	DCE
19	SCA	Secondary request to send	DTE
20	CD	Data terminal ready (DTR)	DTE
21	CG	Signal quality detect	DCE
22	CE	Ring detect	DCE
23	CH	Data rate select	DTE
24	DA	Transmit clock	DTE

pin 3 is the data input line. If the RS-232C port is wired as DCE, the functions of these pins are reversed.

RS-232C interfaces use two types of handshaking. The first is a hardware method in which the signals "data terminal ready" (DTR) and "data set ready" (DSR) indicate that the DTE and DCE, respectively, are ready to receive data. For example, consider a printer that is set up as DTE and for hardware handshaking. If the printer's input buffer becomes full, the printer will set the DTR line FALSE, signaling the computer to stop sending data. When the input buffer is empty, the printer will set the DTR line TRUE, indicating that the computer is free to

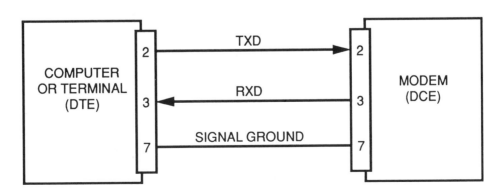

FIGURE 3. A simple RS-232C interface.

send more data. One disadvantage of this method is that the serial interface cable must contain the DTR and DSR lines; hardware handshaking cannot be used with the simple RS-232C interface shown in Figure 3.

The second handshaking method is a software technique that uses ASCII control codes DC1 (XON or Control-Q) and DC4 (XOFF or Control-S) to control the flow of data. For example, consider a printer that is set up as DTE and for software handshaking. When the printer's input buffer becomes full, the printer transmits the Control-S code, indicating that it is no longer able to accept data. When the input buffer is empty, the printer will send Control-Q, which tells the computer that the printer is ready to accept more data. The advantage of the XON/XOFF technique is that dedicated handshaking lines are not required. The computer's RS-232C interface must, however, be designed to respond immediately so that no more data are sent after receiving the Control-S code.

The two most significant shortcomings of RS-232C are its limited transmission distance of 50 feet and maximum baud rate of 20,000. Longer cables and higher bit rates may be used, but only at the risk of data

transmission errors caused by line losses and electromagnetic interference. For the majority of computer-to-printer interfaces, however, 50 feet is more than enough, and few printers can handle data at more than 19,200 baud. For systems that require serial transmission of data over longer distances or at higher speeds, other EIA standards are available such as RS-422A, RS-423A, and RS-499.

The Centronics Parallel Interface
The most widely used parallel interface is the Centronics standard, named after a popular brand of printers. This protocol is not formally defined, but is a de facto standard adopted by the majority of printer manufacturers. The original Centronics Model 737 printer was designed to connect with mainframe computers and used many special-purpose handshaking signals. As applied to microcomputers and other printers, however, the Centronics interface is simplified considerably and consists of eight data lines and only two handshaking lines as shown in Figure 4. Note that this is a one-way interface only; data can be transferred only from the

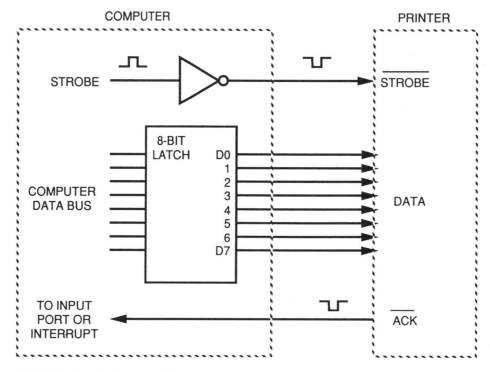

FIGURE 4. Centronics parallel interface.

computer to the printer and not vice versa. All signals in the Centronics interface are transistor-transistor-logic (TTL) compatible.

The data transfer process begins when the computer writes data to an 8-bit latch, as shown. The STROBE signal is then asserted to signal the printer that the data lines contain valid data. The printer acknowledges the transfer of data by asserting the ACK signal, which the computer uses to reset the STROBE line.

The most significant advantage of the Centronics parallel interface is its simplicity and low cost. An entire interface may be implemented with one integrated circuit such as the Intel 8255 Programmable Peripheral Interface chip. On the other hand, the simplicity of the interface prevents its use with intelligent printers or other devices that must pass data in both directions.

The IEEE-488 Parallel Interface

The IEEE-488 parallel interface standard was published in 1975 by the Institute of Electrical and Electronics Engineers. The interface was intended to be a standard for connecting computers to programmable instruments such as data recorders, oscilloscopes, and digital voltmeters. IEEE-488 has since been applied to a wide variety of other devices including conventional peripherals such as disk drives, printers, and plotters. The Hewlett–Packard Corporation's implementation of the IEEE-488 bus, known as the Hewlett–Packard Instrumentation Bus (HPIB), is the most widely used implementation of the IEEE-488 standard. The HPIB standard combines the IEEE-488 hardware standard with a communications system that allows devices on the bus to communicate with one another.

The HPIB consists of eight data lines and eight control lines as shown in Table 2.

Unlike the RS-232C or Centronics interfaces, the HPIB interface allows up to 15 devices to be connected together. All HPIB devices are connected in parallel as shown in Figure 5.

With more than two devices on the bus, some sort of arbitration scheme is necessary. Devices on the HPIB may have the function of "talker", "listener", or "controller," or any combination of the three. Only one device on the bus can be a controller at any particular time. For example, the computer in Figure 5 is a controller, a talker, and a listener because it controls the bus and both sends and receives data. An output-only device such as the printer is a listener because it only receives data from the bus. The digital voltmeter shown in Figure 5 is a talker because it only transmits data to other devices on the bus.

The principal advantage of the IEEE-488 is its wide acceptance in the field of programmable instrumentation. A wide variety of recorders, sensors, and other peripherals are available with HPIB interfaces.

The Small Computer Systems Interface

The small computer systems interface (SCSI) was developed by the American National Standards Institute (ANSI) in response to the need for a sophisticated, high-speed parallel interface capable of serving multiple intelligent peripheral devices. The SCSI (commonly pronounced "scuzzy") standard is an ex-

TABLE 2. IEEE-488 Bus Signals

Signal	Description
DATA BUS	Eight-bit data bus
DATA VALID (DAV)	Indicates valid data on the bus
NOT READY FOR DATA (NRFD)	Device cannot accept data
NOT DATA ACCEPTED (NDAC)	Data were not received
INTERFACE CLEAR (IFC)	Resets the bus interfaces
ATTENTION (ATN)	Sends bus commands
SERVICE REQUEST (SRQ)	Signals bus interrupts
REMOTE ENABLE (REN)	Enables or disables a device
END OR IDENTIFY (EOI)	End of data or poll request

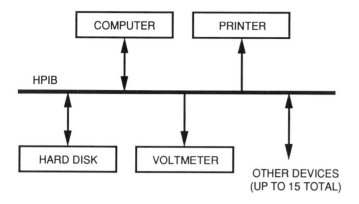

FIGURE 5. Typical IEEE-488 interface.

tension of the Shugart Associates systems interface (SASI), a hard disk controller interface developed in the late 1970s. The SCSI bus is designed to support up to eight devices (including the host computer) with up to 2,048 addressable units per device. Manufacturers have found that having more than one device connected to one interface results in lower hardware costs, less circuit board space required, and simpler driver software. A typical SCSI configuration is shown in Figure 6.

The SCSI standard specifies a bus arbitration scheme that requires one device (usually the host computer) to be the bus controller, directing the flow of data from one device to another. Data may be transferred not only to and from the host computer, but between peripheral devices as well. Asynchronous data transfer rates of up to 1.5 megabytes per

second and synchronous data transfer rates of 4 megabytes per second are possible.

Like the IEEE-488 bus, devices on the SCSI bus are connected together in "daisy chain" fashion with a bus terminator on either end as shown in Figure 6. The bus terminators provide the SCSI bus with the proper electrical characteristics, thereby minimizing the effects of any electromagnetic interference. The total length of the SCSI chain may be up to 6 meters when using open-collector bus drivers, or up to 25 meters when using differential-current line drivers.

The SCSI bus includes eight data lines, one parity line, and nine control lines, as shown in Table 3.

The SCSI standard is designed with the flexibility to accommodate many different system architectures. The simplest architecture consists of two devices, for example, a computer and a hard disk drive. The more complex architectures might include multiprocessing (more than one computer operating simultaneously) or multitasking (one computer performing more than one task simultaneously). The task of designing hardware interfaces for the SCSI bus has been greatly simplified by the development of interface chips such as the NCR 5380. These very large scale integrated circuits contain dedicated processor circuits that are programmed to operate and control the SCSI in even the most complex system architectures.

The flexibility and speed of the SCSI bus have made it one of the most widely accepted

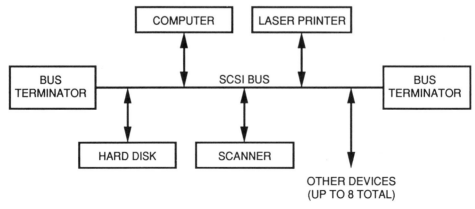

FIGURE 6. Typical SCSI configuration.

TABLE 3. SCSI Bus Signals

Signal	Description
DATA BUS (DB(7)-DB(0))	Eight-bit data bus
DATA PARITY (DB(P))	Odd parity signal
BUSY (BSY)	Indicates that the bus is being used
SELECT (SEL)	Used to select a target device
CONTROL/DATA (C/D)	Indicates type of data on the bus
INPUT/OUTPUT (I/O)	Indicates the direction of data flow
MESSAGE (MSG)	Signal from a target device
REQUEST (REQ)	Request for a data transfer
ACKNOWLEDGE (ACK)	Acknowledgment of a data transfer
ATTENTION (ATN)	Indicates a bus attention condition
RESET (RST)	Indicates a reset condition

standards in the computer industry, one that will remain useful well into the 1990s.

For Further Reading

Ciarcia, S. Ciarcia's circuit cellar. *Byte,* September 1977 through December 1988. This monthly series of hardware construction articles contains many excellent tutorials on hardware interfaces of all types. Highly recommended for the experimenter.

Interface between data terminal equipment and data communications equipment employing serial binary data interchange, EIA Std. RS-232-C. Washington, D.C.: Electronic Industries Association, 1981.

Microprocessor and peripheral handbook, vols. I and II. 1988. Santa Clara, Calif.: Intel Corp. This product guide also contains many design notes on the application of very large scale integrated circuits to hardware interfaces.

Small computer systems interface (SCSI), ANSI X3.131-1986. New York: American National Standards Institute.

Standard codes, formats, protocols, and common commands for use with IEEE/ANSI Std. 488.1-1987, IEEE standard digital interface for programmable instrumentation, IEEE/ANSI Std. 488.2-1987. Piscataway, N.J.: Institute of Electrical and Electronics Engineers.

Standard digital interface for programmable instrumentation, IEEE/ANSI Std. 488.1-1987. Piscataway, N.J.: Institute of Electrical and Electronics Engineers.

Paul Deppe

Computer Systems

The evolution of sophisticated and compact modern computer systems from their crude and gigantic earlier versions undoubtedly ranks as one of the top technological accomplishments of the twentieth century. Remarkable improvements in the performance capabilities of computers, coupled with their miniaturization and steady decline in cost, have resulted in the "computerization" of day-to-day human endeavors. Now the sights are set on the development of truly intelligent computers that will be capable of mimicking the human brain.

This part of the article deals with a brief presentation of computer systems in several sections. The next section defines computers and computer systems and distinguishes between hardware and software subsystems in a computer system. Subsequent sections address the differences between digital and analog computer systems, classification of digital computer systems, and typical organization of microcomputer and mainframe/minicomputer systems. The last section is a summary.

COMPUTERS AND COMPUTER SYSTEMS

A *computer* is essentially an information processing machine. It has the capabilities of accepting information from external devices (input), storing the information, processing/manipulating the information, and displaying the results of processing (output). This definition is broad enough to apply to computers of all sizes, ranging from very large multimillion-dollar mainframes to small inexpensive palm-top personal computers.

A *computer system* can be viewed as a collection of various resources that are interconnected in a way to service the user in an efficient manner. It basically consists of two subsystems, namely, *hardware* and *software,* with each subsystem being made up of several components.

The hardware subsystem refers to physically realizable and visible components such as the keyboard, central processing unit, primary memory, disk drive, monitor, and printers. Although the CPU and the primary memory are considered the internal parts of the computers, the input/output (I/O) devices are referred to as peripherals and include such items as communication devices (e.g., modem), pointing devices (e.g., mouse), and storage devices (e.g., compact-disk read-only memory [CD-ROM]). The organization of the hardware subsystem of a computer system is shown in Figure 1.

The software subsystem is the set of all programs, with each program designed to perform a designated task. Each program in turn contains a series of instructions that control the operation of the computer hardware. There are two types of software: *applications software* and *system software.* Applica-

tion software comprises programs that help a user perform specific tasks such as payroll computation. Programs that assist the user to perform more generalized applications, such as electronic spreadsheets, word processors, and graphics, are also grouped under this heading. System software consists of programs designed to perform tasks associated with directly controlling and using the computer resources. It also contains certain tools that enable the user to use the capabilities of the computer hardware in an effective and "user-friendly" manner. Examples of system software include operating systems, compilers for programming languages, data managers, and utilities.

DIGITAL VERSUS ANALOG COMPUTER SYSTEMS

In digital systems the computers process information coded generally in the binary ("on–off") representation. The two distinct states, namely, 1 ("on") and 0 ("off"), are similar to the states of a mechanical "switch" and are usually represented as two different voltage levels in the system. Computers that use binary representation are known as "binary computers." Various combinations of 1's and 0's represent numbers, letters, and symbols that can be entered into the computer. The processing unit of the computer contains several million "electronic switching circuits" that process the information coded as a sequence of 0's and 1's.

In analog systems, the information is normally represented as voltage levels that correspond to or are "analogous to" some physical quantity. For example, a transducer can transform the temperature of a fluid under observation into a voltage form, with the fluctuations in the temperature being converted continuously as the analogous fluctuations in the output voltage. The circuitry in analog systems is capable of dealing with a continuous range of voltages instead of only two discrete levels as in binary computers. Analog systems are used for such tasks as modeling complex processes in a chemical plant, designing and analyzing control systems, and launching a space shuttle. The input to the system comes from var-

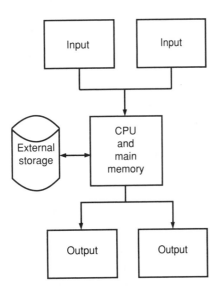

FIGURE 1. Organization of hardware subsystem. *Adapted, with permission, from Anderson and Sullivan 1988.*

ious transducers, and the output of the system is usually displayed in the form of continuous graphs indicating the analogous values of the physical quantities under observation.

Analog systems are normally very limited in their range of tasks, whereas digital systems are more flexible, because they are often general-purpose information processing machines. Another point for comparison is that of accuracy of representation. To illustrate this point let us compare an analog watch with a digital watch. The position of the hands in an analog watch corresponds to the actual time on a continuously changing basis, whereas in a digital watch the time displayed is accurate only at the exact instant the display changes. Thus, a digital watch is accurate at a particular instant of time, whereas an analog watch is accurate "all the time." Nevertheless, human observers, who are not capable of noticing the fine differences in the position of the hands in an analog watch, find the digital display to be "more accurate"! It is possible, of course, to increase the "accuracy" of a digital watch by "coding" even smaller intervals of time, thereby increasing the number of displayed digits. Although analog systems are by nature "more accurate" (within the range of representation of analog signals), the capability of digital systems to increase accuracy "at will" makes the digital systems far superior. With the availability of sophisticated circuits that can perform to the desired level of accuracy, "analog-to-digital conversion" (ADC) and "digital-to-analog conversion" (DAC), it may not be too long before digital systems take over the tasks of the analog systems.

CLASSIFICATION OF DIGITAL COMPUTERS

Modern digital computers, which come in all shapes and sizes, are commonly classified as palm-top computers, lap-top computers, home computers, personal computers, workstations, file servers, minicomputers, superminis, mainframes, and supercomputers. On the basis of such features as size, speed, cost, and number of users serviced, it is possible to classify computers into one of three broad categories: *mainframes, minicomputers, and microcomputers.*

Mainframes are the largest and the most expensive multiuser computer systems. They are found predominantly in large organizations such as government agencies, major corporations, banks, and insurance companies. Very fast mainframes are also called *supercomputers* and are used primarily to perform complex analysis of large amounts of data encountered in scientific and engineering problems. Usually mainframes serve many functions and many users. They are used in situations where extensive computation and processing of voluminous data are required.

Minicomputers are smaller versions of mainframes and are generally used in institutions such as universities, research laboratories, and manufacturing plants. Compared with mainframes, minicomputers provide specific, well-defined services. The hardware subsystems for mainframes and minicomputers are essentially similar in nature, except that in mainframes the components are more numerous, larger, of better quality, faster in operation, and so on.

Microcomputers are the smallest, the least powerful, and the least expensive computers. The heart of a microcomputer is the *microprocessor*. Microprocessors evolved when the semiconductor manufacturers successfully completed and perfected the "computer-on-a-chip" project in the 1980s. Microcomputers frequently appear in the form of *embedded microprocessors* in such devices as microwave ovens, audio/video equipment, clocks, cars, and greeting cards. They also appear in the *personal computer*, which is designed to be used by one person. Typical applications of personal computers include word processors, spreadsheets, and video games. Common folks felt the impact of the computer revolution when the cost of personal computers fell dramatically in the past few years so that they could afford to purchase one for home use.

One of the important programs in the software subsystem of any computer is the *operating system*, which controls and supervises the computer resources and provides services to the users. An operating system may implement one of many processing capabilities such as single-user processing, multiuser processing, single tasking (only one program is allowed to run in the system at a time), and multitasking (several programs are allowed to reside in the memory at the same time and the CPU switches attention from one program to the other).

An operating system that can service multiple users may use *time-sharing* capability, which attempts to provide several users access to the hardware subsystems virtually at the same time. Each user is allocated a *time slice* for processing, and the system maintains a circular list of all the active users. Several users are served on a round-robin basis; that is, all users in the list are served one after another in their allotted time slices until they receive another turn and so on. Users whose jobs are completed are deleted from the list; new users are added to the list. Because of the tremendous disparity in user responses and the processing speed, it appears that each user is serviced continuously by the system.

Most operating systems that are being used in microcomputers, such as DOS, are single-user operating systems. The majority of the operating systems used on mainframes and minicomputers have the capabilities of multitasking and time sharing. Modern operating systems contain many more capabilities to make use of computer systems very efficient for the intended applications and are user-friendly.

In the next two sections, architectures of microcomputer systems are compared with the architectures of mainframe/minicomputer systems. *Architecture of a computer system* is used to mean the organization of interdependent components (hardware as well as software) to accomplish desirable computational and functional efficiency. For a discussion of *computer architecture* in the sense of "the appearance of the computer system to the assembly language programmer," see "Computer Architecture" below.

TYPICAL ORGANIZATION OF MICROCOMPUTER SYSTEMS

In this section, a typical set of hardware/ software components and their organization in a microcomputer system are presented. After understanding the physical limitations of the components of these systems, it is possible to design the architecture of the system by adding or eliminating a few components so that its performance is optimized.

A microcomputer system is designed around a single integrated circuit called a *microprocessor*, which acts as the central processing unit. Usually the cost of a microcomputer system varies from a couple of hundred dollars to a couple of thousand dollars. It uses disk drives for secondary storage, accepts input from a keyboard, and displays output on a screen called a monitor. Figure 2 shows the organization of the various components of a microcomputer system. The microprocessor interacts with other components via a set of parallel conductors called a *bus.* The bus can be thought of as a common pathway; it can be used by a single component to broadcast messages to other components. Rules govern who gets to use the bus when and for whom the message is intended. Rules also govern the manner in which normal messages are interrupted to serve messages of higher priority. The bus interface unit of the microprocessor moderates the activity of the bus.

The microprocessor contains three other parts: the arithmetic and logic unit (ALU), the control unit, and a set of registers. An ALU contains electronic circuitry that performs the arithmetic (add, subtract, multiply, etc.) and logic (*and, or, exclusive-or, coincidence,* etc.) operations on the data supplied. A control unit of the CPU is the actual workhorse of the system, and it is responsible for retrieving instructions from memory, interpreting them, and providing the information and control signals to all units (e.g., ALU, registers, and bus control unit). The set of registers acts as the electronic scratch pad for the microprocessor and is used to store intermediate results during computation.

The primary memory consists of integrated-circuit memory chips, known as random-access memory (RAM) and read-only memory (ROM) chips. The ROM chips usually store the system software and the RAM chips provide space for user programs and data. A part of the primary memory known as display memory is devoted to storing the coded representation of information to appear on the monitor screen. The video driver

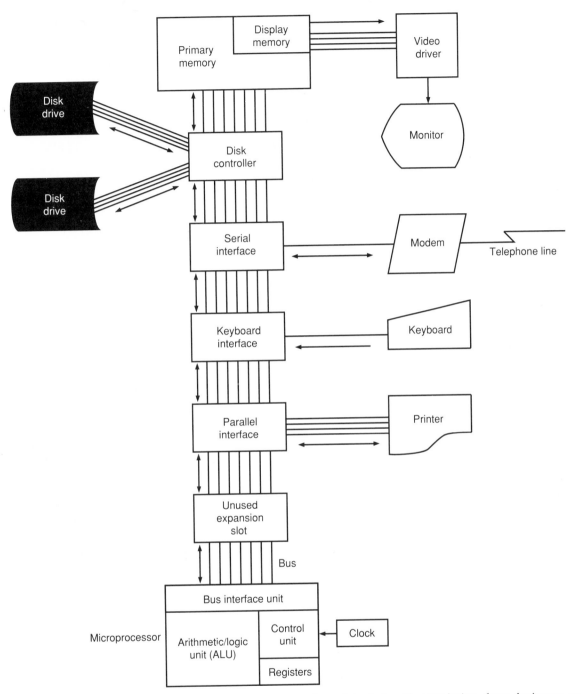

FIGURE 2. Typical organization of a microcomputer system. *Adapted, with permission, from Anderson and Sullivan 1988.*

transforms the digital information stored in the digital memory into appropriate video control signals to enable display of the visual image on the screen.

The secondary storage units are the disk drives, which come in two forms, hard disks and floppy disks. A hard disk is a nonremovable unit and is capable of storing a large amount of information (usual range: 20 to 300 megabytes). The floppy disk drives store information on flexible and removable diskettes, which are stored in protective sleeves.

The storage capacity of these floppy diskettes varies from 200K to 3 megabytes.

Every input, output, and storage device in a microcomputer system must have its own electronic circuitry, or *interface*, linking it to the bus. The interface may conform to the specifications for a standard interface, or it may be a custom interface, like that required for a special-purpose device such as a videodisc or CD-ROM player. A standard interface, which is often called an *I/O port*, makes it easy to connect various devices that adhere to the standards specified. A well-known standard interface is the RS-232 serial port. The RS-232 standard defines the timing and other electrical properties needed to connect a computer to modems, printers, and other serial devices. The information is communicated in a serial fashion (one bit after another) in a serial device, whereas in a parallel device it is communicated in packets of bits in parallel at the same time. Parallel devices are not only faster but more expensive.

An expansion slot is a connector inside a microcomputer, where a custom interface, like those needed for graphic adapters, disk controllers, additional memory, and so on, can be plugged into the system.

A software subsystem for a microcomputer usually contains a disk-based operating system, a BASIC interpreter, compilers for a few high-level languages, and several application software packages (e.g., word processor, spreadsheet, database management system, graphics, video games).

TYPICAL ORGANIZATION OF MAINFRAME/MINICOMPUTER SYSTEMS

The basic functional organization of a mainframe (Figure 3) is essentially similar to that of a microcomputer. Here again, the CPU contains an ALU, a control unit, a set of registers, and bus structures. As in the microcomputer, the data and control signals travel through the bus structures, but the bus struc-

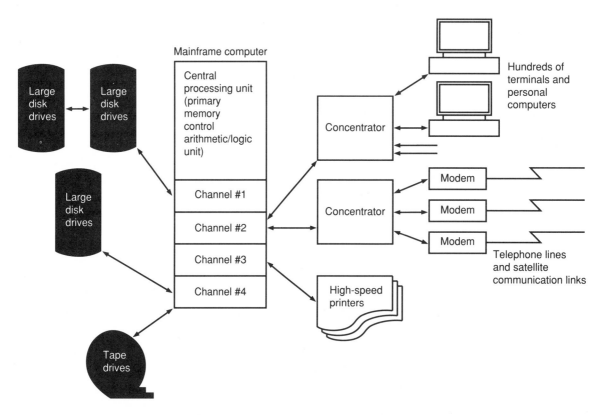

FIGURE 3. Typical organization of mainframe/minicomputer systems. *Adapted, with permission, from Anderson and Sullivan 1988.*

ture is not apparent in the figure because it is hidden inside the CPU and is not directly available to peripheral devices.

The peripheral devices in the mainframe are attached to channels. A channel is a special-purpose computer of limited capacity that takes over the input and output tasks so that the general-purpose mainframe computer can concentrate on handling internal processing tasks. Many devices, such as printers, plotters, terminals, and disk drives, can be attached to a single channel. Channels relieve the mainframe computer of the responsibility of communicating and handling data among hundreds and even thousands of peripherals and thus make possible simultaneous execution of input, output, and internal processing operations. Channels can move the information between the main storage and the peripherals. There are different types of channels: some serving high-speed devices can move the information in larger chunks (blocks of data) and some designed to serve several low-speed devices can transmit information one byte at a time.

The users can access the mainframe systems via user stations, called *terminals.* A typical terminal has a keyboard, a monitor, and a wire that connects the terminal to the computer systems. Most terminals are not capable of processing the information independently. Data are received from the keyboard and transmitted for processing, and any information received from the computer system is displayed on the screen. Such terminals are often referred to as *"dumb terminals."* Sometimes the terminals may be connected to the computer system via telephone.

Microcomputers can act as terminals too. In appearance they look like terminals. In addition to input (keyboard) and output (monitor) capabilities, they have the power to process and store the information because of the presence of the CPU and the primary/secondary storage. These terminals are referred to as *"intelligent terminals."* They can be used to prepare the data in a desired form using the locally available computing capacity, and transmit to the mainframe systems for more complex/high-speed processing purposes. Intelligent terminals can be used

as "standalone" systems when there is no need to access mainframe systems.

Minicomputers, super minicomputers, and the mainframe systems are essentially identical in organization, except for the amount of storage available, the number of peripheral devices, the number of users serviced, and, of course, the cost of the system.

As mainframes and minicomputers need to cater to several users, the software subsystem consists of a multiuser, time-sharing operating system, compilers for several high-level languages, and numerous application packages. The operating system for these machines is responsible for keeping track of the amount of time used by individual users for accounting purposes, for making the system resources available to individual users on demand, for controlling the operations of input/output channels, and other tasks.

SUMMARY

Personal computers have limited computational capabilities, but they are inexpensive. Supercomputers have enormous computational capabilities, and they are expensive. Although it is possible that the modern personal computers may be able to provide as much (or in some cases even more) computing power per dollar as supercomputers, large systems are still needed to handle the needs of several users as well as the demands of complex problems.

There are some problems that cannot be handled by a computer system because of the limitations on the available resources (such as inadequate amount of memory and slower CPU). One would think that if we arbitrarily increase the quality and the quantity of resources made available to a computer system, it would be able to solve all problems. Theory tells us that it is not true. It is sobering to know that computer scientists have identified classes of functions that are not computable by any computer system with any amount of resources. Fortunately, the majority of tasks we wish to handle with a computer fall in the class of computable functions.

For Further Reading

Anderson, R.E., and D.R. Sullivan. 1988. *World of computing.* Boston: Houghton Mifflin.

Augarten, S. 1984. *Bit by bit, an illustrated history of computers.* New York: Ticknor and Fields. This fascinating book traces the history of computers from very early to the birth of personal computers.

Huck, J.C., and M. J. Flynn. 1989. *Analyzing computer architectures.* CS Press Monograph. New York: IEEE Computer Society Press. Excellent technical coverage for advanced readers.

Kimberley, P. 1982. *Microprocessors, an introduction.* New York: McGraw-Hill. Contains a good glossary.

Schechter, P. B., and E. T. Desautels. 1989. *An introduction to computer architecture using VAX machine and assembly language,* Dubuque, Iowa: Wm. C. Brown. Contains an excellent introduction to computer architecture.

Szymanski, R., D. Szymanski, N. Morris, and D. Pulschen. 1991. *Introduction to computers and information systems,* 2nd ed. New York: Macmillan. Excellent text for computer literacy course. Contains good illustrations.

Tanenbaum, A. S. 1990. *Structured computer organization,* 3rd ed. Englewood Cliffs, N.J.: Prentice-Hall. Contains an extensive reading list and bibliography.

S. N. Jayaram Murthy

Computer Architecture

Computer architecture is defined as an area that bridges the gap between digital hardware and computer software by providing close interaction between the two disciplines. The important aspects of computer architecture include the instruction sets and the corresponding hardware structure with respect to the quality of processing units, the software-accessible registers, the memory structures, the data paths, and the ease of hardware–software interactions. As shown in Figure 1, the current research direction in computer architecture has been greatly influenced by recent advances in very large scale integration (VLSI) technology, and has led to many schools of thought. The most important ones are outlined here.

In the 1950s and early 1960s, the cost of logic circuits was very high, and much emphasis was given to implementation of only simple functions in hardware; complex functions were realized with microprogramming and/or subroutine calls. With the advent of

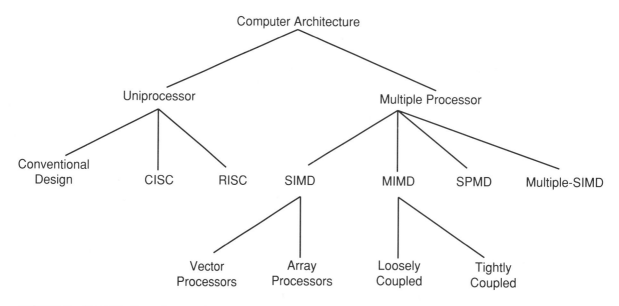

FIGURE 1. Classification of computers.

large-scale integration (LSI) and VLSI technology, it is feasible to fabricate a large complex circuit in one or multiple chips. Many complex arithmetic operations and special functions can be implemented in hardware, and adequate support for the software could be easily provided. The shift to employing logic circuits for numerous software functions has become noticeable and several special-purpose chips are commercially available. Most of the input/output (I/O) controllers are now VLSI-based circuits and designs have been undertaken just to provide efficient interprocessor communication. The idea behind increased use of hardware is to employ them as coprocessors so that special functions can be easily computed. This not only reduces the software complexity, but also makes the programming simpler and the computation faster. The advantage offered by parallel processing has further enhanced the increased desirability of special-purpose hardware.

In VLSI design, off-chip delays are about an order of magnitude larger than signal propagation delays within a chip, and several attempts have been made to limit the digital signals within the chip. This philosophy has led to the design of microprocessors with a large number of complex instructions and many addressing modes. Such a design principle necessitates relatively large decoding delays and forces a typical instruction to take more than one cycle. This led to a controversial and ongoing debate on *reduced instruction set computers* (RISC) versus *complex instruction set computers* (CISC). The basic philosophy behind the RISC concept is to incorporate only simple functions into a processor design, so that the decoder is simple and each instruction can be executed in only one cycle. In addition, compilers for CISC-based machines are much more complex than those for RISC-based systems, as the latter contain fewer, simpler instructions. Thus, for a given application, although a RISC-based processor may require a larger number of instructions as compared with a CISC processor, it may take less time for compilation and fewer clock cycles to execute the instructions. Thus, the RISC-based programs could prove to be faster than the CISC-based ones. The RISC concept has now become widely

acceptable and has been used in the development of all recent processors.

The VLSI design has also influenced memory technology and it is now feasible to have large-size random-access memories (RAMs) at a reasonable cost. Programmable read-only memories (PROMs) serve the purpose of read-only memories (ROMs) that can easily store code for a given application. On the other hand, programmable logic arrays (PLAs) can directly perform any required logic function of reasonable complexity. Thus, PROMs and PLAs are providing flexibility in designing both special-purpose and new experimental digital systems. As any hardware function can be simulated by the software and vice versa, the overall question of the trade-off still remains open: When should the hardware design be preferred over the software implementation, and vice versa? The problem is to determine whether, from cost, speed, and ease-of-fabrication viewpoints, it is appropriate to achieve various complex functions in hardware or to produce the same effect by software.

It is interesting to note that most computer design is based on von Neumann's concept of the stored-program computer, wherein the programs are prestored in the main memory and the execution of instructions is based on the instruction sequencing. Such successive execution is controlled by a program counter, which does not allow parallel processing of instruction and/or programs. Such loss of potential parallelism is known as the *von Neumann bottleneck*. To avoid this, many parallel systems have been introduced and numerous experimental and commercially available parallel machines have been built. Most recent computers contain several multipurpose functional units. To improve the effectiveness of such units, two important architectural concepts, *pipelining* and *vector processing*, are used. Pipelining implies division of an operation or a process into a number of independent steps so that after one stage is finished, partial results can be passed to the next stage, and the current stage can be reused to process another set of operands. Such back-to-back simultaneous processing of operands reduces the total time taken for processing a sequence of operands and therefore increases the speedup and enhances the efficiency. A widely quoted example of a pipeline is an industrial assembly line with many stations, each of which contributes to the partial completion of the product. This allows workers of a factory to perform their tasks concurrently.

In computers, increased efficiency and speedup are achieved from a pipelined unit by employing vector processing, which implies execution of the same operation on all the elements of a single vector or pair of vectors. Such vector processing requires some setup time to configure the pipe for a particular operation. Thereafter, the operands can be fed into the pipe as fast as each stage can process the incoming data, and there is no need to fetch a new instruction. Thus, a pipeline unit can repeatedly perform one simple operation or a combination of a few simple operations over a block of data called a vector. A sequence of such operations is typically represented by loops in a program.

The use of pipelining as a feature of computer architecture is not limited to vector processing. Because of its transparency to the computer programmer, pipelining is widely employed as a model of parallel computation at a higher level. To achieve this, a task could be divided into several stages, with each stage requiring approximately the same amount of time. Each stage could vary in capability, ranging from many instructions to a few subroutines, with output of each stage fed to the successive stage and all the stages executed concurrently on different elements. Another type of multiprocessor that possesses more flexibility and avoids the constrained pipeline operation of a vector processor is known as an array processor. Such an array processor executes the programs in *single instruction stream, multiple data stream* (SIMD) mode, and consists of many identical processing elements, each with its own data memory, but all executing exactly the same program. Obviously, such a machine can achieve very high performance by incorporating a large number of processors, but only if the task is such that all the processors have to execute the same sequence of an algorithm. The model of computation on an SIMD computer is very much

like that of a vector processor: a single operation is performed over a large block of data. The usual manifestation of an SIMD machine is about the same as the vector operations, with loops ranging over the elements of arrays.

In a more powerful general class of multiprocessor, called the *multiple instruction stream, multiple data stream* system (MIMD), each processing element (PE) executes its own program, relatively independent of the other elements. The PEs are connected together in some way to have a mechanism for interprocessor communication, which subdivides MIMD machines into shared memory and distributed memory systems. In a shared memory multiprocessor, a bank of data memory is accessible to all PEs through a common bus or an interconnection network. In contrast, a private memory machine divides storage among the PEs, and each processor can only access its associated memory unit while a communication network connects all the PEs together. There could be distributed memory MIMD systems, with one or more modules shared by a group of processors; these are known as closely coupled systems.

Many newer parallel machines offer multiple processors, each of which possesses a vector or SIMD parallel execution capability. Such machines can be classified as *multiple SIMD* (MSIMD). High-level constructs are typically provided in such machines so that the programmer can specify parallelism at the level of grouping of instructions known as coarse-grain. Within each task, the compiler can automatically vectorize the loops. The MSIMD machines can be seen as a way of getting the best of both worlds: fine-grain vector operation for those parts of a program that are appropriate for the same, and flexible MIMD operation for other parts of the program.

In another common class of computation mode in parallel machines, known as the *same-program* ("single-code") *multiple data* (SPMD) system, every processing element executes the same program on a different portion of the data. Such machines are attractive because massive parallelism is easily obtained by the partitioning of operations over a massive data set. Yet the SPMD model is not as restrictive as the lock-step instruction synchronization of the array and vector processor. In SPMD, the same high-level computation is performed on each piece of data, but the same low-level machine instructions may not be. Processing elements may take conditional branches independent of each other.

The other two important terms used to characterize parallel architectures are *loosely coupled* and *tightly coupled* systems. These terms represent the types of coupling between the processors of a parallel system. In tightly coupled systems, processors share a common memory, which does not necessitate any need for actual data transfer between processors. A simple exchange in memory access control enables a processor to obtain data from any of the memory modules. The term *loose coupling* simply implies that there is no shared memory and, therefore, information exchange has to be achieved by processors through an interconnection network. Thus, in a loosely coupled system, some kind of interconnection network is needed to provide data paths between the processors. Such information transfer is an overhead and needs to be taken into account when determining system performance. The interconnection network, providing data paths between various functional modules of a parallel system, plays a very important role. All hypercube machines constitute loosely coupled systems and the interconnection network is called static, as each link provides a dedicated path between two adjacent processors. Another popular class of networks, known as dynamic networks, are designed using a number of small programmable switches, interconnected in a prespecified way. Important characteristics of many static and dynamic networks and their relative advantages and disadvantages have been widely covered in the literature.

OTHER ARCHITECTURAL STRATEGIES:

Three important strategies used in enhancing system performance are interleaving, memory hierarchy, and caching. *Interleaving* is a common technique employed to reduce the effective access time to main memory.

The idea is to partition the memory into independent modules and do parallel access to the same address in all modules. The read/write cycle to each module is skewed by a factor given by the degree of interleaving (or the number of memory modules), so that each module can supply a word in each fraction of the memory cycle. In this way, parallel read/write memory cycles reduce the effective memory access time by a factor equal to the degree of interleaving.

Memory hierarchy is the ranking of memory devices and systems from high to slow speed, and is employed to provide a match between a relatively high-speed central processing unit and slower memory units by passing on information (instructions and data) from slow to fast memory units before reaching the central processing unit (CPU). The memory hierarchy, in order of decreasing speeds, is

- CPU registers
- Cache memory
- Main memory
- On-line secondary storage (disks, etc.)
- Off-line magnetic storage (e.g., tapes, floppy disks, etc.)

Caching technique is used to make a small but fast memory appear as the main memory. This is achieved by copying a portion of a currently executed program segment into the cache. The processor keeps accessing the cache memory as long as the information is there. If the desired word is not found in the cache because of out-of-range access or jump conditions, a *cache miss* is said to occur and the cache is updated by copying an appropriate segment from the main memory. In a multiple processor, it is possible to have multiple shared caches, all accessible by any processor, or private caches with each accessible by only one processor. There are relative advantages and disadvantages to the two cache organizations, and the choice totally depends on the application in hand. A common difficulty with multiple caches is maintaining all versions of the same data exactly identical at all times; this is known as *cache consistency*. Many strategies have been introduced to minimize this problem.

ARCHITECTURAL PERFORMANCE PARAMETERS

Many parameters are used to characterize and to measure the performance of parallel systems architecture. Some of the widely used attributes follow.

Turnaround time. The time elapsed between the initial submission of a job and the time at which the result is available is the turnaround time. This includes all the delays in initial setup, communication time, synchronization time, idle time, and input/output time.

Effective time delay. Effective time delay is usually applicable to a system with several successive pipeline stages. In such a system, delay of the slowest stage determines the effective time delay of the system and is used in computing the system speedup.

Efficiency. Efficiency is defined as the ratio of the time during which the processors do useful jobs to the total time all the processors have to be kept occupied until the final results are out (i.e., the number of processors multiplied by the turnaround time). In general, it is difficult to keep all the processors busy all the time. Consequently, the efficiency of a multiprocessor is usually less than one.

Speedup. Speedup is defined as the ratio of time taken to run an application on a uniprocessor divided by the time to run the same application on a parallel system.

Cost/performance. The performance of a uniprocessor is often expressed in terms of millions of instructions per second (MIPS), millions of floating point operations per second (MFLOPS), or millions of operations per second (MOPS).

Programmability. Programs have to be written in such a way that the parallel hardware and other resources are utilized effectively so that the system throughput could be maximized.

Scalability. The term *scalability* is applied to both hardware and software. In hardware, scalability indicates how easily the number of elements (processors and/or memory modules) in a parallel system can be increased. In software, scalability indicates how comfortably a program can be run on a larger system (or for a larger problem).

For Further Reading

Recent Books

Agrawal, D. P. 1986. *Advanced computer architecture.* Washington, D.C.: IEEE Computer Society Press.

———. 1991. *Self study guide on parallel processing.* Piscataway, N.J.: IEEE Press.

Hayes, J. P. 1988. *Computer architecture and organization,* 2nd ed. New York: McGraw-Hill.

Hennessy, J. L., and D. A. Patterson. 1990. *Computer architecture: A quantitative approach.* San Mateo, Calif.: Morgan Kaufmann.

Hwang, K., and F. A. Briggs. 1984. *Computer architecture and parallel processing.* New York: McGraw-Hill.

Ibbett, F. N., and N. P. Tophan. 1989. *Architecture of high performance computers,* vol. 2. Berlin: Springer-Verlag.

Kain, R. Y. 1989. *Computer architecture,* vols. 1 and 2. Englewood Cliffs, N.J.: Prentice-Hall.

Proceedings of the Annual International Symposium on Computer Architecture. 1986–1991. Washington, D.C.: IEEE Computer Society Press.

Proceedings of the International Conference on Parallel Processing. University Park: Pennsylvania State University Press.

Stone, H. S. 1990. *High-performance computer architecture,* 2nd ed. Reading, Mass.: Addison-Wesley.

Selected Reference Papers

Flynn, M. J. 1972. Some computer organizations and their effectiveness. *IEEE Transactions on Computers* 21(9):948–60.

Mauney, J., D. P. Agrawal, Y. K. Choe, E. A. Harcourt, S. Kim, and W. J. Staats. 1989.

Computational models and resource allocation for supercomputers. *Proceedings of the IEEE* 77(12):1859–74.

Dharma P. Agrawal

HAZARDOUS WASTE MANAGEMENT, COMPUTERS IN

Hazardous waste management in the United States is based on a set of regulations promulgated from Subtitle C of the Resource Conservation and Recovery Act (RCRA). This statute was enacted in 1976, was amended significantly in 1984, and is currently being considered for major revisions. The act authorized the U.S. Environmental Protection Agency (EPA) to develop hazardous waste regulations. It also empowered EPA headquarters and the ten EPA regional offices to monitor and enforce the regulations governing generation, transportation, treatment, storage, and disposal of hazardous waste. On request, the EPA shall authorize eligible states to develop programs to implement RCRA Subtitle C regulations as long as the state program is equivalent to and no less stringent than the federal program.

The Resource Conservation and Recovery Act defines hazardous waste as a solid waste that, because of its quantity, concentration, or physical, chemical, or infectious characteristics, may pose potential hazard to human health and the environment when improperly managed (U.S. EPA 1986). This definition shows that hazardous wastes are determined in terms of properties of a solid waste. The term *solid waste* is broadly used by the EPA to refer to any discarded material, including solid, semisolid, liquid, or contained gaseous material, irrespective of whether the waste is disposed of, used or reused, recycled, or stored. Solid waste and hazardous waste characteristics are described in detail in the RCRA regulations codified in Title 40 of the Code of Federal Regulations (40 CFR) Part 261. This part of Title 40 CFR Part 261 specifies that a solid waste is hazardous if it has been determined as a hazardous waste by the EPA and listed in Title 40 CFR Part 261, or if it exhibits any of the four hazardous waste characteristics: ignitability, corrosivity, reactivity, and toxicity. In Title 40 CFR Part 261, hazardous wastes are identified in a four-digit coding system, known as the EPA waste code. There are approximately 700 waste codes in the EPA system.

The Subtitle C program developed under RCRA is designed to ensure that hazardous waste is managed properly and safely. The law accomplishes this by creating a "cradle-to-grave" management system that sets forth statutory and regulatory requirements for all hazardous waste handlers. In particular, hazardous waste generators and treatment, storage, and disposal facilities are required to report to the state at least once every 2 years. This mandatory provision is known as the biennial report requirement. The objective is to monitor the flow of each hazardous waste stream from the point of generation ("cradle") to its ultimate disposition ("grave").

When hazardous wastes are transported off-site, manifests are required that specify information on the type and quantities of hazardous waste hauled, the identification of the generator, the receiving facility, the transporter(s) used, the hazard potential if the waste is spilled, and special handling requirements. The receiving facility may store the wastes collected from the generators, treat the wastes, or recycle them. Depending on their chemical constituents, the remaining wastes are ultimately sent to disposal or incineration facilities. Hazardous waste can also be shipped directly from generating sources to disposal facilities for burial in hazardous waste landfills or for burning in hazardous waste incinerators. The regulations require that these treatment, storage, and disposal (TSD) facilities be permitted by the EPA and/or a state regulatory agency; consequently, the EPA has established design and performance standards for such facilities.

The Resource Conservation and Recovery Act has placed demands on both the private and public sectors to develop information systems to meet the compliance requirements. To help industries effectively manage hazardous waste, dozens of specialized software packages are available that aid industries in waste determination and other waste compliance requirements. For the public sector, information needs have been directed at two management areas: (1) monitoring the generation of hazardous wastes by generators and hazardous waste management activities at TSD facilities, and (2) tracking hazardous waste handlers' compliance activities.

SOFTWARE FOR INDUSTRY

The development of software programs for managing hazardous waste in industrial plants has received much attention during the last few years and has been stimulated by RCRA regulations, Occupational Safety and Health Act (OSHA) requirements, and provisions in the Superfund Amendments and Reauthorization Act (SARA) Title III, which is also known as the "emergency response and community right-to-know" law. The software programs can be categorized into several groups based on common usage:

1. *Software to catalog each chemical's name and the associated waste code:* The waste code that appears in the program may or may not include the EPA waste code. The software is used mainly as a quick reference to respond to chemical and hazardous waste spills and to train employees for emergency response.

2. *Software to track a company's off-site hazardous waste shipment based on data provided in the hazardous waste manifest:* The software is able to track the shipments by trip, by waste type, and by destination. The information can be used to analyze the cost of hazardous waste disposal to be paid by the company to different TSD facilities.

3. *Software to track a company's environmental regulatory compliance:* This may include air and water quality compliance and industrial safety and chemical spill prevention, in addition to hazardous waste management regulatory compliance. The information is essential for analysis of potential problem areas in the firm's environmental management.

4. *Software to assist users in implementing waste minimization programs:* The software provides analysis of various waste streams related to waste minimization potential or cost analysis of waste minimization techniques.

SOFTWARE FOR GOVERNMENTAL AGENCIES

The development of integrated software programs for managing hazardous waste nationally or by state has been the EPA's focus of attention for several years. Two significant accomplishments in this area are the development and improvement of the Biennial Reporting System and the Resource Conservation and Recovery Information System databases.

Biennial Reporting System

As specified in the RCRA regulations, the completed biennial report forms must be submitted by hazardous waste generators and TSD facilities to the state by March 31 of the reporting year. The generator report form consists of data on the type and quantities of hazardous waste generated during the previous year, the disposition of the hazardous waste generated, efforts undertaken to reduce the volume and toxicity of waste generated, and changes in the volume and toxicity of waste actually achieved during the reporting year in comparison with previous years. The TSD report form consists of data on the type and quantities of hazardous wastes received from various generators and the type of technology used to treat the waste.

The EPA developed the biennial reporting format in November 1985 as a revision to a format developed in May 1980, which is known as EPA Form 8700-13A/B. The 1985 form was revised again in December 1987, November 1989, and March 1991 to obtain more detailed information from the two regulated communities, that is, the generators and the TSD facilities.

To accompany its reporting format, EPA developed an automated data processing system called the Biennial Reporting System (BRS) to assist states and EPA regional offices in the process of compiling the biennial report data. The data collected on the biennial report forms can be entered directly into the BRS or into other database management systems. Eventually the data in the latter systems will be transferred to the BRS because a built-in "translator" in the BRS has the capability to transfer data from other databases into the BRS database system.

Four main reports can be generated by the BRS:

1. The generator report displays the amount of waste generation by generator, by waste type, and by county.

2. The TSD report describes the quantities of waste handled by TSD facility, by waste type, and by county.

3. The import–export report provides information on the amount of waste imported and exported by individual handlers, or all handlers, in a state.

4. The treatment/disposal report shows the identity of facilities using each of the different treatment/disposal methods, by waste type and by amount of waste. In the BRS, the treatment/disposal methods are grouped into fifteen classes representing a variety of waste management techniques ranging from solvent recovery and sludge treatment to incineration and landfill. These fifteen classes are known as "SARA management categories."

To install and run the BRS, the proper hardware and system configuration are necessary. The required hardware and software include the following (U.S. EPA 1991):

1. IBM PC-AT 80386 or 100-percent-compatible personal computer with a central processing unit (CPU) speed of at least 16 MHz

2. A 1.2-megabyte 5¼-inch floppy disk drive

3. A 30-megabyte hard disk drive with fast access speed

4. 640K random-access memory (RAM) memory with at least 594K of unused RAM

5. A printer capable of printing 132 characters per line

6. MS-DOS or PC-DOS version 3.3 or higher

7. PC-FOCUS version 4.01

The EPA acknowledges that the preceding description of hardware and software requirements does not suggest that the EPA recommends or endorses any particular brand of personal computer or personal computing products.

Resource Conservation and Recovery Information System

The RCRA regulatory program issues TSD permits, inspects facilities, monitors and enforces compliance, prescribes corrective action where releases of hazardous waste in a facility have occurred, oversees closure of facilities, and reports on its findings at the state and national levels. The EPA developed an "activity log system" to be completed by the regulatory agencies during the processing of permit applications and when undertaking inspection and compliance activities. The log system is necessary to obtain a wide range of information to manage effectively the RCRA enforcement programs.

The EPA also developed an automated management information system to accompany the log system. This information system is called the Resource Conservation and Recovery Information System (RCRIS) and is designed to track a wide range of data related to handlers of hazardous waste. The tracking operation is performed by RCRIS's eight modules: (1) handler identification, (2) permit status, (3) compliance evaluation, (4) corrective action, (5) data quality assurance, (6) program management, (7) database administration (U.S. EPA 1989), and (8) facility management planning.

To install RCRIS on a personal computer, the hardware and software required for the BRS are also requested by RCRIS; however, RCRIS demands a larger hard disk, that is, 40 megabytes instead of 30 megabytes ("Putting RCRIS on your PC," 1989). In addition, the new RCRIS release, version 2.1.1, is compatible only with PC-FOCUS 5.5 ("New RCRIS releases," 1991).

References

New RCRIS releases 1991. *RCRIS Reporter*, April, p. 1.

Putting RCRIS on your PC. 1989. *RCRIS Reporter*, September, p. 1.

U.S. Environmental Protection Agency. 1986. *RCRA orientation manual.* Washington, D.C.: U.S. EPA.

U.S. Environmental Protection Agency. 1989. *RCRIS user manual.* Washington, D.C.: U.S. EPA.

U.S. Environmental Protection Agency. 1991. *Biennial reporting system (BRS) user guide and training exercises.* Washington, D.C.: U.S. EPA.

J. Andy Soesilo
David Pijawka

HEALTH AND FITNESS, COMPUTER APPLICATIONS IN

In 1900 the primary cause of death in the United States was infectious respiratory disease. In the 1990s the primary cause of death in the United States is cardiovascular disease, with the largest percentage of deaths from coronary heart disease (CHD). Basically, this change represents the effect of modern medicine and its ability to eradicate infectious disease through the use of vaccines and antibiotics. Americans and individuals in the industrialized world live longer and suffer death and illness from the diseases associated with increasing age and lifestyle. The American Heart Association and the National Heart, Lung, and Blood Institute have identified a set of risk factors associated with the development of CHD. The primary risk factors are high blood pressure, high serum cholesterol, and tobacco smoking. Secondary risk factors are heredity, age, gender, stress level, obesity, diabetes, and physical activity or fitness level (Pollock et al. 1984). Several scientifically valid research studies have demonstrated that higher levels of physical fitness are associated with a significant reduction in the risk of death from CHD (Ekelund et al. 1988, Blair et al. 1989). Increased physical activity and fitness have been shown to reduce obesity and blood pressure, and to improve serum cholesterol profiles. In this context, physical fitness is actually improved aerobic capacity or cardiovascular endurance. Other fitness components— strength, flexibility, local muscular endurance, and body composition (body fat)—are also considered to be important to preventing disease and improving the general quality of life (Lamb 1984). Thus, health-related fitness has a broad definition that generally includes cardiovascular endurance, local muscular endurance, strength, flexibility, and body composition. In the modern industrial world, the civilian populations have become sedentary and have low levels of physical activity and fitness. This has contributed to the increase in CHD, obesity, and musculoskeletal disease and injury. Increased health-related fitness should have positive effects on the disease rates.

The computer and the millions of individuals whose main occupation deals with its use have contributed to the health problem that has been described; however, as in most areas of modern life, the computer and its applications have a very useful role to play in promoting and implementing health-related fitness programs. The study of the human body's acute and chronic responses to exercise is the study of exercise physiology and the computer plays an ever-increasing role in that field. This article attempts to provide an overview of those applications and a direction for further study of this interesting area. The computer applications to be covered in the rest of the article are outlined here:

1. A comprehensive series of programs for fitness evaluation, exercise recording, nutritional analysis, and CHD risk evaluation

2. A physical fitness assessment program in youth

3. Body composition analysis in youth

4. Computer simulation of exercise physiology experiments

5. Computerized measurement of aerobic capacity and strength in the exercise physiology laboratory

6. Additional sources of information

GENERAL HEALTH AND FITNESS ASSESSMENT

CSI Software (Houston, Tex.) has developed a series of over 20 computer programs for use in health, fitness, exercise, and nutritional facilities. These programs run on many types of microcomputers and are menu-driven, user-friendly types of applications. The programs cover a full range of commercial, fitness, and educational applications. They are designed to be purchased by commercial and educational facilities with the resources to cover the expenses of computer and software procurement. They are capable of dealing with large numbers of participants on an interactive, time-sharing basis. Storage and retrieval of data for continuing evaluation of the participants' progress are possible. The programs specifically related to health and fitness applications are General Fitness Assessment, Exerlog, Exerdiet, Exerrisk, and Exerlife. The General Fitness Assessment program is used to evaluate fitness, monitor changes, and prescribe exercise. The Exerlog program is used to record the participants' physical activity and calculate energy expenditure. Exerdiet can be used to conduct a nutritional analysis and compute the calories consumed. Exerrisk and Exerlife are used in the assessment of cardiovascular disease risk and life expectancy. This software operates from direct keyboard input of data (i.e., fitness test results), performs necessary calculations, and provides reports either on the computer monitor or in printed form.

As an example of the software, General Fitness Assessment provides a complete health-related fitness profile for each participant in the exercise program. This assessment includes aerobic capacity or cardiovascular endurance, body composition, flexibility, muscular strength, and muscular endurance. It provides a comparison of test results with normative or normal values appropriate to the age and gender of the participant. Written interpretation of the test results are given along with specific recommendations for an exercise program to improve fitness status. Figure 1 provides an example of the test results and their comparison with normative standards.

CSI Software health and fitness programs are currently in use in a number of educational, medical, and corporate settings. Summary and database analysis can be conducted by facility personnel to provide for evaluation of the health and fitness facility's operations. The company provides an operations manual, installation, and service. The advantages—data storage, manipulation, and interpretation—of the software are obvious. More importantly, this application is potentially beneficial to the individual user. First, by providing instant feedback through the interactive nature of the program, retention or adherence to the exercise program is increased. Second, this process improves understanding of exercise and fitness concepts, which enhances the educational experience of the participant.

YOUTH FITNESS EVALUATION

The status of youth fitness in the United States has been one of the most controversial and important issues in the area of health and fitness. Several events in the twentieth century have influenced the national prospective of physical fitness in youth. During both World Wars I and II, large numbers of young American men were classified as physically unfit for military service. This obviously has a negative effect on the national security of the United States. In the early 1950s American youth appeared to be less physically fit when compared with European youth in fitness research studies. These negative observations led to the development of several national youth fitness testing programs. The President's Challenge (President's Council on Physical Fitness and Sports 1987), Physical Best (American Alliance of Health, Physical Education, Recreation and Dance [AAHPERD] 1988), and the Fitnessgram (Institute for Aerobics Research 1987) are examples of these fitness testing programs. The Fitnessgram developed by the Institute for Aerobics Research and sponsored by the Campbell Soup Corporation has a test battery that includes tests of cardiovascular endurance (one-mile run/walk), body composition (skinfolds or body mass index), hamstring and low back flexibility (sit and reach test), upper body strength and

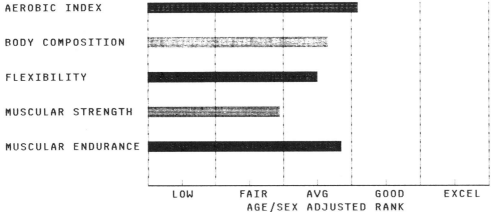

FITNESS PROFILE
YOUR CLUB NAME HERE

Evaluation of: Date: 02/10/88
Member Number: 4593

Age: 33   Sex: Male   Height: 5 ' 10 "   Weight: 185.0
% Body Fat: 17.1 Ideal Weight (16 - 19 %): 182.4 - 189.2   Wt Diff: -0.

AEROBIC INDEX

BODY COMPOSITION

FLEXIBILITY

MUSCULAR STRENGTH

MUSCULAR ENDURANCE

          LOW   FAIR   AVG   GOOD   EXCEL
               AGE/SEX ADJUSTED RANK

BODY MEASUREMENTS

HEIGHT	70
WEIGHT	185
CHEST	42
ARM	16
WAIST	36
HIPS	40
THIGH	22
CALF	16

CARDIOVASCULAR

RESTING BP	120/80
RESTING HR	63
VO2 MAX ml/kg/min	42
TM/3.4MPH/8% (HR)	135

SKIN FOLDS

CHEST	14
THIGH	17
ILIUM	
TRICEPS	
ABDOMEN	25
SCAPULA	
AXILLA	
SUM OF SKIN FOLDS	56

FLEXIBILITY

		NORMS
SIT & REACH	16	15.2
HIP ABDUCTION	38	40
BACK EXTENSION	2	2

(SUM OF SKIN FOLDS ... 56 ... 2)

MUSCULAR STRENGTH

		NORMS
BENCH PRESS	100	100
LEG PRESS	150	179.9
COMB HAND GRIP	90	87.3

MUSCULAR ENDURANCE

		NORMS
SIT UPS	45	36.5
PUSH UPS	30	30
3rd ENDURANCE		

FIGURE 1. CSI Software fitness profile. From CSI Software. Copyright CSI Software. Reprinted by permission.

endurance (pull-ups), abdominal strength and endurance (sit-ups), and running agility (shuttle run). The Fitnessgram includes the fitness tests and standards of evaluation, a fitness awards system, exercise prescription recommendations, and computer software to aid in the administration of the fitness program. The Fitnessgram is designed for application to school situations with mass testing requirements.

The computer software is menu driven and has three basic parts. First, data entry of test results is accomplished with entry screens. Second, calculations and evaluations are completed. Third, printed output can be provided via the computer monitor or directed to a variety of printers for hard copy. The software is available in Apple and IBM-PC compatible forms. The IBM-PC version requires a computer with dual 360K disk drives or a hard disk drive and at least 256K of memory. An effective instruction manual is available with the program. The software allows user-friendly data entry, storage, and retrieval capability, and a variety of useful reports. The reports include a summary of entire test administration results, a student listing, a listing of fitness award qualifiers, a statistical analysis of test results, and an individual Fitnessgram report that is provided for parents. Figure 2 provides an example of this individual report. The key feature to this report is the feedback to the students and parents as to which and the number of test items the student has passed or failed.

BODY COMPOSITION ANALYSIS IN YOUTH

Obesity or overfatness is one of the secondary risk factors for the development of CHD in adults. In adults, obesity is associated with

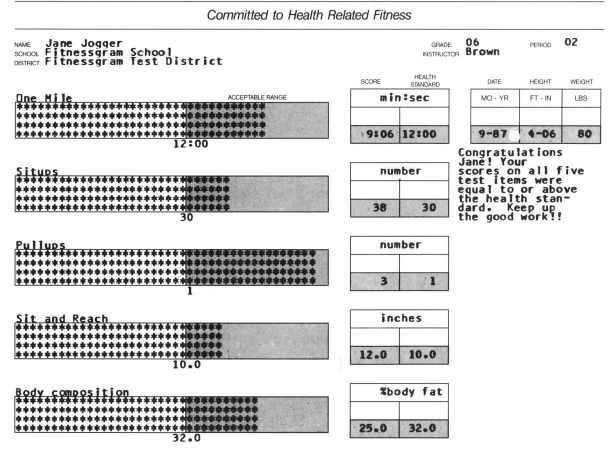

FIGURE 2. Fitnessgram fitness profile. Detailed information accompanies the printout on the actual form. Copyright Institute for Aerobics Research. Reprinted by permission.

diabetes, high cholesterol, and hypertension. In children, obesity levels have increased through the last 20 years. Obese parents tend to have obese children and obese children tend to become obese adults. Thus, body composition analysis in children is a very important component in the assessment of the health and fitness of an individual child. It is also very important for the teacher or health professional to understand the body composition of the entire group of children who may be involved in a health and fitness program. In the two previous applications that have been described, body composition analysis was included. Lohman (1989) has developed computer software to aid in the analysis of body composition in children. The program entitled Body Composition Estimation in Children is to be used with skinfold caliper measurements of fat directly under the skin. The program is menu driven and user friendly. It calculates the body composition based on the child's age, gender, height, weight, and skinfold measurements. It generates a report for each student, compares individual scores with national norms, calculates an optimal weight range, and computes group statistical summaries. Figure 3 presents an example of the output of a report for an individual child. In this example the child is a male, 10 years of age, 90 pounds in weight, 55 inches in height, with a 9-mm triceps skinfold and a 10-mm calf skinfold. The top part of the output indicates the child has 16.2 percent body fat (potential range 13.2–19.2 percent). He is in the optimal or desired range of percentage body fat and the fiftieth percentile on national norms. The second part of the output indicates the optimal weight range for this child is 83.8 to 94.3 pounds. Therefore, this child is in the desired weight range.

The program is provided in Apple and IBM-PC versions. It is menu driven and very user friendly. Lohman, the author, is a leading researcher in the area of body composition in children. A companion videotape entitled Measuring Body Fat Using Skinfolds is available from the publisher. This video demonstrates the techniques for obtaining accurate skinfold measurements. Combining the skinfold caliper, the videotape, and the program provides for a very effective package in assessment of body composition in children.

SIMULATIONS OF EXERCISE PHYSIOLOGY LABORATORIES

Exercise physiology is the study of the acute and chronic responses of the body to exercise. An example of an acute response would be the increase in heart rate when an individual leaves a resting state and begins running, an exercise state. A chronic response would be the decrease in resting heart rate in an individual after 12 weeks of endurance exercise training (Lamb 1984). Scientific research in this area has provided the knowledge on the nature of improved physiological function that results from increased levels of exercise. This improved physiological function or physical fitness has been associated with improved health. There are numerous physiological responses that must be measured and evaluated to develop an understanding of the principles of exercise physiology. Some of the variables are heart rate, blood pressure, maximal oxygen consumption, ventilation, stroke volume of the heart, and cardiac output. The measurement and study of these variables require many hours of testing with complex and expensive equipment in the exercise physiology laboratory.

Morrow and Pivarnik (1989) have developed a software application entitled Simulated Exercise Physiology Laboratories. The purpose of this application is to provide simulated learning or laboratory experiences in exercise physiology. The computer laboratories interact with a laboratory manual to provide the total learning experience. There are twenty laboratories. Table 1 lists these laboratories. Each laboratory follows a step-by-step procedure. The manual provides definitions, terminology, and basic information on the physiological principles to be studied in each laboratory. The software allows for multiple-trial experiments to be conducted during each laboratory. Thus, a student can develop an understanding of the relationships between the physiological variables and how changes in one variable cause changes in other variables. As an example

BODY COMPOSITION   AN ESTIMATE OF PERCENT FAT

Name: Gender: Male

Age: 10.0 years old   Weight: 90.0 lbs   Height: 55.0 in

Skinfolds: Triceps: 9.0 mm   Calf: 10.0 mm

YOUR PERCENT FAT FROM SUM OF TRICEPS AND CALF SKINFOLDS IS 16.2%

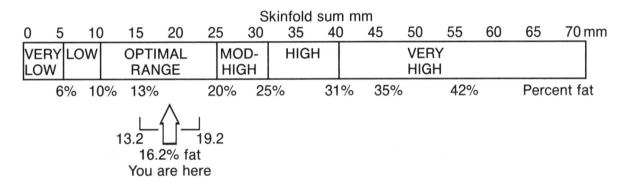

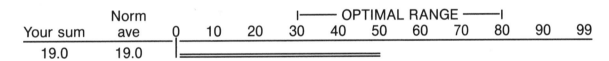

You are in the 50th percentile.

OPTIMAL WEIGHT RANGE

From your present body weight and percent fat, we can calculate a more optimal body weight range for your age. If you stay within this range, it will help you become a healthier person. As you grow each year in muscle and bone, this optimal weight range will increase until you stop growing. The chart below shows a minimal, optimal, and maximal weight based on your body fatness.

MINIMAL WEIGHT		OPTIMAL RANGE		MAXIMAL WEIGHT
80.2	83.8	(in pounds)	94.3	100.6

Your weight is 90.0 lbs.

FIGURE 3. Body composition estimation for children: body composition analysis. From *Body Composition Estimation for Children* by T. G. Lohman, 1987, Champaign, Ill.: Human Kinetics. Copyright 1987 by Tim and Mike Lohman. Reprinted by permission.

TABLE 1. Simulated Exercise Physiology Laboratories

Disk A	Disk B
1. Blood pH	11. Body volume
2. Blood pressure	12. Skinfolds
3. Blood volume	13. Underwater weight
4. Cardiac output	14. Astrand female
5. Gas laws	15. Astrand male
6. Lung function	16. $VO_{2\,max}$ female
7. O_2 consumption	17. $VO_{2\,max}$ male
8. Exercise efficiency	18. Training heart rate
9. Body temperature	19. Weight loss
10. WBGT	20. Weight training

the results from conducting an experiment in the blood pressure laboratory are given in Figure 4. Three measurements—systolic blood pressure, diastolic blood pressure, and

BLOOD PRESSURE LAB

TRIALS

	1	2	3	4
Systolic BP mm Hg	120	145	165	
Diastolic BP mm Hg	80	95	97	
Heart Rate b/min	100	100	100	
Hypertension Evaluation	NORMAL	BORDER	ABSOL	
Maximum Normal BP mm Hg	139/89	139/89	139/89	
Pulse Pressure mm Hg	40	50	68	
Mean Arterial Pressure mm Hg	93.3	111.7	119.7	
Double Product HR X SBP/100	120	145	165	

Use the following key to evaluate hypertension:
    NORMAL = Normal blood pressure
    BORDER = Borderline hypertension
    ABSOL. = Absolute hypertension

FIGURE 4. Simulated exercise physiology laboratories: blood pressure analysis. From *Simulated Exercise Physiology Laboratories* by J. R. Morrow, Jr., and J. M. Pivarnik, 1989, Champaign, Ill.: Human Kinetics. Copyright 1989 by James R. Morrow, Jr., and James M. Pivarnik. Reprinted by permission.

heart rate—are input to the program and the other variables are calculated from those values. The first trial demonstrates a blood pressure of 120/80, which is normal and not indicative of a health problem with hypertension. The second and third trials represent blood pressure evaluated as borderline and absolute hypertensive.

This application is available in Apple and IBM-PC compatible formats. It is designed to operate with a two-floppy-disk drive system but can function with one drive. The program cannot be copied to a hard disk. It is menu driven and user friendly. It provides output to the monitor, and printed output can be obtained. Morrow and Pivarnik, the authors, are recognized leaders in the areas of exercise physiology and computer applications in this field.

METABOLIC ASSESSMENT IN THE EXERCISE PHYSIOLOGY LABORATORY

In the previous section, a computerized simulation of experiments and measurements that can be directly performed in the exercise physiology laboratory was examined. An example of direct assessments made in the laboratory that have a direct relationship to health is the measurement of maximal oxygen consumption. Maximal oxygen consumption is the accepted measure of aerobic capacity or cardiovascular endurance. It is the maximum amount of oxygen that can be consumed by an individual during exercise. To determine maximal oxygen consumption, an individual must undergo a maximal exercise stress test. Work ergometers such as motor-driven treadmills and stationary cycles are used with exercise test protocols to bring a test subject to exhaustion. While the subject exercises, he or she breathes into an automated gas analysis system that continuously measures the oxygen and carbon dioxide inhaled and exhaled. The maximal or peak oxygen consumption measured occurs near exhaustive levels of exercise. This maximal oxygen consumption is expressed in liters per minute or in milliliters per kilogram body weight per minute. The maximal oxygen consumption is a direct measure of the heart's and cardiovascular system's ability to supply oxygen-rich blood to the exercising muscles and for the muscles to use the oxygen for energy production. During such a test other physiological variables such as ventilation (total air inhaled or exhaled), carbon dioxide, and heart rate are also monitored. The automated systems used in the modern exercise physiology laboratory combine gas sensors, electronics, computers, and software to formulate the metabolic measurement system.

An example of such a computerized system is the MedGraphics System 2001 developed by Medical Graphics Corporation, Saint Paul, Minnesota. The system represents state-of-the-art technology in the laboratory measurement and evaluation of cardiorespiratory variables in resting, exercise, and recovery from exercise conditions. It can also be used to measure lung function and to assess nutritional status. The software is menu driven and provides a complex environment for the acquisition, storage, retrieval, display, and analysis of the cardiorespiratory variables. Measurements can be

reported on a breath-by-breath basis or can be based on an average across a number of breaths or a chosen length of time. Measurements can be displayed in tabular format or in a graphics mode. Measurements are reported on a real-time basis during the exercise test and on retrieval from data storage for final test reports. The options available with the system are varied and complex.

Figures 5 and 6 provide examples of the output that is available. Figure 5 is a graph of measurements of cardiorespiratory variables in rest (indicated by the first perpendicular line), in exercise with increasing work load (between the perpendicular lines), and in recovery (after the second perpendicular line). The four variables graphed are oxygen (VO_2), carbon dioxide (CO_2), heart rate (HR), and ventilation (VE). The graph displays the typical increase in metabolic response from rest to increasing exercise work load and the gradual decrease during the recovery phase. Figure 6 provides the tabular results for the same exercise test. It includes the previously noted variables and other physiological responses.

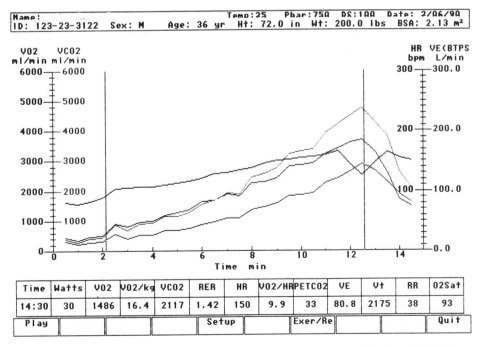

FIGURE 5. MedGraphics System 2001 metabolic response results (graphics). From Medical Graphics Corporation. Copyright Medical Graphics Corporation. Reprinted by permission.

```
-----------------------------------------------------------------------------
MEDGRAPHICS CARDIOPULMONARY EXERCISE TEST                    CPX - TABULAR REPORT
-----------------------------------------------------------------------------
Name:                          Temp:25   Pbar:750   DS:100   Date: 2/06/90
ID: 123-23-3122   Sex: M    Age: 36 yr   Ht: 72.0 in   Wt: 200.0 lbs   BSA: 2.13 m²
-----------------------------------------------------------------------------
    Time   Work   VO2/kg    VCO2      VO2      RER      HR    VO2/HR      RR       VE

    1:00     0      3.7      295      335     0.88      78      4.3       11     10.6
    2:00     0      5.9      471      534     0.88      91      5.9       14     16.1
>>>>>>>>>>>>>>>>>>>>>>>>>>>>> Start of Exercise <<<<<<<<<<<<<<<<<<<<<<<<<<<<<
    3:00    25      9.6      713      870     0.85     106      8.2       15     22.0
    4:00    54     10.9      929      990     0.94     107      9.3       18     27.3
    5:00    84     14.6     1207     1322     0.91     114     11.6       21     35.0
    6:00   115     17.6     1560     1601     0.97     123     13.0       23     44.1
    7:00   145     21.3     1951     1932     1.01     131     14.8       27     54.7
    8:00   175     25.2     2510     2289     1.10     140     16.4       30     69.4
    9:00   203     26.1     2682     2372     1.12     151     15.7       35     77.2
   10:00   234     32.5     3424     2951     1.16     156     18.9       35     95.0
   11:00   262     36.1     3969     3277     1.21     161     20.4       41    114.4
   12:00   294     40.1     4569     3637     1.26     134     27.4       43    134.1
>>>>>>>>>>>>>>>>>>>>>>>>>>>>> Start of Recovery <<<<<<<<<<<<<<<<<<<<<<<<<<<<<
   13:00    48     34.2     4002     3101     1.29     142     22.1       40    125.8
   14:00    30     19.1     2789     1737     1.59     157     11.1       40    100.1
   14:39    30     16.7     2107     1514     1.39     143     10.6       33     77.0
```

FIGURE 6. MedGraphics System 2001 metabolic response results (tabular). From Medical Graphics Corporation. Copyright Medical Graphics Corporation. Reprinted by permission.

This system is truly an example of the application of modern computerized technology to exercise response and fitness assessment. Medical applications in pulmonary disease and cardiac rehabilitation are prevalent. The system is expensive and requires substantial financial support. It is a complex system requiring training and practice to operate proficiently. The basic computer system includes a hard disk, MS-DOS operating system, color monitor, and color printer. Other hardware configurations are available.

LABORATORY ASSESSMENT OF MUSCULAR STRENGTH AND ENDURANCE

Computerized measurement of muscular strength and endurance under laboratory or clinical conditions is accomplished with a computerized dynamometer. The dynamometer is a machine that can control resistance during a movement and or speed in a movement. These systems allow the measurement of force, torque (force × length of the lever arm), work (force × distance), and power (work/time). Such systems are in wide use in exercise physiology laboratories and in orthopedic clinics for physical therapy. Examples of these dynamometers are the Cybex (Lumex, Inc., Ronkonkoma, N.Y.), the Kin/Com (Chattecx Corp., Chattanooga, Tenn.), and the Omnitron (HydraFitness Industries, Belton, Tex.). These systems are used not only for testing purposes but for strength and endurance training in therapeutic situations.

The Omnitron is a dynamometer that can be used in typical arm-and-shoulder and leg exercise applications. The dynamometer uses hydraulic cylinders to provide resistance. Sophisticated electronic sensors and computer software are combined to provide the necessary measurements and calculations of force, power, and work. The system is menu driven and allows storage and retrieval of test data, a variety of exercise and test protocols, and a variety of optional test output that is available on the computer monitor and in printed hard copy. Figure 7 provides examples of tabular and graphical output of a test. This test output includes two exercises, PRS (chest press) and PUL (horizontal pull),

```
MACHINE: KNEE PLUS                      NAME:
CHEST     - BOTH                        AGE: 28 SEX: M
SETTINGS: PRS= 7 PUL= 5                 BODY WEIGHT: 180
LIMITS: PRS=20  PUL=10    (SET BY IBM)  HEIGHT:  6 ft.  1 in.
ANATOMICAL ADJ:   0                     DATE: Sep 02, 1990
```

REP #		PEAK FORCE (Lb)	TIME TO PK (Sec)	PEAK DIST (In)	REP POWER (Watt)	REP WORK (FtLb)	START END (In)	ROM (in)	AVG VELOC (in/sec)
1	PRS	153	0.75	20	31	211	0:27	27	3
	PUL	124	0.82	23	50	162	27:0	26	6
2	PRS	146	0.35	20	10	203	0:27	26	1
	PUL	135	0.03	23	66	169	27:1	25	7
3	PRS	155	0.07	19	29	209	0:28	27	3
	PUL	135	0.18	24	211	179	28:0	28	24
AVG	PRS	151	0.39	19	23	207	0:27	26	2
	PUL	131	0.34	23	109	170	27:0	26	12

```
TOTAL WORK FOR 3 REPS: Press:  623   Pull:  510<MORE>
```

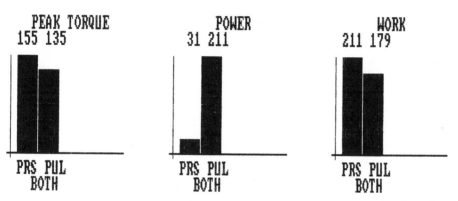

FIGURE 7. Omnitron strength test results. From Hydrafitness Industries. Copyright Hydrafitness Industries. Reprinted by permission.

which were performed in three consecutive repetitions (REP). The tabular results include values for each repetition and the average (AVG) for the three repetitions. Measurements for eight variables, including the important assessments of peak force, power, and work, are given. The graphs illustrate the maximum repetition values for peak torque (force), power, and work for each exercise during the three repetition exercise tests.

The Omnitron interfaces with an IBM-PC compatible computer that includes a hard disk. The software allows a variety of options in test protocol, results reporting, and data management. Similar to the MedGraphics

System 2001, this sophisticated system is complex, and training and practice are required for proper operation.

ADDITIONAL SOURCES OF INFORMATION

The California State University, Fresno, in cooperation with the Western Society for Physical Education of College Women, has sponsored a project entitled Softshare. The purpose of this project is to make available inexpensive, practical software useful in physical education situations. Applications are available for Apple, Macintosh, and IBM-

PC computers. Many of these public-domain programs are useful in health and fitness situations. These programs are provided at nominal cost and are easily ordered through the mail.

Ross and Jackson (1989) have written a text, *Exercise Concepts, Calculations and Computer Applications,* that provides a conceptual framework for understanding exercise, the numerous calculations used in determining metabolic responses, and the role of the computer in the overall process.

References

AAHPERD. 1988. *Physical best.* Reston, Va.: AAHPERD.

Blair, S., et al. 1989. Physical fitness and all-cause mortality: A prospective study of healthy men and women. *Journal of the American Medical Association* 262(17): 2395–401.

Ekelund, L., et al. 1988. Physical fitness as a predictor of cardiovascular mortality in asymptomatic North American men. *New England Journal of Medicine* 319(21):1379–84.

Institute for Aerobics Research. 1987. *Fitnessgram.* Dallas, Tex.: Institute for Aerobics Research.

Lamb, D. 1984. *Physiology of exercise: Response and adaptions.* New York: Macmillan.

Lohman, T. 1989. *Body composition estimation for children.* Champaign, Ill.: Human Kinetics.

Morrow, J., and J. Pivarnik. 1989. *Simulated exercise physiology laboratories.* Champaign, Ill.: Human Kinetics.

Pollock, M., J. Wilmore, and S. Fox. 1984. *Exercise in health and disease: Evaluation and prescription for prevention and rehabilitation.* Philadelphia: Saunders.

President's Council on Physical Fitness and Sports. 1987. *President's challenge.* Washington, D.C.: Department of Health and Human Services.

Ross, R., and A. Jackson. 1989. *Exercise concepts, calculations and computer applications.* Carmel, Ind.: Benchmark.

Allen Jackson

HETEROGENEOUS DATABASES

See Distributed and Heterogeneous Databases

HIERARCHICAL DATABASES

See Database Management

HIGH-LEVEL LANGUAGES

See Languages, Computer; Languages, Very-High-Level

HISTORY OF COMPUTING

Computing is generally thought of as being a very new phenomenon and is frequently referred to as a revolution with wide-ranging implications for the entire society. However, it is based on the work of many people, some known and some relatively unknown, and has developed over centuries. Not only the basis for computer hardware but also the many applications of computing have a long history. Computing is undoubtedly more evolutionary than revolutionary.

HARDWARE

The oldest aid to calculation of which we are aware is the abacus, which was used in China for centuries before Christ. This simple though enormously effective device was widely used throughout the East and Middle East for centuries and continued to be used in the Orient well into the twentieth century. In Europe in the seventeenth century a number of devices were developed that aided computation. John Napier (1550–1617) invented Napier's Bones, sticks that moved back and forth to multiply and divide. He also developed the concept of logarithms, which led to the development of the slide rule. Within a few years William Schickard (1592–1635), a German whose work was lost in a fire, and then Blaise PASCAL (1623–62) developed mechanical calculators with wheels and gears, which implemented carrying in addition and subtraction. Gottfried LEIBNIZ (1646–1716) invented a device that also performed multiplication and division and became the model for mechanical calculators in use worldwide through the mid-twentieth century. During the mid-twentieth century Burroughs, NCR (National Cash Register Company), and Monroe were the prominent U.S. manufacturers of desktop calculators. IBM (International Business Machines) developed and marketed an accounting machine and a calculator that performed certain arithmetic operations on numeric values that had been punched into cards. The accounting machine could develop and print totals and subtotals from groups of cards and print the results. Besides addition and subtraction, the calculator could multiply or divide one number by another and punch the result into a specified location on the card.

During the 1970s, very powerful hand-held calculators became available. In the 1980s, hand-held calculators decreased in price so that they were widely available for $10 or less, and tiny calculators, the size of a credit card, with the capabilities of computing square roots and logarithms, became widely available. Though early calculators were manipulated by hand, calculators in the mid-twentieth century were powered by electricity; and toward the end of the century hand-held and pocket calculators were often battery- or solar-powered. After the development of microcomputers, the use of mechanical calculators declined rapidly.

The essential concepts of modern computers, including the stored program, were first developed by Charles BABBAGE (1791–1871). He borrowed the idea of using punched cards to control the program from Joseph JACQUARD (1752–1834), who developed an automatic loom in 1801 with punched cards controlling the weaving sequences. Much of what we know about Babbage and his work comes from the writings of Augusta Ada BYRON, Countess of Lovelace (1815–52).

At the end of the nineteenth century Herman HOLLERITH (1860–1926) built the machines to tabulate from punched cards (see CARDS, JACQUARD AND HOLLERITH) the information collected in the 1890 census. He went on to develop a group of machines to process data using punched cards, often called "unit records," since each card contained the information about one person or item. The company he formed and later sold eventually became IBM. In the early years of digital computers, IBM punched-card machines were the main input and output devices.

Knowledge about the early history of electronic digital computers is incomplete, and there are continuing disputes about some of the details. The development of computers took place primarily in the United States. Though several important developments occurred in Europe, World War II was going on during these crucial early years of development. Konrad Zuse (1910–), a German engineer, built a program-controlled electronic calculator in 1941, but it was destroyed in an air raid. The British developed a computer, Colossus, which broke the German cipher codes in 1943. Unfortunately, information about Colossus is still classified.

The 1940s was a period of intense activity in electronic and electromechanical calculators in the United States. The Mark I, developed at Harvard by Howard Aiken, is the best known of the electromechanical calculators. John V. Atanasoff (1903–) developed an electronic computer at Iowa State College from 1939 to 1942 with his colleague Clifford Berry. John W. MAUCHLY (1907–80) and J. Presper ECKERT (1919–) developed the Electronic Numerical Integrator And Calculator (ENIAC), a general-purpose electronic digital computer, between 1943 and 1946 with funding from the U.S. Army. The ENIAC and the Atanasoff machines are generally considered to be calculators, not true computers, because they were externally programmed. There is continuing controversy among computer scientists about who should receive the most credit for the electronic computer. Even before the ENIAC was completed, Mauchly and Eckert began work on their next project, the Electronic Discrete Variable Automatic Computer (EDVAC), the first stored-program, electronic digital computer. John VON NEUMANN (1903–57) was a consultant on the EDVAC project and in 1945 he wrote a report on the project. Though unpublished, this report and von Neumann's report on his work on the IAS computer, which he designed with Arthur Burks and Herman Goldstine for the Institute for Advanced Studies, were widely disseminated. Thus von Neumann is credited with the modern development of the stored-program concept. To this day most computers have this same architecture and are called von Neumann–type machines. During the 1950s many universities began to build their own one-of-a-kind computers.

COMMERCIAL COMPUTERS

Mauchly and Eckert were forced by financial problems to sell their company to Remington-Rand, which in 1951 produced the first commercial computer, UNIVAC I, which was sold to the U.S. Census Bureau. IBM began to deliver computers in 1952. Other companies developed and sold computers, but from the mid-1950s IBM dominated the U.S. computer market, and indeed the world market. IBM revenues exceed those of all other computer companies combined. At one time IBM controlled over 75 percent of the world market in computing. The major competition for IBM has been in the minicomputer area, where Digital Computer Company (DEC) has dominated, with its PDP-8s and PDP-11s. Very recently, among supercomputers, the CRAY has dominated, and before IBM entered the microcomputer arena scores of companies were building and selling personal computers. Among the more successful were Apple, Radio Shack (TRS-80), Commodore (Pet), and AMIGA. After IBM entered the microcomputer field, a plethora of companies, including Zenith and Compaq, began to market IBM-compatibles. Recently the market for laptop or notebook computers has grown rapidly. These truly portable computers, weighing only a few pounds, were envisioned by Alan Kay when he was a graduate student at the University of Utah in the late 1960s. A notebook computer fits neatly into a briefcase and is attractive for working while traveling or at home. Such a system generally has a removable diskette, runs on AC or battery power, and has a modem for easy communication with other computer systems, and frequently has a hard disk and an optional portable printer.

COMPUTER GENERATIONS

Electronic, stored-program, digital computers are now in their fourth generation. The first generation (1951–58) was characterized by vacuum tubes for circuitry, magnetic drums for main memory, and punched cards for input/output (I/O) and external storage. In general, these early computers failed frequently. They were unreliable, slow, expensive, and programmed in machine or assembly language. In second-generation computers (1959–64) transistors replaced vacuum tubes, magnetic cores were usually used for main memory, and magnetic tape was used for most secondary storage and I/O. These computers were more reliable, faster, and less expensive and could be programmed in high-level languages such as FORTRAN and COBOL. Operating systems took over many of the duties, including job scheduling, that operators had handled earlier.

In third-generation computers (1964–70) integrated circuits replaced transistors. In addition to magnetic tape, magnetic disks, disk packs, and mass storage devices were used for secondary storage, and the operating systems supported time sharing, which allowed multiple, simultaneous use. These computers were more reliable, faster, and less expensive than those of previous generations. IBM announced its third-generation family of computers in 1964. This family of computers was upwardly compatible—that is, customers could upgrade their computers and still use their applications software without modification. Computers of this generation processed up to 10 million instructions per second and had memory capacities of up to 4 million characters.

Fourth-generation computers (1971–)

began with large-scale integrated (LSI) circuits and today have very-large-scale integrated (VLSI) circuits, sometimes with millions of transistors. These computers have very sophisticated operating systems; virtual memory allows them to run extremely large programs and support up to several thousand users at the same time; and they can be equipped with an extremely wide variety of highly sophisticated I/O devices. With each generation computers have become easier to use, less expensive per instruction executed, more reliable, and smaller, and have provided a wider variety of I/O options. Common I/O options include optical scanners, color graphics printers, laser printers, and touch screens. More unusual I/O devices include those that sense and respond to eye movements or to voice commands; monitor patients in hospitals; monitor and control spacecraft, production of goods, and military weapons; and design and build computers.

A fifth generation, the computer technology of the 1990s, includes new logic-based languages, new architecture, and ultra-large-scale integration (ULSI; e.g., 2–64 million transistors per chip). (See also INTERACTIVE COMPUTER SYSTEMS; PARALLEL COMPUTING.)

MINICOMPUTERS

The classification of computer hardware into generations generally refers to mainframes and minicomputers. The central processing units (CPUs) of the first minicomputers were generally small enough to be placed on a 16-inch-deep shelf. They were easily distinguishable from mainframe computers. Also, early minicomputers were frequently dedicated to a particular application. Now the lines between mainframes, minicomputers, and microcomputers are somewhat blurred, and precise definitions have become difficult. Today minicomputers are usually defined as smaller in size, slower in speed, and less expensive than mainframe computers. Minicomputers, sometimes called superminis, have an increased number of bits per word, have sophisticated operating systems, support a variety of high-level languages, and serve many users simultaneously. For many

years DEC has been the leader in this segment of the market, although there were and are many minicomputer manufacturers, including Hewlett-Packard, Prime, and Data General.

MICROCOMPUTERS

Since the 1970s, when microcomputers were introduced, their influence on computing has been tremendous. Robert Noyce and Gordon Moore established Intel in 1968 and in 1970 produced a 1,024-bit random-access memory (RAM) chip. Later in that same year they produced the first microprocessor, the Intel 4004. This early microprocessor was used as a special-purpose computer in many small appliances and toys. In 1972 they marketed their 8-bit chip, the 8008, and in 1974 the 8080, which was used in many of the early microcomputers. During these early years Intel was the only company in the world manufacturing integrated chips (ICs). In the 1970s the Japanese began to manufacture ICs and became dominant in this area by the mid-1980s. There is great competition in this field as companies in the United States and Japan vie to put more bits on a chip and to corner the market for ICs.

In 1974 *Popular Electronics* magazine published a feature article about the MITS Altair 8800 computer kit. The company was soon inundated with orders from hobbyists, who enthusiastically assembled their kits and programmed their Altairs in machine language. By 1977 fully assembled microcomputers were being sold in stores. The Apple II, developed by Stephen WOZNIAK and Steven JOBS, was the most successful example of this, though the Radio Shack division of Tandy Corporation and Commodore Business Machines both introduced microcomputers in 1977. Wozniak and Jobs formed Apple Computer Company in 1976. Soon A. C. Markkula, a venture capitalist, bought into the company. They introduced the Apple II in 1977 for just under $2,000. Sales for 1977 were just over $750,000. By 1981, annual sales exceeded $300 million, and when the company went public in 1983, annual sales were just under $1 billion. In addition to the appeal to hobbyists, these early microcomputers were purchased for use in a wide variety of academic institutions and some small businesses. The National Computer Conference (NCC) had a special exhibit hall for microcomputers in Anaheim, California, at their 1978 annual conference. At times over fifty companies were manufacturing microcomputers.

Companies came and went almost overnight. In the early 1980s DEC and IBM entered the microcomputer market. Convinced that these personal computers could increase worker productivity, many businesses began to purchase microcomputers. In the mid-1980s hardware prices fell, many of the early microcomputer companies failed, Apple announced the Apple Lisa and then the Macintosh, IBM added the greatly enhanced, multitasking IBM PC AT, and the marketplace was flooded with "IBM-AT-compatible" microcomputers. IBM had attracted the majority of the business market for microcomputers.

Apple was more successful in schools. In the late 1980s, desktop publishing appeared to be the fastest-growing segment of personal computing, and many businesses turned to the Apple Macintosh or the Macintosh II, which was announced in 1987. These machines had outstanding graphics capability, high-capacity floppies, hard-disk storage, and main memory up to 8 million bytes, and were commonly networked. IBM also announced a new computer in 1987, the PS/2, with most of the features of the Macintosh except its graphics capabilities. This shortcoming was substantially remedied by 1989. Though there are still many microcomputer manufacturers, IBM and IBM-compatible machines dominate the business and university markets. Apple computers are popular in the schools, largely because of the installed base of educational software and hardware. Apple Macintosh computers are also popular in certain business segments and at some universities.

Workstations, sometimes called supermicrocomputers, are desktop computers for scientists and engineers. They are used by one person and generally linked to a mini- or mainframe computer to allow the user to take advantage of the facilities of these computers and to communicate easily with co-workers. Sun and Apollo are the major manufacturers of workstations.

SOFTWARE

Just as there are generations of computer hardware, so there are generations of computer software, the programs that cause the hardware to process data and produce the desired results. Every computer has a machine language, and with first-generation computer hardware the software was written in machine language. Programmers quickly realized that the computer could be used to make their job easier, and assembly language, the second generation of programming language, was developed. Assembly language allows the programmer to write mnemonic codes for computer operations instead of having to remember a numeric code; for example, the programmer could remember "A" for add instead of having to remember that some particular number—say, 11—stands for add. Further, the programmer could refer to values by names—for example, "Total"—in assembly language instead of having to keep track of the exact computer address where each variable is stored. Each computer or family of computers has its own assembly language, so software written in machine or assembly language could not be moved from one computer model to another.

Third-generation languages, sometimes called high-level languages, were developed so programmers would not have to learn a new assembly language each time they moved from one computer to another, and so software could be used on a variety of computers. The first widely used third-generation language was FORTRAN (FORmula TRANslation), which was developed for IBM by John Backus in the mid-1950s. FORTRAN was originally designed for use on mathematical and scientific problems. It was standardized in 1966 and updated in 1977; though great effort has been expended on the next revision, no agreement has yet been reached on a new FORTRAN standard, long referred to as FORTRAN 8X and now known as

FORTRAN 9X. COBOL was developed in the late 1950s by computer manufacturers and users, especially the Department of Defense. Commodore (Ret.) Grace Murray HOPPER (1906–), who worked with Mauchly and Eckert for many years, and Jean Sammet, originally with GE and recently retired from IBM, were both active participants in the development of COBOL. This is the most widely used language in business computing today. It was the first standardized programming language and has been updated several times.

BASIC, the language used by more people than any other programming language, was developed at Dartmouth College by John KEMENY and Thomas KURTZ with the intention that the language should be easy to learn and would thus allow large numbers of students to learn about computers and computing. The original BASIC ran on a mainframe computer in batch mode. With the advent of time sharing, BASIC quickly became popular on college campuses across the country. However, the coming of the microcomputer really pushed BASIC to the forefront. In 1974 Bill GATES quit Harvard and with Paul Allen founded Microsoft Corporation. They developed a version of BASIC for the MITS Altair 8800. BASIC was implemented on virtually all early microcomputers and was for some years the first computer language that students learned both in and out of school. BASIC is still popular in schools, though Pascal is now the most widely taught first computer language in colleges and universities. Pascal is also the basis for the Advanced Placement Examination in computing and therefore is taught in many high schools. LOGO is the most popular programming language in elementary schools. It was developed by Seymour Papert at MIT and allows very young children to develop programs of their own. While there are hundreds of high-level languages, many of them widely used, COBOL and FORTRAN continue to be the most widely used programming languages in business and industry. C, developed at Bell Labs, is becoming popular for commercial software development for operating systems. Ada is the language developed for the Department of Defense (DoD) after it was discovered in the mid-1970s that the software for the DoD was written in over 400 different languages and as a result was almost impossible to maintain. Today most contracts for software for DoD specify that Ada is required.

Fourth-generation languages (4GL) are less widely used but are powerful as query languages and for developing programs to extract information from databases. The 4GL languages are easy to learn. Someone with an understanding of computing can become a productive 4GL programmer in a day or two. Productivity is said to be about ten times greater than when programs are written in a third-generation language. The reason that 4GLs are not more popular is that while they may perform some tasks efficiently, programs written in a 4GL do not on average run as efficiently as those written in third-generation languages. Popular 4GLs include NOMAD, Occam, and SQL, the last being the most popular.

SOFTWARE PACKAGES

From the early days of computing, the manufacturers were interested in the development of software. With second- and early third-generation computers, the manufacturer delivered a certain amount of software with the computer. This software included the assembler program and usually some high-level language translator or translators. IBM developed and distributed a great amount of specialized software to its customers until 1970. At that time IBM "unbundled" its software—that is, IBM agreed to charge separately for hardware and for software. Immediately software developers began to develop and market software packages in competition with the hardware manufacturers. This was the beginning of a business that has grown immensely in the past twenty years. While many companies are developing software for mainframe and minicomputers, the most visible market for software packages today is the microcomputer market. While some microcomputer users develop or tailor their own software, the vast majority rely on software packages.

COMPUTER APPLICATIONS

Computers were developed primarily to carry out scientific computations. During World War II a great deal of effort was expended on developing computers for ballistics calculations. Though the first commercial computer, UNIVAC I, was used for data processing by the Bureau of the Census, most early computers were employed for scientific calculations—for example, weather forecasting and mathematical models of physical phenomena. In 1952 the UNIVAC computer was used to predict the U.S. presidential election. At 9:00 P.M. EST, the computer prediction of a landslide victory of Dwight Eisenhower over Adlai Stevenson was within four electoral votes of the final result. Because those running the machine feared an error, Walter Cronkite on CBS Television did not announce the prediction until 10:00 P.M. EST. Later in the 1950s many of the large accounting departments of companies that had computers realized the power of these new machines to automate large, routine tasks such as payroll, accounts payable, and accounts receivable. Point-of-sale (POS) and inventory application, banking, and air traffic control systems were implemented.

By the early 1960s computers were widely used by banks and insurance companies and by business, industry, and universities for individual data processing applications. By 1967 banks required that all checks in the United States be encoded with machine-readable characters in magnetic ink so they could be quickly and easily processed by computers. Minicomputers became common in small scientific laboratories, for operation of factory tools, and in the monitoring of chemical flows in refineries. In the early 1970s, many grocery and drug product manufacturers agreed to put bar codes on their products. By the late 1970s scanners were seen at many supermarket checkout counters. Checkout clerks no longer needed to know the prices of items and could scan and bag the grocery orders quickly. In addition to greater productivity in checkout, this system also kept an up-to-date inventory and in many cases incorporated an automatic reor-

dering system. As banks came to rely more and more on computers and as account balances were immediately available, banks installed automatic teller machines (ATMs), where customers could deposit or withdraw funds twenty-four hours a day, seven days a week, using their special banking card and punching in their personal identification number (PIN) along with information regarding the transaction or transactions they wished to carry out. These ATMs were first located at banks and usually were accessible without entering the building. Now ATMs are available at remote sites, including airports and supermarkets. While the early data processing applications involved one single application, as the users developed sophistication and as the I/O and secondary storage facilities became faster, more reliable, and capable of holding more information, integrated systems were developed. No longer did every department that dealt with a customer or an employee have to have all the information about the person; now such data could be shared. This was particularly advantageous when some item of information, such as an address, needed to be changed. Instead of having to be sure that the change was reflected in the data held by every department, one could make the revision in a single place, and all departments would use the updated, correct information. This was made possible by large integrated databases and the appropriate software and hardware to support such systems. Although many experimental robots had been built earlier, during the 1980s robots became popular in many manufacturing plants—for example, in automobile and computer assembly.

The U.S. government has been the largest user of computers since the early 1950s, with the DoD the largest user of all. The Persian Gulf war in 1991 brought to public attention the many weapons systems controlled by computers. The Social Security Administration and the Internal Revenue Service have complex computer systems, with very detailed information about most people in the country. The space program would be impossible without the use of computers in nearly every facet of the operation, including planning, designing, testing, operation, and evaluation.

Nearly every adult deals directly or indirectly with computers every day. The telephone system is controlled by computers. Medical systems use computers not only for record keeping and billing but also for diagnosis and monitoring of patients. White-collar workers frequently spend some portion of each day using a computer to assist them in their work—for example, analyzing sales, preparing reports and presentations, communicating with co-workers or clients, and obtaining information from company or external databases. Many homes have computers. Originally computers in the home were largely used for computer games. Today computer systems control security systems, regulate interior climate control, assist in personal finances, and have replaced the in-home typewriter.

Large scientific computation includes evaluation of seismic studies and satellite data to determine likely locations for mineral resources, development of computerized mathematical models of various physical phenomena such as subatomic reactions, optimization of delivery patterns for international parcel distribution, weather forecasting, and design of aircraft.

In 1950 only a very small number of people had any idea what a computer was. In 1960 there were very few schools or colleges where students could see or use a computer. By 1970 the Association for Computing Machinery had defined a college curriculum for computer science, and some colleges and universities were offering degree programs in computer science and/or engineering. By 1980 nearly every college and university and most schools had computers, and a majority of college graduates had experience with computers and computing. Today it is not uncommon for college students to have their own microcomputers; in fact, since the mid-1980s some colleges have required each student to purchase his or her own microcomputer. This has been a period of rapid change, and change will continue for the foreseeable future as insightful people devise applications whereby computers can augment human abilities.

For Further Reading

American National Standard COBOL (ANSI X3.23-1974). 1974. New York: American National Standard Institute.

American National Standard FORTRAN (ANSI X3.9-1966). 1966. New York: American National Standard Institute.

Annals of the History of Computing (quarterly). New York: Springer Verlag. For detailed scholarly articles on the history of computing, this is an excellent source. Vol. 11, No. 1, is devoted to computing in France.

Augarten, S. 1984. *Bit by bit: An illustrated history of computers.* New York: Ticknor and Fields.

Backus, J. 1978. Can programming be liberated from the von Neumann style? A functional style and its algebra of programs. *Communications of the ACM* 21(8): 613–41.

Cortada, J. W. 1987. *Historical dictionary of data processing: Biographies.* Westport, Conn.: Greenwood.

——— 1987. *Historical dictionary of data processing: Organizations.* Westport, Conn.: Greenwood.

——— 1987. *Historical dictionary of data processing: Technology.* Westport, Conn.: Greenwood.

Finerman, A., ed. 1990. The origins of modern computing. *Computing Reviews* 31(9): 449–81.

Goldberg, A., and D. Robson. 1983. *Small-Talk-80: The language and its implementation.* Reading, Mass.: Addison-Wesley.

Goldstine, H. H. 1972. *The computer: From Pascal to von Neumann.* Princeton, N.J.: Princeton University Press.

Hopcroft, J. 1989–90. Reflections on computer science. *Annual Review of Computer Science* 4.

Kemeny, J. G., and T. E. Kurtz. 1985. *Back to BASIC.* Reading, Mass.: Addison-Wesley.

Sammet, J. E. 1969. *Programming languages: History and fundamentals.* Englewood Cliffs, N.J.: Prentice-Hall.

Doris K. Lidtke

HOLLERITH, HERMAN

Herman Hollerith was born in Buffalo, New York, on February 29, 1860, the son of a German immigrant couple. Immediately after graduating from the Columbia University's School of Mines in 1879, he became an assistant to one of his former teachers in the U.S. Census Bureau. During the next few years, he taught briefly at the Massachusetts Institute of Technology in Cambridge, experimented on air brakes, and worked for the patent office in Washington, D.C. During all of this time, Hollerith was occupied with the problem of automating the tabulation work of the census.

When the tenth decennial census was taken in 1880, the country had grown to 50 million people, and 5 years later the Census Bureau was still struggling to compile the results. It was not hard to foresee a situation where a given census would not be published before it was time to take the next one.

Hollerith, inspired by watching a conductor punch tickets with a basic description of each passenger, started work on a machine for mechanically tabulating population and other statistics. In 1884, he applied for his first patent on a machine for counting population statistics. He was eventually issued thirty-one patents.

Hollerith's most important innovations were the sensing of the holes through electrical contacts and the design of electrically operated mechanisms for incrementing the proper register in the tabulating machine. He also provided for one step in an electric sort. Each card was coded to fall into the proper pocket in a sorting box. From this point on, sorting had to be done by hand, but it was easier to sort punched cards than handwritten cards because the sorter could sight through the wanted hole or use a sorting needle. The card used in Hollerith's machine was $6\frac{5}{8} \times 3\frac{1}{4}$ inches and had twenty-four columns, each with twelve punching places. Hollerith worked as an independent inventor, with no commitment from the census authorities to the use of his invention; however, he planned his system keeping in mind the requirements for tabulation of the population census.

In 1889, a committee was appointed to consider the means of tabulation to be used in the 1890 census. Three systems were tested, one of them Hollerith's. His system took only about two thirds as long as its nearest competitor to transcribe information. The commission estimated that on a basis of 65,000,000 population, the savings with the Hollerith apparatus would reach nearly $600,000. Hollerith's invention was adopted and an arrangement was entered into by the government with its inventor.

Hollerith subcontracted the development and construction of the keyboard punches to the Pratt and Whitney Company of Hartford, Connecticut, and of the tabulator to the Western Electric Company.

In 1890, three major events occurred in Hollerith's life: (1) he married the daughter of Dr. John Billings; (2) he received his doctor of philosophy degree from Columbia's School of Mines; (3) the United States conducted its eleventh census using his system. Dr. Billings was in charge of the work on vital statistics for both the 1880 and 1890 censuses, especially the collection and tabulation of data. While working at the Census Bureau, Billings, who was Hollerith's superior, also suggested to Hollerith that Jacquard-like punched cards might be the answer to the massive tabulation problems of the census.

In 1896, Hollerith formed the Tabulating Machine Company. Word of his success spread rapidly. Insurance companies used his machines for actuarial work, department stores used them for sales analysis, and the New York Central used them to keep track of their railroad cars. The Tabulating Machine Company became world famous.

Hollerith continued to modify and improve his machines, which were used for the 1900 census. In 1910, even though Hollerith had developed a system of hopper-fed machines that eliminated hand feeding of cards, he was unable to reach an agreement with the Census Bureau for their use.

When his Tabulating Machine Company became too large for individual control, Hollerith sold it. In 1911, the company became part of the Computing-Tabulating-Recording (C-T-R) Company. The C-T-R Company was a holding company and in 1924 was renamed the International Business Machines (IBM) Corporation.

On November 17, 1929, in Washington, D.C., a heart attack ended his life at the age of 69. What Henry Ford did for manufacturing, Herman Hollerith accomplished for data processing—a means for standardization and a format for the interchangeability of information.

For Further Reading

Austrian, G. 1982. *Herman Hollerith.* New York: Columbia University Press.

Donald D. Spencer

HOME, COMPUTERS IN THE

Compared with other types of information technologies in the home, computers may seem relatively rare. For example, only 15 percent of the 90 million households in the United States had a personal computer in 1990, compared with the 75 percent of homes that had a video recorder; radios and televisions are almost universal. On a deeper level, however, the computer is already changing the home. At the start of the industrial revolution, the wealthy in Victorian England discussed how many motors they had in their houses; today, few of us would know because the motor has become invisible, buried in many common objects. As they become smaller, faster, and cheaper, computers also are becoming invisible; most people do not realize how many microprocessors they have in their homes (in microwaves, video recorders, clocks), not to mention the number under the hoods of their cars.

Computers have the potential to transform many aspects of individual lifestyle. The computer has already reshaped the office and the factory; now, microprocessors and personal computers in the home are beginning to alter where we work, how we play, and what we learn. The radio, the television, and the video recorder are information technologies that have changed people's experience by creating "surrogate travel": we can hear and see things beyond our immediate vicinity. The personal computer provides a richer, interactive virtual environment for its users, opening up the possibility of "surrogate experience."

ACCESSING THE WORLD

Home computers can be used as an electronic window on the world, empowering remote access to a wide spectrum of resources. One example of this capability is the "virtual bookshelf." From a variety of vendors, one can purchase books with their contents stored on disk rather than printed on paper. When needed, these electronic volumes load into the computer's memory, allowing quick access without using shelf space. Disk-based versions of reference works such as a dictionary or a thesaurus are particularly popular; when these resources are in electronic form, searches through their contents are much faster and easier.

For example, using an inverted index that lists almost all the words in a book, a computer can quickly find paragraphs that contain key phrases. In less than 3 seconds, a computer can search through an encyclopedia to find all instances of the words *apple trees* that occur in the same paragraph as the word *orchards,* excluding those paragraphs that include the phrase *Garden of Eden.* Electronic storage has other advantages beyond facilitating searches. As an illustration, if the user has a modem, disk-based telephone directories can automatically dial the selected number and log the time and length of the call.

Users with sufficient money can augment their information access by purchasing a compact-disk read-only memory (CD-ROM) drive for their home computer. Read-only memory compact optical disks hold vast amounts of electronic information; 275,000 pages can be stored on a 4.7-inch plastic platter. One vendor offers a virtual bookshelf on a single disk: a dictionary, a thesaurus, an almanac, a zip code directory, a volume of familiar quotations, a style manual, and a compendium of forms and letters. Multivolume works such as encyclopedias, guides to the periodical literature, statistical compendia, collections of government documents, compilations of books in print, and even the complete Sherlock Holmes canon by Sir Arthur Conan Doyle with the original illustrations are available in CD-ROM form. Users can quickly locate key phrases in disks that combine multiple resources because the entire electronic version can be scanned as if it were a single document. In contrast, searching paper copies of diverse volumes can be very time consuming when each has its own individual index.

These capabilities of electronic data storage do not mean that the home library is likely to disappear. Similar predictions of the "paperless office" have been far off target; the more a business uses information technology, the more paper it consumes. Paper has many advantages: Reading text from the printed page is faster than reading from the computer screen, documents are more portable than computers, and part of the pleasure of the reading experience is the tactile sensations books offer. The virtual bookshelf and the home library are complementary rather than competitive.

Work at Home

Beyond displaying virtual documents in the home, computers can access the resources of the world's libraries through electronic information services. Legal documents, business data, financial information, and scientific/technical publications are a few of the many types of specialized material available from on-line searching and retrieval services. In scientific and technological fields alone, over 5,000 reports per day are added to more than 1,000 computerized databases, so practitioners need sophisticated tools to help them keep current with advances in knowledge. Home computers can now access these specialized data sources without requiring the elaborate resources of full-scale research information systems.

Home-based businesses are increasing as these sophisticated data services become more readily available. Powerful personal computers are now sufficiently inexpensive that standard office automation peripherals and applications—laser printers, fax boards, word processors, databases, spreadsheets—are affordable for the home. Many of these business tools have simplified versions for novice users, so that no special expertise is needed to master the product's capabilities quickly. Applications such as spelling, grammar, and syntax checkers take advantage of the electronic nature of the data these tools produce; mistakes can be easily corrected in the electronic version of a document version before a paper copy is created.

Work-at-home ventures based on telecommuting are attractive in several ways. The time and expense of transportation to and from a business site are eliminated, as are the overhead costs of office space. Home-based workers enjoy greater freedom and flexibility and have more time with their families; however, telecommuting has not increased as rapidly as forecasters expected, largely because of psychosocial factors (discussed in Kraut 1987; see also REMOTE WORK). Many marriages cannot stand the strain of constant contact, and home-based employees often miss the varied relationships and expanded interpersonal contact their workplace provided. People go to their offices for many reasons beyond the fact that their desks are located there; a future in which most workplaces are "virtual businesses" staffed by people who work primarily from their residences seems unlikely.

Videotex

The typical home user may be less interested in work-related data sources than in interactive access to leisure-oriented services. Videotex delivers a mixture of consumer information, purchasing options, and messaging services through a personal computer and modem. In contrast to shop-at-home broadcasts that present a predetermined, sequential set of products to television viewers, videotex allows users to browse through a broad menu of choices at their own pace. How subscribers are billed varies; for-profit providers generally assess a flat fee per month plus charges per minute of access.

The largest current videotex service is

France's Minitel, with approximately 4½ million subscribers in 1989. Minitel was subsidized by the French government, which both built an installed base and provided incentives for usage by giving away terminals instead of paper telephone directories. Minitel has about 8,000 participating retailers purveying a wide variety of wares, plus elaborate messaging facilities, financial data, weather reports, sports information, travel services, health advice, computer clubs, airline schedules, restaurant reservations, and many other consumer features.

No other country has implemented a comparable videotex system, and attempts by private consortia to develop videotex services have generally been unsuccessful in attracting enough subscribers to become profitable. The major problems seem to be building consumer awareness that elaborate leisure services can be provided to the home and tapping into an installed base of equipment that can access videotex. Like a telephone system, a videotex service is more valuable the more subscribers it has; a large base of users means that extensive and specialized information sources can be funded, volume discounts can be obtained on products purchased through the system, and messaging services have access to a wide range of people.

At present, several information services have a substantial installed base in the United States. Prodigy, CompuServe, and The Source are examples of major vendors; they provide reports (financial, weather, sports), a variety of travel and consumer services, messaging capabilities, and business-related data. No single enterprise seems likely to dominate the market, and purveyors are wrestling with emerging issues of privacy and censorship.

Some providers are supplying proprietary terminals to obviate the need for a home computer with a modem; a few video game companies are building extra capabilities into their devices to provide a potential installed base for videotex. Eventually, optical fiber cables into every home will provide plenty of bandwidth for data services: 500 megabytes (the capacity of a CD-ROM disk) per second. In the meantime, the number of home computers with modems is rapidly increasing; for example, about 8 million householders in the United States had the installed capability to receive videotex in 1990, with a growth rate of 30 percent per year.

As access and awareness barriers diminish, videotex may expand to create "information utilities." Imagine sitting at the breakfast table, watching the morning news. If an interesting issue is being discussed, push a button, and articles from major newspapers on that topic are downloaded to the home computer. A second command scans those articles for key phrases and initiates a search for periodical articles covering that issue. An automatic electronic message to the author of a journal article could be triggered by yet another command.

Like a conventional utility, such all-encompassing information sources will provide vital services for society and will necessitate careful regulation to prevent abuse of their power. Information utilities are difficult to monitor because people can agree more easily on what constitutes pollution (e.g., impure water) than on what constitutes bias and propaganda (e.g., inaccurate news). Careful regulation will be important because, as civilization moves to economic systems increasingly centered on knowledge rather than on industrial production, sophisticated home-based information systems will become vital for people's roles as workers and citizens.

ENTERTAINMENT

Beyond occupational, informational, and consumer services, home computing opens up the possibility of access to "virtual communities." In his classic science fiction novel *Neuromancer*, Gibson (1984) coined the term *cyberspace* to describe real-time, multiperson, on-line simulated worlds. An entertainment-oriented cyberspace provides users with the opportunity to interact, go on shared adventures, get married or divorced, start businesses, found religions, wage war, hold elections, construct legal systems, tailor their physical appearances, and assume alternative personal identities and interpersonal styles. Each player accesses this electronic environment through a personal computer and modem; the virtual world is maintained by a large centralized computer that downloads a real-time animated display to the home machine.

"Avatars" (animated figures, usually humanoid in appearance) carry out the actions of the players in these electronic contexts. The regions in a virtual world contain scenery and objects with which avatars can interact. For example, in Lucasfilm's "Habitat" (a prototype virtual world), its designers Morningstar and Farmer (1991) enabled avatars to utilize automatic token machines that allowed players access to their virtual bank accounts. At present, QuantumLink's "Club Caribe" is the major virtual community in the United States, with 15,000 participants; Fujitsu's "Habitat" is a comparable system in Japan. Such systems are likely to supplant the current use of home machines for single-user computer games, as shared "artificial realities" with other human participants are more motivating and intriguing than complex, but mindless simulations. Video games will likely evolve to include the capability of interactions in cyberspace; already, some sets being sold have unused power and connectors that could provide an installed base for virtual communities.

Users' interaction with cyberspace will become more realistic through interface innovations such as gesture technology and head-mounted displays. Computerized clothing can sense the physical actions of its wearer and translate those commands into equivalent operations in the electronic environment (Foley 1987). For example, a person wearing a gesture glove could "throw" a virtual ball; if the clothing incorporated force-feedback technology, pressure would be applied to the person's hand to suggest the weight of the ball. Head-mounted displays present their wearers with stereoscopic images across a wide visual field, mimicking how the eye sees the real world. Such interface devices help to remove the cognitive load that computer users now experience: infusing depth and size into a small, two-dimensional screen, mastering the unusual eye–hand coordination required by a pointing device.

In addition to innovations such as recreational cyberspaces, more traditional entertainment media are being reshaped by home computing. Brand (1988) coined the term *broadcatch* to describe information and entertainment services with content-specific selectivity and repackaging at the receiving end. Newspapers, magazines, and books could be manufactured in the home via laser printers rather than printed centrally and shipped. This would allow the content of each issue to vary from user to user depending on personal interest; a reader who wanted 40 percent sports, 40 percent entertainment, 10 percent financial, 5 percent comics, and 5 percent headlines could get that mixture of topics.

Televisions could incorporate powerful computers utilizing advanced image processing technology to make high-resolution, full-motion pictures without shadowing or ghosting. Such an approach would generate higher-quality images than broadcast or cable television signals can produce—better pictures even than the proposed high-definition television (HDTV) standard. A "knowbot" (an intelligent, computer-based agent programmed by the user) could tailor entertainment based on individual preferences. Imagine programming your television set: "I want to see a cowboy movie tonight, made before 1950, but not with John Wayne. Then show me 5 minutes of headlines, tomorrow's weather, and any recent documentaries on computer graphics." The knowbot in the television would then construct your evening's entertainment, time-shifting cable programs and editing broadcasts as appropriate.

As Lai and Malone (1988) propose, a knowbot could also process incoming videotex messages proposing meetings, using a scheduling system that accesses an electronic calendar. Journals arriving in electronic form could be scanned by the knowbot for articles of particular interest; the agent would automatically excerpt and file that material for future reading. At its extreme, a knowbot would become an intelligent partner in mediating human communication. As Schmandt and Arons (1986) have demonstrated, each person in a virtual community could interact through an intelligent device that recognized restricted single-user human speech, took messages through digital voice input/output, filtered phone calls, and scanned databases (weather, traffic, airport) to aid planning.

LIFESTYLE MANAGEMENT

Beyond providing sophisticated sources of information and entertainment, home computers have the capability to enrich many aspects of a user's lifestyle. For example, "expert systems" (knowledge-based applications that can imitate human problem solving in narrow, but complex fields) can provide advice on a variety of lifestyle-related topics: dressing for success, infant nutrition, resume and career counseling, basic medical care, gourmet food preparation, dieting, bartending, selecting the right wine, investments, gardening and landscaping, car care, route planning for trips, and interior and architectural design. Household record-keeping applications can tabulate and summarize medical, financial, educational, and employment data; inventories of possessions; automotive maintenance records; appliance warranties; even information on family pets. Specialized programs can provide advice and keep performance records for various recreational sports (e.g., bowling, running, golf) and hobbies (e.g., stamps, coins, astronomy).

Computers can also enhance the performance of other information technologies in the home. For example, a computer connected to a camcorder can provide sophisticated graphics and editing capabilities for home videos. Digital cameras with embedded chips can store high-resolution still images for later display or printing. Through computers, stereos can be programmed to play elaborate sequences of music from different media.

As discussed earlier, microprocessors are becoming so small and inexpensive that they can be built into home appliances to create "smart" objects. Already, homes contain programmable processors embedded in clocks, televisions, and video recorders. In the future, microwaves and ovens could be programmed to activate and deactivate on a preset schedule. Refrigerators could maintain a lower temperature in the meat section

than in the vegetable bin. Stereos could lower their volume when the doorbell or phone rings. Appliances could be activated remotely, through a central control, to accommodate shifts in the homeowner's plans. Self-diagnostic panels could alert users to potential problems.

A logical extension of smart appliances would be the "intelligent" house. Computerization and automation can change a dwelling from a passive structure to an interactive partner in the homeowner's lifestyle. As an illustration, a color video screen could serve as a centralized control panel. Icons would represent rooms, doors, windows, and appliances; touching the icon for a light would remotely turn it on or off. Sensors scattered around the house and grounds would relay information to the control screen. Heat and motion detectors could sense a person's location and movement. A malfunctioning appliance could be deactivated. Temperature detectors could change thermostat settings and could open and close skylights, unless countermanded by a moisture sensor indicating rain. Power dampers could activate or deactivate to control air flow; such sophisticated energy management would minimize heating and cooling costs.

Utilities could be continuously monitored: lawns watered as needed, electrical outlets activated only if a device is plugged in (to minimize the chances of accidental shock). Voice-recognition systems could lock and unlock doors, aiding the elderly or handicapped in coping with mobility problems. The user could program "scenarios" into the control panel; for example, a bedtime scenario could arm the security system, turn out most lights, and lower the hot water heater's temperature until early morning. (One feature unlikely to appear in intelligent houses is mobile, intelligent robots with vision systems; the technical challenges involved are very difficult.)

How rapidly intelligent houses will become available depends on how much extra consumers are willing to spend for these amenities and on how fast an industry standard emerges. Competing home automation approaches may keep any system from developing the critical mass of customers needed for economic viability. Rival systems in the United States include Electronics Industries Association's Consumer Electronics bus (CEbus), the National Association of Home Builders' Smart House, and AT&T's Discovery House.

EDUCATION

Harnessing the power of the computer to facilitate learning can enable us to stay smarter than our houses. Many of the emerging capabilities described above for home computers have an educational component. Virtual bookshelves, virtual communities, videotex, and telecommuting all involve their users in learning. In addition, significant advances in instructional computing have been made in the last decade; these offer the potential to enhance education in home settings.

As Dede (1988) describes, several types of emerging instructional applications can readily be transported from classrooms to households. For example, intelligent tutoring systems (ITSs) are supplementing computer-assisted instruction (CAI) as a standalone educational tool. Intelligent tutoring systems add capabilities from artificial intelligence to CAI, enabling the instructional device to understand what, whom, and how it is teaching. As with the expert systems discussed earlier, ITSs can instruct only in narrow content areas and lack the emotional motivation that human teachers can bring to learning. Even with these limitations, preliminary data on ITSs in classroom situations indicate that in conjunction with a skilled teacher they can be more effective than any other educational approach except individualized human tutoring.

Microworlds are another promising innovation in educational computing that has potential applications to the home. A "microworld" is an interactive subset of the world, limited to a particular domain, in which the user can change the rules by which the virtual environment functions. Simulations merely model what is; they provide practice with a simplified version of reality. Microworlds enable the learner to see how a particular subject might alter if its underlying principles were to change. For example, a gravity microworld could allow its users to play baseball first at Earth gravity, then at the Moon's gravity, Jupiter's gravity, and even a very short game at zero gravity. Then constant by constant, variable by variable, operator by operator, one could vary Newton's and Einstein's laws to illustrate how baseball (or cooking, or any other activity) would change if the rules determining the behavior of gravity were to shift. This provides a powerful means of learning because students can reflect on the underlying meaning of what they are experiencing.

Hypermedia is a knowledge representation system that enables the nonlinear interconnection of multimedia materials. All prior media (speech, text, still images, video) have been linear and sequential; one concept follows another in a steady stream. Hypermedia presents information in a manner closer to how human long-term memory stores knowledge: as networks of concepts linked by association. For example, the term *apple* conjures up connotations of pies, orchards, Isaac Newton, the Beatles, the Garden of Eden, and a computer corporation—all interrelated through a web of associations. Enthusiasts believe that the widespread availability of a nonlinear medium, empowered by the computer's ability to represent networks of nodes and links, will transform how people think and communicate. In particular, many educators are excited about the instructional potential of hypermedia: as a means of imaging mental models, as an authoring language for creating educational materials, and as a method of sharing ideas among learners.

Emerging applications for collaborative learning also may migrate from the classroom to the home. In parallel with ideas developing in the field of computer-supported cooperative work, these tools support group processes embedded in educational software. Cooperative learning and computer-based learning are complementary instructional approaches. The computer provides a compelling focus with embedded structure that allows small groups of pupils to learn with minimal teacher facilitation, while peer learning and teaching supply the emotional motivation and interpersonal experience that machine-centered education lacks. A well-prepared parent could assume the teacher's role to guide computer-based cooperative learning in home settings.

The ultimate impact of ITSs, microworlds, hypermedia, and computer-supported cooperative learning on education in the home may be fairly minor. Experience with educational technologies has shown that a skilled and knowledgeable teacher is essential to the success of even relatively standalone instructional devices such as ITSs. Only in families that choose to play an active and informed role in learning will home-based educational devices be more than marginally effective. At present, educational applications constitute only a small proportion of home computing usage, and few companies that market instructional software have been profitable.

The one exception to this discouraging assessment is distance learning technologies, which import a virtual human teacher into the home environment. Dede (1990) discusses how the coming synthesis of computing and telecommunications is driving the evolution of technology-mediated interactive learning. Digital video technology enables skilled teachers to establish "telepresence" through "proximity enhancers" that transcend barriers of distance and time. As with virtual communities, emotional bonding, establishment of a shared purpose, and development of common practices of interaction and communication can then occur among virtual teachers and students, as in a successful conventional classroom. Because sophisticated distance learning technologies do not require parental involvement, they may have a much greater impact on enhancing home-based education than the other innovations discussed earlier, even though all have tremendous potential to empower effective classroom instruction.

IMPACT ON FAMILIES AND COMMUNITIES

How much computers are used in homes during the next decade will depend partially on advances in computer–human interface technology. Many people have difficulty programming the clock on their video recorders, a much simpler technique than the elaborate incantations currently required for many aspects of personal computer usage. Direct manipulation interfaces with icons that mimic real-world objects are helping to improve this situation; this approach allows people to apply in the virtual environment their commonsense knowledge about the real world. The interface innovation most likely to open up the home market is gesture technology (discussed above under Entertainment). When people can manipulate a virtual representation by physical actions identical to those with which they interact with the corresponding real-world object, a major barrier to home use will erode.

The increasing use of computers in the home inevitably will have many subtle psychosocial consequences. Computers are so flexible that how this particular medium shapes its message and its users is not well understood. The discussion above implies that home computers are likely to push the balance between direct and virtual human experience even farther into artificial realities than have television, radio, video games, movies, and videotapes.

Most analysts agree that televised media have weakened interpersonal interaction in families. Because television is a passive medium, even when family members share a viewing experience they are often isolated, mute spectators. Computers have the potential to change this situation because they are active media; users constantly interact with the device to shape their experiences. However, personal computers are currently not designed for multiperson use; the microprocessor has one keyboard and monitor configured for a single individual. Unless the architecture of home machines changes to facilitate group interaction, personal computers could further isolate family members by drawing them deeper into individual virtual environments.

Because people's knowledge and values are both enhanced and constrained by the characteristics of technological communications channels, the cultural consequences of technology-mediated physical/social environments are mixed. As Dede (1991) suggests, the technologies themselves do not dictate content that creates a "couch potato" mentality or implies all of life's problems can be solved in 30 minutes. For example, know-bots and smart houses can remove drudgery from our lives, leaving more time for creative activities, or they can filter reality to present a distorted, static vision of our environment that ultimately becomes dangerously out of touch with the real world. As pervasive interpreters of reality, information technologies mirror our own psychological, economic, political, and cultural identities. Influencing the evolution of home computing to maximize its potential benefits and to minimize undesirable side effects is a difficult and important challenge.

[*See also* Microcomputers (Personal Computers).]

References

Brand, S. 1988. *The media lab: Inventing the future at MIT.* New York: Penguin Books.

Dede, C. 1988. The probable evolution of artificial intelligence based educational devices. *Technological Forecasting and Social Change* 34:115–33.

———. 1990. The evolution of distance learning. *Journal of Research on Computing in Education* 22(3):247–64.

———. 1991. Emerging information technologies: Implications for distance learning. *Annals of the American Academy for Political and Social Science* 514(March):146–58.

Foley, J. D. 1987. Interfaces for advanced computing. *Scientific American* 257(4):126–35.

Gibson, W. 1984. *Neuromancer.* New York: Ace Books.

Kraut, R. E. 1987. Predicting the use of technology: The case of telework. In R. E. Kraut, ed. *Technology and the transformation of white-collar work*, pp. 113–34. Englewood Cliffs, N.J.: Erlbaum Associates.

Lai, K., and T. Malone. 1988. Object lens: A "spreadsheet" for cooperative work. In *Proceedings of the 1988 Conference on Computer-Supported Cooperative Work*, pp. 115–24. New York: Association for Computing Machinery.

Morningstar, C., and F. R. Farmer. 1991. The lessons of Lucasfilm's Habitat. In M. Benedikt, ed. *Cyberspace: First steps.* Cambridge, Mass.: MIT Press.

Schmandt, C., and B. Arons. 1986. A robust parser and dialog generator for a conversational office system. In *Proceedings of the 1986 American Voice Input/Output Conference*, pp. 87–94. Palo Alto, Calif.: American Voice Input/Output Society.

For Further Reading

Alber, A. F. 1985. *Videotex/teletext: Principles and practices.* New York: McGraw-Hill.

Lambert, S., and S. Ropiequet, eds. 1986. *CD ROM: The new papyrus.* Redmond, Wash.: Microsoft.

Christopher J. Dede

HOPPER, GRACE BREWSTER MURRAY

Grace Brewster Murray Hopper was born on December 9, 1906, in New York. She earned her bachelor of arts degree in 1928 at Vassar College, where she was elected to Phi Beta Kappa. She did graduate work at Yale University receiving both her masters (1930) and doctoral (1934) degrees in mathematics. Her dissertation, entitled "New Types of Irreducibility Criteria," was written under the supervision of the algebraist Oystein Ore.

Hopper returned to Vassar as an assistant in mathematics in 1931, becoming, successively, instructor, assistant professor, and associate professor. In December 1943, she entered the U.S. Naval Reserve, was commissioned Lieutenant (JG), and ordered to the Bureau of Ordnance Computation Project at Harvard University. Here she learned to program the Mark I computer.

In 1946, she resigned from her leave-of-absence from Vassar and joined the Harvard Faculty as a Research Fellow in Engineering Sciences and Applied Physics at the Computation Laboratory, where work continued on the Mark II and Mark III computers for the Navy.

In 1949, Hopper joined, as senior mathematician, the Eckert–Mauchly Computer Corporation in Philadelphia, then building the UNIVAC I, the first commercial large-scale electronic computer. She remained with the company as a senior programmer when it was bought by Remington Rand (later to become Sperry Rand Corporation, Sperry Corporation, and Unisys Corporation). There she pioneered in the development of the COBOL compiler and later became one of the prime movers in the development of COBOL programming language in the 1950s. The Common Business Oriented Language (COBOL) was based on Hopper's FLOMATIC, the first English-language data processing language. Her reason for developing the business compiler was, simply, why start from scratch with every program you write when a compiler could be developed to do much of the basic work for you over and over again.

Throughout her business life, Hopper was affectionately anchored to the Navy. She chose to retire in 1966, but the Navy called her back to active duty a year later, when she was 60. She finally left the fleet with the rank of rear admiral in 1986 at the age of 79. Grace Hopper was one of the U.S. Navy's greatest public relations assets. She traveled widely, speaking about computers on the Navy's behalf, exhibiting an honest pride in the Navy and her country, and talking vividly and forthrightly about the work she loved. She encouraged people to be innovative. One of her favorite pieces of advice was, "It is easier to apologize than to get permission."

In her lectures, Hopper lashed out at the computer industry on several counts. Its lack of standards—for programming languages, computer architecture, data structure, and networks—was costing the government hundreds of millions of dollars a year in hardware and software that had to be thrown out because of incompatibility.

Hopper also condemned the notion that larger computers were automatically superior. As an analogy, she pointed out that when a farmer had to move a big, heavy boulder, and one of his oxen was not strong enough to do the job alone, he did not try to raise a bigger ox. He added another ox. Likewise, large volumes of data were better handled by multiple users than by a larger machine.

On September 1, 1986, just over 2 weeks after she retired from the Navy, she began working as a roving speaker for Digital Equipment Corporation. She died in January 1992.

Hopper's achievements in the design and preparation of problem solutions for digital computers distinguished her as one of the major contributors to program development throughout a period spanning three computer generations. She disseminated her thoughts and ideas not only through her writings, but also through numerous lecture tours.

For Further Reading

Reflections. 1988. Manhasset, N.Y.: CMP Publications.
Williams, M. 1985. *A history of computing technology.* Englewood Cliffs, N.J.: Prentice-Hall.

Donald D. Spencer

HUMAN RESOURCES, USE OF INFORMATION TECHNOLOGY IN

Extensive governmental regulatory compliance reporting requirements and increased demands of operating management for fast and easy access to information about their employees are driving forces behind the automation of human resources (HR) records. The need for automated HR systems clearly exists in any organization with more than fifty employees, but even smaller organizations may benefit from simple HR automation. As the size of the organization and its level of HR management sophistication increases, the need for automation of HR records also increases.

The HR information that is automated includes not only extensive biographical, skills, education, and experience information about current employees, but also the information needed to automate budgeting, manpower planning, and succession planning. This includes information covering not only current but also projected positions within the company. In addition, to meet staffing needs in the most cost-effective manner possible and to track affirmative action progress properly, it is also increasingly necessary to automate information about applicants for employment. Complexities in benefits and compensation administration and a wide range of social responsibility issues have also become factors in the need to automate.

Prior to the 1960s, organizations either relied on limited HR data contained in their automated payroll system or faced the challenge of recovering employee data from manually maintained personnel records. Advancements in computer hardware and software technology in the 1960s opened the door for automation of the full range of HR information.

The first HR systems commercially introduced in the mid-1960s were available for operation only on very large-scale, expensive mainframe computers. As a result, only large organizations could afford to automate their HR function. Since the 1960s technology has continued to advance and, today, that limit is no longer applicable. Not only are very powerful HR systems available on mainframes and midframe computers, but high-quality systems are also available on microcomputers. Human resource systems are now available on all hardware platforms to meet the full spectrum of organizational needs, budgetary limits, and levels of HR sophistication.

WHY ARE HUMAN RESOURCE SYSTEMS NECESSARY?

To understand why organizations need automated HR systems, it is necessary to review the types of tasks and activities that are performed in the personnel or human resources department. Over the past three decades, the personnel department has evolved from a role as a clerically oriented function having little impact on the organization into the new human resources department.

As part of this transition, HR responsibilities have expanded radically and, in most organizations, the HR function has evolved into a vital role as an essential and highly valuable member of management. Today, HR professionals not only participate in setting the strategic directions and plans for the enterprise, but also contribute in meaningful ways to the smooth functioning of the business. The range of HR activities is shown in Figure 1.

The expansion of HR activities and responsibilities has come about as a result of three primary causes:

1. Governmental compliance and reporting demands have increased.
2. Management's need for data on which to base planning, review, and control decisions has increased.
3. Employers' direct involvement and responsibility in employee relations and social responsibility matters has increased.

WHAT CHOICES ARE AVAILABLE IN HUMAN RESOURCE SYSTEMS?

In response to differing organizational needs, a wide range of automated HR systems are available that operate on differing hardware and operating systems, offering differing capabilities, features, and functionality to the user. But, regardless of the technological framework, HR systems generally fall into two primary categories: (1) integrated, full-capabilities systems and (2) standalone, special-purpose systems.

Integrated, full-capabilities systems cover all functional areas of human resources. These are commonly referred to as either HRIS (human resource information systems) or HRMS (human resource management systems). The two terms are essentially interchangeable and do not necessarily indicate greater or lesser capabilities. Because these systems are fully integrated, all information is shared and all users have immediate access to the most recently updated information.

Standalone, special-purpose systems are of a more limited scope, addressing needs in a single area or activity of the HR function. These systems may address a particular need such as job evaluation, benefits administration, attitude surveys, manpower planning, and organization charting. Because these systems operate independently of other systems and because there is not real-time sharing of data, regular updating must be performed on each system.

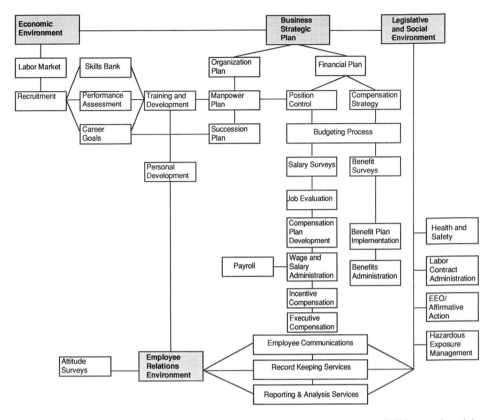

FIGURE 1. Overview of major human resource management responsibilities and activities.

WHAT PURPOSES DOES A FULLY INTEGRATED HUMAN RESOURCE INFORMATION SYSTEM ADDRESS?

As an organization grows, it becomes increasingly essential that key information about employees be shared and accessible to authorized individuals performing different tasks. The most productive and efficient way to achieve this degree of accessibility is through an integrated automated system. With the complexities of HR today, it is not reasonable or practical to rely on manual systems with pieces of paper flowing from place to place and from function to function as the means of notifying differing parts of the HR function of changes to employee records.

In large operations, most of the functions shown in Figure 1 will be performed by individuals and staffs in each specialty area. In organizations that are sensitive and responsive to their HR needs, an HRIS is used to help establish and manage compensation levels, benefits programs, training programs, and the other areas shown. A fully integrated HRIS provides assistance in each HR area. The extent to which the HR department is involved in each of these functional areas or activities varies depending on the size of the organization and its level of HR sophistication.

HOW DOES A HUMAN RESOURCE INFORMATION SYSTEM WORK?

An integrated HRIS consists of a database that contains all information about the employees of an organization. The various pieces of information about each employee are stored in specific files within the HRIS. These separate, but related, files are tied together by a data management system so that the user is able to access the desired information for the desired employees.

In an integrated HR system, each piece of information is entered only once. For example, an employee in the compensation section may be responsible for receiving, processing, and entering all changes in salary. Another employee in the benefits section may be responsible for reviewing all benefits enrollments and changes and for processing them into the system. In the training section, other employees may be responsible for approving and entering requests for enrollment in training classes or for reviewing and recording tuition reimbursement requests. Other individuals in the HR department might be responsible for entering basic information concerning newly hired employees. Once information is entered by the appropriate person or function, any authorized person requiring this information has access to it.

A typical processing of a newly hired person is an excellent example of why an integrated system is essential in a large organization. When a newly hired person arrives for work on the first day she or he is asked to complete a variety of forms. The information on the forms is then entered into the computer. When the employee arrives at the actual workplace within the department, her or his manager identifies specific training needs and calls the training department to enroll the new person in a particular class.

The training coordinator uses a computer terminal to call up the record of the new employee. The essential information that the training person needs about the new person —name, address, job function, and work location—is already in the system and is immediately displayed. The training person only needs to enter enrollment information for the desired class. Everything else is automatically available.

The new employee may also be eligible to eventually participate in certain medical or other insurance benefits after completing a required length of time with the company. When he or she contacts the benefits section to enroll in the desired benefits programs, the benefits administrator has immediate access to the needed information about the employee's age, date of hire, employment status, family status, home address, and other necessary information through the HRIS. A few keystrokes are all it takes to verify eligibility and enroll the employee in the desired benefit choices. Nearly all of the

needed information is accessed from the shared database.

Even after a person has been with the organization a long time, the importance of shared data continues. When a change is made to the person's job or rate of pay, that change may automatically result in changes in the amount of life insurance that a person has through the organization's fringe benefit programs. In an integrated system that change and other changes occur automatically and the life insurance benefit increases without any effort on the part of the employee or the benefits administrator.

As another example of how an HRIS can be used, a company has a critical position suddenly and unexpectedly become open. At the time the opening occurs, there is no candidate within that particular department who is properly qualified and ready to move into the position; however, as information about all employees is available in the company's HRIS, the executive with responsibility for that area is able to give the HR system administrator a summary of the desired qualifications and the administrator is able to easily conduct an automated search of the automated records of all employees, and is able to identify candidates who have the desired educational background, skills, experience, and other qualifications.

The aforementioned examples show how information about a person, once entered into an integrated HR system, can be readily shared by other *authorized* individuals.

SECURITY CONSIDERATIONS IN A HUMAN RESOURCE SYSTEM

The word *authorized* in the previous paragraph is important because security of data in an HR system is a major concern. Much of the information in an HRIS is sensitive and confidential. Therefore, access to data must be carefully controlled. All of the commercially available integrated HR systems, regardless of the hardware on which they operate, provide some level of security.

Though almost every system provides some level of security, there are many different approaches to how security is handled. In the more advanced systems, each user is assigned a specific security profile that enables her or him to see only specific fields within certain employee records and to access only designated segments of the data in the system.

A user may also have the ability to view ("read") only certain information and to update other selected information. For example, a person in the benefits section may be able to view information about an employee's job and department assignment, but is restricted from changing that information. He or she may be able to change only information concerning benefits enrollments.

WHAT INFORMATION IS INCLUDED IN AN INTEGRATED HUMAN RESOURCE INFORMATION SYSTEM AND HOW IS THAT INFORMATION USED?

The amount of information maintained in different systems varies substantially. A basic level HRIS may contain fewer than 100 fields of data on an employee. At the other extreme, a full-featured HRIS may enable users to maintain several thousand fields of information about a person.

Nearly all HR systems allow the user to maintain basic biographical information on each employee. This includes such information as name, address, date of birth, date of hire, and basic job and pay information. Increasingly comprehensive systems offer expanded capabilities and provide users with the ability to include data on education, work experience, performance ratings, skills, qualifications, special training, medical history information, and family and dependent information as well as career goal and career path information.

The amount of information that an HRIS is capable of maintaining varies greatly in each of the following areas:

- Biographical and administrative information
- Compensation information
- Benefits administration data
- Training and development planning information
- Organizational planning information
- Performance and skills tracking
- Career path planning
- Productivity measurement
- Modeling and forecasting
- Business planning
- Graphical presentation of data (charts and graphs)
- Organization charts

In addition, systems offer different historical tracking capabilities. In some basic-level systems, historical records for each person may cover only the most recent two or three changes in position within the organization, rates of pay, or performance ratings. The more powerful HR systems are capable of storing a complete history of all events, changes, and actions.

STANDALONE SPECIAL FUNCTION SYSTEMS IN HUMAN RESOURCES

In addition to the fully integrated systems described in the preceding section, certain types of HR information may be effectively maintained in separate, specialized systems. A variety of such systems are used in HR management to address focused, narrow subject area information and reporting and analysis needs. For example, a special-function system may be used to track only applicant information or job evaluation information.

In these instances, there is usually minimal need for access to "up-to-the-minute" information from other sources. When there are needs for information from another system it is normally easy to "import" the desired information periodically into the standalone special-function system. For example, in a standalone job evaluation system, the listing of job codes and job descriptions could be "imported" electronically into the system periodically or entered manually and then the details of the evaluation of each job would be maintained as evaluations occur.

Standalone systems have achieved particularly wide usage in applicant management. As skilled labor shortages continue to develop, and as the cost of recruiting continues to increase, it is essential that organizations be able to identify, quickly, easily, and effectively, existing internal and external applicants who possess the needed skills. Applicant management systems, or applicant tracking systems, provide an easy solution by allowing basic information on applicants to be stored in a system. An applicant system allows educational information, work experience, job skills, salary requirements, and other qualifications to be entered and quickly searched for desired qualifications as openings occur.

Specialized standalone systems may also be helpful in meeting special governmental reporting and compliance needs. For example, in preparing or updating an equal opportunity affirmative action plan, it is necessary to relate internal statistical information with external census information concerning the availability of minorities in the local population. A standalone affirmative action program can be very well used in such circumstances.

USE OF HUMAN RESOURCE SYSTEMS IN THE INTERNATIONAL OR TRANSNATIONAL ORGANIZATION

Human resource systems are currently in use throughout the world. Many data elements such as name, address, birth date, and birth place are commonly maintained regardless of national environment, although the language used on the screens and as column headings in reports or the currency in which the person's compensation is expressed vary significantly. Translation of screen prompts, field names, and report headings meets these needs.

Similarly, job titles vary from country to country as do benefit types, pay levels and frequencies, currencies of payment, and other aspects such as benefits administration. Systems can readily handle these variations. Several major HRIS vendors offer locally appropriate versions of their systems in the major countries of the world.

When operating on an international level, it is necessary at times to be able to consolidate certain information from all locations. Whether the consolidation includes information from divisions, plants, or regional offices in the home country or whether it involves information from company sites in other countries, HR systems provide the answer. This type of data exchange and consolidation throughout worldwide operations of a company is now performed on a routine basis by users of some of the leading commercially available HR systems.

WHAT ARE HUMAN RESOURCE SYSTEM ALTERNATIVES?

A quality-integrated HR system is a sizable and complex system, often as large or larger than an accounting or manufacturing planning system. Because of this size and complexity, it is not realistic for most organizations to develop their own system. Fortunately, organizations needing an HR system have a wide variety of alternatives available. Quality systems, proven in hundreds or thousands of organizations, are commercially available. These systems operate on hardware configurations from personal computers to midframes to mainframes. The choice of hardware platform is usually determined by a combination of organizational size and complexity, available budget, the organization's computing strategic direction and philosophy, and the desired implementation time frame.

Alternatives also exist in the software and programming environment of systems. Although many early HR systems were written in programming languages such as COBOL, since the 1980s most systems have been developed using generally available and well-accepted databases and relational database software.

WHO CONTROLS THE HUMAN RESOURCE SYSTEM AND WHO ARE THE USERS?

Early HR systems were focused, to a major extent, on essential payroll and basic bio-demographic information. Because of their hard-coded structure, these early systems were controlled by programmers. End users simply interacted with screens for data entry and received printed output reports from a standard library of available hard-coded reports. Once the listing style report was received by the HR department, the data were reformatted by the HR specialist and forwarded in other forms to the line management end user.

With the evolution of high-level, easy-to-use, relational systems and reporting tools, many organizations are putting control of their HR system into the hands of the HR end user. Some provide line managers with direct access to selected information on their employees. This major step enables line managers to conduct modeling, reporting, and analysis without need for HR or programming support.

HUMAN RESOURCE SYSTEM ADMINISTRATOR

The evolution of HR systems using higher-level languages and database systems and the corresponding increase in end-user access and control have put responsibility for implementation, maintenance, and operation of the HR system in the position of the HR system administrator in the HR department. The system administrator not only controls the system's overall operation, but also provides the focal point for all requests for modification and customization. In addition, the administrator manages the security aspects of the system, ensures that the system is properly and regularly backed up, and provides support and training to the actual end users.

For Further Reading

Advanced Personnel Systems, P.O. Box 1438, Roseville, CA 95661; (916) 781-2900. *The Personnel Software Census,* 1989; *Microcomputers in Human Resource Management,* 1990, annual.

American Management Association, 135 W. 50th Street, New York, NY 10020; (212) 586-8100. 1990 Directory of Human Resource Services, Products, and Suppliers; *Personnel* (annual).

Association of HRSP, P.O. Box 8040-8202, Walnut Creek, CA 94596; *Survey of Human Resource Systems,* 1987.

Bartol, K. M. 1987. Making compensation pay. *Computers in Personnel,* Winter, pp. 35–40.

Cerello, V. 1984. Computerizing the personnel department: How do you choose a vendor? *Personnel Journal,* December, pp. 33–38.

———. 1984. Computerizing the personnel department: Make or buy? *Personnel Journal* 63:47–48.

———. 1991. *Human resource management systems.* Lexington, Mass.: Lexington Books.

Dyer, L. D. 1982. Human resource planning. In K. M. Rowland and G. R. Ferris, eds. *Personnel management,* pp. 52–77. Boston, Mass.: Allyn & Bacon.

Frantzreb, R. 1988. *The personnel software census.* Roseville, Calif.: Advanced Personnel Systems.

HRMagazine (formerly *Personnel Administrator*), Reprint Services, P.O. Box 1183, Minneapolis, MN 55458; (612) 633-1214. *The microcomputer-based HRIS: A directory,* December 1987.

Human Resource Executive, 747 Dresher Road, P.O. Box 980, Horsham, PA 19044-0980; (212) 784-0860. "1988 HRIS Buyers' Guide," October 1988; "What's Hot in Specialty Software," April 1989; "Specialty Software Buyers' Guide," April 1989.

Kavanagh, M. J., H. G. Gueutal, and S. I. Tannenbaum. 1990. *Human resource information systems: Development and application.* Boston, Mass.: PWS-KENT.

Magnus, M., and M. Grossman. 1985. Computers and the personnel department. *Personnel Journal,* April, pp. 42–48.

Mathys, N. J., H. LaVan, and G. Nogal. 1984. Issues in purchasing and implementing HRIS Software. *Personnel Administrator,* August, p. 92.

Personnel Journal, 245 Fischer Avenue, No. B2, Costa Mesa, CA 92626; (714) 751-1883. "HRIS Software Buyer's Guide," April 1989.

Schmiedicke, R. J. 1987. Keep it simple. *Computers in Personnel,* Spring, pp. 45–47.

VCR Consulting Group, 289 S. San Antonio Road, Los Altos, CA 94022; (415) 948-

1513. *Microcomputer applications for HRMS: A comparative analysis,* April 1990. Directory produced on a semiannual basis.

Walker, A. J. 1980. A brief history of the computer in personnel. *Personnel Journal* 16:33–36.

———. 1982. *HRIS development: A project team guide to building an effective personnel system.* New York: Van Nostrand Reinhold.

———. 1991. Human resource systems—A milestone reached. *The Review* 7(2):8–12.

James E. Spoor

HYPERCARD

See Authoring Languages, Systems, and Environments; Hypermedia

HYPERMEDIA

Hypermedia refers to an extension of hypertext (see HYPERTEXT) that can add graphics, sound, video, music, animation, and synthesized voice to the capabilities of hypertext. In a hypertext system, links are made from words or phrases of text in one document to related text in another document. In a hypermedia system, however, links may include not only text but also graphics, images, sounds, or full-motion video. With hypermedia, the user is free to pursue associated ideas in the program by branching to related or supplementary materials in a variety of formats in nonlinear ways. If this article were presented in hypermedia format on the computer, for example, clicking the computer's mouse on the word "hypermedia" could link the user to a digitized speech file containing a recording of the word, and the reader would then hear the word pronounced via a speaker or speech attachment connected to the computer. In another example, the user of a hypermedia version of this article could click on a word and see a picture, a video sequence, a map, line drawing, cartoon, or any related information about hypermedia that could be digitized. Hypermedia programs can also be used to access and control such peripheral devices as compact-disk read-only memory (CD-ROM) drives, audio compact disc players, and laser videodisc players.

HISTORY OF HYPERMEDIA

Vannevar Bush was among the first to conceive of using a machine to provide connections among several pieces of information. In 1945 he looked forward to a time when computers could make all the numbers, words, sounds, visuals, and records accessible randomly and quickly. His vision was called "memex," and although it was never developed, it provided the basis for hypermedia. In the 1950s Douglas Engelbart built the first practical hypertext system, although the term "hypertext" was not used until coined by Ted Nelson in the 1960s. In the 1970s the Xerox Palo Alto Research Center (PARC) developed and tested Dynabook under the leadership of Alan Kay. The Dynabook prototypes combined interactive graphics, object-oriented programming, interactive text editing with a mouse, and elements of hypermedia. Additional work during the 1970s and 1980s included linking not only text but also graphics, sounds, video sequences, and photographs. With the inclusion of a variety of formats, the term *hypertext* became a misnomer, and the term *hypermedia* was applied to such applications.

The introduction of Apple's Macintosh computer and its use of graphics, a mouse, consistent user interface, and direct-manipulation metaphors provided impetus for further exploration of hypermedia concepts. In the late 1980s HyperCard by Bill Atkinson, the first hypermedia program for personal computers, was introduced. This was quickly followed by similar applications for other environments, including Owl International's Guide, IBM's Linkway, Asymetrix's ToolBox, TechWare's TutorTech, and Silicon Press's SuperCard.

APPLICATIONS OF HYPERMEDIA

Thousands of commercially available freeware and shareware applications are available that run under one or more of the hypermedia programs mentioned. Although each product has its own unique features and terminology, there are common elements. Each screen is a page or card. Pages or cards may contain objects such as graphics, fields that contain text, and buttons that initiate action and provide the links between pieces of information regardless of the format. Cards, fields, and buttons may have scripts, written in an appropriate programming language, that control the action on the screen as well as the links. For example, HyperTalk is the scripting language for HyperCard, and OpenScript is the scripting language for ToolBox. These scripts also provide controls for laser videodiscs and other peripheral devices. Although use of a scripting language may enhance hypermedia programs, most hypermedia applications are easy to use and are based on a "point and click" system using the computer's mouse. Pointing and clicking will not only link the information but also will automatically create a simple script to do so. A group of related pages or cards becomes a stack or a folder, and these stacks or folders may be linked to one another or to specific pages, cards, or buttons. The creation and importation of graphics is an integral part of all the systems. Hypermedia programs may be used to run applications created by others, or may be used to create applications for the user or for others.

Applications in Education

One of the earliest applications of hypermedia for education was the Grapevine Project in California. A school library media specialist and a classroom teacher used HyperCard to organize and access information about the Depression. The materials linked in the project included moving pictures and photographs recorded on a laser disk, sound recordings, voice narration, fiction written during and about the 1930s, essays, poems, and nonfiction materials. The database was useful to teachers in a variety of disciplines, and both teachers and students could access information and add materials to the database. The Intermedia Project at Brown University included drawings, photographs, portraits, paintings, and three-dimensional models as well as text.

Hypermedia packages available commercially include a number of combinations of media formats. A hypermedia program may contain text, sound, and picture files on a computer disk. Clicking a mouse on a word in the text of one program may provide an illustration for further study. Clicking the mouse on various parts of a picture may show labels for the parts, an explanation of each part, or the audible pronunciation of the name of the part in Spanish, French, or Italian. *Compton's Multimedia Encyclopedia* includes hypermedia buttons that provide access to audio, animation, photographs, and related text.

Hypermedia packages may include laser disks as well. For example, one hypermedia program about Beethoven contains HyperCard stacks and an audio compact disc recording of Beethoven's *Ninth Symphony*. Using the HyperCard program, one student may watch the score on the computer screen while listening to the entire symphony. Another student may choose to listen to specific movements selected from a menu on the computer screen. A third student may choose to read about Beethoven's life and times with segments of the audio used to augment and clarify the text. Other students may use the program in different ways.

Hypermedia programs provide access to visual databases as well as to text. A hypermedia biology package will let a student or teacher select by kingdom, class, phylum, species, or common name from over 50,000 slides stored on a videodisc. The user can save a list of slides selected in a computer file, then use the file to recall and project the images to accompany a lesson or a report at a later date. Another stack provides access to thousands of paintings, sculptures, drawings, and prints in the collections of the National Gallery of Art through the National Gallery videodisc. The user can browse through the gallery or search for a specific style, artist, or period of time. Other currently available hypermedia programs allow students to relive historical events such as a presidential election, the life and works of Martin Luther King, Jr., or recent events in the Holy Land. Some information is contained in the computer program itself, including text, maps, and drawings; other information is provided through links to video sequences and stills on the videodisc. These programs also allow users to combine text and images into a documentary they write and produce themselves, using special features of the hypermedia program.

Hypermedia programs are changing the way information is stored and retrieved. Current hypermedia application programs are easy to learn and to use. They require little or no programming experience. Students, teachers, and researchers can use the programs to create or modify applications and databases. Hypermedia programs can be used by teachers to create lessons, integrating text, sound, and images. They can also be used by students to create electronic, multimedia term papers. Visuals can be created within the program or imported from painting or drawing programs. Images can be digitized or scanned, or computer clip art can be used. Hypermedia programs can also be used to repurpose CD-ROMs, videodiscs, and audio discs.

For Further Reading

Ambron, S., and K. Hooper, eds. 1988. *Interactive multimedia: Visions of multimedia for developers, educators, and information providers*. Redmond, Wash.: Microsoft.

Bush, V. 1945. As we may think. *Atlantic Monthly* 176(1):101–8.

Flynn, L. 1987. HyperCard steals show at Macworld Exposition. *InfoWorld* 9(33):1+.

Goodman, D. 1987. *The complete HyperCard handbook*. New York: Bantam.

Harrington, R., B. Fancher, and P. Black. 1990. *IBM Linkway: Hypermedia for the PC*. New York: Wiley.

Marchionini, G. 1988. Hypermedia and learning: Freedom and chaos. *Educational Technology* 28(11):8–12.

Ofiesh, G. 1986. The seamless carpet of knowledge and learning. In S. Lambert and S. Ropiequet, eds. *CD-ROM: The new papyrus*, pp. 299–319. Redmond, Wash.: Microsoft.

Young, J. 1986. Hypermedia. *MacWorld* 3(3): 116–21.

Donna Baumbach

HYPERTEXT

Hypertext refers to the dynamic linking of concepts or chunks of information in one document to related concepts or chunks in other documents, with the reader controlling movement through the written material. (See Figure 1.) With hypertext, the reader is free to pursue associated thoughts and ideas in the text by branching to related or supplementary materials. In traditional sequential text such as a book, this is attempted through indexes, footnotes, margin comments, and references, each a crude hypertext model. Index cards or note cards that reference other note cards and are arranged sequentially or hierarchically are another primitive model of hypertext.

Computers have made the concept of hypertext a reality. For example, if this encyclopedia were presented in hypertext on a computer, one could select any term or reference by clicking on it with the computer's mouse, and a related article would appear in a window on the computer screen. In addition, any term or reference in the related text could be selected in the same manner, and another window with another related article would appear. Users can also use hypertext to make annotations or comments linked to the original text; these may be accessed by future users. A keystroke or click of the mouse allows the reader to return to the point in the original text where the branching occurred, although the reader may not return at all, continuing to read the related materials. Through hypertext, each reader can create a unique path through text materials.

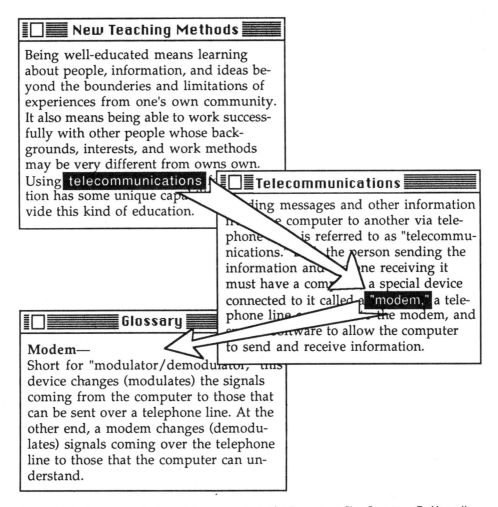

FIGURE 1. A representation of the operation of a hypertext file. *Courtesy R. Norvelle.*

HISTORY OF HYPERTEXT

In 1945 Vannevar Bush, director of the White House Office of Scientific Research under President Roosevelt, was concerned with information overload in the government. It was Bush who first described a tool for linking pieces of information. Bush's "memex" was never actually developed, but he is credited as the first to conceive of using the computer to make and store connections between pieces of information and to make the links accessible with speed and flexibility. In the 1950s and 1960s Douglas Engelbart, influenced by Bush, pioneered a system called NLS (oNLine System), which utilized many hypertext concepts. Engelbart's research group designed and demonstrated the first

mouse, and he conceived the notion of screen windows. Utilizing these innovations, Engelbart built the first practical hypertext system.

Visionary Ted Nelson coined the term "hypertext" in the 1960s to describe a "non-sequential piece of writing" that "only the computer display makes practical." He also described "fresh" or original hypertext; "anthological" hypertext, composed from a variety of sources; and "grand" hypertext, a collection of everything known on a topic. According to Nelson, the document is the fundamental unit of hypertext. Superdocuments are created when links between documents are created, and when documents become highly interconnected, we approach a "docuverse." Nelson began to develop

Xanadu, a computer system that would link large bodies of information and record associated thoughts for future users. Nelson worked with Andy van Dam at Brown University to design the File Retrieval and Editing System (FRESS), a hypertext system used by Brown students for document preparation. Additional work during the 1970s and 1980s included linking not only text but also graphics, sounds, video sequences, and photographs. The term *hypermedia* was applied to such applications.

APPLICATIONS OF HYPERTEXT

Several commercial hypertext programs are available to assist in authoring and managing hypertext documents on desktop computers. These programs include Apple's HyperCard, Owl International's Guide, IBM's Linkway, Asymetrix's ToolBox, TechWare's TutorTech, and Silicon Press's SuperCard. (These programs are actually hypermedia programs, but they can manage text-only applications as well.) In addition, thousands of commercially available, public-domain, and shareware applications are available that run under one or more of these programs. Although each product has its own unique features and terminology, there are common elements. Each screen is a page or card. Pages or cards may contain objects such as fields that contain text, and buttons that initiate action and provide the links between the chunks of information. Cards, fields, and buttons may have scripts, written in an appropriate programming language, that control the action on the screen as well as the links. A group of related pages or cards become a stack or a folder, and these stacks or folders may be linked to one another or to specific pages, cards, or buttons.

Applications in Education

One of the largest research projects utilizing hypertext in education has been the Intermedia Project at Brown University. The Intermedia Project built on decades of hypertext work at Brown. The Institute for Research in Information and Scholarship (IRIS) at Brown began work with Intermedia in 1985 in an effort to assist the academic community at Brown in teaching, learning, and research through hypertext. Intermedia provides instructors with a way to organize and present their courses via computer; it also gives students an interactive medium to study the materials and add their own reports and comments. Running on a network of IBM RT/PCs using the UNIX operating system and Sun workstations that support Sun's Network File System, two courses were initially developed: Plant Cell Biology, and English Literature from 1700 to the Present. Students explore these databases for their reading and research assignments and may contribute notes and comments that remain part of the databases as well.

In Project Jefferson at the University of Southern California, students in freshman writing courses are able to link technical information, library searches, and computer-assisted instruction with literature, the humanities, and instructors' notes and comments. The system requires little training time for students and, although powerful, is easy to use.

Today's compact-disk read-only memory (CD-ROM) encyclopedias used in elementary and secondary schools commonly employ hypertext features to link information between or among articles. Grolier's *New Electronic Encyclopedia*'s articles contain highlighted ''link words.'' Placing the cursor on one of the link words and pushing Enter on the computer keyboard will open the referenced material in an active window, allowing other windows to remain in view to show the path of inquiry. *World Book*'s *Information Finder* uses hypertext to link words in the text of the encyclopedia articles to their dictionary definitions. A click of the mouse over a word in question will make the dictionary entry appear in a windowed overlay.

Hypertext applications can facilitate the retrieval and exchange of information, allowing users to query, browse, link, and create related pieces of information. Using hypertext, students and researchers can access needed information without physically locating indices, volumes, notes, references, glossaries, and articles. Recent developments in hypertext applications, such as those listed above, make it possible for teachers and students to create their own hypertext documents to assist in teaching and in learning.

CRITICISMS OF HYPERTEXT

With the increased use of hypertext, developers face several issues. There is some concern that readers who are familiar with traditional text sources can easily become lost in their own links while navigating through documents. Some programs provide a chronological listing of paths taken so that steps may be retraced; other applications provide visual maps of all the links possible in a hypertext document. Another concern is related to this disorientation, and it concerns cognitive overload. Articles contain many links that can be followed, and each link leads to more links; the amount of information available, though easily accessed, may be overwhelming to the reader. Finally, standards and compatibility among hypertext systems must be addressed.

For Further Reading

Bevilacqua, A. 1989. Hypertext: Behind the hype. *American Libraries* 20(2):158–62.

Bush, V. 1945. As we may think. *Atlantic Monthly* 176(1):101–8.

Conklin, J. 1987. Hypertext: An introduction and survey. *Computer* 20(9):17–41.

Engelbart, D. 1963. A conceptual framework for the augmentation of man's intellect. In P. W. Howerton and D. C. Weeks, eds. *Vistas in information handling, Vol. 1: The augmentation of man's intellect by machine,* pp. 1–29. Washington, D.C.: Spartan Books.

Karon, P. 1987. The Xanadu project: A new era in publishing. *PC Week* 4(40):60.

Manes, S. 1987. Hypertext: A breath of air freshener. *PC Magazine* 6(11):91+.

Nelson, T. H. 1980. Replacing the printed word: A complete literary system. In S. H. Lavington, ed. *Information processing 80,* pp. 1013–23. New York: North-Holland.

———. 1982. A new home for the mind. *Datamation* 28(3):169–80.

———. 1986. The tyranny of the file. *Datamation* 32(24):83–84+.

———. 1987. *Computer lib: You can and must understand computers now!* Redmond, Wash.: Microsoft.

Yankelovich, N., N. Meyrowitz, and A. Van Dam. 1985. Reading and writing the electronic book. *Computer* 18(10):15–30.

Donna Baumbach

ICONS

An icon is a small picture or image that appears on a computer monitor to represent an application, file, or command. For example, a picture of a file folder could represent a filing or storage location on the computer that can be accessed simply by clicking a mouse-controlled screen pointer at that spot. Several examples of icons are shown in Figure 1. Icons, when used properly, can increase the user friendliness of a computer system or application by offering an alternative to typing in textlike commands at the keyboard.

The development of the icon was a complex process that took 30 years of combined research and development efforts of engineers, computer scientists, and research organizations. Each of these groups cooperated (and competed) with one another to make the iconic user interface a practical system. In the 1970s Xerox Corporation's Palo Alto Research Center (PARC) was the center for the development and refinement of various computer user interfaces, one of which was the iconic user interface. PARC also researched and expanded windows, mice, and menus.

In 1973, the research center pioneered the development of the Alto computer and, later, the Star computer, a model that resulted from the refinement of the Alto (Perry 1989). These two computers, which were instrumental in research and experimentation on iconic interfaces and which forged the trail for hundreds of early computer pioneers, were forerunners of the highly successful, low-cost Macintosh computers produced by Apple Computer in 1984. During the mid-1980s the price of random-access memory (RAM) chips fell while the storage capabilities of computers increased, which allowed for the economical implementation of iconic computer interfaces requiring complex graphics (Roe 1990). Using icons, Macintosh brought user friendliness to the personal computer market economically.

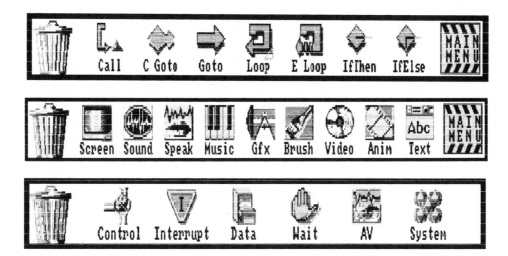

FIGURE 1. Icon examples.

THE EARLY YEARS

Although icons began in the late 1960s, they were not defined or actively investigated until the 1970s. The Flex computer, which was built in 1967 at the University of Utah by Alan Kay and Ed Cheadle (Perry 1989), had boxes on the screen to represent programs and data. Although these boxes were rudimentary and cumbersome, they did lay the groundwork for future computer icons. The Sketchpad, an application program for the Alto, used on-screen graphic objects to represent rules and restraints for the Sketchpad system (Perry 1989). The Flex and the Sketchpad were the grandfathers of the iconic interfaces of the late 1980s.

The first research into the uses of on-screen graphic representation of computer applications and functions was completed by David Canfield Smith in 1973 for a doctoral thesis at the suggestion of his academic advisor, Alan Kay. Kay suggested that Smith look into the powers of the Alto computer as a tool to increase programmer efficiency (Perry 1989). Smith called the on-screen tools *icons*, a term he borrowed from the Russian Orthodox Church (Perry 1985).

The Russian Orthodox Church considers an icon, a picture or artistic rendering of a saint, to be holy and powerful. As Smith's icons represented functions and uses of a computer, contained all the properties of a program, and could be linked and acted on as if they were real programs or data (Perry 1989), Smith felt that they paralleled the icons of the Russian Church.

After receiving his Ph.D. in 1975, Smith joined Xerox and began converting his ideas about icons from the Alto to the Star. One conversion was to redefine his idea of icons in office terms. Smith stated, "I looked around my office and saw papers, folders, file cabinets, a telephone and bookshelves, and it was an easy conversion to icons" (Perry 1989, p. 50). Thus, Smith modeled the appearance of his icons on images of file folders and other office equipment, such as a file cabinet to symbolize a storage area in the computer.

Although early icon research was fueled by scientific curiosity, the later research was driven by the huge demand for a user-friendly computer; however, some early efforts at user friendliness were misguided. Elizabeth R. Regan of Massachusetts Life Insurance Company stated, "We did things like try to personify programs so that communicating with the machine was like having a conversation. Users were greeted by things like, 'Good morning, I am your user friendly computer. I am easy to use and I will lead you step by step in how to use me." (Yovovich 1990). This user friendliness in the interface was annoying to many computer users and only reinforced many people's idea that computers would replace the user (Yovovich 1990). Because of the confusion over user friendliness, icon researchers were called on to create an interface that would be simple to use, but not demeaning or patronizing to the user. They discovered that combining text with graphics was far superior for training purposes (Jeffries 1990) and they began to direct their efforts toward using text and graphics to enhance iconic interfaces.

TECHNICAL RESEARCH CENTER

Xerox developers tested and researched various applications and design problems for iconic interfaces. At first, the tendency was to make icons detailed and precise, similar to a photograph of the object (Perry 1989). After 3 years of research Xerox reached several conclusions, one of which was "make it simple." The researchers found that detailed icons were not as effective, were harder to create, and were not as easily understood as simple, concise icons.

Xerox also decided on standards for both the visual size and the memory size of icons. The early developers used a 16-bit (64 × 64-pixel) representation for icons that left a ragged right margin. To make the icons more visually appealing, the icon size was increased to 64 × 65 pixels; however, the programmers did not immediately appreciate the change in icon size because the 16-bit representation was easier to program. Xerox added more "white space" to the icons to improve appearance, and this alleviated many of the complaints about icon memory size (Perry 1989).

Before reaching the final design of the icons, Xerox compared the ideas of two graphics designers and two software engineers. Xerox had previously attempted to develop a self-explanatory appearance for the icons on the Star, but they met with little success. Eventually, an outside graphics designer, Norman Cox, was employed to redesign the appearance of icons for the Star (Perry 1989).

RESEARCH IN THE 1980s

Icon designers of the 1980s struggled to make icons transferable between different computer systems; various problems were involved. Each system might display an icon in a different size, color, or various shades of gray.

Color became a controversial subject in the mid-1980s. The tendency was to overuse color, which resulted in a jumble of multiple colors that distracted the user and blurred the meaning of an icon. For example, an icon with too much red could be interpreted as dangerous or something to be avoided. To avoid costly mistakes, it was important to test the impact of different forms and symbols on different groups (Feucht 1989). Because it took more time for a programmer to design and program an icon if multiple colors were used, computer manufacturers felt that the increased time and cost for color icons could not be justified in the final cost for the system.

The end of the 1980s resulted in an additional challenge for icon designers: internationalization. The icons that were in use did not allow for the longer words or the vertical orientation of many foreign languages and color was still a design factor. Although the color white is generally used to symbolize "good" in the American culture, in most Oriental cultures, white is used to symbolize death and evil. Conflicts like this had to be resolved.

SUMMARY

The road to the development of the iconic interface was both intriguing and frustrating. In the early years, icons were so revolutionary that entire systems were built with the expansion of icons as their primary goal. As the knowledge about icons grew, so did their uses. In the mid-1980s Apple brought user friendliness to thousands of computer users by implementing icons as part of their standard user interface. Since that time, other computer manufacturers have created their own interfaces using icons as their centerpiece. The road to the iconic interface of the future still lies largely unexplored, but the researchers and developers of the past have given us the passport to the twenty-first century: icons.

References

Feucht, F. N. 1989. It's symbolic. *American Demographics* 13(122):30–33.

Jeffries, R. 1990. Real world graphics. *CBT* 12(2):17–21.

Perry, T. S. 1989. Of mice and menus: Designing the user friendly interface. *IEEE Spectrum* 25(9):46–51.

Roe, S. 1990. VLSI predict the future of computer graphics. *Computer Graphics Review* 18(6):44–46.

Yovovich, B. G. 1990. Easy street. *CIO* 5(6):64–71.

For Further Reading

Anderson, B. 1988. Making sense of multimedia. *Computer Graphics Review* 5(12):7+. Points out that systems that meld video, sound, computer graphics, and scanned images place formidable demands on the hardware and people that can create these complex systems.

Cornish, M. 1990. Four principles of user interface design. *Computer Languages* 7:67–70. Offers some steps to follow to ensure that today's design decisions do not drag down tomorrow's applications.

Curtis, B. 1990. Engineering computer "look and feel": User interface technology and human factors engineering. *Jurimetrics* 30(13):51–78. Presents the developmental history of user interface design and the human factors engineering on which it is based.

Hoadley, E. D. 1990. Investigating the effects of color. *Communications of the ACM*

33(120):5+. Looks at laboratory experiments that study the effects of color on a decision maker's ability to extract information from different graphical and tabular presentations. Thirty references.

Marsan, C. D. 1990. Graphical user interfaces. *Federal Computer Week* 4(14):6+. Tells why many federal users are selecting graphical user interfaces for government systems.

1990 Directory and Resource Issue. 1989. *Computer Graphics Review* 4(56). Presents an ongoing database of computer graphics companies and products including hardware, software, and services relating to computer graphics applications.

Sutcliffe, A. 1989. *Human computer interface design.* New York: Springer-Verlag. Describes general guidelines for the development of software with good human–computer interface, including concepts from psychology and structured systems.

Wadland, K. R. 1990. Graphical user interfaces: A window to the future. *Computer Graphics Review* 5(14):36–40. Presents an analysis of graphical user interfaces other than Apple's and Microsoft Windows.

Ken Brumbaugh

IMAGE PROCESSING

The age-old Chinese proverb "A picture is worth a thousand words" summarizes the motivation for undertaking the study and development of computer systems for processing imagery: The amount of information conveyed in visual data is prodigious. The processing of visual data has two complementary aspects. One treats the visual data as an input with the goal of extracting new information from the data, that is, image processing (Rosenfeld and Kak 1982), our primary concern here. The second treats the visual data as output with the goal of conveying prior information (stored in arbitrary data structures) to a user through image displays, that is, computer graphics (Foley and van Dam 1989). The intent, therefore, of building image processing systems is to provide general computer systems with practical and effective *access* to the enormous quantity of information available in visual data.

Let us look first at the usual form of the raw visual data. Taking photographic cameras as the archetype, visual data are considered to be arranged on a plane, the image plane. For digital systems the arrangement is specified most often to be a rectilinear grid, a checkerboard of picture elements called *pixels.* The grid can be directly stored in a two-dimensional array or a frame buffer, and as such corresponds to the image data structure used in computer graphics systems and referred to as the normalized device coordinate system.

The data encoded at each pixel are an aggregate measure of the radiant energy projected from a volume of the three-dimensional environment onto the pixel (Horn 1986). The shape of the volume is determined by the area of the pixel in the image plane and the projection scheme. For example, with a square pixel area under perspective projection, the volume is a skewed pyramid having the apex at the projection point and the four edges extending indefinitely in the direction away from the image plane.

The type of radiant energy detected and the form of the aggregate measure yielding the pixel data are determined by the sensor mechanism in the image plane. A standard video camera has a photosensitive semiconductor sensor that, for each pixel, integrates the total energy over the visible and near-visible wavelengths—for example, over the range of 350 to 750 nanometers. The integrated value represents the total light intensity irradiating the pixel area and is usually quantized for digital storage to 8 bits—that is, as a nonnegative integer in the range of 0 to 255.

For color imagery each pixel encodes a three-component value. Numerous different encodings have been developed, with the most straightforward being red-green-blue (RGB). As with the video intensity, each RGB component is an integrated energy value, but the wavelength ranges are more restricted (e.g., R:500 to 700, G:450 to 640, B:380 to 520) (Wyszecki and Stiles 1967). Some applications extend the concept of multicomponent pixels by increasing both the number of components and the wavelength range. For example, LANDSAT imagery has four bands—a red and a green component plus two infrared (above 700 nanometers) components [Gonzalez and Wintz 1987, p. 269]—while some sensor systems have as many as twenty bands.

Thus the basic input data structure can be considered to be a two-dimensional array, $P(i,j)$, where i and j are the image coordinates in the spatial domain. Note that alternative image structures have been considered (Samet 1990), including nonrectangular pixels (e.g., a hexagonal array was used in an early commercial system [Golay 1969]), variable arrays (e.g., the log-spiral array motivated by the varying density of photoreceptors in the retina of the human eye [Levine 1985, pp. 71–81]), and hierarchical imagery (e.g., quad trees and image pyramids [Bell et al. 1983]). For our discussion here, however, we will consider the square array image structure, and in the following sections we will discuss techniques that result in more and more abstract output—output progressing from direct images through to detailed semantic structures. As the output of a system becomes more abstract it is more likely to be called a computer vision system (Ballard and Brown 1982).

IMAGE TRANSFORMS

Figure 1 shows a general system configuration for what is often referred to as low-level image processing. The adjective form "low-level" does not imply any lack of power or importance to the processing but relates to the degree of semantic information required or assumed in the processing. A low-level image processing system typically takes images as input and yields images as output—that is, performs image transformations (Gonzalez and Wintz 1987)—and rarely in the processing are the data considered to be more than arrays of numbers. Note that

these systems join with computer graphics because the goal is almost always to create images that better convey certain information to a user.

Some of the most widely known applications of image transformation are with regard to satellite and space exploration imagery (Landgrebe 1981). For example, a process called contrast stretching (Rosenfeld and Kak 1982, vol. 1, p. 233) is a common image enhancement. The effect is to transform dull, rather fuzzy images into apparently sharper and more vivid images. Consider P, a small black-and-white image, a 20×20 array of 4-bit pixels, for which the values in P happen to range only from 3 to 10. There are several definitions of "contrast," and here it is taken to mean the maximum difference in intensity for any pair of pixels in the image. This contrast in P is 7. A convenient way to show the intensity range is via a plot called a histogram. In a histogram the abscissa is the range of possible pixel values (e.g., 0 to 15 for 4-bit pixels), while the ordinate is the frequency of the given intensity, the number of pixels in the image that have the specified pixel value. Figure 2A displays a possible histogram for the image P and shows that the low and high intensity values are not present in P. The contrast in P could be increased by transforming P into P' using the mapping shown in Figure 2B so that P' has the histogram displayed in Figure 2C and has a contrast of 15.

One of the most common applications of image transformation is coding images for transfer and storage (Rosenfeld and Kak 1982, Horn 1986). The codes are not selected for security in the sense of encryption; rather they are chosen to reduce the total number of bits required to represent the image. Thus this sort of coding is often referred to as compression. Figure 3 displays a general process diagram, with the central rectangle representing an image transfer (e.g., communication from a remote site) or long-term storage (e.g., digital photograph archives).

Compression techniques are called lossless and lossful, the former indicating that the exact pixel values can be determined by the decoder, and the latter indicating that error may be made by the decoder. Errors may be tolerable in order to increase the

FIGURE 1. General image processing scheme.

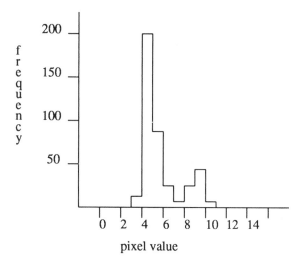

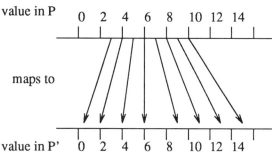

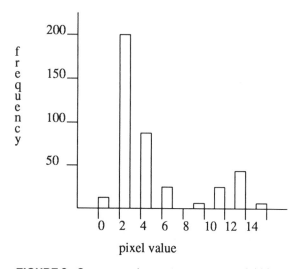

FIGURE 2. Contrast enhancement process: (**a**) histogram of original image; (**b**) pixel mapping; and (**c**) histogram of resulting image.

compression ratio—the ratio of the number of bits of the original to the encoded form—for applications in which only large features in the final image are important. For example, if one transfers an image of a signboard having large block characters, numerous pixels can be received incorrectly with the words still being readable in the final image.

One of the simplest compression techniques is called run-length coding and works well on images such as the signboard mentioned above. Run-length coding is based on the standard raster scan of an image—scanning through the image array row by row, starting in the upper left corner. For each row, the encoding process records that pixel value, counts the number of consecutive pixels having the same value, records that count, and then skips the counted pixels. Thus the run-length code is a sequence on intensity-count pairs. This coding is lossless.

Figure 3 also shows the general process diagram for image filtering—another important class of image transform techniques; one derived from the field of signal processing (Oppenheim and Schafer 1975). For filtering, the encode/decode become transform/inverse-transform, respectively, with the central rectangle being the filter step. The most common transform is the Fourier Transform, in which the visual data are transformed from the spatial domain into the frequency domain. This transform is important for two reasons: First, it is mathematically invertible, and second, many desirable effects in the spatial domain can be obtained by simple operations in the frequency domain. An example of the latter is edge enhancement, in which a high-pass filter—high-frequency components of the transformed image are maintained, while low-frequency components are attenuated—is used to make more evident the boundaries between regions of homogeneous intensity. This example illustrates an important system development approach: If one wants to highlight a type of

FIGURE 3. Coding process for storage and transmission.

image feature that has a simple signature in an alternative domain—for example, region boundaries are a feature corresponding to high-frequency components under the Fourier Transform—then design a filter that passes the signature and attenuates other elements in the transform domain. The concept of "signature" leads to the topic of detection, discussed in the next section.

DETECTION

The simplest form of detection system accepts an image and yields a YES/NO response indicating whether a specific feature is present in the image. A photosensor switch for turning on streetlights at night could be considered such a system. Although the image is extremely small and the signature being detected is only the average light level striking the sensor, it is a clear example of one of the most common image processing techniques: thresholding. For the photosensor switch, a threshold value is set; then the light level is continuously tested. If the level is less than the threshold, the light is turned on (or left on).

The processing of a LANDSAT image to determine the probable yield of a given crop is a more sophisticated example. For discussion purposes, assume that the light reflected from the crop has a distinctively high value, for example, greater than t, under a particular linear combination of the two infrared-band values. The detection step scans the image and for each pixel computes $s = \alpha P(i,j,3) + \beta P(i,j,4)$, where the third index selects the infrared bands and α and β are the coefficients forming the linear combination. If $s>t$ for the pixel at location i,j, then the corresponding pixel in a result image, $R (i,j)$, is set to 1; otherwise it is set to 0. Finally, the estimate of the crop yield is based on the area in the image R that has the value of 1. The image area can be converted to earth surface area through knowledge of the camera's focal length and altitude at the time the image was acquired. Note that R can be considered a characteristic vector for the set of pixels corresponding to the detected crop. One can also count the number of fields planted in the crop by counting the connect-

ed components in R (Rosenfeld and Kak 1982, vol. 2, p. 241). Since R is a binary image—there are only two possible values at any pixel—it can be said to have connected components of 1s. Each connected component is a set of pixels such that each pixel has the value 1, and for any two pixels in the set there is an unbroken chain of pixels in the set—a path connecting the two pixels. For the crop example, each connected component is considered to be a distinct, though contiguous, field.

Thresholding based on individual pixel-by-pixel measurements is referred to as context-independent detection because the decision at a given pixel is made without considering any of the neighboring pixels (e.g., s in the example above gets no contribution from adjacent pixels). Otherwise the operation is context-dependent.

One of the most extensively studied context-dependent operations is edge detection (Rosenfeld and Kak 1982, vol. 2, p. 96). An edge is considered to be a discontinuity—a relatively abrupt change in intensity value. Intensity discontinuities are found by spatial differencing or derivative operations. Here we will discuss an operation that detects pixels through which a horizontal edge passes—that is, pixels at which the maximum gradient vector points up or down. The context-dependent measure computes

$$h = |b - a|,$$

where

$$b = P(i-1,j-1) + 2P(i,j-1) + P(i+1,j-1)$$

and

$$a = P(i-1,j+1) + 2P(i,j+1) + P(i+1,j+1),$$

which is the absolute difference between the summed intensities just below and just above $P(i,j)$. A horizontal edge detector can be implemented by thresholding on this h value—that is, at each location i,j compute h on the adjacent pixel values, and if $h>t$, record a 1, otherwise a 0. The major problem then becomes selecting t, the threshold.

Clearly, the areas summed over for h can be rotated by 90 degrees to yield v, a measure of a vertical edge at location i,j. Also, rotations of 45 and 135 degrees yield *rd* and *ld*, respectively, right and left diagonal edge measures. These four operations can be incorporated in a complete edge detector by applying at every $P(i,j)$ each operation, determining the maximum of the computed values, and if the maximum is above threshold, then setting $R(i,j)$ to 1, otherwise to 0. Alternatively, $R(i,j)$ can have two components: one the computed maximum and the other a code indicating the direction yielding the maximum. This representation approximates a gradient vector having both a magnitude and a direction.

RECOGNITION

Line segments, not necessarily straight, can be extracted from a result image, such as R above, by edge tracing (or edge linking). Often edge tracing attempts to find a closed-line segment—a line segment topologically equivalent to a circle. These closed-line segments are considered to be the boundaries of significant regions in the image (e.g., the outlines of the block characters in the signboard example). Edge tracing begins at an arbitrary edge pixel—that is, at location i,j such that $R(i,j)=1$—and builds a chain of edge pixels. A chain is a connected component in which each pixel (except the endpoints if the chain is not closed) has exactly two of its immediately adjacent pixels also in the chain. To simplify edge tracing, a binary-image transformation called thinning—the image morphology operation called erosion (Schalkoff 1989)—is applied to R. For example, thinning might reduce a rectangle 3 pixels wide by 50 pixels long to a rectangle 1 pixel wide and 44 pixels long, that is, a chain of forty-four elements.

Line segments constitute an initial form of abstract information and as such can be the basis for recognition (Duda and Hart 1973). Here recognition is taken to be a process that has access to information, often called a library, about a set of given objects or classes of objects (e.g., letters of an alphabet). The process is to extract features of interest from the image and then determine if one of the library objects is present. Some of the most widely used image processing systems are recognition systems that have carefully designed libraries—for example, optical character reader (OCR) fonts and bar codes.

Recognition is the process by which the connection is made between visual data and semantic structures. As such, work in recognition via image processing is closely related to perception and cognition in artificial intelligence (AI) (Tanimoto 1990).

References

Ballard, D. H., and C. M. Brown. 1982. *Computer vision.* Englewood Cliffs, N.J.: Prentice-Hall.

Bell, S. B. M., B. M. Diaz, F. Holroyd, and J. J. Jackson. 1983. Spatially referenced methods of processing raster and vector data. *Image and Vision Computing* 1(4):211–20.

Duda, R. O., and P. E. Hart. 1973. *Pattern classification and scene analysis.* New York: Wiley.

Foley, J. D., and A. van Dam. 1989. *Fundamentals of interactive computer graphics.* Reading, Mass.: Addison-Wesley.

Golay, M. J. E. 1969. Hexagonal parallel pattern transformations. *IEEE Transactions on Computers* TC-18(8):733–40.

Gonzalez, R. C., and P. Wintz. 1987. *Digital image processing.* 2nd ed. Reading, Mass.: Addison-Wesley.

Horn, B. K. P. 1986. *Robot vision.* Cambridge, Mass.: The MIT Press; New York: McGraw-Hill.

Landgrebe, D. A. 1981. Analysis technology for land remote sensing. *Proceedings of the IEEE* 69(5):628–42.

Levine, M. D. 1985. *Vision in man and machine.* New York: McGraw-Hill.

Oppenheim, A. V., and Schafer, R. W. 1975. *Digital signal processing.* Englewood Cliffs, N.J.: Prentice-Hall.

Rosenfeld, A., and A. C. Kak. 1982. *Digital picture processing,* 2nd ed., vols. 1 and 2. New York: Academic Press.

Samet, H. 1990. *The design and analysis of spatial data structures.* Reading, Mass.: Addison-Wesley.

Schalkoff, R. J. 1989. *Digital image processing and computer vision.* New York: Wiley.

Tanimoto, S. L. 1990. *The elements of artificial intelligence.* New York: Computer Science Press.

Wyszecki, G., and W. S. Stiles. 1967. *Color science.* New York: Wiley.

For Further Reading

Marr, D. 1982. *Vision.* San Francisco: W. H. Freeman.

Martin, W. N., and J. K. Aggarwal. 1988. *Motion understanding: Robot and human vision.* Norwell, Mass: Kluwer Academic.

Uhr, L. 1987. *Parallel computer vision.* Boston: Academic Press.

Worthy Martin

IMAGING

See Electronic Document Image Processing and Management; Medical Imaging, Computer-Assisted

INDEXING

See Query Processing in Databases

INFORMATION REQUIREMENTS DETERMINATION

The objective of an information system application is to support organizational objectives and satisfy organizational requirements. A vital part of the process of designing, developing, and implementing an application is the determination of correct and complete information requirements. If the requirements are wrong or incomplete, the information system will not be successful.

There are usually two roles in or parties to information requirements determination: the user who is knowledgeable about the uses for the system and the analyst who has expertise in system design and development. There are advantages to having these two parties with their different roles. Many requirements are implicit and users may understand them but leave them out when talking about requirements. In discussions with users, the analyst frequently will notice the existence of implicit assumptions and draw them out. Also, the need to describe requirements to an outsider will help users clarify their thinking and make requirements explicit.

There are also disadvantages in having an analyst from information systems doing the information requirements determination process. It takes time to educate the analyst in key features of the function for which the application is being designed. There are opportunities for errors when requirements are provided by one person and documented by another.

There is a communications problem associated with the documentation of information requirements. The requirements need to be documented so that they are clear and unambiguous to the programmers and other development personnel who will build the system. The documentation also needs to be understandable to the users who provided the requirements, so they can validate the requirements as being correct and complete. (See also USER DOCUMENTATION.)

This article assumes a requirements determination process in which there is a systems analyst who is separate from the person who will use the application. In some small end-user-developed systems, the user will perform both roles. There are some advantages to this setup, but there are some dangers in eliminating the independent analyst. One way to overcome the disadvantages of a single person performing both user and analyst roles is for the person to follow systematic procedures in formulating and documenting requirements and to employ review processes with colleagues to detect incomplete or incorrect requirements.

It is useful to divide information requirements determination into high-level general requirements determination and detailed application requirements determination. The high-level general requirements determination process identifies organizational requirements for the entire organization or for some subunit or process. The discovery process at this level is designed to identify a set of applications and databases that are desirable for the management and operations of the organizational unit or organizational process. Once an application has been identified by a high-level requirements process (or requested by potential users), the specific, detailed requirements for the application must be identified. The detailed requirements include logic, stored data, input and output documents or screens, and reports.

These two levels of requirements determination are termed *unit requirements* and *application requirements.* The term *unit* encompasses the entire organization, an organizational function, a division or other organizational subdivision, or an organizational process. An *application* refers to the set of programs and related data that provide information system support for an organizational process, control, or decision making. An organizational unit or organizational process will usually use several applications.

At both unit and application levels of requirements determination, the question "What are your requirements?" will elicit some responses, but the responses are usually not complete and in some cases may not be entirely correct. The reason this question will not usually suffice for a complete set of requirements is that users on a daily basis do not think in terms of information requirements; instead, they are concerned with operations, analyses, decisions, and outcomes. They must be prompted to think about the information required for these activities. Information requirements determination methods are designed to overcome the limitations in asking users the direct question, "What are your requirements?" The methods generally employ indirect questions and other analysis and discovery procedures.

UNIT INFORMATION REQUIREMENTS DETERMINATION

Requirements determination at the level of an organization, organizational subunit, or process is directed at identifying types or classes of operational support, reports, analyses, and data retrieval requests that are important for the unit. When identified, these requirements can be grouped into applications and databases for detailed requirements analysis and development.

The basic method of information requirements determination at the unit level is to ask indirect questions and use the answers to elicit information requirements. The questions elicit the types of decisions, objectives, and outcomes that are important to the unit. Each of the responses can then be examined to derive information requirements.

Requirements elicitation can be performed with a single person; however, when several persons have a stake in the performance of a unit, there may be a group elicitation process with all interested parties. The nature of most large information systems in organizations is that they cross functional boundaries. This supports the recommendation that the elicitation process involve all interested stakeholders rather than be limited to the most obvious user.

Some unit information requirements methods use one or two questions. The following set of questions represents a synthesis of questions that are contained in different methods. Although each question evokes some unique responses, the questions overlap in coverage. Humans have constraints on their ability to process questions and formulate responses; asking more than one overlapping question aids in overcoming this human constraint. If one question does not elicit a certain requirement, another question may do so. If both questions elicit the same requirements, there is reinforcement.

For each question, there is a follow-up to the response to elicit the information requirements. When requirements are stated, additional data about current availability and usefulness may also be obtained.

Questions	Information Question
What problems do you need to solve?	What information do you need in solving these problems?
What decision do you make?	What information do you need in making these decisions?
What factors are critical to the success of your unit?	What information is needed to tell you whether you are successful in these critical factors?
What are you supposed to achieve with your unit (ends, goods, or services) and what makes these effective to recipients or customers?	What information is needed to tell you whether you are effective in the outputs of your unit?
What are the means or processes used to generate or provide goods or services? How do you measure efficiency in the use of these resources?	What information is needed to evaluate efficiency?

The following examples illustrate the responses and the information requirements elicited from the responses.

Problem: goods not available when ordered (out of stock) This is solved by better inventory management, which requires information on production, suppliers, reorder times, and other items.

Decision: grant credit to customer A credit history, credit rating information, information on status of customer (new, long-standing, reliable, unreliable, etc.), profit margin on goods ordered, and so forth are required.

Critical success factor: order fulfillment time that meets or exceeds customer expectations Order fulfillment times, customer expectations by major customers and major classes of customers, comparison of actual times with customer expectations, and so forth are required.

Effectiveness: match or exceed customer expectations for percentage of items in stock (by major items and major lines) Information is needed on customer expectations relative to shipping from stock and tracking of performance. Also, data on industry performance and performance of major competitors may be required.

Efficiency: cost of maintaining inventory by major lines and major items Information on inventory levels and holding costs broken down by major items and lines is required.

The overlap in the scope of the questions allows for greater assurance that all unit requirements have been identified correctly and completely. These illustrative questions establish the need for one or more applications designed for inventory management. The next step is to identify more detailed requirements for the applications identified.

APPLICATION INFORMATION REQUIREMENTS DETERMINATION

There are four approaches or methods for application-level information requirements determination. One approach will normally dominate, but more than one of these methods may be used for an application.

In using the methods, the analyst may do one-on-one interviews, but a more effective method may be to involve groups of interested persons. The need is similar to that explained under Unit Information Requirements Determination. In the case of application requirements, the group includes all stakeholders—those who will interact with the application or use directly or indirectly the information provided by it. The use of group interviews and group elicitation processes is often referred to as joint application design (JAD). Each of the following four methods of application requirements determination is described briefly and illustrated with a simple example.

1. Ask users directly.
2. Derive from existing applications.
3. Derive from characteristics of system needing the information processing.
4. Discover through experimentation during development.

Ask users directly.   In some cases, users can define the application information requirements without difficulty. For example, an existing report may need to be redesigned or a government report may be required in a certain format. In such cases, it is most efficient to ask the users to define the information requirements.

Derive from existing applications.   A common approach to eliciting requirements is to examine existing applications either in the same organization or in other organizations. The new application requirements can be derived from the existing applications with changes as necessary. Examples in textbooks or trade journals may also provide examples from which requirements may be derived.

Derive from system characteristics.   Although existing applications may be useful for derivation of requirements, many applications are quite different from those already in existence. In fact, in many cases, an important consideration is to rethink the application. The organizational procedures or processes requiring the application may be redesigned; this means that the information requirements must fit the new system that will use the information. The approach is to analyze the operations, decisions, control, reporting, and so forth that support the user system and derive and synthesize the information requirements that are needed. For example, an application to support decision making can be analyzed in terms of the decision-making factors and the decision-making approach. Once these are defined, the information requirements can be derived.

Discover through experimentation during development.   In some cases, it is very difficult to establish complete and correct requirements because users cannot visualize the operation of the application. Users need to experiment with the application before they can think of many requirements. The most common method for experimentation during development is to develop a prototype application that is employed by users. There is discovery of requirements through trial and error as the prototype is used. For example, an application to do consumer loan approval analysis may be difficult to specify in advance. An initial, simple system is built and then users employ this application to discover what is useful and what needs to be dropped, added, or altered.

The question as to which of the four methods should be used in a given circumstance is difficult to answer in the abstract; however, the methods are arranged in terms of their ability to deal with requirements determination uncertainty. In other words, if the requirements are well understood and well formulated, asking directly may be sufficient. If the users and developers both have a high degree of uncertainty about the requirements (what requirements and how to formulate them), then the method that deals best with a highly uncertain requirements situation is prototyping. Other conditions such as number of units, size of applications, existence of legal requirements, standard development methodology, and development tools available will also govern the choice of primary method for application requirements elicitation.

SUMMARY

Information requirements are critical to information systems development. Knowledge of high-level unit requirements is needed to identify the information system applications for the unit. When applications have been identified, detailed requirements for each of them must be elicited and documented. Correct and complete requirements must be found if functional, useful information system applications are to be developed and implemented. The basic problem of information requirements is that correct and complete requirements are usually not obvious, and merely asking the expected users of the application to specify the requirements will frequently fail to achieve satisfactory results. The article describes an approach using five overlapping questions to elicit unit requirements. It then describes four methods for application requirements determination. The properties of the four methods relative to the conditions of development will suggest the most appropriate method to use.

For Further Reading

Davis, G. B. 1982. Strategies for information requirements determination. *IBM Systems Journal* 21(1):4–30.

Davis, G. B., and M. H. Olson. 1985. Strategies for the determination of information requirements. In *Management information systems,* 2nd ed., Ch. 15, pp. 473–500. New York: McGraw-Hill. See also Chapter 16, Database Requirements, pp. 501–28, and Chapter 17, User Interface Requirements, pp. 529–59.

Rockart, J. F. 1979. Critical success factors. *Harvard Business Review,* March–April, pp. 81–91.

Wetherbe, J. C. 1991. Executive information requirements: Getting it right. *MIS Quarterly* 15(1):51–65.

Gordon B. Davis

INFORMATION SCIENCE

See Information Storage and Retrieval

INFORMATION SERVICES

An information service is a large database, maintained on a network of interconnected mainframe computers, accessible to its members or subscribers by modem. Most can be reached by calling a local telephone number, either connected directly to the information service or connected to a supplementary network such as Tymnet, Telenet, or Datapac that allows connections to many services. An information service may be general-purpose, providing its users with data on a wide range of topics and areas of interest, or it may concern itself with only one subject. Some information services are available to anyone, with any type of computer, modem, and general-purpose telecommunications program; a few are set up to use proprietary software that will run only on a particular type of computer. But whatever its size or scope, an information service makes it possible for its subscribers to have access to far more information than could be contained in any single home computer or library.

Information services got their start in the 1970s, when a few companies began allowing *time sharing* use of their mainframe computers to people outside their own businesses. Many firms' computers were heavily used during the day, but after business hours sat idle. The computer owners realized that if there were a system whereby others could use the computers after business hours, the costs of computer time could be reduced and the computers themselves could be used more efficiently. In the early days, it was necessary to use terminals connected directly to the mainframe, but when modems became generally available the computers were linked to telephone lines so that the direct connection was no longer required.

Eventually, the formerly time-shared portion of the computers' use grew to the point where it became a full-time business of its own and was separated from the parent network. Services such as CompuServe (originally known as MicroNET) got their start in this fashion. As the concept became more popular, other services such as The Source, GEnie, Delphi, and QuantumLink were founded without the time-sharing aspect, as information services in their own right. Many of the services founded in the late 1970s and early 1980s still flourish today, as more and more people have come to realize the value of being able to use home computers to tap into nationwide (or in many cases worldwide) sources of information.

The original information services were

set up primarily for experienced computer users and serious hobbyists who wanted access to the power of mainframe computers, and who were willing to do a fair amount of experimentation to make the system work. Commands were cryptic, services were minimal, a certain amount of "hacking" was expected, and there were few areas of interest other than those supporting programmers. As time went by, and as more people bought home computers and became aware of the vast possibilities in the home-computer-to-mainframe connection, the information services responded by making access and navigation easier and by expanding to include an ever wider variety of choices. The "hobbyist" aspects were gradually pushed aside, changed, or eliminated. Today on most of the major information services it is very easy for anyone, with any level of computer literacy, to connect with people of similar interests and find data on a nearly infinite range of subjects.

USING AN INFORMATION SERVICE

To use an information service, one must have a modem and an appropriate telecommunications program (either a general-purpose program or the special proprietary program required by some services), as well as an account with that service. Accounts can be established in several ways: by buying information service "starter kits" from software dealers; through offers packed with hardware or software; by calling special telephone numbers published in magazine advertisements; or by having someone who is already a subscriber to the service ask to have membership information sent to a new subscriber. Most information services provide a certain amount of free connect time for new subscribers as part of the subscription package.

The printed instructions that new members receive (besides an account number, a temporary password, and a list of local telephone numbers) range from a small pamphlet that contains the minimum amount of information needed to log on, to extensive manuals covering every aspect of the service. As nearly all information services charge for

connect time by the minute, the subscriber should have complete instructions on how to navigate the system. If the initial subscription package does not include a full system manual, the subscriber can purchase one once the account has been established (each service has an area where system manuals can be ordered).

After acquiring an account number, by whatever method, a new subscriber should follow the instructions to have the telecommunications software dial the appropriate telephone number and, once connected, follow the on-screen prompts to log in to the information service. Some services begin by asking subscribers to type in an identification number and password. The password will not appear on the screen, for security reasons, so it is important to type it carefully. And, also for security reasons, no one but the subscriber or persons authorized to use that account should know what the password is. Information service instructions are quite emphatic about the importance of changing one's password on a regular basis and of keeping it safe; indeed, if at all possible, the password should not even be written down. The password should be easy to remember, but not something that another person would find easy to guess (nothing so obvious as a nickname, child's name, pet's name, favorite sport, or the like).

Other services, especially those that use proprietary software, automate the log-in process and there are no prompts for account number or password. In many cases, the account number and password are stored on the system software disk, which should be kept protected as well. Anyone using the disk without authorization can easily run up an extremely large bill.

Once connected to the service for the first time, the new subscriber will find instructions for supplying personal information such as choice of billing method and address. Providing some of the information is optional, but most (such as the method that will be used to pay for the connect charges) must be supplied. After the new subscriber has completed the sign-in procedure, the rest of the system is open to exploration. Some commands and system areas will be off limits until the subscriber's financial information is verified, as a security measure.

Most information services have special areas for new subscribers and do their best to make learning the system easy. There are tutorials, files containing useful information for newcomers, special areas to practice using the system commands, and hundreds of people who are more than willing to help the newcomer. Finding help or instruction, or an area of interest, is as simple as making a choice from an on-screen menu. It is generally a good idea to take advantage of all the services provided for new users, many of which are available free or at substantially reduced connect charges. Once familiar with the system, the subscriber can then explore other areas of particular interest.

INFORMATION SERVICE FEATURES

The major information services all have areas of interest to users of particular brands of computers; indeed, some information services such as QuantumLink, PC-Link, and America Online are accessible only by users of a particular brand of computer. People using a general-access system should check the menu for areas of interest to users of their own particular computer systems; those areas will have data libraries full of shareware and public-domain software, as well as message areas where help with particular computer problems is available. Users of a computer-specific system may find a small amount of software designed for other brands of computers, but the system's primary purpose is support and information for the computers for which its software was designed.

Many of the major software companies and computer manufacturers are also directly accessible through information services, and users of their programs and hardware can ask questions or help other users. The companies maintain their own data libraries where one can download software updates and enhancements and find hints and tips for better use of their products.

In addition, information services have separate areas (called Forums, RoundTables, Special Interest Groups, and the like) for people interested in various hobbies, occupations, and pastimes such as sports, science fiction, collecting, desktop publishing, medicine, gardening, and genealogy (to name a few of the hundreds of choices available). There one can exchange messages with people who have similar interests and share help and information. These special areas also have their own data libraries, and will have one or more people commonly known as *Sysops* (a contraction for *system operator*, a term held over from the old computer-hobbyist days) whose purpose is to help subscribers find information, keep the area in order, keep conversations flowing smoothly, and generally make life easier for everyone who enters the group. Subscribers who need help can get it quickly by leaving a message for the Sysops.

Some systems now have "autonavigational" programs available for many types of computers, which make it possible to get the maximum amount of information from the service with the minimum amount of connect time. The program will whiz through the system, collect messages and information, and allow the subscriber to read everything at leisure after disconnecting from the information service, then compose any replies to messages while off-line and send them all to the information service at once. As these programs become more popular, efficient use of information systems will increase. To find such programs, one generally has only to ask about them and mention the particular type of computer one uses.

In addition to finding information on computers and hobbies, any information service subscriber can connect to travel agencies and airline, hotel, and car-rental reservation systems; read news from national wire services; look things up in an on-line encyclopedia; do research through specialized bibliographic databases; look for other users in an on-line user directory; look up toll-free telephone numbers in an on-line telephone directory; look in a database of U.S. telephone directories to find long-lost friends; shop in on-line "malls" with a wide variety of stores; order products offered by the information services themselves; get weather maps and information; and play a number of interactive games, from shoot-'em-up adventures to trivia contests to chess. All information services also provide electronic mail, and many of them allow subscribers to connect to other services such as MCI Mail, Bitnet, and Internet. Some information services make it possible to send telex, fax, and even U.S. Postal Service mail through their regular electronic mail system as well, although it is not yet possible for mail and fax messages to be returned electronically.

One of the most popular features available through information services is real-time interactive conferencing (called "Chat," "People Connection," "Conference," "CB Simulator," or something similar). Subscribers from all over the world can type short messages and "talk" with each other at the same time. As the instructions for each system's interactive conference area are different, a newcomer should read the manual to get a general idea of how the commands are used before signing in. It is also advisable to use a baud rate that incurs the lowest connect-time charge, especially at the beginning, because interactive chatting often occupies one's attention for long periods.

THE IMPORTANCE OF INFORMATION SERVICES

Unlike books and reference materials in a library, which remain static until rewritten, on-line information can be kept continually up-to-date. Using an information service for research can be remarkably convenient and efficient; the home, school, or business computer user can find a vast store of knowledge available for the price of a few minutes' connect time. Data can be gathered with a local phone call, then stored in a form convenient for the user (electronically or on a paper printout). Searching an electronic database is far easier than wading through a card catalog or a pile of books to gather information, because the computer, given instructions on what to search for, can scan far faster than even the most experienced human researcher.

Many information services provide electronic access to reference materials usually found in public libraries, such as encyclopedias, the *Books in Print* catalog, bibliographic

lists of periodicals, financial data about major corporations, government publications, and guides to colleges and universities. The manual provided by the information service will list what is available, as well as any additional commands one must know to navigate. Some of the reference services carry an extra charge, so it is prudent to check the manual and to make sure the commands and extra charges are clearly understood.

Businesspeople will find an information service subscription to be of especial benefit, as many business-related services are available. (Indeed, one service, Dow-Jones News-/Retrieval, is entirely devoted to business and financial information.) Stock quotes, financial data, demographics, economic forecasts, business news, and databases devoted to business periodicals are all available on-line. In addition, on-line travel services (including airline schedules; reservations for tickets, car rentals, and lodging; and up-to-date restaurant guides) can make business travel easier and more pleasant.

But the real strength of the information services, and of far more value than the bare information contained in the databases, lies in person-to-person communications. There is an old saying that no matter how much one person may know, there is always someone else who knows more. A subscription to an information service is one of the very best ways to share one's knowledge and to benefit from the knowledge of others. Each information service offers the opportunity to make contact with thousands of other subscribers. In many cases a question or a description of a problem will elicit dozens of helpful replies in a very short time. And if the information one needs is not available on the system itself, chances are extremely good that another subscriber will know where else to look. Information networks also make it possible to connect directly with the people who design hardware and software, to get answers to thorny problems and to suggest improvements.

Information services are helping to forge a global community; information service connections transcend national boundaries and provide an excellent gateway for international cooperation and understanding and for broadening one's perspective on the world. People who otherwise would never have met can become close friends through messages exchanged on electronic networks. Indeed, quite a number of romances and even marriages have come about through on-line connections. It is not uncommon to see well-known names on one's screen; celebrities use information services too.

Perhaps most important of all, because each person's personality appears only through the messages he or she leaves, the normal visual and physical clues that might lead to prejudices are eliminated. The information service connection is a great equalizer, linking mind to mind without physical barriers. This is the aspect of electronic networking that holds the most promise for the future.

For Further Reading

General Reference

Burstein, J. S., and J. Ralya. 1986. *Computers and information systems.* New York: Holt, Rinehart and Winston.

Glossbrenner, A. 1985. *The complete handbook of personal computer communications.* New York: St. Martin's Press.

Glossbrenner, A. 1987. *How to look it up online.* New York: St. Martin's Press.

Humphrey, S. M., and B. J. Melloni. 1986. *Databases: A primer for retrieving information by computer.* Englewood Cliffs, N.J.: Prentice-Hall.

Specific Reference

System manuals for individual information services (definitely worth the purchase price).

Bowen, C., and D. Peyton. 1989. *How to get the most out of CompuServe*, rev. 4th ed. New York: Bantam.

Out of date, but worth reading for information and historical perspective:

Glossbrenner, A. 1984. *How to get free software.* New York: St. Martin's Press.

Stone, M. D. 1984. *Getting on-line: A guide to accessing computer information services.* Englewood Cliffs, N.J.: Prentice-Hall.

Marte Brengle

INFORMATION STORAGE AND RETRIEVAL

The techniques of information storage and retrieval deal with the collection, analysis, and organization of information, and the searching and distribution of information. Systems for performing these functions began as traditional library operations, but have become increasingly computer-based as electronic technology has advanced. The role of information has increased with the growth of this technology, resulting in an "information explosion" or overload. In the past, the flow of information was largely paper-oriented; today, the new technology is creating huge quantities of computer-readable material. The sheer volume of computer-based data compounds the traditional problem of sifting useful information from a base of material that is uneven in quality. Reductions in the cost of storing, processing, and retrieving information have only added to this dilemma. The consequence is that we are faced with the increasingly difficult problem of selecting critical information from mountains of data.

To cope with the information explosion, information storage and retrieval systems have focused on two main types of tasks: *information analysis* and *information organization and searching*. Information analysis is the process of assigning indicators that accurately reflect the content of stored data. In conventional library systems, such indicators include subject headings and Dewey Decimal or Library of Congress codes. As information and data become more complex, however, simple indicators are no longer adequate. Consequently, today's information retrieval systems feature a blend of sophisticated methods for automatically characterizing the data stored in computer files and matching retrieved responses with user queries. The second task, information organization and searching, deals with the manner in which the stored information is structured so as to permit efficient searching by computer. This process is also undergoing evolutionary change as electronic technology continues to provide the means for representing more and more information at lower and lower cost.

The development of information storage and retrieval systems closely follows the direction that library automation has taken in the United States and the European library community. We can trace the major steps in this development by briefly describing the principal features of the automated library systems that have evolved.

LIBRARY AUTOMATION

An automated library is generally regarded as one that can describe the status of a book or periodical through a computer query and generate reports concerning the use of library holdings. The scope of early systems was limited to the conventional library activities of acquisition, cataloging, circulation, and serials control. The Library of Congress has established a library standard, MARC (for "MAchine Readable Catalog"), which enables cooperating libraries to catalog their holdings in a unified manner (McCoy 1986). Such standard cataloging permits libraries to share their holdings in interlibrary loan networks. This protocol has proved essential to library automation both locally and nationally and has greatly increased access to all kinds of stored information. Of particular importance is the ability of otherwise incompatible computer systems to communicate with each other through MARC.

As library automation progressed, and computers became more powerful, attention turned away from library management activities and began to focus upon the end user of information. On-line search services appeared in direct response to the need to access the contents of technical journals in a cost-effective and efficient manner. In the mid-1960s, publishers started converting book and journal publication from linotype machines using metal slugs to computerized photo-offset equipment. The spinoff of this conversion was a wealth of computer-readable text that could be stored and retrieved on demand. So-called on-line search services allowed users to search this text, usually in the form of abstracts through remote terminals over a telephone network. The first versions of these on-line systems were relatively crude devices that required users to construct searches in the form of Boolean expressions. For example, a request for material dealing with the use of titanium in the design of nose cones or leading edges might have been phrased thus:

(TITANIUM) .AND. (NOSE_CONE .OR. LEADING_EDGE).

Such expressions could be used to retrieve bibliographic references to stored abstracts dealing with the desired subject matter. A defect of this retrieval technique is that it failed to filter out irrelevant references, such as documents that dealt with aspects other than the *design* of the desired components. The above example could just as easily have retrieved data concerning the cost of titanium nose cones.

Despite these deficiencies, on-line services flourished during the 1970s and 1980s, and several commercial systems were offered to the public.

ON-LINE RETRIEVAL SERVICES

During the 1980s, the use of on-line retrieval services by end users increased substantially. An end user is a "processor of information who uses information sources directly" (Buntrock and Valicenti 1985). End users are thus consumers of information, often scientists, engineers, and business people who require access to up-to-date sources of information. Librarians, by contrast, are intermediaries who retrieve information as a service to others. This shift in the user population marked an important change in the way information retrieval was performed.

The predominant mode of retrieval provided by on-line services continued to be bibliographic, such as document citations by author, title, and subject. Several problems were encountered, including the following:

- differences in format among the commercial vendors
- the number of available databases within given areas
- the awkwardness of search strategies based on Boolean logic

- the variations in command languages from vendor to vendor
- the absence of standards
- on-line search costs.

Despite these drawbacks, on-line bibliographic retrieval services still flourish. Major vendors include Dialog and BRS, on the commercial side, and the National Library of Medicine, which provides the MEDLINE service within the public sector (Mischo and Lee 1987).

(See also DATABASES, ON-LINE; INFORMATION SERVICES.)

NONBIBLIOGRAPHIC RETRIEVAL

Most of the databases that are accessed through library-supported on-line systems are bibliographic. That is, they contain records that describe the contents of documents but not the text of the documents. There are also systems that provide access to the full text of documents. Airline reservations, bus schedules, airline departure and arrival information, bulletin boards, and campus directories are examples of full-text systems. College students make widespread use of these facilities. High school students can also find encyclopedia articles in full-text databases.

The primary advantage of full-text systems is that end users can browse through them in search of answers to questions that cannot be readily formulated in Boolean logic terms. The user is in control of the search process at all times, which constitutes a considerable advantage over bibliographic services that provide only references to documents instead of answers to specific questions. Furthermore, the retrieval process in full text is far more flexible, enabling the end user to navigate around the text in any way desired.

CD-ROM SYSTEMS

Full-text databases are mostly available in the compact-disk read-only memory (CD-ROM) configuration. These are used with personal computers and greatly increase their utility as end user retrieval devices. The growth of personal computing has had a profound impact on information retrieval by making available bodies of information heretofore accessible only through on-line services. Frentzen (1988) lists almost 250 CD-ROM databases, many of them derived from U.S. Government sources. These include Census data, the Monthly Catalog of U.S. Government Publications, and federal and state environmental documents. The U.S. Government is also considering putting a large number of different publications on CD-ROM in order to alleviate the problems of depository libraries and also to provide end users with improved retrieval capabilities.

ELECTRONIC REFERENCE BOOKS

Publishers are now beginning to use the computer to produce texts that are themselves computer-readable. The CD-ROM format and hypertext have had a strong influence on this development. Hypertext is a recently developed technology for storing text in an associative fashion, so that related subject matter can be automatically linked in a nonserial manner. Hypertext provides a novel way of organizing information for subsequent retrieval. Hypertext and CD-ROM together provide the means for developing computer-readable references such as dictionaries.

Word processing systems usually include software for checking and correcting spelling errors. Spelling checkers are helpful but prone to error themselves, since incorrect spellings can be incorporated and promulgated throughout the system. The NeXT computer developed by Steven Jobs includes the entire *Webster's Ninth New Collegiate Dictionary* on its CD-ROM system. Computer-readable dictionaries have several important features. The end user who is writing or reading on-line text will find it very helpful to be able to summon up spelling information or definitions by pressing a key.

The CD-ROM technology makes it possible to store large amounts of dictionary information (as much as 650 megabytes) on a small surface. This means that the complete set of twelve volumes of the *Oxford English*

Dictionary could be stored on a compact disk that can be used on a personal computer. Oxford University Press in fact provides a CD-ROM version of its dictionary. The requirements for reading the dictionary are an IBM-compatible personal computer with 640K of random-access memory (RAM), a hard disk drive or twin floppies, and any CD-ROM drive that supports the Microsoft CD-ROM extensions. There are additional retrieval features included with the dictionary. There is an etymological index enabling users to retrieve words of given origins, a label index for retrieving words of a certain type (for example, scientific terms), and a quotation date index for retrieving all citations between two specified dates.

Computer-readable dictionaries are being used for information retrieval of all kinds, text generation, speech synthesis and recognition, and machine translation from one language to another.

INFORMATION RETRIEVAL IN SCIENCE AND ENGINEERING

Engineers have at their disposal a wide variety of computer tools, including workstations, computer-aided design (CAD) and computer-aided manufacturing (CAM) tools, spreadsheets, calculation software packages, and high-speed telecommunications facilities for text, voice, and video. Engineering information systems are combinations of data and equipment that have been designed, integrated, and implemented to perform specific information functions in support of engineering activities. Technical literature, tables of data, on-line databases, CAD, CAM, computer-integrated manufacturing (CIM), technical specifications, project management, and inventory systems all form part of engineering information systems.

A distinctive feature of these information systems is that the specific retrieval function that began as an independent system, conducted largely on on-line bibliographic databases running on mainframe computers, has been interfaced with other system modules into a coherent whole. Information retrieval, once a self-contained

function, is now a component of an overall integrated system that acts as an assistant to scientists and engineers. This combination of functions by way of "seamless" interfaces is characteristic of the expert systems that are becoming an important ingredient in scientific, technological, and business decision making. An expert system is a problem-solving system designed to attain human expert levels of performance. Its goals are to integrate new information and knowledge, retrieve relevant knowledge and display it in an easy-to-understand form, provide explanations, reason about the nature of a task, and support a natural interface with end users.

Information retrieval is much more efficient when it functions as part of an expert system and can communicate with other system components. The retrieved information, for example properties of semiconductor materials, can be fed to CAD subsystems for designing computer chips with those materials, and the performance of the chips can be simulated on another subsystem. Thus information retrieval has undergone a significant transformation from standalone bibliographic services to incorporation in powerful integrated systems for decision making in fields ranging from science and engineering to business and law. Both the methods and the role of information retrieval have changed significantly and will continue to evolve as computers and communication technology become more and more interdependent.

INFORMATION SCIENCE

The term *information science* was first used about 1960 to stand for the scientific basis of information storage and retrieval. Although there have been many attempts to define information science, there is little consensus on a definition. In many universities, the topic is combined with computer science in departments of computer and information science. In such cases, information science could be said to be concerned with the study, design, and use of data structures and their manipulation by computer means.

References

Buntrock, R. E., and A. K. Valicenti. 1985. End-users and chemical information. *Journal of Chemical Information and Computer Sciences* 25(3):203–207.

Frentzen, J., comp. 1988. Commercial CD-ROM titles. *CD-ROM Review* 3(9):28–38.

McCoy, R. W. 1986. The Linked Systems Project: Progress, promise, realities. *Library Journal* 111(16):33–39.

Mischo, W. H., and J. Lee. 1987. End-user searching of bibliographic databases. *Annual Review of Information Science and Technology* 22:227–63.

Donald J. Hillman